W9-BLM-325

PRINCIPLES
OF
ADMINISTRATIVE
LAW

by

David Phillip Jones

B.A. (Hons.) (McGill), B.C.L., M.A. (Oxon.)
of the Faculty of Law, The University of Alberta
Edmonton

and

Anne S. de Villars

B.Sc. (Southampton), LL.B. (Alberta)
of McCuaig, Desrochers, Barristers and Solicitors
Edmonton

1985

CARSWELL

Toronto   Calgary   Vancouver

Canadian Cataloguing in Publication Data

Jones, David P. (David Phillip), 1949-
    Principles of administrative law

(Carswell's legal classics)
Includes index.
ISBN 0-459-37760-4 (bound). — ISBN
    0-459-37770-1 (pbk.)

1. Administrative law — Canada.   2. Administrative
law — Alberta.   3. Judicial review of administrative
acts — Canada.   4. Judicial review of administrative
acts — Alberta.   I. De Villars, Anne S., 1946-
II. Title.   III. Series.
KE5015.J66 1985   342.71′06   C85-091319-5

Copyright © 1985
The Carswell Company Limited

To our families

FOREWORD

Thirty or forty years ago, when Administrative Law in Britain was conspicuously feeble, the Canadian courts were setting a more encouraging example in several different ways. Fortunately a great deal was about to happen, the initiative was seized by the British courts, and it became Canada's turn to catch up. That Canada has been doing so in her own distinctive way is well shown in this book. Keeping their eyes firmly on the main principles, both constitutional and administrative, and skilfully arranging their material, the authors have provided a text which presents a crisp and lucid picture of the state of the subject in Canada.

This is a propitious time for their undertaking. Canada has at last taken control of her own constitution and said an overdue farewell to the British North America Act, 1867. There is now a wholly Canadian framework within which Administrative Law can develop. An outstandingly important part of it is the Charter of Rights and Freedoms, now given full constitutional status. The Charter will both give a lead to the judges and at the same time present them with a host of new problems, many of which are bound to concern Administrative Law. The solutions which the judges will have to find will be observed with great interest from Britain, where there is much talk about a Bill of Rights but a conspicuous lack of action.

Like any other growth area of the law, Administrative Law is producing a crop of technicalities and subtle distinctions which can be traps for unwary litigants. We can read in this book how the Canadian courts are grappling with them, and how they are not necessarily following some of the more extreme and sophisticated English doctrines. In the problematical area of error of law, for instance, the "patently unreasonable" criterion is a specifically Canadian development, being applied in quite a different manner from the corresponding *Wednesbury* principle now so prominent in England. It is interesting also to see that the authors disapprove of the radical stance of the House of Lords, or at least some members of it, who now hold that any error of law must vitiate an administrative or tribunal decision and render it *ultra vires*. Remedies are another subject containing too much technicality, but this book shows that they can be discussed in a way which is both clear and compact.

As to the future, the authors make a series of suggestions in chapter 17. The art of prophecy is not easy, neither is that of law reform, but I hope that in future editions they will be able to point to some fulfilments, perhaps inspired by the work of the Alberta Institute of Law Research and Reform. Meanwhile they are to be congratulated on an important contribution to the literature of Administrative Law.

H.W.R. Wade
Cambridge, England.
20th March 1985

PREFACE

The purpose of this book is to state the principles of Administrative Law. Our goal is to provide a conceptual analysis which will be useful to lawyer and layman alike as a tool for approaching problems which arise in this ever-expanding field.

The use of the word "principles" is deliberate. First, in our experience, very few senior members of the Bar and Bench appear to realize that Administrative Law is a coherent system of principles. This may well result from the fact that Administrative Law is a relatively new addition to the curriculum of Canadian law faculties. In addition, this unfamiliarity may reflect the slow and sometimes erratic evolution of the constitutional philosophy underlying the phenomenon of judicial review of administrative action, and the relationship between the legislature, the executive and the judiciary in a parliamentary democracy.

Secondly, we contrast "principles" with the "rules" which in most areas of law give definite answers to the legal problems arising from particular fact patterns. In Administrative Law, as in other areas of public law, there frequently is no single correct answer to a problem. Rather, competing principles of public policy are involved, and must be weighed against each other to reach a solution to the particular case.

Thirdly, the contexts in which an Administrative Law case can arise are so varied that it is almost impossible to develop a statement of the law without a great deal of generality. Indeed, one of the most difficult aspects of the practice of Administrative Law arises from the necessity of applying general principles to fact patterns which are complicated, frequently unique, and which involve adversaries who each may reasonably claim to have the law on his side. It is difficult, therefore, to glean precedential dicta from such cases without referring to general principles.

Fourthly, Parliament and the legislatures often appear to forget the principles of Administrative Law in enacting increasingly complex schemes of legislation. Without challenging the legislators' sovereign right to abolish, alter, amend, or displace any part of Administrative Law, it nevertheless would be exceedingly helpful if the intent to do so were clearly articulated in the statutes; and this can probably only be done if legislators clearly understand and continuously measure their enactments against the principles of Administrative Law.

Fifthly, any democratic state requires informed citizens. The Rule of Law not only implies a judiciary capable of declaring what the law is, and granting a remedy for infractions thereof; it also implies that citizens generally understand the principles underlying their relationship with governmental officials, and how to assert their rights. It is not reasonable to expect every citizen to be an administrative lawyer, but it is possible for them to understand when their rights and interests have been affected in a manner which Administrative Law would remedy.

Sixthly, we acknowledge that this text deals principally with judicial review of administrative action. This is the focus for most lawyers' contact with Administrative Law. It would simply be impossible to try to describe the detailed statutory schemes within which each of the particular administrative tribunals operate, and it does not seem particularly useful to try to single out any one administrative body in an attempt to use it to try to demonstrate the general principles of Administrative Law. Accordingly, this text may not refer to the particular statute which a practitioner must consider. Similarly, this text does not purport to refer to every Administrative Law case which has ever been decided — any more than a torts text could do so.

Finally, we make no apology for our heavy reliance on Alberta cases and statutory provisions. It would, of course, be possible to refer to similar matters from other provinces, but little would be gained from merely attempting to list every Canadian case on every point. Our aim has been to describe a coherent set of principles; particular cases and statutory provisions are merely used as illustrations. We recognize that cases from other jurisdictions could frequently be used interchangeably. As in so many areas of Canadian law, it is necessary and desirable to refer to English authorities. We have tried whenever possible to take account of decisions of the Supreme Court of Canada, but necessarily also refer to decisions of lower courts which succinctly illustrate the principles under discussion.

These, then, are our reasons for trying to articulate the principles of Administrative Law as a textbook, and not as a digest of cases.

We have tried to state the law as of February 1985.

D.P. Jones
Anne de Villars
St. Valentine's Day 1985
Edmonton

ACKNOWLEDGMENTS

The authors gratefully acknowledge the considerable assistance which they have received in the course of writing this text.

Professor Jones thanks the University of Alberta for a McCalla Research Professorship in 1983-84 and a year's study leave in 1984-85. These allowed him freedom from teaching and administrative duties.

Anne de Villars thanks the members of her law firm, McCuaig Desrochers, for their moral and financial encouragement and support for this project.

Both authors acknowledge the usefulness of the casebook prepared by Professor F.A. Laux from the Faculty of Law at the University of Alberta. Other members of the Bar and Bench provided helpful comments and references, including: Mr. Justice David C. McDonald of the Court of Queen's Bench of Alberta; Andrew C.L. Sims, a practitioner in the labour field in Edmonton; Professor Timothy Christian of the Faculty of Law at the University of Alberta; and Professor Julius Grey of the Faculty of Law at McGill University.

We also thank Kim Graf, who provided invaluable assistance in reading the text and checking all the footnotes — first as Professor Jones's researcher and then as an articling student with McCuaig Desrochers.

Finally, we thank those involved in the technical production of the text: the word processor operators who typed and retyped the manuscript, Cheryl Seavers, Annabell Lui, and Mildred; as well as the publisher's representatives, Leslie McGuffin and John McDermid.

Professor D.P. Jones.
Anne de Villars

CONTENTS

PART II
GROUNDS FOR JUDICIAL REVIEW

PART III
REMEDIES

TABLE OF CASES

I

GENERAL PRINCIPLES

1

Introduction: What is Administrative Law?

1. What Is Administrative Law?

Administrative Law deals with the legal limitations on the actions of governmental officials, and on the remedies which are available to anyone affected by a transgression of these limits. The subject invariably involves the question of the lawful authority of an official to do a particular act which, in the absence of such authority, might well be illegal (or *ultra vires*) and give rise to an actionable wrong.[1] In our legal system, the mere fact that the govern-

---

1 Is there a right without a remedy? Much of substantive Administrative Law derives from the availability of the prerogative remedies, and it is not surprising that some authorities first consider the nature and ambit of the remedies in Administrative Law, and only then look at the grounds for obtaining those remedies. See, for example, Professor Frederick A. Laux's approach in *The Administrative Process*, 6th ed. (Edmonton: The Faculty of Law, University of Alberta, 1983).

ment *is the government* does not give it any particular rights or powers. On the contrary, all governmental actions must be specifically authorized by either legislation or the Royal Prerogative.[2] This need for governmental officials to be able to point to the lawful authority permitting their actions makes Administrative Law a close cousin to Constitutional Law.

2. The Relationship of Administrative Law to Constitutional Law

In its broadest sense, Constitutional Law comprises all of the fundamental rules for determining who and which institutions have the right to make laws for the government of our society; it is "a law for the making of laws".[3] Administrative Law, on the other hand, deals with the actions of administrators to whom powers have been granted by laws which have been validly enacted under the constitution. Logically, therefore, a finding that a particular law is unconstitutional will deprive the administrator (or "statutory delegate") of the legal basis upon which to justify his actions, which may give rise to a legal remedy in the hands of a person adversely affected thereby. Accordingly, any possible constitutional defect in legislation will be relevant to Administrative Law for the purpose of determining the legal validity of the governmental action complained of. Chapter 2 deals with "Constitutional Aspects of Administrative Law in Canada", and considers both the pure form of the doctrine of Parliamentary Sovereignty which exists in the United Kingdom, and the modifications which must be made to that doctrine in light of the federal nature of Canada, section 96 of the Constitution Act, 1867[4] and our newly entrenched Canadian Charter of Rights and Freedoms.[5]

3. Statutory Delegation of Governmental Powers

Once the constitutional validity of the legislation in question has been established, it is then necessary to determine the existence and exact scope of powers which that legislation delegates to the administration. The doctrine of Parliamentary Sovereignty gives the legislative branch authority to delegate powers, and the vast bulk of the business of government in fact takes place by virtue of delegated authority instead of being contained in laws passed by either the Federal Parliament or one of the provincial legislatures. The need to delegate authority can be justified in terms of the following factors, among others:

---

2 On the ambit of the Royal Prerogative, and the ability to override it by legislation, see O. Hood Phillips and Paul Jackson, *O. Hood Phillips' Constitutional and Administrative Law*, 6th ed. (London: Sweet & Maxwell, 1978), chapter 14.
3 A phrase coined by Professor F.R. Scott from McGill.
4 30 & 31 Vict., c. 3; reproduced with amendments in R.S.C. 1970, App. II.
5 Part I of Sched. B to the Canada Act, 1982 (U.K.) (31 Eliz. 2, c. 11); also the Constitution Act, S.C. 1982, Pt. I.

(a) The sheer magnitude of the business of government means that not everything could be dealt with by Parliament or a legislature.

(b) Much of governmental activity is technical in nature, and only broad principles should be contained in legislation.

(c) Delegating power to an administrator allows greater flexibility in applying broad statutory provisions to changing circumstances.

(d) It may not be possible to devise a general rule to deal with all cases, which may be more conveniently determined in the discretion of a delegate.

(e) The need for rapid governmental action may require faster administrative response than can be accommodated by the necessity of legislative amendment.

(f) Innovation and experimentation in solving social problems may not be possible if legislation is required.

(g) Someone actually has to apply legislation, and that person has to have authority to do so.

(h) Emergencies may require broad delegation of powers with respect to a wide range of matters which would normally be dealt with by legislation.

It is not surprising, therefore, to discover that virtually all of the laws passed by the Federal Parliament or the provincial legislatures[6] delegate certain powers and duties, whether to the cabinet, a particular minister, a particular civil servant, a judge, or someone else.[7] Although there are political conventions as to what types of powers should be delegated, there is no legal rule for determining what types of powers should be exercised by the legislative branch itself.[8] To some extent, these conventions are reflected in the rules of statutory construction, which assist in determining the exact meaning of legislation. The doctrine of Parliamentary Sovereignty, however, means that there is no legal — as opposed to political — limit on the ability of the legislative branch to use clear words to delegate virtually any power[9] to someone else. An important part of Administrative Law, therefore, deals with the controls which the Federal Parliament or the provincial legislatures themselves devise to supervise the exercise of *their* powers which they have delegated to administrators. One particular aspect of such controls is examined in chapter 3 dealing with "The Existence and Control of Delegated Legislation".

---

6 Because of the federal nature of Canada, it is necessary to refer to both the Federal Parliament and the provincial legislatures when speaking of the primary level of legislators in Canada. This is not the case in a unitary state such as the United Kingdom, and English textbooks speak of the Sovereignty of Parliament to refer to one legislative body. It is important to remember this distinction when referring to English textbooks on Administrative Law.

7 Or to private individuals, for that matter.

8 In other words, legislation which delegates powers will generally be valid, provided its intent to do so is clear.

9 Whether legislative, judicial, executive or administrative in nature.

4. Delegation, Jurisdiction, and the Doctrine of *Ultra Vires*

Judicial review is probably the most important means of controlling illegal governmental actions. To the extent that such actions may constitute wrongs otherwise known to law, the delegate will have to demonstrate some statutory provision authorizing him to take the impugned action. The delegate must be able to demonstrate that his actions fall squarely within the power granted to him by the Federal Parliament or the provincial legislatures. If they do not, his actions are *ultra vires*, that is, beyond the delegate's jurisdiction. Most of Administrative Law involves the close scrutiny of the jurisdiction or authority of a particular governmental official to do a particular action which affects the rights or interests of another person, and this inevitably involves the application of rules of statutory construction[10] to determine precisely what the legislative branch meant to enact.

"Jurisdiction" is a difficult term of art in Administrative Law, and has a number of different meanings. It is frequently very difficult to determine whether the legislation does grant a particular delegate the "jurisdiction" to do the impugned act, or to do it in some particular way. Lack of jurisdiction makes the act *ultra vires*, and may make available a legal remedy. Chapter 4 examines both the concept of jurisdiction and the concomitant doctrine of *ultra vires*.

5. Grounds for Judicial Review

The superior courts have the inherent power to review the legality of administrative actions. On the one hand, this power is the natural consequence of the courts' role to interpret the meaning of statutes, including determining the ambit of statutes which delegate powers to administrators. In other words, the courts decide which administrative actions are *ultra vires*. On the other hand, the superior courts have historically used the prerogative remedies[11] such as *certiorari*, *mandamus*, prohibition, *quo warranto* and *habeas corpus* to exercise supervisory jurisdiction over inferior courts and other tribunals. As a result, there is considerable judicial review of administrative action in Canada.

"Judicial review" is not the same as an appeal. In general, the superior courts do not have the right to substitute their appraisal of the merits for any

---

10 See J.A. Corry, "Administrative Law and the Interpretation of Statutes", (1935) 1 U.T.L.J. 286.

11 The remedies are called "prerogative" because they were historically available at the instance of the Crown. Hence, all such applications were made in the name of the Crown, on the instance of the applicant. Therefore, the proper style of the cause is *R. v. Commr. of Police of the Metropolis; Ex parte Blackburn*, [1968] 2 Q.B. 118 (C.A.). This nomenclature has for some reason fallen into disuse in Alberta, and the current usage would (incorrectly?) style the same case as *Blackburn v. Commr. of Police of the Metropolis*.

lawful action taken by an administrator. On the contrary, one of the consequences of the doctrine of Parliamentary Sovereignty is the right of the legislative branch to delegate powers to administrators without any right of appeal, whether to another administrator or to a court. Of course, legislation frequently does provide one or more levels of appeal, but there is no obligation for it to do so.

Judicial review, therefore, is generally limited to the power of the superior courts to determine whether the administrator has acted strictly within the powers which have been statutorily[12] delegated to him. Judicial review concentrates almost completely on jurisdictional questions, and on the application of the *ultra vires* doctrine to the particular fact pattern surrounding the impugned administrative action.

For example, if legislation gives a municipality the power to expropriate private property for the purpose of redeveloping an area for the provision of houses, an attempt to expropriate for the purpose of developing a governmental or commercial centre will be void. The superior court can declare the expropriation scheme to be *ultra vires*, and no transfer of property will have occurred as the result of the city's filing the Notice of Intention to Expropriate against the title to the property in the Land Titles Office.[13]

Similarly, the revocation of a restaurant's liquor licence was struck down by the courts in *Roncarelli v. Duplessis*[14] because the Premier of Quebec had ordered the liquor licensing board to revoke the licence in light of Mr. Roncarelli's posting bond for bailing Jehovah's Witnesses out of jail. There were two jurisdictional errors in the administrative action taken in this case. First, the legislature had not delegated power to revoke liquor licences to the premier of the province, but rather to the board. As a result, only the board could exercise that discretionary power, and it had not done so, but had rather simply ratified or implemented the order of the premier, without considering the matter itself. Secondly, the courts held that the legislation did not allow the statutory delegate, the board, to exercise its discretion to revoke licences by referring to the licensee's unrelated activities of posting bond for arrested members of a religious group. That was an irrelevant consideration or an improper motive for the exercise of the power granted to the delegate by the provincial legislature. Accordingly, the delegate's purported action was *ultra vires*, and Mr. Roncarelli was in law entitled to keep his licence (and to damages).[15]

---

12 Judicial review may also be available against certain actions taken pursuant to the Royal Prerogative (e.g., *R. v. Criminal Injuries Comp. Bd.; Ex parte Lain*, [1967] 2 Q.B. 864), and to correct breaches of the principles of natural justice committed by certain non-statutory domestic tribunals.
13 See *Re Ritchie and Edmonton*, (1980) 108 D.L.R. (3d) 694 (Alta. Q.B.).
14 [1959] S.C.R. 121.
15 Indeed, the action was for damages, not for a prerogative remedy or a declaration that the licence was still in effect.

Judicial review of administrative action can occur for the following jurisdictional defects:

(a) substantive *ultra vires*, such as building a highway when the legislature has authorized building a park;[16]

(b) exercising a discretion for an improper purpose,[17] with malice,[18] in
bad faith,[19] or by reference to irrelevant considerations,[20] as exem-
plified in the *Alberta Hotel* case[21] and in *Roncarelli v. Duplessis*
referred to above;

(c) not considering relevant matters;[22]

(d) making serious procedural errors;[23]

(e) making an error of law,[24] in certain circumstances.

The inherent right of the courts to review the legality of administrative
action almost completely depends on the application of the *ultra vires* doctrine
to examine the jurisdiction of the statutory delegate whose action has been
impugned. It must be noted, however, that the courts' right to review certain
errors of law (ground (e) above, technically called "errors of law on the face of
the record") is not necessarily jurisdictional in nature, and has been explained
by Lord Denning in *Shaw v. Northumberland Compensation Appeals Tribunal*[25]
as an important historical anomaly.

Similarly, it has sometimes been suggested that the courts' right to review
administrative proceedings for serious procedural errors (technically called
breaches of the "principles of natural justice" or the "duty to be fair") is not
jurisdictional in nature. With respect, we submit that this view of the courts'
supervisory power is historically wrong, wrong in principle and dangerous in
the face of a privative clause purporting to deprive the courts of their inherent
power to review the merits of administrative action. The better view, we
submit, is that the legislation in question incorporates the common law relating to fair procedures, and any serious deviation from fair procedure takes the
statutory delegate outside the ambit of the powers granted to him, even if he
otherwise had the power to take the particular action in question. In other
words, procedural error goes to jurisdiction, and entitles the superior courts to
review the legality of the delegate's actions.

---

16 See *Re Ritchie and Edmonton* (the "Alberta Hotel" case), *supra*, note 13.

17 *Ibid.*

18 See *Roncarelli v. Duplessis, supra*, note 14.

19 See *Campeau Corp. v. Calgary*, (1979) 7 Alta. L.R. (2d) 294 (C.A.).

20 See *Padfield v. Min. of Agriculture, Fisheries and Food*, [1968] 2 W.L.R. 924 (H.L.), and *Re
Ritchie and Edmonton, supra*, note 13.

21 *Re Ritchie and Edmonton, supra*, note 13.

22 Which may be only the reverse of considering irrelevant matters.

23 *Alliance des Professeurs Catholiques de Montréal v. Que. Lab. Rel. Bd.*, [1953] 2 S.C.R. 140;
Ridge v. Baldwin, [1964] A.C. 40 (H.L.); *Cooper v. Wandsworth Bd. of Works*, (1863) 14 C.B.
(N.S.) 180, 143 E.R. 414.

24 See the *Shaw* case, *infra*, note 30.

25 *Infra*, note 30.

The concept of jurisdiction is discussed in chapter 5, and the jurisdictional nature of a procedural error is discussed in both chapters 6 and 8.

6. Historical Development of Judicial Review of Administrative Action

Dicey observed many years ago that Britain, unlike France, had no "Administrative Law" because the ordinary courts — and not specialized administrative ones — determine the validity of governmental actions.[26] Even when made, this statement was deceptive, because English common law for centuries has provided for judicial review of the lawfulness of governmental actions, which surely puts the administration under the Rule of Law (which Dicey recognized). On the other hand, in recent years the administrative structure in common law countries has frequently included appeals from one administration to another, thereby making our system resemble the continental one much more closely than in Dicey's time. Further, at least one common law jurisdiction, Australia, has now established a specialized Administrative Law Court[27] to exercise the traditional judicial remedies for reviewing the legality of governmental actions. Still, the three central features of our system of Administrative Law would be recognized by Dicey, and remain (a) the Rule of Law (that is, the requirement for all governmental action to be expressly permitted by validly enacted laws); (b) the denial of any special status to the government merely because it *is* the government; and (c) the right of the ordinary courts to determine such questions of legality.

Where do the ordinary courts get their authority to review the lawfulness of governmental action? Nothing in the written constitutions of either the United Kingdom or Canada specifically gives the courts this important power. On the contrary, the superior courts have from time immemorial simply asserted their "inherent" jurisdiction to supervise the legality of actions taken by other officials, tribunals or delegates, which supervision was facilitated procedurally by the development of the prerogative remedies.

Historically, much of the administration of government in England was conferred on the local justices of the peace. When these officials were exercising judicial powers they were subject to the prerogative remedies (such as *certiorari, mandamus* and *habeas corpus*) issued by the superior courts. Perhaps illogically, the same prerogative remedies were used by the superior courts to control and review the administrative (as opposed to judicial) activities which Parliament delegated to these same justices of the peace. Later, the British Parliament created independent bodies (such as the Sewer Commissioners[28]) to exercise many of the administrative functions previously granted

---

26 A.V. Dicey, *Introduction to the Study of the Law of the Constitution*, 10th ed. by E.C.S. Wade (London: Macmillan Papermac, 1961).

27 See *infra*, chapter 4.

28 See, for example, *Arthur v. Yorkshire Sewer Commr.*, (1724) 8 Mod. 331, 88 E.R. 237.

to the justices of the peace, as well as a vast array of new administrative powers. Again, the superior courts simply assumed that the prerogative remedies would be available to review actions taken by these non-judicial administrators, some of whom indeed exercised precisely the same functions which had previously been performed by the justices of the peace. In time, however, the theoretical error of this convenient historical development was recognized, and the superior courts restricted the availability of judicial review (in particular *certiorari*[29]) to those administrative functions which could be characterized as being "quasi-judicial" instead of "merely administrative" in nature. Although this distinction has recently become much less important, it will be necessary to examine the different types of functions which can be delegated, in order to understand the development of modern Administrative Law.

7. Remedies and Standing

Most of Administrative Law involves applications for one of the prerogative remedies, a declaration, damages or a statutory appeal to a court or to another administrative body. Considerable attention must be given to choosing the right remedy, and to making certain that the applicant has the proper standing to apply for it. A number of jurisdictions in the Commonwealth have recently modernized the procedures for seeking judicial review.

The prerogative remedies consist of *certiorari*, prohibition, *mandamus*, *habeas corpus* and *quo warranto*. *Certiorari* is an order from the superior court compelling an inferior tribunal or other statutory delegate to render up all of the record of its proceedings to permit the superior court to determine the lawfulness thereof. If the superior court's review indicates a jurisdictional error (or, in some circumstances, some other error of law on the face of the record[30]), it will quash the proceedings of the inferior body and remit the matter back to the statutory delegate to be determined according to law. An order of prohibition is similar to *certiorari*, except that it occurs prior to the final conclusion of the proceedings by the inferior body, and prohibits it from proceeding in a manner which would take it outside its jurisdiction (or would cause it to commit some other error of law on the face of the record).

Mandamus is a command by the superior court compelling an inferior body to fulfill a statutory duty delegated to it. Thus, an order of *mandamus* can be used to compel an immigration officer to permit a Canadian citizen to enter Canada, because the citizen has that right and the officer has a corresponding duty to permit him to do so. While *mandamus* can be used to compel a delegate to comply with a statutory duty to exercise his discretion, it generally cannot be used to make the delegate exercise his discretion in a particular way (unless,

---

29 See the discussion of the development of the duty to be fair in chapter 8, *infra*.
30 *R. v. Northumberland Comp. App. Trib.; Ex parte Shaw*, [1952] 1 K.B. 338.

in the circumstances, there is only one way the discretion can lawfully be exercised: see the *Vic Restaurant* case[31]).

Habeas corpus is the most glorious prerogative remedy, with high constitutional importance going back to the Magna Carta.[32] It compels the respondent to bring the person of the applicant before the superior court in order to permit the court to determine the lawfulness of the respondent's detention of the applicant.

Quo warranto requires the respondent to demonstrate by what authority he exercises the powers of a particular statutory office. In practice, applications for *quo warranto* are rare, because alternative statutory procedures have been enacted, for example, those dealing with contested elections.[33]

A declaration[34] can be used to determine the lawfulness of an administrator's actions, or the validity of parent action. In Alberta, a statement of claim can list a declaration as all or part of the relief sought in an action, and in certain other circumstances a declaratory order can be obtained by the more summary notice of motion proceedings under Rule 410. While declaratory relief may be useful in many circumstances involving illegal administrative action, it does not itself directly coerce the respondent, but merely declares rights; neither does it quash a decision or "speaking order" of an inferior tribunal.[35] Accordingly, a declaration may not always be an effective remedy in Administrative Law.

Because governmental officials in Canada have no general immunity from legal liability for their actions, a claim for damages may succeed whenever an illegal administrative action causes harm of a kind otherwise known to the private law of property, tort or contract. Difficult questions frequently arise as to the precise type of action to take to claim redress successfully, and it may be hard to determine who is the correct party to sue.[36] Nevertheless, it is important to remember that damages were awarded in two great Administrative Law cases: *Roncarelli v. Duplessis*,[37] and *Cooper v. Wandsworth Board of Works*.[38]

In addition to these methods of obtaining what might be called "inherent judicial review", the courts are sometimes expressly granted either review or appellate powers by the legislation setting up the administrative machinery in question. For example, the Planning Act in Alberta[39] delegates the power to

---

31 *Vic Restaurant Inc. v. Montreal*, [1959] S.C.R. 58.
32 25 Edw. 1, c. 36. See R.J. Sharpe, *The Law of Habeas Corpus* (Oxford: Clarendon Press, 1976).
33 See, *e.g.*, the Local Authorities Election Act, R.S.A. 1980, c. L-27.5. Note that *quo warranto* is still sometimes used for this purpose in Quebec.
34 See Sarna, *The Law of Declaratory Judgments* (Toronto: Carswell, 1978).
35 See, *e.g. Pyx Granite Co., Ltd. v. Min. of Housing and Loc. Govt.*, [1960] A.C. 260 (H.L.).
36 Not all governmental bodies have legal status, and therefore may not be amenable to legal process, which may have to be taken against the individuals involved personally.
37 [1959] S.C.R. 121.
38 (1863) 143 E.R. 414.
39 R.S.A. 1980, c. P-9.

approve developments of land to municipal Development Appeal Boards (or in certain circumstances to the provincial Planning Appeal Board). Section 152[40] of the Act specifically gives the Court of Appeal the right to hear an appeal on any question of law or jurisdiction, providing leave to appeal has been granted by a single judge of that court. Indeed, the court is given power to make inferences from the facts before the board, and has power to confirm, vary, reverse or vacate the board's decision.[41] Such statutory rights of review or appeal are quite common, and it is important to read the legislation in question to determine their precise ambit.

Some Commonwealth jurisdictions have recently implemented reforms to the method by which courts control the legality of administrative action.

---

40 Am. 1984, c. 33, s. 8.

41 Sections 152 and 153 provide as follows:

152(1) Subject to subsection (2), on a question of law or on a question of jurisdiction, an appeal lies to the Court of Appeal from the Board or a development appeal board.

(2) An application for leave to appeal pursuant to subsection (1) shall be made
  (a) to a judge of the Court of Appeal, and
  (b) within 30 days after the issue of the order, decision, permit or approval sought to be appealed,
  and notice of the application shall be given to the Board or the development appeal board, as the case may be, and such other persons as the judge may direct.

(3) On hearing the application and the representations of those persons who are, in the opinion of the judge, affected by the application, the judge may
  (a) grant leave to appeal,
  (b) direct which persons or other bodies shall be named as respondents to the appeal,
  (c) specify the question of law or the questions of jurisdiction to be appealed, and
  (d) make any order as to the costs of the application that he considers appropriate.

(4) If an appeal is from a development appeal board, the municipal corporation shall be given notice of the application for leave to appeal and shall be a respondent to the application and, if leave is granted, a respondent to the appeal.

(5) If a decision of the Board is appealed, the Board
  (a) shall be respondent in the application and appeal, if any, and
  (b) is entitled to be represented by counsel at the application and appeal, if any.

153(1) On the hearing of the appeal
  (a) no evidence other than the evidence that was submitted to the Board or the development appeal board, as the case may be, shall be admitted, but the Court may draw any inferences
    (i) that are not inconsistent with the facts expressly found by the Board or the development appeal board as the case may be, and
    (ii) that are necessary for determining the question of law or the question of jurisdiction,
  and
  (b) the Court shall either confirm, vary, reverse or vacate the order, decision, permit or approval.

(2) In the event that the Court vacates an order, decision, permit or approval, the Court shall refer the matter back to the Board or the development appeal board, as the case may be, and the Board or the development appeal board, as the case may be, shall rehear the matter and deal with it in accordance with the opinion of the Court on the question of law or the question of jurisdiction.

(3) No member of the Board or a development appeal board is liable to costs by reason or in respect of an application for leave to appeal or an appeal under this Act.

For example, the Ontario Judicial Review Procedure Act[42] creates a new remedy called an "application for judicial review" which can be used whenever a prerogative remedy or a declaration would have been available. This reform has been widely copied in other jurisdictions, whether by statute[43] or by amendments to the rules of court (as originally in England[44]). Some reforms have also altered the court before whom such applications may be made; for example, in Ontario they are dealt with by a three member Divisional Court,[45] and in New Zealand there is now an Administrative Division of the High Court.[46] The Federal Court Act[47] in Canada has transferred virtually all applications for judicial review against federal boards, tribunals or commissions from the superior courts of the provinces to the Federal Court (except *habeas corpus*[48]). In addition, that misguided legislation sends some of these applications directly to a three-member panel of the Federal Court of Appeal, while sending others to a single judge of the Trial Division.

Finally, some reforms have increased the grounds for judicial review of administrative action beyond those recognized by the common law. For example, section 28 of the Federal Court Act specifically permits the Court of

---

42 S.O. 1971, c. 48 [now R.S.O. 1980, c. 224].
43 In the Commonwealth of Australia, see Administrative Decisions (Judicial Review) Act, 1977 (No. 59 of 1977 as amended by No. 66 of 1978 and No. 111 of 1980), which was the outcome of the *Report of the Committee of Review on Prerogative Writ Procedures* (Parliamentary Paper No. 56, 1973, the "Elliott Committee Report") and the *Report of the Commonwealth Administrative Review Committee* (Parliamentary Paper No. 144, August 1971, the "Kerr Committee Report").
   In the Australian State of Victoria, see Administrative Law Act, 1978, No. 9234, 1978 (preceded by the Victoria Statute Law Revision Committee's *Report on Appeals from Administrative Decisions*, 1968).
   In British Columbia, see the Judicial Review Procedure Act, R.S.B.C. 1979, c. 209 (first enacted in 1976), and based on recommendations of the British Columbia Law Reform Commission in *A Procedure for Judicial Review of the Actions of Statutory Agencies* (Report No. 18, 1974).
   In New Zealand, see Judicature Amendment Act, 1972, No. 130 of 1972, as amended by No. 32 of 1977, ss. 10-15 (based on recommendations in the Fourth Report of the Public and Administrative Law Reform Committee entitled *Administrative Tribunals: Constitution, Procedure and Appeals*, January 1971, on a draft statute contained in the Fifth Report, January 1972 and on the Eighth Report, September 1975). See also J.F. Northey, "An Administrative Law Division of the New Zealand Supreme Court — A Proposal for Law Reform", (1969) 7 Alta. L. Rev. 62, and J.F. Northey, "The Administrative Division of the New Zealand Supreme Court — A Postscript", (1977) 17 Alta. L. Rev. 186.
44 Order 53 of the Rules of the Supreme Court as substituted in 1977 by the Rules of the Supreme Court (Amendment No. 3) 1977, s. 1. 1977 No. 1955 and enacted subsequently in statutory form in Supreme Court Act, 1981 (U.K.), c. 54, s. 31.
45 *Supra*, note 42.
46 *Supra*, note 43.
47 R.S.C. 1970, c. 10 (2nd Supp.), s. 18.
48 *Habeas corpus* remains available only in the provincial superior courts, even against federal boards, tribunals or commissions. This can work hardship when other remedies, such as *certiorari*, are required to make *habeas corpus* effective because only the Federal Court can issue those other remedies against a federal body, thereby requiring one to go to two separate courts.

Appeal to quash any decision or order which a federal administrative body has made "on an erroneous finding of fact that it has made in a perverse or capricious manner or without regard to the material before it", as well as for any error of law whether or not it appears on the face of the record.[49] Undoubtedly, more reforms will be made in the years to come to both the procedure and the grounds for judicial review of administrative action.

Finally, one should note the existence and importance of non-judicial remedies against administrative action, even if it lies within the delegate's jurisdiction. First, the administration itself is sensitive to well-founded criticism, and may correct errors or unfair action. Secondly, statutory delegates receive their authority from legislation and are therefore responsible to the legislative body which enacted that legislation. Members of Parliament or of provincial legislative assemblies may be useful in drawing attention to unfair administrative action, particularly in light of the constitutional collective responsibility of cabinet members to the legislature for all actions taken by the various government departments. Finally, most provinces (but not the Federal Government) have created ombudsmen for the purpose of reviewing the propriety and fairness of governmental actions, even when clearly within the jurisdiction provided for by statute. Although the ombudsman's only real sanction is to report to the legislative assembly, with all of the attendant publicity which that would generate, in practice this office performs a very useful service and should not be overlooked in seeking to correct administrative errors or unfairness.[50] All of these non-judicial means of reviewing and perhaps changing administrative action are important, but lie outside the scope of this text.

8. Privative Clauses

Judicial review of illegal administrative action can effectively be abolished under our system of government. In the first place, there is no constitutional requirement in Canada that courts exist, and no constitutional guarantee of their jurisdiction.[51] Although the Canadian courts have consistently held that neither federal nor provincial legislation can prevent judicial determination of the constitutional validity of legislation itself,[52] the doctrine

---

49 See David J. Mullan, *The Federal Court Act: Administrative Law Jurisdiction* (Ottawa: Law Reform Commission of Canada, 1977). See also "Proposals to amend the Federal Court Act", by the Hon. Mark MacGuigan, Minister of Justice, 29th August 1983.

50 In Alberta, the Office of the Ombudsman is governed by the Ombudsman Act, R.S.A. 1980, c. O-7. The Ombudsman's annual reports are useful reading, and further information can be obtained from the International Ombudsman Institute located at the Law Centre, The University of Alberta, Edmonton. Although the ombudsman institution has spread widely throughout Canada, it has still not been adopted at the federal level.

51 See David Phillip Jones, "A Constitutionally Guaranteed Role for the Courts", (1979) 57 Can. Bar Rev. 669.

52 See B. Strayer, *Judicial Review of Legislation in Canada* (Toronto: University of Toronto Press, 1968), pp. 206-11; Edward McWhinney, *Judicial Review*, 4th ed. (Toronto: University of

of the Sovereignty of Parliament means that the legislative branch could oust the courts' right to review actions taken by statutory delegates. Such legislative provisions are often called "privative clauses" because they deprive the courts of their inherent jurisdiction to review the *vires* of actions taken by delegates pursuant to statute.

The effect of privative clauses can be obtained in several different ways. As discussed above, the most obvious way is for the legislation to state expressly that the administrator's action shall not be reviewed in any court. The legislation could either specifically prevent the court from issuing any of the remedies available for judicial review, or could specifically abolish the grounds for judicial review, or both. Alternatively, the legislation could extend the jurisdiction of the delegate so far that the ambit for judicial review is reduced to virtually nothing. This results from the exact but inverse relationship between the ambit of the delegate's jurisdiction and the scope of the *ultra vires* doctrine. In particular, the possibility of judicial review becomes minimal if the legislation delegates powers in very subjective terms, such as the British courts held in *Liversidge v. Anderson*[53] where the Secretary of State was given power to intern anyone whom he suspected of being an enemy alien. Short of an out-and-out malicious formation of the suspicion,[54] it would be virtually impossible for the courts to say that the delegate had transgressed the ambit of the discretionary power granted to him by the legislation.

Astonishingly, privative clauses do not always achieve their objective. In particular, the courts have consistently held that jurisdictional errors mean that no lawful decision has been taken by the delegate, so that there is nothing to be protected from judicial review by the privative clause.[55] Indeed, this view has frequently been applied to strike down breaches of natural justice which could only be done if such breaches are jurisdictional in nature and therefore incapable of being preserved by a privative clause.[56]

Toronto Press, 1969), especially chapter 4; *Amax Potash Ltd. v. Sask.*, [1977] 2 S.C.R. 576; *A.G. Can. v. Law Soc. of B.C.* (the *Jabour* case), [1982] 5 W.W.R., 289 at 306-308 (S.C.C.).

53 [1941] 3 All E.R. 338 (H.L.). The actual wording of delegation of power was in much more objective terms than the decision of their Lordships would lead one to believe, *viz*. [at p. 341]:

"If the Secretary of State has *reasonable cause* to believe any person to be of hostile origin or associations . . . and that by reason thereof it is necessary to exercise control over him, he may make an order against that person directing that he be detained". [Emphasis added.]

For an interesting postscript on the controversy caused by this case, and particularly by Lord Atkin's famous dissent, see Heuston, "*Liversidge v. Anderson* in Retrospect", (1970) 86 L.Q. Rev. 33.

54 Which would generally be very difficult to prove, particularly in a proceeding for a prerogative remedy where discovery is not available. Compare the situation in *Roncarelli v. Duplessis*, [1959] S.C.R. 121, which was an action for damages in delict (tort), where the premier's malice came out in cross-examination.

55 See, *e.g., Metro. Life Ins. Co. v. Int. Union of Operating Engineers*, [1970] S.C.R. 425; *Anisminic Ltd. v. Foreign Comp. Comm.*, [1969] 2 A.C. 147.

56 *Alliance des Professeurs Catholiques de Montréal v. Que. Lab. Rel. Bd.*, [1953] 2 S.C.R. 140; *Toronto Newspaper Guild v. Globe Printing Co.*, [1953] 2 S.C.R. 18.

The Supreme Court of Canada has recently recognized the tension created by the desirability for judicial review of administrative action and the sovereign ability of the legislative branch to enact privative clauses.[57] In the end, the "perfect" privative clause would prevent all judicial review, even on jurisdictional grounds.[58] Taken to the extreme, this suggests that the legislative branch could abolish the superior courts outright, notwithstanding the inclusion of section 96 in the Constitution Act, 1867. The solution to this problem may well put limits on the permissible content of privative clauses, thereby effectively constitutionalizing the courts' right to review the legality of administrative actions on jurisdictional grounds.[59]

9. Summary

Administrative Law deals with the legal remedies available to a person affected by administrative action. In our system the government has no special rights or powers, but derives all of its authority either from statute or from the Royal Prerogative. Much of Administrative Law involves determining the precise ambit of the powers which the Federal Parliament or provincial legislatures have granted to a particular statutory delegate. This frequently involves the principles of statutory interpretation. Similarly, the remedies generally available from the normal superior courts to correct administrative action which is *ultra vires* are subject to the doctrine of Parliamentary Sovereignty, and can be modified or abolished by validly enacted legislation. In the end, statutory construction is exceedingly important to determine precisely what the sovereign legislator has done.

In summary, virtually all of Administrative Law flows from two great principles: first, the Sovereignty of Parliament, and second, the right of the ordinary courts to determine the meaning of legislation and the corresponding lawfulness of governmental action. A consideration of these two great principles is necessary to appreciate the constitutional content of Administrative Law, and to understand the judges' reasoning processes in trying to determine whether a particular governmental action is legal or illegal.

---

57 *Crévier v. A.G. Que.*, [1981] 2 S.C.R. 220.

58 See, *e.g.*, the British Columbia Labour Code, R.S.B.C. 1979, c. 212, s. 33, which provides as follows:

> 33. The board has and shall exercise exclusive jurisdiction to determine the extent of its jurisdiction under this Act, a collective agreement or the regulations, to determine a fact or question of law necessary to establish its jurisdiction and to determine whether or in what manner it shall exercise its jurisdiction.

59 See the article referred to in note 51, *supra*.

10. Selected Bibliography

(a) The standard texts to which the reader might make reference are as follows:

Allen, *Law and Orders*, 3rd ed. (1965).

Benjafield, *Principles of Australian Administrative Law*, 4th ed. (1971).

Borrie, *Elements of Public Law*, 2nd ed. (1970).

Clarke, *Constitutional & Administrative Law* (1971).

Davis, *Administrative Law Treatise*. n.d.

de Smith, *Constitutional & Administrative Law*, 2nd ed. (1973).

de Smith, *Judicial Review of Administrative Action*, 4th ed. (1980) ed. J.M. Evans.

Evans, Janisch, Mullan and Risk, *Administrative Law Cases, Text & Materials* (1980).

Foulkes, *Introduction to Administrative Law*, 3rd ed. (1972).

Garner, *Administrative Law*, 4th ed. (1974).

Garrett, *Administrative Reform: The Next Step* (1973).

Griffith and Street, *Principles of Administrative Law*, 4th ed. (1967).

Jennings, *The Law and the Constitution*, 5th ed. (1959).

2 L.S.U.C. Special Lectures (1971).

Phillips, *Constitutional & Administrative Law*, 5th ed. (1973).

Pitblado Lectures, Manitoba Continuing Legal Education Series (1971).

Reid, *Administrative Law and Practice* (1971).

Reid and David, *Administrative Law and Practice*, 2nd ed. (1978).

Wade, *Administrative Law*, 5th ed. (1982).

Wade and Bradley, *Constitutional Law*, 8th ed. (1970).

Yardley, *Source Book of English Administrative Law*, 2nd ed. (1970).

(b) On the historical origins of judicial review:

de Smith, *Judicial Review of Administrative Action*, 4th ed. (1980), App. I, "The Prerogative Writs: Historical Origins".

Jenks, "The Prerogative Writs in English Law", (1923) 32 Yale L.J. 523.

Rubinstein, "On the Origins of Judicial Review", (1964) 1 U.B.C.L. Rev. 1.

(c) Some review articles of a general nature are:

Couture, "Introduction to Canadian Federal Administrative Law", (1972) 22 U.T.L.J. 47.

Hendry, "Some Problems in Canadian Administrative Law", (1967) 2 Ottawa L. Rev. 71.

Hogg, "The Supreme Court of Canada and Administrative Law 1949-1971", (1973) 11 Osgoode Hall L.J. 187.

McAllister, "Administrative Law", (1963) 6 Can. Bar J. 439.

Millward, "Judicial Review of Administrative Authorities in Canada", (1961) 39 Can. Bar Rev. 351.
Molot, "Annual Surveys of Canadian Law: Part 2, Administrative Law", (1969) 3 Ottawa L. Rev. 465; (1970) 4 Ottawa L. Rev. 459; (1971) 5 Ottawa L. Rev. 435; (1975) 7 Ottawa L. Rev. 515.
Morden, "Recent Developments in Administrative Law", (1967) L.S.U.C. Special Lectures 275.
Reid, "Administrative Law: Rights and Remedies", (1953) L.S.U.C. Special Lectures 1.
Rutherford, "Legislative Review of Delegated Legislation", (1969) 47 Can. Bar Rev. 352.
Scott, "Administrative Law 1923-1943", (1948) 26 Can. Bar Rev. 268.
Smillie, "Jurisdictional Review of Abuse of Discretionary Power", (1969) 47 Can. Bar Rev. 623.
Wade, "Anglo-American Administrative Law: Some Reflections", (1965) 81 L.Q. Rev. 357.
Willis, "Administrative Law in Canada", (1939) 53 Harvard L. Rev. 251.
Willis, "Administrative Law in Canada", (1961) 39 Can. Bar Rev. 251.
Willis, "Civil Rights — A Fresh Viewpoint", (1965) 13 Chitty's L.J. 224.
Willis, "Three Approaches to Administrative Law", (1935) 1 U.T.L.J. 53.

(d) Government studies:

Alberta Institute of Law Research and Reform, Report No.40, *Judicial Review of Administrative Action: Application for Judicial Review* (1984).
English Law Commission, Working Paper No. 40, *Remedies in Administrative Law* (1971).
Ontario Royal Commission: *Inquiry into Civil Rights, Report No. 1* (3 vols. 1968), especially vol. 1 and parts of vol. 3 (the "McRuer Commission").
Report of the Committee on Administrative Tribunals and Enquiries (England, 1957) (the "Franks' Committee Report").
Report of the Committee on Minister's Powers (England, 1932) (the "Donoughmore Committee").
Report of the Committee on the Organization of the Government of Ontario (1959) (the "Gordon Report").
Report of the Special Committee on Boards and Tribunals to the Legislative Assembly of Alberta (1966) (the "Clement Committee").
Royal Commission on Government Organization (5 vols., 1963) (the "Glassco Commission").
Scottish Law Commission, Memorandum No. 14, *Remedies in Administrative Law* (1970).
Third Report of Special Committee on Statutory Instruments, (1969) (the "MacGuigan Committee").

2

Constitutional Aspects of Canadian Administrative Law

1. Introduction: The Relevance of British Law

The preamble to the Constitution Act, 1867 proclaimed that Canada was to have a Constitution "similar in principle to that of the United Kingdom". It is not surprising, therefore, that much of our Constitutional and Administrative Law derives from English sources, although certain important differences arise because of our federal system of government, certain specific provisions of the Constitution Act, 1867 (such as the s. 96 problem, and the office of the

Lieutenant Governor) and the new Canadian Charter of Rights and Freedoms.[1] Because so much of Administrative Law focuses on the doctrine of Parliamentary Sovereignty, it is useful to examine the operation of this doctrine in the United Kingdom, to recognize that a modern state such as the United States can function without such a doctrine, and then to identify the extent to which the Sovereignty of Parliament has been modified in Canada. All limitations on the Sovereignty of Parliament raise the potential of constitutionally invalid law, and all administrative actions taken under such invalid laws are themselves illegal. Accordingly, the constitutional limitations on the ability to enact legislation in Canada provide an extremely important backdrop to Canadian Administrative Law.

2. The Sovereignty of Parliament in Britain

The hallmark of British Constitutional Law is the Sovereignty of Parliament, which entails a number of consequences to the operation of the legal system which has been adopted widely throughout the common law world.

(a) The British Parliament is Omnipotent

First, the British Parliament is omnipotent. There is no limitation, therefore, on the content or subject matter of an Act of the British Parliament.[2] This differs from the situation in the United States, where the Bill of Rights[3] prevents either Congress or the state legislatures from enacting law with respect to certain enumerated subjects, and from the situation in Canada after the entrenchment of the Canadian Charter of Rights and Freedoms in our Constitution in 1982.

(b) The British Parliament may not Bind Itself for the Future

Secondly, the Sovereignty of Parliament necessarily implies that Parliament may not bind itself to act in a particular way in the future. If such undertakings were enforceable, a future Parliament would not be sovereign. The better view, therefore, is that commitments by one Parliament as to how it will act in the future have no legal or constitutional force, and that a subsequent

---

1 Technically cited as Pt. I of Sched. B to the Canada Act, 1982 (U.K.) (31 Eliz. 2, c. 11); also the Constitution Act, S.C. 1982, Pt. I.

2 Does the membership of the United Kingdom in the European Common Market change the accuracy of this statement? See F.A. Trindade, "Parliamentary Sovereignty and the Primacy of European Community Law", (1972) 35 Mod. L. Rev. 375; O. Hood Phillips, "Has the 'Incoming Tide' Reached the Palace of Westminster?", (1979) 95 L.Q.Rev. 167; J.P. Warner, "The Relationship between European Community Law and the National Laws of Member States", (1977) 93 L.Q.Rev. 349; H.W.R. Wade, "Sovereignty and the European Communities", (1972) 88 L.Q.Rev. 1.

3 *I.e.*, the first ten amendments to the Constitution of the United States.

contradictory Act is nevertheless valid (although perhaps morally wrong).[4]

(c) The Courts Must Apply Acts of Parliament

Thirdly, the courts are bound to apply Acts of Parliament.[5] The courts must fulfill this duty regardless of their dislike, disapproval or disagreement with the provisions enacted by Parliament. Indeed, Parliament can pass an Act reversing any decision of any court.[6] Yet clear words are required in an Act of Parliament to override certain maxims of common law or certain methods of statutory construction applied by the courts.[7] This power of the courts to interpret the exact words used by Parliament is the fountain of Administrative Law in the United Kingdom because the only real question inevitably comes to: "Has Parliament authorized this delegate to do this action in this manner?"

(d) All Delegates Derive Their Powers from Statute or the Royal Prerogative

Fourthly, aside from a few prerogative powers of the Crown, all of the powers exercised by the executive derive from Parliament. Acts of Parliament frequently grant power to particular persons to do particular things: to make rules or regulations, to decide individual cases, to perform various duties. Because Parliament is omnipotent, it may constitutionally grant powers to various delegates to perform assorted functions, as well as impose duties on those or other persons.[8] Note that the source of the delegates' powers (or of their obligation to perform certain duties) derives from Parliament. Parliament may delegate powers or impose duties on anyone — whether or not that person is a Member of Parliament, an advisor to the Crown (such as a minister), the cabinet, a person permanently employed as a civil servant, or a perfect stranger. Whoever is the delegate, the source of his power or duty is Parliament. In particular, members of the executive (whether the cabinet, the "government" or civil servants) do not possess any inherent power due to their position or office. The only exception to this rule is the very limited ambit of the Royal Prerogative,[9] which historically permits the Crown in certain

---

4 Hood Phillips and Paul Jackson, *O. Hood Phillips' Constitutional and Administrative Law*, 6th ed. (London: Sweet & Maxwell, 1978), especially chapter 3. See also Chijioke Dike, "The Case Against Parliamentary Sovereignty", [1976] P.L. 283.

5 Hood Phillips, *ibid.*, pp. 50-54.

6 See *Burmah Oil Co. v. Lord Advocate*, [1965] A.C. 75 (H.L.).

7 J. Willis, "Statutory Interpretation in a Nutshell", (1938) 16 Can. Bar Rev. 1; and see the bibliography on this topic in G. Gall, *The Canadian Legal System*, 2nd ed. (Toronto: Carswell, 1983), pp. 268-79.

8 For the distinction between powers and duties, see W.N. Hohfeld, *Fundamental Legal Conceptions* (New Haven: Yale University Press, 1919).

9 See Hood Phillips and Paul Jackson, *supra*, note 4, chapter 14 for a discussion of the Royal Prerogative. See also George Winterton, "The Prerogative in Novel Situations", (1983) 99 L.Q. Rev. 407.

restricted circumstances to perform certain acts (such as declaring war, prohibiting entry of aliens into the realm, dismissing the government or dissolving Parliament) independently of Parliament and without its consent. Parliament, however, being sovereign, may clearly abolish any of the prerogative powers of the Crown. Failing such statutory abolition, though, the prerogative powers represent the one exception to the rule that the lawful authority for all actions taken by the executive derives from Parliament, and not from the executive itself.

(e) No Constitutional Separation of Powers in the United Kingdom

Finally, the doctrine of the Sovereignty of Parliament necessarily implies that there is no constitutional separation of powers in the United Kingdom.[10] To the extent that Acts of Parliament are "legislation" (that is, have the force of law and will be applied by the courts), Parliament may be considered to be the legislative branch of government. But it is tautological to assume that every Act of Parliament is necessarily legislative in nature. The difficulty arises when one wishes to distinguish "legislative" functions from judicial or executive ones, all of which may be contained in an Act.[11] Broadly speaking, of course, a legislative function involves making general rules or regulations; a judicial function involves settling a dispute by applying existing rules; an administrative or executive function involves carrying out the law. As will be seen later,[12] closer examination reveals great difficulty in clearly separating these three functions — as demonstrated, for example, when the concepts of quasi-judicial or discretionary functions are considered. For now, it is adequate to note that Parliament may pass any Act, whether its provisions are in substance legislative, judicial or executive in nature.[13] And all governmental powers[14] in the end derive from the authority of Parliament, whether they are legislative, judicial or executive in nature.

3. The United States: A Contrasting Model

In the United States, the written Constitution distributes governmental powers to three separate branches: legislative, executive and judicial, and

---

10 Although in fact the legislative, executive and judicial powers are largely allocated to separate entities, there is no constitutional requirement for these institutional arrangements. By convention, great independence is granted to the judicial branch in particular.

11 *E.g.*, Bills of Attainder or Acts of Indemnity.

12 See chapter 3, *infra*.

13 Similarly, there is no constitutional prohibition in the United Kingdom against one person's being a member of two or more of the legislative, judicial or executive branches of government. Indeed, by convention, all members of the cabinet (part of the executive) must be members of one of the Houses of Parliament, and the Lord Chancellor not only sits in Parliament as a member of cabinet but is also the chief judicial officer of the realm.

14 Except prerogative ones.

prohibits any overlapping between these branches.[15] Thus the President and cabinet ministers in the United States do not sit in Congress[16] and may not be judges. Congress is omnipotent within its sphere, but the independent courts can determine whether it is operating within that sphere. There is also a federal division of powers, with the courts as final arbiters of whether Congress or the state legislatures are operating within their prescribed areas of legislative competence. Thirdly, there is an entrenched Bill of Rights contained in the written Constitution[17] which prevents any state legislature or Congress from passing laws dealing with certain matters, and again, the courts are the final arbiters of what is prohibited by the Bill of Rights. Finally, the U.S. courts (like their British or Canadian counterparts) also apply certain maxims of common law and certain principles of statutory construction in determining whether various actions taken under a particular (and valid) Act of Congress or state legislature fall within the terms of that Act.[18]

4. The Canadian Model

The original Constitution of Canada was the British North America Act, 1867,[19] whose preamble provided that our Constitution should be "similar in principle to that of the United Kingdom," and which therefore makes the British model of government relevant to Administrative Law in Canada. The B.N.A. Act, however, not only created a federal system for governing Canada but contains other provisions which have important implications for Canadian Administrative Law. In addition, the incorporation and entrenchment of the Charter of Rights and Freedoms[20] in certain ways limits the legislative powers of both the Federal Parliament and the provincial legislatures. This undoubtedly makes the American model of government relevant to the future development of Canadian Administrative Law, because constitutional limitations on the power of our governments[21] to enact particular laws necessarily imply judicial review of whether such a prohibition has been breached in a specific case. All of these differences in the Canadian system of government

---

15 See arts. I, II and III of the Constitution of the United States of America.

16 Although the Vice-President has the right to preside over the Senate.

17 As the first ten amendments thereto.

18 See, *e.g., Cleary v. Cardullo's, Inc.*, 198 N.E. 2d 281 (Mass. S.C.) (1964).

19 30 & 31 Vict., c. 3; reproduced with amendments in R.S.C. 1970, App. II, now the Constitution Act, 1867.

20 *Supra*, note 1.

21 Any government, whether federal or provincial (including municipal governments, which derive their authority from provincial legislation), and whether legislative or executive in nature (as held by Cattanach J. in rejecting the Federal Government's attempt to strike out the statement of claim filed by the peace groups attacking the right of the federal cabinet under the Charter to permit testing of the Cruise missile in Alberta: see *Operation Dismantle v. R.*, [1983] 1 F.C. 429, reversed [1983] 1 F.C. 745, which was affirmed S.C.C. No. 18154, 9th May 1985 (not yet reported).

add more arrows to the citizen's quiver for attacking governmental action than would exist under British Administrative Law. Let us therefore now examine the differences between the British and Canadian models of government, and the consequences which these differences have on the application in Canada of the doctrine of absolute Parliamentary Sovereignty which we have inherited from the United Kingdom.

(a) Federalism and the Division of Legislative Powers

Unlike the United Kingdom, Canada is a federal state, so that the power to legislate is divided between the Federal Parliament, on the one hand, and the several provincial legislatures on the other. Before the Constitution Act, 1982, it might have been possible to state that between them, the Federal Parliament and a particular provincial legislature possessed in aggregate all of the sovereign powers of the British Parliament. This may not have been strictly true prior to 1982,[22] but it is certainly no longer true in light of the entrenched Charter of Rights and Freedoms under our revised Constitution.

In any event, the federal nature of Canada means that the right to legislate is split between two levels of government.[23] If the wrong level purports to enact legislation on a subject matter which is not within its responsibilities under the Constitution, that legislation is unconstitutional, that is, illegal and void.[24] The courts have the duty — and the right — to determine whether particular legislation is unconstitutional, and neither the Federal Parliament nor a provincial legislature can deprive the courts of this power.[25]

Similarly, it logically follows that neither the Federal Parliament nor a provincial legislature may attempt to enact legislation which purports to delegate powers which are not assigned to it under the Constitution. Thus, the validity of delegated legislation or of any other form of delegated powers depends upon the constitutional validity of the parent Act itself. Accordingly, the division of legislative competence under our federal system provides a

---

22 Yet, the "implied Bill of Rights theory" developed by Chief Justice Rand in the 1960's brought the accuracy of this statement into question. See, *e.g., Switzman v. Elbling and A.G. Que.,* [1957] S.C.R. 285.

23 The Constitution Act does not recognize municipal governments as one of the partners in the federal system, but rather as the creature of provincial legislatures, who delegate some of their legislative powers to municipalities.

24 *E.g.,* the attempt by the Quebec Legislature to padlock premises used for propagating communism; see *Switzman v. Elbling and A.G. Que., supra,* note 22. Although there is a presumption that all legislation is constitutionally valid, this presumption is only provisional in nature. Thus, when the courts have determined that the legislation is unconstitutional, it will be held always to have been unconstitutional. Accordingly, the better view is that such legislation is void and not voidable. See also Magnet, "Jurisdictional Fact, Constitutional Fact and the Presumption of Constitutionality", (1980) 11 Man. L.J. 21.

25 See *B.C. Power Corp. v. B.C. Elec. Co.,* (1962) 34 D.L.R. (2d) 196 at 274, and also *Laskin's Canadian Constitutional Law,* 4th ed. (Toronto: Carswell, 1973), p. 96.

fundamental departure from the British model of complete Parliamentary Sovereignty; and provides a limitation on the ability of either the Federal Parliament or a provincial legislature to delegate particular powers to the administration. Canadian Administrative Law is, therefore, correspondingly broader than its British counterpart, and overlaps to this extent into Constitutional Law. This feature of Canadian government is generally discussed fully in courses on Constitutional Law,[26] and will not be considered in any greater detail here.

(b) The Ability to Delegate

Within their respective spheres of legislative competence, both the Federal Parliament and the provincial legislatures are supreme or "sovereign".[27] Neither is the delegate of the Imperial Parliament, so that the maxim *delegatus non potest delegare* does not apply to limit the ability of either the Federal Parliament or provincial legislatures from delegating their respective powers to members of the executive government (or to anyone else). For example, in *Re Montmorency (Can.); Valin v. Langlois,*[28] the Supreme Court of Canada upheld the ability of the Federal Parliament to delegate the power to determine controverted federal elections to provincial superior courts, and the *ratio decidendi* of this case clearly validates Parliament's ability to delegate its powers. Similarly, in *Hodge v. R.*[29] the Privy Council upheld the right of a provincial legislature to delegate matters lying within its sphere of legislative competence. Accordingly, one can conclude from these two cases that each level of the legislative branch in Canada has the same power to delegate as is possessed by the British Parliament, subject only to the obvious restriction inherent in a federal system that the matter dealt with must lie within its respective sphere of legislative competence.

The delegation of powers is increasingly necessary in the modern state where governments control so vast a segment of human activity. It would be virtually impossible for the Federal Parliament or a provincial legislature to spell out in each Act all of the detailed rules applicable to every situation, particularly if these rules are technical or likely to change rapidly. Similarly, it may not be possible to deal with every situation in terms of *rules*, and it may be desirable to delegate to a particular person the power to exercise his discretion to determine a matter perhaps within the broad outlines of policy set down by statute. In any event, virtually all of Administrative Law deals with determining the nature and limits of powers delegated for whatever reason by the legislative branch to someone else.

---

26 See *Laskin's Canadian Constitutional Law*, *supra*, note 25; and Peter W. Hogg, *Constitutional Law of Canada* (Toronto: Carswell, 1977).

27 Although one speaks about parliamentary "sovereignty", that word has other connotations generally reserved for members of the international community.

28 (1879) 3 S.C.R. 1.

29 (1883) 9 App. Cas. 117 (P.C.).

(c) Delegation, But Not Abdication

Although the Federal Parliament and the provincial legislatures may delegate their powers, they may not abdicate their legislative functions, nor efface themselves. This limitation on the ability to delegate is inherent in the doctrine of the Sovereignty of Parliament itself: the sovereign may not abolish itself; nor may it create another sovereign. However, it is extremely difficult to draw the line between proper delegation and improper abdication of legislative powers, and the courts appear to lean in favour of the former. Nevertheless, the general lack of success in applying this principle to strike down legislation does not detract from the extreme importance in Constitutional Law of having some idea of which matters (such as the imposition of taxes) should be dealt with by the legislators themselves and not be delegated to others. Indeed, there is considerable current concern about the volume and great breadth of delegated powers which have been authorized by all levels of the legislative branch. If Parliament and the legislatures are not to become mere formalities delegating all of their real powers to the executive (who generally lead the political party which controls a majority in the legislative body), some attempt must be made to determine the proper limits on delegation. The theoretical existence of such limits has been recognized in the cases. Even though it has seldom been applied in practice, this doctrine does provide one (perhaps theoretical) limitation on power granted to the administration.

Before considering the cases, it is important to re-emphasize that not all delegations constitute an improper abdication of Parliament's power. As the Privy Council said in *Hodge v. R.*:[30]

> It was argued at the Bar that a legislature committing important regulations to agents or delegates effaces itself. That is not so. It retains its powers intact, and can, whenever it pleases, destroy the agency it has created and set up another, or take the matter directly into his own hands. How far it shall seek the aid of subordinate agencies, and how long it shall continue them, are matters for each legislature, and not for Courts of Law, to decide.

(i) Cases dealing with provincial delegation

Curiously, the prohibition against abdication has particularly arisen in a number of cases where *provincial* legislation has been struck down by the courts, although the *ratios* of these cases should apply equally to the Federal Parliament. In *Re Initiative and Referendum Act*,[31] the Privy Council indicated that the courts might indeed strike down an Act if the powers delegated

---

30 *Ibid.*, at p. 132.
31 (1919) 48 D.L.R. 18 (P.C.).

therein were so broad as to constitute an abdication of a provincial legislature's powers. In that case, the legislation[32] provided a method by which the
electors of the province could directly either institute or repeal legislation
themselves, without necessarily involving the provincial legislature. Although
the Privy Council disposed of the case on the basis that the legislation unconstitutionally interfered with the office of the Lieutenant Governor, Viscount
Haldane's *obiter dicta* specifically recognized the existence of the doctrine
against abdication when he noted that the ability of a provincial legislature to
delegate power does not mean "that it can create and endow with its own
capacity a new legislative power [or institution] not created by the [B.N.A. or
Constitution] Act to which it owes its own existence".[33]

Similarly, in *Credit Foncier Franco-Can. v. Ross and A.G. Alta.; Netherlands Invt. Co. of Can. v. Fife and A.G. Alta.*,[34] Chief Justice Harvey of the
Appellate Division of the Supreme Court of Alberta indicated that it might be
an unconstitutional abdication for the provincial legislature to delegate to the
Lieutenant Governor in Council the ability to determine which particular
debts were governed by the Reduction and Settlement of Debts Act.[35] Again,
while the legislation was in fact struck down because it interfered with the
functions of the Lieutenant Governor, and also because it trenched on federal
legislative powers with respect to bankruptcy and interest, Chief Justice
Harvey did note[36] that the legislature could not constitutionally abdicate its
legislative power to anyone else.[37]

It is quite common for both the Federal Parliament and the provincial
legislatures to grant very broad discretionary powers to their delegates. In
Canada, the delegation almost invariably goes either to the Governor in
Council or to the Lieutenant Governor in Council, and not to a particular
minister, which is the general practice in the United Kingdom. Short of an out-
and-out abolition of the legislative branch itself, it is probably beyond argument that very broad delegations are lawful.

(ii) Cases dealing with federal legislation

Nevertheless, wherever the frontier between valid delegation and invalid
abdication is located, this rule logically ought to apply identically to the

---

32 S.M. 1916, c. 59.
33 *Supra*, note 31 at p. 25.
34 [1937] 3 D.L.R. 365 (Alta. C.A.).
35 S.A. 1936 (2nd Sess.) c. 2.
36 *Supra*, note 34 at p. 368.
37 Note, however, that His Lordship went so far as to suggest that: "If there could be legislation
   by Orders in Council or in some other way than by Act of the Legislature there would be no
   power reserved in the Governor-General to disallow it". (*ibid.*, p. 369). It is now accepted that
   all delegated legislation is legislation (see *A.G. Que. v. Blaikie*; *A.G. Que. v. Laurier*, [1981] 1
   S.C.R. 312), and there is now no real argument that delegated legislation —whether by Order

Federal Parliament as well as to the provincial legislatures. Although it appears that no federal legislation has ever been struck down for this reason, the principle prohibiting abdication has been considered in four important federal cases in the federal context, some of which may be explained by the wartime context in which they arose.

In *Re Gray (Grey)*,[38] one of the issues involved the ability of the Federal Parliament to delegate to the cabinet the power to amend other Acts of Parliament. This, surely, is a very broad power to legislate. As Fitzpatrick C.J.C. said:[39]

> The practice of authorizing administrative bodies to make regulations to carry out the object of an Act, instead of setting out all the details in the Act itself, is well-known and its legality is unquestioned. But it is said that the power to make such regulations could not constitutionally be granted to such an extent as to enable the express provisions of a statute to be amended or repealed; that under the constitution parliament alone is to make laws, the Governor-in-council to execute them, and the court to interpret them; that it follows that no one of these fundamental branches of government can constitutionally either delegate or accept the functions of any other branch.

> In view of *Rex v. Halliday*, [1917] A.C. 260, I do not think this broad proposition can be maintained. Parliament cannot, indeed, abdicate its functions, but within reasonable limits at any rate it can delegate its powers to the executive government. Such powers must necessarily be subject to determination at any time by parliament, and needless to say the acts of the executive, under its delegated authority, must fall within the ambit of the legislative pronouncement by which its authority is measured. . . .

> There are obvious objections of a political character to the practice of executive legislation in this country because of local conditions. But these objections should have been urged when the regulations were submitted to parliament for its approval, or better still when the War Measures Act was being discussed. Parliament was the delegating authority, and it was for that body to put any limitations on the power conferred upon the executive.

In *Reference Re Regulations in Relation to Chemicals*,[40] the question again arose whether Parliament could lawfully delegate such vast powers to

---

in Council or otherwise — must necessarily by definition constitute an improper abdication by the legislature of its legislative powers, even if it could not be disallowed (if that power is ever used again).

38 (1918) 42 D.L.R. 1 (S.C.C.).
39 *Ibid.*, pp. 2-3, 5.
40 [1943] 1 D.L.R. 248 (S.C.C.).

the Governor in Council. Although the Supreme Court of Canada upheld the validity of the particular delegation in question, Duff C.J.C. clearly stated that "not . . . every matter within the jurisdiction of the Parliament of Canada, even in ordinary times, could be validly committed by Parliament to the Executive for legislative action in the case of an emergency".[41] His Lordship went on to say that ". . . the War Measures Act does not, of course, attempt to transform the Executive Government into a Legislature, in the sense in which the Parliament of Canada and the Legislatures of the Provinces are Legislatures".[42]

Both of these are wartime cases, and the necessities of such an emergency may require the courts to uphold broader delegation of legislative powers to the executive than might otherwise be the case: in effect to roll back the frontier of illegal abdication. Nevertheless, it is useful to note the limitations which the courts have indicated separate lawful delegation from the unlawful abdication of legislative power, even in wartime: (1) the delegation must be reasonably limited; (2) the legislative branch must always be able to terminate the delegate's authority and thereby resume its own legislative power; and (3) the doctrine of *ultra vires* must apply to permit the courts to determine the lawfulness of the delegate's actions. In summary, the ability of Parliament or the legislature to supervise or review the delegate's actions may tip the scales in favour of validating the delegation.

In a peacetime context, the Appeal Side of the Court of Queen's Bench of Quebec held in *R. v. Picard; Ex parte Int. Longshoreman's Assn., Loc. 375*[43] that the Federal Parliament had not abdicated its powers by providing that:

> . . . each collective agreement to which this Act applies shall be deemed to be amended by the incorporation therein of the conclusions [set forth in the Picard Commission's] report, with respect to each of the following matters concerning which [an] inquiry is to be made by [the Commission].[44]

Note that here the Federal Parliament was not merely incorporating into legislation the recommendations of a report *which had already been made*. On the contrary, Parliament constituted a commission of inquiry, gave it *carte blanche ex ante* to regulate the longshoremen's strike and purported to incorporate into the legislation a report which had not yet been written.

A similar problem arose tangentially in *Reference Re Proclamation of Section 16 of the Criminal Law Amendment Act, 1968-69.*[45] Section 16 of that Act required drivers whom the police suspected of being impaired to breathe

---

41 *Ibid.*, p. 253.
42 *Ibid.*, p. 256.
43 (1968) 65 D.L.R. (2d) 658.
44 *Ibid.*, p. 661, quoting the St. Lawrence Ports Working Conditions Act, S.C. 1966-67, c. 49.
45 (1970) 10 D.L.R. (3d) 699.

into a breathalyzer. It also required the policeman to provide the suspected driver with a sample of his breath which the driver could have had analyzed himself. However, no satisfactory and economical container had been developed to hold the driver's own sample. Section 120 of the Act provided that:[46]

> 120 This Act *or any of the provisions of this Act* shall come into force on a day or days to be fixed by proclamation.

The Governor General proclaimed that part of section 16 which required a driver to blow into the breathalyzer; he did not proclaim the requirement for the police officer to provide such a driver with a sample for the driver's own analysis. The question before the court was whether Parliament had, in fact, granted the Governor in Council power to proclaim *part* of a section. To a large extent, the answer depended upon the proper meaning to be attached to the word "provisions" used in section 120. If "provisions" meant any section, subsection, or paragraph, then the Governor General's proclamation was valid; otherwise, it was *ultra vires*.[47] The majority of the Supreme Court of Canada upheld the validity of this delegation to the executive, and dealt with the problem as a strict matter of statutory construction, even though the whole import of section 16 as enacted was changed by the action of Parliament's delegate. Indeed, Laskin J. (as he then was) specifically stated[48] that there was no "constitutional" issue in question in this case, obviously using the word "constitutional" to refer only to the division of legislative powers contained under sections 91 and 92 of the Constitution Act, 1867, and not in the broader sense to refer to those rules and conventions similar in principle to the Constitution of the United Kingdom. With respect, it would appear to be dangerous to assume that this case stands for the proposition that there are no limits on the ability of the Federal Parliament to delegate (or abdicate) its powers.

Indeed, it is important to note that Martland J. dissented[49] because he construed "provision" in such a way that the Governor in Council could not proclaim only part of the relevant section. Although the technical *ratio decidendi* of this case focuses upon the proper interpretation to be given to the word "provision" and therefore deals only with the question whether the delegate's actions were *ultra vires* the proclamation power contained in section 120, it does seem clear that at least Martland J. recognized the broader concern that there are some limits to the ability of Parliament itself to delegate powers to the executive to make autonomous laws, apart altogether from the question of whether the delegate's actions are *intra vires* the power pur-

---

46 S.C. 1968-69, c. 38. Emphasis added.
47 One might ask how the Governor General's proclamation power here differs from the Lieutenant Governor in Council's power in the *Credit Foncier* case, *supra*, note 34.
48 *Supra*, note 45, at p. 717.
49 *Ibid.*, at p. 708.

portedly delegated to him. In particular, if Parliament had expressly said that the executive could proclaim any provision of the Criminal Law Amendment Act, even if the proclamation changed the meaning of the entire Act as passed by Parliament, Martland J. seemed to indicate that that might have been unconstitutional (in the broader British sense of the word).

The same division in judicial philosophy was also apparent in the 1981 Constitutional Reference[50] to the Supreme Court of Canada. That case involved the ability of the Federal Parliament to pass a resolution asking the British Parliament to amend the British North America Act, 1867 without the consent of all (or any) of the provincial legislatures. The majority[51] of the court held that such a resolution breached constitutional conventions, but was not illegal. The minority,[52] however, held that it would be illegal for the Federal Parliament to take action which would have the effect of unilaterally altering its position with respect to the provincial legislatures.

Note that the minority judgments in both of these last two cases clearly indicate that there are constitutional limitations on the type of laws which can be enacted by either level of the legislative branch in Canada. The prohibition against abdicating their sovereign legislative powers is one such constitutional limitation. Any action taken by a person to whom the legislative branch has unconstitutionally abdicated its powers must be as illegal as the abdication itself, and therefore is subject to judicial review in Administrative Law on this ground. Although few examples can be found in the cases where the no-abdication principle has been applied to strike down illegal delegation and actions taken pursuant thereto, this ground for questioning the validity of legislation should not be forgotten by the administrative lawyer.

(d) A Provincial Legislature May Not Interfere with the Office of the Lieutenant Governor

Section 92(1) of the Constitution Act, 1867 prevents a provincial legislature from amending the constitution of the province in any manner which would affect the office of the Lieutenant Governor, who is appointed by the federal Governor in Council. This provision in the Constitution Act has occasionally been used by the courts to strike down various attempts by provincial legislatures to delegate their powers.

Indeed, it was the *ratio decidendi* of the Privy Council's judgment in *Re The Initiative and Referendum Act*,[53] referred to above:

> The references their Lordships have already made to the character of the office of Lieutenant-Governor, and to his position

---

50 *A.G. Man. v. A.G. Can.; A.G. Can. v. A.G. Nfld.; A.G. Que. v. A.G. Can.; A.G. Can. v. A.G. Que.*, [1981] 1 S.C.R. 753.

51 Laskin C.J.C., Dickson, Beetz, Estey, McIntyre, Chouinard and Lamer JJ.

52 Martland and Ritchie JJ.

53 (1919) 48 D.L.R. 18 at 23-25.

as directly representing the Sovereign in the Province, renders natural the exclusion of his office from the power conferred on the Provincial Legislature to amend the constitution of the Province. The analogy of the British constitution is that on which the entire scheme is founded, and that analogy points to the impropriety, in the absence of clear and unmistakable language, of construing s. 92 as permitting the abrogation of any power which the Crown possesses through a person who directly represents it. For when the Lieutenant-Governor gives to or withholds his assent from a Bill passed by the Legislature of the Province, it is in contemplation of law the Sovereign that so gives or withholds assent. . . . It follows that if the *Initiative and Referendum Act* has purported to alter the position of the Lieutenant-Governor in these respects, this Act was insofar *ultra vires*.

Their Lordships are of opinion that the language of the Act cannot be construed otherwise than as intended seriously to affect the position of the Lieutenant-Governor as an integral part of the Legislature, and to detract from rights which are important in the legal theory of that position. For if the Act is valid it compels him to submit a proposed law to a body of voters totally distinct from the Legislature of which he is the constitutional head, and renders him powerless to prevent its becoming an actual law if approved by a majority of these voters. . . . S[ection] 11 of the Initiative and Referendum Act is not less difficult to reconcile with the rights of the Lieutenant-Governor. It provides that when a proposal for repeal of some law has been approved by the majority of the electors voting, that law is automatically to be deemed repealed at the end of 30 days after the Clerk of the Executive Council shall have published in the "Manitoba Gazette" a statement of the result of the vote. Thus the Lieutenant-Governor appears to be wholly excluded from the new legislative authority.

These considerations are sufficient to establish the *ultra vires* character of the Act.

Similarly, in *Credit Foncier v. Ross*,[54] section 12 of the Alberta Debt Reduction Act gave the Lieutenant Governor in Council the power to declare that the Act did not apply to certain kinds of debts. Harvey C.J.A. held this to be an unconstitutional provincial interference with the office of the Lieutenant Governor:

No doubt the Lieutenant-Governor is an integral part of the Legislature but his function is not to initiate or to enact legislation but merely to authorize the introduction to the Legislative Assembly

---

54 [1937] 3 D.L.R. 365 (Alta. C.A.).

of certain classes of legislation and to assent to or withhold assent from legislation proposed by the Legislative Assembly. What is intended by s. 12 is to confer a quite different function from any of those recognized by the Constitution. . . . *This case is different* [from the *Initiative and Referendum* case] *only in that it adds to rather than subtracts from the Lieutenant-Governor's functions. That difference is in my opinion of no importance.* In Lefroy's Canada's Federal System, p. 387, is a note giving the opinion of Sir John Thompson, Minister of Justice, in pursuance of which an Act of the Quebec Legislature declaring the Lieutenant-Governor a corporation sole was disallowed. His opinion was that "It is immaterial whether a Legislature by an Act seeks to add to or take from the rights, powers or authorities which by virtue of his office a Lieutenant-Governor exercises, in either case it is legislation respecting his office."[55]

Notice, however, the manner in which the impugned Alberta Act affected the powers of the Lieutenant Governor: he and his council were delegated the power[56] to determine the debts to which the Act applied. This additional delegated power differed completely from the situation in the Manitoba Act, which purported to permit laws to be made *without* the Lieutenant Governor's assent. It is submitted that Harvey C.J.A. incorrectly ignores this difference. In the first place, the delegation would apparently have been valid if the legislature had granted the power to someone other than the Lieutenant Governor, say to a particular named minister. Such a limitation on the ability of a provincial legislature to delegate is untenable today, particularly in light of the general practice in Canada to delegate powers to the Lieutenant Governor in council provincially and to the Governor in Council federally. There appears to be no other case where the courts have found such delegations to the Crown to be an unconstitutional interference with the office of the Lieutenant Governor, and we submit that this practice is too strongly entrenched now to be challenged. Indeed, in *Shannon v. Lower Mainland Dairy Products Board*,[57] Lord Atkin said:

> The third objection is that it is not within the power of the Provincial Legislature to delegate so-called legislative powers to the Lieutenant-Governor in Council, or to give him powers of further delegation. This objection appears to their Lordships subversive of the rights which the Provincial Legislature enjoys while dealing with matters falling within the classes of subjects in relation to which the constitution has granted legislative powers. Within its appointed sphere the Provincial Legislature is as supreme as any other

---

55 *Ibid.*, at p. 368.
56 Under the Act, to which he gave Royal Assent.
57 [1938] A.C. 708 at 722 (P.C.).

Parliament; and it is unnecessary to try to enumerate the innumerable occasions on which the Legislatures, Provincial, Dominion and Imperial, have entrusted various persons and bodies with similar powers to those contained in this Act.

Accordingly, short of an attempt by a provincial legislature to abolish or restrict the traditional rights of the Lieutenant Governor, it is unlikely that the courts will interfere with delegations made to the Lieutenant Governor personally or in Council.[58]

(e) No Interdelegation

Parliament may not delegate its legislative powers to the legislature of a province, and the reverse is also prohibited. In *Attorney General of Nova Scotia v. Attorney General of Canada*,[59] it was held that such a delegation was invalid because it would permit a readjustment of the respective spheres of legislative authority, contrary to the essentially federal nature of Canada.

Nothing, however, prohibits the Federal Parliament from delegating powers to a person named by a provincial legislature. That person then becomes the delegate of the Federal Parliament when he is exercising the powers granted to him by Parliament, and remains the legislature's delegate when exercising the powers granted to him by the legislature. The legality of this delegation was established in *Prince Edward Island Potato Marketing Board v. H.B. Willis Inc. and Attorney General of Canada*,[60] and provides a very useful method for dealing with a problem which transcends federal and provincial legislative competence. Such a device will also permit a provincial legislature to delegate powers to a person nominated by the Federal Parliament.[61]

(f) The Section 96 Problem

Section 96 of the Constitution Act, 1867, requires the federal Governor in Council to appoint all superior, district and county court judges.[62] This effec-

---

58 For more on this subject, see Saywell, *The Office of the Lieutenant-Governor* (Toronto: University of Toronto Press, 1957), especially chapter 8.
59 [1951] S.C.R. 31.
60 [1952] 2 S.C.R. 392.
61 See G.V. La Forest's article on "Delegation of Legislative Power in Canada", (1975) 21 McGill L.J. 131.
62 See the discussion paper by Hon. Mark MacGuigan entitled "The Constitution of Canada: A Suggested Amendment Relating to Provincial Administrative Tribunals", August 1983, which proposes a constitutional amendment to change section 96 by adding section 96B:

> 96B(1) Notwithstanding section 96, the Legislature of each Province may confer on any tribunal, board, commission or authority, other than a court, established pursuant to the laws of the Province, concurrent or exclusive jurisdiction in respect of any matter within the legislative authority of the Province.

tively limits the ability of either a provincial legislature or the Federal Parliament to delegate to other persons the powers which properly belong to a superior court. Thus, for example, while a provincial legislature can constitutionally establish an administrative board or body which exercises the powers or functions of a superior court, it cannot appoint the members of such an administrative body. Note that the effect of section 96 applies to federal as well as provincial boards: if they constitute superior courts, only the Governor in Council (and not even Parliament itself) may appoint the persons who exercise these powers. In fact, however, almost all federal appointees are coincidentally named by the Governor in Council, and it is therefore unlikely, as a matter of practice, that section 96 will be invoked against a federal board or official.

If a person exercising the powers of a superior court has not been correctly appointed under section 96, his actions are complete nullities. Section 96 therefore provides a particularly fertile means for attacking the validity of actions taken by a provincial delegate.

What constitutes a "superior, district or county court" for the purposes of section 96? Clearly, the phrase includes the courts having those names which were in existence at Confederation in 1867. However, merely because a provincial legislature delegates powers to a body which is *not* called a superior, district or county court does not necessarily prevent its offending section 96. The question is, do the impugned functions belong to such a court? The jurisprudence appears to lay down two tests for answering this question. On the one hand, section 96 has been interpreted historically: were the impugned powers exercised by a superior, district or county court at Confederation? Thus, in *Seminary of Chicoutimi v. Attorney General of Quebec*,[63] the Supreme Court of Canada struck down an attempt by the Legislature of Quebec to confer jurisdiction on provincially appointed judges to determine whether municipal by-laws were discriminatory, because this power had in fact been exercised at Confederation by the Circuit Court (a division of the Superior Court which no longer exists).

On the other hand, the courts have sometimes applied a functional test to determine whether a particular delegation contravenes section 96. Thus, in *Labour Relations Board of Saskatchewan v. John East Iron Works Ltd.*,[64] the Privy Council upheld the validity of provincial appointments to the board, even though it clearly exercised certain judicial functions. Thus, it is possible to assert that not all judicial functions are necessarily only exercised by superior, district or county courts, and thus the characterization of a function

---

(2) Any decision of a tribunal, board, commission or authority on which any jurisdiction of a superior court is conferred under subsection (1) is subject to review by a superior court of the Province for want or excess of jurisdiction.

63 [1973] S.C.R. 681.
64 [1948] 4 D.L.R. 673 (P.C.).

as judicial is a necessary, but not a sufficient factor for a particular appointment to run afoul of section 96. In determining whether the judicial power of the Labour Relations Board corresponded to that exercised by superior courts, Lord Simonds made five observations:[65] (a) that the board created rights while a superior court merely applies already existing law; (b) that the board could appeal in its own name, while a superior court cannot; (c) that the board could investigate matters on its own initiative, while a superior court must wait for an interested party to commence an action; (d) that membership in the board was representative of both management and labour, while a court is independent of the parties before it; and (e) that there was no reason to require members of the board to be members of the Bar, while judges are required so to have been. The *John East Ironworks* case does not indicate, however, how many of these five aspects must exist before the board would constitute a superior court within the meaning of section 96, or whether other *indicia* are also important in making this determination. In the recent *Residential Tenancies* case,[66] Dickson J. (as he then was) re-examined this problem in light of the Supreme Court's decisions in the *Tomko*,[67] *Mississauga*[68] and *Farrah*[69] cases:

> It is no longer sufficient simply to examine the particular power or function of a tribunal and ask whether this power or function was once exercised by s. 96 courts. This would be examining the power or function in a "detached" manner, contrary to the reasoning in *Tomko*. What must be considered is the "context" in which this power is exercised. *Tomko* leads to the following result: it is possible for administrative tribunals to exercise power and jurisdiction which once were exercised by the s. 96 courts. It will all depend on the context of the exercise of the power. It may be that the impugned "judicial powers" are merely subsidiary or ancillary to general administrative functions assigned to the tribunal (*John East; Tomko*) or the powers may be necessarily incidental to the achievement of a broader policy goal of the legislature (*Mississauga*). In such a situation, the grant of judicial power to provincial appointees is valid. *The scheme is only invalid when the adjudicative function is a sole or central function of the tribunal* (Farrah) *so that the tribunal can be said to be operating "like a s. 96 court".*

Whatever the precise test for determining what constitutes a superior court, section 96 has particular importance in Administrative Law for two

---

65 *Ibid.*, at p. 682.
66 *Re Residential Tenancies Act of Ont.*, [1981] 1 S.C.R. 714 at 735-36, emphasis added.
67 *Tomko v. Lab. Rel. Bd. (N.S.)*, [1977] 1 S.C.R. 112.
68 *Mississauga v. Peel*, (1980) 97 D.L.R. (3d) 439.
69 *A.G. Que. v. Farrah*, [1978] 2 S.C.R. 638.

reasons. First, it may prevent an attempt by the legislative branch to delegate certain judicial powers to an administrative tribunal, thereby retaining the historically important distinction between "judicial" and "administrative" matters which has been eroded in another context by the new "duty to be fair".[70] Secondly, because one of the hallmarks of a superior court is its inherent power to determine the jurisdiction of statutory (or "inferior") tribunals, any attempt by the legislative branch to grant such a supervisory power (as opposed to an administrative appeal) to an administrative agency may well convert it into a superior court to which section 96 applies. Indeed, this latter proposition can be used to argue that a statutory provision (or "privative clause") which purports to oust the ordinary courts' inherent power to review a decision of an administrative tribunal effectively gives that tribunal power to determine its own jurisdiction, and thus makes that tribunal into a superior court whose members must be appointed in accordance with section 96. This argument can be used either to strike down the privative clause or to strike down every action taken by the administrative tribunal because its members have not been appointed correctly. In theory, the latter view appears to be better, because there is no doubt that the legislative branch could lawfully (i) enact a stringent privative clause provided (ii) the members of the administrative tribunal are appointed by the federal Governor in Council under section 96. Thus, the privative clause would appear to be valid; only the appointment of the delegates could be questioned.

The Supreme Court of Canada has recently considered this argument about the constitutional importance of section 96 for determining the validity of privative clauses. In *Crévier v. Attorney General of Quebec*,[71] sections 194 and 195 of the Professional Code of Quebec[72] purported to preclude the availability of any of the remedies normally available from the superior court for the purpose of questioning the validity of any action taken by a wide range of officials and tribunals to whom various powers had been granted under the Code. Apart altogether from the question whether any of the provincially appointed officials and tribunals were themselves exercising the power of superior courts contrary to section 96 of the Constitution Act,[73] Laskin C.J.C. held that the mere attempt to deprive the superior courts of their traditional supervisory function over the jurisdiction of these inferior delegates itself contravenes the spirit of section 96. In other words, the Supreme Court of Canada has recognized that our Constitution protects some of the Administrative Law jurisdiction of the superior courts against privative clauses, and to that extent thereby limits the legislative sovereignty of both Parliament and the legislatures. As Laskin C.J.C. said:[74]

---

70 See chapter 8, *infra*.
71 [1981] 2 S.C.R. 220.
72 R.S.Q. 1977, c. C-26.
73 *Supra*, note 71, at p. 230.
74 *Ibid.*, at p. 236.

It is true that this is the first time that this Court has declared unequivocally that a provincially constituted statutory tribunal cannot constitutionally be immunized from review of decisions on questions of jurisdiction. In my opinion, this limitation, arising by virtue of s. 96, stands on the same footing as the well-accepted limitation on the power of provincial statutory tribunals to make unreviewable determinations of constitutionality. There may be differences of opinion as to what are questions of jurisdiction but, in my lexicon, they rise above and are different from errors of law, whether involving statutory construction or evidentiary matters or other matters. It is now unquestioned that privative clauses may, when properly framed, effectively oust judicial review on question of law and, indeed, on other issues not touching jurisdiction. However, given that s. 96 is in the *British North America Act* and that it would make a mockery of it to treat it in non-functional formal terms as a mere appointing power, I can think of nothing that is more the hallmark of a superior court than the vesting of power in a provincial statutory tribunal to determine the limits of its jurisdiction without appeal or other review.

Distinguishing matters which go to jurisdiction — as opposed to those which lie within it[75] — may be exceedingly difficult, and will be considered in more detail in a later chapter.[76] Nevertheless, it is clear that the Supreme Court of Canada has recently expanded and reinforced the importance of section 96 in Administrative Law, and struck a blow against the unfettered ability of the legislative branch to enact broad privative clauses ousting judicial review of administrative actions.

(g) The Canadian Charter of Rights and Freedoms

Prior to the enactment of the Canadian Charter of Rights and Freedoms

---

75 Note the following sources quoted by Laskin C.J.C., *ibid*, at p. 237:

There has been academic concern with the permitted scope of privative clauses referable to determinations of provincial adjudicative agencies. Opinion has varied from a position that even errors of law cannot validly be immunized from review (see J.N. Lyon, "Comment" (1971), 49 Can. Bar Rev. 365), to a position that at least jurisdictional review is constitutionally guaranteed (see W.R. Lederman, "The Independence of the Judiciary" (1956), 34 Can. Bar Rev. 1139, at p. 1174) to a position that jurisdictional determinations may, constitutionally, also be denied judicial review (see P.W. Hogg, "Is Judicial Review of Administrative Action Guaranteed by the British North America Act?" (1976), 54 Can. Bar Rev. 716, and see also Dussault, *Le contrôle judiciare de l'administration au Québec* (1969), especially at pp. 110-13).

See also Mullan, "The Uncertain Constitutional Position of Canada's Administrative Tribunals", (1982) 14 Ottawa L.Rev. 239, as well as *A. G. Que. v. Farrah, supra*, note 69, and *Tomko v. Lab. Rel. Bd (N.S.), supra*, note 67.

76 See chapter 10, *infra*.

on 17th April 1982, the Canadian Constitution recognized no restriction[77] on the content of laws which could be enacted by either the Federal Parliament or the provincial legislatures, provided that the law-making body was exercising its legislative competence according to the division of powers contained principally in sections 91 and 92 of the Constitution Act, 1867. This state of affairs resulted from the doctrine of the Sovereignty of Parliament inherited from the United Kingdom, and stood in contrast with the prohibitions contained in the Constitution of the United States against the enactment of certain kinds of laws (such as those which abridge freedom of speech or religion). The effect of the Charter is to limit the right of both the Federal Parliament and the provincial legislatures to enact certain types of legislation. Accordingly, any governmental action — whether pursuant to statute, regulation or prerogative[78] — which contravenes the Charter will be void.[79] The Charter therefore provides one further weapon in Canadian Administrative Law for attacking governmental actions.[80]

Further, one may speculate that the wording of section 7 of the Charter may extend the procedural requirements (called the "principles of natural justice" or the "duty to be fair")[81] which Administrative Law imposes on delegates to whom the legislative branch has granted power. Section 7 provides as follows:

> 7. Everyone has the right to life, liberty and security of the person and the right not to be deprived thereof *except in accordance with the principles of fundamental justice.*[82]

This phrase is borrowed from the earlier Canadian Bill of Rights[83] and undoubtedly was intended to elevate the procedural aspects of natural justice to constitutional status in any matters dealing with life, liberty and the security of the person. Indeed, one of the federal government's legal advisors so testified to the joint parliamentary committee during its hearing on the constitutional package.[84] Nevertheless, there are at least two reasons to suspect that the reference in section 7 to the "principles of fundamental justice" may ripen into a substantive (as opposed to procedural) limitation on both the content of

---

77 Except the "implied Bill of Rights theory", discussed *supra*, note 22.

78 See Cattanach J.'s decision with respect to the Cruise missile in *Operation Dismantle v. R.*, [1983] 1 F.C. 429 (T.D.), referred to in note 21, *supra*.

79 Notwithstanding the decision in the *Gandam* case (*Gandam v. Min. of Employment and Immigration*, [1982] 6 W.W.R.. 378 (Sask. Q.B.)).

80 See H.N. Janisch, "Beyond Jurisdiction: Judicial Review and the Charter of Rights", in *Judicial Review of Administrative Rulings*, (Montreal: Canadian Institute for the Administration of Justice, Les editions Yvon Blais Inc., 1983), pp. 273-79.

81 See chapter 8, *infra*.

82 Emphasis added.

83 R.S.C. 1970, App. III.

84 Dr. B.L. Strayer, Assistant Deputy Minister of Justice, in *Minutes of Proceedings and Evidence* of the *Special Joint Committee on the Constitution of Canada*, 1980-81, at pp. 46:32 and 46:36.

parent legislation which can be enacted, as well as to provide a method to scrutinize the merits of a delegate's decision.

First, the very words used in section 7 are not restricted to procedural matters, but are equally capable of referring to substantive circumstances in which it would be fundamentally "unjust" to deprive someone of life, liberty or security of the person. Indeed, to insist upon restricting this phrase to procedural questions would largely nullify the institutional protection accorded to life, liberty and the security of the person, because it would imply that all of these could be extinguished provided a proper procedure was followed. For example, suppose that Parliament passes a law stating that "Mr. X shall be executed tomorrow at twelve noon", and further provides that Mr. X shall be informed of this law (after enactment), and shall be given the opportunity to say anything he likes about his prospective demise. Mere procedural fairness in this context will be meaningless, because there is no discretion granted under the law to alter its application in light of anything Mr. X may say at his "hearing". Undoubtedly, the common law principles of natural justice apply even in these circumstances to the delegate upon whom Parliament has imposed the duty to execute Mr. X,[85] but the requirement for a fair hearing is little guarantee that "fundamental justice" will be done to Mr. X. Faced with a patently unjust law that is peremptory and not discretionary in its application, what Canadian court will not be sorely tempted to strike down the substance of the law on the strength of the reference in section 7 to "fundamental justice"?

Secondly, it is relevant to note that this has been precisely the experience of the United States courts in construing the Fifth and Fourteenth Amendments to their Constitution, which provide that "no person shall . . . be deprived of life, liberty, or property, *without due process of law* . . ".[86] and "nor shall any State deprive any person of life, liberty or property, *without due process of law*. . .".[87] Even though the literal wording of the United States provisions is much weaker than the reference to the "principles of fundamental justice" contained in section 7 of our Charter, the United States courts have interpreted these two amendments to require not only procedural fairness but also "substantive due process" in certain circumstances.[88] In other words, the substance of legislation has been struck down by courts where it is unfair. This could, it is submitted, become the case in Canada; and it almost certainly follows that the Canadian courts will also be tempted to look at the merits of discretionary decisions taken by statutory delegates, as well as the content of the parent legislation itself for substantive fairness.

---

85 *Cooper v. Wandsworth Bd. of Works*, (1863) 143 E.R. 414.
86 Emphasis added.
87 Emphasis added.
88 *E.g.*, see *Shapiro, Commr. of Welfare of Connecticut v. Thompson*, 394 U.S. 618 (1969); *Oyama v. California*, 332 U.S. 633 (1948); *Roe v. Wade*, 410 U.S. 113 (1973); *Shelton v. Tucker*, 364 U.S. 479 (1960).

Finally, on a different point, note that section 7 of the Charter at its very narrowest interpretation not only specifically imports procedural fairness into any decision affecting life, liberty and the security of the person, but also eliminates the sovereignty of the legislative branch expressly to oust the two principles of natural justice, at least so far as any question of life, liberty and the security of the person is involved. This differs markedly from the pre-Charter situation, when the legislative branch could specifically exercise its sovereignty to state that the principles of natural justice or procedural fairness were not to apply to the exercise of a particular delegated power. Any attempt to do so now will be unconstitutional with respect to the matters listed in section 7 of the Charter.

5. Summary

The constitutional limitations on the Sovereignty of Parliament which exist in Canada provide an important backdrop to Canadian Administrative Law. To the extent that these limitations mean that a law is unconstitutional, that law cannot validly delegate power to the administration and cannot provide any legal justification for acts done thereunder. Accordingly, Canadian Administrative Law contains these constitutional grounds for challenging the validity of governmental action, which are additional to the grounds which exist in English Administrative Law.

3

Statutory Delegation of Governmental Powers

1. Institutions of Government

On an institutional level, it would be almost inconceivable to expect Parliament by itself to deal with all aspects of the laws it makes without the assistance of other governmental agencies. It is not surprising, therefore, to discover that legislation regularly delegates powers to the executive[1] and judicial[2] branches of government. One must, therefore, take account of the

---

1 *E.g.*, the School Act, R.S.A. 1980, c. S-3, s. 11.
2 *E.g.*, the Rules of Court.

existence of these other two governmental institutions, even if the scope and very existence of their functions theoretically derive from Parliament,[3] which is pre-eminent in our constitutional system.

(a) The Judicial Branch

Let us first consider the position of the judicial institution in the British system of government which we have inherited in Canada. Because there is no entrenched constitutional separation of powers in the United Kingdom similar to the situation in the United States,[4] virtually all of the functions exercised by the British judiciary depend either upon authority statutorily delegated from the legislative branch, or upon common law tradition which can be specifically overridden by statute.[5] As a matter of practice, it is of course true that British constitutional convention has maintained a strongly independent judiciary, but there is no constitutional impediment to prevent the legislative branch from abolishing the courts entirely. Nor do the British courts have any inherent jurisdiction which could not be abolished by clear legislation. Therefore, the *de facto* independence of the judiciary in Britain is really a political matter, not a legal or constitutional necessity.[6]

The position of the judicial branch in Canada is similar, although complicated somewhat by both the Canadian Charter of Rights and Freedoms[7] and certain other provisions of the Constitution Act, 1867.[8] In theory, either the Federal Parliament or a provincial legislature could abolish the courts or abridge all or any part of their jurisdiction. Unlike the position under the Constitution of the United States, there is no constitutional guarantee in Canada that there will be independent courts with an irreducible minimum

---

3 The Crown itself, of course, predates Parliament, and the Royal Prerogative is an independent source of lawful power. On the other hand, legislation enacted by the Queen in Parliament can abridge all or any part of the Royal Prerogative, so that the better view seems to be that the Royal Prerogative continues to exist on the sufferance of Parliament. Further, the Queen herself does not constitute the entirety of the executive branch of government, most of which derives its powers from statutes. Even if the statutes delegate powers to the Queen (or the Queen in Council), the Queen is like any other statutory delegate in the exercise of those powers, who is subject to the doctrine of *ultra vires*, and the legality of which is capable of judicial review in the courts. In other words, one must identify the source of the Crown's powers, and not be content merely to identify the fact that it is the Crown which is exercising the power in question.

4 See arts. I, II and III of the Constitution of the United States of America.

5 Some judicial functions may derive from the Royal Prerogative, which can of course also be overriden by statute.

6 See David Phillip Jones, "A Constitutionally Guaranteed Role for the Courts", (1979) 57 Can. Bar Rev. 669.

7 Part 1 of sched. B to the Canada Act (1982) (U.K.) (31 Eliz. 2, c. 11); also the Constitution Act, S.C. 1982, Pt. I.

8 (30 & 31 Vict.), c. 3; reproduced with amendments in R.S.C. 1970, App. II, as further amended and renamed by the Canada Act, *ibid.*

jurisdiction.[9] Thus, in Canada, at least certain "judicial functions" can be created by legislation but delegated to someone other than a judge sitting in a courtroom.[10] Against this theoretical position, however, it is important to note the existence in Canada of a political convention acknowledging the desirability of the existence of courts which in fact are independent,[11] and to whom a very wide range of judicial[12] and administrative[13] functions are delegated.

(b) The Executive or Administrative Branch

Similarly, no one can deny the *de facto* existence of a separate executive branch of government to which the legislative branch has delegated the power to administer its laws. The exact ambit of the executive may be difficult to identify with precision. It certainly includes the Crown, the Governor in Council (which in practice generally means the cabinet), and individual ministers[14] to whom particular powers have been delegated by legislation. All of the foregoing statutory delegates sit in Parliament and are directly answerable to the legislative branch for the exercise of the powers which have been granted to them (and may of course be answerable in judicial proceedings to determine the lawfulness of their actions[15]). The doctrine of ministerial responsibility applies in these circumstances, even if some assistant or civil servant has in fact exercised the power in the name of the minister, the cabinet, or the Governor in Council.

On the other hand, the executive branch also includes independent

---

9 It is true that s. 96 of the Constitution Act, 1867 requires all functions of a superior, district or county court to be exercised by a judge named by the federal Governor in Council. On the other hand, there is no requirement for legislation to create judicial functions at all. It is conceivable — though obviously inconvenient — that all disputes between citizens could be settled by legislation. In such a case, s. 96 would clearly be inapplicable. See Jones, *supra*, note 6.

10 As noted by the Privy Council in *Labour Rel. Bd. of Sask. v. John East Iron Works Ltd.*, [1948] 4 D.L.R. 673.

11 Maîtres chez eux/Masters in their Own House (the Deschênes Report) (Edmonton: Canadian Institute for the Administration of Justice, 1981).

12 *I.e.*, the vast bulk of judges' functions.

13 *E.g.*, the discretion to permit wire-tapping; taxing a lawyer's fee accounts; decrees absolute of divorce; approving the dissolution of corporations.

14 *E.g.*, the Minister of National Revenue under the Income Tax Act.

15 All statutory delegates are subject to judicial review for a breach of the *ultra vires* doctrine. Sometimes, however, the fact that a statutory delegate sits in the legislature and is subject to the doctrine of ministerial responsibility may cause the courts to give a rather broader construction to the ambit of discretionary powers delegated to that person. See *Liversidge v. Anderson*, [1942] A.C. 206 (H.L.). Similarly, prior to the recent development of the duty to be fair, the applicability of the doctrine of ministerial responsibility sometimes inclined the courts to characterize a particular delegated function as merely administrative instead of being quasi-judicial (and therefore escaping the application of the principles of natural justice). See *Franklin v. Min. of Town & Country Planning*, [1948] A.C. 87 (H.L.).

boards and tribunals which are not part of the organized departmental structure of the civil service,[16] but to whom the legislative branch has nevertheless
delegated powers. Examples from Alberta include the Energy Resources
Conservation Board, the Public Utilities Board, the Provincial Planning
Appeal Board, the Surface Rights Board, and the Alberta Assessment Appeal
Board. Federal examples include the Canadian Transportation Commission,
the National Energy Board, and the Canadian Radio-Television and Telecommunications Commission. All of these might be called "regulatory or
administrative agencies", "tribunals", or "boards". Crown corporations such
as Air Canada or Alberta Housing Corporation provide an example of
governmental activities which are removed even further from political or civil
service control by the government. These arrangements provide varying
distances between the political executive which controls the departmentalized
government and the independent boards, and relieves the former of direct
political responsibility and accountability for the actions of the latter.
Unfortunately, there is no legal or constitutional rule for determining which
executive or administrative functions should be externalized to independent
agencies. From time to time, the political government of the day reconsiders
how independent particular agencies should be. Thus, legislation may provide
for appeals to the cabinet from decisions of an independent administrative
agency[17] or permit the cabinet to give policy directives to one of the agencies.[18]
Or, new legislation may be enacted to reorganize the administrative structure
to move a particular function into one of the departments of state, or out to a
totally or semi-independent agency.[19] It must also be remembered that the
political executive (that is, the cabinet, and perhaps in practice the Prime

---

16 These independent boards or tribunals may report to Parliament directly (*e.g.*, the Ombudsman and the Auditor-General in Alberta) and have their budgets set by the House itself.
Alternatively, there may be a reporting relationship through a particular minister (*e.g.*, the
Law Reform Commission reports to Parliament through the Minister of Justice, who also has
some responsibility for the funding and staff of the agency). There is no single paradigm.

17 Such as the Canadian Radio-Television and Telecommunications Commission. See, *e.g.*,
Inuit Tapirisat of Can. v. A.G. Can. on this point: (1980) 115 D.L.R. (3d) 1 (S.C.C.).

18 *E.g.*, see:
Canadian Wheat Board Act, R.S.C. 1970, c. C-12, s. 11(1):

> (1) The Governor in Council may by order not inconsistent with this Act, direct the
> Board as to the manner in which any of its operations, powers and duties under this
> Act shall be conducted, exercised or performed.

National Transportation Act, R.S.C. 1970, c. N-17, s. 25(2), which provides an appeal to a
minister where the Commission suspends or cancels any licence:

> (2) . . . the carrier . . . may appeal to the Minister, and the Minister shall thereupon certify
> his opinion to the Commission and the Commission shall comply therewith.

19 *E.g.*, the transfer of employer's liability from tort law determined by the courts to an administrative matter dealt with by the Worker's Compensation Board. Conversely, note the
privatization of the post office.

Minister) almost invariably leads the party which has a majority in the legislative branch, and therefore is generally in a position to cause legislation to be enacted to alter the institutional arrangements for performing executive functions. Thus, in practice, it may be the executive which controls the legislative branch, although our constitutional philosophy states the reverse.

In summary, there are three great institutions of modern government: the legislative, the judicial and the executive. In the Anglo-Canadian tradition, the latter two institutions ultimately are subordinate to the legislature, although this is probably not strictly true in Canada under our written constitution and Charter of Rights and Freedoms.[20] It is important, however, to remember that the existence of three separate institutions of government does not mean that each institution exercises only one particular type of function.

2. Institutions Versus Functions of Government

Altogether apart from the governmental institution involved, it is possible to identify three principal *functions* of government: (a) the legislative, which involves making general rules and regulations (such as the Criminal Code[21]) applicable to a wide range of people and fact patterns; (b) the executive, which involves the application and enforcement of the legislation to particular people in particular circumstances (such as an immigration officer's determination whether a particular person is a Canadian citizen entitled to enter Canada as of right[22]); and (c) the judicial, which involves the independent determination by a judge whether a person has contravened the law. As noted earlier, however, the Canadian and British systems of government do not rigorously allocate the exercise of each of these three functions to the corresponding governmental institutions, as is done constitutionally in the United States. Thus, members of the departmentalized civil service form part of the executive branch of government but may be delegated powers that are not really executive in nature, such as powers (a) to make subordinate legislation; (b) to determine disputes in a judicial or quasi-judicial manner; or (c) to do some merely administrative act (such as issuing drivers' licences or admitting returning Canadian citizens to the country). Conversely, all Acts of Parliament are by their very nature "legislation", even if they are functionally judicial or administrative in nature and not general at all. Thus, a Bill of Attainder is legislation which declares a person to be guilty of a criminal offence and may forfeit his property — both of which would generally be considered to be judicial functions. Similarly, divorces granted prior to the 1968

---

20 Because the Charter imposes certain limitations on the ability of either the Federal Parliament or provincial legislatures to enact certain types of laws, and gives the right to judicial redress for breaches of these limitations, thereby implying some irreducible role for the judicial branch of government.

21 R.S.C. 1970, c. C-34.

22 Immigration Act, S.C. 1976-77, c. 52, s. 4; Citizenship Act, S.C. 1974-75-76, c. 108, s. 3.

Divorce Act[23] were incorporated into Acts of Parliament, although they affected only two parties — very much the way that private Acts exempt particular persons from the operation of the general law.[24] All of these functions could have been delegated to judges or members of the executive, and the mere fact that Parliament itself exercises these functions through the vehicle of parent legislation does not really make them "legislative" in nature. Similarly, municipal by-laws which re-zone particular land have been held to be quasi-judicial in nature, even though they are delegated legislation in form.[25] These examples demonstrate the impossibility of characterizing a function as "legislative", "judicial" or merely "administrative" in nature simply by identifying the person or branch of government to whom the power has been delegated by the legislation in question, although some broad correlation may exist between institutions and functions of government.

---

23 R.S.C. 1970, c. D-8.

24 Although the Federal Parliament or a provincial legislature may enact legislation exempting a particular person from the general law, neither the Crown nor any other member of the executive has power to dispense from the general law of the land.

25 *Wiswell v. Winnipeg*, (1964) 48 W.W.R. 193, reversed on other grounds [1965] S.C.R. 512. As Freedman J.A. of the Manitoba Court of Appeal said at pp. 194-95:

> Counsel's argument here is double-pronged. First, he contends that the Metropolitan council, when it was enacting bylaw No. 177, was engaged in a legislative function and not in a *quasi*-judicial act. If that were indeed the case, then it would have had the right to proceed without notice. But to say that the enactment of bylaw No. 177 was simply a legislative act is to ignore the realities and substance of the case. For this was not a bylaw of wide or general application, passed by the Metropolitan council because of a conviction that an entire area had undergone a change in character and hence was in need of reclassification for zoning purposes. Rather this was a specific decision made upon a specific application concerned with a specific parcel of land. . . . In proceeding to enact bylaw No. 177 Metro was essentially dealing with a dispute between Dr. Ginsberg, who wanted the zoning requirements to be altered for his benefit, and those other residents of the district who wanted the zoning restrictions to continue as they were. *That Metro resolved the dispute by the device of an amending bylaw did indeed give to its proceedings an appearance of a legislative character. But in truth the process in which it was engaged was quasi-judicial in nature; and I feel I must so treat it.*
>
> Then counsel argues as well that the governing statute does not call for notice. Hence, he says, notice was not required. I am unable to accept this contention. *A long line of authorities, both old and recent, establish that in judicial or quasi-judicial proceedings notice is required unless the statute expressly dispenses with it. The mere silence of the statute is not enough to do away with notice. In such cases, as has been said, the justice of the common law will supply the omission of the legislature.* Some of the authorities dealing with this subject are referred to by Kirby, J. in the recent case of *Camac Exploration Ltd. v. Oil and Gas Conservation Board of Alta.* (1964) 47 WWR 81. [Emphasis added.]

Cf. the decision of the Alberta Court of Appeal in *Campeau Corp. v. Calgary* (No. 1), (1978) 7 Alta. L.R. (2d) 294, and subsequent decision (No. 2), (1980) 12 Alta. L.R. (2d) 379, and the decision in *Harvie v. Calgary Reg. Planning Comm.*, (1978) 8 Alta. L.R. (2d) 166, reversing 5 Alta. L.R. (2d) 301 (C.A.).

3. Reasons for Characterizing Delegated Powers: "Legislative", "Judicial" or "Administrative"

The characterization of the function is important for determining the ambit of the power granted to the delegate,[26] the procedure which the delegate must follow in exercising that power and the remedies which may be available to challenge the legality of the delegate's action in court. Thus, the general rule is that both delegated legislative and judicial powers must be exercised by the very person to whom they have been granted, whereas merely administrative powers can be sub-delegated quite freely to others. For a long time, the principles of natural justice[27] were thought to be applicable only to the exercise of a judicial (or quasi-judicial) power, and not to the enactment of delegated legislation or to the exercise of a merely administrative action. Similarly, the availability of prerogative remedies of *certiorari* and prohibition was long restricted to correct procedural errors involved in the exercise of judicial (or quasi-judicial) powers, but not legislative or merely administrative ones.[28] So the functional characterization of delegated powers has been extremely important in Administrative Law.

In recent years, the necessity to characterize the nature of delegated functions has become considerably less important. In particular, the development of the general duty to be fair — whether comprised within the principles of natural justice, or in addition to them — has removed the distinction between judicial (or quasi-judicial) functions and merely administrative ones for the purpose of applying rules of fair procedure, as well as for determining the availability of *certiorari* and prohibition. This is a welcome advance, and is considered in detail in later chapters. Nevertheless, important distinctions still exist, particularly if the delegated power is characterized as being legislative in nature, because the principles of natural justice still do not apply to the exercise of such functions. Thus, considerable attention must be given throughout the study of Administrative Law to the courts' historical attempts to characterize the type of delegated powers impugned in litigation before them as being (a) legislative; (b) judicial (or quasi-judicial); or (c) executive (or merely administrative).[29]

---

26 It is submitted that, in applying the doctrine of *ultra vires*, the courts are likely to give a broader content to delegated legislative or administrative powers than they are to delegated judicial or quasi-judicial powers — always bearing in mind that there may be no doubt as to the ambit of the delegated power, however it is characterized.

27 See chapter 6, *infra*.

28 See David Phillip Jones, "Administrative Fairness in Alberta", (1980) 18 Alta. L.Rev. 351.

29 See S.A. de Smith's *Judicial Review of Administrative Decisions*, 4th ed., chapter 2, entitled "Classification of Functions".

4. Discretionary Powers

In addition to identifying the governmental institution involved and characterizing the type of function being exercised, it is also necessary to note the distinction between (a) delegated powers which are really duties; and (b) those which are discretionary in nature.[30] It is obvious why legislation frequently imposes duties on delegates to enforce rules which are contained in the legislation itself, for example, the duty on a policeman to enforce the provisions of the Criminal Code. Frequently, however, it is not possible for Parliament to lay down a rule of general application in the legislation itself. On the contrary, it may be necessary for Parliament to provide the vehicle through which particular decisions are to be made by its delegates, rather than making those decisions itself. Such delegation of discretionary power may be necessary for a variety of reasons, including:

(a) the difficulty of providing a rule which is applicable to all cases;
(b) the difficulty of identifying all of the factors to be applied to a particular case;
(c) the difficulty of weighing those factors;
(d) the need to provide an easy vehicle for changing the considerations to be applied to the problem over time;
(e) the complexity of the issue; and
(f) the desire not to confer vested rights on a particular party (which might be called the "short leash" principle).

The delegate may be authorized to exercise his discretion in each particular case or to enact subordinate legislation governing all such cases (which itself can be changed more easily than the parent legislation). There is no general rule to determine when Parliament should enact a general rule governing all cases, or should delegate discretionary powers, or for determining whether the delegate should be required to exercise his discretion to enact a rule contained in subordinate legislation, or should be permitted to deal with each case individually.[31]

The rest of this section considers: (a) duties compared with discretionary powers; (b) the ambit of discretion; (c) pre-conditions to the exercise of discretion; and (d) the concept of a quasi-judicial power.

---

30 See J.H. Grey, "Discretion in Administrative Law", (1979) 17 Osgoode Hall L.J. 107.
31 It is clear, however, that a delegate who has been authorized to make subordinate legislation cannot validly create a discretionary scheme for dealing with the matter in question; that is, converting a subordinate legislative power into a sub-delegated discretionary power is *ultra vires* because the parent legislation contemplated a system of rules being put in place, not a system of discretionary powers: see the *Brant Dairy* case, [1973] S.C.R. 131.

(a) Duties Compared with Discretionary Powers

Many delegated powers do not involve the exercise of discretion at all, but are really duties imposed upon the statutory delegate. Thus, an immigration officer has the duty to admit Canadian citizens into Canada; he has no discretion to refuse entry to any citizen.[32] It is, of course, true that the officer must make certain preliminary determinations, for example, whether the person is indeed a citizen. He may be right or wrong on that determination, but any error can be corrected by a court, because there is only one correct answer to this question. In other words, the immigration officer has no discretion to decide — as a matter of law — who is a citizen, or whether that citizen can be excluded from Canada; on the contrary, he has a duty to admit citizens into the country.

On the other hand, a law enacted by the legislative branch may grant the executive officer (or "delegate") the power to do or not do something as he, in his discretion, thinks appropriate. For example, the Public Utilities Board has the power to set the price of natural gas supplied to consumers in Alberta; it has discretion as to the actual price to be charged. The price cannot be determined merely by reading the legislation itself, although it is the legislation which creates and delegates the discretion to the board to make such determinations from time to time.

(b) The Ambit of Discretion

It is extremely important to identify the ambit of the discretion[33] which legislation has delegated to the particular executive office in question. Very few discretions are completely unfettered. On the contrary, most legislation lays down at least general guidelines within which the delegate must exercise his discretion. Thus, section 55 of the Public Service Employee Relations Act[34] of Alberta delegates the power to a three-member arbitration board to settle the collective agreement between the provincial government as employer and a union, bearing in mind the following factors:

(a) the interests of the public;
(b) the terms and conditions of employment in similar occupations outside the employer's employment including any geographic, industrial or other variations that the arbitration board considers relevant;
(c) the need to maintain appropriate relationships in the terms and conditions of employment as between different classification levels within an occupation and as between occupations in the employer's employment;

---

32 *Supra*, note 22.
33 See J.H. Grey, *supra*, note 30 at pp. 110 and 114-28.
34 R.S.A. 1980, c. P-33, as amended by S.A. 1983, c. 34, s. 5(7).

(d) the need to establish terms and conditions of employment that are fair and reasonable in relation to the qualifications required, the work performed, the responsibility assumed and the nature of the services rendered;

(e) any other factor that to it appears to be relevant to the matter in dispute.

The enumeration of these factors delimits the ambit of the discretion delegated by the legislature to the arbitration board. Thus, an arbitration board has no lawful power to go outside the area delegated to it, and any attempt to do so will be *ultra vires*.[35] Nevertheless, within the area delegated to it, an arbitration board is entitled to exercise its own discretion. Again, the discretionary nature of the power delegated to the arbitration board makes it impossible to determine from the legislation itself the precise terms of each collective agreement. The legislation merely creates the vehicle within which the statutory delegate will make its decision, within a certain area of discretion.

(c) Pre-Conditions to the Exercise of Discretion

It is important to note that some legislative provisions only delegate discretionary powers to the executive provided certain circumstances exist. For example, in *Bell v. Ontario Human Rights Commission*,[36] the commission could only exercise its powers if there was an allegation of discrimination with respect to the renting of a "self-contained domestic establishment". In the *Bell* case, the accommodation had shared bathroom and kitchen facilities. The Supreme Court of Canada decided that this meant that the property was not "self-contained", and therefore the commission had no jurisdiction to determine whether there had been unlawful racial discrimination involved by the owner's refusal to rent it to a particular applicant. In other words, the commission's discretionary jurisdiction could only be exercised if certain facts or pre-conditions existed, but not otherwise.

Similarly, in *Anisminic v. Foreign Compensation Commission*,[37] the

---

35 Although the discretionary nature of a statutory power may make the courts slow to interfere with the way in which the statutory delegate exercises his discretion, no discretion (indeed, no statutory power) is unlimited, and those limits demarcate the beginning of the doctrine of *ultra vires*.

36 [1971] S.C.R. 756. See also Peter Hogg, "The Jurisdictional Fact Doctrine in the Supreme Court of Canada: *Bell v. Ontario Human Rights Commission*", (1971) 9 Osgoode Hall L.J. 203; *R. v. Nat Bell Liquors Ltd.*, [1922] A.C. 128 (P.C.); *Parkhill Furniture & Bedding Ltd. v. Internat. Molders etc. Union*, (1961) 26 D.L.R. (2d) 589 (Man. C.A.); *R. v. Lab. Rel. Bd. (B.C.); Ex parte Lodum Hldgs. Ltd.*, (1968) 3 D.L.R. (3d) 41 (B.C.S.C.); *R. v. Bd. of Indust. Rel. (Alta.); Ex parte Eastern Irrigation Dist.*, (1970) 17 D.L.R. (3d) 192 (Alta. C.A.); H.W.R. Wade, "Anglo-American Administrative Law; More Reflections", (1966) 82 L.Q.R. 226; D.M. Gordon, "Jurisdictional Fact: An Answer", (1966) 82 L.Q.R. 515; D.M. Gordon, "The Relation of Facts to Jurisdiction", (1929) 45 L.Q.R. 459.

37 [1969] 2 A.C. 147 (H.L.).

legislation granted the commission jurisdiction to determine, in its discretion, how much compensation to pay British nationals or their successors-in-title for assets nationalized by the Egyptian government during the Suez affair. The commission refused even to entertain Anisminic's claim on the basis that it was not a successor-in-title to a person whose property had been nationalized. The House of Lords ruled that Anisminic was indeed a successor-in-title and that it had a right to file a claim which the commission must consider, although the commission could then exercise its discretion to determine how much (if anything) to pay Anisminic.

Both of these examples illustrate the conditional delegation of discretionary powers to the executive. This phenomenon is sometimes referred to as the "jurisdictional fact", "collateral fact", or "preliminary fact" doctrine. All of these phrases indicate that a certain state of affairs must exist before the delegate can exercise the power (generally discretionary in nature[38]) which the legislative branch has delegated to him. Further, the courts — and not the statutory delegate — are entitled to determine whether the relevant pre-conditions do in fact exist which would permit the delegate to exercise the discretion in question.

(d) The Concept of a "Quasi-Judicial" Power

The phrase "quasi-judicial" refers to discretionary powers which are essentially judicial in nature, but which are exercised by officials other than judges in their courtrooms. Historically, quasi-judicial powers have been subject to procedures which more or less resemble the formal ones used in litigation. As one moves further away from the judicial paradigm,[39] it becomes difficult to determine when the discretionary power can more properly be described as "merely administrative" or "ministerial". Nevertheless, the distinction was formerly very important, because the procedural principles of natural justice were thought not to apply to the exercise of "merely administrative" discretionary powers. In recent years, however, the development of the "duty to be fair" when exercising merely administrative powers has largely obliterated the importance of the distinction between them and quasi-judicial powers. Nevertheless, it is difficult to understand current Administrative Law without some familiarity with the old concept of a quasi-judicial power, its great (but not limitless) elasticity, and the procedural consequences of characterizing a particular discretionary power as being "quasi-judicial" in nature.

The concept of a quasi-judicial power takes its point of reference from the type of function exercised by a judge in litigation between two parties. The formal procedures which have been developed over the centuries by the courts

---

38 Sometimes a non-discretionary power or duty is involved, once the pre-conditions have been met.
39 For a discussion of various tests for determining whether a function is judicial, see S.A. de Smith, *Judicial Review of Administrative Action*, 3rd ed., chapter 2, pp. 64-76.

epitomize "natural justice" in its strongest form: there are pleadings; each side brings forward formal evidence; each side makes submissions of law and can answer the other's submissions; and the judge renders a decision in light of the law and the facts which have been proven before him in open court. These procedures are the hallmark of the judicial function. Many of these procedures have been made applicable to quasi-judicial functions exercised by officials who are not judges, although the exact content of the procedural requirements may differ with the type of quasi-judicial power involved.

It is important to remember that not all of a court's functions fit the model referred to above. On the one hand, many court functions are purely administrative in nature, and may not even involve the exercise of discretion, for example, the issuance of a writ or other proceedings. Other judicial proceedings do involve a formal hearing, but give the judge no discretion.[40] In yet other cases, the judge has a great deal of discretion under the applicable law.[41] In general, the procedural requirements of natural justice apply, in their strongest form, to all functions exercised by judges, whether or not discretionary in nature.

Over the years, the superior courts have been asked to review the procedures used by other officials in the exercise of powers delegated to them by legislation. The more closely those powers resembled ones exercised by judges in their courtrooms, the more likely it was that the superior courts would require some form of curial procedure to be used by the officials in the exercise of their powers; hence, the development of the phrase "quasi-judicial" powers. On the one hand, the content of the procedural requirements for exercising such non-curial powers differed enormously with the type and content of the power involved. The less the non-curial power resembled something done by a court, the less stringent was the requirement that court-like procedures be used to exercise that power. On the other hand, the concept of a quasi-judicial power is not infinitely elastic, and at some point it becomes impossible to characterize a particular non-curial power as being quasi-judicial instead of merely administrative — no matter how important it is, or how much it affects people, or how much discretion is involved. Although it was previously thought that no procedural safeguards were required for the exercise of merely administrative powers, Administrative Law has now developed the "duty to be fair"[42] in the method used to exercise even a merely administrative power. Accordingly, the distinction between quasi-judicial and merely administrative powers has become much less important. Nevertheless,

---

40 *E.g.*, the mandatory 25-year minimum sentence for first-degree murder.

41 *E.g.*, in deciding what is the appropriate sentence for certain offences; whether to exercise the court's discretion under the Law of Property Act to relieve against a penalty or forfeiture with respect to land (particularly in the foreclosure context), or to exercise its discretion to refuse one of the prerogative remedies.

42 See chapter 7, *infra*, for a description of the development of the duty to be fair, and the varying content of natural justice in different circumstances.

it is probably accurate to state that the further one moves from the judicial model of decision-making, the less are the procedural requirements involved in adopting a "fair" procedure for the exercise of a statutory power delegated to someone who is not a judge.

Before leaving the topic of quasi-judicial functions, it is important to note two points: first, that section 96 of the Constitution Act prohibits the delegation of any judicial powers exercised by a superior, district or county court to anyone not appointed by the federal Governor in Council, and this constitutional limitation is still important today;[43] secondly, that there is no talisman to guide Parliament in determining whether it should (a) itself enact parent legislation containing all of the rules to govern a particular situation; (b) delegate discretion to an official to deal with each case, within broader or narrower policy guidelines contained in the Act; (c) provide specifically for some sort of procedure to be followed by such a delegate, or provide for an appeal to another official or to the courts; or (d) delegate the power to someone else to make rules and regulations which govern every case.[44] Although these choices are largely political matters, they are important both to good government and to the legal rights which arise as a result of the institutional framework within which the legislative branch chooses to delegate power.

5. Delegated Legislation

One of the most important methods of delegating power is the ability to enact subordinate legislation. Although discretion is obviously involved in determining the content of subordinate legislation, the courts have generally held that the procedural requirements of natural justice do not apply to the exercise of such legislative powers. Because subordinate legislation is as valid as if contained in the parent legislation itself, most legislatures have created systems for registering and publishing the subordinate legislation which has been enacted under their authority. Again, because delegation of power is involved, the ambit of that power can always be questioned and the doctrine of *ultra vires* permits judicial review to determine whether the delegate in fact has exercised the specific legislative power which has been granted to him. In addition, the Federal Parliament and some provincial legislatures have instituted standing "scrutiny" committees to review both the content and legality of the subordinate legislation which their servants have enacted with their authority. The great volume and importance of subordinate legislation makes this topic extremely important in Administrative Law, and it is discussed in detail in the next chapter.

---

43 See the discussion on this point in chapter 2, *supra*.
44 But see the *caveat* discussed in note 31, *supra*, on the ability of a delegate to convert a legislative power into a discretionary one.

Subordinate Legislation

1. Introduction

The previous chapter considered various types of statutory powers which can be delegated: duties, discretionary powers, judicial powers and the power to enact subordinate legislation. In fact, the sheer volume of subordinate legislation greatly exceeds parent legislation enacted in most years.[1] Because subordinate legislation derives its effect from the Sovereignty of Parliament, it is important to examine in some detail the applicability of the *ultra vires*

---

1 In 1977, the Joint Standing Committee of Parliament on Regulations estimated that there were more than 14,000 federal regulations in force. In Alberta, it has been estimated that there are 7,000 regulations in force.

doctrine to the enactment of subordinate legislation, as well as the systems which many jurisdictions have created for the registration, publication and parliamentary scrutiny of at least some subordinate legislation.

2. Reasons for Subordinate Legislation

The need for delegated legislation can be justified in terms of the following factors, among others:

(a) The sheer magnitude of the business of government means that not everything can be dealt with in parent legislation.

(b) The technical nature of much of governmental activity requires that only broad principles should be contained in legislation.

(c) Delegating power to an administrator allows greater flexibility in applying broad statutory provisions to changing circumstances.

(d) The need for rapid governmental action may require faster administrative response than can be achieved by the necessity of amending parent legislation.

(e) Innovation and experimentation in solving social problems may not be possible if legislative amendments are required.

(f) Emergencies may require broad delegation of legislative powers with respect to a wide range of matters which would normally be dealt with in parent legislation.

As seen earlier,[2] the ability of the legislative branch in Canada to delegate legislative powers is constitutionally somewhat more restricted than in the United Kingdom. Thus, our federal system means that one level of the legislative branch (for example, the Federal Parliament) cannot delegate its law-making powers to the other level (for example, a provincial legislature). Similarly, the legislative branch cannot delegate such broad powers that it effectively effaces itself, nor can a provincial legislature delegate its legislative powers in such a way as to affect the office of the Lieutenant Governor to breach section 96 of the Constitution Act.[3] Otherwise, however, there are no legal or constitutional limitations on the ability of the legislative branch in Canada to delegate its legislative or law-making powers, although again political conventions do provide some common sense guide to what types of matters should be dealt with in parent legislation rather than being delegated.

---

2 See chapter 2, *supra*.

3 30 & 31 Vict., c. 3; reproduced with amendments in R.S.C. 1970, App. II, as further amended by the Canada Act, 1982 (U.K.) (31 Eliz. 2, c. 11); also the Constitution Act, 1982 (Can.).

3. Examples of the Power to Enact Subordinate Legislation

Virtually all parent legislation now contains provision for the enactment of regulations or other subordinate legislation. The ambit within which the delegate may make regulations varies greatly from Act to Act.

Sometimes, the delegate is only empowered to make regulations on a relatively narrow range of topics — for example, the ability of the Lieutenant Governor in Council to designate the dates within which daylight saving time is to be observed each year in British Columbia;[4] the establishment of the Classification Appeal Tribunal to settle disputes about the classification of civil service jobs under the Public Service Act[5] in Alberta.

Some Acts delegate quite broad regulation-making powers, such as section 221(1) of the Income Tax Act,[6] which provides:

221(1) The Governor in Council may make regulations

(a) prescribing anything that, by this Act, is to be prescribed or is to be determined or regulated by regulation,

(b) prescribing the evidence required to establish facts relevant to assessments under this Act,

(c) to facilitate the assessment of tax where deductions or exemptions of a taxpayer have changed in a taxation year,

(d) requiring any class of persons to make information returns respecting any class of information required in connection with assessments under this Act,

(e) requiring a person who is, by a regulation made under paragraph (d), required to make an information return to supply a copy of the information return or of a prescribed portion thereof to the person or persons in respect of whose income the information return or portion thereof relates,

(f) authorizing a designated officer or class of officers to exercise powers or perform duties of the Minister under this Act,

(g) providing for the retention by way of deduction or set off of the amount of a taxpayer's income tax or other indebtedness under this Act out of any amount or amounts that may be or become payable by Her Majesty to him in respect of salary or wages,

---

4 Interpretation Act, R.S.B.C. 1979, c. 206, ss. 25(7), 26(a).

5 R.S.A. 1980, c. P-31, s. 11 [am. 1983, c. 45, s. 3].

6 R.S.C. 1952, c. 148, as amended by S.C. 1970-71-72, c. 63.

(*h*) defining the classes of persons who may be regarded as dependent for the purposes of this Act,

(*i*) defining the classes of non-resident persons who may be regarded for the purposes of this Act

(i) as a spouse supported by a taxpayer, or

(ii) as a person dependent or wholly dependent upon a taxpayer for support,

and specifying the evidence required to establish that a person belongs to any such class, and

(*j*) generally to carry out the purposes and provisions of this Act.

The taxpayer's right to deduct capital cost allowance or depreciation is governed entirely by regulations enacted under section 221(1), although previously there was no entitlement to such deductions, which instead were left entirely to the discretion of the Minister.[7] Under the present system the Governor in Council must enact regulations, which may be changed frequently, but which give rights to all taxpayers to whom they apply.

At the extreme, the legislature may delegate such broad regulation-making power that it is impossible to determine how the administrative system in question operates without reference to volumes of regulations dealing with substantive matters. The Liquor Control Act[8] is a good example of this type of bare-bones legislation.

Finally, all by-laws enacted by municipal corporations are a form of delegated legislation, because local governments derive their powers from the provincial Municipal Government Act.[9] Not all by-laws, however, are in fact legislative in nature, and certain procedural requirements must be observed if they are properly characterized as being quasi-judicial.[10]

4. Subordinate Legislation as Effective as Parent Legislation

One must not be misled by its name into supposing that subordinate legislation is inferior, less important or less effective than parent legislation. On the one hand, the doctrine of *ultra vires* does apply to require the delegate to enact subordinate legislation within the constraints prescribed by the

---

7 Under the Income War Tax Act, R.S.C. 1927, c. 97, until 1952.

8 Liquor Control Act, R.S.A. 1980, c. L-17. See also the federal Petroleum Administration Act, S.C. 1974-75-76, c. 47, the Energy Supplies Emergency Act, S.C. 1978-79, c. 17, s. 33 establishing the Energy Supplies Allocation Board, or the Fisheries Act, R.S.C. 1970, c. F-14.

9 In Alberta, the Municipal Government Act, R.S.A. 1980, c. M-26.

10 See note 25 in chapter 3, *supra*.

parent legislation.[11] On the other hand, if this requirement is met, the subordinate legislation is as valid and effective as if it had been enacted by the legislative branch itself.

Under the federal Interpretation Act,[12] all regulations are specifically included in the definition of "enactment", and must therefore be given the same force, effect and interpretation as if contained in parent legislation. Thus, "enactment" is defined to mean "an Act *or regulation* or any portion of an Act or regulation . . ."[13] and "regulation" is defined to include

> an order, regulation, order in council, order prescribing regulations, rule, rule of court, form, tariff of costs or fees, letters patent, commission, warrant, proclamation, by-law, resolution or other instrument issued, made or established
>
> (*a*) in the execution of a power conferred by or under the authority of an Act, or
>
> (*b*) by or under the authority of the Governor in Council.[14]

The Alberta Interpretation Act[15] is not quite so clear on this point because it does not specifically contain a definition of "enactment", although it does deal extensively with the interpretation of regulations. In any event, the authority to make regulations derives from the legislative branch (whether federal or provincial) and in principle regulations which have been validly enacted must have the same legal force as though contained in an Act itself.

---

11 *E.g.*, see:

    (1) *Keough v. Memorial Univ. of Nfld.*; *Caravan v. Memorial Univ. of Nfld.*, (1980) 26 Nfld. & P.E.I.R. 386 (Nfld. T.D.), where the university was held not to have the power to make by-laws restricting parking;

    (2) *Herman Bros. Ltd. v. Regina*, [1978] 1 W.W.R. 97 (Sask. C.A.), where by-laws charging for services delivered outside the city were held to be invalid;

    (3) *R. v. Knapp*, [1971] 5 W.W.R. 727 (B.C.S.C.), where the city's power to regulate use of streets was held not to encompass the right to prohibit distribution of written material;

    (4) *Affleck v. Nelson*, (1957) 23 W.W.R. 386 (B.C.S.C.), where there was no power to declare a street a monument;

    (5) *Can. Freightways Ltd. v. Calgary*, (1967) 58 W.W.R 601 (Alta. S.C.), where the power to license businesses was held not to give the right to license vehicles used by the business;

    (6) *Alaska Trainship Corp. v. Pac. Pilotage Authority*, [1981] 1 S.C.R. 261, where a requirement for compulsory pilots for U.S. ships was struck down.

    For an example of an *ultra vires* exercise of delegated power which might or might not be legislative in nature, see the Fifteenth Report of the Joint Standing Committee on Regulations and Other Statutory Instruments to the First Session of the 32nd Parliament, 1980-81-82-83, dated 5th May 1983, relating to the exercise by the Minister of Indian and Northern Affairs of his power under s. 12(1)(*a*)(iv) of the Indian Act, R.S.C. 1970, c. I-6, to exempt certain persons from various provisions of the Act, thereby effectively amending the Act.

12 R.S.C. 1970, c. I-23.

13 Section 2(1), emphasis added.

14 *Ibid.*

15 R.S.A. 1980, c. I-7.

The constitutional relationship between parent and subordinate legislation bothered Harvey C.J.A. in *Credit Foncier Franco-Canadien v. Ross*; *Netherlands Investment Company of Canada v. Fife*:

> It is important also to note that s. 92 [of the Constitution Act, 1867] authorizes and therefore makes valid only legislation by a Provincial Legislature and it is no doubt because of that fact that the power of disallowance given to the Governor-General in Council has reference only to Acts of Provincial Legislatures [as opposed to subordinate legislation]. If there could be [subordinate] legislation by Orders in Council or in some other way than by Act of the Legislature there would be no power reserved in the Governor-General to disallow it.[16]

The full force of this logic would be to prevent any use of subordinate legislation by provincial legislatures. This view is simply not sustainable in light of the recognition by the Privy Council in *Hodge v. R.*[17] of the right of provincial legislatures to delegate all or some of their powers even if legislative in nature. Nevertheless, it does point out the concern that some legislative enactments are so important that they should be debated openly in Parliament before enactment, and should not be contained in subordinate legislation.

5. The Doctrine of *Ultra Vires* Applies to Subordinate Legislation

The doctrine of *ultra vires* applies to the power of a delegate to enact subordinate legislation.[18] In other words, the delegate can only enact rules or regulations within the area granted to him by the parent legislation. To determine that ambit often requires close scrutiny of the particular statutory provision which creates the regulation-making power, as interpreted in light of the entire legislative scheme. As a corollary, the courts are entitled to review whether there is statutory authority for the enactment of any impugned regulations, just as the courts in general can review whether any other type of delegated action is *ultra vires*. It is unusual for legislation to contain a privative clause preventing judicial review of the *vires* of regulations.[19] Indeed,

---

16 [1937] 3 D.L.R. 365 at 369 (Alta. C.A.).

17 (1883) 9 App. Cas. 117.

18 *McEldowney v. Forde*, [1969] 2 All E.R. 1039 (H.L.). See also note 11, *supra*. The McRuer Report discusses various ways in which subordinate legislation may be *ultra vires* the parent enactment at pp. 343-55 and pp. 380*ff*. The common law presumed that subordinate legislation could only validly do the following with specific authority in the parent act: amend another Act (or regulations passed thereunder); amend the parent Act; impose penalties; sub-delegate; impose taxes or fees; operate retroactively; reverse the onus of proof; or exclude the jurisdiction of the courts.

19 As opposed to a privative clause preventing judicial review of a discretionary action by a delegate, *e.g.*, a decision of the Public Utilities Board setting natural gas prices.

such a privative clause might itself be unconstitutional because it would in effect endow the delegate with autonomous legislative authority, thereby arguably effacing the Federal Parliament or a provincial legislature.

It is sometimes difficult to determine the specific statutory provision under which a particular regulation has been made. On the one hand, it is often not enough to learn that the regulation has been enacted pursuant to some Act, without having the specific section in the Act identified. At the federal level, the Joint Standing Committee on Regulations and Other Statutory Instruments[20] has insisted that each regulation identify the specific statutory provision which is being relied upon by the delegate for authority to enact the regulation. This provides an opportunity for the delegate to consider carefully the specific statutory terms governing those regulations prior to the enactment of them, as well as a similar opportunity for the committee when reviewing them, or for an individual who might be affected by them.[21]

On the other hand, legislation sometimes contains both specific regulation-making powers and an omnibus clause purporting to authorize the delegate to enact regulations "for any purpose connected with this Act".[22] In general, the courts have given little scope to such vague powers, requiring delegates to found the validity of regulations on the provisions of the legislation authorizing regulations for specific purposes.

6. Procedure Required Prior to Enacting Regulations

A difficult problem arises when considering the procedure to be followed by a person to whom the power to legislate has been delegated by the Federal Parliament or a provincial legislature. At first glance, the delegate is in precisely the same position as any other delegate who exercises discretionary powers to which the duty to be fair applies. After all, the content of the delegated legislation is a matter of discretion. Almost always, its quality will be improved as a result of publicity and comment by those likely to be affected by it. The public policy rationale underlying both the *audi alteram partem* rule and the duty to be fair appears to apply to subordinate legislation as well as to judicial, quasi-judicial or other discretionary powers which are subject to judicial review on procedural grounds. Indeed, the desirability of prior

---

20 See section 10 of this chapter, *infra*, for a discussion of the "Scrutiny Committee".

21 It is equally difficult to find all of the regulations on a particular topic, since they are generally not well indexed. See Recommendation 22 of the Report of the Select Committee of the Legislative Assembly on Regulations in the Province of Alberta (the "Zander Committee") November 1974, and discussion at pp. 84-90 thereof. See also David S.M. Huberman, "Searching for Delegated Legislation or How to Find Your 'Red Tape,' " (1966) 2 U.B.C.L. Rev. 467.

22 E.g., s. 227 of the Highway Traffic Act, R.S.A. 1970, c. 169; s. 12(1) of the Workmen's Compensation Act, R.S.A. 1970, c. 397; s. 25 of the Social Development Act, R.S.A. 1970, c. 345.

consultation with affected parties appears to have been recognized recently by the legislative branch in a number of Acts where *draft* rules and regulations must be published and circulated prior to their final implementation: for example, under Bill 101 in Quebec;[23] both the Canada[24] and Alberta[25] Business Corporations Acts; the Canada Post Act;[26] the Broadcasting Act;[27] and the Grain Futures Act.[28] Further, this system has long been the standard practice of the United States federal government under their Administrative Procedures Act.[29]

Some parent legislation requires regulations to be tabled in the House of Commons or a provincial legislature. In some cases, the legislative branch must specifically affirm the regulations in order to bring them into force.[30] In other cases, the regulations will automatically come into force after a certain delay unless vetoed by a negative resolution of the parent body.[31] To some extent, each of these systems provides a limited measure of pre-publication, and an opportunity for interested parties to make comments on the content

---

23 R.S.Q. 1977, c. O-5.

24 S.C. 1974-75, c. 33, s. 254(2).

25 S.A. 1981, c. B-15, s. 254(2).

26 S.C. 1980-81, c. 54, ss. 17(3)-17(7).

27 S.C. 1967-68, c. 25, s. 16(2) [now R.S.C. 1970, c. B-11].

28 R.S.C. 1952, c. 140, s. 5(2) [now R.S.C. 1970, c. G-11]. The Broadcasting Act and the Grain Futures Act were the only examples of this type of pre-publication requirement which the MacGuigan Committee could find in the federal statutes.

29 The U.S. Federal Administrative Procedure Act, 5 U.S.C.A., ss. 551-556. See W. Gellhorn and C. Byse, *Administrative Law*, (Mineola: The Foundation Press, 1974), pp. 731*ff.* and App. A. See also K.C. Davis, *Administrative Law*, (St. Paul: West Publishing Co., 1973), chapters 11 and 12. And see also the discussion of the operation of the U.S. Act in App. V of the Fourth Report of the (Canadian) Federal Joint Standing Committee of the Senate and House of Commons on Regulations and Other Statutory Instruments (the "Scrutiny Committee") (17th July 1980), and contained in *Hansard* at pp. 328*ff.* as App. B to the proceedings of that day (hereinafter referred to as the "Fourth Report"). Note that both the Fourth Report and the Second Report were published under separate cover. Page references here are to the versions published in *Hansard*.

30 The Scrutiny Committee states that it could only find two examples of federal statutes requiring positive affirmation by Parliament to bring subordinate legislation into force: s. 18 of the Government Organization Act, R.S.C. 1970, c. 14 (2nd Supp.); and s. 4(2) of the Unemployment Insurance Act 1971, S.C. 1970-71-72, c. 48. See the Fourth Report at p. 340.

31 The federal Scrutiny Committee could only find twenty-one instances in all federal legislation in force at the end of the 1976-77 Session where Parliament was afforded the opportunity to disallow a statutory instrument or to prevent its coming into or continuing in force by refusing to affirm it: see the Fourth Report, pp. 337, 368-70. Other jurisdictions, such as the United Kingdom and Australia, have general rules permitting motions to disallow subordinate legislation to be brought to the floor of Parliament quite easily: see App. III to the fourth Report, pp. 382-84. Indeed, in 1975-76, the British House of Commons debated 92 motions for disallowance of subordinate legislation (Fourth Report, p. 342). Finally, note that R.S.C. 1970 (2nd Supp.), c. 29, s. 1(3), amends the federal Interpretation Act, R.S.C. 1970, c. I-23, to specify the procedure to be used for affirmative or negative resolutions of Parliament or of the House of Commons, and the effect of such a resolution.

and form of the proposed regulations.[32] It appears, however, that this type of parliamentary approval of delegated legislation is falling into disuse, in favour of more systematic *ex post facto* scrutiny of regulations which have been enacted under the authority of parent legislation.

Section 3 of the Canadian Bill of Rights[33] requires the federal Minister of Justice (or, in practice, one of his legal officers) to examine every regulation submitted in draft form to the Clerk of the Privy Council

> in order to ascertain whether any of the provisions thereof are inconsistent with the purposes and provisions of this Part [of the Bill of Rights] and he shall report any such inconsistency to the House of Commons at the first convenient opportunity.

In effect, this is an executive check on the exercise by another member of the executive of his discretion to enact subordinate legislation; it only indirectly permits the Federal Parliament to become involved in the supervision of the legislative powers which it has delegated. A similar provision is not generally encountered in provincial legislation.[34]

Notwithstanding the absence of a specific statutory requirement for consultation or pre-publication of proposed regulations, many delegates in practice do so. In 1969, the MacGuigan Committee[35] asked all federal departments and agencies the following questions:

> Does your Department or Agency consult interested or affected persons when preparing regulations so as to obtain their views with respect to the scope and content of the regulations? If so, please advise as to the procedures used, formal or otherwise, for obtaining or implementing this consultation.

The MacGuigan Committee discovered that the departments and agencies almost invariably consult interested and affected persons and representative parties through meetings, correspondence, telephone calls and even formal hearings. In some cases, the proposed regulations are published in draft form for comment and criticism by those affected. This particular method of obtaining assistance exhibits, perhaps, one advantage of making regulations

---

32 The Scrutiny Committee called the procedure for determining the substance of subordinate legislation "truly the secret garden of the Crown" (Fourth Report at p. 343). It noted the increased requirement of pre-publication of draft subordinate legislation, and also the study by the Economic Council of Canada as to the need to know the impact of proposed subordinate legislation of a "social nature". It also noted how the U.S. system operates, and that the U.K. had abandoned its pre-publication scheme with the enactment of its Statutory Instruments Act, 1946 (9 & 10 Geo. 6, c. 36), in favour of a more comprehensive *ex post facto* scrutiny.

33 R.S.C. 1970, App. III.

34 No similar provision exists in the Alberta Regulations Act, R.S.A. 1980, c. R-13.

35 Third Report of the Special Committee of the House of Commons on Statutory Instruments ("the MacGuigan Committee") (1968-69).

compared to statute laws, since it is not the practice to circulate draft government bills prior to their first reading in the House. One may suppose that similar informal consultation still occurs, both federally and provincially, though this may be of no comfort to a person affected by a regulation about which he was not consulted, and which is nevertheless legally valid and enforceable against him.

In the absence of a specific statutory requirement for pre-publication of proposed regulations, judicial review is not available against the procedure used in implementing any form of legislation, whether parent or subordinate in nature. Indeed, in the sequel to the *Campeau* case,[36] the Alberta Court of Appeal specifically excluded the availability of judicial review because a *legislative* function was involved in the enactment of a municipal by-law. The same point was made by D.C. McDonald J. in *R. in Right of Alberta v. Beaver*,[37] involving the unsuccessful attempt to quash first reading of a municipal by-law, and by Megarry J. in *Bates v. Lord Hailsham of St. Marylebone*,[38] which involved the proclamation of a new tariff of solicitors' fees.

It is imperative to note the distinction between delegated powers which are legislative in function and those which are merely legislative in form. Not all Orders in Council, for example, constitute subordinate legislation.[39] Con-

---

36 *Campeau Corp. v. Calgary*, (1980) 112 D.L.R. (3d) 737 (Alta. C.A.).

37 (1982) 20 Alta. L.R. (2d) 78 (Q.B.).

38 [1972] 1 W.L.R. 1373 (Ch. D.).

39 See App. I to the federal Scrutiny Committee's Fourth Report, entitled "Subordinate Law, Orders in Council, 'Ministerial Orders', Regulations, Statutory Instruments and Official Documents", pp. 376-81. It sets out the following Table for 1976:

Pursuant to Statute	3,265
Under the Royal Prerogative	61
Total number of orders in Council made in 1976	3,326

Description of Orders In Council for the Year 1976

	Number	Percentage
Appointments (includes re-appointments, resignations and fixing salaries)	750	22.55
Regulations and other Statutory Instruments	653	19.63
Lands and other property (includes exchanges, acquisitions, transfers to or from a Province, sales of lands under the surplus Crown Assets Act and under the Veterans' Land Act)	481	14.46
Contracts and other agreements	289	8.70
Pardons and Revocations (under Criminal Records Act)	234	7.03
Foreign Investment Review Act	232	6.97
Payments, loans, contributions, grants and gifts	161	4.84
Remission Orders	82	2.46
Satisfied Securities	75	2.25

versely, not all subordinate legislation is enacted by an Order in Council[40] (even if the power is granted to the Governor in Council, or to someone else entirely such as the Benchers of the Law Society[41]). Further, it is important to remember that all municipal actions take place pursuant to either a by-law or a resolution, both of which are legislative in form. Nevertheless, the courts have long held that by-laws which are quasi-judicial in nature (for example, those dealing with re-zoning, subdividing or granting permission to develop an individual's land[42]) are subject to the procedural requirements of natural justice, even though these discretionary decisions are cast in legislative form.[43]

	Number	Percentage
Judges Act, other than appointments (annuities to widows, approving residence, retirements, etc.)	55	1.65
Railways	41	1.23
Ex gratis payments	35	1.05
Other	238	7.18
TOTAL	3,326	100.00

40 The Scrutiny Committee noted at p. 337 of its Fourth Report:

> In Canada most regulations, and hence subordinate laws, are made by Order in Council of the Governor in Council. It is, therefore, commonly said that the regulations are made by the Cabinet. Your Committee thinks it important to place on public record that this is not strictly so. Since the Governor General does not preside at his Council, his assent to an Order in Council follows upon its earlier approval by Cabinet members. Very few draft regulations are actually considered by the Cabinet as a deliberative body. Some of these are first considered by Cabinet Subcommittees. By far the greatest number of regulations is recommended for His Excellency's approval by the Special Committee of Council which consists of ten Ministers with a quorum of four. The extent to which draft regulations are scrutinized as to policy, legality and propriety by the Special Committee will depend upon its membership. The decision as to whether a regulation should be considered by a Cabinet Committee or direct by the Cabinet rests fundamentally with the sponsoring Minister according to his view of the regulation's importance and implications. Occasionally, the Cabinet itself may decide that particular regulations when drafted should come before it. Your Committee records this information merely to disabuse the Houses and the public, if that be necessary, of the notion that all the Cabinet members turn their collective attention to each of the thousand and more regulations made each year. The way in which regulations by Order in Council are in fact made gives but little support to the view that there are safeguards in vesting subordinate law making powers in the Governor in Council rather than in individual Ministers. Furthermore, it does nothing to satisfy the need for scrutiny of subordinate laws both as proposed and as made, by the public and particularly by Parliament.

41 The Legal Profession Act, R.S.A. 1980, c. L-9. Sometimes the delegate can only enact subordinate legislation if it is approved by the Lieutenant Governor in Council, *e.g.*, the Nursing Profession Act, S.A. 1983, c. N-14.5; the Engineering Geological, and Geophysical Professions Act, S.A. 1981, c. E-11.1.

42 *Wiswell v. Winnipeg*, (1964) 45 D.L.R. (2d) 348, reversed on other grounds [1965] S.C.R. 512; *Camac Exploration Ltd. v. Oil & Gas Conservation Bd. of Alta.*, (1964) 47 W.W.R. 81 (Alta. T.D.). See quotation contained in note 25 to chapter 3.

43 Indeed, the legislature has considerably broadened the notice and hearing requirements for

In principle, the same type of argument ought to be available to seek judicial review of the procedure adopted for the enactment of other forms of regulations or subordinate legislation which really involve quasi-judicial functions.

The circumstances in which Parliament or a provincial legislature chooses to delegate legislative powers are many and varied. While it may not be possible to establish one model procedure for consulting in advance parties who might be affected by a particular type of subordinate legislation, it is clear that the legislative branch should carefully consider whether such consultation should take place, and in what form, when considering the parent legislation itself.[44]

Unlike parent legislation which is enacted after at least three readings in a public forum, subordinate legislation is generally enacted relatively privately. It is important, therefore, to devise a method whereby the public can determine the existence and content of subordinate legislation. Virtually all jurisdictions[45] in Canada require at least some of their subordinate legislation to be registered in one place, as well as to be published in an official gazette, before coming into force. Different jurisdictions, however, adopt somewhat different definitions of which "regulations" are subject to registration and publication, and provide certain exceptions to both of these general requirements. Let us therefore examine the applicable federal and Alberta legislation with respect to: (a) the filing of regulations in a central public registry; (b) the publication of regulations, or the exemption therefrom; and (c) the definition of the "regulations" to which such systems apply.

7. The Filing or Registration of Regulations

Both Alberta and federal legislation require the filing of regulations in a central public registry. Thus, section 2 of the Alberta Regulations Act,[46] provides as follows:

> 2(1) Every regulation or a certified copy of it shall be filed in duplicate with the registrar.
>
> (2) Unless a later day is provided, a regulation comes into force on the day it is filed with the registrar and in no case does a regulation come into force before the day of filing.

---

the enactment of *general* zoning by-laws, which do not affect only one person's land and which therefore might not have been subject at common law to the principles of natural justice. See the Planning Act, R.S.A. 1980, c. P-9, ss. 139, 140.

44 See Pt. E of the Fourth Report of the Scrutiny Committee, entitled "Drafting of Enabling Powers and of Subordinate Laws", pp. 357*ff.*, where the Scrutiny Committee recommends that all enabling clauses in parent legislation should be referred to it prior to enactment.

45 But not the Northwest Territories: see *Catholique v. R.*, [1980] 1 W.W.R. 166 (N.W.T. S.C.). Also, Quebec no longer has a central system for filing and publishing regulations. For a description of the situation in other provinces and countries, see the Zander Report, *infra*, note 114, and the McRuer Report, Vol. 1, s. 3, especially c. 26.

46 R.S.A. 1980, c. R-13.

(3) Unless expressly provided to the contrary in another Act, a regulation that is not filed as herein provided has no effect.

(4) If, before its filing, a regulation has been amended by any subsequent regulation, the filing of the first mentioned regulation with the amendment so made embodied therein or added to it is deemed compliance with this section in respect of all those regulations.

The filing requirements under the federal Statutory Instruments Act[47] are similar, with three exceptions. First, the federal scheme requires a pre-implementation examination of each federal regulation[48] by the Clerk of the Privy Council and the Deputy Minister of Justice to ensure that:

3. . . .
    (2) . . .
        (*a*) it is authorized by the statute pursuant to which it is to be made;
        (*b*) it does not constitute an unusual or unexpected use of the authority pursuant to which it is to be made;
        (*c*) it does not trespass unduly on existing rights and freedoms and is not, in any case, inconsistent with the purposes and provisions of the *Canadian Bill of Rights*; and
        (*d*) the form and draftsmanship of the proposed regulation are in accordance with established standards.

The Deputy Minister of Justice is required to draw the attention of the regulation-making authority to any problem arising under these headings. There is, however, no legal power requiring the regulation-making power to take account of such criticisms, although in practice the draft regulations probably would be amended before being made in final form. In any event, no regulation is invalid only because it was not examined prior to implementation by the Deputy Minister of Justice, although the Governor in Council has the power to revoke such a regulation in whole or in part.[49]

Secondly, all federal regulations are required to be registered within seven days of their having been made[50] unless an exemption has been granted. In Alberta, there is no time limit for registration, although lack of registration will generally prevent the regulation from coming into effect.[51]

---

47 S.C. 1970-71-72, c. 38.
48 *Ibid.*, s. 3 [am. 1976-77, c. 28, s. 42]. But note the exception provided for by s. 3(4) [re-en. 1976-77, c. 28, s. 42].
49 *Ibid.*, s. 8.
50 *Ibid.*, s. 5.
51 Section 2(2) of the Alberta Regulations Act, *supra*, note 46, provides that no regulation comes into force prior to being filed. However, s. 8(1)(*e*) of the Alberta Act provides a method for avoiding the filing requirement in certain circumstances, which has the effect of permitting such exempted regulations to come into effect prior to filing.

Thirdly, unlike the case under the Alberta Act,[52] the federal scheme specifically provides a method for permitting regulations to come into force prior to the date of registration. This may occur provided one of the following two conditions is met:[53]

9(1) . . .
>   (a) [the regulation] expressly states that it comes into force on a day earlier than that day and it is registered within seven days after it is made, or
>   (b) [the regulation] is of a class that . . . is exempted [from filing] . . .[54]

In either of these cases, the regulation-making authority is required to advise the Clerk of the Privy Council in writing of the reasons why it was not practical to wait to bring the regulation into force with registration.[55]

It sometimes becomes necessary to consider the legal effect of failure to register or file a regulation in accordance with the applicable legislation. In Alberta it is clear that an unfiled regulation has no effect whatever and will not be recognized by a court. As Dechene J. said in *Civil Service Association of Alberta v. Solicitor General of Alberta*:[56]

> It has not been filed and promulgated as a Regulation under the *Regulations Act* [R.S.A. 1970 c. 318], the filing of which is a prerequisite to its effectiveness under s. 3 of the *Regulations Act*. It is, in my view, merely an internal document for the guidance of members of the Public Service. Indeed, the evidence before me indicates that it can be altered or disregarded, at least in part, on verbal or written instructions from the Commissioner.

A different result, however, was reached by the Federal Court of Appeal in *Melville v. Attorney General of Canada*,[57] which held the corresponding obligation under the federal Act to be merely directory and not mandatory, so that failure to register did not invalidate the Order in Council in question. It may be possible to distinguish these two lines of cases in light of the much weaker filing requirement contained in the federal Act, which permits *ex post facto* filing as well as retroactive regulations, unlike the peremptory terms of the Alberta Act, which specifically states that no regulation has any effect

---

52 *Ibid.*
53 *Supra*, note 47, s. 9(1)(a).
54 In which case it comes into effect on the day it was made, or on such later date as is specified in the regulation.
55 *Supra*, note 47, s. 9(2).
56 2 A.R. 500 at 504, affirmed [1979] 3 W.W.R. 385 (C.A.). A similar result was reached in the decision by Hope J. in *Her Majesty The Queen upon the Information of Ranganathan Marayanan*, February 1978 (unreported).
57 (1983) 141 D.L.R. (3d) 191, reversing 129 D.L.R. (3d) 488 (Fed. C.A.).

until filed. Certainly, the position adopted by the Alberta courts reinforces the policy of the Act.

Finally, the Alberta Act contains a provision[58] which permits the Lieutenant Governor in Council to enact regulations exempting any other regulations, rules, orders or by-laws from the provisions of the Regulations Act. While such exempting regulations must themselves be filed and otherwise comply with the Regulations Act,[59] they clearly could be used to exempt other regulations from the filing requirements, and therefore from the consequences of non-filing. The ability to pass such exempting regulations therefore reinforces our view that the Alberta courts have correctly construed the mandatory nature of the filing requirement where no such exemption order has been enacted.

Obviously, the date of filing a regulation will generally precede the date of its publication, and may also precede the date upon which it is brought to the actual notice of a person affected by it. To this extent, therefore, it may be true that a person cannot be affected retroactively by a regulation if it cannot take effect prior to filing.[60] On the other hand, it is possible for a regulation to affect matters or to change the law with respect to a point in time prior to the date of filing. Although such a regulation will only become effective on the date of filing, it seems that it will from that moment validly alter the preceding law — in effect, retroactively.[61] Accordingly, it is not quite accurate to say that the Alberta Act does not permit retroactive regulations — apart altogether from ones exempted from the filing requirements.

---

58 R.S.A. 1980, c. R-13, s. 8(1)(e).

59 Section 18 of Alta. Reg. 377/68 (filed 22nd November 1968) lists the regulations generally exempted from the provisions of the Regulations Act. It has been frequently amended: see Reg. 62/69, 206/69, 310/69, 314/72, 95/78, 248/78, 193/81, 203/83, 296/84, 392/84. In addition, other regulations have been exempted from publication (although they must be filed). All of these are now listed in the Index to The Alberta Gazette.

60 Unless exempted from filing pursuant to s. 8 of the Act. Also, it is fairly common for an effective date to be different from the date of filing:

(1) A regulation may specify an effective date in the future *after* filing (s. 2(2) of the Regulations Act).

(2) Under the Interpretation Act, R.S.A. 1980, c. I-7, s. 7, regulations can be made and filed under an unproclaimed Act, but will only come into force on proclamation of the Act.

(3) If the regulation specifies no date for effectiveness, it becomes effective on filing (s. 2(2) of the Regulations Act).

61 *E.g.*, a regulation made and filed on 4th January 1984 may alter the rate of capital cost allowance available under the Alberta Corporate Income Tax Act for the 1973 taxation year. Under s. 2 of the Regulations Act, the regulation only comes into effect on 4th January 1984. Nevertheless, the consequence of that regulation is to change the law as it stood at some previous point in time, namely, 1973.

8. Publication of Regulations and Exemption Therefrom

In principle, the maxim that "ignorance of the law is no excuse" should apply as much to subordinate legislation as to an Act of Parliament itself. However, as noted in *R. v. Ross*,[62] there are important differences in the manner of enacting parent legislation compared to the exercise of delegated powers:

> Briefly, amongst other things, before a public Act can receive the Royal assent and become law it must first, in the form of a bill, be presented to and deliberated upon and conveyed or passed, through its different stages at different times and on different days, by the action of the members of the Legislative Assembly in concourse duly assembled in the proper place designated for that purpose, at which the public, including representatives of the press, are generally permitted to be present. Therefore the proceedings necessary to enact and bring into force an Act or law binding upon the public give to it a certain measure of publicity, and it is not difficult to understand why it is a general rule of law that one cannot successfully plead ignorance of such an Act or law.
>
> But, on the other hand, an order made by a Minister, such as the one under discussion, is on a different footing than is an Act of the Legislature. The making of such an order is at the discretion of the Minister himself, as appears by the provisions of s. 119 of the *Forest Act* [R.S.B.C. 1936, c. 102], and is drawn up and signed in his private office or some other private place, as I assume was the case with the order in question.
>
> There does not appear to be any provisions in the *Forest Act*, or any other Act, that I can find, requiring promulgation of such an order, nor *any provisions excluding such a requirement.*
>
> I think it hardly compatible with justice that a person may be convicted and penalized, and perhaps lose his personal liberty by being committed to jail in default of payment of any fine imposed, for the violation of an order of which he had no knowledge or notice at any material time.
>
> I think this view of the matter, without the necessity of further enlargement, is fairly in accord with the decisions rendered, respectively, in *Johnson v. Sargant & Sons*, [1918] 1 K.B. 101, and *Brightman & Co. v. Tate*, [1919] 1 K.B. 463, 35 T.L.R. 209.

A similar result was reached by Tallis J. in the Supreme Court of the Northwest Territories in *Catholique v. R.*,[63] which was decided on common

---

62 [1945] 3 D.L.R. 574 at 576-77 (B.C.Co.Ct.) *per* Harrison Co. Ct. J.
63 Ont. C.A., 9th March 1979 (unreported), affirmed [1980] 1 W.W.R. 166 (N.W.T. S.C.). See

law principles because no Territorial Ordinance dealt with the effect of publi-cation. Indeed, His Lordship referred to the decision by Martin J.A. in *R. v. Molis*[64], who expressly left open the question of whether ignorance of a regulation which has in fact been duly published might nevertheless in some circumstances still be a defence.

Under the Alberta Regulations Act, a regulation must either be published or actual notice of it must be given for a person to be bound by a regulation governed by the Act. Thus, section 3 provides

3(1) Subject to subsection (2) and (3), the registrar shall, within one month of the filing of the regulation, publish the regulation in The Alberta Gazette.

(2) The Minister may, by order, extend the time for publication of a regulation, and if the regulation is subsequently published a copy of the order or a notice of the order shall be published with the regulation.

(3) If a regulation, in the opinion of the Lieutenant Governor in Council,

(*a*) has been available in printed form to all persons who are likely to be interested therein, and

(*b*) is of such length as to render its publication in The Alberta Gazette unnecessary or undesirable,

the Lieutenant Governor in Council, by order, may dispense with the publication thereof and the regulation on registration is as valid against all persons as if it had been published.

(4) When, by order of the Minister or of the Lieutenant Governor in Council, the time for publication of a regulation is extended or its publication is dispensed with, the registrar shall publish the order or a notice of the order in The Alberta Gazette within one month after the making thereof.

(5) Unless expressly provided to the contrary in another Act, and subject to subsection (3), a regulation that is not published is not valid as against a person who has not had actual notice of it.

In theory, of course, another Act of the legislature could alter this general rule.[65] In addition, the Regulations Act itself provides two different ways to get around this general rule.

First, the Lieutenant Governor in Council may waive publication of a

---

also *Johnson v. Sargant & Sons*, [1918] 1 K.B. 101; *Jones v. Robson*, [1901] 1 K.B. 673; *Simms Motor Units v. Min. of Labour*, [1946] 2 All E.R. 201; *Simmonds v. Newell*, [1953] 1 W.L.R. 826; *R. v. Sheer Metalcraft Ltd.*, [1954] 1 Q.B. 586; *R. v. Villeneuve*, (1968) 2 C.R.N.S. 301 (N.S. Co. Ct.); *Blackpool Corp. v. Locker*, [1948] 1 K.B. 349 (C.A.).

64 [1980] 2 S.C.R. 356.

65 See note 91, *infra*.

specific regulation.[66] If this is done, the Act effectively provides that the mere filing of such an exempted regulation makes it as valid against all persons as if it had been published. Accordingly the lack of actual notice of such an exempted regulation would not appear to provide any legal defence to any matter which depends upon the regulation for its validity. The Lieutenant Governor's power to make exempt a particular regulation from publication is subject to the specific terms of section 3(3), which requires the regulation

(a) [to have] been available in printed form to all persons who are likely to be interested therein, and

(b) [to be] of such length as to render its publication in The Alberta Gazette unnecessary or undesirable.

If both of these conditions are met, the exempted regulation is effectively deemed to have been published.

Secondly, the Lieutenant Governor in Council can pass a regulation[67] to exempt any other regulation, rule, order or by-law from publication. A regulation exempted from publication by this method is not deemed by the Act to have been published, and therefore the better view[68] appears to be that actual notice of this type of exempted regulation must be given to the person to be affected by it.

Similarly, the federal Act requires all regulations to be published in the Canada Gazette within twenty-three days of registration of the regulation in both official languages.[69] Although a regulation is not invalidated by lack of publication,[70] the federal Act specifically provides that no person shall be convicted of an offence consisting of a contravention of the regulation which occurred while the regulation was unpublished, unless both of the following conditions obtain:

11. . . .

(2) . . .

(a) the regulation was exempted from [publication by a general regulation enacted by the Governor in Council,[71] or specifically on its face] provides that it shall apply . . . before it is published in the *Canada Gazette*,[72]

and

---

66 See s. 3(3).

67 Under s. 8(1)(c), which regulation would itself have to comply with the Act. See note 59, *supra*, for reference to regulations exempted from publication.

68 No cases appear to have been reported on this point.

69 The Statutory Instruments Act, S.C. 1970-71-72, c. 38, s. 11(1).

70 *Ibid.*, s. 11(2).

71 Pursuant to s. 27(c) [am. 1980-81-82-83, c. 111, s. 5 (Sched. IV, item 6)] of the federal Act, the general regulation would itself have to be published.

72 Thereby permitting the regulation-making authority to decide whether to exempt it from

(*b*) it is proved that at the date of the alleged contravention reasonable steps had been taken to bring the purport of the regulation to the notice of those persons likely to be affected by it.

Finally, one must consider the effect of non-publication on the validity of a regulation. Although no one can be convicted of an offence created by an unpublished regulation,[73] not all regulations create offences, and people may therefore be affected in quite substantial ways by such unpublished regulations. The Saskatchewan courts have reached this conclusion by upholding the validity of an unpublished Order in Council declaring California to be a reciprocal jurisdiction under the Saskatchewan Reciprocal Enforcement of Maintenance Orders Act, 1968.[74] This approach follows the English decision in *R. v. Sheer Metalcraft Ltd.*,[75] which, however, deals with the English Statutory Instruments Act, 1946, which implies that unpublished regulations are nevertheless in existence and therefore may have some legal effect.[76]

9. The Type of "Regulations" Subject to These Systems

Exactly what types of regulations are subject to the filing and publication requirements of these two Acts may be difficult to determine.

The word "regulation" is defined in the Alberta Act to mean[77]

any regulation, rule, order or by-law, *of a legislative nature* made or approved under the authority of an Act of the Legislature, including those made by any board, commission, association or similar body, whether incorporated or unincorporated, all the members of which, or all the members of the board of management or board of directors of which, are appointed by an Act of the Legislature or by the

---

publication. Compare this with the provision in s. 3 of the Alberta Act which grants a similar power to the Lieutenant Governor in Council (who may not be the regulation-making authority).

73 Unless one of the exceptions to publication applies.

74 S.S. 1968, c. 59 [now S.S. 1983, c. R-4.1]; see *Santa Clara v. Hudson*, [1978] 6 W.W.R. 124 (Sask. Dist. Ct.).

75 [1954] 1 Q.B. 586.

76 9 & 10 Geo. 6, c. 36. See s. 3(2) of the English Act, which specifically provides a defence for infringements of an unpublished statutory instrument. Because one can only infringe a prohibition which has existence, the wording of the English Act implies that the regulation is valid, and creates an offence, although a defence is available. If no offence is created, there is no need for a defence, but is it correct to assume that the unpublished regulation must therefore be in existence and valid? Such reasoning certainly flies in the face of the policy of the Act requiring publication.

77 Section 1(1)(*f*) of the Alberta Act, emphasis added.

> Lieutenant Governor in Council, but does not include any regu-
> lations, rule, order, by-law or resolution made by a local authority,[78]
> or except as hereinbefore otherwise provided, by a corporation
> incorporated under the laws of Alberta.

The requirement that a regulation must be "of a legislative nature" implies the existence of other regulations which are not subject to the filing, publication and other provisions of the Alberta Act. It may not be easy to determine whether a particular regulation is "of a legislative nature". As the Ontario Court of Appeal said in *Rose v. R.*,[79] dealing with a virtually identical provision:

> We are all of the opinion that the Order in question in this
> appeal is an act of a legislative and not of an administrative charac-
> ter. We have come to that conclusion upon a consideration of the
> terms of the Order in Council and of the legislation pursuant to
> which it was enacted. . . .
> The action of the Lieutenant-Governor in Council, as set out in
> the Order in Council referred to, in our opinion, clearly is of a legis-
> lative nature as I have said. We think that to an extent generally
> applicable to the public or large segments thereof it alters rights and
> responsibilities and even the nature and extent of those responsi-
> bilities. Upon that ground alone we think sufficient has been said to
> indicate the legislative nature of the action taken by the Lieutenant-
> Governor in Council as set out in the Order in Council referred to.
> . . . In coming to a conclusion as to the nature of the act performed,
> not only must one look at the substance rather than the form but
> indeed in the inquiry upon which one must embark, all the sur-
> rounding circumstances must be looked at and by that I include the
> nature of the body enacting the Order in question, the subject-
> matter of the Order, the rights and responsibilities, if any, altered or
> changed by that Order. Significant in our opinion among these
> indicia to be considered in a determination of the legal question, is
> the fact that the Order here under review is an Order made formally
> by the Lieutenant-Governor in Council upon the recommendation
> of one of the Ministers of the Crown. That is to say it is an Order
> made by the executive of the Government and an Order that the
> executive could not have made unless the power to make it had been
> delegated to it by the Legislature. While this is not decisive it is, as I

---

78 "Local authority" is defined in s. 1(1)(*b*):

> "local authority" means a city, town, village, municipal district, county, improvement
> district, hospital district, irrigation district, drainage district, special area, school
> division or school district.

79 (1960) 22 D.L.R. (2d) 633 at 634-36 (Ont. C.A.).

have said, one of the factors not without importance in the determination of the question.

While one must bear in mind that not all Orders-in-Council are regulations,[80]
the criteria laid down in the *Rose* case indicate that most regulations would
qualify as being "of a legislative nature", and therefore subject to the provisions of the Alberta Regulations Act.

Further, the definition of a "regulation" is extended under the Alberta
Act as follows:[81]

> **1** . . .
>
> > (2) Where a regulation, rule, order, or by-law is made or
> > approved, pursuant to an Act of the Legislature, by the Lieu-
> > tenant Governor in Council, a member of the Executive
> > Council, or any board, commission, association, or similar
> > body, of the kind mentioned in subsection (1)(f), if it
> > prescribes, fixes or designates
> >
> > (*a*) a district, area, person, animal or other thing, or
> > (*b*) a period of time,
> >
> > within, to, during, or in respect of, which the Act or any pro-
> > vision thereof does or does not apply, in whole or in part,
> > generally or in a restricted manner, or within, to, during, or in
> > respect of, which the Act provides that a thing specified in the
> > Act may or may not be done, or shall or shall not be done, *the
> > regulation, rule, order, or by-law shall be deemed to be a
> > regulation as defined in subsection (1)(f).*

The effect of the wording of this provision appears to deem such a regulation
to be "of a legislative nature" as well. Accordingly, all such regulations are
subject to the filing and publication provisions of the Regulations Act.

On the other hand, the Act also deems certain matters not to constitute
regulations. Thus, the definition excludes:

> . . . an order of the Lieutenant Governor in Council directing the
> issue of a proclamation bringing into force, suspending or repealing
> an Act of the Legislature or any provision thereof;[82]

and

> A regulation, rule, order, by-law or resolution made by a corpora-
> tion incorporated by a private Act of the Legislature, or by the board
> of directors or board of management of such a corporation.[83]

---

80 See note 39, *supra.*
81 Section 1(2), emphasis added.
82 Section 1(3).
83 Section 1(4).

The registrar is given authority to determine[84]

> whether any regulation, rule, order or by-law that has been presented to him for filing is a regulation within the meaning of this Act.

He is required[85] to report to the Lieutenant Governor in Council[86] at least monthly concerning anything which he has decided is not a regulation, and the Lieutenant Governor in Council has the authority to reverse the registrar's decision and to require the document to be registered and published as a regulation.[87] On the other hand, as noted before, the Lieutenant Governor in Council may make regulations exempting any other regulations, rules, orders or by-laws[88] from all of the provisions of the Regulations Act.[89] This power is additional to the more restricted provision permitting the Lieutenant Governor in Council to exempt a particular regulation from publication.[90] In particular, it provides a means to exempt particular regulations from filing, or from the invalidity which would otherwise result from failure to file. Finally, some statutes themselves contain specific provisions to the effect that the regulations, by-laws or rules made thereunder are *not* subject to the Regulations Act.[91]

The federal Statutory Instruments Act has a much more complicated scheme for determining which instruments must be filed and published. The federal definition of "regulation" reads as follows:[92]

> **2(1)** . . .
>
> > (*b*) "regulation" means a statutory instrument
> >
> > > (i) made in the exercise of a legislative power conferred by or under an Act of Parliament, or
> > > (ii) for the contravention of which a penalty, fine or imprisonment is prescribed by or under an Act of Parliament,
> >
> > and includes a rule, order or regulation governing the practice or procedure in any proceedings before a judicial or quasi-judicial body established by or under an Act of

---

84 Under s. 5(1).
85 Under s. 5(2).
86 But not to the legislature!
87 Under s. 5(4). Note, however, that the Lieutenant Governor in Council does not have the reverse power, and therefore cannot direct the registrar to treat something as not being a regulation.
88 Or any class thereof.
89 Section 8(1)(*e*).
90 Section 3(3).
91 See, *e.g.*, s. 149 of the Workers' Compensation Act, R.S.A. 1980, c. W-16; s. 8(3) of the Alberta Government Telephones Act, R.S.A. 1980, c. A-23; s. 19(4) of the Engineering, Geological and Geophysical Professions Act, R.S.A. 1980, c. E-11.1.
92 S.C. 1970-71-72 c. 38. s. 2(1)(*b*).

Parliament, and any instrument described as a regulation in any other Act of Parliament.

With one exception,[93] a regulation must be a "statutory instrument", which in turn is defined in the following manner:[94]

2(1) . . .

(*d*) "statutory instrument" means any rule, order, regulation, ordinance, direction, form, tariff of costs or fees, letters patent, commission, warrant, proclamation, by-law, resolution or other instrument issued, made or established

(i) in the execution of a power conferred by or under an Act of Parliament, by or under which such instrument is expressly authorized to be issued, made or established otherwise than by the conferring on any person or body of powers or functions in relation to a matter to which such instrument relates, or

(ii) by or under the authority of the Governor-in-Council, otherwise than in the execution of a power conferred by or under an Act of Parliament,

but does not include

(iii) any such instrument issued, made or established by a corporation incorporated by or under an Act of Parliament unless

(A) the instrument is a regulation and the corporation by which it is made is one that is ultimately accountable, through a Minister, to Parliament for the conduct of its affairs, or

(B) the instrument is one for the contravention of which a penalty, fine or imprisonment is prescribed by or under an Act of Parliament,

(iv) any such instrument issued, made or established by a judicial or quasi-judicial body, unless the instrument is a rule, order or regulation governing the practice or procedure in proceedings before a judicial or quasi-judicial body established by or under an Act of Parliament,

(v) any such instrument in respect of which, or in respect of the production or other disclosure of which, any privilege exists by law or whose contents are limited to

---

93 *Ibid.*, s. 2(2).
94 *Ibid.*, s. 2(1)(*d*).

advice or information intended only for use or assistance in the making of a decision or the determination
of policy, or in the ascertainment of any matter necessarily incidental thereto, or

(vi) an ordinance of the Yukon Territory or the Northwest
Territories or any instrument issued, made or established thereunder.

The federal scheme is therefore more complicated than the Alberta method of
identifying the types of subordinate legislation governed by the filing and
publishing system.[95] On the other hand, the federal Statutory Instruments Act
goes considerably further in providing a vehicle for parliamentary scrutiny of
delegates' actual exercise of Parliament's authority to legislate.

10. Parliamentary Scrutiny of Subordinate Legislation

Undoubtedly the most important aspect of the federal Statutory Instruments Act is the provision[96] for the systematic review and scrutinizing of
virtually every federal statutory instrument by a standing joint committee of
the Senate and House of Commons. In effect, this innovation provides a
mechanism for Parliament to examine and supervise the exercise of those
legislative powers which Parliament has delegated. Although the permanent
existence of the joint committee itself is not provided for by the federal Act,[97]
in practice a joint committee has been established each session with the following criteria for reviewing statutory instruments.[98]

Whether any Regulation or other Statutory Instrument . . .

1. (a) is not authorized by the terms of the enabling statute, or, if it
is made pursuant to the prerogative, its terms are not in conformity with the common law; or

(b) does not clearly state therein the precise authority for the
making of the Instrument;

---

95 The Fourth Report of the Scrutiny Committee strongly criticizes the federal definition of a
"statutory instrument" and the distinction between it and a "regulation", and recommends a
new definition along the lines originally proposed by the MacGuigan Committee: see paras.
56-65.

96 *Supra*, note 92, s. 26.

97 Section 26 does not establish the Scrutiny Committee, nor does it require one to be
established in each session of Parliament. The Fourth Report recommends that the Scrutiny
Committee be put on a permanent statutory basis: see Recommendation No. 3.

98 Appendix II to the Fourth Report. The Scrutiny Committee noted that these criteria cover
the question of the legality of subordinate legislation (*i.e.*, *ultra vires*) and fourteen instances
of impropriety not necessarily involving illegality — a point apparently lost on many
government draftsmen and statutory delegates. See para. 81 of the Fourth Report.

2. has not complied with the provisions of the *Statutory Instruments Act* with respect to transmittal, recording, numbering or publication;

3. (*a*) has not complied with any tabling provision or other condition set forth in the enabling statute; or

   (*b*) does not clearly state therein the time and manner of compliance with any such condition;

4. makes some unusual or unexpected use of the powers conferred by the enabling statute or by the prerogative;

5. trespasses unduly on the rights and liberties of the subject;

6. (*a*) tends directly or indirectly to exclude the jurisdiction of the Courts without explicit authorization therefor in the enabling statute; or

   (*b*) makes the rights and liberties of the subject dependent on administrative discretion rather than on the judicial process;

7. purports to have retroactive effect where the enabling statute confers no express authority so to provide or, where such authority is so provided, the retroactive effect appears to be oppressive, harsh or unnecessary;

8. appears for any reason to infringe the rule of law or the rules of natural justice;

9. provides without good and sufficient reason that it shall come into force before registration by the Clerk of the Privy Council;

10. in the absence of express authority to that effect in the enabling statute or prerogative, appears to amount to the exercise of a substantive legislative power properly the subject of direct parliamentary enactment, and not merely to the formulation of subordinate provisions of a technical or administrative character properly the subject of delegated legislation;

11. without express provision to the effect having been made in the enabling statute or prerogative, imposes a fine, imprisonment or other penalty, or shifts the onus of proof of innocence to the person accused of an offence;

12. imposes a charge on the public revenues or contains provisions requiring payment to be made to the Crown or to any other authority in consideration of any license or service to be rendered, or prescribes the amount of any such charge or payment, without express authority to that effect having been provided in the enabling statute or prerogative;

13. is not in conformity with the *Canadian Bill of Rights* [or the *Canadian Charter of Rights and Freedoms*[99]];

---

99 Constitution Act, 1982, Pt. I [am. SI/84-102].

14. is unclear in its meaning or otherwise defective in its drafting;
15. for any other reason requires elucidation as to its form or purport.

The joint committee has observed[100] that it has objected to a far higher proportion of the regulations which it has scrutinized than have its counterparts in the United Kingdom, Australia and Ontario. In addition to looking beyond mere questions of *ultra vires* to the substance of delegated legislation, the joint committee has insisted that each statutory instrument identify the specific legislative provision which is being relied upon for the enactment of the subordinate legislation.[101] The entire record of the proceedings of the joint committee is an excellent source for studying problems of subordinate legislation and compels one to question why Ontario is the only province to adopt such a scrutiny committee, particularly in light of the fact that all who exercise delegated powers derive their authority from the Sovereignty of Parliament. As one of the joint committees said:[102]

> The maintenance of parliamentary supremacy and of parliamentary democracy is imperative. The inability of Parliament to consider or to make all the laws necessary in the modern state should not lead to a decrease in accountability to Parliament for law making. Delegated law making is far too wide-spread a practice to be without democratic participation, procedural safeguards and parliamentary accountability. Yet, our present practices are based on the premises that delegated legislation is abnormal, and that it is confined to matters of detail. There can be no doubt that delegated legislation is now the ordinary and indispensible way of making the bulk of the non-common law of the land. It is beyond question that subordinate legislation is not confined to detail and more often than not embodies and effects policy. The making and control of subordinate law must therefore be regularized and brought into harmony with our constitutional order.

Indeed, the joint committee's work has gone far beyond merely scrutinizing delegated legislation *ex post facto*. The Federal Parliament empowered the joint committee

> to conduct a comprehensive study of the means by which Parliament can better oversee the government regulatory process and in particular to enquire into and report upon:

---

100 At p. 336 of the Fourth Report.
101 As recommended in the Second Report of the Committee to the 1976-77 session of Parliament, paras. 56-69.
102 Second Report for the 1976-77 Session of Parliament (also published separately from *Hansard*). See App. VI to the Fourth Report for a list of the government's (non-)action on the recommendations contained in the Second Report.

1. the appropriate principles and practices to be observed,

   (a) in the drafting of powers enabling delegates of Parliament to make subordinate laws;
   (b) in the enactment of statutory instruments;
   (c) in the use of executive regulation — including delegated powers and subordinate laws;

   and in the manner in which Parliamentary control should be effected in respect of the same;

2. the role, functions and powers of the Standing Joint Committee on Regulations and other Statutory Instruments.[103]

The overall thrust of the joint committee's report was to reiterate the need to reinforce Parliamentary control over both the content and the process for making delegated legislation — matters which go far beyond merely requiring registration and, publication as conditions precedent to the enforcement of subordinate legislation. Its recommendations include:[104]

1. Greater care in the use of legislative phrases which delegate powers, by instituting a procedure for referring all Bills containing such provisions to the Joint Committee after second reading but prior to enactment.[105]

2. Greater care in drafting subordinate legislation, in particular to prevent undue discretionary action by administrators which is incapable of judicial review.[106]

3. Developing a system for parliamentary scrutiny of the content of delegated legislation before it is enacted, perhaps by reference to the appropriate standing committees of the two Houses.[107]

4. Providing for a standard method for Parliament to disallow subordinate legislation, along the lines adopted in Australia.[108]

5. Recognize that the scrutiny of delegated legislation provided for in the *Act* and in the *Canadian Bill of Rights* is really an internal administrative procedure, and not an independent parliamentary review of the draft subordinate laws.

6. Encourage the publication of draft versions of delegated legislation, along the lines of the system in use under the U.S. federal *Administrative Procedures Act*.[109]

---

103 In the fourth session of the 30th Parliament, in the first session of the 31st Parliament and subsequently.
104 Fourth Report, Summary of Recommendations, pp. 366*ff.*
105 *Ibid.*, pp. 332, 357.
106 *Ibid.*, pp. 360-62.
107 *Ibid.*, p. 334.
108 *Ibid.*, pp. 335, 338.
109 *Ibid.*, pp. 338*ff.*

7. The definition of "regulations" should be expanded to include departmental directives, circulars and guidelines which direct public servants how to exercise discretions which have been delegated to them.[110]

8. A method should be devised to make certain that all regulations in fact are remitted to the Joint Committee for scrutiny.

9. The Joint Committee should be entitled to obtain copies of the legal opinions rendered by members of the Department of Justice advising as to the legality of proposed regulations.[111]

10. The complicated definitions of "regulation" and "statutory instrument" be replaced by a simpler, more comprehensive definition of "regulations", as recommended by the MacGuigan Committee in 1969.[112]

11. The Joint Committee should be put on a permanent, statutory basis, and its criteria for scrutinizing delegated legislation should be contained in that new *Subordinate Legislation Act*.

In summary, the federal joint committee is doing excellent work on two separate fronts: one, on reviewing the legality and appropriateness of the content of the vast flow of particular subordinate laws enacted each year; the other, on finding methods to improve the Federal Parliament's conscious control over the circumstances in which it delegates powers to the administration, and over the administration's use of that delegated power.[113] Both of these goals represent a re-assertion of the supremacy of Parliament. It is regrettable that the Alberta Government has to date rejected the need for a provincial scrutiny committee, even for the first purpose of scrutinizing the actual use of powers which the provincial legislature has delegated to the provincial executive.[114]

---

110 *Ibid.*, p. 356.

111 *Ibid.*, pp. 363-64.

112 *Ibid.*, paras. 57, 61.

113 The reader may also usefully refer to the following appendices to the Fourth Report: App. III, which describes the scrutiny systems used in the United Kingdom and in the Commonwealth of Australia for parliamentary control of delegated legislation; App. IV, which refers to the administrative requirement adopted by the federal Treasury Board for passing any "health, safety or fairness" regulation; App. V, which refers to the experience in the United States under the federal Administrative Procedures Act; App. VI, which lists the government's disposition of the recommendations made in the committee's Second Report (for the 1976-77 Session).

114 In November 1974, a Select Committee of the Legislative Assembly on Regulations in the Province of Alberta (the "Zander Committee") tabled its report in the legislature. It made 41 recommendations, including: (a) the establishment of a provincial scrutiny committee; (b) pre-publication of draft regulations, if possible accompanying the introduction of bills into the legislature; (c) the adoption of the guidelines set out in the McRuer Report (Ont.) for drafting regulations and the proper role and content thereof; (d) that regulation-making powers in legislation should be as specific as possible; (e) that regulations should be void if

11. Municipal By-laws: A Particular Type of Subordinate Legislation

Municipal by-laws are an important species of subordinate legislation, which possibly affect more people more directly than other types of regulations. It is useful, therefore, to consider the procedures required for the enactment, filing, publication, and validity of municipal by-laws, particularly as these differ somewhat from those contained in the Regulations Act.

In the first place, all municipal by-laws are *subordinate* legislation because municipalities are the creatures of provincial legislation under our constitutional system. This has two principal consequences. On the one hand, it means that municipal by-laws can only be valid if they fall within an area constitutionally allocated to the provinces under section 92 of the Constitution Act. Thus, many by-laws have been struck down for trenching on areas of federal legislative authority.[115] On the other hand, the doctrine of *ultra vires* applies to restrict by-laws to areas which the provincial legislatures have validly delegated to municipalities.[116] These legal constraints, therefore, affect the validity of municipal legislation, even though municipalities are granted sweeping powers to make laws for the peace, order and good government of the municipality, its health, safety, morality and welfare.[117]

Secondly, section 1(1)(*f*) of the Alberta Regulations Act specifically excludes municipal by-laws from the definition of a "regulation", with the result that the filing and publication system of that Act does not apply to municipal by-laws. Nevertheless, the Municipal Government Act[118] contains provisions requiring public hearings prior to the enactment of many types of by-laws, which must also be made generally available to the public.[119] Indeed,

---

not published within 30 days of filing; (f) that all regulations should be published by the Queen's Printer; (g) that the indexing system for regulations should be improved; (h) that the regulations should be regularly revised and consolidated, like the statutes. Unfortunately, the report has not been adopted by the government or the legislature, and no reference can be found of its even having been debated. Nevertheless, it is an extremely useful source, particularly on the history of the control of regulations in Alberta, Canada, the United Kingdom, and various other Commonwealth jurisdictions.

One should also note the Report of the Special Committee on Boards and Tribunals to the Legislative Assembly of Alberta (the "Clement Committee") (1965), which also relates to the exercise and control of delegated statutory powers, although not always of a legislative nature.

115 *E.g.*, attempts to regulate prostitution have been held to infringe on the federal power to enact criminal law.

116 See the cases listed in note 11, *supra*.

117 See, *e.g.*, s. 112 of the Municipal Government Act, R.S.A. 1980, c. M-26; the Municipal Taxation Act, R.S.A. 1980, c. M-31; and the School Act, R.S.A. 1980, c. S-3.

118 See note 117, *supra*.

119 Although there is no general province-wide registry of municipal by-laws, and it may frequently be difficult to determine the exact extent of by-laws in force in a particular municipality. This problem was considered by the Zander Committee Report to the Alberta

other legislation, such as the Planning Act, requires a municipality to give specific notice to certain parties prior to the enactment of certain types of by-laws likely to affect those persons.[120] These statutory provisions generally exceed and supplant any common law requirement on the municipality to follow the principles of natural justice or fairness in enacting particular types of by-laws. In principle, the effect of a failure to comply with these statutory procedures should render the by-law void.[121]

Thirdly, the common law has long required notice and hearings prior to the enactment of certain types of by-laws — apart altogether from any statutorily imposed procedures. Although all municipal by-laws and resolutions are legislative in form, the courts have long recognized the quasi-judicial nature of by-laws affecting the rights or property of particular individuals. Accordingly, a municipality can only pass such by-laws if it complies with the principles of natural justice or procedural fairness.[122] The exact content of these common law procedural requirements may be difficult to determine in particular circumstances,[123] as may be the border line between by-laws which are quasi-judicial in nature and those which are truly legislative.[124] In any event, the better view is that a breach of these common law procedural requirements renders the by-law void, not merely voidable.[125]

12. Summary

The purpose of this chapter has been to focus attention on those delegated powers which are of a legislative nature. On the one hand, the doctrine

---

legislature in 1974, which recommended "a centralized agency for the recording, reviewing and distribution of all municipal by-laws and resolutions in the Province of Alberta", much like the Ontario Municipal Board. To date, however, this recommendation has not been implemented.

120 See ss. 139 and 140 of the Planning Act, R.S.A. 1980, c. P-9.

121 See *Harvie v. Calgary Regional Planning Comm.*, (1979) 8 Alta. L.R. (2d) 166, reversing 5 Alta. L.R. (2d) 301 (C.A.). A question may arise whether such statutory procedures are mandatory or merely directory, in which case a failure to comply with them might not render the decision void. In such a case, however, what authority would the court have to strike down the by-law, even if flagrant injustice had been done by not notifying a particular person affected by the by-law?

122 See, *e.g.*, *Wiswell v. Winnipeg*, (1964) 48 W.W.R. 193, reversed on other grounds [1965] S.C.R. 512, quoted from at note 25 in chapter 3, *supra*; *Camac Exploration Ltd. v. Oil & Gas Conservation Bd. of Alta.*, (1964) 43 D.L.R. (2d) 755 (Alta. T.D.); *Campeau Corp. v. Calgary*, (1979) 7 Alta. L.R. (2d) 294, reversing (1978) 8 A.R. 77 (C.A.). In *Campeau Corp. v. Calgary (No. 2)*, (1980) 12 Alta. L.R. (2d) 379, the Court of Appeal declined to interfere with council's actions, which it specifically held to be legislative and not quasi-judicial in nature.

123 See chapter 6, *infra*.

124 See, *e.g.*, *Campeau (No. 1)* and *(No. 2)* on this point, *supra*, note 122.

125 See H.W.R. Wade, "Unlawful Administrative Act: Void or Voidable?", Pt. I at (1967) 83 L.Q. Rev. 499; Pt. II at (1968) 84 L.Q. Rev. 95; Wade's *Administrative Law*, 4th ed. (1977) especially pp. 296-301 and 447-50. See also D.P. Jones, "Discretionary Refusal of Judicial Review in Administrative Law", (1981) 19 Alta. L. Rev. 483.

of *ultra vires* applies to subordinate legislation as it does to all delegated powers. On the other hand, if the delegate exercises his legislative powers correctly, the subordinate legislation is as valid as though it were contained in a parent Act. It is not surprising, therefore, to note that most jurisdictions have created systems for filing and publishing a large part of their subordinate legislation. These systems are not perfect, and particular items of subordinate legislation can be exempted from filing or publication. We also observed a certain movement (not yet adopted everywhere) towards re-asserting effective control by the legislative branch of the subordinate legislation enacted in its name. In the future, one might expect an increased role for parliamentary scrutiny committees, as well as greater statutory procedures applicable prior to the enactment of subordinate legislation. In summary, subordinate legislation is an extremely important legal phenomenon affecting vast portions of the life of every citizen. No study of Administrative Law would be complete without examining it.

13. Selected Bibliography

Most of the standard works referred to in the previous chapter have sections dealing with problems associated with delegation of powers. In addition, the reader might refer to:

Driedger, "Subordinate Legislation", (1960) 38 Can. Bar Rev. 1.

Fairweather, "The Attitude of the Supreme Court of Canada toward Inter-delegation: *Coughlin v. Ontario Highway Transport Board*", (1970) 5 U.B.C. L. Rev. 43.

Fourth Report of the Joint Standing Committee on Regulations and Other Statutory Instruments (Canada), for the 1st Session of the 32nd Parliament (Statutory Instruments No. 10).

Friedmann, "Statute Law and Its Interpretation in the Modern State", (1948) 26 Can. Bar Rev. 1277.

Hewitt, *The Control of Delegated Legislation* (1953).

Janisch, H.N., "What is Law?", 55 Can. Bar Rev. 576.

Kerwell, *Parliamentary Supervision of Delegated Legislation* (1960).

Lanham, "Delegated Legislation and Publication".

Lanham, D.J., "Delegated Legislation and the Alter Ego Principle", (1984) 100 L. Q. Rev. 587.

McCormick on Evidence, 2nd ed., pp. 757 *et seq.*

McIntosh, "Controls on Federal Legislation", (1970) 35 Sask. Bar Rev. 63.

Mallory, "Parliamentary Scrutiny of Delegated Legislation in Canada", [1969] P.L.

Mullan, "Recent Developments in Nova Scotian Administrative Law", (1978) 4 Dalhousie L. J. 467 at 555.

Powe, "The Georgia Straight and Freedom of Expression in Canada", (1970) 48 Can. Bar Rev. 410.

Report of the McRuer Royal Commission (Ontario), especially Vol. 1.

Report of the Second Commonwealth Conference on Delegated Legislation, Vol. 1 (Report), Vol. 2 (Documents), Vol. 3 (Transcript of Proceedings), Ottawa, April 1983.

Report of the Select Committee of the Alberta Legislature on Regulations (the "Zander Committee"), November 1974.

Report of the Special Committee on Boards and Tribunals to the Legislative Assembly of Alberta (the "Clement Committee"), 1965.

Rutherford, "Legislative Review of Delegated Legislation", (1969) 47 Can. Bar Rev. 352.

Second Report of the Joint Standing Committee on Regulations and Other Statutory Instruments (Canada) (Statutory Instruments No. 1), 1976-77.

Third Report of the Special Committee of the House of Commons on Statutory Instruments (the "MacGuigan Committee"), 1968-69.

Wigmore on Evidence, 3rd ed. (1940), vol. 9, pp. 551 *et seq.*

Williams, "The Making of Statutory Instruments", (1970) 8 Alta. L. Rev. 324.

Willis, "*Delegatus Non Potest Delegare*", (1943) 21 Can. Bar Rev. 257.

Willis, "Statutory Interpretation in a Nutshell", (1938) 16 Can. Bar Rev. 1.

14. Reports of the Federal Scrutiny Committee

Substantive Reports of the Standing Joint Committee on Regulations and Other Statutory Instruments have been numbered in a series stretching over the several sessions and Parliaments since January 1977. The substantive reports presented to the two Houses to date are as follows:

Statutory Instruments No. 1 — General Report (1977), Second Report for the Second Session of the Thirtieth Parliament.

Statutory Instruments No. 2 — Postal Rate Increases (1977), SOR/76-552, Domestic First Class Mail Regulations, SOR/76-553, Second Class Mail Regulations, amendment, and SI/76-101, Postmaster General Authority to Prescribe Fees Order, Third Report for the Second Session of the Thirtieth Parliament.

Statutory Instruments No. 3 — Postal Rate Increases (1978), SOR/78-297, Domestic First Class Mail Regulations, SOR/78-298, Second Class Mail Regulations, amendment, and SI/78-60, Postmaster General Authority to Prescribe Fees Order, Fourth Report for the Third Session of the Thirtieth Parliament.

Statutory Instruments No. 4 — Destruction of Natural Growth on lands adjoining Airports (1978), SOR/76-311, SOR/76-312, SOR/76-350, SOR/76-474, SOR/77-414, SOR/77-470, SOR/77-724, SOR/77-796, SOR/77-797, SOR/77-798, SOR/77-806, SOR/77-807, SOR/77-808, SOR/77-809, SOR/77-810, SOR/77-868, SOR/78-657, SOR/78-771, Third Report for the Fourth Session of the Thirtieth Parliament.

Statutory Instruments No. 5 — Absence of Legal Rules governing Import Quotas on Footwear and Other Goods (1979), SOR/77-1058, Import Control List, amendment, SOR/77-1059, General Import Permit No. 57, Fourth Report for the Fourth Session of the Thirtieth Parliament.

Statutory Instruments No. 6 — Special Terms of Reference (1979) Fifth Report for the Fourth Session of the Thirtieth Parliament.

Statutory Instruments No. 7 — Postal Rate Increases (1979), SOR/79-159, Domestic First Class Mail Regulations, amendment, SOR/79-161, Second Class Mail Regulations, amendment, and SI/79-20, Postmaster General Authority to Prescribe Fees Order, Sixth Report for the Fourth Session of the Thirtieth Parliament.

Statutory Instruments No. 8 — Criteria and Special Terms of Reference (1979), First Report for the First Session of the Thirty-First Parliament.

Statutory Instruments No. 9 — Criteria, and Special Terms of Reference Renewed (1980), First Report for the First Session of the Thirty-Second Parliament.

Statutory Instruments No. 10 — Report under Special Terms of Reference (1980), Fourth Report for the First Session of the Thirty-Second Parliament.

Statutory Instruments No. 11 — Cancellation of Licences to sell Postage Stamps (1980), SOR/72-263, Sale of Postage Stamps Regulations, Section 14, Fifth Report for the First Session of the Thirty-Second Parliament.

II

GROUNDS FOR JUDICIAL REVIEW

5

Introduction
to the Grounds
for Judicial
Review

1. General

Part II of this book deals with the grounds upon which superior courts may review the legality of a delegate's actions. It does not deal with the remedies or vehicles available for obtaining such judicial review; these are discussed in Part III.

Because most Administrative Law deals with the right of the superior courts to review the legality of actions allegedly taken by delegates pursuant to statutory authority, a great deal of attention must be focused on the precise limits of the statutory power being exercised. Although the doctrine of Parliamentary Sovereignty generally means that specific legislation can be enacted to delegate virtually any power, the corollary is that any action taken outside of the area (or "jurisdiction") specifically delegated by statute will be *ultra vires*. In the end, the superior courts have the inherent right to construe the statutory language to determine whether the impugned administrative action is in fact authorized or instead is *ultra vires*.

This part examines possible jurisdictional defects from two aspects. First, chapter 6 examines defects which prevent a delegate from acquiring jurisdiction "in the narrow sense". Secondly, other errors which may cause the delegate to lose or exceed his jurisdiction are examined. Thus, chapter 7 considers the abuse of discretion; chapter 8 deals with breaches of the *audi alteram partem* rule and the duty to be fair; and chapter 9 examines the rule against bias (*nemo judex in sua causa debet esse*).

Although all of the previous grounds for judicial review are jurisdictional in nature, the superior courts have also historically asserted the anomalous power to issue *certiorari* to correct many *intra* jurisdictional errors of law on the face of the record. This ground for judicial review has, however, recently been restricted to only those errors of law which are "patently unreasonable". These developments are discussed in chapter 10.

The examination will begin with a consideration of the various meanings which have been given to "jurisdiction".

2. The "Narrow" and "Wide" Meanings of "Jurisdiction"

"Jurisdiction" is one of the most elusive concepts in Administrative Law. In its broadest sense, "jurisdiction" means the power to do every aspect of an *intra vires* action. In a narrower sense, however, "jurisdiction" means the power to commence or embark on a particular type of activity. A defect in jurisdiction "in the narrow sense" is thus distinguished from other errors — such as a breach of natural justice, considering irrelevant evidence, or acting for an improper purpose — which take place *after* the delegate has lawfully started his activity, but which cause him to leave or exceed his jurisdiction. Lord Reid's analysis of these difficulties in defining "jurisdiction" in *Anisminic Ltd. v. Foreign Compensation Commission* is particularly useful:[1]

> It has sometimes been said that it is only where a tribunal acts without jurisdiction that its decision is a nullity. But in such cases the word "jurisdiction" has been used in a very wide sense, and I have come to the conclusion that it is better not to use the term except in the narrow and original sense of the tribunal being entitled to enter on the inquiry in question. But there are many cases where, although the tribunal had jurisdiction to enter on the inquiry, it has done or failed to do something in the course of the inquiry which is of such a nature that its decision is a nullity. It may have given its decision in bad faith. It may have made a decision which it has no power to

---

1 [1969] 2 A.C. 147 at 171.

make. It may have failed in the course of the inquiry to comply with the requirements of natural justice. It may in perfect good faith have misconstrued the provisions giving it power to act so that it failed to deal with the question remitted to it and decided some question which was not remitted to it. It may have refused to take into account something which it was required to take into account. Or it may have based its decision on some matter which, under the provisions setting it up, it had no right to take into account. I do not intend this list to be exhaustive. But if it decides a question remitted to it for decision without committing any of these errors it is as much entitled to decide that question wrongly as it is to decide it rightly. I understand that some confusion has been caused by my having said in *Reg. v. Governor of Brixton Prison, Ex parte Armah* [1968] A.C. 192, 234 that if a tribunal has jurisdiction to go right it has jurisdiction to go wrong. So it has, if one uses "jurisdiction" in the narrow original sense. If it is entitled to enter on the inquiry and does not do any of those things which I have mentioned in the course of the proceedings, then its decision is equally valid whether it is right or wrong subject only to the power of the court in certain circumstances to correct an error of law. I think that, if these views are correct, the only case cited which was plainly wrongly decided is *Davies v. Price* [1958] 1 W.L.R. 434. But in a number of other cases some of the grounds of judgment are questionable.

It is important to remember that virtually all grounds for judicial review of administrative action depend upon an attack on some aspect of the delegate's jurisdiction to do the particular activity in question. Consequently, it is equally important to remember that any behaviour which causes the delegate to *exceed* his jurisdiction is just as fatal as any error which means that he never had jurisdiction "in the narrow sense" even to commence his action.

3. Judicial Review, Jurisdiction and Privative Clauses

The jurisdictional nature of most of judicial review is extremely important when the statute authorizing the delegate's action contains a privative clause.[2] Although such a clause purports to insulate the delegate's action from judicial review, the courts have consistently held that privative clauses cannot protect decisions taken outside the delegate's jurisdiction. The court can declare such decisions to be *ultra vires* and void. In other words, the exact ambit of the delegate's jurisdiction is an objective matter to be determined by the court's construction of the statute in question, and the delegate's jurisdiction is not extended by the mere presence of a privative

---

2 For a discussion of the different types of privative clauses, and their legal effect, see Part III, *infra*. See also the discussion of the "patently unreasonable" test for determining which errors of law go to jurisdiction in chapter 10, *infra*.

clause in the legislation.[3] By contrast, a privative clause will prevent judicial review only where the delegate has made an error of law *within* his jurisdiction[4] — which is the one ground for judicial review which is not jurisdictional in nature. If the error of law lies within jurisdiction, a privative clause has the effect of ousting the superior court's anomalous common law jurisdiction to correct the error, because the delegate's decision or action is not *ultra vires*, that is, it legally exists, and therefore there is something which can be protected by the privative clause. No infallible test has been developed, however, for distinguishing errors of law which deprive a delegate of his jurisdiction from those which lie within it.[5]

4. Problems in Determining the Ambit of Jurisdiction

(a) Implied Statutory Intent

A precise delimitation of the ambit of the delegate's jurisdiction is frequently a very difficult matter of statutory interpretation. In most cases, the particular objection to the delegate's behaviour is not specifically dealt with by the authorizing statute; if it were, no argument could arise. For example, questions frequently arise as to specific aspects of the procedure to be adopted by the delegate in reaching his decision or prior to his taking action. In the absence of a comprehensive and specific statutory code of procedure,[6] the courts must determine whether the principles of natural justice or the duty to be fair apply to the governmental activity in question, and if so what their precise content is in all of the circumstances of the case. In the end, the resolution of most jurisdictional questions involves application of the generally accepted rules of statutory construction,[7] which are, nevertheless, difficult to apply to particular statutes. Accordingly, it is extremely important to read the statute under which the delegate purports to act!

(b) Discretion

The concept of discretion sometimes compounds the difficulty in determining the precise ambit of the delegate's jurisdiction. Lord Morris referred to this in his decision in *Anisminic*:[8]

---

3 Although the existence of a privative clause may make the courts less inclined to interfere with decisions of the statutory delegate, so that they more readily exercise their discretion to refuse to issue a remedy even though grounds for judicial review exist.

4 See chapter 10, *infra*.

5 *Ibid.*, section 9.

6 The Administrative Procedures Act, R.S.A. 1980, c. A-2, is a partial code of procedure, but only applies to a very few provincial tribunals. No corresponding federal code exists to govern the procedure of federal tribunals. On procedural fairness, see chapter 8, *infra*.

7 For a discussion of the rules of statutory interpretation, see *Maxwell on The Interpretation of Statutes*, 10th ed. (1953); and E.A. Driedger, *The Construction of Statutes* (Toronto: Butterworths, 1974).

8 [1969] 2 A.C. 147 at 182, emphasis added.

In all cases similar to the present one it becomes necessary, therefore, to ascertain what was the question submitted for the determination of a tribunal. What were its terms of reference? What was its remit? What were the questions left to it or sent to it for its decision? What were the limits of its duties and powers? Were there any conditions precedent which had to be satisfied before its functions began? *If there were, was it or was it not left to the tribunal itself to decide whether or not the conditions precedent were satisfied?* If Parliament has enacted that provided a certain situation exists then a tribunal may have certain powers, it is clear that the tribunal will not have those powers unless the situation exists. The decided cases illustrate the infinite variety of the situations which may exist and the variations of statutory wording which have called for consideration. Most of the cases depend, therefore, upon an examination of their own particular facts and of particular sets of words. It is, however, abundantly clear that questions of law as well as of fact can be remitted for the determination of a tribunal.

In some circumstances, therefore, the discretionary nature of the delegate's power may have the effect of widening his jurisdiction — and thereby reducing the ambit for judicial review on the ground of jurisdictional error.[9]

5. Is an Ultra Vires Action Void or Voidable?

The question sometimes arises whether an *ultra vires* act is void or merely voidable.[10] The answer is important in order to determine whether the delegate's action has any legal effect prior to the declaration by the court that it is *ultra vires*. In principle, all *ultra vires* administrative actions are void, not voidable, and there are no degrees of invalidity. This is clearly true where the delegate is not even purporting to deal with the matter which the legislation grants to him: such substantive errors of jurisdiction "in the narrow sense" identified by Lord Reid are clearly void, and are not even arguably voidable. Similarly, Lord Reid indicated that subsequent errors which cause a delegate to exceed or lose his jurisdiction (*e.g.*, abuse of discretion, breaches of natural justice, certain errors of law) make his actions a nullity. Although people may have acted on the assumption that the delegate did have authority to do the impugned action, the effect of the court's granting of judicial review must be to declare that that was an erroneous state of affairs, that the delegate never had

---

9 *Liversidge v. Anderson*, [1942] A.C. 206, is probably the most striking example of this. There a majority of the House of Lords construed a delegation of internment powers in subjective terms, not objective ones, thereby making judicial review virtually impossible.

10 For a complete discussion of this point, see H.W.R. Wade, "Unlawful Administrative Action: Void or Voidable?", Part I at (1967) 83 L.Q. Rev. 499, Part II at (1968) 84 L.Q. Rev. 95; Wade's *Administrative Law*, 4th ed., especially at pp. 296-301 and 447-50; and D.P. Jones, "Discretionary Refusal of Judicial Review in Administrative Law", (1981) 19 Alta. L. Rev. 483.

jurisdiction to do the particular action in the manner complained of. Contrary to the *dicta* by the Supreme Court of Canada in *Harelkin v. The University of Regina*[11] to the effect that a breach of natural justice merely renders the delegate's action voidable, theoretical considerations require one to conclude that all of the types of excess of jurisdiction discussed in chapters 7, 8, 9 and 10 render the decision or action void. This theoretical conclusion is of practical importance if there is a privative clause, because then the courts can only review errors of *jurisdiction* (whether "narrow" or "wide"), *which can only occur if the action is void, not voidable.*

6. The Discretion to Refuse a Remedy Where Grounds for Judicial Review Exist

It has been noted that the courts have a discretion to refuse at least some of the remedies for illegal administrative action even if grounds for judicial review have been established. Although the proper ambit for the exercise of this judicial discretion is discussed in Part III, it is important to remember that the existence of this discretion does not restrict the grounds for judicial review of illegal administrative action. Those cases in which the courts exercise their discretion to refuse a remedy even though grounds for judicial review undoubtedly exist should be identified and distinguished from those cases which refuse judicial review because no grounds for relief have been disclosed.

7. Summary

With the exception of the anomalous use of *certiorari* to correct certain intra-jurisdictional errors of law on the face of the record, all grounds for judicial review depend upon a defect in the delegate's jurisdiction to do the particular act in question. This defect may occur in his acquisition of jurisdiction. Alternatively, the abuse of discretion or breach of natural justice may cause him to lose jurisdiction. All of these constitute grounds for judicial review. However, because the courts have the discretion to refuse certain remedies, a remedy may not be granted in every case where there are grounds to review an illegal administrative action.

The following chapters examine in some detail the separate grounds for judicial review of illegal administrative action.

---

11 [1979] 2 S.C.R. 561. In the *Olds College* case (Re *A.U.P.E. and Olds College Bd. of Govs.*, [1982] 1 S.C.R. 923, discussed in chapter 10, *infra*), Chief Justice Laskin attempted to correct the dicta from *Harelkin* by saying: "Jurisdictional errors, *including want of natural justice...*". This position must be correct in theory.

8. Selected Bibliography

Akehurst, M.B., "Void or Voidable? — Natural Justice and Unnatural Meanings", (1968) 31 M.L.R. 138.

Arthurs, H.W., "Protection Against Judicial Review", in Canadian Institute for the Administration of Justice, *Judicial Review of Administrative Rulings*. Montreal: Les Editions Yvon Blais Inc. (1983), p. 149.

David, H., "Some Consequences of Procedural Error", in Canadian Institute for the Administration of Justice, *Judicial Review of Administrative Rulings*. Montreal: Les Editions Yvon Blais Inc. (1983), p. 335.

Macdonald, R.A., "Absence of Jurisdiction: A Perspective", Canadian Institute for the Administration of Justice, *Judicial Review of Administrative Rulings*. Montreal: Les Editions Yvon Blais Inc. (1983), p. 179.

Oliver, D., "Void and Voidable in Administrative Law: A Problem of Legal Recognition", (1981) 34 Current Legal Problems 43.

Peiris, G.L., "Natural Justice and Degrees of Invalidity of Administrative Action", [1983] P. L. 634.

Rubinstein, A., *Jurisdiction and Illegality*. Oxford: Clarendon Press, 1965.

Wade, H.W.R., "Unlawful Administrative Action: Void or Voidable?", Part I at (1967) 83 L.Q. Rev. 499.

Wade, H.W.R., "Unlawful Administrative Action: Void or Voidable?", Part II at (1968) 84 L.Q. Rev. 95.

6

Defects in Acquiring Jurisdiction

1. Introduction

Adopting Lord Reid's narrow meaning of jurisdiction,[1] one must focus on the acquisition of the delegate's jurisdiction to do the particular act in question. This requires an examination of the statute to determine: (a) precisely what sort of thing the delegate is authorized to do, outside of which his actions are clearly *ultra vires*; (b) that the delegate has been validly constituted, by identifying who is the delegate, whether he can sub-delegate his responsibilities and powers, and has in fact been validly appointed; (c) whether the delegate has complied with all statutory requirements, such as

---

1 In *Anisminic Ltd., v. Foreign Compensation Comm.*, [1969] 2 A.C. 147 at 171, quoted in chapter 5, *supra*.

advertising or giving notices to particular people; and (d) whether any other preliminary or collateral matters have been complied with in order to bring the delegate into the jurisdiction granted to him by statute. Errors on any one of these matters may prevent the delegate from acquiring jurisdiction in Lord Reid's narrow sense of the word, will render the delegate's actions *ultra vires*, and will provide grounds for judicial review.

2. Substantive *Ultra Vires*

It is obvious that a delegate can only acquire jurisdiction to do the type of activity authorized by the statute, and any other activity will be *ultra vires*. Thus, a delegate authorized to build a park has no jurisdiction to build a highway instead, and any attempt to do so will be *ultra vires* and therefore susceptible to judicial review.

3. Constitution of the Delegate

Jurisdiction can only be acquired by the person contemplated by the statute to do the particular activity in question. Accordingly, questions can always be raised as to whether the delegate has been properly constituted, which really breaks down into two separate questions: (a) in what circumstances can the delegate sub-delegate all or any of his powers and responsibilities to another person; and (b) what formalities, if any, must be observed in appointing a particular delegate?

(a) Sub-delegation

The maxim *delegatus non potest delegare*[2] states the general rule that a delegate may not sub-delegate statutory powers. The policy underlying the general rule reflects the Sovereignty of Parliament, which after all chose the specific delegate to whom it granted the statutory power in question.

Parliament may, of course, specifically authorize the sub-delegation of powers, and this has the effect of ousting the applicability of the maxim *delegatus non potest delegare* altogether. Thus, the Universities Act[3] creates the Universities Co-ordinating Council to co-ordinate degree programmes given by universities in Alberta as well as to determine the equivalence of non-Alberta degrees relating to various professions. The Universities Act specifically permits the council to delegate these latter powers to a Professional Examination Board in each subject, and further authorizes each board to sub-sub-delegate any or all of its powers to an executive committee of the board.[4] Because the legislation specifically permits these instances of sub-delegation,

---

2 "A delegate cannot sub-delegate".
3 R.S.A. 1980, c. U-5.
4 *Ibid.*, s. 64 [re-en. 1984, c. 41, s. 2].

no question of *ultra vires* can arise if it occurs.[5]

A more difficult question of statutory interpretation arises when Parliament does not use express language, but may nevertheless arguably be said to have intended to permit sub-delegation. Professor John Willis described the court's task in such a case as follows:[6]

> [If] the language of the statute does not, ex hypothesi, help it [a court], it is driven therefore to the scope and object of the statute. Is there anything in the nature of the authority to which the discretion is entrusted, in the situation in which the discretion is to be exercised, in the object which its exercise is to achieve to suggest that the legislature did not intend to confine the authority to the personal exercise of its discretion? This question is answered in practice by comparing the *prima facie* rule with the known practices or the apprehended needs of the authority in doing its work; the court enquires whether the policy-scheme of the statute is such as could not easily be realized unless the policy which requires that a discretion be exercised by the authority named thereto be displaced; it weighs the presumed desire of the legislature for the judgment of the authority it has named against the presumed desire of the legislature that the process of government shall go on in its accustomed and most effective manner and where there is a conflict between the two policies it determines which, under all the circumstances, is the more important.

The courts adopted this approach in *Reference re Regulations in Relation to Chemicals*[7] to permit sub-delegation of the power to make regulations by the Governor in Council to the Controller of Chemicals, and a similar result occurred in *Fort Frances Pulp & Paper Co. v. Manitoba Free Press*.[8] On the other hand, this approach does not necessarily result in validating the impugned sub-delegation. For example, in *Ex parte Brent*,[9] the Ontario Court of Appeal struck down regulations made by the Governor in Council which had the effect of sub-delegating to special inquiry officers the power to exercise their discretion to determine which immigrants should be granted landed immigrant status in Canada. As Aylesworth J.A. said:[10]

> In short, those limited powers of [subordinate] legislation, wide though the limits of the subject-matter be, which Parliament has

---

5 On the other hand, if sub-delegation has been validly done, only the sub-delegate can exercise the power; the delegate has given away his power and can no longer lawfully exercise it. For other examples of specific statutory authority to sub-delegate powers, see: ss. 7 and 8 of the Public Service Act, R.S.A. 1980, c. P-31; s. 224 of the Income Tax Act, R.S.C. 1952, c. 148, as amended by S.C. 1970-71-72, c. 63, and subsequently.

6 "Delegatus Non Potest Delegare", (1943) 21 Can. Bar Rev. 257 at 260-61.

7 [1943] S.C.R. 1.

8 [1923] 3 D.L.R. 629, affirming [1923] 3 D.L.R. 199 (P.C.), especially at p. 200, per Riddell J. (Ont. C.A.).

9 [1955] 3 D.L.R. 587 (Ont. C.A.).

10 *Ibid.*, p. 593.

delegated to His Excellency in Council have not been exercised by the delegate at all, but, on the contrary, by him have been re-delegated bodily, for exercise not merely by some one other individual but, respectively and independently of each other, by every Special Inquiry Officer who sees fit to invoke them and according to "the opinion" of each such sub-delegate.

I can find nothing in the Act expressly (or by inference, if that is permissible) manifesting any intention to permit or authorize any such procedure. On the other hand, it is reasonable to suppose that what Parliament had in contemplation was the enactment of such Regulations relevant to the named subject-matters, or some of them, as in His Excellency in Council's own opinion were advisable and as, therefore, would be of general application to persons seeking entry into Canada regardless of the particular port of entry involved. Surely, what was intended was legislation enacted by His Excellency in Council according to his wisdom and broad experience, prescribing standards for the general guidance of Immigration Officers and Special Inquiry Officers operating at or near the borders of the country, not a wide divergency of rules and opinions ever changing according to the individual notions of such officers. The Regulation is invalid and the order of deportation based upon it is invalid likewise, *delegatus non potest delegare* . . .

Other good examples of cases where the courts have applied the maxim include: *Re Behari Lal et al.*,[11] where it was held that the power conferred on the Governor in Council by section 30 of the Immigration Act[12] to prohibit the landing of immigrants of a specified class could not be delegated to the Minister of the Interior, because the exercise of power depended upon the *Governor's* opinion about the necessity and expediency of such a prohibition, and *Geraghty v. Porter*,[13] which required express words in the legislation before sub-delegation could be permitted.

Two particular circumstances, however, appear to incline the courts to conclude that Parliament must have intended sub-delegation to occur, even in the absence of express words permitting it. The first arises where the legislation delegates a power to a person who clearly will not be able to exercise it himself personally, such as to a minister of the Crown who could not possibly personally exercise all of the statutory powers delegated to him.[14] Our constitutional practice generally permits ministers to delegate most of their powers

---

11 (1908) 13 B.C.R. 415.
12 R.S.C. 1906, c. 93.
13 [1917] N.Z.L.R. 554.
14 But compare this reasoning with that in *Re Behari Lal, supra*, note 11. Query: was the power to prohibit a particular immigrant so rarely used that Parliament must have intended the Governor in Council to do so itself? See also *Reference re Regulations in Relation to Chemicals, supra*, note 7.

to the civil servants in their department, who exercise the powers in the minister's name. This practice is specifically recognized in sections 17 and 18 of the former Alberta Interpretation Act, which provided as follows:[15]

> 17(2) Words directing or empowering a public officer to do any act or thing, or otherwise applying to him by his name or office include his successors in the office *and his or their deputy.*
>
> (3) Words directing or empowering a Minister of the Crown to do an act or thing, or otherwise applying to him by his name of office, include a Minister acting for him, or, if the office is vacant a Minister designated to act in the office by or under the authority of an order in council, and also his successors in the office, *and his or their deputy. . . .*
>
> 18(1) In an enactment, . . .
>
> (*b*) where power is given to the Lieutenant Governor in Council or a public officer to do or enforce the doing of any act or thing, all such powers shall be deemed to be also given as are necessary to enable him to do or enforce the doing of the act or thing; . . .
>
> (*d*) where any act or thing is required to be done by more than two persons, a majority may do it;

Politically, the minister remains responsible for all actions taken in his name. Thus, the better view may be that civil servants merely act as agents helping the minister himself to exercise his powers, instead of acting as sub-delegates in the place and stead of the minister. Certainly, the minister is politically responsible for all actions taken in his name, whether or not he even knew about them. And it is quite clear that the proper construction of some legislation may require the minister himself to exercise the particular statutory power in question, for example, deciding to prosecute for tax evasion under

---

15 R.S.A. 1970, c. 189, emphasis added, repealed by S.A. 1980, c. 70 [now R.S.A. 1980, c. I-7]. Section 21 [am. 1981, c. 50, s. 2] of the new Act reads as follows:

> 21(1) Words in an enactment directing or empowering a Minister of the Crown to do something, or otherwise applying to him by his name of office, include
>
> (*a*) a Minister designated to act in the office, and
> (*b*) the deputy of the Minister or a person appointed as acting deputy,
>
> but nothing in this subsection authorizes a deputy or acting deputy to exercise any authority conferred on a Minister to enact a regulation as defined in the *Regulations Act.*
>
> (2) Words in an enactment directing or empowering a person to do something, or otherwise applying to him by his name of office, include
>
> (*a*) a person acting for him or appointed to act in the office, and
> (*b*) his deputy or a person appointed as his acting deputy
>
> (3) This section applies whether or not the office of a Minister or other person is vacant.

the Income Tax Act.[16] So provisions similar to those in the Interpretation Act really do not permit sub-delegation in all circumstances,[17] but rather only add one more factor to be considered by the courts in construing legislation to try to eke out the implied intent of Parliament on this point.

Secondly, the courts appear to be more prepared to accept that Parliament intended to permit sub-delegation of merely administrative functions, but not legislative or judicial ones. This approach necessarily involves characterizing the function whose sub-delegation is in doubt — a futile process which has been made obsolete in other aspects of Administrative Law.[18] To some extent, however, this distinction makes good sense, because many merely administrative matters do not require the exercise of discretion or personal judgment, and it really does not matter which particular person in fact does the action in question. On the other hand, to the extent that the phrase "merely administrative" has been used in Administrative Law to encompass some discretionary functions which cannot be characterized as judicial or quasi-judicial, the policy underlying the rule against sub-delegation applies to require that particular administrator to exercise his own discretion. In short, it is submitted that the real question is whether discretion must be exercised by the delegate. If so, there should be a strong presumption against sub-delegation, whatever the appellation of the function involved.

It may not always be easy to determine when sub-delegation has occurred. For example, the decisions in *Ex parte Brent*[19] and in *Brant Dairy Company v. Milk Commission of Ontario*[20] demonstrate an improper attempt to sub-delegate the power to enact subordinate legislation by converting it into a discretionary power to be exercised by sub-delegates. A similar situation arose in *R. v. Horback*,[21] where a municipal by-law purported to delegate judicial or discretionary power to the Superintendent of Motor Vehicles to determine which automobiles were unsafe, without setting out in the by-law the standards for what constituted safety. In *Lab. Rel. Bd. (Sask.) v. Speers*,[22] the Saskatchewan Court of Appeal found there to be an illegal sub-delegation when the board had its administrator determine how many of the employees wished to be represented by the respondent union instead of undertaking this task itself. Although the line between sub-delegation and

---

16 *Granby Const. & Equip. Ltd. v. Milley*, (1974) 47 D.L.R. (3d) 427, reversed (1975) 50 D.L.R. (3d) 115 (B.C.C.A.).

17 *E.g.*, see *Ex parte Brent, supra*, note 9.

18 See chapter 8, *infra*, for a discussion of the previous need to characterize functions as "judicial" or "quasi-judicial" (as opposed to "administrative" or "executive") in order to make the rules of natural justice applicable, or to make *certiorari* available to correct a breach of those rules. This need to characterize has been supplanted by the development of the "duty to be fair".

19 *Supra*, note 9.

20 [1973] S.C.R. 131.

21 (1967) 64 D.L.R. (2d) 17 (B.C.S.C.).

22 [1948] 1 D.L.R. 340.

using an agent or servant may be difficult to determine, stepping over it will generally be fatal to the validity of the administrator's action.

Altogether apart from determining whether sub-delegation is permitted in a particular context, it may frequently be difficult for the citizen to verify whether the governmental official with whom he is dealing has in fact been sub-delegated the powers being exercised. On the one hand, some statutes specifically require some formal method by which the delegate must indicate that he is sub-delegating his statutory powers. Thus, section 224 of the Income Tax Act[23] specifically permits the Minister of National Revenue to delegate certain of his powers to other departmental officials, which must be done by regulation. Accordingly, one can look at the regulation to determine whether a particular departmental officer has been sub-delegated the particular power[24] being used. To some extent, such formality will only help the citizen after the fact, because he is not likely to be able to delay a search-and-seizure raid by police and officials from the tax department while he roots around to find the regulation delegating the minister's authority to the person who in fact authorized the expedition. On the other hand, most federal and provincial statutes do not provide a formal method for recording sub-delegation of powers, nor is there often a written record of informal sub-delegation. For example, section 25 of the Public Service Act[25] of Alberta permits the department head to discipline or dismiss a member of the public service in certain circumstances, and section 7 authorizes the deputy head to exercise all of the powers of the department head. Section 8 in effect permits either of these to delegate any of their powers to any other designated officer of the department. It may be valid for the deputy to instruct such an officer verbally to discipline a particular public servant, even though the latter has no way at the time to determine that a sub-delegation has occurred.

To the extent that the sub-delegate's activity would otherwise constitute an actionable wrong known to law, he — and not the citizen — will have to bear the burden of proving the validity of the sub-delegation in order to raise a valid defence to the citizen's lawsuit. In other circumstances, however (such as getting a permit),[26] the burden of attacking the sub-delegation will lie on the citizen, and this burden will be compounded by the lack of any formal system of recording or registering sub-delegation of particular powers.

Sub-delegation may also effectively result where the delegate fetters his discretion by adopting a policy or contractually undertaking to exercise it

---

23 R.S.C. 1952, c. 148, as amended by S.C. 1970-71-72, c. 63 and subsequently.
24 Generally discretionary in nature.
25 R.S.A. 1980, c. P-31, which provides as follows:

    7(2) For the purposes of this Act a deputy head has the powers and may perform the duties of his department head.

    8 A department head may, subject to the regulations, delegate any of the powers and duties granted to him by this Act to designated officials of his department.

26 See *Vic Restaurant Inc. v. Montreal*, (1959) 17 D.L.R. (2d) 81 (S.C.C.).

only one way. Although "fettering discretion" is recognized as a separate ground for judicial review,[27] the practical result is the same as illegal sub-delegation because the discretion is not in fact exercised by the very delegate whom the legislation has designated. Thus, in *Vic Restaurant Ltd. v. Montreal*,[28] the Supreme Court of Canada struck down the city's practice of always accepting the advice of the police to refuse a restaurant licence to anyone whom the police had identified as undesirable. Adopting such a policy not only fettered the discretion specifically granted by statute to the city council, it effectively amounted to an illegal sub-delegation to the police, thereby making the administrative action *ultra vires*.

One must also consider the effect of a valid sub-delegation on the ability of the delegate himself to exercise the statutory power. Although the delegate may generally at any time rescind the sub-delegation, the better view appears to be that the delegate himself cannot exercise the statutory powers so long as the sub-delegation subsists. What one has given away, one cannot continue to exercise! To this extent, therefore, delegation and sub-delegation operate differently from the law of agency, and the two concepts must be distinguished.

One must also distinguish between sub-delegation and agency when considering the applicability of the principles of natural justice or the duty to be fair. These procedural rules require the very person who is making a decision to give a fair hearing to anyone affected thereby. In sub-delegation situations, the sub-delegate clearly is making the decision and will be the one required to adopt a fair procedure. On the other hand, if the statutory delegate uses agents to help him exercise his power, the delegate himself — and not merely his agents — must comply with natural justice.[29] The coupling of natural justice considerations to the question of sub-delegation, therefore, may expand the ambit of judicial review of administrative actions.

In summary, the difficulties surrounding sub-delegation may affect the jurisdiction of the person purporting to exercise a statutory power. To the extent that there is a defect in that person's acquisition of jurisdiction, there is a ground for judicial review.

(b) Appointment of Members of the Delegate Body

Sometimes defects in the appointment of the members of a statutory body will render its actions void. Examples of fatal defects have included: failing to appoint persons with proper professional qualifications; appointing members for the wrong term of office;[30] not complying with a mandatory step

---

27 See the discussion in chapter 7, section 6, *infra*.
28 *Supra*, note 26.
29 See *Arlidge v. Islington Corp.*, [1909] 2 K.B. 127, for a discussion of this problem.
30 *Hollenberg v. B.C. Optometric Assn.*, (1967) 61 D.L.R. (2d) 295 (B.C.C.A.).

in the appointment process;[31] adding unauthorized additional members to a tribunal;[32] and the lack of a quorum.[33]

4. Compliance with Statutory Requirements

Sometimes legislation prescribes specific matters that the delegate must attend to in the exercise of his powers. For example, the delegate may be required by statute to give notice to certain persons of his intended actions;[34] to give a hearing prior to acting;[35] to obtain someone else's approval;[36] to keep a written record of his proceedings;[37] or to do certain things within a pre-scribed period of time.[38] Questions often arise as to the legal consequence of

---

31 *Wetaskiwin Mun. Dist. No. 74 v. Kaiser*, [1947] 4 D.L.R. 461 (Alta. T.D.), where the minister had the right to nominate one member for appointment by the council of one member of the Agricultural Services Board, which was struck down because the *council* did not make the appointment but let the minister do it directly.

32 *R. (Rogers) v. Council of College of Physicians & Surgeons of B.C.*, [1942] 3 W.W.R. 510 (B.C.S.C.), where the executive committee added a county court judge as one of its members.

33 At common law, a quorum probably exists where half of the members are present: *Herring v. Mexia, Texas*, 290 S.W. 792 at 794 (Tex. C. Civ. A.) (1927). This rule has been enacted in s. 17 of the new Alberta Interpretation Act, R.S.A. 1980, c. I-7. Sometimes legislation specifically deviates from this rule: see *County of Strathcona No. 20 v. Provincial Planning Bd.*, (1970) 75 W.W.R. 629 at 642-43 (Alta. S.C.), where s. 7 of the Planning Act, S.A. 1963, c. 43, specifically permitted the board to fix its own quorum. See *R. v. Hatskin*, [1936] 3 D.L.R. 437 (Man. C.A.), for a case requiring all members to sit on an appeal under the Minimum Wage Act, 1924 (Man.), c. 128; or whether a member of a board can vote if he was not present at its proceedings: *Inter-City Freightlines Ltd. v. Swan River-The Pas Transfer Ltd.*, [1972] 2 W.W.R. 317 (Man. C.A.); and McFadyen J.'s decision in *Hoyda v. Edmonton*, Alta. T.D. No. 7903-13252 (unreported), subsequently altered by an amendment to the Municipal Government Act.

34 Such a provision was held to be mandatory in *Re Nor. Ont. Natural Gas Co. and La Rocque*, (1959) 18 D.L.R. (2d) 73 (Ont. H.C.), where the applicant had never in fact received a notice sent by double registered mail, even though the board was given power to direct the manner of service of such notice. This provision, therefore, required the board to give *actual* notice to persons affected by its proceedings, and failure to do so resulted in the invalidity of its proceedings.

35 Such a provision was held to be mandatory in *R. Ex rel. Mikklesen v. Highway Traffic Bd.*, [1947] 2 D.L.R. 373 (Alta. T.D.), where a *mandamus* was issued to require a hearing at which competitors could be heard prior to the issuance of an initial certificate of operation under s. 19 of the Public Service Vehicles Act, R.S.A. 1942, c. 276. Note that the specific statutory hearing provided for here was a pre-condition to the board's power to issue the certificate, and not necessarily implied by the common law requirement to follow the principles of natural justice.

36 Such a provision was held to be mandatory in *Ross (Twp.) v. Cobden and Eganville Dist. High School Bd.*, (1967) 63 D.L.R. (2d) 390 (Ont. H.C.), where the minister's approval had not been obtained prior to the enactment of the by-law, as required under the Act. See also *Moshos v. Min. of Manpower & Immigration*, [1969] S.C.R. 886.

37 Such a provision was held to be mandatory in *Re Fitzpatrick and Calgary*, (1964) 47 D.L.R. (2d) 365 at 369 (Alta. C.A.).

38 The statutory requirement that arbitrators issue their decisions within a certain time was held to be merely directory in *Re Metro. Toronto Police Commrs. Bd. and Metro. Toronto Police*

the delegate's failure to comply with such matters. On the one hand, if the statutory requirement is mandatory, failure to comply therewith will render the delegate's action void.[39] On the other hand, breach of a merely directory statutory provision does not affect the validity of the delegate's action.

Distinguishing between mandatory and directory statutory provisions can be an exceedingly tricky task. Although the Interpretation Act provides[40] that "shall" has an imperative meaning, and "may" is generally to be read as being directory, this rule is specifically stated not to apply if the context of a particular statute requires some other construction. Accordingly, the true construction of a particular statute may be subject to considerable debate. As noted by *Maxwell on The Interpretation of Statutes*,[41] the courts have sometimes taken the view that procedural requirements for public duties should generally be read as being directory, not mandatory:

> A strong line of distinction may be drawn between cases where the prescriptions of the Act affect the performance of a duty and where they relate to a privilege or power. Where powers, rights or immunities are granted with a direction that certain regulations, formalities or conditions shall be complied with, it seems neither unjust nor inconvenient to exact a rigorous observance of them as essential to the acquisition of the right or authority conferred, and it is therefore probable that such was the intention of the legislature. But when a public duty is imposed and the statute requires that it shall be performed in a certain manner, or within a certain time, or under other specified conditions, such prescriptions may well be regarded as intended to be directory only in cases when injustice or inconvenience to others who have no control over those exercising the duty would result if such requirements were essential and imperative.

On reflection, it may not be any easier to identify a public duty than to distinguish a mandatory statutory requirement from a merely directory one. It is clear that the courts in the end must make these distinctions in exercising their (public?) duty to construe the particular statute in question, having

---

Assn., (1973) 37 D.L.R. (3d) 487 (Ont. Div. Ct.); *Assn. Catholique des Institutrices v. Commissaires d'Ecoles de St. Pascal*, [1948] R. L. 97 (C.A.); *Re Lincoln County R. C. Sep. Sch. Bd. and Buchler*, [1972] 1 O.R. 854 (C.A.). By contrast, time periods under the Expropriation Act (Alta.) have been held to be mandatory.

39 Although the superior court may in an appropriate case exercise its discretion to refuse one of the prerogative remedies to a person attacking the delegate's action.

40 R.S.A. 1980, c. I-7, s. 25(2)(*e*).

41 10th ed. (1953), pp. 376-77, quoted by Edmund Davies J. in *Cullimore v. Lyme Regis Corp.*, [1962] 1 Q.B. 718 at 726-27. See also: *Montreal Street Ry. Co. v. Normandin*, [1917] A.C. 170 at 174 (P.C.); *Re Metro. Toronto Police Commrs. and Metro. Toronto Police Assn.*, *supra*, note 38; *Anderson v. Stewart*, (1921) 62 D.L.R. 98 at 109-10 (N.B.C.A.); *Liverpool Borough Bank v. Turner*, (1860) 2 De G.F. & J. 502, 45 E.R. 715 (Ch.).

regard to the policy of the Act, all of its provisions, the reason for including the specific statutory requirement in question, whether any statutory consequence is provided for failure to comply, and what the practical effect of non-compliance is on the complainant or any other person.

5. Preliminary or Collateral Matters

Sometimes, legislation only delegates powers to an administrator in conditional terms: if a certain state of affairs exists, then, but only then, does the administrator have authority to act or make a decision. It is important, therefore, to determine whether the delegate's jurisdiction depends upon any preliminary or collateral matter. If so, a defect or error in such a preliminary or collateral matter will prevent the delegate from having jurisdiction.

Let us examine a few examples of preliminary or collateral errors of jurisdiction. In *Anisminic v. Foreign Compensation Commission*,[42] the commission was delegated authority to determine what compensation to pay British nationals or their successors-in-title for property confiscated by the Egyptian government during the Suez affair. The commission decided that Anisminic Ltd. was not a British successor-in-title to a British owner of expropriated property, and declined to consider Anisminic's claim for recompense. The House of Lords, however, held that Anisminic was indeed in law a successor-in-title, with the result that the commission was bound to consider its claim. In other words, the status of being a successor-in-title was a pre-condition to the commission's jurisdiction to consider claims for compensation. Further, by making an erroneous determination of Anisminic's status as a successor-in-title, the commission could not deprive the company of its right to be considered for compensation. In short, the jurisdiction of the commission did not include the right to determine conclusively whether an applicant was a successor-in-title, but was consequent upon the right determination of that preliminary matter.

Similarly, in *Bell v. Ontario Human Rights Commission*,[43] the statutory delegate had certain powers if there was illegal racial discrimination with respect to renting a "self-contained domestic establishment". The Supreme Court of Canada upheld the issuance of an order of prohibition to stop the commission from exercising its powers with respect to a residential unit which was not self-contained. Again, the fact of being self-contained was preliminary to the jurisdiction of the statutory delegate. As Martland J. said:[44]

---

42 [1969] A.C. 147 (H.L.).

43 [1971] S.C.R. 756.

44 *Ibid.*, p. 775. Query: if the Act *had* purported to place the determination of whether there was a self-contained domestic establishment within the exclusive jurisdiction of the commission, would this have breached s. 96 of the Constitution Act, 1867? See discussion, *supra*, in chapter 2.

The Act does not purport to place that issue [of whether there is a self-contained domestic establishment] within the exclusive jurisdiction of the board, and a wrong decision on it would not enable the board to proceed further.

Accordingly, there was only one right answer to this question — and it was for the courts to determine that right answer.

As a final example, the decision in *Parkhill Furniture & Bedding Ltd. v. International Molders and Foundry Workers Union of North America, Local 174*,[45] illustrates a collateral error of law which deprived the statutory delegate of jurisdiction.

The legislation provided that a collective agreement continued to apply to "any new employer to whom passes the ownership of the business of an employer who has entered into the agreement. . . ." The issue arose whether Parkhill was bound by the agreement when it purchased assets from the receiver of another company which had been party to the agreement. Section 59(1)(c) of the Manitoba Labour Relations Act provided as follows:[46]

> 59(1) Where in any proceeding before the board or otherwise in the course of the administration of this Act a question arises under this Act as to whether . . .
>
>> (c) in any case, a collective agreement has been entered into, and the terms thereof, and the persons who are parties to or are bound by the collective agreement or on whose behalf the collective agreement was entered into. . . .
>
> the board shall decide the question and its decision shall be final and conclusive for all the purposes of this Act.

As Freedman J.A. said:[47]

> [T]he issue which the Board had to consider was whether the collective agreement was binding on Parkhill, and the Board came to the conclusion that it was. It must be remembered that neither Bastin, J., nor this Court can sit in appeal on the Board's decision. The Board has a right to be wrong, provided it acts within its jurisdiction. Did it so act in this case? That is the only question properly arising on this *certiorari* application.
>
>   In my view the Board's order was made without jurisdiction. It is obvious that before the Board could make a final decision under s. 59(1)(c) it had to address itself to the question raised in s. 18(1)(c), namely, whether Parkhill was a new employer to whom the ownership of the business of Trysson had passed. Was this latter question,

---

45 (1961) 26 D.L.R. (2d) 589 (Man. C.A.).

46 R.S.M. 1954, c. 132, quoted *ibid.*, p. 592.

47 *Ibid.*, pp. 593-94.

in the circumstances of this case, one that could properly be classified as preliminary or collateral, in the sense in which those terms are used in *certiorari* matters? Or was it part of the main issue which the Board had to decide? If it was the latter, then clearly the Board had exclusive jurisdiction to deal with it, and its decision would not be subject to review. If, on the other hand, it was the former, a different situation would arise. For the Board cannot give itself jurisdiction by a wrong decision on such a preliminary or collateral point upon which the limit to its jurisdiction depends (*Bunbury v. Fuller* (1853), 9 Exch. 111 at p. 140, 156 E.R. 47). An error by the Board on such a point is reviewable by the Court on *certiorari*.

I am aware that I am now entering upon fighting ground. Classification of a matter as preliminary or collateral is not always easy. Nor has an expanding jurisprudence on this branch of the law altogether removed its difficulties. For cases may be found on both sides of the question. Although the matter has been dealt with by the Supreme Court of Canada it has not come before it in circumstances which in my view are comparable to those of the present case. To the extent, however, that any general principles may be extracted from the decisions, the cases have been most helpful to me in the present controversy.

His Lordship noted[48] that the courts had intervened whenever "the point for determination involved an examination of legal principles and considerations that went beyond the simple confines of the statute under which the Board operated." Thus, in the present case:[49]

[b]efore the Board could determine whether the collective agreement was binding on Parkhill it had first of all to consider whether Parkhill was a "new employer" to whom had passed the business of Trysson. That question involved something more than the provisions of the *Labour Relations Act*, including specifically s. 59(1)(*c*) and s. 18(1)(*c*) thereof. It involved a consideration of the law pertaining to bankruptcy, to the effect of an assignment in bankruptcy upon the contracts of workmen, to the powers of a Trustee in Bankruptcy to sell, with the consent of inspectors, assets belonging to the bankrupt estate and to the title which a purchaser of assets from such Trustee acquires — including, in the latter question, whether such title is to be deemed encumbered by obligations under a collective agreement which had been entered into by the assignor in bankruptcy. These are matters entering into the determination of the question whether Parkhill was a "new employer" within the

---

48 *Ibid.*, p. 596.
49 *Ibid.*, pp. 597-98.

meaning of the Act. How can it be said that consideration of those matters is within the exclusive jurisdiction of the Board? Rather they are matters touching upon the status of Parkhill — a preliminary or collateral matter which the Board had first to deal with before it could proceed to adjudicate on whether the collective agreement was binding. On such a question the Board could be right or wrong. But since this was a preliminary or collateral matter the Board's decision thereon would be subject to review. If the Board were wrong and by its error assumed a jurisdiction it did not possess, *certiorari* would lie, and the Court could correct the error, as in *Re Workmen's Compensation Act and C.P.R.* and as in the *Lunenburg* case. If the Board were right, a *certiorari* application could still be brought — because the matter involved was preliminary or collateral —but in that case the Court, once it agreed that the Board's jurisdiction had been established, could not interfere with whatever adjudication was made therein.

I do not wish to be taken as having attempted to lay down a definition of the phrase "a preliminary or collateral question", least of all an exhaustive definition. I am merely saying that the cases in Group B appear to possess a common factor that is also present in the case before us — namely, that before it can determine whether the Act applies at all, the Board must first consider legal principles that are outside the scope of the Act. Other forms of preliminary or collateral questions have arisen and doubtless will arise, but that is a field which I need not enter at this time.

Being of the view, then, that when the Board began to examine the status of Parkhill it entered upon a question that was truly preliminary or collateral to its jurisdiction, I must now ask whether the Board on that question arrived at the right or wrong decision. With respect, I believe its decision was wrong.

Accordingly, because a jurisdictional point was involved, the privative clause had no effect.

It is not always easy to determine from the legislation whether a particular matter is preliminary or collateral to a delegate's jurisdiction on the one hand, or lies within it on the other hand. As de Smith commented:[50]

No satisfactory test has ever been formulated for distinguishing findings which go to jurisdiction from findings which go to the merits; and in some cases the courts, impressed by logical difficulties, have appeared to ignore the distinction altogether. . . . It is hardly surprising, however, that many of the reported decisions on

---

50 *Judicial Review of Administrative Action*, 2nd ed. (1968), p. 100.

the jurisdiction of inferior courts and tribunals are manifestly contradictory, or that prolonged reflection on those decisions tends to induce feelings of desperation.

The Supreme Court of Canada, however, has clearly indicated recently that the court will not be hasty to characterize a particular matter as being jurisdictional in nature if there is any doubt. As Dickson J. said in the C.U.P.E. case:[51]

> The question of what is and is not jurisdictional is often very difficult to determine. The Courts, in my view, should not be alert to brand as jurisdictional, and therefore subject to broader curial review, that which may be doubtfully so.

Dickson J.'s reference to "broader curial review" is to compare review of juris-dictional matters with the much more limited ambit of judicial review of intra-jurisdictional errors of law, to which the new "patently unreasonable" test has been applied. In principle, the "patently unreasonable" test should not be applied once it has been determined that a jurisdictional matter is in question.[52]

How can one demonstrate a preliminary or collateral jurisdictional defect? In some cases, it may be possible to demonstrate the defect from the face of the record of the proceedings. But, unlike the case involving intra-jurisdictional errors of law, a person alleging a jurisdictional error is not restricted to the record, but can lead any relevant evidence (usually in the form of affidavits) to cast light on the defect.[53]

In summary, therefore, preliminary and collateral matters operate to restrict the jurisdiction of statutory delegates. By definition, a statutory dele-gate has no discretion to make an error on a preliminary or collateral question upon which his jurisdiction depends. Although in practice it may be difficult to determine whether preliminary or collateral matters are involved, the conse-quence of such a characterization is to bring that jurisdictional matter within the ambit of judicial review.

---

51 C.U.P.E., Loc. 963 v. N.B. Liquor Corp., (1979) 97 D.L.R. (3d) 417 at 422 (S.C.C.).

52 See the discussion on this point in chapter 10, section 9, *infra*.

53 This was recognized by Lord Denning M.R. in *R. v. Northumberland Compensation Appeal Tribunal; Ex parte Shaw*, [1952] 1 K.B. 338 (C.A.). It also arose in *Anisminic Ltd. v. Foreign Compensation Comm.*, [1969] 2 A.C. 147, where the commission's erroneous determination that Anisminic was not a successor-in-title was not disclosed on the face of the record but only in a subsequent affidavit explaining the basis of the commission's decision. Martland J. also refers to the admissibility of affidavits to show jurisdictional errors in the *Bell* case, *supra*, note 43.

6. Summary

This chapter has examined the following types of defects which prevent a statutory delegate from acquiring jurisdiction: (a) substantive *ultra vires*; (b) improper constitution of the delegate; (c) lack of compliance with mandatory procedural requirements; and (d) errors on a matter preliminary collateral to the delegate's jurisdiction. All of these errors prevent the delegate from acquiring jurisdiction "in the narrow sense" of the word used by Lord Reid. Each of these errors results in a nullity, makes the delegate's actions *ultra vires*, and provides grounds for judicial review.

The next three chapters examine errors which the delegate can commit after having acquired jurisdiction "in the narrow sense", but which take him outside his jurisdiction and therefore also provide grounds for judicial review. Chapter 10 deals with the sole exception to the rule that all judicial review is jurisdictional in nature: the anomalous use of *certiorari* to correct errors of law *within* jurisdiction.

7. Selected Bibliography

Gordon, D.M., "Conditional and Contingent Jurisdiction of Tribunals", (1960) 1 U.B.C.L. Rev. 185.

Gordon, D.M., "Jurisdictional Fact: An Answer", (1966) 82 L.Q. Rev. 515.

Gordon, D.M., "The Observance of Law as a Condition of Jurisdiction", (1931) 47 L.Q. Rev. 386, 557.

Gordon, D.M., "The Relation of Facts to Jurisdiction", (1929) 45 L.Q. Rev. 459.

Hogg, P.W., "The Jurisdictional Fact Doctrine in the Supreme Court of Canada: *Bell* v. *Ontario, Human Rights Commissions*", (1971) 9 Osgoode Hall L.J. 203.

Jaffe, L., "Judicial Review: Constitutional and Jurisdictional Fact", (1957) 70 Harv. L. Rev. 953.

Jaffe, L., "Judicial Review: Question of Fact", (1956) 69 Harv. L. Rev. 1020.

McRuer, "Objective Conditions Precedent to the Existence of the Power of Decision", Report of the Royal Commission, pp. 71*ff*, pp. 250*ff*.

7

Losing Jurisdiction Through an Abuse of Discretion

1. Introduction

The doctrine of Parliamentary Sovereignty permits legislation to delegate very broad discretionary powers,[1] which Professor Julius Grey has described as follows:[2]

> Discretion may best be defined as the power to make a decision that cannot be determined to be right or wrong in any objective way. A university that interviews prospective students has the power to admit some applicants and reject some; an executive may choose a secretary out of a field of applicants; the sovereign may pardon some convicts and not others. While one could disagree with any of these decisions, there is no body or person entitled, as a general rule, to correct them and declare them wrong. Lord Diplock put it well in a recent case when he said:
>
> > "The very concept of administrative discretion involves a right to choose between more than one possible course of action upon which there is room for reasonable people to hold differing opinions as to which is to be preferred".[3]
>
> It would not be incorrect to say that discretion involves the creation of rights and privileges, as opposed to the determination of who holds those rights and privileges.

Nevertheless, unlimited discretion cannot exist. The courts have continuously asserted their right to review a delegate's exercise of discretion for a wide range of abuses. It is possible to identify at least five generic types of abuses, which can be described as follows. The first category occurs when a delegate exercises his discretion with an improper intention in mind, which subsumes acting for an unauthorized purpose, in bad faith, or on irrelevant considerations. The second type of abuse arises when the delegate acts on inadequate material, including where there is no evidence or without considering relevant matters. Thirdly, the courts sometimes hold that an abuse of discretion has been committed where there is an improper result, including unreasonable, discriminatory or retroactive administrative actions. A fourth type of abuse arises when the delegate exercises his discretion on an erroneous view of the law. Finally, it is an abuse for a delegate to refuse to exercise his discretion by adopting a policy which fetters his ability to consider individual cases with an open mind.

---

1 See chapter 2 for a discussion of constitutional limitations on the ability to delegate discretionary powers.

2 In "Discretion in Administrative Law", (1979) 17 Osgoode Hall L.J. 107, footnote renumbered.

3 *Secretary of State for Educ. & Science v. Thameside Metro. Borough Council*, [1977] A.C. 1014 at 1064.

An abuse of discretion is an error which is jurisdictional in nature, even though the statutory delegate is properly constituted, has complied with all mandatory requirements, is dealing with the subject matter granted to him by the legislation, and undoubtedly has the right to exercise the discretionary power in question. Again to quote from Lord Reid's decision in *Anisminic*:[4]

> [T]here are many cases where, although the tribunal had jurisdiction to enter on the inquiry, it has done or failed to do something in the course of the inquiry which is of such a nature that its decision is a nullity. It may have given its decision in bad faith. It may have made a decision which it had no power to make. It may have failed in the course of the inquiry to comply with the requirements of natural justice. It may in perfect good faith have misconstrued the provisions giving it power to act so that it failed to deal with the question remitted to it and decided some question which was not remitted to it. It may have refused to take into account something which it was required to take into account. Or it may have based its decision on some matter which, under the provisions setting it up, it had no right to take into account. I do not intend this list to be exhaustive.

Thus, these errors make the delegate's action a nullity. Because it is nonsensical to say that anyone has jurisdiction to commit a nullity, these errors must deprive the delegate of his jurisdiction to exercise his discretion in that particular manner. And this brings into play the doctrine of *ultra vires*, which provides the theoretical basis upon which the courts are entitled to review[5] the manner in which the delegate has exercised the discretion which the sovereign legislature has conferred upon him.

It is also important to note that Lord Reid specifically states that his list of abuses of discretion and other errors is not meant to be exhaustive. The underlying theme connecting all of these errors is that they make the delegate's action so outrageous, unreasonable or unacceptable that the courts decide that the legislative branch could never have intended to grant the statutory delegate the power to act in such a manner. But this implied statement of legislative intent must necessarily yield whenever the legislative branch has used sufficiently specific words to indicate that the statutory delegate does in fact have the power to proceed in the manner complained of, for example, by specifically ousting the applicability of the procedural requirements of natural justice,[6] or permitting a delegate to exercise his discretion in a discriminatory

---

4 [1969] 2 A.C. 147 at 171 (H.L.).

5 Even in the face of a privative clause purporting to oust the court's supervisory jurisdiction. See the discussion on this point in chapters 10 and 14.

6 The principles of natural justice are not directly related to the proper exercise of discretion, and may apply even to the exercise of non-discretionary powers. These principles are dealt with in chapters 8 and 9, *infra*. Nevertheless, judicial review for a breach of natural justice occurs for precisely the same reason as judicial review for an abuse of discretion: the

or retroactive manner. As Lord Reid suggests, it is possible that the courts will in the future find some other type of action by the statutory delegate so contrary to the presumed intention of the legislative branch that it takes the delegate outside of his jurisdiction, and therefore is susceptible to judicial review.

The labels used by the courts to describe various types of abuse of discretion may be unduly precise and may sometimes overlap. Thus, it may be difficult to determine whether a particular discretionary action is void because the delegate acted in bad faith, or for an improper purpose, or on irrelevant considerations — all of which phrases could be used to describe Mr. Duplessis's motivation in ordering the cancellation of Mr. Roncarelli's liquor permit because he posted bail for Jehovah's Witnesses charged with various offences.[7] As Lord Greene M.R. said in *Associated Provincial Picture Houses, Ltd., v. Wednesbury Corporation*:[8]

> Lawyers familiar with the phraseology commonly used in relation to the exercise of statutory discretions often use the word "unreasonable" in a rather comprehensive sense. It is frequently used as a general description of the things that must not be done. For instance, a person entrusted with a discretion must direct himself properly in law. He must call his own attention to the matters which he is bound to consider. He must exclude from his consideration matters which are irrelevant to the matter that he has to consider. If he does not obey those rules, he may truly be said, and often is said, to be acting "unreasonably". Similarly, you may have something so absurd that no sensible person could ever dream that it lay within the powers of the authority. WARRINGTON, L.J., I think it was, gave the example of the red-haired teacher, dismissed because she had red hair. That is unreasonable in one sense. In another sense it is taking into consideration extraneous matters. It is so unreasonable that it might almost be described as being done in bad faith. In fact, all these things largely fall under one head.

And Lord MacNaughten put it similarly in *Westminster Corporation v. London and Northwestern Railway Company*:[9]

> There can be no question as to the law applicable to the case. It is well settled that a public body invested with statutory powers such as those conferred upon the corporation must take care not to exceed or abuse its powers. It must keep within the limits of the authority

---

legislation is presumed not to permit that particular type of administrative action. This presumption, of course, must yield in the face of a specific statutory provision to the contrary, in all cases.

7 *Roncarelli v. Duplessis*, [1959] S.C.R. 121.

8 [1947] 2 All E.R. 680 at 682-83 (C.A.).

9 [1905] A.C. 426 at 430 (H.L.).

committed to it. It must act in good faith. And it must act reasonably. The last proposition is involved in the second, if not in the first. But in the present case I think it will be convenient to take it separately.

Whatever the label used, the result is the same: judicial review of the delegate's jurisdiction to exercise his discretion in the manner complained of.

Finally, many of the cases referred to in this chapter deal with the content of delegated legislation, and not with the exercise of other forms of discretionary administrative actions. Nevertheless, it is submitted that the same principles of Administrative Law apply to determine the legality of all forms of delegated powers. First, one must of course acknowledge that the power to enact delegated legislation is discretionary in nature; after all, discretion is involved in determining the content of those legislative rules. Accordingly, the rules governing the exercise of this type of discretion should be applicable to other types as well. Secondly, one can indeed find examples where discretionary administrative decisions have in fact been struck down on these grounds, even though no legislative function is involved. Thus, all of these types of discretionary powers are dealt with together in this chapter.

Let us now consider the nature of these categories of abuse which the courts have held take a statutory delegate outside of his jurisdiction "in the narrow sense" used by Lord Reid.

2. The Abuse of an Improper Intention: Unauthorized or Ulterior Purpose, Bad Faith, Irrelevant Considerations

The courts have frequently held that it is *ultra vires* for a statutory delegate to use a power for some unauthorized or ulterior purpose, in bad faith, or acting on irrelevant considerations.

A clear example would be an attempt by a delegate who has been given power to expropriate land for creating a park to expropriate for the purpose of making a highway instead. Although the delegate undoubtedly has the power to expropriate land, he can only lawfully do so for the purpose for which that power was granted to him by the legislation; any other purpose is unauthorized, and therefore *ultra vires*. Of course, it will frequently be a nice question of statutory interpretation as to whether the particular purpose for which the statutory power is being exercised has been authorized or not by the legislation. Similarly, it may be difficult in some cases to establish precisely what the purpose is for which the statutory delegate is exercising the power in question.[10] However, this difficulty is somewhat alleviated by the fact that

---

10 A nice question arises if there were more than one motive for an administrative action, if at least one were improper. The courts seem to weigh the motives to determine whether the improper one tainted the others. See H.W.R. Wade's description of the cases in *Administrative Law*, 5th ed. (Oxford: Clarendon Press, 1982), p. 390.

because a jurisdictional question is involved, extrinsic evidence is admissible concerning the purpose of the statutory delegate.[11]

"Bad faith", "unauthorized purpose", and "irrelevant considerations" are sometimes used interchangeably by the courts to describe the same defect. Thus, the use of a statutory power for an ulterior purpose may well constitute bad faith, and may also have resulted from irrelevant considerations. The *Roncarelli*[12] and *Padfield*[13] cases are examples of this type of interchangeability of terms. On the other hand, only one of these phrases may be applicable to describe the particular error committed by the statutory delegate. In particular, the courts may be reluctant to find the existence of bad faith, even where the delegate has acted for an improper purpose or on irrelevant considerations. Bearing in mind this terminological difficulty, it is useful to consider examples of each one of these categories.

(a) Unauthorized or Ulterior Purpose

Examples where the courts have struck down a delegate's actions on the ground that they were being taken for an unauthorized purpose include: the payment by a municipal council of higher wages than necessary in order to be a model employer even though the council was entitled to pay "such wages as [council] may think fit";[14] the enactment of a by-law[15] prohibiting pharmacists from advertising their professional services or fees, even though the association was entitled to enact by-laws concerning discipline of members, as well as any other matter requisite for carrying out the objects of its Act;[16] the refusal of a licence to carry on the business of a salvage yard on the ground that a prospective zoning by-law would prohibit the use of that particular land for that purpose;[17] or that the use of land for a restaurant would create traffic problems;[18] the exercise of a statutory provision to "refuse in any particular case to grant the request of an applicant for a [business] licence . . . but the granting or renewal of a licence shall not be unreasonably refused" where members of the municipal council were apparently concerned about the morality of a sex shop. In the last case, Dickson J. stated that the

---

11 As occurred in the *Anisminic* case, *supra*, note 4, which dealt with a preliminary error of law. Indeed, the improper purpose in *Roncarelli v. Duplessis*, *supra*, note 7, only came to light during examinations for discovery in a damage action, and probably never would have been disclosed on any record of the proceedings revoking the liquor licence.

12 *Supra*, note 7.

13 *Padfield v. Min. of Agriculture, Fisheries and Food*, [1968] A.C. 997 (H.L.), discussed *infra*.

14 *Roberts v. Hopwood*, [1925] A.C. 578 (H.L.).

15 Approved by the Lieutenant Governor in Council pursuant to the statute.

16 *Bass v. Pharmaceutical Assn. of B.C.*, (1965) 51 D.L.R. (2d) 552, affirmed 55 D.L.R. (2d) 476 (B.C.C.A.).

17 *Wilcox v. Pickering Twp.*, (1961) 29 D.L.R. (2d) 428 (Ont. H.C.).

18 *Re Henry's Drive-In and Hamilton Police Bd.*, [1960] O.W.N. 458; and see also *Brampton Jersey Ent. Ltd. v. Milk Control Bd. of Ont.*, (1956) 1 D.L.R. (2d) 130 (Ont. C.A.).

specific statutory power delegated to the municipal council to refuse a licence in "any particular case"could not be construed to extend to refusing licences for any particular type of business, such as "adult boutiques" which were not *ex hypothesi* illegal.[19]

The courts' approach to this problem is well illustrated by the decision in *Tegon Developments Ltd. v. Edmonton City Council*.[20] The case involved a resolution by city council prohibiting any development or demolition which might conflict with the historical character of the Old Strathcona area of Edmonton. Although the Planning Act[21] specifically provided that a municipal council might make resolutions respecting "(a) the use of land in specific areas, or (b) any special aspects of specific kinds of development and the manner of their control", Moir J.A. held that the resolution in question purported to use this statutory power for an unauthorized purpose:[22]

> In my opinion council has the right to pass a resolution dealing with the "use" of land or "any ... aspects of specific kinds of development". This resolution is not for that purpose but it is for the stated and express purpose of preserving the historical structures pending designation of certain sites in the area under the provisions of The Alberta Heritage Act, 1973 (Alta.), c. 5.
>
> That statute empowers the Lieutenant-Governor in Council to designate any heritage site where preservation is in the public interest (s. 18). This is a procedure to safeguard the interest of the owner and of the public and it allows the owner to be heard. There is no power delegated to any municipal council to designate any area of building under that statute.
>
> Further, the avowed purpose of the resolution is to enable the city to obtain contributions from Heritage Canada and the Devonian Foundation. It is said that the obtaining of such grants is "conditional, in part, on the adoption of the Resolution". Thus, in the guise of planning, the city has passed a resolution to freeze development in the area until the Lieutenant-Governor in Council acts and to enable the city to obtain grants from Heritage Canada and the Devonian Foundation.
>
> The Old Strathcona Resolution is not concerned with the "use" of land as such but with preserving the existing structures. Neither can it be said that they set out "special aspects of specific kinds of development". The resolution in its latter aspect deals with all development and not with "specific kinds of development". The

19 *Prince George v. Payne*, [1978] 1 S.C.R. 458.
20 (1977) 5 Alta. L.R. (2d) 63, affirmed without written reasons (1979) 7 Alta. L.R. (2d) 292 (S.C.C.).
21 R.S.A. 1970, c. 276 [now R.S.A. 1980, c. P-9], s. 106(1).
22 *Tegon Dev. Ltd. v. Edmonton City Council*, (1977) 5 Alta. L.R. (2d) 63 at 68-69 (C.A.).

legislature of the province empowered the municipal council of the city of Edmonton to pass resolutions dealing with the use of land and in respect of "special aspects of specific kinds of development". However, the council, in purporting to act under that power, expressed other purposes, namely, to impose a freeze on land so that the powers given to the Lieutenant-Governor in Council by the Alberta Heritage Act could be exercised by the Lieutenant-Governor in Council. They also expressed the hope that funds would be forthcoming from Heritage Canada and from the Devonian Foundation. The freeze continues in effect as council has re-enacted the resolution for 1976 and again in 1977.

The power given to the council of the city of Edmonton must be exercised for the purpose for which it is given. It is not a valid exercise of the power to use it to preserve historical sites and to induce others to advance money to preserve historical sites. This division recently reviewed the authorities in respect of the right of the executive council of the province of Alberta to exercise a power given to it by the legislature of the province for a purpose not coming within the statute: *Heppner v. Min. of Environment of Alta.* (1977), 4 Alta. L.R. (2d) 139 (C.A.). The court has the right and the duty to ascertain if the power given was used for a proper purpose. Here the material before the council of the city of Edmonton, as produced in the affidavit filed on behalf of the city, clearly establishes the purpose. It was not a planning purpose.

It is a trite law that municipal governments are the creatures of statute. They can only do what they are authorized to do by statute. If there is no legislative authority for their actions, then those actions are beyond the competence of the municipal council. Here the resolution setting up the rules does not deal with the use of land but constitutes a freeze on the present development of the land and makes rules to preserve the existing development rather than dealing with the use of land as such. In my opinion the Old Strathcona Resolution is beyond the legislative competence of the council of the city of Edmonton.

Similarly, in *Columbia Estates Co. Ltd. v. Burnaby*,[23] the British Columbia Supreme Court struck down the re-zoning of private land to parking lot use when it was demonstrated that the true purpose of the re-zoning was to ensure that the land would be readily available for use in conjunction with a publicly operated transit system.

In all of these cases, the statutory delegate undoubtedly had the power in certain circumstances to take the impugned actions. The question in each case, however, was whether the purpose for which the action was taken was

---

23 (1974) 49 D.L.R. (3d) 123. (B.C.S.C.).

authorized by the legislation in question. In other words, a power granted by legislation for one purpose cannot be used by a delegate for another purpose.

(b) Bad Faith

The phrase "bad faith" is frequently used to describe an abuse of a discretionary power. Such an abuse may be dishonest, malicious, fraudulent or *mala fides*. As Rand J. said in *Roncarelli v. Duplessis*:[24]

> In public regulation of this sort there is no such thing as abso-
> lute and untrammeled "discretion", that is that action can be taken
> on any ground or for any reason that can be suggested to the mind of
> the administrator; no legislative Act can, without express language,
> be taken to contemplate an unlimited arbitrary power exercisable
> for any purpose, however capricious or irrelevant, regardless of the
> nature or purpose of the statute. Fraud and corruption in the Com-
> mission may not be mentioned in such statutes but they are always
> implied as exceptions. "Discretion" necessarily implies good faith in
> discharging public duty; *there is always a perspective within which a
> statute is intended to operate*; and any clear departure from its lines
> or objects is just as objectionable as fraud or corruption. Could an
> applicant be refused a permit because he had been born in another
> province, or because of the colour of his hair? The ordinary language
> of the legislature cannot be so distorted.

It may well be that it is impossible for a tribunal to act in bad faith without doing so for an improper purpose, or without taking into account extraneous considerations. As Pennell J. said in *Re Smith and Vanier*, where there was an allegation of bad faith:[25]

> In the house of good faith there are many mansions. Good faith or
> want of it is not an external fact but rather a state of mind that can be
> judged by verbal or physical acts. To my mind good faith is a
> composite thing referable to all the relevant circumstances. Included
> in the circumstances is the manner in which the discretion was
> exercised.

---

24 [1959] S.C.R. 121 at 140, emphasis added. See also the decision in *Gershman v. Man. Vegetable Producers' Marketing Bd.*, [1976] 2 W.W.R. 432, affirmed [1976] 4 W.W.R. 406 (Man. C.A.).

25 (1973) 30 D.L.R. (3d) 386 at 390-91 (Ont. H.C.). A similar result was reached in *Re Burns and Haldimand Twp.*, (1966) 52 D.L.R. (2d) 101 (Ont. C.A.), where bad faith was found to exist when a city council purported to expropriate the applicant's lands for park purposes (which they undoubtedly had the power to do) when their real motive was to settle a law suit which the applicant had commenced against the municipality. It is submitted that this is the real *ratio decidendi* of the decision of the Alberta Court of Appeal in *Campeau Corp. v. Calgary (No. 1)*, (1979) 7 Alta. L.R. (2d) 294. See also *Re Multi-Malls Inc. and Min. of Tpt. and Communications*, (1976) 14 O.R. (2d) 49 at 60*ff* (C.A.).

In that case, the respondent had refused a building permit for renovations to construct a mini-cinema. On an application for *mandamus*, the respondent set forth only three defects in the application's compliance with the relevant by-law. When the applicant had remedied these three deficiencies, the respondent again refused to issue the licence. Although Pennell J. held that the members of the municipal council believed that refusing the licence would be for the public benefit, and noted that the council was not bound to give any reason for refusing the licence, His Lordship issued a second order of *mandamus* compelling the issuance of the licence because:[26]

> Good faith in law is not to be measured always by a man's own standard of right, but that which the law has prescribed as the standard for the observance of all men in their dealings with each other. The good faith must be determined by what has been done. Would not a reasonable man be entitled to assume from the posture of the Municipal Council on return of the first motion [for *mandamus*] that approval would be forthcoming if he remedied the deficiencies? In the present case the applicant ordered his affairs accordingly. Then, after completing the deficiencies with the financial consequences which that entailed he finds that the Council refused to issue the licence.
>
> Under such circumstances I believe a Court is entitled to look beyond the resolution to refuse the licence. I am of opinion that there was a want of good faith in law and accordingly an order of *mandamus* may issue.

On the other hand, although the courts have given a very broad definition to what constitutes "bad faith" in Administrative Law and particularly in Municipal Law, it nevertheless may be unwise to plead bad faith unless actual *mala fides* or malice can be demonstrated conclusively. In private law, the courts have tended to place a heavy onus on a person pleading bad faith,[27] and it is unnecessarily dangerous to count on the courts to remember that the term has taken on a much less odious meaning in public law. Because "unauthorized or ulterior purpose" or "irrelevant considerations" probably apply as well to virtually every abuse of discretion which could qualify as "bad faith", the latter phrase should be avoided whenever possible.

(c) Irrelevant Considerations

A third category of improper intention arises when a delegate bases his decision on irrelevant considerations.

---

26 *Re Smith and Vanier, ibid.*, p. 392. See also *McIntyre Ranching Co. v. Cardston 6*, (1983) 28 Alta. L.R. (2d) 206 (C.A.).

27 See *Holt Renfrew & Co. v. Henry Singer Ltd.*, (1983) 135 D.L.R. (3d) 391, affirming (1981) 118 D.L.R. (3d) 645 (Alta. C.A.).

In *Associated Provincial Picture Houses, Ltd. v. Wednesbury Corporation*,[28] the English Court of Appeal upheld the decision of a municipal corporation to prohibit children under the age of fifteen years from being admitted to a cinema on a Sunday, pursuant to a statutory provision which permitted cinemas to stay open on Sunday "subject to such conditions as the [council] think fit to impose. . . ". In determining whether this was a proper exercise of the municipality's discretion, Lord Greene M.R. said:[29]

> When an executive discretion is entrusted by Parliament to a local authority, what purports to be an exercise of that discretion can only be challenged in the courts in a very limited class of case. It must always be remembered that the court is not a court of appeal. The law recognizes certain principles on which the discretion must be exercised, but within the four corners of those principles the discretion is an absolute one and cannot be questioned in any court of law.
>
> What, then, are those principles? They are perfectly well understood. The exercise of such a discretion must be a real exercise of the discretion. If, in the statute conferring the discretion, there is to be found, expressly or by implication, matters to which the authority exercising the discretion ought to have regard, then, in exercising the discretion, they must have regard to those matters. Conversely, if the nature of the subject-matter and the general interpretation of the Act make it clear that certain matters would not be germane to the matter in question, they must disregard those matters. Expressions have been used in cases where the powers of local authorities came to be considered relating to the sort of thing that may give rise to interference by the court. Bad faith, dishonesty — those, of course, stand by themselves — unreasonableness, attention given to extraneous circumstances, disregard of public policy, and things like that have all been referred to as being matters which are relevant for consideration. In the present case we have heard a great deal about the meaning of the word "unreasonable". It is true the discretion must be exercised reasonably. What does that mean? Lawyers familiar with the phraseology commonly used in relation to the exercise of statutory discretions often use the word "unreasonable" in a rather comprehensive sense. It is frequently used as a general description of the things that must not be done. For instance, a person entrusted with a discretion must direct himself properly in law. He must call his own attention to the matters which he is bound to consider. He must exclude from his consideration matters which are irrelevant to the matter that he has to consider. If he does not obey those rules, he

---

28 [1948] 1 K.B. 223, [1947] 2 All E.R. 680 (C.A.).
29 *Ibid.*, at pp. 682-83, 685 (All E.R.). This quotation is reported in a somewhat different form in K.B. (see pp. 228-30, 233-34).

may truly be said, and often is said, to be acting "unreasonably". Similarly, you may have something so absurd that no sensible person could ever dream that it lay within the powers of the authority. WARRINGTON, L.J., I think it was, gave the example of the red-haired teacher, dismissed because she had red hair. That is unreasonable in one sense. In another sense it is taking into consideration extraneous matters. It is so unreasonable that it might almost be described as being done in bad faith. In fact, all these things largely fall under one head. . . .

In the result, in my opinion, the appeal must be dismissed. I do not wish to repeat what I have said, but it might be useful to summarise once again the principle, which seems to me to be that the court is entitled to investigate the action of the local authority with a view to seeing whether it has taken into account matters which it ought not to take into account, or, conversely, has refused to take into account or neglected to take into account matters which it ought to take into account. Once that question is answered in favour of the local authority, it may still be possible to say that the local authority, nevertheless, have come to a conclusion so unreasonable that no reasonable authority could ever have come to it. In such a case, again, I think the court can interfere. The power of the court to interfere in each case is not that of an appellate authority to override a decision of the local authority, but is that of a judicial authority which is concerned, and concerned only, to see whether the local authority have contravened the law by acting in excess of the powers which Parliament has confided in it.

Similarly, in *Smith & Rhuland Ltd. v. R.; Ex rel. Andrews,*[30] the Supreme Court of Canada held that it was not a relevant consideration for a Labour Relations Board to exercise its discretion to reject an application for certification of a union as a bargaining unit on the basis that the secretary-treasurer of the union was a communist. Rand J. said that he was unable to agree that[31]

the Board has been empowered to act upon the view that official association with an individual holding political views considered to be dangerous by the Board proscribes a labour organization. Regardless of the strength and character of the influence of such a person, there must be some evidence that, with the acquiescence of the members, it has been directed to ends destructive of the legitimate purposes of the union, before that association can justify the exclusion of employees from the rights and privileges of a statute designed primarily for their benefit.

---

30 [1953] 2 S.C.R. 95.
31 *Ibid.*, p. 100.

In light of the presumption that legislation is presumed not to infringe upon fundamental liberties, such as the freedom of speech and association, without specifically saying so, His Lordship held that the communist leanings of the secretary-treasurer of the union were an irrelevant consideration upon which the statutory delegate could exercise the discretionary powers which the legislature had undoubtedly granted to it. Cartwright and Taschereau JJ. each dissented, asserting that such political views were relevant to the exercise of the board's discretion. Unfortunately, none of the judges indicated a test for determining what matters are or are not relevant. Perhaps such a test could never be devised, and one must rest content with the ability to canvass the matter before the courts.

More recently, the Alberta Court of Appeal in *Campeau Corporation v. Calgary (No. 1)*[32] held that the city's exercise of its power to enact a by-law zoning particular land as agricultural reserve could not be exercised for the improper purpose of creating a park without complying with the strict requirements of the Planning Act[33] requiring the city to purchase land designated as a park. Again, the *ratio* of the case rests on the exercise of a power which the legislative branch has undoubtedly granted to the statutory delegate, but for an unauthorized or improper purpose, or on irrelevant considerations. Similarly, in *Re Dallinga and Calgary*,[34] the court held that a development appeal board should not have considered evidence about the applicant's business methods in running an auto-wrecking yard when it exercised its statutory powers to determine whether to grant a development permit. And in *Re Doctors Hospital and Minister of Health*,[35] an order of the provincial Cabinet exercising a statutory power to revoke the hospital's approval under the Public Hospitals Act[36] as part of an economy drive was struck down on the basis that budgetary considerations were irrelevant to the public health purposes for which the legislation had delegated that power to the Cabinet.

(d) Improper Intention Applies to all Types of Delegated Discretionary Powers

It is important to note that this ground for judicial review is available regardless of the characterization of the function exercised by the statutory delegate. In particular, it is not necessary to characterize the delegate's function as being judicial or quasi-judicial in nature; even a purely administrative or ministerial action must not be based on an irrelevant consideration,

---

32 (1978) 7 Alta. L.R. (2d) 294.
33 R.S.A. 1980, c. P-9.
34 (1976) 62 D.L.R. (3d) 433 (Alta. C.A.).
35 (1976) 68 D.L.R. (3d) 220 (Ont. Div. Ct.).
36 R.S.O. 1970, c. 378.

made in bad faith, or done for an improper or unauthorized purpose.[37] This point was made by Lord Denning M.R. in *Padfield v. Minister of Agriculture, Fisheries and Food*:[38]

> It is said that the decision of the Minister is administrative and not judicial. But that does not mean that he can do as he likes, regardless of right or wrong. Nor does it mean that the courts are powerless to correct him. Good administration requires that complaints should be investigated and that grievances should be remedied. When Parliament has set up machinery for that very purpose, it is not for the Minister to brush it on one side. He should not refuse to have a complaint investigated without good reason.
>
> But it is said that the Minister is not bound to give any reason at all. And that, if he gives no reason, his refusal can not be questioned. So why does it matter if he gives bad reasons? I do not agree. . . . If the Minister is to deny the complainant a hearing — and a remedy — he should at least have good reasons for his refusal: and, if asked, he should give them. If he does not do so, the court may infer that he has no good reason. If it appears to the court that the Minister has been, or must have been, influenced by extraneous considerations which ought not to have influenced him — or, conversely, has failed, or must have failed, to take into account considerations which ought to have influenced him — the court has power to interfere. It can issue a mandamus to compel him to consider the complaint properly.

This reasoning applies equally to all types of delegated discretionary powers: they must be exercised by the delegate for a proper purpose, in good faith, and on relevant considerations only.

3. The Abuse of Acting on Inadequate Material: No Evidence; Ignoring Relevant Considerations

The courts have tended to strike down purely arbitrary exercises of discretion. Thus, judicial review will occur where the delegate has acted upon no evidence whatever,[39] or has ignored relevant considerations.[40] On the other hand, the courts are reluctant to attack the weight to be given to

---

37 See *Shawn v. Robertson*, [1964] 2 O.R. 696 (H.C.); *R. v. Brixton Prison Gov.; Ex parte Soblen*, [1963] 2 Q.B. 248 (C.A.); *Calgary Power Ltd. v. Copithorne*, (1959) 16 D.L.R. (2d) 241 at 251 (S.C.C.), per Martland J.

38 [1968] 2 W.L.R. 924 at 928-29 (H.L.). Lord Reid noted that the words "if the Minister in any case so directs" are sufficient to show that he has some discretion, but they give no guide as to its nature or extent. That must be inferred from a construction of the Act read as a whole, which is the court's task.

39 See D.W. Elliott, "No Evidence — A Ground for Judicial Review in Canada?", (1972-73) 37 Sask. L.R. 48.

40 *R. v. Alta. Lab. Rel. Bd.*, (1983) 27 Alta. L.R. (2d) 338 at 343 (Q.B.). See also *Service*

evidence or considerations which are clearly relevant. As Robins J. said in *Innisfil v. Barrie; Oro v. Barrie*:[41]

> Once it is recognized that the Board is entitled to accept the policy statement, it follows, in my view, that it is for the Board to determine the weight to be given to it. It is not for the Court to enter the arena in such proceedings and judge the effect to be given material before the body charged with the decision. If a matter may properly be considered it is, I think, "scarcely possible for a court ever to say that too much weight was given to it or that it ought not to have been allowed to outweigh other considerations", to adopt the words of Windeyer, J. in *R. v. Anderson, Ex p. Ipec-Air Pty. Ltd.* (1965), 113 C.L.R. 177 at p. 205.

4. The Abuse of Improper Result: Unreasonable, Discriminatory, Retroactive or Uncertain Administrative Actions

Sometimes the court will look to the effect of the exercise of a discretion to determine whether an abuse has occurred. Thus, there is a presumption that discretionary powers should not be exercised unreasonably, discriminatorily, retroactively, or in an uncertain manner. As with all jurisdictional defects, extrinsic evidence is admissible to demonstrate whether one of these states of affairs exists.

(a) Unreasonableness

"Unreasonableness" has a very broad meaning in Administrative Law, as Lord Greene M.R. noted in *Associated Provincial Picture Houses, Ltd. v. Wednesbury Corporation*:[42]

> Lawyers familiar with the phraseology commonly used in relation to the exercise of statutory discretions often use the word "unreasonable" in a rather comprehensive sense. It is frequently used as a general description of the things that must not be done. For instance, a person entrusted with a discretion must direct himself properly in law. He must call his own attention to the matters which he is bound to consider. He must exclude from his consideration matters which are irrelevant to the matter that he has to consider. If he does not obey those rules, he may truly be said, and often is said,

Employees Int. Union v. Nipawin Dist. Staff Nurses Assn., (1975) 41 D.L.R. (3d) 6 at 11-12 (S.C.C.), and the cases cited therein.
41 (1977) 17 O.R. (2d) 277 at 287 (Div. Ct.). See also *R. v. Nat Bell Liquors Ltd.*, [1922] A.C. 128 (P.C.).
42 [1948] 1 K.B. 223 at 229, [1947] 2 All E.R. 680 at 682-83 (C.A.).

to be acting "unreasonably". Similarly, you may have something so absurd that no sensible person could ever dream that it lay within the powers of the authority. WARRINGTON, L.J., I think it was, gave the example of the red-haired teacher, dismissed because she had red hair. That is unreasonable in one sense. In another sense, it is taking into consideration extraneous matters. It is so unreasonable that it might almost be described as being done in bad faith. In fact, all these things largely fall under one head.

As Lord MacNaughton said in *Westminster Corporation v. London and North Western Railway*:[43]

> It is well settled that a public body invested with statutory powers such as those conferred upon the corporation must take care not to exceed or abuse its powers. It must keep within the limits of the authority committed to it. It must act in good faith. *And it must act reasonably*. The last proposition is involved in the second, if not in the first. But in the present case I think it will be convenient to take it separately.

It is important to note — again! — that reasonableness is an implied limitation on the ability of a statutory delegate to exercise the discretion which undoubtedly has been granted to him by legislation. Because it is probably impossible to give a fool-proof litmus test to determine what particular results would constitute unreasonable exercises of statutory discretion, a few examples may be illuminating. In *Roberts v. Hopwood*,[44] the House of Lords held that it was an unreasonable and therefore *ultra vires* exercise of a municipal council's statutory discretion to pay its workers substantially more at a time of falling cost of living, even though the council wished to be "model employers". Coke reports a case where the court struck down charges levied by the commissioners of sewers against one owner of land adjacent to the river bank which they had repaired, instead of levying it against all of the owners who benefitted.[45]

It may well be that unreasonableness can in some circumstances be treated as a synonym for the exercise of a discretion for an improper purpose, in bad faith, or on irrelevant considerations. Nevertheless, it is possible that a delegate can act in good faith, closing his mind to irrelevancies and considering all relevant factors, but still come up with a result which the court might characterize as being unreasonable. In such circumstances, the court will probably be slow to strike down the decision which the legislation has clearly granted to the delegate and not to the courts.[46] Of course, legislation

---

43 [1905] A.C. 426 at 430 (H.L.), emphasis added.
44 [1925] A.C. 578 (H.L.). See H.W.R. Wade's account of the subsequent history of the case in *Administrative Law*, 5th ed. (Oxford: Clarendon Press, 1982), p. 378.
45 *Rooke's Case*, (1598) 5 Co. Rep. 99b.
46 Whether in first instance, or in appeal *de novo*.

can put this matter beyond dispute, as is demonstrated by section 108 of the Alberta Municipal Government Act:[47]

> **108** A by-law or resolution passed by a council in the exercise of any of the powers conferred and in accordance with this Act, and in good faith, is not open to question, nor shall it be quashed, set aside or declared invalid, either wholly or partly, on account of the unreasonableness or supposed unreasonableness of its provisions or any of them.

This statutory provision, of course, presumes that unreasonableness is different from bad faith. Further, this provision only insulates a by-law or resolution from attack on the ground of unreasonableness; it does not prevent attacking a discretionary action taken by a municipal officer pursuant to a by-law (or any other legislation) on the grounds of unreasonableness.

Unreasonableness has been dealt with here as a separate heading from the earlier one dealing with improper intentions[48] because unreasonableness — at least in one sense[49] — does not really go to the state of mind of the statutory delegate in the exercise of his discretion, but rather to the objective effect of the exercise of his discretion.

(b) Discrimination

There is also a presumption that a statutory delegate must not exercise his discretion in a discriminatory manner. Chief Justice McKeigan stated the test for what constitutes discrimination in *Lacewood Development Co. v. Halifax*[50] as follows:

> Wrongful discrimination involves two elements, both of which must be present before a by-law should be condemned on this ground:
>
> (1) The by-law must discriminate in fact. To use the words of Middleton, J. in the "classic definition", by-laws discriminate if they "give permission to one and refuse it to another".
> (2) The factual discrimination must be carried out with the improper motive of favouring or hurting one individual and without regard to the public interest.

Most of the cases on discrimination deal with the exercise of the delegated discretionary power to enact legislation. For example in *Calgary v. S. S.*

---

47 R.S.A. 1980 c. M-26, s. 108.
48 Including improper or ulterior purpose, bad faith, and irrelevant considerations.
49 Not the sense used by Lord Greene M.R. in the quotation from the *Associated Picture Houses* case, *supra*, note 42.
50 (1976) 58 D.L.R. (3d) 383 at 395-96 (N.S.C.A.).

Kresge Company Ltd.; Calgary v. Super S Drugs Ltd.,[51] the court struck down a by-law requiring certain stores to close but permitting other stores to stay open on Sundays. Nevertheless, the presumption against discrimination should in theory also apply to all forms of discretionary powers, and not just legislative ones.

Again, legislation may specifically permit discrimination with respect to certain matters.[52]

(c) Retroactivity

There is also a presumption that a delegated discretionary power shall not be exercised retroactively, unless the legislation expressly authorizes retroactivity. Most of the cases in this area deal with the discretion to enact delegated legislation, and not to other forms of discretionary action, but in theory the presumption against retroactivity should also apply to all other forms of discretionary powers.

For example, in *Canuck Holdings Western Ltd. v. Fort Nelson Improvement Dist.*,[53] the court held that a by-law levying a hook-up charge with respect to service from a district's utilities could not be applied retroactively to require the plaintiffs to pay when they had completed the construction of their building and hooked it up to the utilities prior to the passage of the by-law. This reasoning is consistent with the principles set out in both the Alberta Regulations Act and the federal Statutory Instruments Act, which provide

---

51 (1965) 51 W.W.R. 747 (Alta. T.D.). See also: *Sanbay Dev. Ltd. v. London*, [1975] 1 S.C.R. 485, dealing with discriminatory spot zoning; *Rodenbush v. North Cowichan*, (1977) 76 D.L.R. (3d) 731 (B.C.S.C.); *Neilson Enrg. Ltd. v. Toronto*, [1968] 1 O.R. 271 (H.C.).

52 See, *e.g.*, s. 224 of the Municipal Government Act, R.S.A. 1980, c. M-26, which provides:

> 224 (1) A council may by by-law do all things with respect to the regulation of any business or industry including the licensing thereof, the restriction and limitation of its operations and any other matter considered necessary with respect to the business or industry including the right to impose a penalty and to prohibit the carrying on of any business or industry without a licence.
> (2) The power under subsection (1) extends within the municipality to persons who carry on any business or industry partly within and partly outside the municipality.
> (3) A licence fee may be in the nature of a reasonable tax for the privilege conferred by the licence or for the purpose of raising revenue and may be computed in any manner accepted by the council.
> (4) In fixing a licence fee the council shall, when applicable, have regard for the business tax payable by similar businesses in the municipality.
> (5) In establishing licence fees the council may charge a greater licence fee to a person who does not maintain a place of business within the municipality or reside in the municipality or both.
> (6) The power to license a business or industry includes the power to specify the qualifications of the persons carrying on the business or industry and the conditions on which the licences shall be granted.

53 (1963) 42 D.L.R. (2d) 313 (B.C.S.C.).

quite strict limitations on the ability to make delegated legislation retroactive.[54]

A problem does sometimes arise, however, in determining whether a decision has a retroactive effect. In the first place, a complaint about retro-activity can only arise where rights have already vested so as to be affected by the impugned retroactive decision.[55] Secondly, not every change in a rule is truly retroactive. For example, the implementation of a rule prohibiting an articling student from writing the bar admission examination more than three times is not necessarily retroactive if applied to students who have not yet written the examination three times (but, for example, only once and failed). In all likelihood, the student does not have a vested right to sit the examina-tion an unlimited number of times, and therefore his rights have not been affected by the imposition of a three-time rule. By contrast, if the three-time rule is subsequently amended to a two-time rule, it is conceivable that the application of that rule to anyone registered in the bar course who had not yet written three examinations might be a retroactive amendment to his right to write the examinations three times.

(d) Uncertainty

Administrative actions whose results are uncertain have also been held to be void on review by the superior courts. Again, most examples of this ground for judicial review relate to the content of delegated legislation. In *McEldowney v. Forde*,[56] a regulation was attacked for being uncertain. The legislation granted the government of Northern Ireland wide powers to preserve peace and maintain order, and a regulation was passed making it a criminal offence to belong to a "republican club" or "any like organization however described". Serious doubt was expressed by the courts about whether these phrases were so vague as to be incapable of enforcement. Of course, mere ambiguity is not sufficient to constitute uncertainty. On the contrary, the court's task is to resolve the ambiguity, to choose the one correct meaning — which in most cases would not itself be uncertain. Accordingly, the ambit within which uncertainty will be a useful ground for reviewing delegated legislation is likely to be narrow.

In principle, uncertainty should also be a ground for attacking the exercise of other discretionary administrative powers which are not legislative in nature; however, it is difficult to find a good example of this.

---

54 See the discussion on this point in chapter 4, *supra*.

55 See *Wilkin v. White*, (1980) 11 M.P.L.R. 275 (B.C.S.C.), where the rules relating to subdivision were changed after an application had been made but no right had vested; *Hunter v. Surrey*, (1980) 108 D.L.R. (3d) 557 (B.C.S.C.), where the applicants were charged higher development cost charges under a new by-law passed after an application for subdivision had been made.

56 [1971] A.C. 632 (H.L.). See also *Tpt. Min. v. Alexander*, [1978] 1 N.Z.L.R. 306; *Hotel & Catering Indust. Training Bd. v. Automobile Pty. Ltd.*, [1969] 1 W.L.R. 697 (H.L.).

5. The Abuse of Misconstruing the Law

Certain errors of law will cause a delegate to lose his jurisdiction. Unfortunately, no satisfactory test has ever been devised to distinguish between those errors which constitute jurisdictional defects and those which are intra-jurisdictional in nature. Nevertheless, the distinction between these two types of legal errors is important for at least five reasons. First, a privative clause cannot effectively prevent judicial review where the jurisdiction of the delegate is in question, but will be effective to prevent the superior courts from using *certiorari* to correct mere errors of law on the face of the record. Secondly, affidavits and other evidence are admissible, if necessary, to prove the existence of a jurisdictional error, but they cannot be considered by the court if a non-jurisdictional error of law is involved. Thirdly, the court's anomalous power to correct intra-jurisdictional errors is limited to errors of law only, and does not apply to errors of fact, whereas factual matters may give rise to a jurisdictional error, particularly in the context of the preliminary or collateral fact doctrine. Fourthly, this anomalous use of *certiorari* can only correct errors of law which appear on the face of the record, however that is defined, whereas jurisdictional errors do not have to be so disclosed. Finally, it may not be possible to correct intra-jurisdictional errors by any remedy other than this anomalous use of *certiorari*, although other remedies may frequently be available to review jurisdictional errors.

In theory, a distinction should be made between two kinds of jurisdictional errors of law. On the one hand, certain preliminary or collateral questions of law sometimes have to be determined correctly in order to bring the delegate within the jurisdiction granted to him by statute.[57] Errors on these preliminary matters constitute defects in the delegate's acquisition of jurisdiction, and are discussed more fully in chapter 6. On the other hand, the delegate may undoubtedly have acquired jurisdiction to do the matter remitted to him by statute, but may subsequently make an error of law which causes him to lose jurisdiction. This type of error is discussed here and in chapter 10.

Further, a theoretical distinction must be made between errors of law which cause a delegate to lose jurisdiction and intra-jurisdictional errors. Because of the jurisdictional nature of the former category, extrinsic evidence is admissible on any application for any remedy to correct such an error. By contrast, only an anomalous use of *certiorari* is available to quash an intra-jurisdictional error of law, and then only if the error is disclosed on the face of the record of the proceedings of the statutory delegate.[58]

---

57 See *Anisminic Ltd. v. Foreign Compensation Comm.*, [1969] 2 A.C. 147 (H.L.); *Jacmain v. A.G. Can.*, [1978] 2 S.C.R. 15; *Parkhill Furniture & Bedding Ltd. v. Int. Molders etc. Union*, (1961) 34 W.W.R. 13 (Man. C.A.); and *Jarvis v. Assoc. Medical Services Inc.*, [1964] S.C.R. 497. See also the discussion in section 6 of chapter 10, *infra*.

58 See chapter 10, *infra*.

The distinction between jurisdictional and intra-jurisdictional errors of law is brought into sharp relief if the legislation contains a privative clause which purports to prevent judicial review of a delegate's action. The courts have long held that such clauses only apply to administrative actions which are *intra vires*. Accordingly, a privative clause will not protect a jurisdictional error of law. The courts have recently adopted the phrase "patently unreasonable" to determine whether an error of law is jurisdictional or intra-jurisdictional in nature.[59] This recent development is discussed more fully in chapter 10.

6. The Abuse of Fettering Discretion

Because Administrative Law generally requires a statutory power to be exercised by the very person upon whom it has been conferred,[60] there must necessarily be some limit on the extent to which the exercise of a discretionary power can be fettered by the adoption of an inflexible policy, by contract, or by other means. After all, the existence of discretion implies the absence of a rule dictating the result in each case; the essence of discretion is that it can be exercised differently in different cases. Each case must be looked at individually, on its own merits.[61] Anything, therefore, which requires a delegate to exercise his discretion in a particular way may illegally limit the ambit of his power. A delegate who thus fetters his discretion commits a jurisdictional error which is capable of judicial review.

On the other hand, it would be incorrect to assert that a delegate cannot adopt a general policy. Any administrator[62] faced with a large volume of discretionary decisions is practically bound to adopt rough rules of thumb. This practice is legally acceptable, provided each case is individually considered on its merits. As Bankes L. J. said in *R. v. Port of London Authority; Ex parte Kynoch, Ltd.*:[63]

> There are on the one hand cases where a tribunal in the honest exercise of its discretion has adopted a policy, and, without refusing to

---

59 See, *e.g.*, *C.U.P.E., Loc. 963 v. N.B. Liquor Corp.*, (1979) 97 D.L.R. (3d) 417 (S.C.C.).

60 See chapter 6 for a discussion of circumstances in which a delegate may validly sub-delegate certain statutory powers.

61 See H.W.R. Wade, *Administrative Law*, 5th ed. (Oxford: Clarendon Press, 1982), pp. 330-31: "It is a fundamental rule for the exercise of discretionary power that discretion must be brought to bear on every case: each one must be considered on its own merits and decided as the public interest requires at the time."

62 Or sometimes many administrators, all faced with exercising the same statutory discretion, *e.g.*, immigration officers deciding whether to grant landed immigrant status, tax inspectors, or prosecutors deciding whether to proceed by way of indictment or summary conviction. There is a natural tendency for the civil service to attempt to codify the way such discretions are to be exercised, to attempt to achieve consistency. Hence the various "guide lines", "interpretation bulletins" and other similar non-statutory material.

63 [1919] 1 K.B. 176 at 184 (C.A.). See also Lord Reid's comments in *British Oxygen Co. v. Min. of Technology*, [1971] A.C. 610 at 625 (H.L.).

hear an applicant, intimates to him what its policy is, and that after hearing him it will in accordance with its policy decide against him, unless there is something exceptional in his case. . . . [I]f the policy has been adopted for reasons which the tribunal may legitimately entertain, no objection could be taken to such a course. On the other hand there are cases where a tribunal has passed a rule, or come to a determination, not to hear any application of a particular character by whomsoever made. There is a wide distinction to be drawn between these two classes.

Similarly, a delegate does not necessarily commit an error by referring to the policy adopted by another governmental agency when deciding to exercise his own discretion.[64] It is true that the principles of natural justice and fairness may in both cases require the delegate to disclose the existence of such policies so that a person affected thereby can intelligently make representations as to why the delegate should exercise his discretion differently in the particular case. Nevertheless, the legal issue boils down to whether the delegate in fact has exercised his discretion or fettered it.

(a) Inflexible Policy Fetters on the Exercise of Discretion

The adoption of an inflexible policy almost certainly means that the delegate has not exercised the discretionary power granted to him.[65] Accordingly, an order for *mandamus* in principle will issue to compel the delegate to decide the particular case on its own merits. This situation arose in *Lloyd v. Superintendent of Motor Vehicles*,[66] where the Court of Appeal of British Columbia struck down the superintendent's invariable policy of suspending the licence of every driver convicted of driving while impaired. Bull J. A. dealt with the legal issues as follows:[67]

---

64 *Innisfil v. Vespra*, [1981] 2 S.C.R. 145, varying (1978) 95 D.L.R. (3d) 298, which reversed in part (sub nom. *Re City of Barrie Annexation*) 4 M.P.L.R. 83; *R. v. Anderson; Ex parte Ipec-Air Pty. Ltd.*, (1965) 113 C.L.R. 177 (Aus. H.C.).

65 On the contrary, the adoption of an inflexible policy constitutes converting a discretionary power into a rule applicable to all cases, rather similar to enacting delegated legislation with no discretionary element. This is the reverse of the problem in *Ex parte Brent*, [1955] 3 D.L.R. 587 (Ont. C.A.), and *Brant Dairy Co. v. Milk Comm. of Ont.*, [1973] S.C.R. 131, discussed in the text accompanying note 9 to chapter 6, where the delegate purported to create a discretionary power by enacting delegated legislation. Both errors are fatal because they depart from the form of power delegated by the legislation to the administrator, who has no authority to make such changes.

66 (1971) 20 D.L.R. (3d) 181 (B.C.C.A.). See also *Jackson v. Beaudry*, (1969) 70 W.W.R. 572 (Sask. Q.B.); and *Wimpey Western Ltd. v. Dept. of Environment, Dir. of Standards & Approvals*, (1983) 28 Alta. L.R. (2d) 193, affirming (1982) 21 Alta. L.R. (2d) 125 (C.A.); *R. v. Bowman*, [1898] 1 Q.B. 663 at 667 (Div. Ct.); *R. v. London County Council; Ex parte Corrie*, [1918] 1 K.B. 68 (Div. Ct.); *Alden v. Gaglardi*, [1971] 2 W.W.R. 148, affirmed [1973] S.C.R. 199; *Alkali Lake Indian Band v. Westcoast Transmission Co.*, [1984] 4 W.W.R. 263 (B.C.C.A.).

67 (1971) 20 D.L.R. (3d) 181 at 188-89, emphasis added.

With respect, I do not agree, but I prefer to base my conclusion on a somewhat different approach. As the proceedings are for *certiorari*, we are concerned with jurisdiction. Did the respondent Superintendent exceed or reject or decline the jurisdiction provided him by the statute, or put in another way, did he determine the question which he was required to determine? To my mind, the question of the justification for a blanket policy decision as to unfitness is irrelevant in these proceedings. Once the Superintendent is carrying out his duties within his jurisdiction as required of him, it matters not how wrong or right he may be in the decisions he makes or the discretion he exercises. But where, as in *Board of Education v. Rice*, [1911] A.C. 179 [H.L.], and in *Toronto Newspaper Guild v. Globe Printing Co.*, [1953] 2 S.C.R. 18, 106 C.C.C. 225, [1953] 3 D.L.R. 561, the inferior tribunal, board or official has declined to enter upon, or has not entered upon, an inquiry upon which he was bound to enter, or where, as in numerous decisions of the Supreme Court of Canada and of this Court, having entered upon such inquiry the tribunal, board or official has exceeded the authority or jurisdictional boundary which the statute gave, a superior Court will interfere by the issue of one of the appropriate prerogative writs.

In my view it is crystal clear that the respondent Superintendent did not enter into any inquiry at all as to whether or not the appellant was or was not, by virtue of any reason, unfit to drive a motor vehicle. *He formed no opinion of the appellant's fitness at any time, and never at any time put his mind to that question. A pre-existing policy decision formed at some unknown earlier time would unquestionably, have bearing upon the formation of his opinion, had he put his mind to the appellant's fitness or otherwise, but that policy decision is not what the section required the Superintendent to make or to apply. He was required to form an opinion of fitness or unfitness as at the time of the formation of the opinion. Put simply, there never was any inquiry or consideration given to the situation of the person aggrieved by the official charged by the Legislature with judicial or quasi-judicial duties*. I fail to see on what valid grounds it can be said that the respondent Superintendent judicially formed an opinion of the appellant's unfitness to drive at the time of the opinion and which unfitness had been satisfactorily proved to him, when he did nothing more than give directions at some unknown earlier date to his staff to send out suspension notices to all persons who had been convicted of a violation of s. 222 of the *Criminal Code* and to place his stamped name thereon.

On the other hand, it is sometimes possible for a delegate to adopt a general policy without thereby fettering the exercise of his discretion in a particular case. At the minimum, it appears that the delegate must consider fairly those cases which run counter to the policy.[68] Fair consideration might require disclosure of the existence of the policy to the person seeking to be exempted[69] therefrom. Provided that the policy is relevant to the purpose for which the discretion was granted,[70] the courts have upheld the validity of using a flexible policy in determining how to exercise the discretion. In such a case, the delegate has not relentlessly refused or declined to exercise his discretion on account of the policy, but rather has exercised his discretion in the very case before him.

It has been suggested that the administrator's natural desire for consistency may sometimes amount to an illegal fettering of discretion, as may adopting a policy of only acting on the recommendation of a third party.[71] This not only fetters discretion but also constitutes illegal sub-delegation.[72]

(b) Contractual Fetters on the Exercise of Discretion

A statutory delegate cannot validly contract to exercise his discretion in a particular way. As Lord Birkenhead said,[73] there is

> a well-established principle of law, that if a person or public body is entrusted by the legislature with certain powers and duties expressly or impliedly for public purposes, those persons or bodies cannot divest themselves of these powers and duties. They cannot enter into a contract or take any action incompatible with the exercise of their power or the discharge of their duties.

Thus, any contract which compels a municipality to re-zone land in a particular way is illegal, whether reliance is placed upon it by the municipality, the

---

68 *R. v. Port of London Authority; Ex parte Kynoch, Ltd.*, *supra*, note 63; *R. v. Sylvester* (1862), 31 L.J. M.C. 93, 95.

69 *Innisfil v. Vespra*, *supra*, note 64.

70 *Ibid*. See also the *Wimpey Western* case, *supra*, note 66, especially at pp. 198-204 (C.A.), and pp. 134-38 (Q.B.).

71 See D.J. Mullan, "Natural Justice and Fairness — Substantive as well as Procedural Standards for the Review of Administrative Decision-Making?", (1982) 27 McGill L.J. 250; D.J. Mullan, "Recent Developments in Nova Scotian Administrative Law", (1978) 4 Dalhousie L.J. 467 at 538; H. Wade MacLauchlan, "Some Problems with Judicial Review of Administrative Inconsistency", (1984) 8 Dalhousie L.J. 435. See also *Merchandise Tpt. Ltd. v. British Tpt. Comm*; *Arnold Tpt. (Rochester) v. British Tpt. Comm.*, [1962] 2 Q.B. 173 at 193; *Capital Cities Communications Inc. v. C.R.T.C.*, (1977) 81 D.L.R. (3d) 609 at 629 (S.C.C.); *Re Hopedale Dev. Ltd. and Oakville*, [1965] O.R. 259 (C.A.).

72 See *Vic Restaurant Inc. v. Montreal*, (1958) 17 D.L.R. (2d) 81 (S.C.C.), discussed in the text accompanying note 26 to chapter 6.

73 *Birkdale Dist. Elec. Supply Co. v. Southport Corp.*, [1926] A.C. 355 at 364 (H.L.). See also *Cobalt v. Temiskaming Tel. Co.*, (1919) 59 S.C.R. 62, where Anglin J. said at p. 79: "A municipal corporation cannot validly contract not to use discretionary powers committed to it for the public good".

land-owner, or any third party.[74] Of course, a statute may specifically permit such contractual agreements on how a discretionary power is to be exercised.[75]

(c) Reference to Other Governmental Policies

A statutory delegate sometimes exercises his discretion by reference to a policy articulated by some other governmental body. On the one hand, such an external policy must clearly be relevant to the statutory question in issue.[76] If it is irrelevant or improper, the exercise of the delegated power is invalid for this reason.[77] On the other hand, even if the external policy is relevant, the rule against fettering requires the delegate to exercise his own discretion in deciding whether and how to accept the policy. In particular, the delegate cannot simply treat the external policy as a given, and may be required to permit cross-examination and refutation of that policy.[78] The expectation that a delegate will exercise his discretion in a manner so as to accommodate other governmental policies raises difficult legal issues about the relationship between apparently independent administrative bodies and more centralized government agencies,[79] which are only occasionally dealt with specifically by the legislature.[80]

In theory, all fetters on the ability of a delegate to exercise his discretion are an abuse, and result in a loss of jurisdiction[81] which can be reviewed by the courts, even in the face of a privative clause.

---

74 *Vancouver v. Reg. of Vancouver Land Registration Dist.*, [1955] 2 D.L.R. 709 (B.C.C.A.), where the illegality was asserted against the city when the registrar refused to register an agreement which gave it an interest in land which it undertook to re-zone. See also *Osborne v. Amalgamated Soc. of Ry. Servants*, [1909] 1 Ch. 163, affirmed [1910] A.C. 87 (H.L.), where this principle was applied to strike down an agreement as to how trustees were to vote; *Egerton v. Earl Brownlow*, (1853) 4 H.L. Cas. 1 at 160-61.

75 Under s. 10 [re-en. 1974-75-76, c. 51, s. 4] of the Northern Canada Power Commission Act, R.S.C. 1970, c. N-21, the commission is given broad discretion to determine the rates to be charged for power supplied by it. However, under s. 11, the commission may also enter into long-term contracts for the supply of power, and any such contract lawfully derogates from the commission's ongoing discretionary rate-setting power.

76 As it was held to be in both *Innisfil v. Vespra*, [1981] 2 S.C.R. 145, and the *Wimpey Western* case, *supra*, note 66.

77 See the discussion of this abuse in section 2 of this chapter, *supra*.

78 This was the issue in the *Innisfil* case, *supra*, note 76.

79 See *Parliament and Administrative Agencies*, prepared by F.F. Slatter as a Study Paper for the Law Reform Commission of Canada (1982); and *Public Participation in the Administrative Process*, prepared by David Fox as a Study Paper for the Law Reform Commission of Canada (1979).

80 See, *e.g.*, s. 27 of the Broadcasting Act, R.S.C. 1970, c. B-11, which permits the cabinet to give broad policy guidelines to the Canadian Radio, Television and Telecommunications Commission, and s. 54 of the Public Service Employee Relations Act, R.S.A. 1980, c. P-33, as amended by the Labour Statutes Amendment Act, 1983 (Alta.), c. 34, s. 5(7), which requires a board of arbitration to consider the Provincial Treasurer's written statements of fiscal policy.

81 The error is jurisdictional in nature because the policy fetter prevents the delegate from exercising *his* discretion at all. In the *Innisfil* case, however, some of the judges in the lower

7. Summary

This chapter has considered the legal limitations on the ability of a statutory delegate to exercise discretionary powers. Although the essence of a discretionary power is that it can and should be exercised differently in different cases, this does not mean that discretionary administrative actions can never be challenged successfully in court. In the first place, the courts can review whether the legislation in fact grants the delegate authority to exercise the impugned discretion at all.[82] Even if the court upholds the ambit of the discretionary power upon which the delegate relies, judicial review nevertheless lies to ensure that there has been no abuse of that power in a particular case. Although the courts have frequently elided them together, this chapter has for convenience grouped possible abuses into the following categories:

(a) improper intention in exercising a discretionary power for an unauthorized or ulterior purpose, in bad faith, or for irrelevant considerations;

(b) acting on inadequate material where there is no evidence or by ignoring relevant considerations;

(c) exercising discretionary power so as to obtain an improper result, which may be unreasonable, discriminatory, retroactive or uncertain in operation;

(d) exercising discretionary power under a misapprehension of the law; and

(e) fettering the exercising of discretion by adopting a policy or entering into a contract.

In theory, all these abuses cause the delegate to lose jurisdiction,[83] and therefore are susceptible to judicial review even in the face of privative clauses.[84]

8. Selected Bibliography

Brun, H., "La Mort de la discretion administrative", (1974) 52 Can. Bar Rev. 426.

Davis, K.C., *Discretionary Justice*. Baton Rouge: Louisiana State Press, 1969.

Galligan, D.J., "The Nature and Function of Policies Within Discretionary Power", [1976] P. L. 332.

Ontario courts treated this type of error as one *within* jurisdiction: *supra*, note 76. With respect, this approach is theoretically incorrect, as Estey J. recognized in the Supreme Court of Canada.

82 *E.g.*, see *Petrashuyk v. Law Soc. of Alta.*, (1983) 29 Alta. L.R. (2d) 251, reversed (1984), 35 Alta. L.R. (2d) 259, leave to appeal to S.C.C. granted [1985] A.W.L.D. 445; and *Liversidge v. Anderson*, [1942] A.C. 206 (H.L.).

83 *Ibid.*

84 See chapter 14, *infra*.

Grey, J.H., "Discretion in Administrative Law", (1979) 17 Osgoode Hall L. J. 107.

Law Reform Commission of Canada, *A Catalogue of Discretionary Powers in the Revised Statutes of Canada 1970*, prepared by Philip Anisman, 1975.

MacLauchlan, H.W., "Some Problems with Judicial Review of Administrative Consistency", (1984) 8 Dalhousie L.J. 435.

Molot, H., "The Self-Created Rule of Policy and Other Ways of Exercising Administrative Discretion", (1972) 18 McGill L.J. 310.

Mullan, D.J., "Natural Justice and Fairness — Substantive as well as Procedural Standards for Review of Administrative Decision-Making", (1982) McGill L.J. 250.

Mullan, D.J., "Recent Developments in Nova Scotian Administrative Law", (1978) 4 Dalhousie L.J. 467 at 538*ff*.

Rogerson, P., "On the Fettering of Public Powers", [1971] P. L. 288.

Smillie, J.A., "Review of Abuse of Discretionary Power", (1969) 47 Can. Bar Rev. 623.

Wade, H.R.H., *Administrative Law*, 5th ed. Oxford: Clarendon Press, 1982.

Wilson, H.J., "Discretion in the Analysis of Administrative Process", (1972) 10 Osgoode Hall L. J. 117.

8

The Principles of Natural Justice and the Duty to be Fair

1. Introduction

This chapter describes the principles of natural justice and the newer doctrine of procedural fairness as they apply to the work of administrative tribunals and other statutory delegates.

We start with an historical review of the law as it related to the principles of natural justice in England and Canada. In particular, the first part of this century saw the gradual erosion of the vigour of the principles, in Canada culminating with *Calgary Power Ltd. v. Copithorne.*[1] The restoration of the principles of natural justice began in England with *Ridge v. Baldwin,*[2] which in turn developed such momentum that it led to a tremendous extension of the principles into a new doctrine of procedural fairness. This "duty to be fair" has now been extended to cover both quasi-judicial and executive decisions, thus frequently eliminating the need to characterize the nature of the delegate's function before determining whether the procedure used in exercising it must be "fair" and thereby amenable to *certiorari* or another remedy. The content of procedural fairness in any given circumstance may be very difficult to determine without litigation. It is considered later in this chapter.

Finally, a word about terminology: A discussion of the principles of natural justice and procedural fairness necessarily entails the characterization of a delegate's function. Traditionally, the categories of legislative, judicial or quasi-judicial, and administrative (or ministerial, or executive) have been

1 [1959] S.C.R. 24.
2 [1964] A.C. 40 (H.L.).

used. In this chapter, the term "executive" is used to describe the governmental function of applying and enforcing legislation to particular people in particular circumstances. The term "administrative" will often be found in the cases used synonymously with "executive", but it has so many other meanings that we have tried to avoid it wherever possible.[3]

This chapter draws substantially on two articles written by Professor D.P. Jones: "Administrative Fairness in Alberta";[4] and "Natural Justice and Fairness in the Administrative Process".[5]

2. Historical Development

(a) Origins of the Phrase: "Judicial or Quasi-judicial"

"Natural justice" connotes the requirement that administrative tribunals, when reaching a decision, must do so with procedural fairness. If they err, the superior courts will step in to quash the decision by *certiorari* or prevent the error being made by prohibition. Such an error is jurisdictional in nature and renders the decision void.[6]

The prerogative writs of *certiorari* and prohibition were originally used by the superior courts to control the decisions of inferior courts. In other words, the writs were originally used in a purely judicial context. Historically, not only the administration of justice but also other governmental functions were delegated by Parliament to local justices of the peace. They were originally legal officers who ran courts within a limited jurisdiction. But the justices of the peace also became administrators of local government in the sense that they had duties in connection with the administration of the Poor Laws, the upkeep of roads and bridges, and the licensing of ale houses, for example. The two functions — judicial and executive — were not separated. As a result, administrative decisions were arrived at by a process similar to a trial of the issue.

With the growth of local government and statutory tribunals in the 19th century, many of the administrative powers of the justices of the peace were transferred to these new creations. Curiously, these transferred governmental

---

3 See J.M. Evans, "Classification of Functions" in de Smith's *Judicial Review of Administrative Actions*, 4th ed. (1980), c. 2, pp. 68-89.

4 (1980) 18 Alta. L. Rev. 351.

5 Published as a chapter in *Judicial Review of Administrative Rulings* arising out of the 1982 Annual Conference of the Canadian Institute for the Administration of Justice; also printed in (1983) 43 *Revue du Barreau* 441.

6 See H.W.R. Wade, "Unlawful Administrative Action: Void or Voidable?", Part I at (1967) 83 L.Q. Rev. 499; Part II at (1968) 84 L.Q. Rev. 95; Wade's *Administrative Law*, 5th ed. (1982), pp. 310*ff.*; M.B. Akehurst, (1968) 31 M.L.R. 2, 138; J.F. Northey, [1977] N.Z.L.J. 284; D. Oliver, [1981] C.L.P.; G.L. Peiris, "Natural Justice and Degrees of Invalidity of Administrative Action", [1983] P.L. 634; *Harelkin v. Univ. of Regina*, [1979] 2 S.C.R. 561, and comment by D.P. Jones "Discretionary Refusal of Judicial Review in Administrative Law", (1981) 19 Alta. L. Rev. 483.

tasks retained the characterization as "judicial" because they had previously been performed by judicial officers. Loosely, this meant that the new decision-makers were also required to proceed fairly (that is, they had to observe the principles of natural justice); and, secondly, of course, they were required to stay within their limited respective areas of jurisdiction. The new label "quasi-judicial" appeared in an effort to distinguish between the judicial decision-making of the judges on the one hand, and on the other hand the decision-making of members of administrative tribunals who were not judicial officers, but who were nevertheless required to adopt at least some of the procedures reminiscent of those used in a courtroom.

Although the label "judicial" originally applied to all administrative acts, the courts subsequently narrowed the meaning. As a result, the characterization of powers as either "legislative", "judicial" or "executive" became a necessary prerequisite to judicial review because the principles of natural justice did not apply unless the power was characterized first as judicial or quasi-judicial in nature. Similarly, prohibition and *certiorari* came to be available only against judicial or quasi-judicial functions. This restriction omitted the wide range of decision-making in the legislative and executive areas which could then proceed unimpaired by considerations of natural justice.

Natural justice was comprised of two main sub-rules: *audi alteram partem*[7] — that a person must know the case being made against him and be given an opportunity to answer it; and *nemo judex in sua causa debet esse*[8] — the rule against bias (which is discussed in chapter 9). Until recently in Canada, these two great principles were held not to apply to a vast number of decisions said to be legislative or executive in nature. As a result, procedural error in those cases was generally not subject to judicial review.

In the last few years, the concept of the "duty to be fair" has developed. The result has been to re-assert the power of the courts to review governmental decisions which cannot be characterized as judicial or quasi-judicial in nature, and to eliminate some of the need for extreme care in choosing the correct remedy before seeking judicial review. It is possible to view the "duty to be fair" as being either an extension of the principles of natural justice, or as another way of stating those principles;[9] probably nothing hangs now on this distinction.

(b) Early English Cases Applying Natural Justice

The late 19th and early 20th centuries saw a huge increase in the number of statutory bodies and regulatory agencies created at all levels of government. The courts expected them to be no less governed by the principles of natural

---

7 "Hear the other side."

8 "No man can be a judge in his own cause."

9 For a discussion of this point, see D.P. Jones, "Administrative Fairness in Alberta", (1980) 18 Alta. L. Rev. 351.

justice than the justices of the peace had been before them, since the powers they exercised in the administration of government were the same. This view was plainly stated by Earle C.J. in *Cooper v. Wandsworth Board of Works*:[10]

> It has been said that the principle [to give notice to and allow the party affected to be heard] . . . is limited to a judicial proceeding, and that a district board ordering a house to be pulled down cannot be said to be doing a judicial act. I do not quite agree with that; . . . I think the appeal clause would evidently indicate that many exercises of the power of a district board would be in the nature of judicial proceedings. . . .

And *per* Willes J.:[11]

> I am of the same opinion. I apprehend that a tribunal which is by law invested with power to affect the property of one of Her Majesty's subjects, is bound to give such subject an opportunity of being heard before it proceeds: and that that rule is of universal application, and founded upon the plainest principles of justice. Now, is the board in the present case such a tribunal? I apprehend it clearly is. . . .

The case stands for the proposition that the right to be heard is a fundamental principle of justice and of universal application even where the power in question is purely executive, even where it is not exercised by a judicial officer, and even where there is no requirement for a hearing in the enabling legislation. This view was subsequently applied in many decisions. In doing so, the courts characterized as judicial or quasi-judicial many powers which might more properly be considered executive. Why the courts felt the characterization was necessary is not clear. It could have been merely an unthinking linkage between the old functions of the justices of the peace as judicial officers and the new tribunals, or a justification of the court's desire to maintain jurisdiction over government officials. Unfortunately, as a result, emphasis came to be placed on the characterization dichotomy rather than on a universal application of the principles of natural justice whenever persons were adversely affected by any form of governmental decision. The results achieved may have been correct in some cases, but the process of reasoning involved led the development of the law astray.

Still, in 1911, the courts had not yet started to confuse themselves. In *Board of Education v. Rice*,[12] Loreburn L.C. in the House of Lords said:

> Comparatively recent statutes have extended, if they have not originated, the practice of imposing upon departments or officers of State the duty of deciding or determining questions of various kinds.

---

10 (1863) 143 E.R. 414 at 418.
11 *Ibid.*, p. 418.
12 [1911] A.C. 179 at 182 (H.L.).

In the present instance, as in many others, what comes for determination is sometimes a matter to be settled by discretion, involving
no law. It will, I suppose, usually be of an administrative kind; but
sometimes it will involve matter of law as well as matter of fact, or
even depend upon matter of law alone. In such cases the Board of
Education will have to ascertain the law and also to ascertain the
facts. I need not add that in doing either they must act in good faith
and fairly listen to both sides, for that is a duty lying upon everyone
who decides anything. But I do not think they are bound to treat
such a question as though it were a trial. They have no power to
administer an oath, and need not examine witnesses. They can
obtain information in any way they think best, always giving a fair
opportunity to those who are parties in the controversy for correcting or contradicting anything prejudicial to their view.

The declamation that to hear both sides "is a duty lying upon everyone
who decides anything" could, if taken to its logical but ridiculous extreme,
have gone too far. Certainly, there are thousands of decisions made every day
which affect persons and which could not be made without prior notice and
the opportunity to be heard having been given. The problem was to set the
boundaries of the duty but, in attempting to do so over the next 50 years, the
courts so severely narrowed the scope of natural justice that it appeared they
had wrought its demise.

The erosion of the principles of natural justice took place in England
mainly between the two World Wars and can be seen primarily in the plethora
of cases arising out of the large number of slum clearance schemes which were
instituted; and, secondarily, in the area of town and country planning. In the
minds of the courts, the greater public advantage seen to be inherent in these
schemes far outweighed the danger to individual rights which followed from
the almost wholesale denial of the right to be heard.

By the time the Supreme Court of Canada caught up with the trend in
England in the *Copithorne*[13] case, the English courts had already seen the error
of their ways. It took the Supreme Court of Canada nearly 20 more years to
restore natural justice to its rightful place in the scheme of Administrative Law
in the *Nicholson* case.[14]

(c) The First Erosion of Natural Justice:
Concentrating on the Identity of the Decision-maker

The beginning of the erosion of the principle that there is a right to be
heard whenever a person is affected by a tribunal's decision, be it executive or
quasi-judicial in nature, occurred in *Local Government Board v. Arlidge*.[15]

---

13 [1959] S.C.R. 24.
14 *Nicholson v. Haldimand-Norfolk Police Commr. Bd.*, [1979] 1 S.C.R. 311.
15 [1915] A.C. 120 (H.L.).

The House of Lords, reluctant to interfere with the sovereign power of Parliament, determined that the nature of the tribunal making the decision should (in modern times) determine the procedure to be followed. On the one hand, courts of law traditionally followed a procedure characterized as judicial. On the other hand, administrative tribunals, having been given power over other governmental matters by Parliament, must (in the absence of any express intention to the contrary) have been intended by Parliament to follow procedures which were their own and which were necessary to obtain efficiency. This was the beginning of an emphasis on the identity of the decision-maker, instead of on the substance of the decision being made.

Secondly, the court expressly recognized the right of Parliament to delegate governmental powers to members of the executive, with no right of appeal to the courts. In the end Parliament was responsible for the exercise of these powers which it had delegated and for the procedures adopted by the non-judicial persons to whom they had been granted. Thus, the courts yielded their traditional supervisory power over the procedure adopted by such delegates to the doctrine of complete Parliamentary Responsibility — the ultimate in judicial deference!

Thirdly, this court was concerned about administrative efficiency, delay and expense. A full-blown court procedure, or something akin to it, offended against all of these worthwhile aims. Again, therefore, Parliament could not have intended this procedure to be followed. This was how individual rights were eroded in the face of administrative efficiency. The courts lost sight of the fact that government should serve the needs of the governed, and not the other way around.

In summary, the House of Lords fell into the error of regarding the identity of the decision-maker as determinative of what procedure should be applied, rather than looking at the nature of the decision itself and its effect on a subject. The error lay in the assumption that it was because administrative officials had previously been justices of the peace that they had to follow the principles of natural justice. In truth it was because the questions being determined by them were of such a nature as to require procedural fairness. When these powers were transferred from the inferior courts, only the identity of the decision-makers, and not the nature of the questions, changed.

This first and fundamental misunderstanding by the courts was continued, fossilized and compounded in subsequent cases.

(d) The Second Erosion of Natural Justice: The "Super-added Duty to act Judicially"

The second misunderstanding had its origin in *R v. Electricity Commissioners; Ex parte London Electricity Joint Committee Company*,[16] where the issue was whether the proceedings of the electricity commissioners were of an

---

16 [1924] 1 K.B. 171 (C.A.).

executive rather than judicial character. On the one hand, Banks L.J. cited authorities showing that the court would issue prohibition or *certiorari* to a body exercising judicial functions, even though the body could not be described as a court in the ordinary sense. On the other hand, while Atkin L.J. agreed that the operation of prohibition and *certiorari* had extended to control the proceedings of bodies which were not courts of justice, he went on to say that:[17]

> Wherever any body of persons having legal authority to determine questions affecting the rights of subjects, *and having the duty to act judicially*, act in excess of their legal authority they are subject to the controlling jurisdiction of the King's Bench Division exercised in these writs.

Unfortunately, these words of Lord Atkin took on a life and meaning far beyond anything intended by him and were to cause the law in this area to stray far from its proper course.

In 1927 the King's Bench Division adopted these words in *R. v. Church Assembly Legislative Committee; Ex parte Haynes Smith*,[18] where the issue was whether writs of prohibition and *certiorari* would lie against the church assembly or its legislative committee to prohibit them from proceeding further with the Prayer Book Measure, 1927. As a preliminary question, the court considered what kinds of bodies were involved, and whether either was[19]

> [a] body of persons having legal authority to determine questions affecting the rights of subjects, *and having the duty to act judicially....*

This was a direct quote from Atkin L.J.'s judgment in the *Electricity Commissioners*. Lord Hewart L.C.J. emphasized that this was a double test, the two parts being joined by "and" not "or". He interpreted this to mean that:[20]

> In order that a body may satisfy the required test it is not enough that it should have legal authority to determine questions affecting the rights of subjects; *there must be superadded to that characteristic the further characteristic that the body has the duty to act judicially.* The duty to act judicially is an ingredient which, if the test is to be satisfied, must be present. As these writs in the earlier days were issued only to bodies which without any harshness of construction could be called, and naturally would be called Courts, so also today these writs do not issue except to bodies which act or are under the duty to act in a judicial capacity.

---

17 *Ibid.*, p. 205, emphasis added.
18 [1928] 1 K.B. 411.
19 *Ibid.*, p. 415, emphasis added.
20 *Ibid.*, emphasis added.

Note that he also made the *Arlidge* mistake of looking at the decision-maker, not the nature of the decision; and he compounded his error by adopting Atkin L.J.'s careless reference to the "superadded duty" test. He then went on to hold that the church assembly and the legislative committee did not have the duty to act judicially. Rather, he characterized their function as legislative and held that therefore *certiorari* was not available.[21]

The decision of the Privy Council in *Nakkuda Ali v. Jayaratne*,[22] graphically illustrates the degree to which the principles of natural justice had been eroded. The case involved the question of whether the Controller of Textiles in Ceylon was required to hold a hearing before revoking Nakkuda Ali's textile licence. The Privy Council held that the double test of (a) affecting rights, and (b) the existence of a superadded duty to act judicially had to be met before the principles of natural justice applied. Although the words of the statute[23] imposed a condition that there must in fact exist such reasonable grounds known to the controller before he could validly exercise the power of cancellation (which undoubtedly affected the rights of the subject), the court held that this requirement did not of itself mean that the controller was under any superadded duty to act judicially. After all, the controller could have reasonable grounds for his belief without ever confronting the licence holder, and it could not be said that he could only arrive at this conclusion by a process analogous to the judicial process. As a result, the Privy Council held that *certiorari* was unavailable. In so deciding, the Privy Council relied on Atkin L.J.'s test in *Electricity Commissioners*, as interpreted by Hewart L.C.J. in *Church Assembly*.

(e) The Development of the Law in Canada

The Supreme Court of Canada was also wrestling with this knotty problem. However, at least until the *Copithorne* case,[24] Canadian courts did not veer as far off the path as the English courts had done.

(i) The Alliance case

In *Alliance des Professeurs Catholiques de Montréal v. Labour Relations Board of Quebec*,[25] the question was whether the Labour Relations Board had exceeded its jurisdiction in acting without notice to the union in cancelling the union's certificate of representation for calling an illegal strike.

The Quebec Labour Relations Act permitted the dissolution of a union

---

21 Compare the decision of the Alberta Court of Appeal in *Campeau (No. 2)* and the decision of the Supreme Court of Canada in the *Inuit Tapirisat* case, both discussed below.

22 [1951] A.C. 66 (P.C.).

23 "Where the Controller has reasonable grounds to believe. . . ."

24 [1959] S.C.R. 24.

25 [1953] 2 S.C.R. 140.

but "après lui avoir donné l'occasion d'être entendue et de faire toute la preuve tendant à se disculper".[26]

The Supreme Court rejected the view that silence by the legislature with respect to the requirement to give notice to a party affected by any decision must be taken to mean that the legislature intended no notice to be given. Rather, it reasoned that since the legislature may be presumed to know the general law, which requires such notice, it would be necessary for it in explicit terms to absolve the board from the necessity of giving notice.

Throughout the judgments, there is no mention of the *Electricity Commissioners*[27] case, the superadded duty test, or of *Nakkuda Ali*.[28] Indeed the court was following the principles enunciated early in the century to provide litigants with a fair procedure in the course of administrative decision-making.

(ii) Saltfleet v. Knapman

The Supreme Court continued its adherence to these principles in *Board of Health of Saltfleet v. Knapman*,[29] where it was argued that the board's function was executive in deciding whether certain conditions precedent, which had to be met before the board could acquire jurisdiction, had been met. The court held that[30]

in deciding whether or not such condition exists a duty to act judicially rests upon the board. It would, I think, require the plainest words to enable us to impute to the Legislature the intention to confer upon the local board the power to forcibly eject the occupants of a building for certain specified causes without giving such occupants an opportunity to know which of such causes was alleged to exist or to make answer to the allegation and I find no such words in the statute or the schedule.

Although the characterization of the function occupied the court's time, the double test was not used — so far, so good!

(iii) Calgary Power v. Copithorne

Something went seriously wrong when the case of *Calgary Power v. Copithorne*[31] came before the Supreme Court of Canada. By now the Supreme Court of Canada knew what was happening in England.[32]

---

26 R.S.Q. 1941, c. 162A, article 50. An unofficial translation: ". . . after having given it the opportunity to be heard and to prove anything tending to exculpate it."

27 [1924] 1 K.B. 171 (C.A.).

28 *Supra*, note 22.

29 [1956] S.C.R. 877.

30 *Ibid.*, p. 879.

31 *Supra*, note 24.

32 Martland J. had been to Oxford.

The question before the court was the characterization of the Minister's powers under the Alberta Water Resources Act[33] to order the expropriation of land for a transmission line right of way. If quasi-judicial, he was bound to give notice and hear the respondent; if purely executive, then there was no provision in the Act requiring him to give notice or to hold a hearing.

On the one side, it was argued that these powers must be characterized as quasi-judicial because they extinguished or modified private rights or interests in favour of another person. However, Martland J. held that this effect was not sufficient to label the power as quasi-judicial; there must be additionally imposed a duty to act judicially. In support of this proposition he cited the *Church Assembly*[34] case, *Nakkuda Ali*,[35] and (through the latter), the *Electricity Commissioners*[36] and *Robinson v. Minister of Town and Country Planning*.[37]

The legislation in *Copithorne* contained no requirement as to the giving of notice, nor the holding of an inquiry in relation to the expropriation itself, although there were requirements regarding the arbitration proceedings which would determine fair compensation. The Act gave the Minister sole power to decide whether the lands were necessary for the authorized undertaking and there was no appeal provision from his decision.

Martland J. therefore concluded that the minister's decision was taken as a minister of the Crown and was therefore a policy decision for which he was answerable only to the legislature, and was made necessarily in consideration of the public interest. (Compare this to the reasoning adopted by the House of Lords in the *Arlidge* case.) Martland J. adopted the trial judge's extraordinary view that there was no contest here between Calgary Power and Mr. Copithorne to be decided by the Minister, nor that there was any specific issue between them which the Minister was called upon to settle. Therefore, His Lordship held that none of the hallmarks of a quasi-judicial proceeding was present, nor was there a *lis inter partes*. He found a vast difference between a minister so acting and the position of some inferior administrative board called upon to decide a dispute between parties in particular circumstances which would be quasi-judicial. He gave no reasons or rationale for saying there was a vast difference.

Thus the Supreme Court held that the power of the Minister was executive, not quasi-judicial. The Minister's decision was to be made in accordance with the statutory requirements, and was to be guided by his own views as to policy. Since the court characterized the Minister's function as executive, there was no requirement to apply the principles of natural justice, *certiorari*

---

33 R.S.A. 1942, c. 65.
34 [1928] 1 K.B. 411.
35 [1951] A.C. 66 (P.C.).
36 [1924] 1 K.B. 171.
37 [1947] K.B. 702.

was not available, and Mr. Copithorne lost his land without benefit of an opportunity to state his case.

Thus, Canadian jurisprudence was provided with a standard to be followed that was to colour the next 20 years. Ironically, shortly afterwards, the English courts began a reversal of the process which had been strangling natural justice.

3. The Duty to be Fair

(a) *Ridge v. Baldwin*

In England, the principles of natural justice were restored to their rightful place in administrative decision-making beginning in the 1960's with a line of cases in which the old authorities once more held sway. The damage done to Canadian jurisprudence took more time to repair.

The restoration began with *Ridge v. Baldwin*,[38] when the House of Lords considered the case of Chief Constable Ridge of Brighton, who was dismissed by the Watch Committee without notice or a hearing.

Lord Reid found it necessary to state that "the authorities on the applicability of the principles of natural justice are in some confusion . . .".[39] He went on:[40]

> In modern times opinions have sometimes been expressed to the effect that natural justice is so vague as to be practically meaningless. But I would regard these as being tainted by the perennial fallacy that because something cannot be cut and dried or nicely weighed or measured therefore it does not exist. . . . It appears to me that one reason why the authorities on natural justice have been found diffi-cult to reconcile is that insufficient attention has been paid to the great difference between various kinds of cases in which it has been sought to apply the principle. What a minister ought to do in considering objections to a scheme may be very different from what a watch committee ought to do in considering whether to dismiss a chief constable.

He divided the various cases on dismissal into three classes: (a) dismissal of a servant by a master; (b) dismissal from offices held at pleasure; (c) dismissal from an office where there must be something against a man to warrant his dismissal. The present case, he held, fell into category (c). Lord Reid then referred to an unbroken line of authorities which required the officer to be told of the case against him and be given an opportunity to be heard. On the other hand, the statutory authority relied on a number of more recent cases which

---

38 [1963] 2 All E.R. 66 (H.L.).
39 *Ibid.*, p. 71; a masterpiece of understatement!
40 *Ibid.*

dealt with decisions by ministers, officials and bodies of various kinds which adversely affected property rights or privileges of persons, and which found no fault with the lack of a proper hearing afforded to such persons. Lord Reid grouped these cases into three categories:

(a) There were many cases where attempts were made to apply the principles of natural justice to wider duties imposed by modern legislation on ministers and other organs of government. The principles were given limited application in these situations. For example, where the functions of a minister or department were more to do with questions of public interest and the merits of alternative schemes of action than with the effect on individuals, then the minister might attach more importance to public policy than to the fate of individuals. In such circumstances, he might adopt a different procedure, as did the Board of Works in *Cooper*. Further, as in *Arlidge*, the minister could not do everything himself and an individual could not complain if the ordinarily accepted methods of doing public business did not give him as much procedural protection as he would be given by the principles of natural justice in a different kind of case. However, Lord Reid pointed out that it would be incorrect to extrapolate this restriction on the applicability of natural justice to every circumstance in which a minister was involved.

(b) There were cases involving wartime legislation where the principles had been held to have limited applicability. But this rationale for restricting natural justice cannot be taken to apply to peacetime legislation.

(c) The cases show a misunderstanding of Atkin L.J.'s judgment in the *Electricity Commissioners* as glossed upon by Lord Hewart in the *Church Assembly* case. Lord Reid quoted the latter and said:[41]

> I have quoted the whole of this passage because it is typical of what has been said in several subsequent cases. If Lord Hewart C.J. meant that it is never enough that a body simply has a duty to determine what the rights of an individual should be, but that there must always be something more to impose on it a duty to act judicially before it can be found to observe the principles of natural justice, then that appears to me impossible to reconcile with the earlier authorities. I could not reconcile it with what [various judges had said in various cases]. And, as I shall try to show, it cannot be what Lord Atkin meant.

He referred to the cases considered by Atkin L.J. and found nothing in them "superadded" to the duty itself. Rather, Atkin L.J. inferred the judicial character of the duty involved from the nature of the duty itself. Indeed, the electricity scheme considered many matters, not just the treatment of an individual, yet still Lord Atkin inferred a judicial character to the powers

---

41 *Ibid.*, pp. 77-78.

involved in that legislation. Surely he would hardly have done less where the power involved related solely to the treatment of one individual.

The troublesome decision in *Nakkuda Ali* was summarily dismissed by Lord Reid as follows:[42]

> This House is not bound by decisions of the Privy Council and for my part nothing short of a decision of this House directly in point would induce me to accept the position that, although an enactment expressly requires an official to have reasonable grounds for his decision, our law is so defective that a subject cannot bring up such a decision for review however seriously he may be affected and however obvious it may be that the official acted in breach of his statutory obligation.

Lord Reid continued:[43]

> No case older than 1911 was cited in *Nakkuda Ali v. M.F. de S. Jayaratne* on this question, and this question was only one of several difficult questions which were argued and decided. So I am forced to the conclusion that this part of the judgment in *Nakkuda*'s case was given under a serious misapprehension of the effect of the older authorities and therefore cannot be regarded as authoritative.

As a result, he held that the power of dismissal in the Act of 1882 could neither in 1882 nor now be exercised until the Watch Committee had informed the constable of the grounds on which it proposed to proceed and had given him a proper opportunity to submit his defence. Lord Reid also stated that decisions given without regard to the principles of natural justice are void, a conclusion reached time and time again in the authorities.[44]

Lord Hodson also squarely rebuffed the view that there had to be some superadded characteristic in the process over and above the fact that the decision affected rights. He first noted that the cases clearly showed that the absence of a *lis* or dispute between opposing parties was not a decisive feature in determining whether the principles of natural justice applied, although the presence of one certainly necessitated their application. He went on:[45]

> Secondly, the answer in a given case is not provided by the statement that the giver of the decision is acting in an executive or administra-

---

42 *Ibid.*, p. 79.

43 *Ibid.*, p. 80.

44 See H.W.R. Wade, "Unlawful Administrative Action: Void or Voidable?", Part I at (1967) 83 L.Q. Rev. 499; Part II at (1968) 84 L.Q. Rev. 95; Wade's *Administrative Law* 5th ed. (1982), pp. 310*ff*.; M.B. Akehurst, (1968) 31 M.L.R. 2, 138; J.F. Northey, [1977] N.Z.L.J. 284; D. Oliver, [1981] C.L.P.; G.L. Peiris, "Natural Justice and Degrees of Invalidity of Administrative Action", [1983] P.L. 634; *Harelkin v. Univ. of Regina*, [1979] 2 S.C.R. 561, and comment by D.P. Jones "Discretionary Refusal of Judicial Review in Administrative Law", (1981) 19 Alta. L. Rev. 483.

45 *Supra*, note 38, p. 113.

tive capacity, as if that was the antithesis of a judicial capacity. The cases seem to me to show that persons acting in a capacity which is not on the face of it judicial, but rather executive or administrative, have been held by the courts to be subject to the principles of natural justice.

In effect, therefore, the House of Lords in *Ridge v. Baldwin* restored the reasoning in *Cooper* as the benchmark for the applicability of natural justice, and swept away the damaging confusion of 40 years. Although the scope of government in that time had expanded to cover many areas previously not regulated, the House of Lords found no justification for moving away from the old principles. In Lord Reid's words:[46]

> We do not have a developed system of administrative law — perhaps because until fairly recently we did not need it. So it is not surprising that in dealing with new types of cases the courts have had to grope for solutions, and have found that old powers, rules and procedure are largely inapplicable to cases which they were never designed or intended to deal with. But I see nothing in that to justify our thinking that our old methods are any less applicable today than ever they were to the older types of cases. And, if they are any dicta in modern authorities which point in that direction, then in my judgment they should not be followed.

(b) *Re H.K.*

By 1967, Lord Denning in *Re H.K.*[47] could state:

> At one time it was said the principles [of due process review] only apply to judicial proceedings and not to administrative proceedings. That heresy was scotched in *Ridge v. Baldwin.*

And Lord Parker C.J. in the same case held that there is a duty on an immigration officer to act *fairly* even though his function was not judicial or quasi-judicial in nature:[48]

> That is not, as I see it, a question of acting or being required to act judicially, but of being required to act fairly. Good administration and an honest or bona fide decision must, as it seems to me, require not merely impartiality, nor merely bringing one's mind to bear on the problem, but acting fairly; and to the limited extent that the circumstances of any particular case allow, and within the legislative framework under which the administrator is working, only to that

---

46 *Supra*, note 38, p. 76.
47 [1970] 2 Q.B. 417 at 430.
48 [1967] 2 Q.B. 617 at 630.

limited extent do the so-called rules of natural justice apply, which in a case such as this is merely a duty to act fairly.

Wade summarizes the new approach to the judicial control of administrative action on procedural grounds as follows:[49]

> The courts now have two strings to their bow. An administrative act may be held to be subject to the requirements of natural justice either because it affects rights or interests and therefore involves a duty to act judicially, in accordance with the classic authorities and *Ridge* v. *Baldwin*; or it may simply be held that, "in our modern approach", it automatically involves a duty to act fairly and in accordance with natural justice, without any of the analysis which has been made into such an unnecessary obstacle.

(c) Advantages of the New Approach

The new duty to be fair freed the law from the old tautological strait jacket which provided that *if* there was a quasi-judicial function, then the principles of natural justice applied, and *certiorari* was available to superintend any breach of those procedural requirements. Conversely, that tautology provided that if the function was not quasi-judicial in nature but rather merely executive, then the principles of natural justice did not apply, nor was *certiorari* available. Under this tautology, the question of fairness could only arise to determine the content of natural justice *assuming that a quasi-judicial function was involved.*

Unfortunately, the distinction was never clear between a quasi-judicial function on the one hand and a merely executive one on the other. However, because the availability of *certiorari* depended upon this characterization, a great deal of litigation occurred. Each case had to be determined by itself, and provided virtually no precedent for subsequent litigation. Although there is considerable elasticity in what constitutes a quasi-judicial function (and the courts variously stretched or narrowed the concept), at some point it is simply not possible to characterize something as quasi-judicial, no matter how unfair the procedure used, or how desirable it would be for *certiorari* to issue in the circumstances.

The new concept of the "duty to be fair" is much more robust. In the first place, it avoids premising the availability of judicial review on the existence of a quasi-judicial function, which is not a clear concept in any event. Secondly, the "duty to be fair" openly articulates the question at least subconsciously asked by the courts in determining whether judicial review should issue for procedural reasons. And, finally, it provides an accurate rubric for adminis-

---

49 H.W.R. Wade, *Administrative Law*, 5th ed. (1982), p. 468. For an excellent summary of the English cases on the "duty to be fair" see D.J. Mullan, "Fairness: The New Natural Justice", (1975) 25 U.T.L.J. 281.

trators of all descriptions to bear in mind when exercising their various functions.

Of course there will still be continuous litigation over the question of whether a particular administrator's procedure was in fact fair. It is submitted, however, that this may well not generate any more litigation than that previously arising out of the meaning of "quasi-judicial". Rather, the focus of argument will have shifted to the real question at issue: was this decision arrived at fairly? And the judicial answers to this question should, in each case, provide considerably better guidance about acceptable procedures in particular circumstances. No longer will a court's finding that no quasi-judicial function is involved effectively grant the administrator *carte blanche* to adopt any procedure, no matter how unfair.

It is not possible to dismiss the development of the duty to be fair as a mere fleshing-out of the content of natural justice.[50] On the contrary, it significantly extends the ambit of judicial review beyond the existence of quasi-judicial functions (to which it previously was argued that only natural justice applied). And the recent jurisprudence clearly holds that *certiorari* — which historically only issued to quash a quasi-judicial function — is available to remedy any breach of the duty to be fair, even if no quasi-judicial function is involved.[51] Accordingly, the old trilogy uniting the existence of a quasi-judicial function, the applicability of the rules of natural justice, and the availability of *certiorari* has now been shattered.

4. The Development of the Duty to be Fair in Canada

(a) The *Nicholson* Case

The *Nicholson* case arose in Ontario under the Judicial Review Procedure Act,[52] and concerned the termination of a probationary police constable. Although section 27 of Regulation 680 of the Police Act[53] generally provided that

> [n]o chief of police, constable or other police officer is subject to any penalty under this Part except after a hearing and final disposition of a charge on appeal as provided by this Part . . .

---

50 As has been suggested, while the essence of natural justice may be fairness, the duty to be fair applies even where natural justice may not. In particular, the requirement of fairness is not limited to quasi-judicial functions (however they may be defined).

51 Laycraft J.'s decision in *McCarthy* (discussed, *infra*), unanimously upheld by the Court of Appeal, is clear authority for this proposition. So is the reasoning of Dickson J. in *Martineau (No. 2)*, although Pigeon J.'s majority judgment in that case is less clear on this point. It seems certain, therefore, that the reasoning of the Supreme Court of Canada in *Calgary Power Ltd. v. Copithorne*, [1959] S.C.R. 24, is no longer good law.

52 S.O. 1971, c. 48 (now R.S.O. 1980, c. 224).

53 R.S.O. 1970, c. 351 (now R.S.O. 1980, c. 381), Reg. 680.

there was a specific exception preserving the authority of a police board:

> (b) to dispense with the services of any [probationary] constable within eighteen months of his becoming a constable.

Nicholson was not told why he was dismissed, nor was he given notice or any opportunity to make representations before his services were terminated. He applied for judicial review. This was granted by Hughes J. at first instance,[54] who relied heavily on the reasoning of the House of Lords in *Ridge v. Baldwin*[55] to classify the legal position of a police constable as an "office". Therefore, notwithstanding the existence of section 27(b), His Lordship held that, while the board's[56]

> deliberations may be untrammelled by Regulations made under the *Police Act*, . . . this court should not allow them to proceed as if the principles of natural justice did not exist.

The Court of Appeal, however, reversed the decision, answering the following question in the affirmative:[57]

> Can the services of a police constable be dispensed with within 18 months of his becoming a constable, without observance by the authority discharging him of the requirements of natural justice, including a hearing?

In effect, the Ontario Court of Appeal focused on the statutory provisions dealing with appeals for permanent constables, noted the absence of similar provisions for probationary members who were employed "at pleasure", applied the maxim *expressio unius est exclusio alterius*,[58] and washed their hands of any general judicial responsibility for enforcing the observance of fair procedures by administrative bodies. In a five-to-four decision,[59] however, the Supreme Court of Canada reversed the Ontario Court of Appeal, and reinstated the result reached by Hughes J. — thereby quashing

---

54 (1975) 61 D.L.R. (3d) 36 (Ont. Div. Ct.).

55 [1964] A.C. 40 (H.L.).

56 *Supra*, note 54 at p. 45.

57 (1976) 69 D.L.R. (3d) 13 at 14.

58 *Ibid.*, pp. 17-22: "to state one thing is to exclude others". See also the application of this maxim by the majority of the Supreme Court of Canada in *L.S.U.C. v. French*, [1975] 2 S.C.R. 767. It is submitted that this application of the *expressio unius* rule is wrong in principle. Natural justice is presumed to apply to decisions, unless specifically ousted by Parliament. Specifying certain procedural steps in some circumstances only reinforces the applicability or fleshes out the content of natural justice in those cases; it does not indicate Parliament's intention specifically to exclude natural justice in other circumstances. In short, the onus is on the decision-maker to show Parliament's clear intent to exempt him from complying with natural justice or procedural fairness.

59 Laskin C.J.C.'s judgment was concurred in by Ritchie, Spence, Dickson and Estey JJ.; Martland J.'s dissent was concurred in by Pigeon, Beetz and Pratte JJ.

the termination of Nicholson's employment (which by then had exceeded the 18-month probation period!).

Two principal issues underlie the majority decision of the Supreme Court, written by Laskin C.J.C.:

(a) Was the status of a probationary constable sufficient to attract the principles of natural justice to termination proceedings?
(b) Is there a general duty to be fair even if the principles of natural justice do not apply?

The first question raises the issue of whether a probationary constable occupies an "office" which cannot be terminated without cause (to which the principles of natural justice apply, following *Ridge v. Baldwin*) or whether he is a mere employee who can be dismissed at pleasure. Indeed, this precise issue divided Hughes J. and the Court of Appeal. Laskin C.J.C., however, held[60] that the lower courts' references to the common law position of policemen were inapt in light of the existence of the Police Act, which made no reference whatever to the concept of employment "at pleasure". It was therefore not necessary to rely upon the *Constitutional Reference* case[61] (as Hughes J. had done) to fit Nicholson's employment into the third category adopted by Lord Reid in *Ridge v. Baldwin*, instead of into the second.[62] Nor was it necessary to re-examine whether the law should continue to recognize employment at pleasure, even in light of the decision by the House of Lords in *Malloch v. Aberdeen Corporation*.[63] Rather, Laskin C.J.C. held that the Police Act forms a complete code, "a turning away from the old common law rule even in cases where the full [probationary] period of time has not fully run".[64] Accordingly, his Lordship was[65]

> of the opinion that although the appellant clearly cannot claim the procedural protections afforded to a constable with more than 18 months' service, he cannot be denied any protection. He should be treated "fairly" not arbitrarily.

It is important to note that this reasoning does not necessarily apply to an employee who truly is engaged at pleasure, although that precise issue did arise in the *McCarthy* case.[66] Indeed, this difference in the characterization of Nicholson's employment provides the basis for the dissenting judgment in the Supreme Court. Martland J. simply held that Nicholson was dismissable at pleasure, that that was the very purpose of the 18-month probationary period,

---

60 (1979) 88 D.L.R. (3d) 671 at 677.
61 *Re Reference under Constitutional Questions Act*, [1957] O.R. 28 (C.A.).
62 *Supra*, note 55. Lord Reid's three categories in *Ridge v. Baldwin* were: (a) pure master-servant relationships; (b) offices held at pleasure; and (c) offices terminable only for cause.
63 [1971] 2 All E.R. 1278 (H.L.).
64 *Supra*, note 60 at p. 680.
65 *Ibid*.
66 Discussed *infra*, section 4.

and that, unlike *Malloch*'s case, there were no procedures governing this type of case in the Police Act. According, Martland J. was of the opinion that there was no breach of any legal duty to the appellant in the exercise of this purely executive function.

This led to the second issue facing the court: was there a general duty to be fair even if the principles of natural justice did not apply? Martland J. did not even refer to the "duty to be fair", and it is clear that His Lordship did not recognize it as a concept different from natural justice. Because only an executive (and not quasi-judicial) function was involved in terminating a probationary constable, the rules of natural justice simply did not apply in this case. *Cedit questio.*

On the other hand, Laskin C.J.C. equally clearly recognized a distinction between the "duty to be fair" and the principles of natural justice. He specifically adopted Megarry J.'s *dictum* in *Bates v. Lord Hailsham of St. Marylebone*:[67]

> that in the sphere of the so-called quasi-judicial the rules of natural justice run, and that in the administrative or executive field there is a general duty of fairness.

The chief justice also referred to de Smith's explanation[68] of the relationship between fairness and natural justice, and to the[69]

> realization that the *classification of statutory functions as judicial, quasi-judicial or administrative is often very difficult*, to say the least; and to endow some with procedural protection while denying others any at all would work injustice when the results of statutory decisions raise the same serious consequences for those adversely affected, regardless of the classification of the function in question. . . .

Finally, the chief justice cited several English decisions[70] on the duty to be fair to support his view that this concept is now part of the common law. Because of the unfairness of the method adopted by the board in deciding to terminate Nicholson, its decision was quashed.

It is important to note that Laskin C.J.C. adopted the concept of the duty to be fair as a remedy for procedural unfairness where no quasi-judicial function was involved. He thus tacitly recognized the continuing need to characterize functions as quasi-judicial or merely executive, however difficult that characterization may be. While this approach is consistent with the recent

---

67 [1972] 1 W.L.R. 1373 at 1378 (Ch.D).

68 S.A. de Smith, *Judicial Review of Administrative Action*, 3rd ed. (1973), pp. 208-209.

69 *Supra* note 60 at p. 681, emphasis added.

70 *Pearlberg v. Varty*, [1972] 1 W.L.R. 534 (H.L.); *Furnell v. Whangarei High Schools Bd.*, [1973] A.C. 660 (P.C.); *Russell v. Duke of Norfolk*, [1949] 1 All E.R. 109 at 118; *Selvarajan v. Race Relations Bd.*, [1976] 1 All E.R. 12 (C.A.).

English cases and it undoubtedly permits judicial review of purely executive functions, it perpetuates the need to distinguish between quasi-judicial and merely executive functions, and it does not decide whether *certiorari* is available as a remedy for a breach of the duty to be fair where no quasi-judicial function is involved.[71] Although the seminal importance of *Nicholson* cannot be underestimated, these problems were precisely the issues which arose in *McCarthy*[72] and *Martineau (No. 2).*[73]

(b) The *Campeau* Case

The duty to be fair was also an important element in the decisions of the Appellate Division of the Supreme Court of Alberta in *Campeau Corporation v. Calgary (No. 1),*[74] and *Harvie v. Calgary Regional Planning Commission.*[75]

Campeau involved an application to the city council to have the land use classification of certain lands changed from "agricultural-future residential" to "direct control" for a multiple-family development, pursuant to section 106(2) of the former Planning Act.[76] The lands in question, however, were ideally suited for a park. After lengthy proceedings, city council decided not to approve the requested amendment to the land use classification guidelines, even though it also declined to purchase the land for use as a park. The landowner applied to the Trial Division for an order either (a) approving the reclassification, or (b) directing council to re-hear the matter without taking into account the land's possible use as a park. Milvain C.J.T.D. rejected this application, after having noted that even an affirmative resolution by council to reclassify the land would have required further approval by the provincial planning board:[77]

> Such being the case I am satisfied the decision was no more than an administrative act, done in the performance of a divided concept as to what was a public duty. The decision is not subject to judicial review and the application before me is dismissed.

The Appellate Division unanimously reversed this decision. Lieberman J.A., writing the opinion for the court — one month before *Nicholson* was

---

71 In *McCarthy v. Bd. of Trustees of Calgary Roman Catholic Separate School Dist. No. 1,* [1979] 4 W.W.R. 725 (Alta. T.D.), it was argued by the school board that *Nicholson* should be confined to proceedings under the Ontario Judicial Review Procedure Act, S.O. 1971, c. 48 (now R.S.O. 1980, c. 224), and should not be applied to *certiorari* in Alberta. Laycraft J. rejected this narrow interpretation of *Nicholson,* and Dickson J. in *Martineau (No. 2)* confirms that the broader view is correct.

72 [1979] 4 W.W.R. 725 (Alta. T.D.).

73 *Martineau v. Matsqui Inst. Disciplinary Bd.,* [1980] 1 S.C.R. 602.

74 (1979) 8 A.R. 77, reversed (1980) 7 Alta. L.R. (2d) 302 (C.A.); see also *Campeau (No. 2),* (1980) 12 Alta. L.R. (2d) 379 (C.A.).

75 (1978) 8 Alta. L.R. (2d) 166 (C.A.).

76 R.S.A. 1970, c. 276 (now R.S.A. 1980, c. P-9).

77 (1978) 8 A.R. 77 at 86.

decided by the Supreme Court of Canada — noted the "difficulties and uncertainties inherent" in characterizing functions as quasi-judicial or merely administrative. He went on to note (indeed, predict!) that[78]

> there is a discernible trend in the decisions of the Supreme Court of Canada to examine the conduct of a tribunal's proceedings or even the exercise of ministerial discretion where a person's rights are affected in order to determine whether they were conducted and exercised fairly and in good faith. If not, the court will, wherever possible, intervene and right the injustice suffered by the aggrieved party by the use of one of the prerogative writs.

His Lordship then referred at length to the Supreme Court of Canada's decisions in *Roper v. Royal Victoria Hospital Medical Executive Committee*,[79] *Minister of Manpower & Immigration v. Hardayal*,[80] and *St. John v. Fraser*,[81] as well as to the recent English cases on the duty to be fair in purely administrative proceedings.[82]

Notwithstanding this disquisition on the duty to be fair, Lieberman J.A. nevertheless held[83] that it was unnecessary to characterize the council's function in handling the application for reclassification of the land. The principal basis of His Lordship's judgment does not concern the duty to be fair at all, but rather the use of a statutory power for an improper purpose — namely, to acquire a park without paying full market value for it. Yet a breach of the principles of natural justice (or of the duty to be fair) has traditionally been treated as a separate ground for judicial review from actions made for an improper purpose, or based on irrelevant evidence, or on the lack of relevant evidence, or those which are simply *ultra vires* the governing legislation. Of course, in some circumstances, the procedures used by administrators acting in bad faith or for an improper purpose or on irrelevant evidence *may* also contravene the principles of natural justice (or the duty to adopt fair procedures). But, with respect, this coincidence of grounds for judicial review is precisely that: a coincidence. Accordingly, it is submitted that the real *ratio decidendi* of the *Campeau* decision concerns improper purpose, which is a substantive matter, and not procedural unfairness. Nevertheless, Lieberman J.A.'s *obiter dicta* on the duty to be fair accurately presaged the subsequent development of the law.[84]

---

78 (1979) 7 Alta. L.R. (2d) 294 at 302.

79 [1975] 2 S.C.R. 62.

80 [1978] 1 S.C.R. 470, reversing [1976] 2 F.C. 746.

81 [1935] S.C.R. 441.

82 *Pearlberg v. Varty*, [1972] 1 W.L.R. 534 (H.L.); *Furnell v. Whangarei High Schools Bd.*, [1973] A.C. 660 (P.C.); *Russell v. Duke of Norfolk*, [1949] 1 All E.R. 109 at 118; *Selvarajan v. Race Relations Bd.*, [1976] 1 All E.R. 12 (C.A.).

83 *Supra*, note 78.

84 Particularly in *Nicholson*, decided on 3rd October 1978 — just about a month after Lieberman J.A.'s judgment in *Campeau*, rendered 9th September 1978.

(c) The *Harvie* Case

Although decided after *Nicholson* had been reported, and despite numerous references to the duty to be fair, the *ratio decidendi* of the unanimous judgment of the Appellate Division in *Harvie v. Calgary Regional Planning Commission*[85] clearly characterizes the subdivision process in Alberta as quasi-judicial. Accordingly, the court held that Glenbow Ranches Ltd. had the right to notice and to appear before the planning commission on an application by a neighbouring landowner to subdivide the latter's land. The duty to be fair, in this case, did not stand in contradistinction to the principles of natural justice, but rather was relevant to concluding that there was a quasi-judicial function involved. The judgment, therefore, demonstrates the elastic nature of the concept of a quasi-judicial function.

To reach this conclusion, it was necessary for the court to overcome the judgment in a strikingly similar English case, *Gregory v. London Borough of Camden*,[86] to the effect that a neighbouring landowner had no "rights" affected when subdivision on development approval was granted to the applicant. This precedent, and the perception that subdivision was merely a "mechanical process",[87] had led Quigley J. to refuse judicial review over a purely executive function. Clement J.A., writing for the unanimous court[88] on appeal, came to a different conclusion. First, he noted that it is not possible to compartmentalize judicial and executive functions, and that the "quasi-judicial" label is apt to describe a composite function which involves both judicial and executive duties.[89] Secondly, His Lordship rejected the argument that a quasi-judicial function was not involved because none of Glenbow's *rights* were involved.[90] He quoted the following passage from the judgment of Martland J. in *Calgary Power Ltd. v. Copithorne*:[91]

> With respect to the first point, the respondent submitted that a function is of a judicial or quasi-judicial character when the exercise of it effects the extinguishment or modification of private rights or interests in favour of another person, unless a contrary intent clearly appears from the statute. *This proposition, it appears to me, goes too far in seeking to define functions of a judicial or quasi-judicial character*. In determining whether or not a body or an individual is exercising judicial or quasi-judicial duties, *it is necessary to examine the defined scope of its functions and then to determine whether or not there is imposed a duty to act judicially. . . .*

---

85 (1978) 8 Alta. L.R. (2d) 166 (C.A.).
86 [1966] 2 All E.R. 196 (Q.B.).
87 (1978) 5 Alta. L.R. (2d) 301 at 303.
88 Composed of Clement, Moir and Haddad JJ.A. — the latter two of whom formed the court with Lieberman J.A. in *Campeau*.
89 *Supra*, note 85 at p. 180.
90 *Supra*, note 85 at pp. 180-85.
91 *Supra*, note 85 at p. 180, emphasis added.

Now Martland J.'s judgment in *Calgary Power*[92] has generally been interpreted to mean that there are two necessary requirements for the existence of a quasi-judicial function: first, that *rights* are affected; and, secondly, that there is a superadded duty to act judicially. Indeed, Martland J. in *Calgary Power* goes on to quote Hewart L.C.J.'s famous *dictum* to this effect from *R. v. Church Assembly Legislative Committee; Ex parte Haynes Smith*:[93]

> In order that a body may satisfy the required test it is not enough that it should have legal authority to determine questions affecting the rights of subjects; there must be superadded to that characteristic the further characteristic that the body has the duty to act judicially.

Clement J.A., however, referred to *Nicholson*, and rejected this traditional test. To paraphrase, he said that the traditional proposition that rights must be affected went too far in seeking to define a judicial or quasi-judicial function.[94] He accepted de Smith's view[95] that

> the term "rights" is to be understood in a very broad sense, and is not to be confined to the jurisprudential concept of rights to which correlative legal duties are annexed. It comprises an extensive range of legally recognised interests, the categories of which have never been closed.

Although Glenbow Ranches did not have any cause of action against either the developer or the commission, nevertheless Clement J.A. held that its interests were so affected by the proposed subdivision that judicial review should issue in the circumstances.[96]

> Administrative law in the statutory sense reflects the concepts of legislatures to meet the difficulties in society arising out of increasing population densities, changing relationships between subjects and between subjects and government, and other societal stresses. The new concepts are expressed in a legislative framework in which various rights, interests, duties and powers are created, for varied purposes and objectives, many unknown to the common law and some of far-reaching effect on traditional concepts. All of these must be given their proper effect. Jurisdiction over their administration is entrusted to newly-created tribunals or, in some cases, to existing tribunals. It is, in my view, necessary to the maintenance of the supervisory jurisdiction of the courts in the general public interest that these new rights and interests be viewed and weighed in the light of the legislative concept that created them, not in the

---

92 [1959] S.C.R. 24 at 30-34.
93 [1928] 1 K.B. 411 at 415.
94 *Supra*, note 85 at p. 183.
95 S.A. de Smith, *Judicial Review of Administrative Action*, 3rd ed. (1973), p. 344.
96 *Harvie v. Calgary Regional Planning Comm.*, (1978) 8 Alta. L.R. (2d) 166 at 184-85 (C.A.).

shadow of narrower considerations expressed in times past under different societal conditions. When a new right or interest has been created by statute it must be examined, not in isolation, but in the context of the whole. I am of the opinion that the nature and extent of the right or interest is a vitally important facet of the complex judicial process necessary to determine whether, in a particular case, there is a duty on a tribunal to conform wholly or to some degree to the principles of natural justice in coming to a decision affecting the person asserting the interest.

This passage justifies the extention of the concept of a quasi-judicial function to a process which only affects "interests" and not technical "rights". Unfortunately, it still maintains the distinction between quasi-judicial and merely executive powers, and thus the need to characterize functions. At some point, it simply will not be possible to stretch the elastic concept of quasi-judicial to cover a purely executive function which clearly cries out for judicial review. Thus, with respect, it is unfortunate that Clement J.A. did not follow *Nicholson* (from which he quoted extensively)[97] to its logical conclusion, nor did he in the end give effect to his bold statement of the expanding ambit of judicial review:[98]

In late years there has been an emerging recognition that the supervisory jurisdiction of the court must keep pace with the increasing variety and scope of what are classified as administrative functions of tribunals, when a decision in the exercise of such functions has an appreciable effect on a right or interest of a subject which is, in the view of the court, of sufficient importance to warrant recognition.

The duty to be fair, therefore, in *Harvie* was relevant because its breach constituted a breach of the principles of natural justice, which applied because a quasi-judicial function was involved.

(d) The *McCarthy* Case

A bolder approach to the duty to be fair was taken by the Court of Appeal in unanimously upholding Laycraft J.'s judgment in *McCarthy v. Board of Trustees of Calgary Roman Catholic Separate School District No. 1.*[99] Mr. McCarthy was the superintendent of the Calgary separate school system, and was dismissed by the board without notice and without reasons. He sought (*inter alia*) *certiorari* to quash his purported dismissal, and the board countered by asking for a preliminary determination whether *certiorari* could even apply in these circumstances, which it said involved only a master-

---

97 *Ibid.*, pp. 185-87.
98 *Ibid.*, p. 185.
99 [1979] 4 W.W.R. 725 (Alta. T.D.).

servant relationship. Milvain C.J.T.D. rejected[100] the board's application for a preliminary determination, but this was reversed by the Court of Appeal.[101] Laycraft J.'s judgment, therefore, deals with the availability of *certiorari* in these circumstances.

Laycraft J. held[102] that McCarthy occupied a statutory office under the School Act,[103] and that the reasoning adopted by the majority of the Supreme Court of Canada in *Nicholson* applied squarely to this case. Nevertheless, the board argued that *Nicholson* was decided under the Ontario Judicial Review Procedure Act,[104] and was not authority in Alberta for extending the availability of *certiorari* to supervise the exercise of a purely administrative function. Laycraft J. rejected this argument, even though he specifically held that[105]

> [t]he function of the board in this case must be characterized as administrative and not as judicial or quasi-judicial in the sense that those terms have been distinguished from each other in Canadian cases.

This characterization clearly poses the problem so neatly avoided by Lieberman J.A. in *Campeau* and Clement J.A. in *Harvie*, who both managed to eke a quasi-judicial function out of the statutory powers involved in those cases. By holding that only an executive function was involved in *McCarthy*, Laycraft J. had to consider both (a) whether the duty to be fair had been breached, and also (b) whether *certiorari* was even available as a remedy for such a breach. His Lordship held that *Nicholson* not only recognized the right of the citizen to fairness in administrative procedure, but also necessarily recognized that *certiorari* was available to enforce that right:[106]

> to hold otherwise is to say that, though administrative acts in Alberta are subject to control by the courts, the only means of control is by the declaratory action. In some cases that result may follow as, for example, where the record produced on the motion under the Crown Practice Rules is inadequate or where the court in the exercise of its discretion decides that the case is not appropriate for a prerogative writ. In many cases, however, it would be highly undesirable that there be no power to quash an administrative decision made contrary to statutory power. When the Supreme Court of Canada recognized the right of the citizen to fair treatment

---

100 On 20th November 1978, *ibid.*, p. 727.
101 *Ibid.*, pp. 728-29.
102 *Ibid.*, pp. 731-34.
103 R.S.A. 1970, c. 329 (now R.S.A. 1980, c. S-3).
104 S.O. 1971, c. 48 (now R.S.O. 1980, c. 224).
105 *Supra*, note 99 at p. 735.
106 *Supra*, note 99 at p. 737.

in the exercise of such powers, it must also be taken to have recognized the traditional remedy by which the right might be enforced.

Accordingly, *certiorari* is available to correct a breach of the duty to be fair, even where only an executive function is involved. It is no longer necessary to stretch the concept of a quasi-judicial function to fit the particular facts in which it is alleged that a breach of procedural fairness has occurred. Nor is it necessary to find some other remedy (such as a declaration) for procedural unfairness in a purely executive matter. In other words, the tautology that *certiorari* is available only to correct breaches of the principles of natural justice, which are only relevant to quasi-judicial functions, has been broken.

Laycraft J.'s judgment was unanimously upheld by the Court of Appeal,[107] and must be taken now to represent the law of Alberta — particularly in light of the subsequent decision of the Supreme Court of Canada in *Martineau (No. 2)*.

(e) *Martineau (No. 2)*

Precisely the same question which confronted Laycraft J. and the Alberta Court of Appeal in *McCarthy* was faced by the Supreme Court of Canada in *Martineau v. Matsqui Institution Disciplinary Board (No. 2)*:[108] Is *certiorari* available to remedy a breach of the duty to be fair when a purely executive function is involved? Although the Supreme Court was unanimous in granting *certiorari*, it divided six-to-three[109] in the reasons for this outcome. The reasoning adopted by the court is, therefore, relevant to the Alberta cases on the duty to be fair, even though *Martineau* arose under the peculiar provisions of the Federal Court Act.[110]

Mr. Martineau was sentenced to 15 days in solitary confinement for a "flagrant or serious" disciplinary offence. His application for judicial review under section 28 of the Federal Court Act was rejected by the Supreme Court of Canada in *Martineau (No. 1)*[111] because the "directives" governing the procedure for dealing with disciplinary offences were executive rather than "law", and therefore could not be quasi-judicial in nature. Martineau, therefore, proceeded with his second action, under section 18 of the Federal Court Act, for an order of *certiorari* to quash the disciplinary board's decision.

---

107 October 1979 (unreported).

108 [1980] 1 S.C.R. 602.

109 Martland, Ritchie, Beetz, Estey and Pratte JJ., concurred with Pigeon J.; Laskin C.J.C. and McIntyre J. concurred with Dickson J.'s reasons.

110 R.S.C. 1970, c. 10 (2nd Supp.). See David J. Mullan, *The Federal Court Act: Administrative Law Jurisdiction* (Ottawa: Law Reform Commission of Canada, 1977). See also "Proposals to amend the *Federal Court Act*", by the Hon. Mark MacGuigan, Minister of Justice, 29th August 1983.

111 [1976] 2 F.C. 198, affirmed [1978] 1 S.C.R. 118.

Mahoney J. at first instance, treating the matter as an application for a preliminary determination of a question of law, held that[112]

> a public body, such as the respondent, authorized by law to impose a punishment, that was more than a mere denial of privileges, had a duty to act fairly in arriving at its decision to impose the punishment. Any other conclusion would be repugnant. The circumstances disclosed in this application would appear to be appropriate to the remedy sought. I am not, of course, deciding whether the remedy should be granted but merely whether it could be granted by the Federal Court of Canada, Trial Division. In my view it could.

The Federal Court of Appeal reversed this[113] on the basis that a conviction for a disciplinary offence was a purely executive function with respect to which *certiorari* was not available. The consequence of this view, of course, is that Parliament must be taken to have transferred all supervising jurisdiction over quasi-judicial federal bodies to the Federal Court of Appeal under section 28 of the Act, so that the reference in section 18 to *certiorari* in the Trial Division is hollow, leaving no effective judicial review over purely executive functions.

Pigeon J., writing for the majority of the Supreme Court, refused to accept this view of the law. Rather, he understood *Nicholson* to stand for the "common law principle"[114]

> *that in the sphere of the so-called quasi-judicial the rules of natural justice run, and that in the administrative or executive field there is a general duty of fairness. . . .*

and the further principle that a breach of the duty could be enforced by judicial review. Policy may require that full-blown judicial procedures not be applicable to disciplinary proceedings,[115] thereby preventing their characterization as quasi-judicial for the purpose of judicial review under section 28 of the Federal Court Act. Nevertheless, there is still a general supervisory jurisdiction to ensure that purely executive proceedings are conducted fairly — and, under the Act, that jurisdiction is assigned to the Trial Division under section 18. Although[116]

> [i]t is specially important that the remedy be granted only in cases of serious injustice and that proper care be taken to prevent such

---

112 [1978] 1 F.C. 312 at 318-19.

113 [1978] 2 F.C. 637.

114 *Supra*, note 108 at p. 634, quoting from Megarry J.'s judgment in *Bates v. Lord Hailsham of St. Marylebone*, [1972] 3 All E.R. 1019 at 1024 (H.L.) (emphasis is Pigeon J.'s); and referring specifically to *Nicholson* as the acceptance in Canada of the duty to be fair as a "common law principle".

115 *Supra*, note 108 at pp. 636-37.

116 *Supra*, note 108 at p. 637.

[disciplinary] proceedings from being used to delay deserved punishment so long that it is made ineffective, if not altogether avoided[,]

Pigeon J. upheld[117] Mahoney J.'s ruling that *certiorari* is available under section 18 of the Federal Court Act to supervise a breach of the duty to be fair in purely executive proceedings.

While the remaining three members of the court concurred in the outcome reached by Pigeon J., the reasons written on their behalf by Dickson J. were considerably lengthier, and addressed three specific issues: first, sorting out the respective supervisory jurisdictions of the Trial and Appellate Divisions of the Federal Court under sections 18 and 28 of the Act; secondly, the duty to act fairly; and, finally, the ambit of *certiorari* in Canada.

On the first issue, Dickson J. agreed with Pigeon J., both in the present case and his *dicta* in *Howarth v. National Parole Board*,[118] in rejecting the Federal Court of Appeal's interpretation that section 28 of the Act completely supplants the jurisdiction of the Trial Division to grant *certiorari*. While a breach of the duty to be fair alone is not sufficient to bring an administrative body within the definition of "quasi-judicial" (required to give the Federal Court of Appeal jurisdiction under section 28[119]), the converse is not true either. Therefore, while the lack of a quasi-judicial function may well deprive the Court of Appeal of jurisdiction, it does not mean that the Trial Division cannot remedy a breach of the duty to be fair.[120] The duty to be fair is procedural in nature, and means more than merely good faith.[121]

Dickson J. then turned his attention to the availability of *certiorari* to remedy a breach of the duty to be fair procedurally. He referred to Atkin L.J.'s famous quotation in *R. v. Electricity Commissioners; Ex parte London Electricity Joint Committee Company*:[122]

> Wherever any body of persons having legal authority to determine questions affecting the rights of subjects, and having the duty to act judicially, act in excess of their legal authority they are subject to the controlling jurisdiction of the King's Bench Division exercised in these writs.

---

117 *Supra*, note 108. Note that curiously Pigeon J. referred to the proceedings under s. 28 of the Federal Court Act as being "in the nature of a right of appeal". Is this to be contrasted to judicial review?

118 [1976] 1 S.C.R. 453.

119 [1980] 1 S.C.R. 602 at 613. Note, however, that a breach of the duty to act fairly may predispose the court to characterize an impugned function as being quasi-judicial, as occurred in both *Campeau (No. 1)* and *Harvie* cases discussed above.

120 See also *Min. of Manpower and Immigration v. Hardayal*, [1978] 1 S.C.R. 470 at 479; *Roper v. Royal Victoria Hospital Med. Executive Ctee.*, [1975] 2 S.C.R. 62 at 67.

121 *Supra*, note 119 at p. 614.

122 [1924] 1 K.B. 171 (C.A.), quoted *supra*, note 119, at p. 617.

Dickson J. noted the danger of construing this quotation too restrictively. In particular:[123]

> There has been an unfortunate tendency to treat "rights" in the narrow sense of rights to which correlative legal duties attach. In this sense, "rights" are frequently contrasted with "privileges", in the mistaken belief that only the former can ground judicial review of the decision-maker's actions.

His Lordship thus rejected such a narrow concentration on "rights", and focused instead on the public policy underlying judicial review:[124]

> When concerned with individual cases and aggrieved persons, there is the tendency to forget that one is dealing with public law remedies, which, when granted by the courts, not only set aright individual injustice, but also ensure that public bodies exercising powers affecting citizens heed the jurisdiction granted to them. *Certiorari* stems from the assumption by the courts of supervisory powers over certain tribunals in order to assure the proper functioning of the machinery of government. To give a narrow or technical interpretation to "rights" in an individual sense is to misconceive the broader purpose of judicial review of administrative action. *One should, I suggest, begin with the premise that any public body exercising power over subjects may be amenable to judicial supervision, the individual interest involved being but one factor to be considered in resolving the broad policy question of the nature of review appropriate for the particular administrative body.*

If judicial review will issue even where "rights" are not technically affected, must there nevertheless be a duty to act judicially before *certiorari* is available? Again, Dickson J. rejected such a restriction on the availability of *certiorari* — relying principally upon Lord Reid's judgment in *Ridge v. Baldwin*, and on the now long line of English cases on the duty to be fair.[125] These authorities indicated to His Lordship that[126]

> the application of a duty of fairness with procedural content does not depend upon proof of a judicial or quasi-judicial function. *Even though the function is analytically administrative, courts may intervene in a suitable case.*

---

123 *Supra*, note 119 at p. 618.
124 *Supra*, note 119 at p. 619, emphasis added.
125 In particular, *R. v. Hillington London Borough Council; Ex parte Royco Homes Ltd.*, [1974] Q.B. 720; *R. v. Barnsley Metro. Borough Council; Ex parte Hook*, [1976] 3 All E.R. 452 (C.A.); *Re H.K.*, [1967] 2 Q.B. 617; *R. v. Liverpool Corp.; Ex parte Liverpool Taxi Fleet Operators' Assn.*, [1972] 2 Q.B. 299; *Furnell v. Whangarei High Schools Bd.*, [1973] A.C. 660 (P.C.).
126 *Supra*, note 119 at pp. 622-23, emphasis added.

In my opinion, *certiorari* avails as a remedy wherever a public body has power to decide any matter affecting the rights, interests, property, privileges, or liberties of any person.

What, then, is the relationship of the principles of natural justice to the duty to be fair? As the reader will recall, Laskin C.J.C. in the *Nicholson* case and Laycraft J. in the *McCarthy* case both treated the duty to be fair as quite distinct from the existence of a quasi-judicial power on the one hand, or natural justice on the other. Both Lieberman J.A. in *Campeau* and Clement J.A. in *Harvie*, by contrast, used the concept of fairness to establish that a quasi-judicial function was involved, and that the principles of natural justice had been breached. Dickson J. in *Martineau (No. 2)* deals with this contradiction expressly:[127]

Conceptually, there is much to be said against such a differentiation between traditional natural justice and procedural fairness, but if one is forced to cast judicial review in traditional classification terms as is the case under the *Federal Court Act*, there can be no doubt that procedural fairness extends well beyond the realm of the judicial and quasi-judicial, as commonly understood.

Thus:[128]

In general, courts ought not to seek to distinguish between the two concepts, for the drawing of a distinction between a duty to act fairly, and a duty to act in accordance with the rules of natural justice, yields an unwieldy conceptual framework. The *Federal Court Act*, however, compels classification for review of federal decision-makers.

Finally, Dickson J. had to determine whether the duty to be fair applied in disciplinary cases. He noted that there were a number of precedents for the courts refusing to review disciplinary procedures.[129] Nevertheless, Dickson J. held that, while these may be counsels of caution, the rule of law must run within penitentiary walls:[130]

It seems clear that although the courts will not readily interfere in the exercise of disciplinary powers, whether in the armed services,

---

127 *Ibid.*, p. 623.
128 *Ibid.*, p. 629.
129 In particular, *R. v. Army Council; Ex parte Ravenscroft*, [1917] 2 K.B. 504; *Dawkins v. Lord Rokeby*, (1873) L.R. 8 Q.B. 255; *Re Armstrong and Whitehead*, [1973] 2 O.R. 495 (C.A.); *Fraser v. Mudge*, [1975] 3 All E.R. 78 (C.A.); *R. v. Bd. of Visitors of Hull Prison; Ex parte St. Germain*, [1979] Q.B. 425, reversing [1978] 2 W.L.R. 598 (C.A.); *Daemer v. Hall*, [1978] 2 N.Z.L.R. 594 (S.C.); *R. v. White*, [1956] S.C.R. 154; *R. v. Institutional Head of Beaver Creek Correctional Camp; Ex parte MacCaud*, [1969] 1 O.R. 373 (C.A.); *Wolff v. McDonnell*, 418 U.S. 539 (1975).
130 [1980] 1 S.C.R. 602 at 628.

the police force or the penitentiary, there is no rule of law which necessarily exempts the exercise of such disciplinary powers from review by *certiorari*.

Accordingly, Dickson, J., on behalf of the minority of the court, concurred with Pigeon J.'s conclusion that, in principle, *certiorari* was available to review the disciplinary proceedings complained of by Mr. Martineau.

(f) Conclusion

One must conclude, therefore, that these five cases have significantly extended the ambit of judicial review in Canada. The duty to be fair is now undoubtedly part of our law and a breach of the duty to be fair can be corrected by *certiorari*, even if no judicial or quasi-judicial function is involved.

Instead of characterizing functions as judicial or executive, the courts must now concentrate squarely on the real question which has always been before them: Was the procedure used in this case fair in all the circumstances? While different judges may answer this question differently, and it will be difficult therefore to advise either clients or administrators of the answer, this approach is totally consistent with the policy underlying the historical judicial power to review procedures for breaches of natural justice — to ensure that justice is not only done, but manifestly and undoubtedly perceived to be done. The courts' recognition of the duty to be fair should be welcomed by everyone concerned with Administrative Law.

Alas, however, it is probably too early to forget about quasi-judicial functions. In the first place, there is still the great danger that other courts in the future will unduly narrow the duty to be fair to apply only to those functions which otherwise would be called quasi-judicial. In effect, this would adopt the very same technique used by Lieberman J.A. in *Campeau* and Clement J.A. in *Harvie* — equating the duty to be fair with the existence of a quasi-judicial function — but for the reverse purpose of narrowing judicial review. So long as judges are human, different ones will decide differently whether fairness was or was not breached in a particular case. What must be avoided, however, is attempting to justify those decisions by reference to the obsolete tool of characterizing the function as purely executive.

Secondly, the concept of a quasi-judicial function is likely to remain important for determining whether that function may be delegated without breaching the rule that *delegatus non potest delegare*.[131] Similarly, administrators' immunity from suit is likely to continue to refer to the qualified immunity of a judicial or quasi-judicial officer.[132]

---

131 See, *e.g.*, *Vic Restaurant Inc. v. Montreal*, [1959] S.C.R. 58; *A.G. Can. v. Brent*, [1956] S.C.R. 318; and *Brant Dairy Co. v. Milk Comm. of Ont.*, [1973] S.C.R. 131.

132 See de Smith, *supra* note 68 at pp. 97-98, 106-107, 295-96.

Finally, the duty to be fair does not affect legislative functions at all, as is more fully described below.[133] Those cases which say that the exercise of a legislative function for an improper purpose is *ultra vires* do not relate to the *procedure* used. Hence, *Campeau* is not really on point. Indeed, for some reason the principles of natural justice have never applied to the exercise of a legislative power, and this principle has not been affected at all by the development of the duty to be fair. The distinction between a legislative function on the one hand, and a judicial, quasi-judicial or executive one on the other hand, will continue to be important.

5. The Applicability of the Duty to be Fair to Legislative Functions and to Decisions of the Cabinet

The duty to be fair regulates the procedure adopted by statutory delegates in the exercise of their powers. It generally applies to the exercise of *discretionary* powers.[134] One does not normally think of it in the context of an exercise of a *duty* where peremptory consequences follow the existence of a given state of facts, although *Cooper v. Wandsworth Board of Works*[135] involved precisely this circumstance (as does much of the courts' normal workload). Does the duty to be fair apply to a delegate exercising the power to make delegated legislation?[136] And does the duty to be fair apply to the cabinet,[137] exercising any kind of power which the Federal Parliament or a provincial legislature has delegated to it, or exercising the Royal Prerogative?

---

133 See the decision of the Alberta Court of Appeal in *Campeau (No. 2)*, (1980) 12 Alta. L.R. (2d) 379. *Sed quaere* the duty to be fair should not apply to the exercise of legislative powers — particularly delegated legislative powers.

134 A discretionary power is one granted by the legislative branch to a delegate to exercise his discretion to do (or not do) certain things or to choose among a number of alternatives. Not all delegated powers are discretionary; for example, some are duties. Similarly, some powers involve the promulgation of delegated legislation of general applicability, instead of decisions in individual cases. Finally, not all discretionary powers can be classified as "quasi-judicial" under the old classification of functions; some are "merely administrative".

135 (1863) 14 C.B. (N.S.) 180.

136 Difficulties arise in determining what constitutes "legislation" and "delegated legislation". For example, not all Orders in Council are legislative in nature, nor are all Acts of Parliament of general application. Similarly, land-use by-laws passed by municipalities are legislative in form but sufficiently quasi-judicial in nature that judicial review has frequently issued to strike down such by-laws enacted contrary to the principles of natural justice: see *Campeau (No. 1)*, (1979) 7 Alta. L.R. (2d) 294, and *(No. 2)*, (1980) 12 Alta. L.R. (2d) 379. As a result, the importance of "legislative" functions may give rise to as many characterization problems as the dichotomy between quasi-judicial and administrative functions.

137 Or the Governor in Council, or the Executive Council, or any other group or committee closely related to what we know as the Cabinet.

(a) Legislative Powers

Under the positivistic philosophy of our system of law, it is for Parliament to make the laws and for the courts to enforce them; and the courts will not generally inquire into procedure followed by Parliament in enacting laws, no matter how directly anyone's rights are affected. The only question is whether the Act in fact appears upon the Parliamentary roll.[138]

This blind judicial obedience to legal positivism has never been total under our federal system, for the question could always be raised whether a particular statute lay within the legislative competence of the legislative branch which purported to enact it. The Charter of Rights and Freedoms will increase the ambit of judicial review of parent (and subsidiary) legislation. Nevertheless, neither of these grounds for judicial review has any direct bearing on procedure or the duty to be fair.

A more difficult problem arises when the power to legislate has been delegated to a subordinate. At first glance, the delegate is in precisely the same position as any other delegate who exercises discretionary powers to which the duty to be fair applies. After all, the content of the delegated legislation is a matter of discretion. Almost always, its quality will be improved as a result of publicity and comment by those likely to be affected by it. The public policy rationale underlying both the *audi alteram partem* rule and the duty to be fair appears to apply to delegated legislation as well as to judicial, quasi-judicial or other discretionary powers which are subject to judicial review on procedural grounds. Indeed, this appears to have been recognized recently by the legislative branch in a number of cases where *draft* rules and regulations must be published and circulated prior to their final implementation: for example, under Bill 101 in Quebec,[139] and under both the Canada[140] and Alberta Business Corporations Acts,[141] and under the Canada Post Corporation Act.[142] Further, this appears to be the standard practice of the United States Federal Government.[143]

Nevertheless, the law in Canada appears to be clear that judicial review is not available against the procedure used in implementing delegated legislation. Indeed, in the sequel to the *Campeau* case,[144] the Alberta Court of Appeal specifically excluded the availability of judicial review because a legislative function was involved. The same point was made by McDonald J. in *R. in*

---

138 Or has been printed by the Queen's Printer, and therefore is presumed to be an Act: Alberta Evidence Act, R.S.A. 1980, c. A-21, ss. 29, 33.

139 S.Q. 1977, c. 5, s. 94.

140 S.C. 1974-75-76, c. 33. s. 254(2).

141 R.S.A. 1981, c. B-15, s. 254(2) [repealed 6th June 1983, c. 20, s. 18].

142 S.C. 1980-81-82-83, c. 54, s. 17(3)-(7).

143 The U.S. Federal Administrative Procedures Act, 5 U.S.C.A., ss. 551-556. See W. Gellhorn and C. Byse, *Administrative Law* (Mineola, N.Y.: The Foundation Press, Inc., 1974), p. 731*ff.* and Appendix A. See also K.C. Davis, *Administrative Law* (St. Paul, Minn.: The West Publishing Co., 1973), c. 11 and 12.

144 *Campeau (No. 2), supra*, note 136.

Right of Alberta v. Beaver,[145] involving the unsuccessful attempt to quash first reading of a municipal by-law; and by Megarry J., in *Bates v. Lord Hailsham of St. Marylebone*[146] which involved the proclamation of a new tariff of solicitors' fees.

Still, the concept of procedural fairness is important in the legislative context, and — as with all delegated powers — the legislative branch could pay considerably more attention to specifying the process by which its delegates are to determine the content of the legislation which they enact in the name of Parliament or the legislatures, as well as reviewing *ex post facto* the way the delegated legislative power in fact has been used.[147]

(b) The Cabinet and the Duty to be Fair

In principle, the duty to be fair applies to the exercise of all delegated discretionary powers[148] including those exercised by the Cabinet. The prerogative remedies are traditionally not available against the Crown because they are the Crown's remedies, and the Crown can hardly grant a remedy against Herself. This rationale for restricting judicial review, however, is of an extremely personal and narrow nature, and cannot apply to any circumstance where Parliament has delegated powers to the cabinet or to a particular minister.[149] Such delegations are subject to all of the normal rules of Administrative Law, including the doctrine of *ultra vires* and the principles of natural justice (or the duty to be fair). The executive committee[150] is not immune from judicial review, and the fact that some — but by no means all — of its powers are exercised on behalf of the Crown does not entitle it to Her Majesty's extensive personal immunity from judicial action. Two recent cases deal with the susceptibility of the cabinet to judicial review, and in the particular context of the duty to be fair.

---

145 [1982] 4 W.W.R. 344, reversed [1984] 4 W.W.R. 371 (Alta. C.A.).

146 [1972] 3 All E.R. 1019 (Ch.).

147 As is done by the Joint Committee of the Senate and House of Commons on Regulations and other Statutory Instruments, whose proceedings are well worth reading. Not all provincial legislatures have such standing committees to review how their powers have in fact been used by their delegates.

148 As well as to certain non-discretionary powers. See notes 134 and 135, *supra*.

149 For some unknown reason, the Canadian practice favours delegation to the Cabinet, and, unlike the British practice, not to a particular minister. In principle, the distinction should make no difference to the amenability of the delegate to judicial review. See P.W. Hogg, "Judicial Review of Action by the Crown Representative", (1969) 43 Australian L.J. 215; *Re Toohey (Aboriginal Land Commr.); Ex parte Nor. Land Council*, (1981) 58. A.L.J.R. 164 (Aus. H.C.); and *F.A.I. Ins. Ltd. v. Winneke*, (1982) 56 A.L.J.R. 388 (Aus. H.C.).

150 Not to be confused with Parliament or the legislatures. The distinction is important because only the latter bodies are "sovereign" whereas the executive government has no autonomous power apart from statutory delegation to it or the narrow remnants of the Royal Prerogative.

(i) A.G. (Canada) v. Inuit Tapirisat of Canada

The *Inuit Tapirisat*[151] case has been said — wrongly, it is submitted — to stand for the proposition that the cabinet owes no duty to be fair in exercising a broad appellate power granted to it by statute, and that judicial review is not available against the cabinet if it does not adopt a fair procedure for exercising such a power.

The case arose out of an application to the Canadian Radio-Television and Telecommunications Commission by Bell Canada to raise certain of its rates. The Indian Tapirisat appeared as intervenants before the C.R.T.C., and appealed its decision to the Governor in Council under section 64 of the National Transportation Act.[152] The Cabinet disposed of the appeal after receiving Bell Canada's response thereto, but prior to any further reply by the Tapirisat. The actual written submissions of the parties were not presented to the Cabinet, which instead obtained materials from officials of the department of communication as to: (a) what the department thought were the parties' positions; (b) the department's position on the issues; and (c) whether the appeal should be allowed. In addition, the C.R.T.C. was requested to advise the Cabinet as to its views on the proper disposition of the appeal. The Minister of Communications participated actively in advancing the submissions of both the departmental officials and the C.R.T.C. (which were not communicated to the appellants and who were given no opportunity to reply), but still participated in Cabinet's decision to reject the appeals.

The appellants brought an action in the Trial Division of the Federal Court for a declaration that the Order in Council giving effect to the Cabinet's rejection of the appeal was void, and the Attorney General for Canada moved to strike the statement of claim on the basis that it disclosed no reasonable cause of action. The Trial Division allowed the motion to strike out the statement of claim,[153] but this was reversed by the Appellate Division.[154] Estey J., writing the unanimous judgment of the Supreme Court of Canada, held that there was no reasonable cause of action, and struck out the statement of claim. His Lordship put the question as follows:[155]

> The substance of the question before this Court . . . is this: is there a duty to observe natural justice in, or at least a lesser duty of fairness incumbent on the Governor in Council in dealing with parties such as the respondents upon their submission of a petition under s. 64(1)?

---

151 (1981) 115 D.L.R. (3d) 1 (S.C.C.).
152 R.S.C. 1970, c. N-17 [am. 1970, c. 10 (2nd Supp.), s. 65 (Item 32)].
153 [1979] 1 F.C. 213.
154 [1979] 1 F.C. 710.
155 *Supra*, note 151 at p. 9.

His Lordship then considered[156] the development of the duty to be fair, along the lines set out in section 4 of this chapter.

Estey J. then re-asserted the right of the courts to review the exercise of a statutory power by the Governor in Council, with particular reference to a breach of the terms of a condition precedent.[157] He went on, however, to note that the present case did not deal with a condition precedent, but rather with the proper procedure to be adopted by the statutory delegate. His Lordship specifically stated that it was not necessary to characterize the Cabinet's functions as quasi-judicial in order to permit the court to review its legality.

The Supreme Court then examined the nature of the appeal under section 64, in order to determine what would constitute a fair procedure thereunder. In particular, Estey J. noted that the Act provided a more conventional appeal from the decision of the C.R.T.C. to the Federal Court of Appeal on any point of law or jurisdiction, in addition to the "political route" of appealing to the Cabinet under section 64.[158] Further, the Cabinet's powers under section 64 could be exercised of its own motion, include the power to substitute its own ruling for that of the C.R.T.C., and (unlike the power delegated to the C.R.T.C.) contain no standards or guidelines for their exercise. His Lordship specifically thought that the identity of the delegate (that is, the Cabinet) was relevant in determining the specific procedural requirements which Parliament must have intended the delegate to follow in reaching its decision:[159]

> While the CRTC must operate within a certain framework when rendering its decisions, Parliament has in s. 64(1) not burdened the executive branch with any standards or guidelines in the exercise of its rate review function. Neither were procedural standards imposed or even implied. That is not to say that the courts will not respond today as in the *Wilson* case, *supra*, if the conditions precedent to the exercise of power so granted to the executive branch have not been observed. *Such a response might also occur if, on a petition being received by the Council, no examination of its contents by the Governor in Council were undertaken.* That is quite a different matter (and one with which we are not here faced) from the assertion of some principle of law that requires the Governor in Council, before discharg-

---

156 *Ibid.*, pp. 9-11, 18-19.
157 Note that later in this judgment, Estey J. asserts the right of the courts to review the Cabinet's exercise of the power granted to it by Parliament, even where no condition precedent is involved:

> the Court must fall back upon the basic jurisdictional supervisory role and in so doing construe the statute to determine whether the Governor in Council has performed its functions within the boundary of the parliamentary grant and in accordance with the terms of the parliamentary mandate.

Supra, note 151, p. 19.
158 *Ibid.*, p. 8.
159 *Ibid.*, pp. 15, 17.

ing its duty under the section, to read either individually or *en masse* the petition itself and all supporting material, the evidence taken before the CRTC and all the submissions and arguments advanced by the petitioner and responding parties. The very nature of the body must be taken into account in assessing the technique of review which has been adopted by the Governor in Council. The executive branch cannot be deprived of the right to resort to its staff, to departmental personnel concerned with the subject-matter, and above all to the comments and advice of ministerial members of the Council who are by virtue of their office concerned with the policy issues arising by reason of the petition whether those policies be economic, political, commercial or of some other nature. Parliament might otherwise ordain, but in s. 64 no such limitation has been imposed on the Governor in Council in the adoption of the procedures for the hearing of petitions under s-s.(1).

Under s. 64 the cabinet, as the executive branch of Government, was exercising the power delegated by Parliament to determine the appropriate tariffs for the telephone services of Bell Canada. In so doing the Cabinet, unless otherwise directed in the enabling statute, must be free to consult all sources which Parliament itself might consult had it retained this function. This is clearly so in those instances where the Council acts on its own initiative as it is authorized and required to do by the same subsection. There is no indication in s-s. (1) that a different interpretation comes into play upon the exercise of the right of a party to petition the Governor in Council to exercise this same delegated function or power. The wording adopted by Parliament in my view makes this clear. The Governor in Council may act "at any time". He may vary or rescind any order, decision, rule or regulation "in his discretion". The guidelines mandated by Parliament in the case of the CRTC are not repeated expressly or by implication in s. 64. The function applies to broad, *quasi*-legislative orders of the Commission as well as to inter-party decisions. In short, the discretion of the Governor in Council is complete provided he observes the jurisdictional boundaries of s. 64(1).

Strangely, His Lordship then went on to characterize the Cabinet's powers under section 64 as "legislative action in its purest form where the subject matter is the fixing of rates for a public utility such as a telephone system".[160] His Lordship thought giving notice to everyone potentially affected by such rate-making power would be impractical for the Cabinet, and

---

160 *Ibid.*, p. 15, and see also p. 19, where Estey J. considered the *Bates* case and concluded that

> [i]t is clear that the orders in question in *Bates* and the case at bar were legislative in nature and I adopt the reasoning of Megarry J. to the effect that no hearing is required in

this too was relevant in minimizing the content of the procedural fairness required in the Cabinet's decision.

Estey J. recognized[161] that the obligation to comply with natural justice does not have to be imposed specifically by statute, but will generally be implied by the courts, who will also have to determine the content of such implied procedural requirements.[162] The fact that there is a broad (or, indeed, untrammelled) discretionary power does not — with respect to Estey J. — necessarily have any effect on the duty to adopt a fair procedure in exercising the discretionary power. After all, the discretion goes to the merits of the decision, not to the procedure by which it is reached. Nevertheless, Estey J. kept coming back to this point in reaching his judgment that no procedural unfairness had occurred.[163]

---

such cases. I realize, however, that the dividing line between legislative and administrative functions is not always easy to draw: see *Essex County Council v. Minister of Housing* (1967), 66 L.G.R. 23.

The answer is not to be found in continuing the search for words that will clearly and invariably differentiate between judicial and administrative on the one hand, or administrative and legislative on the other. It may be said that the use of the fairness principle as in *Nicholson, supra*, will obviate the need for the distinction in instances where the tribunal or agency is discharging a function with reference to something akin to a *lis* or where the agency may be described as an "investigating body" as in the *Selvarajan* case, *supra*. Where, however, the executive branch has been assigned a function performable in the past by the Legislature itself and where the *res* or subject-matter is not an individual concern or a right unique to the petitioner or appellant, different considerations may be thought to arise. The fact that the function has been assigned as here to a tier of agencies (the CRTC in the first instance and the Governor in Council in the second) does not, in my view, alter the political science pathology of the case. In such a circumstance the Court must fall back upon the basic jurisdictional supervisory role and in so doing construe the statute to determine whether the Governor in Council has performed its functions within the boundary of the parliamentary grant and in accordance with the terms of the parliamentary mandate.

161 *Ibid.*, p. 17.
162 *Ibid.*
163 *E.g.*, immediately after noting that the duty to observe procedural fairness will generally be implied by the courts, Estey J. notes (at p. 17) that

[u]nder s. 64 the Cabinet, *as the executive branch of Government*, was exercising the power delegated by Parliament to determine the appropriate tariffs for the telephone services of Bell Canada. In so doing *the Cabinet, unless otherwise directed in the enabling statute*, must be free *to consult all sources which Parliament* itself might consult had it retained this function. . . . The wording adopted by Parliament in my view makes this clear. The Governor in Council may act "at any time". He may vary or rescind any order, decision, rule or regulation "in his discretion". The guidelines mandated by Parliament in the case of the CRTC are not repeated expressly or by implication in s. 64 [giving the appeal to Cabinet]. The function implies to broad, *quasi*-legislative orders of the Commission as well as to inter-party decisions. *In short, the discretion of the Governor in Council is complete provided he observes the jurisdictional boundaries of s. 64.* [Emphasis added.]

Note also Estey J.'s reluctance to comment on the desirability of Parliament granting "political" appeals to Cabinet, and his reference to the recommendation of the Law Reform

(ii) The Gray Line case

A different approach was recently taken by the Supreme Court of British Columbia in *Gray Line of Victoria Ltd. v. Chabot; Gray Line of Victoria v. McClelland*.[164] Again, an appeal was made to Cabinet from a licensing body; in this case, the Motor Carrier Commission for licences to operate sightseeing services. The Lieutenant Governor in Council (or a committee thereof) allowed the appeal and granted the licences. A group of objectors applied for judicial review of the Cabinet's decision on two grounds. The first attack dealt with the fact that new evidence had been led on the appeal, contrary to the published rules governing such appeals. McEachern C.J.S.C. clearly asserted[165] the power of the courts to review the procedure used by the Cabinet in exercising the appellate function delegated to it by the legislature. Unlike Estey J. in the *Inuit Tapirisat* case, he did not even suggest that the fact the Cabinet was involved could either preclude judicial review of the delegated power or affect the content of the duty to be fair. On the facts, however, the Chief Justice held[166] that there was no unfairness involved in the procedure used because all the parties adduced new evidence, and all were represented by counsel who could answer the points made by other parties.

On the second point, also dealing with natural justice, McEachern C.J.S.C. struck down the Orders in Council implementing the Cabinet's decision on the appeal. These Orders in Council referred to the entire executive council, but in fact the appeal had been heard by only some members thereof. His Lordship stated that[167]

> [t]he matter may be summarized by saying that in the discharge of its appellate jurisdiction natural justice and fairness requires [sic] the real decision to be made only by a majority of the members of the Executive Council who hear the parties if there is a hearing. Where there is no hearing, the real decision may only be made by a majority of those members of the Executive Council who consider the submissions of the parties and who give the parties the required opportunity to respond to adverse submissions, etc.

Accordingly, His Lordship quashed the Orders in Council, and this case provides an example of judicial review of a cabinet decision for a breach of the principles of natural justice (or fairness).

Commission of Canada that such appeals should be abolished, except in the case of the equivalent of the exercise of the prerogative of mercy of a decision based on humanitarian grounds. See *Independent Administrative Agencies* (Working Paper 25, 1980), especially pp. 87-89.

164 [1981] 2 W.W.R. 635, supplementary reasons (dealing with section 96 of the B.N.A. Act, 1867) [1981] 5 W.W.R. 385.

165 *Ibid.*, pp. 641-42.

166 *Ibid.*, p. 642.

167 *Ibid.*, p. 646.

(iii) The Cruise case

Unlike the previous two cases which dealt with *statutory* powers delegated to the cabinet, the Cruise[168] case appears to deal with the exercise of the Royal Prerogative by the cabinet.[169] While the case focuses principally on the substantive issue as to whether section 7 of the Canadian Charter of Rights and Freedoms provides an absolute right to "life, liberty and security of the person", thereby providing an entrenched constitutional prohibition on the government's actions, it also raises the question whether the exercise of the Royal Prerogative by the cabinet must comply with certain fair procedures (a) at common law, or (b) under section 7 of the Charter. If so, judicial review is in principle available against this type of cabinet decision, apart altogether from any consideration of the content of such procedural fairness in these circumstances.

The case arose from the government's attempt to strike out the plaintiff's statement of claim[170] on the basis that it disclosed no reasonable cause of action. Cattanach J. refused to strike the statement of claim because he thought it raised a justiciable issue as to whether substantive rights were infringed. On the procedural point, Cattanach J. said:[171]

> It is not incumbent upon me to proffer an interpretation of the words [from s. 7 of the Charter], "in accordance with the principles of fundamental justice" other than to hazard the view that the words "fundamental justice" may be synonymous with words such as "natural justice".
>
> In that event should this be a case where national security is involved and the state is endangered then our cherished freedom of the individual and doing justice to him must in the last resort take second place to the security of the country itself.

And:[172]

> The very fundamental contention advanced on behalf of the defendants for striking out the plaintiff's statement of claim is that

---

168 *Operation Dismantle v. Can.*, [1983] 1 F.C. 429, reversed [1983] 1 F.C. 745, affirmed S.C.C., Dickson C.J., Ritchie, Estey, McIntyre, Chouinard, Lamer, Wilson JJ., No. 18154, 9th May 1985 (not yet reported).

169 Query the actual extent of the Royal Prerogative today, in light of the voluminous statutory provisions dealing with the military, external affairs and the like, which therefore no longer can globally be correctly described as falling under the Royal Prerogative.

170 The method of framing the statement of claim was questioned by both Cattanach J. and by members of the Federal Court of Appeal. In particular, it appears that the statement of claim did not squarely attach the procedure used by the Cabinet in deciding to permit testing of the cruise missile in Canada. See [1983] 1 F.C. 745 at 753, where Pratt J.A. specifically states that the statement of claim "nowhere alleges that the impugned decision was not made in accordance with the principles of fundamental justice to which section 7 refers".

171 *Supra*, note 168 at p. 436.

172 *Ibid.*, pp. 433-34, emphasis added.

the decision to permit the testing of the cruise missile in Canada was one made by the Government of Canada in its executive capacity based upon policy and expediency and as such is not subject to control or interference from the judicial branch.

Had the decision here in question been made prior to the enactment and proclamation of the *Canadian Charter of Rights and Freedoms* I could not agree more with the validity of that contention.

In the remote likelihood that any solicitor would have launched such an action, that action would have been summarily dismissed as the present statement of claim is sought to be dismissed.

In the Court of Appeal, the Royal Prerogative issue was clearly raised by the government in its further (and successful) attempt to have the statement of claim struck out. The majority of the court seems to assume that judicial review is not available at common law against the exercise of a prerogative power. As LeDain J. said:[173]

Counsel for the appellants also argued that in view of the very restricted limits at common law of the scope of judicial review of an exercise of the royal prerogative, limits which he submitted reflected a fundamental principle of the Constitution concerning the proper relationship between the executive and the judiciary, it could not have been intended to subject an exercise of the prerogative to the scope of review called for by the application of the Charter, which necessarily involved issues of legislative and executive policy. He invoked, as indicating those limits, what was said in *Blackburn v. Attorney-General*, [1971] 2 All E.R. 1380 (C.A.) concerning the prerogative power to make treaties, and in *Chandler and Others v. Director of Public Prosecutions*, [1962] 3 All E.R. 142 (H.L.) concerning the prerogative power to determine the disposition and armament of the armed forces. The weight of judicial authority as to the scope of judicial review of an exercise of the royal prerogative is summed up in *de Smith's Judicial Review of Administrative Action*, 4th ed. (J.M. Evans), pp. 286-287, as follows:

(3) If it is claimed that the authority for the exercise of discretion derives from the royal prerogative, the courts had traditionally limited review to questions of *vires* in the narrowest sense of the term. They can determine whether the prerogative power exists, what is its extent, whether it has been exercised in the appropriate form and how far it has been superseded by statute; they have not normally been prepared to examine the appropriateness or adequacy of the grounds for exer-

---

173 *Ibid.*, pp. 763-64.

cising the power, or the fairness of the procedure followed before the power is exercised, and they will not allow bad faith to be attributed to the Crown.

The treatise goes on to suggest that there may be no reason to distinguish, in respect of the scope of judicial review, between the exercise of a prerogative discretion and the exercise of a statutory discretion, a view expressed by Lord Denning M.R. in *Laker Airways Ltd. v. Department of Trade*, [1977] 1 Q.B. 643, which was relied on by the respondents in the present case.

LeDain J. therefore did not actually decide that judicial review was not available at common law to control the procedure used for exercising a prerogative power, and three other judges really did not deal with this point squarely. Marceau J., on the other hand, clearly held that judicial review of the Royal Prerogative was almost unheard of.[174]

The question then arose as to whether the procedural requirements of section 7 of the Charter have changed this common law impotence of the judiciary towards the exercise of the Crown's prerogative powers. This required the court to determine whether the Charter even applies to the Crown's prerogatives. Section 32(1) of the Charter reads as follows:

32.(1) This Charter applies

(*a*) to the Parliament and government of Canada in respect of all matters *within the authority of Parliament* including all matters relating to the Yukon Territory and Northwest Territories; and
(*b*) to the legislature and government of each province in respect of all matters *within the authority of the legislature of each province.*

[Emphasis added.]

In other words, does the Royal Prerogative fall "within the authority of Parliament"?[175]

The majority of the Court of Appeal answered this question affirmatively. As LeDain J. said:[176]

A matter which is subject to the prerogative of the Crown in right of Canada is one on which Parliament may legislate so as to restrict or displace the prerogative (cf. *Attorney-General v. De Keyser's Hotel, Limited*, [1920] A.C. 508 (H.L.)), and as such, is in my opinion a matter "within the authority of Parliament", as those words are

---

174 *Ibid.*, pp. 779-82. He relied on Lord Parker's decision in the *Chandler* case in the English Court of Appeal, [1962] 2 All E.R. 314 (which went on to the House of Lords, [1962] 2 All E.R. 142); and *China Navigation Co. v. A.G.*, [1932] 2 K.B. 197 (C.A.).

175 Or of a provincial legislature with respect to prerogatives of the Crown in right of a province.

176 *Supra*, note 168 at pp. 763-64, concurred in by Pratte J. (p. 751), Ryan J. (p. 756). Hugessen J. does not specifically deal with this point. Marceau J. dissented on this point.

used in section 32(1)(*a*). I note also that the French version of the words "any law" in section 52(1) of the *Constitution Act, 1982*, Schedule B, *Canada Act 1982*, 1982, c. 11 (U.K.), is "*toute autre règle de droit*", indicating that not only statutory provisions and any law made in the exercise of statutory authority, but the common law rules of governmental authority are rendered inoperative to the extent of inconsistency with the Constitution of Canada. I am, therefore, of the opinion that the Charter is, on its face, applicable to an exercise of the royal prerogative.

. . . . .

The *Canadian Charter of Rights and Freedoms* imposes new legal limits on the exercise of the prerogative and has thereby enlarged the scope of judicial review of it.

Again, Marceau J. dissented, in very strong terms:[177]

If the act is really an act of prerogative in the sense that it remains within the limits of the prerogative, the courts have no power to interfere with it. The *Canadian Charter of Rights and Freedoms*, introduced to provide a solemn guarantee that private rights and interests will be respected, did not affect the exercise of the royal prerogative powers, especially those associated with defence and national security, powers the continued existence of which is attribu-table strictly to considerations of pure national and collective interest.

The majority of the Court of Appeal, therefore, clearly held that section 7 of the Charter does permit the courts to review the procedure used by the government in the exercise of a Royal Prerogative. Unfortunately, the plaintiffs' explicit disavowal of any reliance on the principles of natural justice allowed the Court of Appeal to avoid ruling on whether the Cabinet's decision was unfair. Indeed, no consideration was ever given to the content of procedural fairness in these circumstances. One can speculate that the court would have minimized the content of procedural fairness in light of the *Inuit Tapirisat* case.

The Supreme Court of Canada, while unequivocally confirming the view of the majority of the Court of Appeal that section 7 of the Charter is applicable to Cabinet decisions, gave no consideration to the content of procedural fairness in the circumstances.[178]

---

177 *Ibid.*, p. 782.
178 *Supra*, note 168, per Dickson C.J.C., p. 16:

      I agree with Madame Justice Wilson that Cabinet decisions fall under s. 32(1)(*a*) of the Charter and are therefore reviewable in the courts and subject to judicial scrutiny for compatability with the Constitution. I have no doubt that the executive branch of the

6. Theoretically Incorrect Attempts to Make the Duty to be Fair Apply to the Merits of a Decision

The phrase "duty to be fair" may give rise to misunderstanding because it does not clearly refer to procedural instead of substantive fairness. Its derivation, however, from the principles of natural justice[179] necessarily links it to questions of fair procedure. The obligation for a statutory delegate to adopt a fair procedure goes to the very terms of the power granted to him, and a breach of the duty to adopt a fair procedure renders the decision void and therefore capable of judicial review.[180] In the absence of a specific appellate power created by statute, the courts themselves have no jurisdiction to review the substantive fairness or any other aspect of the merits of a delegate's actions.[181] In other words, the distinction between judicial review and an appeal (of whatever breadth)[182] clearly endures notwithstanding the development of the duty to be fair.

Of course, certain substantive (as opposed to procedural) errors may sometimes also nullify a decision taken by a statutory delegate. For example, the legislature is generally presumed to have implicitly limited all delegated discretionary powers within the realm of reasonableness.[183] Accordingly, an unreasonable exercise of delegated power[184] will be *ultra vires*, and therefore capable of judicial review (though not of an appeal unless one is specifically created). Similarly, all statutory delegates are assumed to be under an obligation to act in good faith, and for no ulterior purpose,[185] not to act upon irrelevant considerations,[186] and not to ignore relevant ones.[187] All of these are implied substantive limitations which go to the ambit of the power granted by the legislative branch to its delegate. Any breach of these substantive limita-

---

Canadian Government is duty bound to act in accordance with the dictates of the Charter. Specifically, the Cabinet has a duty to act in a manner consistent with the right to life, liberty and security of the person and the right not to be deprived thereof except in accordance with the principles of fundamental justice.

179 See Part 2, *supra*.
180 See Part 8 below.
181 See D.P. Jones, "Discretionary Refusal of Judicial Review in Administrative Law", (1981) 19 Alta. L. Rev. 483, especially pp. 485-87.
182 The word "appeal" does not connote any particular meaning, and in a particular context may mean an appeal *de novo*, an appeal on questions of law or jurisdiction, or (less frequently) a review of the record of the initial decision.
183 See H.W.R. Wade's *Administrative Law*, 5th ed. (1982), pp. 353*ff.* for a discussion of the availability of judicial review on the ground of unreasonableness.
184 *Sed quaere* whether the same rule should apply to unreasonable parent legislation.
185 See *Roncarelli v. Duplessis*, [1959] S.C.R. 121; *Campeau Corp. v. Calgary (No. 1)*, (1979) 7 Alta. L.R. (2d) 294 (C.A.); *Padfield v. Min. of Agriculture, Fisheries and Food*, [1968] A.C. 997 (H.L.).
186 See *Padfield, supra*, note 185; *Dallinga v. Calgary City Council*, [1976] 1 W.W.R 319 (Alta. C.A.); *Smith & Rhuland Ltd. v. R.*, [1953] 2 S.C.R. 95.
187 Which may only really be the reverse of acting on irrelevant evidence, "unreasonableness" or lack of evidence as grounds for judicial review.

tions will render the delegate's action *ultra vires*, and give rise to judicial review (but not necessarily to an appeal).

To some extent, it may be possible to characterize all of these substantive limitations on the delegate's jurisdiction as a duty to be fair, although none of them deals with procedural matters. It is confusing to include these implied jurisdictional limitations on a delegate's powers under the rubric of the "duty to be fair", because there is a tendency to widen the use of that phrase even further to refer to the merits of the case before the delegate. For example, Professor David Mullan has noted four recent cases where the courts may have overstepped their review powers to interfere with a delegate's discretion solely because they found it "unfair" on the merits.[188] Judicial review is not an appeal on the merits and it is dangerous constitutionally for the courts to arrogate to themselves appellate powers which the legislative branch has not given to them.[189]

It may be difficult to distinguish the substance or merits of a delegate's decision from procedural limitations which Administrative Law has implied to circumscribe the ambit of power assumed to have been granted by the legislature.[190] Conversely, the temptation on the courts to interfere with the merits of an administrative decision may indicate that the legislative branch should take considerably more care in defining the relevant factors to be considered by its delegates when exercising the discretion granted to them, when determining the procedures to be followed, and when determining the need for an appeal (including determining to whom the appeal should lie, and the nature of it).

7. Relationship Between the Duty to be Fair and the "Principles of Fundamental Justice" Contained in Section 7 of the Charter of Rights and Freedoms

The "substantive fairness" problem may also now arise under section 7 of the Canadian Charter of Rights and Freedoms, which provides as follows:[191]

---

188 David J. Mullan, "Natural Justice and Fairness — Substantive as Well as Procedural Standards for the Review of Administrative Decision-Making?" (1982) 27 McGill L.J. 250. The four cases are: (a) *R. v. Barnsley Metro. Borough Council; Ex parte Hook*, [1976] 1 W.L.R. 1052 (C.A.); (b) *H.T.V. Ltd. v. Price Comm.*, [1976] I.C.R. 170 (C.A.); (c) *Daganayais v. Min. of Immigration*, [1980] 2 N.Z.L.R. 130 (C.A.); (d) *Min. of Immigration and Ethnic Affairs v. Pochi*, (1980) 31 A.L.J.R. 666 (F.C.). Note also that the question of substantive fairness arose in the *Operation Dismantle* case, discussed in the previous section of this chapter.
189 See D.P. Jones "A Constitutionally Guaranteed Role for the Courts", (1979) 57 Can. Bar Rev. 669.
190 See Mullan, *supra*, note 188.
191 Contained in the Constitution Act, 1982, which is Schedule B to the Canada Act, 1982 passed by the Parliament of the United Kingdom, and proclaimed in Ottawa on April 17, 1982, emphasis added.

Everyone has the right to life, liberty and security of the person and the right not to be deprived thereof *except in accordance with the principles of fundamental justice.*

This phrase is borrowed from the earlier Canadian Bill of Rights,[192] and undoubtedly was intended to elevate the procedural aspects of natural justice to constitutional status in any matters dealing with life, liberty and the security of the person. Indeed, one of the Federal Government's legal advisors so testified to the Joint Parliamentary Committee during its hearings on the constitutional package.[193] Nevertheless, there are at least two reasons to suspect that the reference in section 7 to the "principles of fundamental justice" may ripen into a substantive limitation on the content of parent legislation that can be enacted, as well as providing a method of scrutinizing the merits of a delegate's decision.

First, the very words used in section 7 are not restricted to procedural matters, but are equally capable of referring to substantive circumstances in which it would be "fundamentally unjust" to deprive someone of life, liberty or security of the person. Indeed, to insist upon restricting this phrase to procedural questions would largely nullify the constitutional protection accorded to life, liberty and the security of the person, because it would imply that all of these could be extinguished, provided a proper procedure was followed. For example, suppose that Parliament passed a law stating that "Mr. X shall be executed tomorrow at twelve noon", and further provided that Mr. X would be informed of this law (after enactment), and given the opportunity to say anything he liked about his prospective demise. Mere procedural fairness in this context would be meaningless, because there is no discretion granted under the law to alter its application in light of anything Mr. X might say at his "hearing". Undoubtedly, the principles of natural justice apply to the delegate upon whom Parliament has imposed the duty to execute Mr. X.[194] But the requirement for a fair hearing is little guarantee that

---

192 R.S.C. 1970, App. III. Section 2(e) of the Canadian Bill of Rights stated that no law of Canada shall be construed or applied so as to "deprive a person of the right to a fair hearing in accordance with the principles of fundamental justice for the determination of his rights and obligations". This reference to the "principles of fundamental justice" is clearly procedural. See Fauteux C.J.'s comments on this point in *Duke v. R.*, [1972] S.C.R. 917 at 923. Note further that s. 7 of the new Charter in fact corresponds to s. 1(*a*) — and not to s. 2(*e*) — of the Canadian Bill of Rights. Section 1 recognizes and continues the existence of certain human rights and fundamental freedoms, including "the right of the individual to life, liberty, security of the person and enjoyment of property, *and the right not to be deprived thereof except by due process of law*" (emphasis added). This reference to "due process" is (apart from the American concept of substantive due process) procedural in nature. Nevertheless, the substitution of "principles of fundamental justice" for "due process" in s. 7 of the Charter opens up the question of substantive justice now being protected.

193 See the testimony of Dr. Strayer, Minutes of Proceedings and Evidence of the Special Joint Committee of the Senate and House of Commons on the Constitution of Canada, Issue No. 46, pp. 32-33.

194 *Cooper v. Wandsworth Bd. of Works*, (1863) 14 C.B. (N.S.) 180.

"fundamental justice" would be done to Mr. X.[195] Faced with a patently unjust law, perhaps peremptory and not discretionary in its application, what Canadian court would not be sorely tempted to strike down the substance of law on the strength of the reference in section 7 to "fundamental justice"?

The second reason for suspecting that the reference in section 7 to fundamental justice will limit the content of parent legislation derives from noting that this has been precisely the experience of the United States courts in construing the fifth and fourteenth amendments to their Constitution, which provide that:

> no person shall . . . be deprived of life, liberty or property, *without due process of law* . . . ;

and

> nor shall any State deprive any person of life, liberty or property, *without due process of law.* . . .

Even though the wording of the U.S. version is much weaker than the reference in section 7 of our Charter to the "principles of fundamental justice", the U.S. courts have interpreted these two amendments to require not only procedural fairness, but also "substantive due process" in certain circumstances.[196] In other words, the substance of legislation has been struck down by courts where it is unfair. This could, it is submitted, become the case in Canada; and the Canadian courts will also be tempted to look at the merits of discretionary decisions taken by statutory delegates, as well as the content of the legislation itself.

Finally, on a different point, it is important to note that section 7 of the Charter at its very narrowest interpretation not only specifically imports procedural fairness into any decision affecting life, liberty and the security of the person, it also eliminates the sovereignty of the legislative branch with respect to ousting the principles of natural justice, at least so far as any question of life, liberty and the security of the person is involved, and any attempt to do so will be unconstitutional.

8. Effect of a Breach of the Duty to be Fair

Notwithstanding heretical *dicta* to the contrary,[197] a breach of natural justice (or of the duty to be fair) renders the decision void, not voidable, and

---

195 See Julius H. Grey's comment on "Can Fairness be Effective?", (1982) 27 McGill L.J. 360, for a good consideration of the extent to which requirements of procedural fairness ensure substantive justice on the merits.

196 See Gerald Gunther, *Constitutional Law*, 10th ed. (Mineola N.Y.: The Foundation Press, Inc., 1980), especially c. 9, and Lawrence H. Tribe, *American Constitutional Law*, (Mineola, N.Y.: The Foundation Press, Inc. 1978), especially c. 8, 10, 11, and 12.

197 See *Harelkin v. Univ. of Regina*, [1979] 2 S.C.R. 561, per Beetz J.; and the dicta of Kerans J. in *Bridgeland-Riverside Community Assn. v. Calgary*, (1982) 19 Alta. L.R. (2d) 361 (C.A.).

therefore not protected by most privative clauses. The following explanation demonstrates the theoretical and practical importance of this statement.

Virtually all Administrative Law depends upon two maxims: (a) Parliament is sovereign; and (b) a delegate to whom Parliament has granted powers must act strictly within his jurisdiction, and the courts will determine whether his actions are *ultra vires.*

A delegate's jurisdiction may depend upon certain preliminary or collateral matters. Thus, in *Anisminic v. Foreign Compensation Commission,*[198] the commission was bound to consider a claim for compensation filed by a party, or the party's successor-in-title, whose property was sequestrated by the Egyptian Government after Suez. Entertaining a claim from someone who did not meet those conditions would clearly have been *ultra vires* the power or jurisdiction granted to the commission by Parliament. Conversely, refusing even to receive a claim from a person who did meet those conditions would also have been *ultra vires.* Similarly, in *Bell v. Ontario Human Rights Commission,*[199] the commission could only hear complaints of discrimination relating to the rental of self-contained residential premises. The question whether particular premises were self-contained was obviously a jurisdictional one. Again, if Parliament gives a delegate power to make a park, it is *ultra vires* for the delegate to try to use that power to build a highway. All of these are examples of what may be called substantive *ultra vires.*

Even if the delegate is acting substantively within the subject matter granted to him by Parliament (that is, has correctly decided any preliminary or collateral point, or is in fact exercising the power granted to him), his actions may nevertheless be *ultra vires* if he commits any of the following errors:

(a) breaches the principles of natural justice or the duty to be procedurally fair;[200]
(b) considers irrelevant evidence;[201]
(c) ignores relevant evidence;[202]
(d) acts for an improper purpose or out of malice.[203]

In each of these cases, the delegate has jurisdiction to commence his action to deal with the matter, but steps outside his jurisdiction by committing one of the errors listed above. His decision is clearly subject to judicial review. With

---

198 [1969] 2 A.C. 147 (H.L.).
199 [1971] S.C.R. 756.
200 See *e.g., Alliance des Professeurs Catholiques de Montréal v. Lab. Rel. Bd. of Qué.*, [1953] 2 S.C.R. 140; *Ridge v. Baldwin,* [1964] A.C. 40 (H.L.); *Cooper v. Wandsworth Bd. of Works, supra,* note 194.
201 *Smith & Rhuland v. R.*, [1953] 2 S.C.R. 95; *Padfield v. Min. of Agriculture, Fisheries and Food,* [1968] 2 A.C. 997 (H.L.); *Dallinga v. Calgary City Council,* [1976] 1 W.W.R. 319 (Alta. C.A.).
202 See the discussion on this point in section 2 of chapter 7.
203 *Roncarelli v. Duplessis,* [1959] S.C.R. 121; *Campeau Corp. v. Calgary (No. 1),* (1979) 7 Alta. L.R. (2d) 294 (C.A.); *cf.* the *Padfield* case, *supra,* note 201.

one exception,[204] the only theoretical basis upon which the superior courts are entitled to review the legality of a delegate's action is based upon their inherent power to keep inferior tribunals within their respective jurisdictions. The concept of jurisdiction thus underlies these four grounds for judicial review every bit as much as it underlies review of other substantive *ultra vires* actions by a delegate of the legislature. The unstated premise, of course, is that Parliament never intended its delegate to act contrary to natural justice, or to consider irrelevant evidence, or to ignore relevant evidence, or to act maliciously or in bad faith, or unreasonably. Of course Parliament's sovereignty means that it would theoretically permit its delegates to act in any of these ways, and the courts would have to give effect to such specific legislative commandment. But the legislature rarely does this and the courts continue to construe legislation and other powers[205] on the assumption that these four requirements must be complied with in order for the delegate's action to be valid. In short, these requirements go to the substantive jurisdiction of the delegate, and must do so to authorize the courts to interfere with any such defective administrative action.

It is true that, for example, a breach of the principles of natural justice appears to be merely a procedural error, committed after the delegate has validly commenced his exercise of the power which Parliament has granted to him. But it would be incorrect to assume that such a procedural error is somehow less important or less substantive than a clear attempt by the delegate to do something completely unrelated to the power granted by Parliament (for example, to build a highway instead of a park). For more than a century the assumption has been that Parliament intends the procedural requirements of natural justice to be observed by certain delegates, as part and parcel of the power granted to them; any default renders the decision void.[206] Nor is it possible to say that such a decision is voidable. If it were, what would entitle the courts to intervene to correct it? For the decision would — on the voidable assumption — lie within the jurisdiction of the delegate and would not be *ultra vires*. Of course such an error undoubtedly constitutes an error of law[207] which could be corrected by the court under its anomalous power to

---

204 Error of law on the face of the record, even though the error does not go to the delegate's jurisdiction. For an excellent historical explanation of its anomaly, see *R. v. Northumberland Compensation Appeal Tribunal; Ex parte Shaw*, [1952] 1 K.B. 338 (C.A.), *cf.* Lord Reid's judgment in *Anisminic, supra*, note 198.

205 Including delegated legislation such as rules and regulations, as well as delegated discretionary powers and duties.

206 Otherwise the decision in *Cooper v. Wandsworth Bd. of Works*, (1863) 14 C.B. (N.S.) 180, would have been opposite, for the demolition order there would have been valid and therefore a complete defence to the action in trespass (which is not a discretionary remedy). See H.W.R. Wade, "Unlawful Administration Action: Void or Voidable?" Part I at (1967) 83 L.Q. Rev. 499; Part II (1968) 84 L.Q. Rev. 95; Wade's Administrative Law, 4th ed. (1977), especially pp. 296-301 and pp. 447-50. *Cf. Durayappah v. Fernando*, [1967] 2 A.C. 337 (P.C.).

207 Because a breach of the principles of natural justice, or of the duty to be fair, obviously is an error of procedure.

grant *certiorari* to correct even errors of law not going to jurisdiction. But this power to correct errors of law clearly is not available if there is a privative clause depriving the courts of their inherent power to review decisions of such a delegate made within his jurisdiction nor, possibly, even where there is none.[207a] Yet the courts have consistently held that privative clauses do not protect "decisions" which are made outside of the delegate's jurisdiction, because such decisions are void (not voidable), and therefore are not "decisions".[208] Nor is it difficult to find such cases involving breaches of natural justice, improper consideration of the evidence, or malice. None of these cases could have avoided the clear words of a privative clause if the decisions involved were merely voidable instead of being void, because then there would have been a "decision" protected by the privative clause. It must be concluded, therefore, that the rule that a breach of natural justice renders the decision *void* is of high constitutional importance, and must not be permitted to be eroded by loose *dicta* in cases where there is no privative clause.[209]

9. Summary on the Duty to be Fair

In conclusion, it can be seen that judicial review has long been available to control the procedure used to exercise many governmental powers. The ambit of this ground for judicial review has been expanding in recent years, in particular beyond the old category of "quasi-judicial" functions. The effect of a breach of procedural fairness is to render the delegate's actions void, that is, the error is jurisdictional in nature, and should not be insulated from judicial review by either a privative clause or the recently developed judicial deference towards intra-jurisdictional errors of law which are not "patently unreasonable". Many questions still remain, such as the procedural requirements for the exercise of a legislative power, the amenability of cabinet decisions to judicial review, and the actual content of procedural fairness in particular circumstances. The courts will therefore still be very active in this area, but may be able to perform their supervisory function better by asking the question: "Is this procedure fair?"

207a See chapter 10, Errors of Law.

208 See, *e.g.*, *Anisminic, supra*, note 198; *Bell, supra*, note 199; *Toronto Newspaper Guild v. Globe Printing Co.*, [1953] 2 S.C.R. 18. *Cf. Pringle v. Fraser*, [1972] S.C.R. 821.

209 *Harelkin v. Univ. of Regina*, [1979] 2 S.C.R. 561, and *Bridgeland-Riverside Community Assn. v. Calgary*, (1982) 19 Alta. L.R. (2d) 361 (C.A.).

10. The Content of *Audi Alteram Partem* and Fairness

(a) Generally

The content of the *audi alteram partem* principle is difficult to determine in particular circumstances, and what fairness requires has altered over time and circumstance.[210]

At the very least, the rule requires that the parties affected be given adequate notice of the case to be met, the right to bring evidence and to make argument. The application of this procedure to administrative tribunals is an obvious transplant from the courts which reflects the historical fact that justices of the peace did much of the administration of government, and so naturally followed similar procedures in both areas of their jurisdiction.

The rule is an ancient one, known in Greek and even biblical times.[211] It certainly made an appearance in English common law by the 17th century,[212] and often appeared thereafter in cases having to do with restoration to offices. It extended to ecclesiastical matters, to societies and clubs, and later to protect members of trade unions from unfair expulsion. As administrative tribunals proliferated in the 19th and 20th centuries, they were required to follow the same rules of fair procedure as their predecessors, the justices of the peace. The identity of the person who exercised the power was not decisive; rather, what mattered was the character of the power being exercised. If it affected a person's rights and interests, then the power had to be exercised in a fair manner. The subsequent error into which courts fell in determining when the rule was to be applied has been previously described.[213] Just as the rule suffered an eclipse in application in the first part of this century but is now once more in vigorous health, so the content of the rule has ebbed and flowed with the judicial tides.

Two cases illustrate the full force with which the courts have applied the rule to administrative bodies. In 1863, in *Cooper v. Wandsworth Board of Works*,[214] the board was required to proceed judicially and at the very least to have given Mr. Cooper notice of its intention to demolish his house and to have allowed him to be heard on the matter, even though it was exercising an administrative power. This was said to do "substantial justice"[215] and to be "founded on the plainest principles of justice".[216] Indeed, the court asserted

---

210 For an extremely thorough collection of Canadian cases on most aspects of *audi alteram partem* and fairness, see R.F. Reid and H. David *Administrative Law and Practice*, 2nd ed. (Butterworths, 1978), pp. 49-104.

211 In classical Roman law the judge who made a suit his own was liable in *quasi-delict* to the party damnified (Justinian, Inst. 4,5 pr. Justinian, Codex 3.5.1.); see de Smith, *Judicial Review of Administrative Actions*, 4th ed. (1980), p. 248.

212 *Bagg's Case*, (1615) 11 Co.Rep. 93b, concerning the disfranchisement of a freeman for insulting the mayor of Plymouth.

213 *Supra*, section 2.

214 (1863) 143 E.R. 414.

215 *Ibid.*, per Earle C.J., p. 417.

216 *Ibid.*, per Willes J., p. 418.

that where legislation had overlooked adherence to the rule "the justice of the common law will supply the omission of the legislature".[217] Adopting the same approach 90 years later, the Supreme Court of Canada in *Alliance des Professeurs Catholiques de Montréal v. Labour Relations Board of Quebec*[218] held that the principle that no one could be deprived of his rights without being heard and above all without at least being given notice that his rights were being put at risk was "d'une équité universelle et ce n'est pas le silence de la loi qui devrait être invoqué pour en priver quelqu'un".[219] The general law required notice in such cases and express legislative provisions would be required before this principle would be ignored.

(b) The Requirement of a Hearing

The *Cooper*[220] and *Alliance*[221] cases indicate the courts' recognition of the long established rule of common law that a person has a right to know and answer any case to be made against him, whether in a traditional judicial setting or in administrative regulation. In the early 20th century, many areas of activity came to be regulated specifically by statutes. Many of these statutes also contained procedural provisions concerning notice and the right to a hearing. The courts then had to face the question of how far these provisions had gone in replacing the common law: did the absence of procedural provisions in the statute mean that the tribunal was absolute master of its own procedure, or did the common law still operate? If the common law did still operate, to what extent did it supplement the incomplete statutory code of procedure? The question arose at a time when there was great statutory activity to regulate many aspects of citizens' lives which had not previously been the subject of government intervention. It was a time when laissez-faire had been replaced with state interference, considered to be in the interest of the greater public good. In England, this was very apparent in the areas of slum clearance and health legislation. The courts' decisions of those times reflect a reluctance to interfere in this great public enterprise, where the interest of the many gained paramountcy over the rights of individuals.

(i) The Arlidge case

As discussed previously, the case of *Local Government Board v. Arlidge*[222] was the turning point at which administrative efficiency gained the day over individual rights.

The conflicting opinions in the Court of Appeal illustrate clearly the two

---

217 *Ibid.*, per Byles J., p. 420.
218 [1953] 2 S.C.R. 140.
219 *Ibid.*, per Rinfret C.J., p. 154.
220 *Supra*, note 214.
221 *Supra*, note 218.
222 [1915] A.C. 120 (H.L.).

opposing principles which the House of Lords was called upon to resolve — and which did so, wrongly as it turned out. On the one hand, two of the judges felt that administrative decision-makers must be guided, but not bound, by procedures analogous to those used in the court room, in the absence of express legislative direction to the contrary. On the other hand, the third judge held that this analogy was displaced by the statutory scheme of procedure laid down in the 1909 Act. Viscount Haldane L.C., speaking for the House of Lords, summarized the problem as follows:[223]

> Here, as in other cases, we have simply to construe that language and to abstain from guessing at what Parliament had in its mind, excepting so far as the language enables us to do so. There is no doubt that the question is one affecting property and the liberty of a man to do what he chooses with what is his own. Such rights are not to be affected unless Parliament has said so. But Parliament, in what it considers higher interests than those of the individual, has so often interfered with such rights on other occasions, that it is dangerous for judges to lay much stress on what a hundred years ago would have been a presumption considerably stronger than it is to-day.

For Lord Haldane, the crucial part of the 1909 legislation was that Parliament had replaced the previous appeal procedure to courts of law by an appeal procedure to an administrative body, the Local Government Board. The substance of the legislation — the power to close dwelling houses considered unfit for habitation or dangerous or injurious to health — was an old jurisdiction. But the 1909 Act embodied the change of principle that the procedure as to everything, including costs, was solely in the discretion of the board to determine by *its* rules. The statute required the holding of a public local inquiry but set down no other procedural requirements. The consequences of this change of policy, in Lord Haldane's view, was that the procedure laid down by the administrative tribunal in question must be taken to have replaced the previous "judicial" character of the procedure. Nevertheless, in so proceeding, a tribunal must still have an eye to[224]

> deal with the question referred to them without bias, and they must give to each of the parties the opportunity of adequately presenting the case made. The decision must be come to in the spirit and with the sense of responsibility of a tribunal whose duty it is to mete out justice. But it does not follow that the procedure of every such tribunal must be the same. In the case of a Court of law tradition in this country has prescribed certain principles to which in the main the procedure must conform. But what that procedure is to be in

---

223 *Ibid.*, pp. 130-31.
224 *Ibid.*, p. 132, emphasis added.

detail must depend *on the nature of the tribunal*. In modern times it has become increasingly common for Parliament to give an appeal in matters which really pertain to administration, rather than to the exercise of the judicial functions of an ordinary Court, to authorities whose functions are administrative and not in the ordinary sense judicial. Such a body as the Local Government Board has the duty of enforcing obligations on the individual which are imposed in the interests of the community. Its character is that of an organization with executive functions. In this it resembles other great departments of State. When, therefore, Parliament entrusts it with judicial duties, Parliament must be taken, in the absence of any declaration to the contrary, to have intended it to follow the procedure which is its own and is necessary if it is to be capable of doing its work efficiently.

In other words, Lord Haldane relied on the *Rice* decision[225] to hold that an administrative tribunal had a duty to act in good faith and to listen fairly to both sides, but not to treat the question as if it were a trial. There would be no need to examine under oath, nor even to examine witnesses at all. Any other procedure could be utilized which would obtain the information required, as long as the parties had an opportunity to know and to contradict anything which might be prejudicial to their case.

In *Arlidge*, the board had appointed one of its health inspectors to hold a public inquiry, all in accordance with its rules and usual practice. The health inspector's report was not disclosed to Arlidge. Lord Haldane felt that the board was not bound to do so. Although Arlidge and his solicitor had attended the local inquiry and adduced evidence on his behalf there, the inspector submitted his reports and shorthand notes of the proceedings to the board, which then made its decision. Arlidge did not know what was in the report, and therefore had no opportunity "to correct or contradict any relevant statement prejudicial to [his] view".[226] This procedure flies directly in the face of one of Lord Haldane's own principles for the proper procedure to be followed by an administrative tribunal. How, then, he could say that the board was not bound to disclose the report is hard to explain, except in the overriding interests of administrative efficiency and the usual government reaction to keep all its documents secret. Certainly Lord Shaw had this in mind:[227]

> I incline to hold that the disadvantage in very many cases would exceed the advantage of such disclosure [of the inspector's report]. And I feel certain that if it were laid down in courts of law that such disclosure could be compelled, a serious impediment might be placed upon that frankness which ought to obtain among a staff

---

225 *Bd. of Educ. v. Rice*, [1911] A.C. 179 (H.L.).
226 *Supra*, note 222 at p. 133.
227 *Ibid.*, p. 137.

accustomed to elaborately detailed and often most delicate and difficult tasks. The very same argument would lead to the disclosure of
the whole file. It may contain, and frequently does contain, the views
of inspectors, secretaries, assistants and consultants of various
degrees of experience, many of whose opinions may differ but all of
which form the material for the ultimate decision. To set up any rule
that that decision must on demand, and as a matter of right, be
accompanied by a disclosure of what went before, so that it may be
weakened or strengthened or judged thereby would be inconsistent,
as I say, with efficiency, with practice, and with the true theory of
complete parliamentary responsibility for departmental action. This
is, in my opinion, implied as the legitimate and proper consequence
of any department being vested by statute with authority to make
determinations.

This obvious unfairness was rectified by statute some years later in
England as a result of the Franks Committee Report.[228] Inspectors' reports
must now be published, thus removing an overwhelming reason to sense
unfairness. It is interesting to observe that none of the horrors painted by
government ministries as being attendant upon such publication would
appear to have been realized. On the contrary, disclosure has led to a great
deal of good and the public has come to have confidence in the fairness of
inspectors' reports.

In summary, the content of the rule that there be notice and a fair hearing
in *Arlidge* was:

(a) the procedure to be followed need not have the rigour of proceedings in a
court of law; the administrative tribunal may set its own rules;
(b) in setting its own rules, however, there can be no bias;
(c) each party must have an adequate opportunity to present his case;
(d) the tribunal must act in a spirit of responsible justice-giving;
(e) the goal of efficiency is a good reason to deviate from strict procedural
fairness;
(f) evidence need not be given through witnesses, nor need witnesses be
sworn. Evidence may be adduced through any method as long as the
parties have an opportunity to contradict prejudicial evidence;
(g) it is not necessary that the decision-maker be a given and known
individual;
(h) the decision-maker need not hear a party personally — the tribunal can
act through an agent whose decision becomes the tribunal's decision;
(i) the tribunal must act justly and honestly through just and honest means or
the statutory means if they are express.

---

228 Cmnd. 218 (1957; Eng.).

(ii) The Errington case

The content of the hearing required by the *audi alteram partem* rule was refined through a series of cases in the 1930's also dealing with housing matters. The leading case is *Errington v. Minister of Health*.[229]

Under the authority of the 1930 Housing Act,[230] the Jarrow Corporation made a clearance order of certain houses in its area and submitted the order to the Minister of Health for confirmation. As required by the Act, the local authority published notice of its order and served it upon the owners of the affected properties, including Mr. Errington. He and others raised several objections, including the alleged unfitness in fact of the houses for habitation; the expense of the clearance being more than the local authority could bear; the lack of alternative accommodation for those who would be displaced; and demolition not being the most satisfactory method of dealing with the housing conditions. In short, it was Errington's position that the houses could be renovated and repaired and thus be made fit for human habitation.

As required by the Act, a public local inquiry was held by an inspector appointed by the minister. During the course of the inquiry, it was suggested that there might be agreement between the local authority and the owners on the idea of repairing the houses instead of pulling them down, and negotiations proceeded on this basis. Meetings were held and the ministry suggested to the local authority that repair was the right way to proceed. It entirely disagreed and asked the minister to receive a deputation from the town council to reiterate its submission that only demolition would properly deal with the matter.

The minister refused to do this because of the quasi-judicial function which he had to exercise in the situation. He therefore could not hear a deputation from one side only. Subsequently, however, officials from the ministry visited Jarrow and inspected the area together with officials from the local authority in the absence of representatives of the owners. Later the town council wrote to the minister to say that their decision to demolish was unchanged and furthermore, the town engineer advised that repair was impractical and in any event impossible because the foundations and structure of the houses were such as to preclude the possibility of reconstruction. The borough engineer had not given evidence at the local inquiry and therefore the owners had had no opportunity to cross-examine him on this opinion. Indeed, they did not even know that this opinion had been given.

Having received the confirmation he sought that the local authority could bear the expense of the clearance order, the minister then decided to confirm the order and this was duly published. Errington took the matter to court on the following grounds:

(a) the minister's order was *ultra vires* the Act;

---

229 [1935] 1 K.B. 249 (C.A.).
230 1930 (20 & 21 Geo. 5, c. 39).

(b) the requirements of the Act had not been complied with and Errington
    was thereby substantially prejudiced in that between the date of the public
    inquiry and the minister's confirmation, the minister and the town council
    had met and discussed the matter, had inspected the area and communi-
    cated in writing, all without giving notice to Errington, without affording
    him an opportunity to attend or see the written communications, and
    without affording him an opportunity to reply;
(c) the implied requirements of the Act had not been complied with, because
    the minister had to consider the objections of the appellants fairly and
    properly, and to give a fair and proper effect to the result of such con-
    sideration in deciding whether or not to confirm the clearance order.

The action was dismissed at first instance[231] on the ground that the minister was not acting as a judge under the Act, deciding an issue between two
parties. Rather he was acting as an administrative officer with a statutory duty
to perform, which was imposed on him by the legislature for the benefit of the
community. So long as he complied with all the explicit statutory requirements governing his conduct in dealing with objections (that is, that he hold a
local inquiry and consider the objections and the report of the inspector), then
the minister could further inform himself howsoever he wished and reach his
decision in any way which seemed reasonable to him. As such the court held
that the Minister had acted *intra vires*.

The Court of Appeal, however, distinguished between those situations
where no objections are taken to a clearance order and those where there are
objections. In the former case, where the minister confirms the order, he is
acting in a ministerial or administrative capacity and his inquiries would be
confined to a consideration of whether the order was in the public interest or
not. By contrast, however, where the minister has to decide whether to
confirm a closing order in the face of objections, then his function would be
quasi-judicial because it related to the rights of the objecting parties (in this
case by greatly diminishing their property values). Were the court only dealing
with the common law, Greer L.J. had no doubt that *certiorari* should have
been granted.[232]

However, the Court of Appeal had to determine the extent to which this
common law result would be affected by the specific provisions of the statute
governing the power to issue the clearance order. After all, the House of Lords
in *Arlidge*[233] had recently recognized the right of Parliament to enact legislation which derogated from the common law rules of procedure applicable to
quasi-judicial decisions. This approach had been taken further in the *Rice*[234]
case (which involved an administrative tribunal exercising statutory authority)

---

231 Unreported.
232 *Supra*, note 229 at pp. 264-65.
233 [1915] A.C. 120 (H.L.).
234 *Supra*, note 225.

and in the *Electricity Commissioners*[235] case (where the courts considered the applicability of *certiorari* to quasi-judicial tribunals which were not, strictly speaking, courts).

The 1930 Act contained very specific provisions which restricted the courts' power to review clearance orders issued thereunder. These concerned publication of the notice of the minister's confirmation of a clearance order by the local authority; a time limit within which objectors could apply to the court on questions of *ultra vires* and failure to comply with procedural requirements; and a power in the court to quash the decision if it were *ultra vires* or if a failure to comply with a procedural requirement had substantially prejudiced the interests of the applicant. The latter limited the court's powers to quash for any failure to comply with the statutory procedures, and restricted it to the circumstance only where the failure had also had a prejudicial effect on the applicant.

In determining that the minister was acting quasi-judicially, the Court of Appeal defined this to mean that although he was not in the position of a judge having to hold a judicial proceeding, he must nevertheless determine the material law and the facts in the same way as the Board of Education in *Rice*[236] had to do and must proceed as the court found that board had to do. The quasi-judicial characterization was appropriate because here there was a true contest — or *lis inter partes*[237] between two parties who formed the two sides between whom the Minister had to decide. The public local inquiry afforded the parties the opportunity for evidence to be given and cross-examined upon during which "the ordinary principles of fair play have to be observed".[238] To base a decision on *ex parte* evidence was *ultra vires* the authority of the

---

235 *R. v. Elec. Commr.; Ex parte London Elec. Joint Ctee. Co.*, [1924] 1 K.B. 171 (C.A.).

236 [1911] A.C. 179 (H.L.).

237 What Wade calls "the doctrine of the *lis*" only operated once objections were lodged and the *lis* arose. Before that time, the courts refused to set aside orders on the ground that the minister had dealt with the local authority exclusively *(Frost v. Min. of Health*, [1935] 1 K.B. 286) or failed to disclose documents or advice available in the department before objections were filed and upon which he subsequently based his decision (*Errington v. Min. of Health*, [1935] 1 K.B. 249). This was based on a consideration of both the administrative and quasi-judicial duties imposed on the minister by Parliament, which must have deliberately decided that the two functions were compatible. However, once the quasi-judicial state was reached, the courts consistently required that natural justice be observed.

Wade also discusses the difficulties faced by a ministry when it must act as if it were an independent judge. In reality the central and local authorities should be working together and the doctrine of the *lis* is especially weak when the schemes originate with the ministry since then there is no triangle. The absurdity of this was seen in *Re Trunk Roads Act, 1936*, [1939] 2 K.B. 515 ("the Kingston By-pass case"). At the public local inquiry the Minister of Transport, whose scheme it was, read a statement of the proposals and produced plans and documents but produced no witnesses and refused to deal with the objections, and would not answer the objectors' questions. Nevertheless, the courts held this to be a valid public inquiry since its only object was to hear objections, not to call evidence from the ministry. This unfair situation was again dealt with by the Franks Committee.

238 *Supra*, note 229, per Maugham L.J., p. 272.

Minister under the statute.[239] Only the plainest legislative language could permit this procedure; no such language existed. Accordingly, this procedural error was amendable to *certiorari*, and the Court of Appeal quashed the clearance order.

(iii) The Franklin case

The total dilution of what constitutes a "hearing" occurred in *Franklin v. Minister of Town and Country Planning*.[240]

Stevenage was designated as one of the first "new towns" in England after the Second World War. There were strong objections to this and a public inquiry was held. The Minister considered the inspector's report and confirmed the designation order. However, before the inquiry the Minister had visited Stevenage to make a speech during which he told the jeering crowd "It is no good your jeering: it is going to be done". The objectors said that this showed that the Minister's mind was made up beforehand and therefore he could not consider the inspector's report fairly and in an unbiased fashion, and applied to have his decision quashed. The first court held that the law required an impartial consideration and that this had not been given. The Court of Appeal agreed that the law required an impartial consideration, but held that it had been given. The House of Lords, however, held that no impartial consideration was necessary; as long as he followed the statutory procedures, the Minister could be as biased as he wished. Thus, the contents of natural justice were completely diluted by the statutory procedure — to the extent that the House held that the Minister's function was purely administrative and not quasi-judicial in nature.

(iv) The long retreat

Subsequently, the courts further emasculated the rule (from their position in *Franklin* that natural justice did not apply to an administrative decision taken pursuant to statutory procedures) to hold that natural justice did not apply even where there were no statutory procedures. The common law rule was thus finally ousted. Wade says[241] that this arose from "verbal confusion". The courts relied on the premise that if a function were administrative, it could not be judicial or quasi-judicial, and therefore the principles of natural justice did not apply. In so doing they used the term "administrative" in a contrasting sense from judicial or legislative, whereas the term quasi-judicial had previously been invented to apply to all decisions taken in the administration of government in its broadest sense.

---

239 Although Roche L.J. would have allowed an exception to this if it could be shown that what was done by the minister after the inquiry had reference to matters of high policy or finance, not to matters which were the subject matter of the inquiry.

240 [1948] A.C. 87 (H.L.).

241 *Administrative Law*, 5th ed. (1982), p. 436 *ff.*

Such "logic" led to the decisions in cases such as *Nakkuda Ali v. Jayaratne*[242] and *R. v. Metropolitan Police Commissioner; Ex parte Parker*,[243] where people were denied the right to a fair hearing, even though no specific legislation existed to abridge this common law right. Accordingly, little debate could arise as to the content of a fair hearing if no hearing at all was required for the exercise of a "merely administrative" power!

(v) The resurrection: the Gaming Board case

By the time that *R. v. Gaming Board for Great Britain; Ex parte Benaim and Khaida*[244] came before the English Court of Appeal, the decision by the House of Lords in *Ridge v. Baldwin*[245] had corrected the error that only quasi-judicial proceedings attracted the principles of natural justice. In the *Gaming Board* case, the court began the long struggle to define the contents of the rule as applied to all types of governmental actions, whether "judicial", "quasi-judicial" or "merely administrative".

Two French nationals applied to the gaming board for a certificate of consent, which would have allowed them to apply for a licence for the premises of a gaming club in London, Crockford's. The granting of such a certificate was an indication that the person was to be trusted. The licence allowed the operation of a gaming house where gaming could take place without hindrance.

The hearing lasted four hours. The applicants were refused the opportunity to have counsel represent them. The board had acquired much information about Crockford's, the source and content of which was not disclosed to the applicants. They were asked many questions which they answered and were invited to provide any further information they wished, in writing, which they did. In the end, the board refused the certificate. Attempts by the applicants to find out why they were unsuccessful were to no avail, although they were invited to make further submissions. Nevertheless, the board again confirmed its decision, without giving reasons. The applicants moved for *certiorari* and *mandamus* — the first to quash the decision, the second to require the board to give sufficient information so that the applicants would know and could answer the case against them. They alleged that the board had acted unfairly in a manner which would deprive them of their valuable rights of property.

The Court of Appeal considered to what extent the board was bound by the rules of natural justice and noted that the legislation gave the board power to regulate its own procedures. The board's procedures gave an applicant an opportunity to make representations to the board, which would give the best

---

242 [1951] A.C. 66 (P.C.).
243 [1953] 1 W.L.R. 1150.
244 [1970] 2 Q.B. 417 (C.A.).
245 [1964] A.C. 40 (H.L.).

indications possible of the matters which were troubling it. However, where
the source or content of information which the board had was confidential,
the board treated itself as obliged to withhold particulars where their disclosure would be a breach of confidence inconsistent with its statutory duty
and the public interest. Within these confines, the board would advise the
applicant of the matters troubling it.

Despite their counsel's strong urging that this procedure deprived the
applicants of a property right or a right to make a living, Lord Denning M.R.
held that they had no property right of which they were now being deprived.
Rather they were seeking a privilege to carry on gaming for profit, not hitherto
allowed in Britain, and they had to demonstrate they were fit to be trusted with
it. Accordingly, the board's function was not quasi-judicial in the sense used
by the House of Lords in *Franklin*'s case. Nevertheless, the board was not free
to grant or refuse a certificate as it pleased. The board was bound to observe
the rules of natural justice. The real question was the content of those rules.
On this, Lord Denning said:[246]

> It is not possible to lay down rigid rules as to when the prin-
> ciples of natural justice are to apply: nor as to their scope and extent.
> Everything depends on the subject-matter . . . At one time it was said
> that the principles only apply to judicial proceedings and not to
> administrative proceedings. That heresy was scotched in *Ridge v.
> Baldwin* . . . At another time it was said that the principles do not
> apply to the grant or revocation of licences. That too is wrong. *Reg.
> v. Metropolitan Police Commissioner, Ex parte Parker* . . . and
> *Nakkuda Ali v. Jayaratne* . . . are no longer authority for any such
> proposition. . . .
>
> So let us sheer away from those distinctions and consider the
> task of this Gaming Board and what they should do.

Accordingly, the court found that the applicants had a right to be heard
and to have an opportunity to satisfy the tribunal on the matters to which the
statute required the board to have regard. The tribunal had to reveal its
impressions and allow the applicants the opportunity to disabuse the board.
This did not mean that it need "quote chapter and verse against him as if they
were dismissing him from an office . . . or depriving him of his property".[247]
The board was required to inquire into character, reputation, capability, dili-
gence, and financial standing to determine fitness to run a gaming club and to
protect the public interest.

In discharging this duty, the board could obtain information which
would often be confidential. An applicant had to be given a chance to answer
it, subject to the qualification that he need not be told the source if that would
imperil the informant or be contrary to the public interest. (Experience had

---

246 *Supra*, note 244 at p. 430.
247 *Ibid.*

shown that certain disreputable gaming clubs had links with organized crime and no informer would inform if he feared reprisals.) The board was also not bound to disclose every detail as this would again imperil the informer, but sufficient indications of the objections were to be given to allow the applicant to answer them for "[t]hat is only fair. And the board must at all costs be fair. If they are not, these courts will not hesitate to interfere."[248]

(c) Notice of the Hearing

It is obviously impossible to give a fair hearing to a person who has no notice whatever of the action which a statutory delegate proposes to take. Conversely, it is not always possible to effect personal service of actual notice on every person who might potentially be affected by government action. Accordingly, the question often arises whether a person has been given proper notice so that he can participate effectively in administrative procedures affecting him.

Many statutes contain express provisions about how notice is to be given, to whom, and what it shall contain. For example, section 139(2) of the Planning Act[249] is quite specific in requiring a municipal council to give notice of its intention to pass certain types of land use by-laws:

> 139(2) A council shall give written notice to each owner of land that is the subject of a proposed amendment to a land use by-law and summarize its effect.
>
> (3) In addition to the notice to owners required under subsection (2), if any, the council shall
>
> (a) name the one or more dates, places and times it will hold a public hearing with respect to the proposed by-law and provide for the holding of any further public hearings it considers necessary;
>
> (b) outline the procedure to be followed by anyone wishing to be heard at the public hearing;
>
> (c) outline the procedure by which the public hearing will be conducted;
>
> (d) direct the publication in 2 issues of a newspaper circulating in the area to which the proposed by-law relates a notice containing
>
> (i) a statement of the purpose of the proposed by-law;
>
> (ii) the name of one or more places, one of which shall be the office of the council, where
>
> (A) a copy of the proposed by-law, and

---

248 *Ibid.*, p. 431.
249 R.S.A. 1980, c. P-9.

> (B) the documents that a person is entitled to inspect under section 151 of the *Municipal Government Act* and that relate to the proposed by-law,
>
> may be inspected by the public;
> (iii) the one or more dates, places and times the council will hold a public hearing with respect to the proposed by-law;
> (iv) an outline of the procedures referred to in clauses (b) and (c).

Thus, this provision requires actual written notice to be given to each owner of land affected by the proposed re-zoning, and the notice must contain quite detailed information about the way in which the council will proceed to consider the proposed amendments.

Sometimes, however, the statute may relieve the delegate from the obligation to give actual notice of proceedings, permitting a much more general form of publication as, for example, is contemplated in section 43 of the Public Utilities Board Act:[250]

> 43(1) A notice with regard to a matter before or to come before the Board and required or authorized to be given in writing
>
> (*a*) by the Board, may be signed by the chairman, any other member of the Board, or the secretary,
> (*b*) by any person appointed by the Board, may be signed by that person, or
> (*c*) by any other person, may be signed by that other person or his authorized agent or solicitor.
>
> (2) A notice required to be given to a company, a municipal or other corporation, co-partnership, firm or individual, shall be deemed to be sufficiently given by delivering it, or a copy thereof, within the time, if any, limited therefor,
>
> (*a*) in the case of a municipal corporation, to the head of the municipality or to the clerk or secretary,
> (*b*) in the case of any other corporation or company, to the president, vice-president, manager or secretary or to some adult person in its employ at its head office or chief place of business within Alberta,
> (*c*) in the case of a firm or co-partnership, to any member thereof or, at the last known place of abode of any member, to any adult member of his household or, at the office or place of business of the firm, to a clerk employed therein, and

---

250 R.S.A. 1980, c. P-37, emphasis added.

(*d*) in the case of an individual, to him or, at his last known place of abode, to any adult member of his household or, at his office or place of business, to a clerk of his employ.

(3) *if, in a case within the jurisdiction of the Board, it is made to appear to the satisfaction of the Board that service of the notice cannot conveniently be made in the manner provided in subsection (2), the Board may order and allow service to be made by publication in The Alberta Gazette or by publication in a local newspaper, and that publication in each case shall be deemed to be equivalent to service in the manner provided in subsection (2).*

(4) In contentious matters, the Board may require such notice of an application to or hearing by the Board to be given, as it considers requisite.

In the absence of a specific statutory prescription, the general rule is that an administrator must give adequate notice to permit an affected person to know how he might be affected, and to prepare himself adequately to make representations.[251] The exact content of this requirement may be difficult to determine without litigation. Nevertheless, the effect of inadequate or no notice will be to render the delegate's actions void.[252] On the other hand, a person may in some circumstances have an obligation to take reasonable steps to inform himself about proceedings,[253] and certainly cannot use a formal defect in giving notice to attack the validity of proceedings which he in fact knew about.[254] As in most areas of natural justice, the test is whether the alleged lack of notice is so unfair that the proceedings in question should be set aside by the courts.

(d) Knowing the Case to be Met

The courts have consistently held that a fair hearing can only be had if the person affected by the tribunal's decision knows the case to be made against him. Only in this circumstance can he correct evidence prejudicial to his case and bring his own evidence to prove his position. Without knowing what might be said against him, no one can properly present his case. But knowing the case that must be met is not enough, of course: the opportunity to present the other side of the matter must also be allowed. In the *Errington* case,[255] the fact that there had been representations made to the Minister in the absence of

---

251 See the discussion and cases referred to on this point in R.F. Reid and H. David, *Administrative Law and Practice*, 2nd ed. (Butterworths, 1978), pp. 63-70.

252 *Wiswell v. Winnipeg*, [1965] S.C.R. 512.

253 *Tomko v. Lab. Rel. Bd. (N.S.).*, (1975) 9 N.S.R. (2d) 277; affirmed [1977] 1 S.C.R. 112; *Hretchka v. A.G. B.C.*, [1972] S.C.R. 119.

254 Particularly if he waives the right to object to the defect: *Camac Exploration Ltd. v. Oil & Gas Conservation Bd. of Alta.*, (1964) 47 W.W.R. 81 (Alta. T.D.).

255 *Errington v. Min. of Health*, [1935] 1 K.B. 249 (C.A.).

Errington and that an engineer's report had been given to the Minister without making it available to the other side was sufficient for the court to strike down the Minister's decision. The error of the court in *Arlidge*[256] (in failing to allow Arlidge to know the contents of the inspector's report) should not recur, at least in England, since the reforms enacted after the Franks Committee Report.

Nevertheless, there are limits to the requirement of full disclosure. For instance, in the *Gaming Board* case,[257] the intention of the Act under which the tribunal was operating required that the sources of the board's information not be disclosed. To do otherwise would prejudice the operation of the Act. Instead the board was to give sufficient indications of the objections to enable the person affected to answer them.

(i) The Lazarov case

A further example of the limits on disclosure can be found in *Lazarov v. Secretary of State of Canada*[258] where the Federal Court of Appeal set aside the Secretary of State's decision to refuse a certificate of citizenship to Lazarov on the grounds that he had not been advised of pertinent facts alleged against him, so that he had no opportunity to reply to them.

The Canadian Citizenship Act[259] set out several requirements which an applicant had to satisfy before the Citizenship Court could make a finding that the applicant was a fit and proper person to be granted Canadian citizenship. However, the Act also gave a discretion to the minister whether or not to grant the citizenship and in this case the minister refused on the basis of "confidential information recently provided by the Royal Canadian Mounted Police".[260] Lazarov had been given no opportunity to be heard with respect to this information, the contents of which he also did not know.

Lazarov argued that the *audi alteram partem* rule applied so as to entitle him to know this information and to make a reply to it. For the minister, it was submitted that his function was purely administrative in character, and since Lazarov had no right to the certificate and no existing right was being affected or interfered with by the minister's decision, the *audi alteram partem* rule did not apply at all.

On the question of rights, Thurlow J. found for the court that the distinction between a situation where existing rights were affected, as opposed to a situation which would create rights, made no critical difference to the principle involved. Rather the question to be determined was whether the function of the minister, although plainly administrative in nature, neverthe-

---

256 *Loc. Govt. Bd. v. Arlidge*, [1915] A.C. 120 (H.L.).
257 *R. v. Gaming Board for Great Britain; Ex parte Benaim and Khaida*, [1970] 2 Q.B. 417 (C.A.).
258 (1973), 39 D.L.R. (3d) 738 (Fed. C.A.).
259 R.S.C. 1970, c. C-19 [see now S.C. 1974-75-76, c. 108].
260 *Supra*, note 258 at p. 740.

less required him to exercise his power on a quasi-judicial basis. His Lordship relied[261] on the following passage from Lord Upjohn's judgment in *Durayappah v. Fernando*[262] to formulate a test:

> Outside the well-known classes of cases, no general rule can be laid down as to the application of the general principle in addition to the language of the provision. In their Lordships' opinion there are three matters which must always be borne in mind when considering whether the principle should be applied or not. These three matters are: first, what is the nature of the property, the office held, status enjoyed or services to be performed by the complainant of injustice. Secondly, in what circumstances or upon what occasions is the person claiming to be entitled to exercise the measure of control entitled to intervene. Thirdly, when a right to intervene is proved, what sanctions in fact is the latter entitled to impose upon the other. It is only upon a consideration of all these matters that the question of the application of the principle can properly be determined. Their Lordships therefore proceed to examine the facts of this case upon these considerations.

Referring to these three considerations, Thurlow J. held, on the first, that the question of entitlement to Canadian citizenship was of great importance to the person involved. Although the grant of citizenship was in the discretion of the minister on facts determinable by him, nevertheless His Lordship thought that the applicant had some right to be heard:[263]

> In these instances the whole question is thus for him to decide and it seems to me that the right to a hearing for such applicants with respect to all the problems arising upon their applications is clearly to be implied. It would therefore, as I see it, involve no great departure from a course required in such instances nor would it do violence to the language of s-s. 10(1) if a right to answer were implied in respect of facts or information considered to warrant refusal of the application under that provision and particularly so in the case of matters upon which the Citizenship Court has not been called upon to pass.

Given the nature of citizenship and its importance to the individual, he should at least have been given an opportunity to dispute the existence of the grounds of refusal peculiar to him.

On the second consideration concerning when the minister might be entitled to exercise his discretion, the statute in question provided a very broad and unfettered discretion. It arose whenever an application was made.

---

261 *Supra*, note 258 at p. 744.
262 [1967] 2 A.C. 337 at 349 (P.C.).
263 *Supra*, note 258 at p. 747.

However, the width of the minister's discretion did not necessarily determine the procedure which he could adopt to exercise it. If the minister were to consider other facts apart from those appearing on the application, the applicant was to be given an opportunity to be heard with respect to them, prior to the exercise of the minister's admittedly unfettered discretion.

Thirdly, the sanction which could be imposed here was not a case of deprivation but rather more of a delay of the rights and advantages which citizenship confers. Nevertheless, His Lordship held that this did not excuse the lack of a fair hearing:[264]

> It is not a case of depriving a person of his property and it is true that the applicant can apply again after two years, but the status of citizenship carries with it rights and advantages and to refuse the application of a person to whom it would otherwise be granted on the basis of matters of which he is not apprised and which he is given no opportunity to dispute is shocking to one's sense of justice, even though he may lawfully apply again after a comparatively short time. It suggests that the applicant is not being fairly dealt with and that fairness demands that he at least be afforded an opportunity to state his position on them. . . .
>
> In my opinion, therefore, the rule *audi alteram partem* applies whenever the Minister proposes to exercise his discretion to refuse an application on the basis of facts pertaining to the particular applicant or his application and where he has not already had an opportunity in the course of the proceedings before the Citizenship Court he must be afforded a fair opportunity in one way or another of stating his position with respect to any matters which in the absence of refutation or explanation would lead to the rejection of his application. That is not to say that a confidential report or its contents need be disclosed to him but the pertinent allegations which if undenied or unresolved would lead to rejection of his application must, as I see it, be made known to him to an extent sufficient to enable him to respond to them and he must have a fair opportunity to dispute or explain them.

(ii) The Saltfleet case

The exclusion of an applicant or party from the hearing will obviously result in his not knowing the case to be met and having no opportunity to reply, thereby breaching the *audi alteram partem* rule too.

This problem arose in *Saltfleet Board of Health v. Knapman*,[265] where the Supreme Court of Canada considered the proper procedure to be followed by a local board of health in the exercise of its power to force occupants to vacate

---

264 *Ibid.*, pp. 749-50.
265 [1956] S.C.R. 877.

unfit premises. The board delivered the required notices to vacate but then, when it met to discuss the matter, refused to hear the submissions of the owner and several of the occupants who had attended the meeting in order to ascertain the nature of the complaints and to make submissions in answer to them. The board denied them any hearing at all. The board maintained that its action was administrative in nature and not quasi-judicial, so that no hearing was required.

The court found that, under the provisions of the enabling legislation, the board was required, as a condition precedent to the exercise of its authority, to be satisfied that buildings were unfit or a nuisance or dangerous to health in some way. Once so satisfied, the board could proceed to issue its order to vacate. In deciding whether or not a condition of unfitness existed, the court held that the board was required to act judicially and that only very plain words in the statute could oust this requirement. There were none and therefore the board was required to give the occupants an opportunity to know the case against them and to give an answer to the allegations. Since this had not been done, *certiorari* was issued to quash the eviction notices.

(e) Cross-examination of Witnesses

The rules of natural justice do not require that a hearing be oral.[266] However, when an oral hearing is held, rather than a hearing based solely on written submissions and documents, generally the right to call witnesses and to cross-examine them is part of the procedure protected by the rules of natural justice. Of course, even in the case of a written "hearing", the parties must know the case being made by the opposing side and be given an opportunity to reply in written form.

In *R. v. Deputy Industrial Injuries Commissioner; Ex parte Moore*,[267] Diplock L.J. listed certain rules for the tribunal. He first confirmed that, in the absence of any statutory requirement, a hearing need not be held. In that case, a delegate *must* consider all written material submitted to him, including the written decision of the lower tribunal which is being appealed. He *may* also consider material from other sources which constitutes "evidence". Such "evidence" is

> not restricted to evidence which would be admissible in a court of law. For historical reasons, based on the fear that juries who might be illiterate would be incapable of differentiating between the probative values of different methods of proof, the practice of the common law courts has been to admit only what the judges then regarded as the best evidence of any disputed fact, and thereby to exclude much material which, as a matter of common sense, would

---

266 *Stuart v. Haughley Parochial Church Council*, [1935] Ch. 452, affirmed [1936] Ch. 32 (lay electoral commission).
267 [1965] 1 Q.B. 456 at 488, 490.

assist a fact-finding tribunal to reach a correct conclusion: *cf. Myers v. Director of Public Prosecutions* [1964] 3 W.L.R. 145.

These technical rules of evidence, however, form no part of the rules of natural justice. The requirement that a person exercising quasi-judicial functions must base his decision on evidence means no more than it must be based upon material which tends logically to show the existence or non-existence of facts relevant to the issue to be determined, or to show the likelihood or unlikelihood of the occurrence of some future event the occurrence of which would be relevant. It means that he must not spin a coin or consult an astrologer, but he may take into account any material which, as a matter of reason, has some probative value in the sense mentioned above. If it is capable of having any probative value, the weight to be attached to it is a matter for the person to whom Parliament has entrusted the responsibility of deciding the issue. The supervisory jurisdiction of the High Court does not entitle it to usurp this responsibility and to substitute its own view for his.

However, where a person entitled to request a hearing makes such a request, the delegate is obligated:

(a) to consider such "evidence" relevant to the question to be decided as any person entitled to be represented wishes to put before him; (b) to inform every person represented of any "evidence" which the deputy commissioner proposes to take into consideration, whether such "evidence" be proffered by another person represented at the hearing, or is discovered by the deputy commissioner as a result of his own investigations; (c) to allow each person represented to comment upon any such "evidence" and, where the "evidence" is given orally by witnesses, to put questions to those witnesses; and (d) to allow each person represented to address argument to him on the whole of the case. This is in the context of the Act and the regulations fulfils the requirement of the second rule of natural justice to listen, fairly to all sides (see *Board of Education v. Rice*).

(i) The Fernando case

In *University of Ceylon v. Fernando*,[268] a student had been suspended from all university examinations for an indefinite period after allegations of cheating had been found proven against him. The statutory procedure required the vice-chancellor to be satisfied that the candidate for an examination had acquired prior knowledge of a question. If so, he had to report the matter to the Board of Residence and Discipline, which had the power to take

---

268 [1960] 1 W.L.R. 223 (P.C.).

one or more disciplinary measures as it determined. In this case, a fellow student, Miss B., taking the same examination made the allegations and the vice-chancellor set up a board of commission to inquire into them. Fernando was requested to attend some of its meetings.

The commission questioned Fernando. In addition it questioned Miss B., other students and faculty members, but none of them in the presence of Fernando. It concluded that the allegations were correct and reported Fernando to the board. The board found him guilty of an examination offence and suspended him indefinitely.

Fernando applied for a declaration that the commission's finding was contrary to the principles of natural justice, in that the evidence of various witnesses, including his accuser, was taken in his absence. He was not aware of the contents of this evidence and thus the case he had to meet, nor did he have an opportunity to cross-examine. He succeeded on appeal but this was overturned by the Privy Council in the university's favour.[269]

The court remarked that "the question whether the requirements of natural justice have been met by the procedure adopted in any given case must depend to a great extent on the facts and circumstances of the case in point".[270] It cited with approval Lord Loreburn's general definition of the nature of and limits on the requirements of natural justice in *Rice*[271] and followed their previous statement in *De Verteuil v. Knaggs*:[272]

> Their Lordships are of opinion that in making such an inquiry there is, apart from special circumstances, a duty of giving to any person against whom the complaint is made a fair opportunity to make any relevant statement which he may desire to bring forward and a fair opportunity to correct or controvert any relevant statement brought forward to his prejudice.

They also cited with approval Harman J.'s statement in *Byrne v. Kinematograph Renters Society Ltd.*:[273]

> What then are the requirements of natural justice in a case of this kind? First, I think that the person accused should know the nature of the accusation made; secondly, that he should be given an opportunity to state his case; and, thirdly, of course, that the tribunal should act in good faith. I do not myself think that there really is anything more.

With these considerations in mind, the court held that in the absence of precise statutory direction on procedure, the vice-chancellor in proceeding to

---

269 Fernando did not appear and was not represented before the Privy Council, which disquieted their Lordships.

270 *Supra*, note 268 at p. 231, per Lord Jenkins.

271 *Bd. of Educ. v. Rice*, [1911] A.C. 179 (H.L.).

272 [1918] A.C. 557 at 560 (H.L.).

273 [1958] 1 W.L.R. 762 at 784 (Q.B.).

satisfy himself could follow the procedure he thought best. This by necessary implication had to include holding some form of inquiry and acting "honestly and by honest means"[274] in accordance with the principles set out above.

The question was whether the vice-chancellor had satisfied those principles when Fernando was not able to cross-examine the other witnesses. The court held that there was no violation of the requirements of natural justice because the vice-chancellor could obtain information in any way he thought best and did not have to examine witnesses as in a trial. Therefore it was open to him to question witnesses in the absence of the plaintiff. However, he then had to advise the plaintiff of the evidence so the plaintiff might have a fair opportunity to correct or contradict any relevant statement to his prejudice. This he had done in the commission's interviews with Fernando.

As to whether the inability of Fernando to cross-examine Miss B. specifically fell short of the requirements of natural justice, the court found that it did not. As reasons, the court indicated that Fernando had never asked to cross-examine Miss B. If such a request had been refused, there might have been some merit in Fernando's objection. That the commission failed to volunteer the opportunity was not an error on its part.

It must be said that to summarize the evidence of a witness for the prosecution and then invite the accused to correct or contradict it does not afford the kind of opportunity that actual cross-examination of that witness provides. While the tribunal may be master of its own procedure, in the absence of statutory direction, surely once it decides to examine witnesses fairness dictates that the opportunity to cross-examine the original source, and not just a hearsay version must be provided. Cross-examination, if any, by the tribunal in ignorance of all relevant evidence which may be solely within the knowledge of the accused cannot substitute for the challenges to veracity and interpretation which the accused could bring to such a cross-examination.[275]

(f) Hearsay

Not all tribunals are governed by the strict evidentiary rules of a court of law and in many instances hearsay is properly admitted and acted upon.

For example, both the Labour Relations Act[276] and the Public Service Employee Relations Act[277] specifically provide that boards of arbitration constituted thereunder are not bound by the rules of evidence. In fact, arbitrators very frequently admit hearsay to the extent that it is relevant to the issue at hand, giving it whatever weight is appropriate in the circumstances. In

---

274 Quoting *Local Government Board v. Arlidge*, [1915] A.C. 120 at 138 (H.L.).
275 But see *Wolfe v. Robinson*, [1962] O.R. 132, where the Ontario Court of Appeal held that there was no right to cross-examine witnesses at a coroner's inquest, precisely because there is no accused.
276 R.S.A. 1980, c.L-1.1.
277 R.S.A. 1980, c. P-33.

light of the statutory provisions governing their powers, such a procedure is clearly permissible — and may well be appropriate in other contexts, too.

(g) Open Court

The tradition of the common law has always required that judicial proceedings be conducted in public so that justice will manifestly be seen to be done. The exceptions to this rule occur where, for public policy reasons, it has been decided that the case should not be subjected to the full glare of publicity, for example, in adoption cases concerning infants.

The openness of judicial proceedings does not have a general counterpart in the actions of statutory delegates. There is no rule that such proceedings must be held in public. Indeed, a huge number of merely administrative acts are carried out by public servants every day and this is not in a public forum, nor would such a suggestion be made.

But the question becomes more difficult where the nature of the administrative proceedings leans more towards a judicial model. Many statutes provide that deliberations of the various administrative tribunals set up under them be in public. In the absence of such statutory provisions, however, the courts have had to decide when the requirement of a public hearing shall operate and when it shall not.

(i) The Hearts of Oak case

In *Hearts of Oak Assurance Company Limited v. Attorney General*,[278] the House of Lords considered the case of the inquiry by an inspector, appointed under the Industrial Assurance Act 1923,[279] into the affairs of an industrial assurance company. The statute was silent as to whether the inquiry should be held in public. The inspector called for the books and documents of the company and then held a public meeting for the purpose of examining under oath various persons whose evidence he wanted. At the meeting, the inspector made an opening statement during which he revealed information he had obtained from his examination of the company's affairs. The inspector ruled that the inquiry must be held in public because it was a judicial proceeding. The company applied for a declaration that the inspector was neither bound nor entitled to conduct the examination in public.

The purpose of the inquiry was to determine whether an offence had been committed under the Act or was likely to be committed. The inspector's report was to be submitted to the Industrial Assurance Commissioner, who might then proceed as he considered necessary. The inquiry could be called by the commissioner if he had reasonable cause to believe that an offence was in prospect or had occurred. In the opinion of the majority of the court[280] the

---

278 [1932] A.C. 392 (H.L.).
279 13 & 14 Geo. 5, c. 8, s. 17(1).
280 Viscount Dunedin dissented.

solution to the question rested mainly on a consideration of the nature and purpose of the inspector's inquiry.

Lord Thankerton found it to be clear that "the object of the examination is merely to recover information as to the company's affairs and that it is in no sense a judicial proceeding for the purpose of trial of an offence".[281] If the information gathered subsequently caused the commissioner to petition to wind up the company, the company would then have the opportunity to have the whole matter investigated judicially. The main function of the commissioner was to protect the policy holders, and it might well have been the case that admission of the general public to the affairs of the company would have been prejudicial to the policy holders' interests. The affairs of such a company were its own domestic matter, and therefore, in the absence of statutory provision to the contrary, such an examination should not have been conducted in public. It was important to the company that its affairs not be put at risk by the publicity attendant upon such an inquiry, when the result of the investigation might well have been that the commissioner was satisfied that the company was conducting itself quite properly.

Lord Macmillan held that the inspection was a purely preliminary proceeding of a delicate nature and that[282]

> [i]f Parliament had intended that the inspection should or might be conducted as a public inquiry one would have expected to find in the Act the familiar provisions which are inserted when a public inquiry is contemplated. These in the present instance are conspicuously absent.

Lord Macmillan held that two considerations were important: first, to ensure that the efficiency of the procedure for the purpose in view was not impaired; and secondly, to ensure that fair treatment was afforded to all concerned. In his judgment, both of these were satisfied by holding the inspection in private.

Viscount Dunedin, on the other hand, dissented. He could not see that the court could have the power to say that the inquiry, although not a judicial proceeding which must be held in public, must be private simply because expediency pointed that way, although a precedent existed in the analogous investigation of the affairs of joint stock companies under the Companies Act, 1929.[283] From the inception of this legislation some seventy years earlier, the invariable practice had been to conduct such inquiries in private. Despite this, Viscount Dunedin was not prepared to say that Parliament, in the knowledge of this existing practice, intended it to be followed in the present case:[284]

---

281 *Supra*, note 278 at p. 396.
282 *Ibid.*, p. 402.
283 1929 (Eng.), c. 23.
284 *Supra*, note 278 at p. 405.

But the statute does not say whether it is to be in public or in private, and therefore I cannot see how a Court of law can have power to say that it must be in private simply because it thinks that conditions of expediency all point that way.

(ii) Re Millward

In *Re Millward and Public Service Commission*,[285] the Federal Court of Appeal had to determine whether proceedings before an appeal board established under the Public Service Employment Act[286] had to be held in public or private, or whether there was discretion in the board to conduct the proceedings either in public or in private or partly in each. The purpose of the board was to inquire into the appeal of an unsuccessful candidate for a federal government job against the appointment of the successful candidate. The appellant and the deputy head of the federal department concerned had to be given an opportunity to be heard, the board was to make a decision and the Public Service Commission then was to implement it. The deputy head was concerned to show that the appointment of the successful candidate was based on merit, and the appellant wanted to show that this was not the case.[287]

Cattanach J. stated the rule of open court as applied to Courts of Law and Justice and quoted Lord Haldane from *Scott v. Scott*:[288]

If there is any exception to the broad principle which requires the administration of justice to take place in open Court, that exception must be based on the application of some other and overriding principle which defines the field of exception and does not leave its limits to the individual discretion of the judge.

Although no principles have emerged to justify the exception, two principles have been advanced: first, that the public will be excluded when it is necessary to secure that justice is done;[289] and secondly, that the court only hears cases *in camera* in exceptional classes established by judicial decisions and statutes. Cattanach J. then went on to list the rules of common law:[290]

  (1) the fundamental rule is open Court;
  (2) the Court may hear an application for trial *in camera* where justice cannot be administered otherwise;

---

285 (1974) 49 D.L.R. (3d) 295 (Fed. T.D.).

286 R.S.C. 1970, c. P-32.

287 Interestingly, the court held that there was a *quasi-lis* between quasi-parties, so that the board's inquiry had to be characterized as quasi-judicial — a matter which is important under the Federal Court Act, R.S.C. 1970, c. 10 (2nd Supp.) — to determine whether the Trial or Appellate Division had jurisdiction to review the decision under ss. 18 and 28 respectively.

288 [1913] A.C. 417 at 435*ff.* (H.L.), quoted by Cattanach J. at p. 303.

289 Viscount Haldane in *Scott v. Scott, ibid.*; Lush J. in *Ex parte Norman*, (1915) 85 L.J.K.B. 203.

290 *Supra*, note 285 at p. 304.

(3) the Court may hear matters *in camera* in specific cases, such as when a statute so provides, wards, lunacy, secret processes and keeping order;

(4) the Court has no power at common law, beyond these exceptions, to hear cases *in camera* and has no arbitrary discretion, it does not have such power in divorce or nullity proceedings;[291]

(5) at one time the Courts have exercised this power to hear matters *in camera* on consent of the parties but this has been doubted in *Nagle-Gillman v. Christopher*[292] and . . . overruled in *Scott v. Scott, supra.*

However, there is no requirement for non-judicial bodies to sit in public in the absence of statutory direction to the contrary. Where the statute is silent, then the tribunal in question has the discretion to decide in that particular case, it generally being the master of its own proceedings.

In this case, the Public Service Commission had published a "Guide to the Public Service Appeals System" which stated that every appeal hearing was open to the public. The court emphasized that this was merely a guide and not a statement of the law. Indeed it was dangerously misleading to the lay persons who would read it, since it purported to oust the discretion vested in the board.

Having disposed of the guide, the court then sought help in the statute as a whole and found none. As a result, the decision whether to hold the inquiry in public or private was held to be a matter solely in the board's discretion. It may be relevant that the parties consent to one form or another,[293] although this may only govern if the tribunal is a creature of those parties.

(h) Right to Counsel

The right to counsel has not traditionally been part of the principles of natural justice although it may become so as administrative law evolves. Indeed there are situations where the courts have upheld the denial of the right to counsel: where regulations exclude it;[294] where it is excluded in the rules of an association;[295] in disciplinary hearings which require a rapid hearing and decision;[296] or where no oral hearing is required at all.[297]

---

291 *McPherson v. McPherson*, [1936] 1 D.L.R. 321 at 326-27.

292 *Nagle-Gillman v. Christopher*, (1876) 4 Ch.D. 173.

293 If for no other reason than because they would be estopped from later asserting their right to privacy to prevent a public (or private) hearing.

294 *Maynard v. Osmond*, [1976] 3 W.L.R. 711 (C.A.). Query whether the validity of such regulations could be attached on the grounds that Parliament did not grant the delegate power to make regulations excluding this (possible) aspect of natural justice. The same point may be taken under the Canadian Charter of Rights and Freedoms with respect to the validity of parent legislation purporting to remove the right to counsel.

295 *Enderby Town Football Club v. Football Assn.*, [1971] Ch. 591.

296 *Fraser v. Mudge*, [1975] 1 W.L.R. 1132.

297 *R. v. Melbourne; Ex parte Whyte*, [1949] V.L.R. 257.

(i) *Guay v. Lafleur*

The Supreme Court of Canada adopted this approach in *Guay v. Lafleur.*[298] This case involved an investigation which was conducted by a delegate on behalf of a minister, and which was a purely administrative procedure, during which the delegate could neither decide nor adjudicate upon anything. The court held that the respondent was neither entitled to be present if not called nor entitled to be represented by counsel through the proceedings.

The case involved an inquiry under the Income Tax Act[299] into the affairs of the respondent and others. The inquiry officer called a number of witnesses, not including the respondent, to be questioned under oath, and gave them an opportunity to be represented by counsel. The respondent wished to be present and to be represented by counsel. Despite the quasi-judicial trappings of the inquiry, the court held that its nature remained administrative and that the inquiry officer was the master of his own procedure. The *audi alteram partem* maxim did not apply since the inquiry officer was merely collecting information, not imposing a liability or making a decision directly affecting the rights of parties. The majority of the court held that section 2(*e*) of the Canadian Bill of Rights was of no avail either, for the same reason.[300]

Hall J. dissented. He was of the opinion that the inquiry officer was not precluded from making recommendations arising out of the inquiry, and that there would be some judgment by him of the facts and information obtained in his report to the deputy minister. Had the deputy minister himself held the inquiry instead of delegating this task, he would have had to act judicially: that is, fairly and impartially. Such a requirement is even stronger when powers are delegated to a subordinate since the reality of the situation was that the decision was made by the subordinate but was issued in the deputy minister's name.

(ii) *The Pett case*

In *Pett v. Greyhound Racing Association, Ltd.,*[301] the track stewards of a greyhound racing stadium held an inquiry into whether or not drugs had been administered to a dog trained by Pett. An unfavourable decision could have involved Pett in the loss of his licence as a trainer and thus have damaged his reputation and livelihood. When he obtained his licence, he had agreed to abide by the rules of the National Greyhound Racing Club, which did not

---

298 [1965] S.C.R. 12.
299 R.S.C. 1952, c. 148, as amended by S.C. 1970-71-72, c. 63 and subsequent amendments.
300 S.C. 1960, c. 44, s. 2(*e*) provides as follows:

2. . . . no law of Canada shall be construed or applied so as to . . .

(*e*) deprive a person of the right to a fair hearing in accordance with the principles of fundamental justice for the determination of his rights and obligations;

301 [1969] 1 Q.B. 125 (C.A.).

prescribe any procedure to be followed at such an inquiry. The procedure used in fact allowed him to be present, to hear the evidence and cross-examine witnesses, but he also wished to be represented by counsel. The track stewards' refusal of this request was reversed by the High Court.

One of the grounds upon which the stewards appealed the order to allow counsel was that the court should not interfere with the absolute discretion of the track stewards to determine all matters in such inquiries. Secondly, the club alleged that legal representation would cause delay and complications which would frustrate the object of completing inquiries expeditiously and with complete fairness.

Lord Denning M.R. did not accept either of these submissions. He considered the serious consequences to Pett of being found guilty and found that he was entitled to appear himself and to appoint an agent to act for him, as a general principle of law. That agent could be a lawyer, especially so since a lawyer is trained in the arts of cross-examination and advocacy, which are not generally attributes of the average layman. In Lord Denning's view, therefore, when a person's reputation or livelihood is at stake, he has a right to speak by his own mouth or by counsel. He dismissed the view of Maugham J. in *MacLean v. Workers Union*[302] that there was no right of audience to counsel before a domestic tribunal, on the grounds that that finding had been made a long time ago. Secondly, while it might have been true when applied to tribunals dealing with minor matters, it did not apply to those dealing with very serious matters, as in this case. Natural justice therefore required the right to counsel.

(i) Hearing Before the Person Making the Decision

In general, the person upon whom the statutory power to decide has been conferred shall make the decision.[303] No delegation of this power is allowed. However, the rule is relaxed in various circumstances where administrative efficiency and possibility demand it. For instance, many statutes require the minister to make the decision. It would be physically impossible for one person to investigate, hear and decide all the matters which the statute calls upon that person to decide. The courts have therefore often allowed such powers to be exercised by officials in the minister's department who are his subordinates. In most cases, this is a form of valid sub-delegation.[304]

By contrast there are some cases where a subordinate official conducts an investigation, hears submissions, examines witnesses and so on, and then reports everything fully to the person with the statutory power to decide. If

---

302 [1929] 1 Ch. 602.

303 See chapters 3 and 4, *supra*, for a discussion of the maxim *delegatus non potest delegare*.

304 Under the Income Tax Act, specific provision is made to permit the delegation *by regulation* of certain of the minister's powers to various departmental officials. The text does not refer to this formally recognized delegation, but rather to less formal institutional delegation.

that person makes a decision based on the full information, there is no breach of natural justice. It is of course a nice question whether the person affected by that report is entitled to see it.[305]

Notwithstanding these two particular circumstances, the general rule is that the person who makes the decision must himself conduct the hearing, whatever the content of that hearing may be. A breach of this aspect of natural justice in effect constitutes an illegal sub-delegation.

An example of proper sub-delegation occurred in the *Arlidge* case.[306] In reply to Arlidge's contention that he had a right to know who had decided his appeal, the court determined that there was no doubt but that the minister was the head of the local government board and responsible to Parliament for its decisions. The volume of work in the department being what it was, it was impractical to expect the minister to do all the work himself. Instead he worked vicariously through his officials and the minister's responsibility consisted of seeing that this official worked properly. He and the other members of the board could not work efficiently and do everything personally. Therefore when the board was directed to deal with an appeal, this did not mean that any particular official had to deal with it. Provided the work was done in accordance with the principles as laid down by Lord Haldane in this case, only Parliament could review it.

Furthermore, the court held that the board was not bound to hear Arlidge orally although it was the decision-maker. Instead the inspectors' report was vicariously the board's report and decision. In principle, it is submitted that this case is wrongly decided, and may really be a violation of the rule against sub-delegation.

In *Hoyda v. Edmonton*,[307] a person complained that not all members of city council who made the decision had been present at the public hearings. McFadyen J. held that this was a breach of natural justice and that only those who had been present at the public hearings and had had the opportunity to hear all sides of the issue could later vote on the matter. Although this appears to be correct in principle, the legislation was subsequently amended to provide that[308]

> [a] member of council is eligible to vote on a proposed by-law notwithstanding that the member of council was not present at the public hearing held under section 139 with respect to the proposed by-law.

---

305 For affirmative decision, see *Errington v. Min. of Health*, [1935] 1 K.B. 249; for negative decision, see *Loc. Govt. Bd. v. Arlidge*, [1915] A.C. 120 (H.L.).
306 *Supra*, note 305.
307 Alta. Q.B., No. 7903-13252 (unreported). See also *Western Realty Projects Ltd. v. Edmonton*, [1974] 5 W.W.R. 131, affirmed [1975] 1 W.W.R. 681 (Alta. C.A.).
308 *Planning Act*, R.S.A. 1980, c. P-9, s. 140(3).

(j) Availability of an Adjournment

The refusal by an administrative tribunal to grant an adjournment may amount to a denial of natural justice. A fair hearing requires that all sides be heard, and if one side cannot be present but its request for an adjournment is denied, the courts can step in to remedy the situation. Undoubtedly, the tribunal has the jurisdiction to refuse an adjournment on proper grounds

> but in the exercise of that discretion the Court will not permit a Board to act capriciously, or in disregard of the rights of others, or be motivated by bias towards any interested party. And where such conduct appears and results in a denial of natural justice, the Courts will not hesitate to intervene in order that justice may be done.[309]

In the *Piggott* case, the Labour Relations Board in Saskatchewan had refused a request for an adjournment by the employer who wished to bring a witness before the board to testify on the issue. The request was for a one-day adjournment. The court found that the dispute could only have been properly resolved by the board once it had heard this testimony. The request was genuine in this case, entirely reasonable and none of the parties would have been prejudiced if an adjournment had been granted. Therefore, the board's refusal was unjustified and resulted in a denial of natural justice.

In the same case, Davis J. described a situation where a refusal to grant an adjournment did not amount to a denial of natural justice. He referred to the *Brodsky Construction* case,[310] in which the board had sent notices to Brodsky of a certification hearing concerning the company. Everything the board was required to do had been done properly and in its regular fashion. By chance the company had moved offices and did not receive the notices and consequently failed to appear. The company applied to have the certification order set aside on the grounds that there had been a denial of natural justice. This was refused, since everything the board had done was authorized by statute, and having so acted, the board was entitled to proceed in the absence of an interested party.

A request for an adjournment may also be properly refused where the tribunal honestly believes that the request is a stalling tactic or otherwise ungenuine.

The governing principle must be that all interested parties have a right to a fair hearing. If for good reason, one party cannot put its case squarely before the tribunal on the day set for the hearing, then natural justice requires that that party be granted its requested adjournment.

---

309 *Re Piggott Const. Ltd. & United Brotherhood of Carpenters & Joiners of Amer.*, (1972) 31 D.L.R. (3d) 758 at 764, per Davis J., reversed on other grounds [1973] 6 W.W.R. 165 (Sask. C.A.).

310 *R. v. Sask. Lab. Rel. Bd.; Ex parte Brodsky Const. Ltd.*, (1967) 63 D.L.R. (2d) 621 (Sask. C.A.).

(k) Reasons for Decisions

(i) The common law position

At common law, there is no obligation on a judge to give reasons for his decisions, although it is customary to do so and frequently done.[311] Administrative Law adapted this principle to statutory tribunals, with the result that the failure of such a tribunal to give reasons has not generally been regarded as a breach of natural justice.[312]

(ii) Statutory requirements for reasons

Notwithstanding this common law position, fairness (and the perception of fairness) in administrative decision-making dictates that the persons affected by a decision should know why it has been reached. This is all the more true where there is a right of appeal, or where the availability of judicial review depends on the ability to demonstrate that the delegate's reasoning contained either a jurisdictional error or an intra-jurisdictional error of law on the face of the record. Without reasons, it may be impossible to correct a bad result, arrived at on irrelevant evidence, in bad faith, for an improper purpose[313] or as a result of bias (to cite only some examples). This point was one of the great reforms advocated by the Franks Committee on Tribunals and Inquiries[314] in England in 1957, and subsequently by the Clement Committee Report in Alberta in 1966.[315] The latter deals with the issue as follows:

> Individuals have a right to know the reasons for a decision that has been come to by a tribunal.
>
> This point also was the subject of unanimous criticism and complaint in submissions which touched on specific tribunals, and is a matter that has greatly exercised writers and commentators on

---

311 See *R. v. Gaming Board for Great Britain; Ex parte Benaim and Khaida*, [1970] 2 Q.B. 417 (C.A.).; *R. v. Chapman (and Carra)*, (1958) 26 W.W.R. 385 (B.C.C.A.); *Payne v. Lord Harris of Greenwich*, [1981] 1 W.L.R. 754 (C.A.).

312 See *Pure Spring Co. v. M.N.R.*, [1947] 1 D.L.R. 501 at 534 (Ex. Ct.); *K.E. Roessler Const. Co. v. Thiessen*, [1976] 4 W.W.R. 529 (Man.); *Re Gill Lumber Chipman (1973) Ltd. and United Brotherhood of Carpenters etc.*, (1973) 42 D.L.R. (3d) 271 (C.A.); *Lazar v. Assn. of Pro. Engineers of Man.*, (1971) 23 D.L.R. (3d) 614 (Man. Q.B.); *Min. of Highways (B.C.) v. Toop*, [1973] 4 W.W.R. 219 (B.C.S.C.); *Dobson v. Edmonton* (1959), 27 W.W.R. 495 (Alta. S.C.); *Andreas v. Edmonton Hosp. Bd.*, [1944] 3 W.W.R. 599 (Alta. C.A.); M. Akehurst, "Statements of Reasons for Judicial and Administrative Decisions", (1970) 33 M.L.R. 154; G.A. Flick [1978] P.L. 16.

313 *E.g.*, in *Roncarelli v. Duplessis*, [1959] S.C.R. 121, where the premier (in discovery) gave his improper reason for cancelling Roncarelli's liquor licence.

314 Report of the Committee on Administrative Tribunals and Inquiries (the "Franks Committee Report"), (England: 1957, Cmnd. 219). See also the Report of the Donoughmore Committee on Ministers' Powers (England: 1932, Cmd. 4060), pp. 80, 100.

315 Report of the Special Committee on Boards and Tribunals to the Legislative Assembly of Alberta, 1966 (the "Clement Report").

civil liberties. It is interesting to compare the views on this point of three important committees. In the *Franks Report* the following is said:

> 98. Almost all witnesses have advocated the giving of reasoned decisions by tribunals. We are convinced that if tribunal proceedings are to be fair to the citizen reasons should be given to the fullest practicable extent. A decision is apt to be better if the reasons for it have to be set out in writing because the reasons are then more likely to have been properly thought out. Further, a reasoned decision is essential in order that, where there is a right of appeal, the applicant can assess whether he has good grounds of appeal and know the case he will have to meet if he decides to appeal. It is true that, in the simpler types of case, particularly where the decision turns on the expert judgment of the tribunal itself rather than on the application of stated law to proven fact, it may only be possible to give a brief statement of reasons, for example that the evidence of one party has been preferred to the evidence of the other, or that having heard the arguments and inspected the premises the tribunal considers that the rent should be X. But generally fuller reasons for decision can be given.

The Attorney General's Committee on Administrative Procedure (the *Acheson Report*, U.S. Government Printing Office, 1941) contains the following observation:

> For, in the first place, the requirement of an opinion provides considerable assurance that the case will be thought through by the deciding authority. There is a salutary discipline in formulating reasons for a result, a discipline wholly absent where there is freedom to announce a naked conclusion. Error and carelessness may be squeezed out in the opinion-shaping process. Secondly, the exposure of reasoning to public scrutiny and criticism is healthy. An agency will benefit from having its decision run the professional and academic gauntlet. Third, the parties to a proceeding will be better satisfied if they are enabled to know the basis of the decision affecting them. Often they may assign the most improbable reasons if told none.

In a study of administrative law made by the Inns of Court Conservative and Unionist Society it said:

> The single reform which would do most to vindicate the Rule of Law and ensure justice in administrative disputes

would be to insist that a decision, if challenged, should be fortified by a statement of the facts and reasons on which it is based.

The Committee concurs in these views. The Courts acknowledge a right of litigants to be given reasons for judgment, and there can be no doubt that the delivery of reasons has the salutary effects above discussed. The business of an individual before a tribunal is as important as the business of a litigant before a Court, and there is no valid reason why the tribunal should not be subject to the same self-disciplines.

As a result, the English Parliament enacted the *Tribunals and Inquiries Act 1958*,[316] which requires certain administrative bodies[317] to give reasons where requested to do so.[318] Similarly, Alberta enacted section 7 of the Administrative Procedure Act,[319] which provides:

> 7. When an authority exercises a statutory power so as to adversely affect the rights of a party, the authority shall furnish to each party a written statement of its decision setting out
>
> (*a*) the findings of fact on which it based its decision, and
> (*b*) the reasons for the decisions

An "authority" is defined to mean:

> 1(*a*) . . . a person authorized to exercise a statutory power;

and a "statutory power" in turn is defined to mean:

> 1(*c*) . . . an administrative, quasi-judicial or judicial power conferred by statute, other than a power conferred on a court of record of civil or criminal jurisdiction or a power to make regulations, and for greater certainty, but without restricting the generality of the foregoing, includes a power. . . .

The Lieutenant Governor in Council is given power under the Act to prescribe the statutory authorities to whom the procedural requirements of the

---

316 6 & 7 Eliz. 2, c. 66, s. 12; replaced by s. 12 of the consolidated Tribunals and Inquiries Act, 1971 (Eng.), c. 62. See M. Akehurst, *supra*, note 312.

317 The English Act applies to a large number of statutory tribunals listed in the schedule to the Act or added subsequently by ministerial order (see s. 15 of the 1971 Act, *supra*, note 316). Wade's *Administrative Law*, 5th ed. (1982), pp. 824-28 sets out a table showing at least 65 statutory tribunals to whom the Act applies.

318 Section 12 of the 1971 English Act requires the listed tribunals

> to furnish a statement, either written or oral, of the reasons for the decision if requested, on or before the giving or notification of the decision, to state the reasons.

For a discussion of judicial interpretation of this provision, see Wade's, *supra*, note 317 at pp. 812-14.

319 R.S.A. 1980, c. A-2.

Administrative Procedure Act apply.[320] Unfortunately, to date only ten bodies have been brought under this regime.[321]

Similar general legislation exists in a number of other provinces requiring some or all of their statutory delegates to give reasons.[322] Unfortunately, no corresponding general requirement yet exists at the federal level in Canada.[323]

In addition, however, a number of individual Acts contain similar specific provisions requiring the persons to whom statutory powers have been delegated to give reasons for their decisions.[324] As in most of Administrative Law, therefore, it is important to study the particular legislation involved to know what legal obligations are imposed on the administrator.

---

320 *Ibid.*, s. 2.
321 Alberta Regulation No. 135/80 reads as follows:

Authorities Designation Regulation

1. The following authorities are designated as authorities to which The Administrative Procedures Act applies in whole:

(a) the Alberta Agricultural Products Marketing Council when acting under section 26 of The Marketing of Agricultural Products Act;
(b) the Surface Rights Board;
(c) the Alberta Motor Transportation Board;
(d) the Irrigation Council;
(e) the Local Authorities Board;
(f) the Energy Resources Conservation Board;
(g) the Public Utilities Board;
(h) the Provincial Planning Board;
(i) the Alberta Planning Board when it is acting under sections 103, 104 and 105 of The Planning Act, 1977;
(j) the Environment Council of Alberta when it is exercising its authority of making inquiries and determinations with respect to stop orders made pursuant to

(i) The Department of the Environment Act;
(ii) The Land Surface Conservation and Reclamation Act;
(iii) The Clear Air Act;
(iv) The Clean Water Act; and
(v) The Beverage Container Act, 1977.

2(1) Subject to subsection (2), the Alberta Assessment Appeal Board is designated as an authority to which The Administrative Procedures Act applies.
(2) Section 8 of The Administrative Procedures Act does not apply to the Alberta Assessment Appeal Board unless a party to an appeal before the Board requests that it apply.
3. Alta. Reg. 123/70, as amended, is repealed.

322 *E.g.*, see s. 17 of the Statutory Powers Procedure Act, R.S.O. 1980, c. 484, which requires a tribunal to whom the Act applies to "give reasons in writing . . . if requested by a party".
323 See, however, the recent Report of the Law Reform Commission on a Council on Tribunals. For the position in Australia, see s. 13 of the Administrative Decisions (Judicial Review) Act 1977 (affecting federal decisions and s. 8 of the Administrative Law Act 1978 (Victoria).
324 *E.g.*, s. 85(2)(*b*) of the Planning Act, R.S.A. 1980, c. P-9, requires a development appeal board to give reasons in writing. On the other hand, statutes sometimes expressly permit a delegate not to give reasons: see *R. v. Yule* (1962), 33 D.L.R. (2d) 179 (Ont. C.A.); *R. v. Estevan*, [1951] 3 W.W.R. 513, affirmed [1953] 1 D.L.R. 656 (S.C.C.).

(iii) The effect of giving a "wrong" reason

If a statutory delegate gives a reason for his decision (whether required to do so or voluntarily[325]), the possibility exists that the reason will demonstrate some fatal error in the way in which he purported to exercise the power delegated to him — thereby opening the door to judicial review. This is demonstrated extremely well in the *Padfield*[326] case.

The case involved provisions of the Agricultural Marketing Act 1958,[327] which regulated the marketing of milk under the Milk Marketing Board. The board fixed different prices for milk in the eleven regions into which England and Wales were divided, the price differential among the regions reflecting differences in transportation costs. The south east region was unhappy with this and since they could not get a majority on the board, which was made up of representatives from the eleven regions, they asked the minister to appoint a committee of investigation to look into their complaints. He refused to do so and gave certain reasons for his refusal. The House had to consider the lawfulness of these reasons.

Under the Act, a complaint would go to a committee of investigation "if the Minister in any case so directs . . ."[328] The committee had to consider whether any act or omission of the board was "contrary to the interests of any persons affected by the scheme and is not in the public interest".[329]

The minister refused to refer the matter to the committee, for the following stated reasons:

(a) If the complaint were upheld, he would be expected to make a statutory order to remedy the situation.
(b) The complaint would open up too wide an issue.
(c) The decision was one for the board, not the committee of investigation.

On a challenge to this approach, the court first had to consider the nature of the authority given to the minister. It was argued that the minister was subject to *mandamus* since there was a duty imposed on him to refer serious complaints to the committee. The court considered the distinction between a power coupled with a duty and a complete discretion. All five law lords held that this was not a duty but a discretion in the minister. The question was whether he had exercised his discretion lawfully. Lord Denning (dissenting in the Court of Appeal) and four of the five law lords,[330] held that the minister had acted unlawfully. The difference of opinion among the judges lay in the nature and extent of the discretion conferred and whether it was unfettered,

---

325 See the discussion on this point in the *Padfield* case, *infra*, section (v).
326 *Padfield v. Min. of Agriculture, Fisheries and Food*, [1968] 2 W.L.R. 924 (H.L.).
327 6 & 7 Eliz. 2, c. 47.
328 S. 19(3)(*b*).
329 S. 19(6).
330 Lord Borth-y-Gest dissented.

and whether the reasons which the minister had given constituted unlawful conduct.

Lord Denning M.R. considered that Parliament had provided the machinery by which complaints would be dealt with independent of the board. The minister had to consider each complaint and could reject frivolous ones. Every genuine complaint, however, was to be referred to the committee and the minister could not refuse it on arbitrary or capricious grounds, or personal grounds, or any other irrelevant ground. The minister could not do as he liked safe from judicial scrutiny. Parliament had set up the machinery and the minister could not refuse a complaint without good reason. Simply because the minister was not bound to give reasons did not mean that his refusal could not be questioned. If he denied a complainant his only remedy, he had to have good reasons for his refusal. If asked for them, he should give them and if he refused, the court could infer that he had no good reasons. The court had power to interfere where it appeared or could be inferred that the minister was influenced by extraneous considerations or failed to take into account considerations which should have influenced him. The reasons given by the minister were unlawful and thus he stepped outside the bounds of his discretionary power.

In Lord Reid's view, Parliament had conferred the discretion on the minister with the intention that it would be exercised in furtherance of the policy and objects of the Act. It was to the Act as a whole that the court had to look to construe its objects and policy and then it might determine whether the minister had misconstrued the Act or used his discretion to thwart it. If so, those aggrieved were entitled to the court's protection.

In Lord Reid's view, refusing the complaint on the ground that it raised wide issues which he might have to remedy constituted a misdirection by the minister, since the legislation clearly contemplated this very eventuality by providing for amendment and revocation of the scheme first through the means of the committee's investigation.

Secondly, the reason that the issue should be resolved through the board was also insufficient. The minister could not absolve himself from his responsibility. He had a duty to act where the board had acted contrary to the public interest and a duty to investigate complaints.

Lord Reid was also of the view that if the minister was suggesting that the result of the committee's investigation might lead to his later embarrassment, this would be a bad reason.

While the minister was not bound to give reasons, his failure to do so did not mean that his decision could not be questioned by a court. The court could act if it could be inferred from all the circumstances that the effect of the refusal was to frustrate the policy and objects of the Act. Merely because the Act conferred a power (as distinct from a duty) did not prevent the court from going behind the words and determining that the circumstances warranted coupling the power with a duty. In this case, the minister's discretion was not unlimited and it had been used in a manner that did not accord with the intention of the Act which conferred it.

Lord Hodson said:[331]

> The reasons disclosed are not, in my opinion, good reasons for refusing to refer the complaint seeing that they leave out of account altogether the merits of the complaint itself.

Lord Pearce said:[332]

> Thus the independent committee of investigation was a corner-stone in the structure of the Act. It was a deliberate safeguard against injustices that might arise from the operation of the scheme.
>
> . . . . .
>
> It is quite clear from the Act in question that the Minister is intended to have *some* duty in the matter. It is conceded that he must properly consider the complaint. He cannot throw it unread into the waste paper basket. He cannot simply say (albeit honestly) "I think that in general the investigation of complaints has a disruptive effect on the scheme and leads to more trouble than (on balance) it is worth; I shall therefore never refer anything to the committee of investigation." To allow him to do so would be to give him power to set aside for his period as Minister the obvious intention of Parliament, namely that an independent committee set up for the purpose should investigate grievances and that their report should be available to Parliament. This was clearly never intended by the Act.

A general abdication of the minister's power and duty in this fashion was not in accord with Parliament's intention.

Similarly, Lord Upjohn outlined what might constitute unlawful behaviour by the minister:

(a) an outright refusal to consider a relevant matter;
(b) misdirecting himself on a point of law;
(c) taking into account some wholly irrelevant or extraneous consideration; or
(d) wholly omitting to take into account a relevant consideration.

If the reasons disclosed that the minister had committed one of these errors and thereby acted unlawfully, he had exceeded his jurisdiction. Even if his discretion was said to be unfettered, this did not unfetter the control which the judiciary had over the executive, namely that in exercising its powers, the latter had to act lawfully; this the court determined by looking at the scope and purpose of the Act in conferring a discretion. The minister, by failing to

---

331 *Supra*, note 326 at p. 958.
332 *Ibid.*, pp. 960-62.

understand the scope and object of section 19, and of his functions and duties under it, so misdirected himself in law.

(iv) What constitutes "reasons"

As the Alberta Court of Appeal noted in *Dome Petroleum Ltd. v. Public Utilities Board (Alberta)*,[333] the rationale for requiring an administrator to give reasons is

> to enable persons whose rights are adversely affected by an administrative decision to know what the reasons for that decision were. The reasons must be proper, adequate and intelligible. They must also enable the person concerned to assess whether he has grounds of appeal.

This mirrors the approach adopted by the English courts in *Re Poyser and Mills' Arbitration*.[334] The reasons were held to be inadequate because the arbitrator had indicated in his report that certain items were bad and others were good, but he did not identify which was which. As Megaw J. stated:

> I am bound to say this, and again I do not think it was disputed by [counsel for the landlord], that a reason which is as jejune as that reason is not satisfactory, but in my view it goes further than that. The whole purpose of section 12 of the Tribunals and Inquiries Act, 1958, was to enable persons whose property, or whose interests, were being affected by some administrative decision or some statutory arbitration to know, if the decision was against them, what the reasons for it were. Up to then, people's property and other interests might be gravely affected by a decision of some official. The decision might be perfectly right, but the person against whom it was made was left with the real grievance that he was not told why the decision had been made. The purpose of section 12 was to remedy that, and to remedy it in relation to arbitrations under this Act. Parliament provided that reasons shall be given, and in my view that must read as meaning that proper, adequate reasons must be given. The reasons that are set out must be reasons which will not only be intelligible, but which deal with the substantial points that have been raised. In my view, it is right to consider that statutory provision as being a provision as to the form which the arbitration award shall take. If those reasons do not fairly comply with that which Parliament intended, then that is an error on the face of the award. It is a material error of form. Here, having regard to paragraph 3, this

---

333 2 A.R. 453 at 472 (per Sinclair J.A.), affirmed [1977] 2 S.C.R. 822.
334 [1964] 2 Q.B. 467 at 477-78 (per Megaw J.). Even if the duty to give reasons is not mandatory, failure to do so may imply inadequate reasons, which Megaw J. suggested might constitute a reviewable intra-jurisdictional error of law.

award, including the reasons, does not comply with the proper form, and that is, in my view, an error of law on the face of the award. . . . I do not say that any minor or trivial error, or failure to give reasons in relation to every particular point that has been raised at the hearing, would be sufficient ground for invoking the jurisdiction of this court.

Merely parroting the matters which a delegate is required to consider does not constitute a "reason" for his action. For example, a development appeal board is given discretion under the Alberta Planning Act to approve certain non-conforming developments if they do not adversely affect the amenities of the neighbourhood.[335] In *Hannley v. Edmonton*,[336] the Court of Appeal struck down a board's decision which merely repeated that the particular development "would not adversely affect the amenities of the neighbourhood" because that did not constitute a "reason", but rather stated a conclusion. A similar result was reached in both *Morin v. Provincial Planning Board*[337] and *Dome Petroleum Ltd. v. Public Utilities Board (Alberta)*.[338]

The fact that reasons are obscure will not of itself make them bad when an inference can be drawn from them to enable a court to deal with the matter.[339] Similarly, although the reasons must demonstrate (necessarily or by implication) that the delegate considered the matters required by statute,[340] the delegate does not need to enumerate each finding of fact.[341]

In summary, it appears that the test for determining whether the reasons given by a delegate are adequate in law is whether they show why or how or upon what evidence the delegate reached his conclusion. If so, then any statutory requirement to give reasons will be satisfied (although the reasons given may disclose another fatal error); if not, that fact alone will constitute a fatal flaw in the exercise of the delegate's power.

(v) The effect of failing to give reasons

The failure to give reasons may invalidate the statutory delegate's actions in two possible ways.

First, as the House of Lords noted in *Padfield*,[342] the failure of the minister to give a reason may lead the court to conclude that he had no proper reason for his action, and must therefore have acted for some improper purpose. As a result of this influence, the delegate's action is necessarily *ultra*

---

335 R.S.A. 1980, c. P-9, s. 69(5).
336 (1978) 7 Alta. L.R. (2d) 394 (C.A.).
337 [1974] 6 W.W.R. 291 (Alta. T.D.).
338 *Supra*, note 333.
339 *Iveagh v. Min. of Housing and Loc. Govt.*, [1964] 1 Q.B. 395 (C.A.).
340 *Morin v. Prov. Planning Bd.*, *supra*, note 337.
341 *Service Employees' Int. Union v. Nipawin Dist. Staff Nurses Assn.*, [1975] 1 S.C.R. 382; *Woolaston v. Min. of Manpower & Immigration*, [1973] S.C.R. 102.
342 [1968] 2 W.L.R. 924 (H.L.).

vires. This reasoning can apply even where the delegate is under no obligation to give any reasons whatever for his actions — as was the case in *Padfield.* As their Lordships said:

> True it is that the Minister is not bound to give his reasons for refusing to exercise his discretion in a particular manner, but when, as here, the circumstances indicate a genuine complaint for which the appropriate remedy is provided, if the Minister in the case in question so directs, he would not escape from the possibility of control by mandamus through adopting a negative attitude without explanation. As the guardian of the public interest he has a duty to protect the interests of those who claim to have been treated contrary to the public interest.[343]
>
> . . . . .
>
> Nor was it intended that he could silently thwart its intention by failing to carry out its purposes. I do not regard a Minister's failure or refusal to give any reasons as a sufficient exclusion of the court's surveillance. If all the prima facie reasons seem to point in favour of his taking a certain course to carry out the intentions of Parliament in respect of a power which it has given him in that regard, and he gives no reason whatever for taking a contrary course, the court may infer that he has no good reason and that he is not using the power given by Parliament to carry out its intentions. In the present case, however, the Minister has given reasons which show that he was not exercising his discretion in accordance with the intentions of the Act.[344]
>
> . . . . .
>
> [H]e is a public officer charged by Parliament with the discharge of a public discretion affecting Her Majesty's subjects; if he does not give any reason for his decision it may be, if circumstances warrant it, that a court may be at liberty to come to the conclusion that he had no good reason for reaching that conclusion and order a prerogative writ to issue accordingly.[345]

In effect, this reasoning assumes that silence or lack of a proper reason constitutes no lawful reason and an abuse of discretion.[346] However, the court

---

343 *Ibid.,* p. 958, per Lord Hodson.
344 *Ibid.,* p. 962, per Lord Pearce.
345 *Ibid.,* p. 969, per Lord Upjohn.
346 For other examples of this reasoning, see *M.N.R. v. Wrights' Can. Ropes Ltd.,* [1947] A.C. 109 at 123 (P.C.); *Norton Tool Co. v. Tewson,* [1973] 1 W.L.R. 45; *Pepys v. London Tpt. Executive,* [1975] 1 W.L.R. 234 (C.A.). In *Re Poyser & Mills' Arbitration,* [1964] 2 Q.B. 467, Megaw J. considered that lack of reasons could also constitute an intra-jurisdictional error of law reviewable in certain circumstances by *certiorari* (see chapter 10, *infra*) or on appeal.

cannot be counted on always to impugn the integrity of a delegate who emulates the "inscrutable face of the Sphinx", to quote Lord Atkin's famous judgment in the *Nat Bell Liquors* case.[347]

Secondly, the failure to give reasons will more directly deprive the delegate of his jurisdiction if he is under a statutory obligation to do so. Failure to do so renders his decision void.[348] In some cases, it may be both possible (and appropriate) for the delegate to articulate the reasons for his decision afterwards in proper form, without having to recommence his hearing *de novo*.[349]

(l) Summary on the Contents of Fairness

It is now well established that an administrative tribunal must proceed fairly when making its decision. Precisely what this means will be the subject of innumerable cases, all of which will have to seek that fine line between procedural fairness and procedural arbitrariness. It must be remembered that the proliferation of administrative decision-makers throughout the multitude of Canadian federal and provincial statutes represents the intention of legislatures to have the process of governing made fast, efficient, and readily accessible to the general public. In achieving this objective, however, the courts will not allow the decision-makers to lose sight of all those elements of fair procedure contained in the phrase "the rules of natural justice". However, from the above discussion, it can be seen that the contents of the rule are flexible and must be tailored to each situation as it arises. It cannot be said with definition what precisely the content of the rule is in every circumstance. Nevertheless, the courts are and will continue to be called upon to define the rule.

One attempt has been made by Addy J. in *Re Blanchard and Disciplinary Board of Millhaven Institution*.[350] Blanchard was convicted by the prison board of various offences generally having to do with prejudicing good order in the institution. He applied under section 18 of the Federal Court Act[351] to have his convictions quashed on various grounds amounting to a denial of natural justice.

Having held that the hearing was administrative in nature and not quasi-judicial, Addy J. went on to list the general principles inherent in the rules of natural justice:

---

347 [1922] 2 A.C. 128 (P.C.).
348 *Morin v. Prov. Planning Bd.*, [1974] 6 W.W.R. 291 (Alta. T.D.); *Hannley v. Edmonton*, (1978) 7 Alta. L.R. (2d) 394 (C.A.); *Dome Petroleum Ltd. v. Pub. Utilities Bd. (Alta.)*, 2 A.R. 453, affirmed [1977] 2 S.C.R. 822.
349 This procedure may be more apt under the English Act than under the Alberta one which *requires* the tribunal to give reasons in writing, not merely on request. This implies a condition precedent, the non-fulfilment of which could possibly not be cured by a subsequent issuance of reasons. For a discussion of the timing for asking for and giving reasons under the English Act, see Wade's *Administrative Law*, 5th ed. (1982), p. 813.
350 [1983] 1 F.C. 309 (T.D.).
351 R.S.C. 1970, c. 10 (2nd Supp.).

(a) the tribunal is not required to conform to any particular procedure, nor to abide by rules of evidence generally applicable to judicial proceedings, except where the empowering statute requires otherwise;

(b) there is an overall duty to act fairly in administrative matters, that is, the inquiry must be carried out in a fair manner and with due regard for natural justice;

(c) the duty to act fairly requires that the person who is being examined and who may be subject to some penalty:

   (i) be aware of what the allegations are;

   (ii) be aware of the evidence and the nature of the evidence against him;

   (iii) be afforded a reasonable opportunity to respond to the evidence and to give his version of the matter;

   (iv) be afforded the opportunity of cross-examining witnesses or questioning any witness where evidence is being given orally in order to achieve points (i), (ii) and (iii). However, there may be exceptional circumstances which would render such a hearing practically impossible or very difficult to conduct, such as deliberately obstructive conduct on the part of the party concerned;

(d) the hearing is to be conducted in an inquisitorial, not adversarial, fashion but there is no duty on the tribunal to explore every conceivable defence or to suggest possible defences;

(e) nevertheless, the tribunal must conduct a full and fair inquiry which may oblige it to ask questions of the person concerned or of the witnesses, the answers to which may prove exculpatory insofar as the person is concerned. This is the way in which the tribunal examines both sides of the question;

(f) there is no general right to counsel. Whether counsel may represent the person is in the discretion of the tribunal, although matters may be so complicated legally that to act fairly may require the presence of counsel;

(g) the person must be mentally and physically capable of understanding the proceedings and the nature of the accusations and generally of presenting his case and replying to the evidence against him. The tribunal must satisfy itself on this point before embarking on the hearing.

Addy J. then applied these principles to the case before him and concluded that the chairman of the board had not acted unfairly in any way.

(m) Correcting Errors by Re-hearing

The question sometimes arises whether a delegate may correct procedural or substantive errors by holding a re-hearing.[352] Apart from correcting

---

352 For a comprehensive consideration of this topic, see R.F. Reid and H. David, *Administrative Law and Practice*, 2nd ed. (Butterworths, 1978), pp. 105-115. See also R.A. Macdonald,

obvious slips and technical errors,[353] the better view seems to be that a delegate has no power to re-open a matter which has been decided because he is then *functus officio*.[354] On the other hand, a number of statutes specifically permit re-hearings, reconsiderations and variations of previous decisions.[355] For example, section 56 of the Public Utilities Board Act provides that:[356]

> The Board may rehear an application before deciding it, and may review, rescind or vary any order or decision made by it.

In principle, the same components of fairness apply to any such re-hearing as would apply to the board's initial proceedings, including adequate notice of the rehearing and the matters that will be considered, an open hearing, the right to cross-examine witnesses, the obligation to give reasons, and the like. Nevertheless, the precise nature of the proceedings must — as always in Administrative Law — be determined in the context of the specific statutory provisions involved.

It may be tempting for a delegate who has made a procedural error to try to correct it by re-hearing the matter. On the one hand, it is of course true that administrators are not generally bound by the doctrine of precedent, and are entitled to change the basis upon which they exercise their discretionary powers from time to time.[357] This militates in favour of the validity of a re-hearing, or at least in favour of the validity of a new hearing on a new application. On the other hand, a re-hearing by the same decision-maker on the same matter may well raise a reasonable apprehension of the bias that the decision-maker would not in fact be able to approach the matter with an open mind in light of his involvement in the previous decision.[358]

"Reopenings, Rehearings and Reconsiderations in Administrative Law", (1979) 17 Osgoode Hall L.J. 207.

353 *Re Wilkes and Interlake Tissue Mills Co.*, [1970] S.C.R. 441; *Re B.C. Forest Products Ltd.*, (1961) 36 W.W.R. 145 (B.C.S.C.). Sometimes legislation specifically gives the power to correct errors: see *Heller v. Reg., Vancouver Land Registration Dist.*, [1963] S.C.R. 229; and s. 80(2) of the Public Service Employee Relations Act, R.S.A. 1980, c. P-33, which provides that "a tribunal may in any proceeding, award or decision correct any clerical mistake, error or omission".

354 *Windsor Const. (1962) Ltd. v. Int. Union of Operating Engineers Loc. 115*, (1968) 1 D.L.R. (3d) 683 (B.C.S.C.).

355 *E.g.*, the Income Tax Act permits the minister to re-assess a taxpayer within three years after the date of the original assessment. Such a re-consideration will re-verify the taxpayer's right to object or appeal within 90 days.

356 R.S.A. 1980, c. P-37. The refusal to re-hear a matter was considered in *Can. Western Natural Gas Co. v. Pub. Utilities Bd.*, (1984) 33 Alta. L.R. (2d) 185 (C.A.).

357 *Bd. of Dir. of Lethbridge Nor. Irrigation Dist. v. Bd. of Indust. Rel. for Alta.*, [1973] 5 W.W.R. 71 (Alta. T.D.); *Pandurangan v. Alta. Assn. of Architects*, (1981) 14 Alta L.R. (2d) 331 (Q.B.).

358 See chapter 9, *infra*.

(n) Legislative Prescriptions for Administrative Procedures

We have already noted that many statutes contain provisions concerning specific aspects of the procedure to be adopted by the delegate. But more general attempts have also been made to provide an all-encompassing code of procedure for delegates. For example, the Alberta Administrative Procedures Act[359] governs many aspects of the procedure used by the 10 bodies[360] to which it has been applied. The same approach was adopted subsequently in the Ontario Statutory Powers Procedure Act,[361] which is not only more comprehensive in dealing with every aspect of procedure, but also applies to considerably more statutory delegates. Both of these models follow the lead of the American federal Administrative Procedures Act.[362] Just as *ad hoc* statutory provisions as to procedure do not totally supplant the common law rule of fairness and *audi alteram partem*, it is probably true that these uniform procedure acts provide minimum requirements for procedural fairness, leaving the courts with the power to impose the additional procedural requirements of the residual common law if the ends of fairness so require.

The English approach goes considerably further. On the one hand it is true that the 1958 and 1971 Tribunals and Inquiries Acts[363] attempt to provide a comprehensive code of procedure for a large number of statutory tribunals. On the other hand, the Acts also create a Council on Tribunals,[364] which is charged with the task of reviewing and approving the procedures adopted by these tribunals. This allows for considerable attention to adapting general procedural guidelines to the requirements of individual and quite diverse statutory schemes. It also permits close scrutiny of the content of any delegated legislation enacted by the tribunal to govern its own procedures. There is a great deal to be said for the two-pronged English approach to ensuring the adoption of fair administrative procedures.[365]

11. Conclusion

The principles of natural justice have been applied by the courts for many years to determine whether a delegate has adopted a fair procedure in the exercise of his statutory powers. Natural justice and procedural fairness are presumed by the common law to be implied limitations on the exercise of delegated power. The courts have adopted these rules from their own

---

359 R.S.A. 1980, c. A-2, reproduced in Appendix I.
360 *Supra*, note 311.
361 R.S.O. 1980, c. 484, reproduced in Appendix II.
362 5 U.S.C.A.
363 1958 (6 & 7 Eliz. 2, c. 66); 1971, c. 62.
364 *Supra*, notes 316, 317, 318.
365 The Law Reform Commission of Canada has considered the desirability of this approach in Alan Leadbeater's Study Paper entitled *Council on Administration*, 1980. In Ontario, the Statutory Powers Procedure Review Committee performs this function.

procedures, and have applied them to administrators generally, whether or not quasi-judicial functions are involved. Because of the doctrine of the Sovereignty of Parliament, legislation may specifically prescribe the procedure to be adopted by a delegate, but very specific words are required to oust the common law's presumption in favour of fairness.

What constitutes "fairness" may be difficult to determine in particular circumstances. The cases have identified many types of unfair procedures. But what is unfair in one context may be fair in another. Accordingly, it is dangerous to generalize about the nature of a fair hearing in the abstract. Nevertheless, the courts' insistence on a fair procedure is an extremely important vehicle for judicial review of administrative action, and for maintaining regularity and decency in the workings of our large and complicated modern government.

12. Selected Bibliography

Akehurst, C.M., "Statements of Reasons for Judicial and Administrative Decisions", (1970) 33 M.L.R. 154.

Flick, G.A., "Administrative Adjudications and the Duty to Give Reasons — A Search for Criteria", [1978] P.L. 16.

Fox, David, Public Participation in the Administrative Process, Study Paper for the Law Reform Commission of Canada, 1979.

Grey, Julius, "Can Fairness be Effective?" (1982) 27 McGill L.J. 360.

Hogg, P.W., "Judicial Review of Action by the Crown Representative", (1969) 43 Australian L.J. 215.

Jones, D.P., "Administrative Fairness in Alberta", (1980) 18 Alta. L.R. 351.

Jones, D.P., "Discretionary Refusal of Judicial Review in Administrative Law", (1981) 19 Alta. L. Rev. 483.

Jones, D.P., "Natural Justice and Fairness in the Administrative Process" in Judicial Review of Administrative Rulings, arising out of the 1982 Annual Conference of the Canadian Institute for the Administration of Justice.

Leadbeatter, Alan, Council on Administration, Study Paper for the Law Reform Commission of Canada, 1980.

Mullan, D.J., "Fairness: The New Natural Justice", (1975) 25 University of Toronto L.J. 281.

Mullan, D.J., "Natural Justice and Fairness — Substantive as Well as Procedural Standards for the Review of Administrative Decision-Making?" (1982) 27 McGill L.J. 250.

Peiris, G.L., "Natural Justice and Degrees of Invalidity of Administrative Action", [1983] P.L. 634.

Reid, R.F., and David, H., Administrative Law and Practice, 2nd ed., Butterworths, 1978, especially chapters 2 and 3.

Report of the Committee on Administrative Tribunals and Inquiries, (the "Franks Committee Report"), England, 1957, Cmnd. 219.

Report of the Committee on Minister's Powers (the "Donoughmore Report"), England, 1932, Cmd. 4060.

Report of the Special Committee on Boards and Tribunals to the Legislative Assembly of Alberta (the "Clement Report"), 1966.

The Rule
Against Bias

1. Introduction to the Rule

The Latin maxim *nemo judex in sua causa debet esse* literally means that "no man shall be a judge in his own cause", but the phrase is used more widely to focus attention on the second principle of natural justice, which is sometimes referred to as the rule against bias. Although the *nemo judex* rule has not received the same attention which has been given to fairness and the *audi alteram partem* rule,[1] the policy underlying both aspects of natural justice is identical: justice must not only be done, but must manifestly and undoubtedly be seen to be done.[2] Accordingly, a breach of the *nemo judex* rule will generally cause a statutory delegate to lose his jurisdiction, and will render any administrative action void[3] and thereby subject to successful judicial review.

Although the ambit of the rule against bias is generally well understood when applied to courts of law,[4] a number of questions must be considered in attempting to apply the rule to other delegates exercising a wide range of powers under extremely varied statutory provisions: first, whether the impugned activity, behaviour or state of mind of the delegate is capable of constituting "bias" in law; secondly, whether legislation expressly or impliedly alters the accepted concept of what constitutes "bias" for the purposes of the particular statutory scheme in question; thirdly, what test is employed for determining when the *nemo judex* rule is breached (must there be actual bias, a real likelihood of bias, or only a reasonable apprehension of bias?); fourthly, what evidence can be led to demonstrate a breach of the *nemo judex* rule; fifthly, whether the rule applies to all types of delegated powers, or only to those which can be characterized as being "quasi-judicial" in nature; and finally, what the effect is of a decision made in breach of the rule, and whether the rule can be waived in particular cases. All of these points are important in applying the rule against bias in Administrative Law.

---

1 Curiously, however, the Supreme Court of Canada has considered the *nemo judex* rule exhaustively in recent years. See *Ghirardosi v. Min. of Highways (B.C.)*, [1966] S.C.R. 367; *King v. Univ. of Sask.*, (1969) 68 W.W.R. 745; *Blanchette v. C.I.S. Ltd.*, (1973) 36 D.L.R. (3d) 561; *L.S.U.C. v. French*, [1975] 2 S.C.R. 767; *P.P.G. Indust. Can. Ltd. v. A.G. Can.*, (1976) 65 D.L.R. (3d) 354; *Ringrose v. College of Physicians & Surgeons of Alta.*, [1976] 4 W.W.R. 712; *Committee for Justice & Liberty v. Nat. Energy Bd.*, (1976) 68 D.L.R. (3d) 716; *Morgentaler v. R.*, [1976] 1 S.C.R. 616. Of these cases, the invocation of the *nemo judex* rule was only successful in the *National Energy Board* case, *Ghirardosi* and *Blanchette*. In all of the other cases cited above, the impugned decision was upheld.

2 To paraphrase the words of Lord Chief Justice Hewart in *R. v. Sussex Justices; Ex parte McCarthy*, [1924] 1 K.B. 256 at 259.

3 And not merely voidable. See section 4 below for a discussion of the importance of this distinction.

4 See Reid and David, *Administrative Law and Practice*, 2nd ed. (Toronto: Butterworths, 1978), pp. 229*ff.*

2. What Constitutes "Bias" in Law?

The word "bias" is not accurate in a literal sense to describe the ambit within which the *nemo judex* rule has been applied either to the courts or to other statutory delegates. For example, a delegate with a pecuniary interest in the outcome of a matter will almost always be in breach of the *nemo judex* rule, even though no actual or apprehended bias exists. Conversely, the rule may not be breached by a delegate who has previously expressed such a strong opinion on a matter which he must now decide that a non-lawyer might reasonably conclude that there was bias. It is useful, therefore, to consider what constitutes bias in law.

(a) Pecuniary Interest

The courts have consistently held that the existence of a pecuniary interest almost always disqualifies a statutory delegate from acting. In other words, a pecuniary interest constitutes "bias", no matter how open-minded in fact the delegate might be. This rule was applied by the House of Lords in the celebrated case of *Dimes v. Grand Junction Canal*,[5] where the Lord Chancellor had affirmed the order of the Vice-Chancellor granting relief to a company in which, unknown to the defendant, the former had an interest as a shareholder. As Lord Campbell said:[6]

> No one can suppose that Lord Cottenham could be, in the remotest degree, influenced by the interest that he had in this concern; but, my Lords, it is of the last importance that the maxim that no man is to be a judge in his own cause should be held sacred. And that is not to be confined to a cause in which he is a party, but applies to a cause in which he has an interest. Since I have had the honour to be Chief Justice of the Court of Queen's Bench, we have again and again set aside proceedings in inferior tribunals because an individual who had an interest in a cause, took a part in the decision. And it will have a most salutary influence on these tribunals when it is known that this high Court of last resort, in a case in which the Lord Chancellor of England had an interest, considered that his decision was on that account a decree not according to law, and was set aside. This will be a lesson to all inferior tribunals to take care not only that in their decrees they are not influenced by their personal interest, but to avoid the appearance of labouring under such an influence.

---

5 (1852) 3 H.L.Cas. 759. See also *Metro. Properties Co. (F.G.C.) v. Lannon*, [1969] 1 Q.B. 577 (C.A.), concerning a pecuniary interest by the chairman of the appeal board against local taxes; *Re Innisfail By-law No. 724*, (1957) 23 W.W.R. 184 (Alta.)

6 *Ibid.*, pp. 793-94.

Sometimes legislation specifically reiterates the common law view that a pecuniary interest always constitutes bias. Thus, section 30(2) of the Alberta Municipal Government Act[7] provides that:

(2) A member of a council shall not vote in the council

    (*a*) on any question

        (i) affecting a private company of which he is a share-holder,

        (ii) affecting a public company in which he holds more than 1% of the number of shares issued,

        (iii) affecting a partnership or firm of which he is a member, or

        (iv) affecting a company of which he is a director unless he is a director only by reason of being a member of the council and the council, by resolution, authorizes him to vote,

    (*b*) on a contract for the sale of goods, merchandise or services to which he is party,

    (*c*) on a question affecting his selling or leasing land or an interest in land to the municipality, or

    (*d*) on any question in which he has a direct or indirect pecuniary interest.

Obviously, the mere existence of a pecuniary interest may not in fact influence the decision-maker,[8] nor cause anyone reasonably to apprehend that it would do so. Nevertheless, the common law almost invariably equates the existence of pecuniary interest to a breach of the *nemo judex* rule. There are probably only three exceptions: where legislation specifically permits a decision-maker to have a pecuniary interest;[9] where the decision-maker is the only person who

---

7 R.S.A. 1980, c. M-26.

8 *R. v. Sunderland Justices*, [1901] 2 K.B. 357 (C.A.), where the justices had the same pecuniary interest as any other ratepayer.

9 *E.g.*, s. 30(5) of the Municipal Government Act, *supra*, note 7, provides that no disqualification of a member of a local council occurs by reason only of his voting on a question that affects:

    (*a*) the interests or business of a private company, of which the member is a shareholder, in a manner common with all other, or a substantial number of other, persons who carry on business in the municipality and who have interests or business in the municipality and who have interests or business in common with the interests or business of that private company,

    (*b*) the interests or business of a public company in which the member holds more than 1% of the number of shares issued, in a manner common with all other, or a substantial number of other, persons who carry on business in the municipality and who have interests or business in common with the interests or business of that public company,

can make the decision;[10] and, possibly, where the parties have agreed to waive any objections to the decision-maker's interest.[11]

(b) Other Behaviour Constituting "Bias"

Although no exhaustive catalogue can be given, the courts have some-times found the following behaviour to contravene the *nemo judex* rule: where the decision-maker is now or previously has been the solicitor or client of one of the parties in the proceedings;[12] where one party's solicitor or officer has participated in the delegate's deliberations after the hearing;[13] where a person acts as both prosecutor and judge in disciplinary proceedings;[14] where a decision-maker sits on appeal from his own decision;[15] where there is some dealing between the decision-maker and one of the parties prior to the hearing;[16] or where the decision-maker's intervention in the proceedings

---

(c) the interests or business of a partnership or firm, of which the member of council is a member, in a manner common with all other, or a substantial number of other, persons who carry on business in the municipality and who have interests or business in common with the interests or business of that partnership or firm,

(d) the interests or business of a company, of which the member is a director, in a manner common with all other, or a substantial number of other, persons who carry on business in the municipality and who have interests or business in common with the interests or business of that company,

(e) a contract for the sale of any goods, merchandise or services that the member is entitled to buy or sell on terms common with all other, or a substantial number of other, persons in the municipality, or

(f) any thing in respect of which the member has a direct or indirect pecuniary interest if the member's interest in it is one which is in common with all other, or a substantial number of other, persons in the municipality.

10 *Judges v. A.G. Sask.*, (1931) 53 T.L.R. 464 (P.C.); *Martel v. M.N.R.*, [1970] Ex. C.R. 68. Query whether this may have been the situation in *Dimes v. Grand Junction Canal Co., supra*, note 5.

11 See the discussion of waiver in section 7 of this chapter.

12 *Ghirardosi v. Min. of Highways (B.C.)*, [1966] S.C.R. 367.

13 *R. v. Sussex Justices; Ex parte McCarthy*, [1924] 1 K.B. 256; *Cooper v. Wilson*, [1937] 2 K.B. 309 (C.A.); *R. v. Hendon R.D.C.; Ex parte Chorley*, [1932] 2 K.B. 696, *Fooks v. Alta. Assn. of Architects*, (1982) 21 Alta. L.R. (2d) 306 (Q.B.), where the registrar and solicitor of the association met privately with the discipline committee and the council of the association.

14 *Maillet v. Bd. of Gov. of College of Dental Surgeons*, (1919) 58 D.L.R. 210 (Ont. C.A.); but *cf. Re Solicitor*, (1967) 60 W.W.R. 705 (Alta. C.A.).

15 *R. v. Alta. Securities Comm.; Ex parte Albrecht*, (1963) 36 D.L.R. (2d) 199 (Alta. S.C.); *Re Glassman and Council of College of Physicians and Surgeons*, [1966] 2 O.R. 81 (C.A.). Note that there was no common law ban on a member of the Court of Appeal sitting on an appeal from his own decision at trial. See also section (c) below on "Institutional Bias". And *cf. Re Dancyger and Pharmaceutical Assn.*, [1971] 1 W.W.R. 371 (Alta. C.A.); *Ringrose v. College of Physicians & Surgeons of Alta.*, [1976] 4 W.W.R. 712 (S.C.C.).

16 *Cathcart v. Public Service Comm.*, [1975] F.C. 407. See also *Winnipeg Free Press Ltd. v. Man. Lab. Bd.*, [1974] 3 W.W.R. 475 (Man. C.A.), where there was no bias because there was no evidence that the decision-maker would be influenced by fear of dismissal as a result of the communication by the provincial premier and a cabinet minister.

makes him *parti pris*.[17] All of these activities have been held to constitute bias in law in certain circumstances, but do not necessarily always raise a "reasonable apprehension of bias"[18] in every context involving administrative tribunals. To a large extent, each case must be decided on its own merits.

(c) Institutional Bias and Two-Tier Decisions

Legislation very often establishes a hierarchy of administrative proceedings to deal with a particular matter. Thus, a committee which is entitled to exercise a particular power (for example, to discipline a member of a profession) may appoint a sub-committee either (a) to investigate the facts but make no judgment thereon, or (b) to decide the matter tentatively subject to the final hearing (or any appeal) before the parent committee. Is the *nemo judex* rule breached if the members of the sub-committee also participate in the deliberations of the parent committee? Similarly, is the *nemo judex* rule breached where there is an appeal to a person or body which is reasonably apprehended to be unlikely to deviate from the previous decision taken elsewhere in the decision-making institution, even if no actual overlap of personnel occurs between the two different decisions? Both of these fact patterns arise out of two-tier decision-making processes, and might generically be labelled "institutional bias".[19]

Attempts to obtain judicial review of decisions entailing institutional bias have been rare until relatively recently, and, furthermore, the courts have not clearly come to grips with the issues raised by such allegations. For example, in 1969 the Supreme Court of Canada in *King v. The University of Saskatchewan*,[20] rejected an attempt to invoke the concept of institutional bias to strike down a particular decision. There, the appellant argued that he had not been given a fair hearing by a committee of the university senate (which declined to grant him a law degree) because a number of the members of that committee had also been members of at least two previous bodies which had

---

17 *E.g.*, by hostile cross-examination: *Re United Steel-Wkrs. of Amer., Loc. 4444 and Stanley Steel Co.*, (1974) 6 O.R. (2d) 385 (Div. Ct.); *Re Golomb and College of Physicians & Surgeons of Ont.*, (1976) 12 O.R. (2d) 73 (Div. Ct.); but *cf. College of Physicians & Surgeons of Ont. v. Cosullo*, (1976) 67 D.L.R. (3d) 351 (S.C.C.), where the committee was annoyed by the evasiveness of the complainant; and *Re Hawkins and Halifax City Residential Tenancy Bd.*, (1974) 47 D.L.R. (3d) 117 (N.S.T.D.), where the tribunal compelled a person to appear before it.

18 Which is the test for a breach of the *nemo judex* rule, as discussed below.

19 See de Smith, *Judicial Review of Administrative Action*, 3rd ed. (1973), pp. 227-29, for a discussion of the problems raised by the phenomenon of institutional bias, which is sometimes also called departmental bias. Note that Dickson J. used the phrase "institutional bias or participation by association" in the *Ringrose* case, *supra*, note 15, to refer to the second type of bias identified in the text. See also D.P. Jones, "Institutional Bias: The Applicability of the Nemo Judex Rule to Two-Tier Decisions", (1977) 23 McGill L.J. 605.

20 [1969] S.C.R. 678 affirming 67 W.W.R. 126.

considered his petition.[21] Although Spence J. accepted that the *nemo judex* rule was applicable to the senate committee's deliberations, he held that it had not in fact been breached because:[22]

> It was inevitable that there would be duplication as one proceeded from one body to another. . . . of persons carrying out their ordinary duties as members of the faculty of the University. . . .

> I am of the opinion that, in such matters as were the concern of the various university bodies here, duplication was proper and was to be expected, and I am not ready to agree that such duplication would result in any bias or constitute a breach of natural justice.

Thus, Spence J., without referring to any test for determining whether the *nemo judex* rule had been breached, simply rejected the appeal. One must conclude, therefore, that the facts in this case did not disclose any reasonable apprehension of bias.

Three more recent cases demonstrate the serious division in judicial opinion attempting to deal with the concept of institutional bias.

(i) Law Society of Upper Canada v. French

In *Law Society of Upper Canada v. French*,[23] the respondent had been found guilty of professional misconduct by the discipline committee of the law society. Its report was sent to convocation for final decision, along with a recommendation that Mr. French be suspended for three months. All members of the discipline committee were benchers and therefore also members of convocation. Two of them[24] asserted their right to participate in convocation's disposition of the discipline committee's report. At this point, French successfully applied to the High Court for an order quashing convocation's proceedings[25] on the basis of apprehended bias. This was subsequently

---

21 King's "appeal" was first heard by a special committee of faculty council (composed of Messrs. Spinks, Booth, Haslam, Tracey, Mann, Langley and Pepper), which recommended that he be granted his degree. The executive committee of faculty council (including both Dean Lang and Professor Pepper from the College of Law, as well as all of the other members of the special committee except Professor Tracey) then rejected the special committee's recommendation. Finally, the plaintiff appealed to the chancellor of the university, Chief Justice Culliton, who treated it as an appeal to the university senate and set up a five-member senate committee to dispose of the matter. The members of the senate committee included the president of the university as well as two deans (Begg and Currie) who had all been members of the executive committee.

22 *Supra*, note 20 at pp. 690-91.

23 [1975] 2 S.C.R. 767.

24 Messrs. Strauss and Harris. Mr. Maloney (later Ombudsman for Ontario) of his own volition did not sit in convocation on this matter. Mr. Chappel had been defeated at an intervening election for benchers, and therefore had ceased to act as a member of the discipline committee and was not entitled to sit in convocation.

25 [1972] 2 O.R. 766 (Osler J.).

affirmed by the Court of Appeal.[26] The law society took a further appeal to the Supreme Court of Canada, on two principal grounds: first, that the Law Society Act[27] impliedly permitted the two benchers to participate in convocation's decision;[28] and, secondly, that convocation was not really hearing an *appeal* at all, but merely receiving a report from one of its committees, and that the *nemo judex* rule therefore could not be applied to prevent members of the discipline committee from sitting in convocation on the same matter.

The majority of the Supreme Court of Canada held that the legislature had impliedly intended to oust the application of the *nemo judex* rule from the particular kind of disciplinary proceedings which had been taken against French.[29] It reached this conclusion by comparing the wording of the section dealing with professional misconduct with that of other provisions dealing with other disciplinary offences which specifically prohibited members of the

---

26 1 O.R. (2d) 513n.

27 S.O. 1970, c. 238 [now R.S.O. 1980, c. 233].

28 Spence J. rejected the law society's submission that the present proceedings were not subject to the *nemo judex* rule because at common law judges could sit in appeal from their own decisions. He pointed out that the Supreme Court of Judicature Act, 1873 of England (36 & 37 Vict., c. 66) and the Judicature Act of Ontario (R.S.O. 1970, c. 228 [now R.S.O. 1980, c. 223]) now prohibit such judicial overlapping, *supra*, note 23 at pp. 782-83; and specifically held that such overlapping could contain the seeds of bias. Therefore the *nemo judex* rule could arguably be presumed to apply to the present proceedings *unless ousted by statute* — which he held to be the case here. It is interesting to note that Spence J. specifically treated his earlier decision in *King v. Univ. of Sask., supra*, note 20, as "applying only to its particular circumstances", *supra*, note 23 at p. 783.

29 French was charged with professional misconduct under s. 34 of the Law Society Act, which provided:

> If a member is found guilty of professional misconduct or of conduct unbecoming a barrister and solicitor after due investigation by a committee of Convocation, Convocation may by order cancel his membership in the Society by disbarring him as a barrister and striking his name off the roll of solicitors or may by order suspend his rights and privileges as a member for a period to be named or may by order reprimand him or may by order make such other disposition as it considers proper in the circumstances.

One might note that s. 33(12) clearly infers that a person found guilty of professional misconduct under s. 34 by the discipline committee has a right of appeal:

> The decision taken after a hearing shall be in writing and shall contain or be accompanied by the reasons for the decision in which are set out the findings of fact and the conclusions of law, if any, based thereon, and a copy of the decision and the reasons therefor, together with a notice to the person whose conduct is being investigated of his right of appeal within thirty days after the date of the decision.

Although the Act does not specify to whom this *appeal* lies, the Lieutenant-Governor-in-Council, acting under the powers granted to him in s. 55 of the Act, made Regulation 556, R.R.O. 1970, which assumes that the "appeal" lies to convocation, although it refers to the discipline committee's *report*, not to its *decision* (see s. 13.(7) of that regulation). The *vires* of this regulation was not considered by either the majority or the minority in the Supreme Court of Canada — somewhat remarkable in light of Spencer J.'s insistence that there was no strict appeal because the discipline committee was merely investigating and did not decide anything. Osler J., *supra*, note 25, specifically held the regulation to be *intra vires*.

discipline committee from subsequently sitting in convocation on the same matter.[30] Spence J. concluded that this was a proper place to apply the maxim *expressio unius est exclusio alterius*,[31] and that therefore this particular example of institutional bias had been statutorily put beyond the reach of the *nemo judex* rule,[32] whether or not a reasonable person would apprehend that the two benchers would have been biased.

On the other hand, Laskin C.J.C.'s dissent found this to be "a curious, if not inverted view of *expressio unius, exclusio alterius*".[33] He noted that the specific statutory prohibitions against overlapping membership between the discipline committee and convocation dealt with far less serious offences than the charges of professional misconduct against French. He pointed out that a charge of professional misconduct is so grave that the *nemo judex* rule would clearly have been implied by the courts at common law if the statute had been silent. Faced with the absence of an express statutory prohibition against overlapping membership, Laskin C.J.C. considered this to be "a *casus omissus* which cries for judicial intervention in accordance with accepted principles of administrative law".[34]

The majority of the Supreme Court also held that the *nemo judex* rule did not apply to prevent the two benchers from sitting in convocation because it was not, strictly speaking, hearing an *appeal* from a decision of the discipline committee, which decided nothing, but was only an investigator and reporter, not a prosecutor. Therefore, the court held that the *nemo judex* rule did not apply to prevent the two members of the committee from also sitting in convocation.

This decision raises certain questions. It does not follow that the committee made no determination at all. Indeed, the committee did decide that French had been guilty of professional misconduct, and recommended to convocation that he be suspended. Surely, this would give rise to a reasonable apprehension of bias. One may question, therefore, whether the existence of a strict appeal is a necessary, as opposed to a sufficient, requirement for the *nemo judex* rule to apply to prevent overlapping membership of committees in circumstances like that in *French*.

In our opinion, Laskin C.J.C.'s approach is preferable. Clearly, Parliament ought to give closer attention to the details of legislation so as to specify when it does intend to permit or prohibit overlapping membership in multi-

---

30 Spence J., *supra*, note 23 at pp. 781-82, referred to s. 39 of the Act, which permitted the discipline committee itself to impose the lightest penalty — the reprimand — on a recalcitrant member, and which also provided that an appeal from such a decision lay to convocation. S. 39(4) further provided that "no bencher who sat on the committee of Convocation when the order appealed from [*i.e.*, the reprimand] was made shall take any part in the hearing of the appeal in Convocation".

31 Expression of one thing is the exclusion of another.

32 *Supra*, note 23 at pp. 785-86.

33 *Ibid.*, p. 773.

34 *Ibid.*

tiered decisions. But Parliament seems to lack the energy, the will and the time to consider such important procedural details. Although the courts may no longer be prepared to strike down a statutory provision which expressly ousts the *nemo judex* rule, as Coke did,[35] there is still no reason to scrutinize legislation minutely in order to eke out the legislators' "intention" to permit bias.[36] After all, the policy underlying the *nemo judex* rule is to maintain the public's confidence that the affairs of state are administered with integrity and impartiality. The courts have achieved this policy by applying both principles of natural justice to a myriad of decisions where Parliament has made no specific provision whatever for the procedure by which, or the persons by whom, these decisions were to be made. Of course, Parliament may always oust the application of either rule of natural justice, provided it uses clear words to do so. But why should the courts not adopt as robust a method of statutory construction to presume that the *nemo judex* rule does apply as they have when avoiding the effect of privative clauses?[37] Let Parliament state its intentions clearly.

(ii) Ringrose v. College of Physicians and Surgeons of Alberta

In *Ringrose v. College of Physicians and Surgeons of Alberta*,[38] the plaintiff was charged with conduct unbecoming a physician and surgeon. His medical privileges were immediately suspended[39] by the executive committee of the council (or general governing body) of the college, pending the outcome of a formal hearing into his conduct by the discipline committee.

This latter committee subsequently found him guilty and recommended to the council (which had the final decision-making power) that he be

---

35 See *Dr. Bonham's Case*, (1610) 8 Co. Rep. 114a at 118a where Coke said: "[W]hen an Act of Parliament is against common right and reason, or repugnant, or impossible to be performed, the common law will controul [sic] it, and adjudge such Act to be void."

36 De Grandpré J. in *Ringrose v. College of Physicians & Surgeons of Alta.*, [1976] 4 W.W.R. 712 (S.C.C.), discussed *infra*, at p. 718 stated, as a general proposition, that the *nemo judex* rule is ousted whenever the statutory scheme provides for multi-step proceedings where overlapping membership could occur but does not specifically prohibit it. De Grandpré J. said:

> "[N]o reasonable apprehension of bias is to be entertained when the statute itself prescribes overlapping of functions. Such is exactly the situation under the Medical Profession Act. . . . Thus, the same council, the members of which are by law entitled to take part in all its decisions, is by statute authorized to . . . appoint a discipline committee staffed by at least three of its midst. *Thus, it is clear that the legislator has created the conditions forcing upon the members of the council overlapping capacities.*" [Emphasis added.]

37 See, *e.g., Anisminic Ltd. v. Foreign Comp. Comm.*, [1969] 2 A.C. 147 (H.L.); *Metro. Life Ins. Co. v. Int. Union of Operating Engineers, Loc. 796*, [1970] S.C.R. 425. Arguing for a less hostile judicial approach to privative clauses, see Laskin, "Certiorari to Labour Boards: The Apparent Futility of Privative Clauses", (1952) 20 Can. Bar Rev. 986.

38 *Supra*, note 36.

39 The suspension itself was almost immediately quashed (unreported, but referred to in de Grandpré J.'s judgment, *ibid.*, p. 713).

suspended for one year.[40] Dr. Ringrose sought to prevent this report from reaching the council by applying for an order of *certiorari* quashing the discipline committee's report because one of its members (Dr. McCutcheon) was also a member of the executive committee which had earlier temporarily suspended the plaintiff's licence. In fact it turned out that Dr. McCutcheon had not taken part in the first proceedings at all, but only became aware of the charges against the plaintiff when the case later came before the discipline committee. The *Ringrose* case, therefore, does not concern the first type of institutional bias noted above (where the same person actually participates in more than one stage of a multi-step proceeding), but rather the second type in which there is a reasonable apprehension that the final decision-maker is unlikely to deviate from the previous decision taken elsewhere within the decision-making institution, even if no overlap of personnel occurs. Ringrose's application for *certiorari* was dismissed by the Trial Division of the Supreme Court of Alberta, and this was confirmed both by the Appellate Division[41] and the Supreme Court of Canada.[42]

The majority of the Supreme Court held that the executive committee's decision to suspend Ringrose temporarily was[43]

> nothing more than a statement that the common weal on the one hand and the private interest of the medical practitioner on the other have been weighed and . . . the temporary conclusion has been reached that, until the facts are properly investigated, it is preferable to suspend.

On this view, the discipline committee was not hearing an appeal of any kind from the provisional decision of the executive committee to suspend Dr. Ringrose, and the majority of the Supreme Court therefore held that the *nemo judex* rule did not apply to the discipline committee's proceedings.

Dickson J., writing for the majority, strongly dissented from this technical approach. He simply assumed that the principles of natural justice did apply to the discipline committee's proceedings. He then asked whether, on the facts, there was a reasonable apprehension that the discipline committee would have been biased against the plaintiff. The answer to this question obviously depends upon a host of factors in each case:[44]

> *All of the surrounding circumstances must be investigated.* What is the function of each of the committees? Does the first body merely

---

40 The final decision rested with the council, of which Dr. McCutcheon was also a member (as, presumably, were all of the members of both the executive and the discipline committees). The discipline committee also recommended that Dr. Ringrose be required to pay the costs of its investigation.
41 [1975] 4 W.W.R. 43.
42 *Supra*, note 36.
43 *Ibid.*, p. 717.
44 *Ibid.*, p. 720, emphasis added.

find facts, or does it make a preliminary adjudication? What is the effect of one body's decision on the second's decision making? Is one of the committees sitting in appeal, expressly or in effect, from the decision of the other committee? Is the member in the second committee defending, perhaps unconsciously, a decision of the first committee which he helped to make? Did the first committee initiate the proceedings or lay charges with the result that a member of that committee, who later sits on the other committee to hear evidence, is both accuser and judge? What is the size of the respective committees? What was the degree of participation in each committee by the member whose presence on both committees is impugned? These and other questions must be asked and answered.

Dickson J. posed these questions for the sole purpose of determining whether there was a reasonable apprehension of bias. If these questions had been answered in the affirmative, Dickson J. would have held the impugned decision to have been void, without further inquiry. Although the majority also asked these questions, they did so for the completely different purpose of first determining whether the principles of natural justice applied at all; only then would they have asked whether there was a reasonable apprehension of bias.

Although Dickson J.'s approach would not always yield a different solution,[45] it possesses a number of distinct advantages. First, Dickson J. clearly concentrated on the impression created by the particular fact situation in which the *nemo judex* rule is alleged to have been breached, thus bearing in mind the public policy behind the very existence of the rule: that justice should be seen to be done impartially. This has the double advantage of being both a generic approach capable of being applied to all situations in which bias is alleged, as well as recognizing that[46]

> [w]hat may be termed institutional bias or participation by association should not . . . be rejected out of hand as a possible ground for apprehension of bias.

Dickson J. thus acknowledged that both of the types of institutional bias distinguished earlier in this chapter may, in certain circumstances, constitute a breach of the *nemo judex* rule. Secondly, this approach avoids the magical requirement that there be a strict "appeal" before the *nemo judex* rule can apply to the second stage of a two-tier decision. Thirdly, this approach rivets the court's attention on the apprehension of bias at a particular stage in the proceedings, and completely avoids confusing the issue by attempting to characterize the preceding steps in the decision-making process as being "merely investigative" or "administrative" in nature. Finally, such a forth-

---

45 Indeed, in this case, Dickson J. agreed that there was no reasonable apprehension of bias.
46 [1976] 4 W.W.R. 712 at 720.

right judicial appraisal of whether or not the particular facts do generate a reasonable apprehension of bias would encourage the courts to take a far more robust approach to the construction of poorly drafted statutory provisions which may (or may not) inferentially permit institutional bias. As Dickson J. himself said:[47]

> On occasion . . . the governing statute may permit overlapping of functions in a two-stage procedure but such an enabling provision must not be over-extended. The provision contained in the Medical Profession Act . . . permitting a degree of overlapping between the council and discipline committee, does not justify overlapping between the discipline committee and the executive committee. I think that, to avoid criticism, reliance should be placed upon such an overlapping provision as infrequently as the practicalities of the situation permit, since there rests upon the governing bodies of the professions in the exercise of their statutory disciplinary powers the duty to be scrupulously fair to those of their members whose conduct is under investigation and whose reputations and livelihood may be at stake. . . . [T]he investigation of the alleged breach, and the steps taken to determine culpability, must be such that justice is manifestly seen to be done, impartially and, indeed, quasi-judicially.

(iii) Bethany Care Centre v. United Nurses of Alberta

The Alberta Court of Appeal has applied the *nemo judex* rule to a different type of institutional bias in the *Bethany Care Centre* case.[48] Under the applicable labour statutes,[49] three-member arbitration boards dealt with rights[50] grievances filed by workers against their employers. The employer and the union each had the right to nominate one member of the board, and they in turn chose the chairman. The issue was whether there was a reasonable apprehension of bias because one of the nominees was a full-time employee of the parent union whose local was a party to the arbitration. Clearly, the legislature specifically chose a three-man board to resolve this type of dispute, and

---

47 *Ibid.*

48 (1983) 29 Alta. L.R. (2d) 3, reversing 22 Alta. L.R. (2d) 279. Compare *Re Arbitration Act; Re Gainers Ltd. and United Packinghouse Wkrs. of Amer., Loc. 319,* (1964) 47 W.W.R. 544 (Alta. S.C.).

49 Alberta Labour Act, R.S.A. 1955, c. 167, s. 73(8) [re-en 1968, c. 51, ss. 15, 16 (renumbered as s. 73a(4))]; Labour Relations Act, R.S.A. 1980, c. L-1.1, s. 122. Three-member boards also arise under the Public Service Employee Relations Act, R.S.A. 1980, c. P-33.

50 As opposed to "interest arbitrations", which settle the terms of a collective agreement, including monetary issues. The court suggests that its result might have been different if an interest arbitration had been involved, because it is more like a continuation of negotiation than a right arbitration which is clearly adjudicative in nature. See *supra*, note 52 at pp. 5 and 9.

one could not expect "neutrality or impartiality"[51] when the parties each preserved the right to designate an arbitrator. Section 122 of the legislation itself only prohibited two specific types of bias:[52]

> 122   No person shall be appointed as an arbitrator or as a member of an arbitration board or other body who is directly affected by the difference or has been involved in an attempt to negotiate or settle the difference.

The Court of Appeal held that these two statutory examples of bias did not cover the case in question,[53] but also held that they did not provide an exhaustive code of possible circumstances in which the *nemo judex* rule could apply. As Stevenson J.A. said:[54]

> Is there to be a disqualification on the grounds of apprehension of lack of independence? Is it reasonable to assume, to suspect, that the employee of the parent union will not readily displease his employer? He or she has an economic interest in sustaining the good will of that employer. The grievor is a member of that employer. One of the employer's objects is to promote the welfare of nurses, a highly relevant consideration in a policy dispute. Can the other party say with confidence: here is someone partial, but independent? The answer is no.

Thus, the Alberta Court of Appeal in effect adopted the approach advocated by Dickson J. in the *Ringrose* case:[55] determining first whether there was an apprehension of bias, and only then going on to determine whether there was some statutory or other overriding reason for ousting the application of the *nemo judex* rule to permit institutional bias. In the result, the Court of Appeal

---

51 In the words of Riley J. in *Re Arbitration Act; Re Gainers Ltd. and United Packinghouse Wkrs. of Amer., Loc. 319, supra,* note 48, who held that employee/nominees were not disqualified on account of bias. See also *Re J. K. Campbell & Assoc. Ltd. and Int. Assn. of Heat & Frost Insulators & Asbestos Wkrs., Loc. 126,* (1979) 21 L.A.C. (2d) 16 (Sychuk); *Const. & Gen. Wkrs., Loc. 1111 v. Jurisdictional Ctee.,* (1982) 22 Alta. L.R. (2d) 30 (Q.B.); *Const. & Gen. Wkrs. Union, Loc. 890 v. Graham Const. Ltd.,* [1977] 3 W.W.R. 677 (Sask., Q.B.); and *Dalhousie College Gov. v. Dalhousie Staff Assn.,* (1981) 49 N.S.R. (2d) 54 (T.D.).

52 Labour Relations Act, *supra,* note 49.

53 Because the nominee was not directly affected by the difference being arbitrated, nor had he been engaged in an attempt to negotiate or settle the difference. Stevenson J.A. implies, *supra,* note 48 at pp. 8 and 11, that the parties could not waive these two statutory prohibitions, leaving open the possibility that other forms of bias can be waived, notwithstanding the jurisdictional nature of a breach of the *nemo judex* rule. Indeed, the authors understand that some employers and unions have agreed to waive the rule set out in the *Bethany Care Centre* case.

54 *Supra,* note 50 at pp. 8-9.

55 [1976] 4 W.W.R. 712 (S.C.C.).

disqualified the union's employee from being its nominee on the board of arbitration on account of bias.[56]

(iv) Summary on institutional bias

In summary, it appears that the courts recognize that overlapping steps in the government's decision-making process can give rise to a reasonable apprehension of bias, and therefore can constitute a breach, at least in certain circumstances, of the *nemo judex* rule. As is so often the case in Administrative Law, difficulties arise in trying to apply this principle to particular institutional contexts involving two-tiered decisions. In each case, the courts must determine whether Parliament intended to oust or modify the application of the *nemo judex* rule as a natural consequence of the mere creation of overlapping in the decision-making process. Obviously, if the legislation specifically permits duplication, the doctrine of Parliamentary Sovereignty means that the rule against bias must yield. On the other hand, legislation very seldom is so specific, and it is suggested that the courts should not be quick to imply any unnecessary restriction on the application or content of the *nemo judex* rule. In short, it is submitted that the better approach is that advocated by Dickson J. in *Ringrose* and used by the Alberta Court of Appeal in *Bethany Care Centre*: to ask whether the facts demonstrate a reasonable apprehension of bias, and then whether the legislative scheme can be made to work without permitting institutional bias.[57]

(d) Attitudinal Bias

The *Bethany Care Centre*[58] case also raises the possibility that a decision-maker may not be required to be neutral and impartial, but may rather demonstrate a distinct "attitudinal bias" in favour of a particular outcome. In theory, the *nemo judex* rule applies to such cases, but the overwhelming trend in the cases appears to be that no breach of the rule occurs provided the decision-maker is perceived to be able to address his mind openly to the question at hand. As Stevenson J.A. put it in the *Bethany Care Centre* case:[59]

---

56 Thus bringing Alberta law into accord with that in Manitoba: *Simmons v. Man.*, [1982] 1 W.W.R. 140 (Man. C.A.); and in Ontario: *Re Can. Shipbldg. & Enrg. Ltd. and United Steelwkrs. of Amer.*, [1973] O.R. 240 (C.A.); and *R. v. Ont. Lab. Rel. Bd.; Ex parte Hall*, [1963] 2 O.R. 239 (H.C.).

57 *E.g.*, the result in the *Bethany Care Centre* case, *supra*, note 48, clearly does not immobilize the arbitration process because unions and employers can clearly nominate persons other than employees. Similarly, it is difficult to understand the necessity for members of the discipline committee to insist on their right to sit in convocation in the *French* case, [1975] S.C.R. 767, given the size of convocation. In *Ringrose, supra*, note 55, no actual overlapping occurred, and the administrative process worked perfectly well. Indeed, none of the cases considered here involves a situation where the application of the *nemo judex* rule would bring the institution to a grinding stop.

58 (1983) 29 Alta. L.R. (2d) 3 (C.A.).

59 *Ibid.*, p. 9.

I return then to consider what is expected of a labour arbitrator. Is he to stand by the side who nominated him come what may? Is he free to sign a unanimous report against the party nominating him? Is he expected — at least — to form an honest conclusion regardless of his sympathies or loyalties? The answer to that last question must be yes.

This approach is reminiscent of the reasoning adopted by the courts for determining the circumstances in which a delegate may validly refer to a policy when exercising his discretion.[60] Nevertheless, because the test for a breach of the *nemo judex* rule is a reasonable apprehension of bias, it is irrelevant to determine whether the decision-maker in fact has an open mind. On the contrary, all that is required for a breach of the *nemo judex* rule is a reasonable apprehension that the decision-maker's attitudinal bias will prevent him from being open-minded. Thus, Stevenson J.A. prohibited the appointment of a union employee to an arbitration board with the following words:[61]

> The Employers merely say that no one is to inquire into the nominee's independence and in accordance with the fundamental precept that justice must appear to be done, the employers ought not to be required to submit themselves to arbitration boards where one member may be seen not to have independence of mind, where there is an apprehension of bias by reason of that lack of independence.

It is useful, therefore, to examine a number of other cases in which attitudinal bias has been raised.

(i) The National Energy Board case

The *National Energy Board* case[62] arose out of the formation in June 1972 of the Arctic Gas consortium to build a pipeline to transport natural gas from the Arctic to southern markets. The Canada Development Corporation, wholly owned by the Government of Canada, became a shareholder in the new corporation, and contributed some $1.2 million to the pipeline project. Mr. Marshall Crowe was President of the Canada Development Corporation from the date of its entry into the project until October 1973, when he was appointed Chairman of the National Energy Board. During this period, he attended various meetings and took part in numerous decisions made by several of the committees of the consortium.

In 1975, Arctic Gas and a number of competitors made applications to the board for permission to construct pipelines to move natural gas from the

---

60 See chapter 7 for a discussion of the circumstances in which a delegate may validly take into account a policy when exercising his discretion.

61 *Ibid.*, p. 9.

62 *Ctee. for Justice & Liberty v. Nat. Energy Bd.*, [1978] 1 S.C.R. 369, reversing (1976) 65 D.L.R. (3d) 660 (*sub nom. Re Can. Arctic Gas Pipeline Ltd.*).

Arctic to southern markets. In April 1975 the board, which at that time had eight members, assigned Crowe and two others to constitute the panel to hear these competing applications, which were subsequently directed to be heard together at public hearings commencing in October 1975.

In the meantime, counsel for Arctic Gas approached the board's counsel and raised the question whether Crowe should participate in the hearings, since a third party might reasonably apprehend that Crowe was biased in favour of Arctic Gas. Crowe therefore prepared a statement which was sent to all of the applicants and intervenors shortly before the hearings, setting out his previous involvement with the Arctic Gas project. When this was read at the opening of the hearings, five of the intervenors objected to Crowe's participation. The National Energy Board therefore decided to state a case to the Federal Court of Appeal under section 28(4) of the Federal Court Act[63] in the following terms: Would the board err in rejecting the objections and in holding that Mr. Crowe was not disqualified from being a member of the panel on the grounds of reasonable apprehension or reasonable likelihood of bias?

After first considering its own jurisdiction to decide the question put to it, the five members of the Court of Appeal unanimously held that the board would not err in permitting Crowe to participate in the hearings. In giving reasons for the court's decision, Thurlow J. surveyed the wide range of factual circumstances in which bias may be alleged, and noted that there was no suggestion here that Crowe was actually biased or had a pecuniary interest in the outcome of the hearings. He then considered the two submissions made by the intervenors: first, that a third party could reasonably apprehend that Crowe's previous involvement with Arctic Gas would incline him to favour *its* application; or, secondly, that Crowe was in favour of building *a* pipeline (which the intervenors opposed).

Thurlow J. only dealt with the second submission by recognizing that bias might theoretically be established in "predetermination cases, cases where there has been some expression of views indicating . . . prejudgment".[64] But he said that[65]

> [e]ven in such cases *it becomes necessary to consider whether* there is reason to apprehend that *the person* whose duty it is to decide *will not listen to the evidence and decide fairly on it.*

After noting that Crowe's previous participation in the Arctic Gas consortium "might give rise in a very sensitive or scrupulous conscience to the uneasy suspicion that he might be unconsciously biased . . .",[66] the learned judge

---

63 R.S.C. 1970, c. 10 (2nd Supp.).
64 (1976) 65 D.L.R. (3d) 660 at 667.
65 *Ibid.*, emphasis added.
66 *Ibid.*

rejected such a subjective test for bias. Rather, he said the *nemo judex* rule was cast in terms of:[67]

> [W]hat would an informed person, viewing the matter realistically and practically — and having thought the matter through — conclude[?] Would he think that it is more likely than not that Mr. Crowe, whether consciously or unconsciously, would not decide fairly?

Applying this test, the Court of Appeal held that reasonable and right-minded people had no cause to apprehend bias in Crowe. Therefore, the decisions of the National Energy Board over which Crowe was scheduled to preside would be valid.

It is interesting to note that the Court of Appeal buttressed this conclusion by referring to the fact that Crowe's participation in the consortium was of a representative nature only.[68] While he was President of the Canada Development Corporation, he had no financial interest either in it or in the consortium; he "was essentially a person acting in the interest of the Government of Canada . . .".[69] He therefore had nothing to gain or lose from any decision which might be reached by the board. Accordingly, Thurlow J. held that there was no[70]

> reason for apprehension that he would be likely to be unable or unwilling to disabuse his mind of preconceptions he may have in the face of new material [coming before the Board] pointing to a different view of matters considered in the course of his participation in activities of the study group, or that he would be unconsciously influenced by decisions which he had supported as a participant in the study group.

Furthermore, the Court of Appeal noted that a two-year period had elapsed between Crowe's tenure as President of the Canada Development Corporation and the Arctic Gas application to the board, and it held that the issues now to be decided by the board were "widely different from those to which the study group devoted its attention".[71] Thus[72]

> there appear[ed] to be no valid reason for apprehension that Mr. Crowe . . . cannot approach these new issues with the equanimity and impartiality to be expected of one in his position.

This reinforced the court's rejection of the allegations of bias. In summary, the

---

67 *Ibid.*
68 *Ibid.*, p. 668.
69 *Ibid.*
70 *Ibid.*
71 *Ibid.*
72 *Ibid.*, p. 669.

ratio decidendi of the Court of Appeal's judgment centered on its appraisal of Crowe's actual ability to keep an open mind, and not on what a bystander would reasonably perceive.

The Supreme Court of Canada reversed the decision of the Court of Appeal by a five-to-three margin.[73] The analyses adopted by the majority and minority in the Supreme Court were diametrically opposed. On the one hand, Laskin C.J.C., writing for the majority, concentrated almost exclusively on whether the particular facts disclosed a reasonable apprehension of bias. Although he referred fleetingly to the possibility that predetermination or preconception could amount to bias, his judgment was not based on any extension of the *nemo judex* rule to cover what might be called "attitudinal bias". This robust approach mirrors that adopted by Dickson J. in *Ringrose*.

On the other hand, de Grandpré J.'s dissenting judgment not only denied the quasi-judicial nature of the National Energy Board, and therefore even the applicability of the *nemo judex* rule to its proceedings, but also was particularly hostile to the possibility that personal attitudes or previous experiences might ever amount to a disqualifying bias. After pointing out that "the National Energy Board is a tribunal that must be staffed with persons of experience and expertise", he quoted the following passage from *R. v. Picard; Ex parte International Longshoremen's Association, Local 375:*[74]

> Professional persons are called upon to serve in judicial, *quasi-judicial* and administrative posts in many fields and if Governments were to exclude candidates on such ground, they would find themselves deprived of the services of most professionals with any experience in the matters in respect of which their services are sought. Accordingly, I agree with the Court below that this ground was properly rejected.

and emphasized that "mere prior knowledge of the particular case or preconceptions or even prejudgments cannot be held *per se* to disqualify a Panel member".[75] His Lordship then accepted the distinction made in the American decision of *New Hampshire Milk Dealers' Association v. New Hampshire Milk Control Board*[76] between a "predisposed view about . . . public or economic policies" (attitudinal bias) and "a prejudgment concerning issues of fact in a particular case" (bias in law):

---

73 [1978] 1 S.C.R. 369. Note that the Supreme Court did not award costs to the appellants.

74 (1968) 65 D.L.R. (2d) 658 at 661 (Que. C.A.).

75 [1978] 1 S.C.R. 369 at 397, quoting MacKeigan C.J.N.S. in *Tomko v. N.S. Lab. Rel. Bd.*, (1975) 9 N.S.R. (2d) 277 at 298, affirmed (1977) 69 D.L.R. (3d) 250 (S.C.C.). De Grandpré J. also referred to *Re Schabas and Univ. of Toronto*, (1975) 6 O.R. (2d) 271 (H.C.); *U.S. v. Morgan*, 313 U.S. 409 (1940); 1 Hals. (4th) 83, para. 69; *R. v. Commonwealth Conciliation and Arb. Comm.; Ex parte The Angliss Group*, (1969) 122 C.L.R. 546 (Aust. H.C.).

76 222 A. 2d 194 at 198 (1967), quoted in *National Energy Board, ibid.*, pp. 399-400.

It is a well-established legal principle that a distinction must be made between a preconceived point of view about certain principles of law or a predisposed view about the public or economic policies which should be controlling and a prejudgment concerning issues of fact in a particular case. 2 Davis, Administrative Law Treaties, s. 12.01, p. 131. There is no doubt that the latter would constitute a cause for disqualification. However, "Bias in the sense of crystallized point of view about issues of law or policy is almost universally deemed no ground for disqualification." (. . .) If this were not the law, Justices Holmes and Brandeis would have been disqualified as would be others from sitting on cases involving issue of law or policy on which they had previously manifested strong diverging views from the holdings of a majority of the members of their respective courts.

Thus de Grandpré J. rejected the appellant's submission that Crowe should be disqualified because his background would naturally incline him to favour the building of a pipeline, and turned to consider whether any particular incident, involvement or action on Crowe's part would lead one reasonably to apprehend that Crowe could not impartially consider the merits of the particular applications before the board.

It appears that the courts have not enthusiastically embraced the concept of attitudinal bias as a ground for judicial review of administrative action. Reference to two other cases, one Canadian, the other English, illustrates this reticence, even where such strong personal preferences are evident that there must be a reasonable apprehension that the decision-maker has a closed mind.

(ii) The Railway case

In *R. v. Pickersgill; Ex parte Smith*,[77] the Canadian Transport Commission was conducting public hearings in Winnipeg to determine whether the Canadian Pacific Railway should be permitted to discontinue its prestigious transcontinental train, "The Canadian". The chairman of the commission was Mr. J.W. Pickersgill, the former federal Minister of Transport who had been actively involved in the formulation of the controversial National Transportation Act,[78] which permitted the discontinuance of rail services under certain conditions. Two months prior to the Winnipeg hearings, he made a speech to the Canadian Manufacturers' Association in Montreal, entitled "Charting the Course of Canada's New Transportation Policy". Although the speech did not mention "The Canadian" by name, the audience clearly would have understood it to refer to the operations of the C.P.R. When the Manitoba Queen's Bench Division was asked to rule whether Pickersgill would thereby

---

77 (1970) 14 D.L.R. (3d) 717 (Man. Q.B.).
78 S.C. 1966-67, c. 69.

be disqualified from presiding over the commission's hearings, Wilson J. held that the speech would not lead reasonable people to[79]

> conclude that Mr. Pickersgill must be taken to harbour a prejudice, or bias, such as would predispose him to allow the application now pending touching "The Canadian".

The learned judge also rejected the applicants' submission that Pickersgill should be disqualified because he "declared himself in favour of a policy which would equate the railways with other industries generally".[80] Wilson J. said that, taking the speech as a whole, he was[81]

> unable to conclude that reasonable people would decide that, consciously or unconsciously, the speaker is *seized with an attitude, a predilection, or bias, whereby he must be taken to have prejudged the fate of "The Canadian"*.

This judgment does not, however, rule out the possibility that, in other circumstances, "an attitude" or "a predilection" or "a prejudgment" might raise a reasonable apprehension of bias, which might disqualify a person from making this type of decision.[82]

(iii) The Franklin case

An even more striking fact pattern occurred in the English case of *Franklin v. Minister of Town and Country Planning*.[83] There the minister, Mr. Lewis Silkin,[84] had appointed a committee[85] to advise the British government on the future development of metropolitan London. Its report in 1946 recommended the establishment of new towns separated from London by a green belt. Four months later the minister introduced legislation in the House of Commons to expropriate the land required for the new towns. In May, two days before second reading of the Bill, he attended a public meeting at Stevenage, where the following exchange took place:[86]

---

79 *Supra*, note 77 at p. 725.

80 *Ibid.*, p. 728.

81 *Ibid.*, emphasis added.

82 *Ibid.*, p. 729, where Wilson J. clearly contemplated that other facts might have amounted to disqualifying bias: "[M]ore is needed than was here shown before the Court will restrain another tribunal from the exercise of its jurisdiction".

83 [1948] A.C. 87 (H.L.).

84 The father of Mr. Samuel Silkin, a later British Attorney General who refused to permit his name to be used in relator proceedings for an injunction against post office workers threatening an illegal boycott of mail and telegrams destined for South Africa. See "quis custodiet?", *The Economist*, 22nd Jan. 1977, p. 11.

85 The Reith Committee (to advise the U.K. government on future development of London), whose interim report was dated 21st January 1946.

86 *Supra*, note 83 at p. 90. This account of the minister's speech differs slightly from that contained in the statement of facts and argument at p. 104 of the reported case.

> I think you will agree that if we are to carry out our policy of creating a number of new towns to relieve congestion in London we could hardly have chosen for the site of one of them a better place than Stevenage. Now I know that many objections have been raised by the inhabitants of Stevenage, perhaps not unnaturally. . . . I want to carry out a daring exercise in town planning — (*Jeers*). It is no good your jeering: it is going to be done — (*Applause and boos*) (*Cries of "Dictator"*). After all this new town is to be built in order to provide for the happiness and welfare of some sixty thousand men, women and children. . . . The project will go forward. It will do so more smoothly and more successfully with your help and co-operation. Stevenage will in a short time become world famous — (*Laughter*). People from all over the world will come to Stevenage to see how we here in this country are building for the new way of life.

The Bill received Royal Assent on 1st August 1946. A draft expropriation notice concerning the Stevenage property was published (as required by the Act[87]) on 6th August 1946. Formal objections to the expropriation were lodged and a public hearing was conducted in October by an inspector. The minister considered this report, wrote a letter to the objectors stating why he did not accept their views, and on 11th November 1946 confirmed the expropriation order. Thereupon, the plaintiffs successfully applied to the High Court to quash the minister's order. Henn Collins J. held[88] that the minister was bound to consider the inspector's report in a judicial or quasi-judicial manner. Referring to the minister's speech in May 1946 the learned judge said:[89]

> If I am to judge by what he said at the public meeting which was held very shortly before the Bill, then published, became an Act of Parliament, *I could have no doubt but that any issue raised by objectors was forejudged. The Minister's language leaves no doubt about that.* He was not saying there must be and shall be satellite towns, but he was saying that Stevenage was to be the first of them. But, when he made that speech, and gave his answers to questions which were asked, he had no administrative functions in relation to the Act in question, for the Act had not then been passed. Though that was his attitude two days before the Bill received its second reading, it is upon the objectors to prove that the Minister was in a like mind, or at least had not an open mind, from and after, at latest, the inception of the public inquiry, which was held in October, 1946.

---

87 New Towns Act, 1946, (9-10 Geo. 6, c. 68).
88 Unreported.
89 Quoted by Lord Thankerton in the House of Lords, *supra*, note 83 at p. 100.

Disqualifying bias, therefore, had not been proved by the plaintiffs on the facts of this case, although its arguability was clearly recognized by the judge. For other reasons, he struck down the minister's order but was reversed by the Court of Appeal,[90] and this reversal was upheld by the House of Lords.[91]

(iv) Summary on attitudinal bias

The *Bethany Care Centre* case is the only one in which the courts have specifically struck down a decision on the grounds of attitudinal bias. Nevertheless, it is submitted that the courts have frequently recognized the possibility that a prejudgment or preference may be so strong as to raise a reasonable apprehension that the decision-maker does not bring an open mind to the matter at hand. Dickson J.'s approach in *Ringrose* would apply the same test to allegations of attitudinal bias which governs other breaches of the *nemo judex* rule: is there a reasonable apprehension of bias on the facts of this case? Adopting this approach will undoubtedly result in more successful challenges to alleged attitudinal bias and this development would accord with the fundamental principle that justice must be seen to be done.

(e) Conflicts of Interest

Despite the court's reluctance to concede the existence of attitudinal bias, the *National Energy Board* case nevertheless pinpoints one of the weaknesses of our present regulatory system: the interchange of personnel between the bodies regulated and the regulatory agencies. This interchange provides the regulatory agencies with the expertise which they require in order to understand and regulate their respective industries. Unfortunately, however, there are concomitant disadvantages of this convenient arrangement: first, the tendency of these expert members of the regulatory agencies to view the matters before them from the narrow perspective of their experience of the regulated industry, without taking into account the broader public interest; and, secondly, the tendency of persons appointed to regulatory agencies to use their position and experience as a springboard back into the industry at a very high level. However much this flow increases the agencies' expertise, it does not always foster the public's perception of impartiality on their part. It is interesting, therefore, to note former U.S. President Carter's stated policy of prohibiting former members of such agencies from taking employment in the regulated industry for a period of two years after their retirement.[92] This, of

---

90 (1947) 176 L.T. 200.

91 *Supra*, note 83. Lord Thankerton first determined that the minister's function was not quasi-judicial in nature, and then held that there was no breach of the *nemo judex* rule. As discussed in section 6 of this chapter, it is probably now the better view that both *audi alteram partem* and *nemo judex* apply to all types of delegated powers, and are not restricted to ones which can be characterized as quasi-judicial.

92 See "Carter expects . . .", *The Economist*, 8th Jan. 1977, p. 41, where the U.S. President's policy was described as follows:

course, will only stop the flow of personnel in one direction, but it does acknowledge the existence of the problem of maintaining public confidence in quasi-judicial agencies.

Nor is the problem of attitudinal bias restricted to the exercise of judicial or quasi-judicial functions. Similar flows of personnel take place between the public service proper (as opposed to quasi-independent adjudicative or regulatory agencies) and the private sector. How often does a senior civil servant[93] quit his public position only to become, immediately thereafter, a consultant advising private interests on how best to deal with that very part of the government?

Not much can effectively be done to prevent such flows of personnel, given the wide variety of positions in the public service and the differing saleability of any expertise gained by public servants. In the private sector, of course, restrictive covenants often prevent a senior manager from going to work for a competitor within a certain time after leaving his previous employer. By contrast, President Carter's limitations on members of regulatory agencies could not be generalized to apply to people still in the public service whose predispositions to certain courses of action arise from hopes for future career openings. On this point, the conflict of interest guidelines for federal public servants and members of Parliament[94] are aimed at preventing conflicts which arise while the person is acting in a governmental capacity.

Similarly, Parliament may explicitly consider whether particular persons should be excluded from exercising the powers which it delegates, whether or not these powers are delegated to members of the central public service. A good example of such a prohibition is contained in section 251(4) of the Criminal Code,[95] which prevents a doctor who is a member of a hospital's abortion committee from performing any abortions in that hospital. The

---

Mr. Carter has spoken out against the "revolving door" through which outgoing members of regulator agencies pass to join up as lobbyists with the firms they have supervised. The new rules extend to two years the period poachers must wait before handling matters they touched as keepers. Retiring officials will also be barred for a year from formal or informal contact with former colleagues for financial gain. The occasional drink, it seems, is still permitted.

The stricter rules apply only to cabinet members and the most senior officials. Unless written into law they are not easily enforceable. But exacting penalties is hardly the point. Mr. Carter's "code" was felt necessary to dispel public mistrust and has its symbolic side.

93 Or a cabinet member?

94 See the Green Paper, *Members of Parliament and Conflict of Interest*, July 1973, issued on behalf of the government by the Hon. Allan J. MacEachen, then President of the Privy Council. See also *Report of the Senate's Standing Committee on Legal and Constitutional Affairs* (the Hon. H. Carl Goldenberg, Chairman), 29th June 1976 (Issue No. 42). On the law relating to conflicts of interest in municipal politicians in Ontario, see Rogers, "Conflicts of Interest — a Trap for Unwary Politicians", (1973) 11 Osgoode Hall L.J. 537.

95 R.S.C. 1970, c. C-34.

purpose of this provision is clear. However, it does not prevent a doctor from resigning from the committee and immediately thereafter performing an abortion in the same hospital. Indeed, it is understood that, in certain hospitals where abortions are readily available, the membership of the abortion committees rotates very rapidly among the doctors performing the abortions at that hospital. Although this device may well fulfill the technical requirements of the Criminal Code, it frankly defeats the purpose for which Parliament enacted the provision.

Greater awareness by the government of possible or perceived conflicts of interest would cause it to exercise greater care in appointing its various officers, particularly to quasi-judicial bodies. For example, in the *National Energy Board* case, there were eight members of the board, all of whom were presumably competent to hear the applications in question. Why, therefore, was it necessary for Crowe to act as chairman of these hearings? At any rate, if neither Parliament nor the government exhibits much sensitivity to the appearance of justice in appointing high officers of state, the courts should not quail at applying the *nemo judex* rule.

3. The Test for Bias

Because the rationale for the *nemo judex* rule lies in the appearance of justice being done, it has long been established that it is not necessary to demonstrate that a decision-maker is actually biased.[96] Indeed, no evidence can be led to show that the delegate is not in fact biased,[97] because that state of

---

96 Note that the appellants in the *National Energy Board* case, [1978] 1 S.C.R. 369, reversing (*sub nom. Re Canadian Arctic Gas Pipeline Ltd.*) (1976) 65 D.L.R. (3d) 660, specifically disclaimed that Mr. Crowe was in fact biased. Similarly, the House of Lords indicated that no one could have presumed Lord Cottenham to have allowed his financial interest to affect his order in *Dimes v. Grand Junction Canal Co.*, (1852) 3 H.L. Cas. 759. *A fortiori*, however, the existence of actual bias or hostility will nullify a decision: *Pearson v. Anctil*, [1974] C.A. 19 (Que.).

97 As discussed in the *Ringrose* case, [1976] 4 W.W.R. 712 (S.C.C.). In the Alberta Court of Appeal, [1975] 4 W.W.R. 43 at 48, Prowse J.A. said:

> In my view these cases [*Szilard v. Szasz*, [1955] S.C.R. 3; and *Ghirardosi v. Min. of Highways (B.C.)*, [1966] S.C.R. 367] merely support the conclusion that when circumstances exist from which a reasonable apprehension of bias arises *evidence is not admissible for the purpose of establishing that a person the law presumes to be biased was not in fact biased*. They do not purport to deal with the question of the admissibility of evidence for the purpose of having the relevant circumstances before the court so that it may consider whether in those circumstances a reasonable apprehension of bias arises. [Emphasis added.]

> Although de Grandpré J. referred to Laskin C.J.C.'s decision in *P. P. G. Indust. Can. Ltd. v. A.G. Can.*, (1976) 65 D.L.R. (3d) 354 (S.C.C.), he did not appear to notice that the Chief Justice there did quite definitely consider evidence, contrary to principle, which showed that Buchanan had not in fact *participated* in the Anti-Dumping Tribunal's decision, although he had signed one copy of it. Nevertheless, that evidence was not directed to bias, but rather to show non-participation.

affairs is irrelevant to the issue before the court: namely, is there a reasonable apprehension of bias?

Until recently, there was some confusion as to whether the proper test was (a) a real likelihood, or (b) a reasonable apprehension of bias. Although some commentators have suggested that there is no practical difference between these two tests,[98] the law now appears to be correctly settled in favour of the latter.[99] After all, there may well be circumstances in which there is a "reasonable apprehension" of bias when a detailed examination of the facts might demonstrate no "real likelihood" thereof. Perhaps the converse situation can also exist. But the public policy which requires the appearance of justice necessarily focuses on perceptions. Hence, the real likelihood of bias must be as irrelevant as actual bias to the applicability of the *nemo judex* rule.

The courts must determine whether a particular fact pattern gives rise to a reasonable apprehension of bias. On the one hand, because different judges will react differently to similar allegations of bias, it is therefore important not to elevate individual decisions into inflexible rules of law as to the circumstances in which a reasonable apprehension of bias can arise.[100] This flexibility is the importance of Dickson J.'s approach in *Ringrose*.[101] On the other hand, there must be some basis for saying that there is a reasonable apprehension of bias. Thus, a number of cases impose a duty on the person raising the allegation to make reasonable inquiries about the facts which he says make him apprehend bias.[102] Probably this duty is no more than not to be irresponsible in his allegations,[103] for any higher duty to investigate would require him to conclude that there was at least a real likelihood of — if not actual — bias.

---

98 For a discussion of the differences in the tests, see *Metro. Properties Co. (F.G.C.) v. Lannon*, [1969] 1 Q.B. 577 (C.A.), p. 599 *per* Lord Denning M.R., p. 606 *per* Edmund Davies L.J. See also H.W.R. Wade, *Administrative Law*, 5th ed. (Oxford: Clarendon Press, 1982), pp. 430-32; and S.A. de Smith, *Judicial Review of Administrative Action*, 3rd ed., (London: Stevens & Sons Ltd., 1973), pp. 230-32.

99 Accepted by Chief Justice Laskin writing for the unanimous Supreme Court of Canada in *P.P.G. Indust. Can. Ltd. v. A.G. Can.*, (1976) 65 D.L.R. (3d) 354 (S.C.C.), reversing (1974) 39 D.L.R. (3d) 229 (*sub nom. Re A.G. Can. and Anti-Dumping Tribunal*), which reversed on other grounds (1973) 30 D.L.R. (3d) 678; accepted by de Grandpré J. in the *Ringrose* case, *supra* note 97, even though he had dissented on this point in the *National Energy Board* case, *supra* note 96 at pp. 728-29. The test was also accepted in *Szilard v. Szasz*, [1955] S.C.R. 3.

100 *E.g.*, that attitudinal bias could never constitute a breach of the *nemo judex* rule.

101 *Supra*, note 97.

102 *E.g.*, see de Grandpré J.'s comments in the *National Energy Board* case, *supra*, note 96, especially at pp. 741-45.

103 In any event, many people may quite reasonably doubt the impartiality of a decision-maker without feeling the necessity of verifying their suspicions beyond reasonable doubt. The courts, therefore, should not impose the same investigative duty on the person who alleges a breach of *nemo judex* rule as it would on a prudent man who considers making a potentially defamatory statement.

4. A Breach Goes to Jurisdiction

A breach of the *nemo judex* rule causes a delegate to lose jurisdiction. The common law presumes that "no man shall be a judge in his own cause", and any attempt to do so will render the delegate's action void. This is identical to what happens when there is a breach of the other principle of natural justice, *audi alteram partem*. Thus, (a) such a decision has no legal effect whatever; (b) a privative clause would be ineffective to prevent judicial review since there is no "decision" to be protected by the clause; and (c) *certiorari* clearly would operate retrospectively to confirm that the decision never had lawful effect. Because bias involves a loss of jurisdiction, and is not merely an intra-jurisdictional error of law, there is no need to quash the decision, and a declaration should in principle be interchangeable with *certiorari* as a remedy. As Wade has pointed out,[104] the conclusion that a breach of the principles of natural justice goes to jurisdiction is not contradicted by the courts' occasional refusal to grant a remedy because the applicant has no standing or for other discretionary reasons. Such a decision is not thereby validated, although no one may be able to challenge it successfully.

5. Admissibility of Evidence to Show a Reasonable Apprehension of Bias

Evidence is admissible to demonstrate all types of jurisdictional errors, including breaches of the *nemo judex* rule. The policy underlying this rule is to permit the superior courts to apply the *ultra vires* principle to keep inferior tribunals within the ambit of their limited jurisdictions. Thus, the facts supporting an apprehension of bias do not have to appear on the face of the record of the proceedings of the delegate. Indeed, it would be comparatively rare for the record itself to demonstrate why bias might be perceived to exist. On the contrary, affidavits and *viva voce* evidence are unquestionably relevant and admissible to determine whether there is such a reasonable apprehension of bias that the delegate should be deprived of his jurisdiction.

This rationale, however, does not necessarily apply to the converse situation to permit the delegate to lead extrinsic evidence. On the one hand, common sense says that the delegate (or another party) can lead evidence to contradict that introduced by the applicant for judicial review. The purpose of such evidence is to show that there is no reasonable apprehension of bias disclosed by the facts. On the other hand, it would appear to be wrong in principle to permit the delegate (or another party) to lead evidence to show that there was no actual bias, or no actual participation by a disqualified person in the decision. Such evidence is irrelevant to determining whether there is an *apprehension* of bias, and therefore is inadmissible.

---

104 H.W.R. Wade, "Unlawful Administrative Action: Void or Voidable?", Part I at (1967) 83 L.Q.R. 499; Part II at (1968) 84 L.Q.R. 95.

6. The *Nemo Judex* Rule Applies to All Types of Functions

In theory, the rule against bias applies to precisely the same ambit of delegated powers as the first principle of natural justice, *audi alteram partem*. Although it used to be thought that *audi alteram partem* only applied to the exercise of a judicial or quasi-judicial power, the law has recently developed so that the principles of natural justice and fairness apply as well to delegated powers which were formerly characterized as being merely administrative in nature. Although legal analysis has tended to treat the two principles of natural justice separately, the right to be heard by an impartial and unbiased decision-maker is really only one aspect of fairness — and, indeed, of *audi alteram partem*. Accordingly, the recent expansion of the fair hearing rule should logically be matched by an expansion of the *nemo judex* rule beyond judicial or quasi-judicial powers to include merely administrative ones as well.

Unfortunately, the cases do not yet clearly demonstrate this trend. In both *French*[105] and *Ringrose*, there are *dicta* in the Supreme Court of Canada that the *nemo judex* rule did not apply because no quasi-judicial function was involved in the first step of the two-tier decisions involving professional discipline. The court's analysis of what constitutes a quasi-judicial decision has been criticized elsewhere, but the broader question is why the *nemo judex* rule should not be extended to merely administrative functions as well. Certainly this is contemplated by the approach adopted by Dickson J. in his dissent in *Ringrose*, where he simply asks whether there is a reasonable apprehension of bias without first characterizing the nature of the delegated power in question. Dickson J.'s approach contemplates that there can be a reasonable apprehension of institutional or attitudinal bias in certain circumstances, and clearly also contemplates applying the *nemo judex* rule to cases which other judges might not hold to be technically quasi-judicial. In light of the fact that *French* and *Ringrose* were both decided prior to the decisions by the Supreme Court of Canada in *Nicholson*[106] and *Martineau (No. 2)*,[107] one might speculate that the courts will now adopt Dickson J.'s approach to the *nemo judex* rule.

7. Can the Rule be Waived?

Although parties generally cannot extend a delegate's statutory powers by agreement, it is submitted that there is no objection to their waiving the *nemo judex* rule to prevent disqualification of a decision-maker whom they find to be acceptable.[108] After all, a breach of natural justice does not prevent the delegate from obtaining jurisdiction in the narrow sense used by Lord Reid

---

105 [1975] 2 S.C.R. 767.
106 *Nicholson v. Haldimand-Norfolk Police Commr. Bd.*, [1979] 1 S.C.R. 311.
107 *Martineau v. Matsqui Inst. Disciplinary Bd. (No. 2)*, [1980] 1 S.C.R. 602.
108 *Wakefield Loc. Bd. of Health v. West Riding & Grimsby Ry. Co.*, (1865) L.R. 1 Q.B. 84.

in *Anisminic*,[109] but is an error which causes him to lose jurisdiction in the course of his proceedings. If both parties specifically agree to a particular way of conducting that hearing, this does not amount to conferring jurisdiction where none ever existed; rather, it merely prevents the delegate from losing jurisdiction, which might otherwise occur in the absence of that agreement. Indeed, the very fact that both parties specifically agree that a particular person may hear the matter not only estops each of them from subsequently raising the *nemo judex* rule,[110] it also undoubtedly means that neither of them can thereafter have a reasonable apprehension that that decision-maker is biased.[111] Accordingly, there appears to be nothing wrong with the practice wherein both parties specifically agree that a union may appoint one of its own members to an arbitration board affecting itself, notwithstanding the decision in the *Bethany Care Centre* case. Of course, it would be wise to have any such agreement specifically noted in the record. Conversely, a party who does not raise an allegation of bias in a timely fashion may be held to have acquiesced and waived his right to do so subsequently.[112]

8. Summary

The rule against bias has been discussed in this chapter as a separate part of the principles of natural justice and fairness which the common law presumes to apply to the exercise of delegated powers. Parliament may, of course, exercise its sovereignty specifically to exclude the application of the rule in a particular situation.

The content of the *nemo judex* rule is relatively clear when applied to court proceedings, where the judge is a third party who is expected to be impartial. The maxim is more difficult to apply to other delegates exercising statutory powers which take them away from the curial model but which nevertheless seriously affect people. The appearance of justice is an important value in our system of government, and it is not surprising that the courts have often applied the same standards of impartiality to administrators that apply to judges. Nor is it surprising that attempts have been made in recent years to extend the *nemo judex* rule to circumstances involving institutional or attitudinal bias. It would be helpful if legislators could give greater thought to the appearance of justice when drafting laws establishing administrative schemes.

---

109 *Anisminic v. Foreign Comp. Comm.*, [1969] 2 A.C. 147.

110 *MacLean v. Wkrs. Union*, [1929] 1 Ch. 602.

111 Actual bias which was unknown to the party, however, may still permit the application of the *nemo judex* rule: see *Loc. 1571, Int. Longshoremen's Assn. v. Int. Longshoremen's Assn.*, [1951] 3 D.L.R. 50 (N.B.S.C.).

112 *R. v. Nailsworth Licensing Justices; Ex parte Bird*, [1953] 1 W.L.R. 1046; *H. Tulputt & Co. v. Mole*, [1911] 1 K.B. 836; but see *R. v. Williams; Ex parte Phillips*, [1914] 1 K.B. 608, and *R. v. Essex Justices; Ex parte Perkins*, [1927] 2 K.B. 475, where litigants *in personam* were permitted to raise bias later because they did not know its legal effect at the time.

Until then, the courts will have to apply the *nemo judex* rule to each case, on its now facts, as it arises.

9. Selected Bibliography

Arthurs, H.W., "The Three Faces of Justice — Bias in the Tripartite Tribunal", (1963) 28 Sask. Bar Rev. 147.

Jones, D.P. "Comment on *P. P. G. Industries Canada Ltd. v. The Attorney-General of Canada*", (1977) 55 Can. Bar Rev. 718.

Jones, D.P., "Institutional Bias: The Applicability of the Nemo Judex Rule to Two-Tier Decisions", (1977) 23 McGill L.J. 605.

Jones, D.P., "The National Energy Board Case and the Concept of Attitudinal Bias", (1977) 23 McGill L.J. 459.

Report of the Committee on Ministers' Powers, (the "Donoughmore Committee") England (1932), pp. 76-9.

Sedgewick, R.M., Jr., "Disqualification on the Ground of Bias as Applied to Administrative Tribunals", (1945) 23 Can. Bar Rev. 453.

10

Errors of Law
on the Face
of the Record

1. Introduction

The purpose of this chapter is to examine the anomalous use of *certiorari* to correct certain intra-jurisdictional errors of law on the face of the record of proceedings taken by a statutory delegate. This requires consideration of:

(a) the distinction between errors which deprive a statutory delegate of his jurisdiction, and errors which are not jurisdictional in nature;
(b) the general limitations on *certiorari* as a remedy;
(c) the extent of the "record";
(d) the distinction between an error of "law" and other kinds of errors;
(e) the use of the "patently unreasonable" test to avoid the effect of a privative clause; and
(f) the new use of the "patently unreasonable" test upon the exercise of the court's discretion to refuse a prerogative remedy, particularly when there is no privative clause to protect an intra-jurisdictional error of law.

Finally, reference will be made to the similar (but separate) common law power of the superior courts to quash and remit the decision of a consensual arbitrator who has committed an error of law.

2. The Distinction Between Jurisdictional and Non-Jurisdictional Errors of Law

Although almost all grounds for judicial review concentrate on the jurisdiction of a statutory delgate, *certiorari* is also sometimes available to correct any errors of law made by the delegate *within* his jurisdiction. This anomaly was referred to by Lord Sumner in *R. v. Nat Bell Liquors Limited*,[1] and resuscitated by Denning L.J. in *R. v. Northumberland Compensation Appeal Tribunal; Ex parte Shaw*.[2] In theory, this use of *certiorari* permits the court to make sure that all statutory delegates abide by the law of the land. This ground of judicial review is subject to restriction by the enactment of a privative clause, and is also subject to the court's inherent discretion to refuse prerogative remedies. Both of these restrictions seriously complicate this area of the law and they will be considered in detail below. Further, it is often extremely difficult to determine whether an error deprives the delegate of his jurisdiction or lies within it.

No satisfactory test has ever been developed for distinguishing between jurisdictional and non-jurisdictional errors. Nevertheless, the distinction between these two concepts is important for at least five reasons. First, a privative clause cannot effectively prevent judicial review where the jurisdiction of the delegate is in question, but will be effective to prevent the superior courts from using *certiorari* to correct mere errors of law on the face of the record. Secondly, affidavits and other evidence are admissible if necessary to prove the existence of a jurisdictional error, but they cannot be considered by the court if a non-jurisdictional error of law is involved. Thirdly, the court's anomalous power to correct intra-jurisdictional errors is limited to errors of law only, and does not apply to errors of fact, whereas factual matters may give rise to a jurisdictional error, particularly in the context of the preliminary or collateral fact doctrine. Fourthly, this anomalous use of *certiorari* can only correct errors of law which appear on the face of the record, however that is defined, whereas jurisdictional errors do not have to be so disclosed. Finally, it may not be possible to correct intra-jurisdictional errors by any remedy other than this anomalous use of *certiorari*,[3] although other remedies may frequently be available to review jurisdictional errors.

3. Inherent Limitations on the Availability of *Certiorari* as a Remedy to Correct Errors of Law

Because errors of law on the face of the record can sometimes be corrected by *certiorari*, this ground for judicial review will generally only be available to the extent to which *certiorari* is available as a remedy.

(a) The Ambit of *Certiorari* Against Administrative Decisions

Formerly, it was thought that *certiorari* was only available against judicial or quasi-judicial bodies, and not against merely administrative ones.

---

1 [1922] 2 A.C. 128 (P.C.).

2 [1952] 1 K.B. 338, affirming [1951] 1 K.B. 711 (C.A.).

3 *E.g.*, by a declaration, which will not quash the delegate's decision. See *Punton v. Min. of Pensions and Nat. Ins. (No. 2)*, [1964] 1 W.L.R. 226 (C.A.).

However, at least since the *Nicholson v. Haldimand-Norfolk Police Commissioners Board*[4] and *Martineau v. Matsqui Institution Disciplinary Board*[5] cases, the ambit of *certiorari* has been expanded to supervise the procedural fairness of merely administrative bodies. In principle, therefore, *certiorari* should be available to correct errors of law committed by merely administrative bodies, and not be restricted to those which are exercising judicial or quasi-judicial functions.

(b) Is a Statutory Delegate Involved?

Certiorari is also only available against the exercise of a statutory power. Thus, in *Re Minister of Education and Civil Service Association (Alberta)*,[6] the Court of Appeal held that *certiorari* was not available to supervise the exercise of judicial powers created by an agreement. The same difficulty has long plagued attempts to obtain *certiorari* against labour arbitration boards. On the one hand, some labour arbitration boards are established by statute, and *certiorari* will[7] be available to correct at least some errors of law made on the face of their records. On the other hand, other labour legislation merely provides the vehicle through which collective agreements are reached, including a statutory obligation to include an arbitration clause in such agreements. The courts have vacillated about the availability of *certiorari* to correct errors of law committed by such consensual arbitration boards. This point appears to have been recently settled affirmatively by the Supreme Court of Canada in *Roberval Express Ltee. v. Transport Drivers, Warehousemen and General Workers' Union, Local 106.*[8] This decision will in effect convert many labour arbitrations into statutory proceedings, thereby bringing them within the ambit of *certiorari*. Nevertheless, *certiorari* is still not available against non-statutory decisions, and it is important to remember the existence of the

---

4 [1979] 1 S.C.R. 311.

5 [1980] 1 S.C.R. 602.

6 (1976) 70 D.L.R. (3d) 696 at 699. See also the reasoning of Clement J.A. in *Inland Cement Indust. Ltd. v. C.L.G.W., Loc. 359*, [1981] 3 W.W.R. 65 (Alta. C.A.), to the effect that arbitration boards constituted under the Labour Relations Act, S.A. 1980, c. 72 [now R.S.A. 1980, c. L-1.1 (Supp.)], are indeed statutory, following *Re Int. Nickel Co. and Rivando*, [1956] O.R. 379 (C.A.), from Ontario. In 1977 the words "or otherwise" were removed from the Alberta Labour Act, thereby really putting the statutory nature of labour arbitration boards beyond question in this province. This realization would have pre-empted a considerable part of the subsequent judgment by Kerans J.A. in *Suncor Inc. v. McMurray Independent Oil Wkrs., Loc. 1*, [1983] 1 W.W.R. 604 (Alta. C.A.), discussed *infra*.

7 In the absence of an effective privative clause.

8 [1982] 2 S.C.R. 888, reversing its previous decision in *Howe Sound Co. v. Int. Union of Mine etc. Workers*, [1962] S.C.R. 318, which held that there could be a statutory arbitrator only if the parties were compelled by statute to submit their disputes to that person, and did not have the option of settling those disputes by some other method. Such compulsion was the case in *Port Arthur Shipbldg. Co. v. Arthurs*, [1969] S.C.R. 85, and *Re Int. Nickel Co. and Rivando*, *supra*, note 6.

separate common law remedy to quash and remit a consensual arbitrator's decision for misconduct (discussed in section 9 below).

4. The Record

What, then, constitutes the record? Lord Denning said this in the *Shaw* case:[9]

> It has been said to consist of all those documents which are kept by the tribunal for a permanent memorial and testimony of their proceedings: see Blackstone's Commentaries, Vol. III, at p. 24. But it must be noted that, whenever there was any question as to what should, or should not be, included in the record of any tribunal, the Court of King's Bench used to determine it. It did it in this way: When the tribunal sent their record to the King's Bench in answer to the writ of certiorari, this return was examined, and if it was defective or incomplete it was quashed: see *Apsley's* case,[10] *Rex v. Levermore*,[11] and *Ashley's* case,[12] or, alternatively, the tribunal might be ordered to complete it: *Williams v. Bagot*[13] and *Rex v. Warnford*.[14] It appears that the Court of King's Bench always insisted that the record should contain, or recite, the document or information which initiated the proceedings and thus gave the tribunal its jurisdiction; and also the document which contained their adjudication. Thus in the old days the record sent up by the justices had, in the case of a conviction, to recite the information in its precise terms; and in the case of an order which had been decided by quarter sessions by way of appeal, the record had to set out the order appealed from: see *Anon.*[15] The record had also to set out the adjudication, but it was never necessary to set out the reasons (see *South Cadbury (Inhabitants) v. Braddon, Somerset (Inhabitants)*[16]) nor the evidence, save in the case of convictions. Following these cases, I think the record must contain at least the document which initiates the proceedings; the pleadings, if any; and the adjudication; but not the evidence, nor the reasons, unless the tribunal chooses to incorporate them. If the tribunal does state its reasons, and those reasons are wrong in law, certiorari lies to quash the decision.

---

9 *Supra*, note 2 at 352, footnotes renumbered. See also the decision in *Baldwin & Francis Ltd. v. Patent Appeal Tribunal*, [1959] 2 All E.R. 433 at 445; *Bd. of Indust. Rel. (Alta.) v. Stedelbauer Chevrolet Oldsmobile Ltd.*, 59 W.W.R. 269 at 278, affirmed [1969] S.C.R. 137.

10 (1648) Sty. 86.

11 (1700) 1 Salk. 146.

12 (1697) 2 Salk. 479.

13 (1824) 4 Dow. & Ry. K.B. 315.

14 (1825) 5 Dow. & Ry. K.B. 489.

15 (1697) 2 Salk. 479.

16 (1710) 2 Salk. 607.

A nice question arises whether the record includes the evidence presented to a statutory delegate during the course of his proceedings. On the one hand, the decision in *Farrell v. Workmen's Compensation Board*,[17] specifically holds that the record consists only of the initiating document, the pleadings (if any), and the adjudication (including the reasons if incorporated therein), but not the evidence or the supporting documents referred to in the decision. In Alberta, the Rules of Court[18] effectively deem the following documents to be part of the record which the decision-maker is required to return to the Court of Queen's Bench in an application for *certiorari*: the judgment, order or decision (as the case may be) and reasons therefor, together with the process commencing the proceedings, the evidence and all exhibits filed (if any), and all things touching the matter, together with the notice of motion for *certiorari*. Accordingly, it appears that the definition of the record has been extended in Alberta to include all of the evidence.[19] To this extent, therefore, it may be possible to use the extended record in Alberta to demonstrate errors of law which can be corrected by the anomalous use of *certiorari*. On the other hand, administrative bodies often do not make verbatim transcripts or tape recordings of their proceedings, and are generally under no duty to do so.[20] As a result, it may not be possible to show an error of law on the face of even the extended record: the delegate's decision may still be "the inscrutable face of the Sphinx",[21] immune from judicial review.

Secondly, a similar problem relates to whether notes taken by a statutory delegate form part of the record. These notes are not themselves evidence, but may be summaries of the evidence. In *Walker v. Keating*,[22] the Appeal Division of the Nova Scotia Supreme Court declined to include the handwritten notes of the chairman of a three-member tribunal as part of the record. By contrast, the Trial Division of that same court did order the notes of a sole arbitrator to be included in the record in *Construction Association Management Labour Bureau Ltd. v. International Brotherhood of Electrical Workers, Local 625*[23] apparently because there could be no possibility of a difference in the notes taken by the various members of the tribunal. On the other hand,

---

17 26 D.L.R. (2d) 185, affirmed [1962] S.C.R. 48.

18 R. 743 in civil matters; R. 831 in criminal matters.

19 Note: In *Woodward Stores (Westmount) Ltd. v. Alta. Assessment Appeal Bd. Division No. 1*, (1976) 69 D.L.R. (3d) 450 (Alta. T.D.), McDonald J. queried whether such an extension to the record could be accomplished by Rule of Court, in light of the fact that such an extension might affect the substantive law which could not be changed by rule. This possible problem no longer exists because s. 47(2) of the Judicature Act, R.S.A. 1980, c. J-1, validates the Rules of Court notwithstanding that any provision therein may affect substantive rights.

20 If proceedings are tape recorded, the practice in Alberta appears to be to include the tape as part of the record returned to the court. However, the court has held that no jurisdictional error arises where the tape is unintelligible: see *Int. Assoc. of Bridge, Structural & Ornamental Iron Wkrs. Loc. 725 v. Canron Inc.*, (1983) 43 A.R. 299 (Q.B.).

21 *R. v. Nat Bell Liquors Ltd.*, (1922) 65 D.L.R. 1 at 25 (P.C.), per Lord Sumner.

22 (1973) 6 N.S.R. (2d) 1 (C.A.).

23 (1983) 34 C.P.C. 65 (N.S. T.D.).

this last case holds that copies of decisions and other authorities submitted to the tribunal do not form part of its record, even though they are "other papers or documents in the proceeding"[24] and "touch the matter"[25] being questioned by *certiorari*. Oddly, the dissenting decision of a multi-member statutory body has been held not to constitute part of the record.[26] In principle, correspondence between members of a statutory body, written after the hearing for the purpose of discussing the issues, should not form part of the record, because it does not affect the proceedings at the hearing. If such documents exist, the person making the return to the court cannot sign the certificate as drafted in Rule 744,[27] and should probably alter the certificate to reflect that certain documents in his possession are not properly returnable to the court as part of the record. At least such a procedure discloses the existence of such materials, and leaves it open to the judge to determine whether they are part of the record.

---

24 Nova Scotia rule.

25 Alberta rule.

26 *Regina (City) v. Amalgam. Transit Union*, (1976) 61 D.L.R. (3d) 376, affirmed 67 D.L.R. (3d) 533 (Sask. C.A.). However, counsel often puts the dissenting reasons before the court by affidavit. For a different view, see *Milan v. Cominco Ltd.*, N.W.T.S.C. Morrow J., 28th November 1972 (unreported).

27 Alberta Rules of Court, R. 744 provides as follows:

744(1) Upon receiving the notice so endorsed the justice or justices, officer, clerk or tribunal shall return forthwith to the office mentioned therein the judgment, order, warrant or decision together with the process commencing the proceedings, the evidence and all exhibits filed, if any, and all things touching the matter and the notice served upon him with a certificate endorsed thereon in the following form:

"Pursuant to the accompanying notice I herewith return to the Honourable Court the following papers and documents, that is to say —

"(a) the judgment, order, decision (or as the case may be) and the reasons therefor;
"(b) the process commencing the proceedings and the warrant issued thereon;
"(c) the evidence taken at the hearing and all exhibits filed;
"(d) all other papers or documents touching the matter.

"And I hereby certify to this Honourable Court that I have above truly set forth all the papers and documents in my custody and power relating to the matter set forth in the notice of motion."

(2) If the proceedings are not in the possession of the person required to transmit them, he shall in lieu of the certificate, so state and explain the circumstances.

(3) If the proceedings have not been received by the officer to whom or the clerk of the office to which they are by law required to be transmitted, that officer or clerk shall return a certificate of the fact.

(4) The certificate prescribed in subrule (1) or (2) has the same effect as a return to a writ of *certiorari*.

(5) The court may dispense with the return of the evidence or exhibits or part of them.

(6) A copy of this Rule shall appear upon or be annexed to the notice of motion served upon the provincial judge, justice or justices, clerk or officer or tribunal from whom the return is required.

Finally, it is sometimes possible to extend the record by agreement. As Lord Denning noted in the *Shaw* case:[28]

> Notwithstanding the strictness of the rule that the error of law must appear on the face of the record, the parties could always by agreement overcome this difficulty. If they both desired a ruling of the Court of King's Bench on a point of law which had been decided by the tribunal, but which had not been entered on the record, the parties could agree that the question should be argued and determined as if it were expressed in the order. The first case I have found in which this was done was in 1792, *Rex v. Essex*,[29] but thereafter it was quite common. It became a regular practice for parties to supplement the record by affidavits disclosing the points of law that had been decided by the tribunal. This course was only taken if no one objected. It seems to have been adopted by litigants as a convenient alternative to asking the tribunal to make a speaking order. Thus, in the numerous cases on the validity of a sewer's rate, it was the regular course of proceeding for affidavits to be lodged stating the objections in law to the rate; and the case was decided on the objections stated in the affidavits: see, for instance, *Rex v. Tower Hamlets*.[30] Recent cases such as *Rex v. West Riding of Yorkshire Justices*[31] and *General Medical Council v. Spackman*[32] show that the practice continues today. The explanation of all these cases is, I think, that the affidavits are treated by consent as if they were part of the record and make it into a speaking order.

5. Errors of Law Versus Errors of Fact

As its name implies, the anomalous use of *certiorari* to quash errors of law on the face of the record requires there to be an error of law, and not some other type of mistake. Thus, *certiorari* will not issue to correct an error of fact.[33] Nevertheless, what constitutes an "error of law" is to be widely construed, and probably has a meaning similar to the phrase used for determining the right of appeal on a point of law. Wade[34] describes the distinction as follows:

---

28 [1952] 1 K.B. 338 at 353 (C.A.).
29 (1792) 4 Term Rep. 591.
30 (1829) 9 B. & C. 517.
31 [1910] 2 K.B. 192.
32 [1943] A.C. 627, affirming [1942] 2 K.B. 261 (sub nom. *R. v. Gen. Medical Council; Ex parte Spackman*) (H.L.).
33 See *R. v. Criminal Injuries Comp. Bd.; Ex parte Staten*, [1972] 1 W.L.R. 569 (Div. Ct.).
34 *Administrative Law*, 4th ed., (1977), p. 775.

There is only one clear and logical point at which the line [between errors of law and errors of fact] can be drawn, and it has been recognized in many judgments. This is that questions of fact are the primary facts of the particular case which have to be established before the law can be applied, the "facts which are observed by the witnesses and proved by testimony", to which should be added any facts of common knowledge of which the court will take notice without proof. Whether these facts, once established, satisfy some legal definition or requirement is a question of law, for the question then is how to interpret and apply the law to those established facts. If the question is whether some building is a "house" within the meaning of the Housing Acts, its location, condition, purpose of use and so forth are questions of fact. But once these facts are established, the question whether it counts as a house within the meaning of the Act is a question of law.

. . . .

In principle, therefore, an appeal on a point of law should be available on every question of legal interpretation arising after the primary facts have been established. It ought to cover all legal "inferences from facts", as they are often called. It should cover all questions of causation. But the courts have laid down a narrower doctrine, designed to give greater latitude to tribunals where there is room for difference of opinion. The rule is that the application of a legal definition or principle to ascertained facts is erroneous in point of law only if the conclusion reached by the tribunal is unreasonable. If it is within the range of interpretations within which different persons might reasonably reach different conclusions, the court will hold that there is no error of law.

The "unreasonableness' doctrine for defining errors of law is considered in detail in sections 6 and 7 of this chapter.

It would be wrong, however, to assume that errors of fact made by an administrative tribunal can never be the subject of judicial review, although such review clearly would relate to jurisdiction. To the extent that a statutory delegate has discretion to determine the facts, he must exercise his discretion reasonably. If he does so, he is acting within his jurisdiction, and no judicial review can arise (because there is no jurisdictional error, and there is no error of law within jurisdiction). On the other hand, if the statutory delegate exercises his discretion to determine the facts in an unreasonable manner, he has not in law exercised his discretion, but rather has declined jurisdiction. The normal grounds for reviewing a jurisdictional error, therefore, should in principle be available in such a circumstance. This situation sometimes arises in determining whether to review the decision of a statutory delegate on the basis that there was no, or insufficient, evidence before him to support his finding. The courts appear to have adopted the view in *Nat Bell Liquors*[35] that the sufficiency of evidence is not a question of law, and therefore an erroneous appraisal of the evidence by a statutory delegate will not give rise to the anomalous use of *certiorari* to correct an error of law on the face of the record. On the other hand, total lack of evidence appears to be a jurisdictional error capable of judicial review, even in the face of a privative clause. Similarly, it is submitted that an unreasonable appreciation of the facts may constitute a jurisdictional defect in the tribunal's proceedings. This point was clearly recognized by the Supreme Court of Canada recently in *Blanchard v. Control Data Canada Limited*, where Lamer J. provided the following analysis:[35a]

> In looking for an error which might affect jurisdiction, the emphasis placed by this Court on the dichotomy of the reasonable or unreasonable nature of the error casts doubt on the appropriateness of making, on this basis, a distinction between error of law and error of fact. In addition to the difficulty of classification, the distinction collides with that given by the courts to unreasonable errors of fact. An unreasonable error of fact has been categorized as an error of law. The distinction would mean that this error of law is then protected by the privative clause unless it is unreasonable. What more is needed in order that an unreasonable finding of fact, in becoming an error of law, becomes an unreasonable error of law? An administrative tribunal has the necessary jurisdiction to make a mistake, and even a serious one, but not to be unreasonable. The unreasonable finding is no less fatal to jurisdiction because the finding is one of fact rather than law. An unreasonable finding is what justifies intervention by the courts.
>
> Not only is the distinction between error of law and of fact superfluous in light of an unreasonable finding or conclusion, but the reference to error itself is as well. Indeed, though all errors do not lead to unreasonable findings, every unreasonable finding results from an error (whether of law, fact, or a combination of the two), which is unreasonable.
>
> In conclusion, an unreasonable finding, whatever its origin, affects the jurisdiction of the tribunal. I hasten to add that the distinction between an error of law and one of fact is still entirely valid when the tribunal is not protected by a privative clause. Indeed, though all errors of law are then subjected to review, only unreasonable errors of fact are, but no others.

---

35 (1922) 65 D.L.R. 1 (P.C.). See also D.W. Elliott's excellent article entitled "No Evidence — A Ground for Judicial Review in Canada?" (1972-73) 37 Sask. L.R. 48.
35a [1984] 2 S.C.R. 476 at 494-95.

6. The "Patently Unreasonable" Doctrine in the Face of a Privative Clause

Errors of law on the face of the record cannot be corrected by the anomalous use of *certiorari* if there is a statutory[36] privative clause preventing judicial review of errors made within a delegate's jurisdiction. Of course privative clauses[37] cannot constitutionally be effective to oust judicial review of jurisdictional questions, on the rationale that a statutory delegate cannot lawfully make a decision outside his jurisdiction, so there is nothing to be protected by the privative clause. Precisely because intra-jurisdictional errors of law lie within the delegate's jurisdiction, however, there is a decision or action which can be protected by the privative clause. In order to succeed in obtaining judicial review when there is a privative clause, therefore, one must show that a jurisdictional error has been committed by the delegate. A vast number of cases can be used to illustrate attempts to characterize particular errors of law as "going to jurisdiction". Until recently, it was probably true to state that no satisfactory test had ever been devised to differentiate intra-jurisdictional errors of law from those which go to jurisdiction.

A line of cases has recently developed the doctrine that errors of law which are "patently unreasonable" are jurisdictional in nature, and therefore cannot be immunized from judicial review by a privative clause. The clearest statement of this doctrine occurs in the Supreme Court of Canada's very recent decision in *Blanchard v. Control Data Canada Limited*, where Beetz J. said:[38]

> According to the prior decisions of this Court, a patently unreasonable error by an administrative tribunal in interpreting a provision which it has to apply within the limits of its jurisdiction will in itself cause the tribunal to lose its jurisdiction.

and Lamer J. put it this way:[38a]

---

36   *I.e.*, in the same statute as creates the delegate's power to do the act in question. There may be some doubt as to the precise meaning of a privative clause, particularly (as in *Re Alta. Union of Prov. Employees and Bd. of Gov. of Olds. College*, (1982) 21 Alta. L.R. (2d) 104 (S.C.C.); *United Nurses of Alta., Loc. 11 v. Misericordia Hosp.*, [1983] 6 W.W.R. 1 (Alta. C.A.); and *Suncor Inc. v. Fort McMurray Independent Oil Wkrs., Loc. 1*, [1983] 1 W.W.R. 604 (Alta. C.A.); all discussed below) where the Act specifically provides that *certiorari* or some other remedy is available in some short period of time (*e.g.*, 30 days). Does a "no *certiorari*" clause have the same effect as a "final and binding" clause? These are difficult questions of statutory construction. See S. Chumir, "The Rammell and Farrell Cases", (1963) 3 Alta. L. Rev. 124, for a discussion of different types of privative clauses. See also *Pringle v. Fraser*, [1972] S.C.R. 821; *Min. of Fin. v. Woodward*, [1973] S.C.R. 120; and *Toronto Newspaper Guild v. Globe Printing Co.*, [1953] 2 S.C.R. 18.

37   Loosely defined, to include all of those types referred to, *ibid*.

38   *Supra*, note 35a at p. 479.

38a *Ibid.*, pp. 492-93.

In principle, where there is a privative clause the superior courts should not be able to review errors of law made by the administrative tribunals. However, it is now settled that some errors of law can cause the arbitrator to lose his jurisdiction. The debate turns on the question of *which* errors of law result in the loss of jurisdiction. Contrary to the decision of Lord Denning in *Pearlman v. Keepers and Governors of Harrow School*, [1979] 1 All E.R. 365, where he said (at p. 372) that "no court or tribunal has any jurisdiction to make an error of law on which the decision of the case depends" (subsequently disapproved by the Privy Council in *South East Asia Fire Bricks Sdn. Bhd. v. Non-Metallic Mineral Products Manufacturing Employees Union*, [1980] 3 W.L.R. 318, and *Re Racal Communications Ltd.*, [1980] 2 All E.R. 634), this Court has tended since *Nipawin* . . . and *C.U.P.E.* . . . to avoid intervening when the decision of the administrative tribunal was reasonable, whether erroneous or not. In other words, only unreasonable errors of law can affect jurisdiction. The following extract from *C.U.P.E.* . . . has become the classic statement of the approach taken by this Court:

> Put another way, was the Board's interpretation so patently unreasonable that its construction cannot be rationally supported by the relevant legislation and demands intervention by the court upon review?

> This is a very severe test and signals a strict approach to the question of judicial review. It is nevertheless the test which this Court has applied and continues to apply. . . .

Because the doctrine of patent unreasonability has been extended to other circumstances, where it is arguably inappropriate, it is important to examine *C.U.P.E* and subsequent cases in some detail.

(a) The *C.U.P.E.* Case

The *C.U.P.E.*[38b] case dealt with a complaint by a union that the New Brunswick Liquor Corporation was replacing striking employees with management personnel contrary to s. 102(3)(*a*) of the Public Service Labour Relations Act,[39] which provided as follows:

> 102(3) Where subsection (1) and subsection (2) are complied with employees may strike and during the continuance of the strike

---

38b *Can. Union of Pub. Employees Loc. 963 v. N.B. Liquor Corp.*, (1979) 97 D.L.R. (3d) 417 (S.C.C.).
39 R.S.N.B. 1973, c. P-25.

>   (*a*) the employer shall not replace the striking employees or
>   fill their position with any other employee, and
>   (*b*) no employee shall picket, parade or in any manner
>   demonstrate in or near any place of business of the
>   employer.

The question arose as to whether the use of management personnel to perform the functions of striking workers constituted an illegal "replacement" within the meaning of section 102(3)(*a*). The board ruled that it did, and was illegal. However, a majority of the Court of Appeal disagreed with the board's legal interpretation of this section, and went on to hold that this question was preliminary or collateral to the board's jurisdiction under the Act. Accordingly, the Court of Appeal held that there was only one correct interpretation of the section, and it was for the court (or a majority of it) to determine what that correct interpretation was.

The Supreme Court of Canada characterized the matter somewhat differently. In the first place, Dickson J. held that the correct interpretation of s. 102(3)(*a*) was not preliminary or collateral to the board's jurisdiction, which must be determined at the outset of the inquiry.[40] In Dickson J.'s words:[41]

> The question of what is and is not jurisdictional is often very difficult to determine. The Courts, in my view, should not be alert to brand as jurisdictional, and therefore subject to broader curial review, that which may be doubtfully so.

His Lordship noted that the general subject matter of the dispute between the parties unquestionably fell within the confines of the legislation, and the board was asked by the parties to determine whether certain activities of the union and of the employer during the lawful strike were in violation of the prohibition contained in the provision in question. Accordingly, it was not possible to suggest that the board did not have "jurisdiction in the narrow sense of authority to enter upon an inquiry".[42] Accordingly, the Supreme Court rejected the relevance of the *Jacmain*,[43] *Parkhill Bedding*,[44] and *Jarvis*[45] cases, in all of which, at the threshold of the inquiry, the statutory delegate had to determine whether the case before them was one of the kind upon which the empowering statute permitted entering an inquiry.

---

40 See *supra*, note 38 at pp. 421-22.
41 *Ibid.*, p. 422.
42 See *Service Employees' Int. Union v. Nipawin Dist. Staff Nurses Assn.*, [1975] 1 S.C.R. 382 at 389.
43 *Jacmain v. A.G. Can.*, [1978] 2 S.C.R. 15.
44 *Parkhill Furniture & Bedding Ltd. v. Int. Molders etc. Union*, (1961) 26 D.L.R. (2d) 589 (Man. C.A.).
45 *Jarvis v. Assoc. Medical Services Inc.*, [1964] S.C.R. 497.

Dickson J. then noted that s. 101 of the Act[46] contained the following privative clause:

101(1) Except as provided in this Act, every order, award, direction, decision, declaration or ruling of the Board, the Arbitration Tribunal or an adjudicator is final and shall not be questioned or reviewed in any court.

(2) No order shall be made or process entered, and no proceeding shall be taken in any court, whether by way of injunction, *certiorari*, prohibition, *quo warranto*, or otherwise, to question, review, prohibit or restrain the Board, the Arbitration Tribunal or an adjudicator in any of its or his proceedings.

His Lordship referred to the policy reasons for including such a privative clause to protect a labour board's decision within jurisdiction, on the basis that it is a specialized[47] tribunal administering a comprehensive statute regulating difficult labour relations. He also noted[48] the reasons why the superior courts have tended to exercise their discretion to refuse prerogative remedies against such specialized statutory delegates dealing with labour relations. Accordingly, the *ratio decidendi* of the Supreme Court's decision in *C.U.P.E.* is that the legal error, if any, committed by the board lay within its jurisdiction, and was not "patently unreasonable"[49] but was at least as reasonable as the numerous alternative interpretations suggested in the Court of Appeal. In the end, the board could not be said to have so misinterpreted the statutory provision as to "embark on an inquiry or answer a question not remitted to it".

One can summarize the reasoning in the *C.U.P.E.* decision as follows. On the one hand, it is frequently very difficult to determine which errors are jurisdictional in nature, and which lie within the jurisdiction of a statutory delegate. The "jurisdiction" of a statutory delegate is generally to be determined in the narrow sense of authority to enter upon an inquiry, although it includes doing something subsequently to take the statutory delegate outside the ambit of its powers (and therefore outside the protective ambit of a privative or preclusive clause) such as:[50]

acting in bad faith, basing the decision on extraneous matters, failing to take relevant factors into account, breaching the provi-

---

46 *Supra*, note 38 at p. 423.
47 The courts have used other rationales for deferring to statutory delegates' decisions. See section 11 of this chapter, *infra*.
48 (1979) 97 D.L.R. (3d) 417 at 424 (S.C.C.).
49 *Ibid.*, p. 429 (S.C.C.).
50 In the words of the Supreme Court of Canada in *Nipawin*, *supra*, note 42.

sions of natural justice or misinterpreting provisions of the Act so as
to embark on an inquiry or answer a question not remitted to it.

As long as the legislative provisions are not preliminary or collateral in nature
(however that characterization is determined), the *C.U.P.E.* decision seems to
hold that only a patently unreasonable interpretation of the statutory provisions in question will make an arguably incorrect legal interpretation into a
jurisdictional error, which therefore would not be protected by a privative
clause. Thus, the "patently unreasonable" test is used to determine which
legal errors within jurisdiction are so serious as to cause a delegate who has
jurisdiction in the narrow sense to exceed or depart from his jurisdiction.
"Patently unreasonable" is therefore a test for determining which errors are
jurisdictional in nature. The effect of a successful application of the "patently
unreasonable" doctrine is to evade the operation of a privative clause, that is,
to use "patently unreasonable" as a sword for judicial review of administrative action. Conversely, errors of law which are not "patently unreasonable",
and which do not relate to a matter which is preliminary or collateral to the
delegate's jurisdiction in the narrow sense, are intra-jurisdictional in nature
and will be immunized from judicial review whenever there is a privative
clause. This is the result of the doctrine of Parliamentary Sovereignty, under
which the legislative branch may specifically exclude judicial review.

(b) The *Massicotte* Case

A similar result was reached by the Supreme Court of Canada in
Teamsters' Union, Local 938 v. Massicotte.[51] This case dealt with whether the
Canada Labour Relations Board had exceeded or left its jurisdiction after it
had found that a union had violated its duty of fair representation in failing to
permit a part-time employee to grieve his dismissal, and ordered arbitration of
the grievance. Section 122(2) of the Canada Labour Code[52] contains a very
strong privative clause, which goes so far as to prevent judicial review

on any ground, including the ground that the order, decision or proceeding is beyond the jurisdiction of the Board to make or carry on
or that, in the course of any proceeding, the Board for any reason
exceeded or lost its jurisdiction.

Section 122(1) of the Code does provide a narrow range for judicial review by
the Federal Court of Appeal pursuant to section 28(1)(*a*) of the Federal Court
Act,[53] which is restricted to two grounds only: failure to observe a principle of
natural justice; or otherwise acting beyond or refusing to exercise jurisdiction.

---

51 (1982) 134 D.L.R. (3d) 385 (S.C.C.).
52 R.S.C. 1970, c. L-1 [am. 1972, c. 18, s. 1; 1977-78, c. 27, s. 43].
53 R.S.C. 1970, c. 10 (2nd Supp.).

Again, the appellant union tried to characterize the issue as one of a matter that was preliminary or collateral to the board's jurisdiction.[54] The union submitted that a jurisdictional error was involved because of the board's alleged patent unreasonableness in interpreting its powers to order the arbitration at the instance of a member of the union when the union itself had not chosen to go to arbitration.

Laskin C.J.C., writing for a unanimous five-member[55] panel of the Supreme Court of Canada, clearly rejected the notion that any preliminary or collateral matter was involved in this case. As the Chief Justice said,[56] there could be no question of the authority of the Canada Labour Relations Board to deal with the complaint of Massicotte as a part-time employee. His Lordship seems to indicate that an intra-jurisdictional question arises in the following circumstances:[57]

> I do not see . . . any basis for questioning the jurisdiction exercised in the present case by the Canada Labour Relations Board. Essentially, this court has admonished that there must be no failure of natural justice (and there was none here) and that the Board should address itself to an issue arising under the legislation which it is charged to administer. If it has done this (as the Federal Court of Appeal held and, in my opinion , rightly so) there can be no jurisdictional infirmity when the Board is protected in its determinations by a privative clause. It may be wrong in law in interpreting the range of powers confided to it but its decisions are none the less immunized from judicial review.

Again, His Lordship went on:[58]

> [M]ere doubt as to correctness of a labour board interpretation of its statutory power is no ground for finding jurisdictional error, especially when the labour board is exercising powers confided to it in wide terms to resolve competing contentions. In so far as the *Anisminic* and *Metropolitan Life Ins.* cases deal with the so-called "wrong question" test of jurisdiction, they have no relevance here. It is impossible to say that the Canada Labour Relations Board asked itself the wrong question in any sense of departing from the inquiry in which it was engaged. It addressed itself to the issue raised by the complaint and exercised powers in relation thereto which it clearly

---

54 Relying on *Service Employees Int. Union v. Nipawin Dist. Staff Nurses' Assn.*, [1975] 1 S.C.R. 382; *Jacmain v. A.G. Can.*, [1978] 2 S.C.R. 15; *C.U.P.E., Loc. 963 v. N.B. Liquor Corp., supra*, note 48; *Anisminic v. Foreign Comp. Comm.*, [1969] 2 A.C. 147 (H.L.); and *Metro. Life Ins. Co. v. Int. Union of Operating Engineers*, [1970] S.C.R. 425.

55 Composed of Laskin C.J.C. and Dickson, Beetz, Chouinard and Lamer JJ.

56 *Supra*, note 51 at p. 390.

57 *Ibid.*, p. 391.

58 *Ibid.*, p. 395.

had. At bottom, the objection is to the consequential results of that exercise, but this is a long way from any jurisdictional issue.

In the result, I am of the opinion that there is no question of jurisdiction involved in the objection to what the Canada Labour Relations Board did. Its decision and remedial order are hence not reviewable and this appeal therefore fails. . . .

Massicotte, therefore, exactly follows the rule set down in *C.U.P.E.*

(c) The *Volvo* Case

Strictly speaking, the reasoning of the Supreme Court of Canada in *Volvo Canada Ltd. v. International Union, United Automobile, Aerospace and Agricultural Implement Workers of America, Local 720*,[59] does not apply to the test for reviewing errors of law made by a statutory delegate, but rather deals with the grounds for review of a consensual arbitrator. As a result, the case deals with an important side issue of whether a "specific question of law" had been remitted to the consensual arbitrator for determination (in which case judicial review by the common law action to quash and remit is not available, even if the arbitrator has given clauses of the collective agreement an interpretation which their language will not reasonably bear), or whether the submission to arbitration was a "general question" in the determination of which a question of law incidentally arose (in which case judicial review would be available, but only if the arbitrator's interpretation was one which the collective agreement could not reasonably bear). In the result, all nine members of the Supreme Court of Canada declined to interfere with the arbitrator's decision, although for different reasons.[60] The court has returned to this issue in the *Shalansky* decision, which dealt with a consensual arbitration of a general (and not specific) question of construction of a collective agreement.[61]

---

59 (1979) 99 D.L.R. (3d) 193.

60 On the one hand, three members of the court (Laskin C.J.C., Spence and Dickson JJ.) held that a specific question of law had been referred to the arbitrator and could not be reviewed by the courts in any way. On the other hand, five members of the court (Martland, Ritchie, Pigeon, Beetz and Pratte JJ.) declined to hold that a specific question of law had been remitted to the arbitrator, but nevertheless refused to interfere with the arbitrator's award because it was not unreasonable. Estey J. was in favour of rejecting the distinction between a general question and a specific question of law, but would have limited judicial review to those cases where the arbitrator, in answering the question remitted to him, does something he is not by statute or contract authorized to do.

61 *Shalansky v. Regina Pasqua Hosp. Bd. of Gov.*, (1983) 145 D.L.R. (3d) 413. A unanimous five-member panel of the Supreme Court of Canada held that the common law action to remit and quash a consensual arbitrator's decision, at least on a general question, can only arise if it involves an interpretation which the word of a collective agreement could not reasonably bear. See section 9 of this chapter, *infra*.

(d) The *U.N.A.* Case

The "patently unreasonable" test was also adopted by the Alberta Court of Appeal in the *U.N.A.* case.[62] The issue dealt with whether the arbitration board had correctly dismissed a grievance on the basis that the employer had reserved the right to dismiss employees without cause under the terms of the collective agreement, and as such the issue was not arbitrable. The Court of Appeal unanimously held that the question of whether an issue was arbitrable was clearly within the jurisdiction of the board of arbitration pursuant to the very specific wording of section 138 of the Alberta Labour Act,[63] which provided as follows:

> 138 Every collective agreement must contain a method for the settlement of differences arising
>
> > (*a*) as to the interpretation, application or operation of a collective agreement,
> > (*b*) with respect to a contravention or alleged contravention of a collective agreement, and
> > (*c*) as to whether a difference referred to in clause (*a*) or (*b*) can be the subject of arbitration
>
> between the parties to or parties bound by the collective agreement.

Accordingly, the board of arbitration had the power to determine whether a difference could be the subject of arbitration, and such a decision was "final and binding" on the parties.[64] Although in some circumstances the question of arbitrability may undoubtedly be a jurisdictional one, in light of the specific legislation involved in this case, Stevenson J.A. stated as follows:[65]

> I am of the view that the "enquiry in question" here is whether the alleged grievance is arbitrable. True, the board had jurisdiction to decide other questions, notably whether the grievance, if arbitrable was established and, if established, what remedy ought to be granted, but it undoubtedly had "authority to decide" the question of arbitrability. "Authority to decide" is the definition of jurisdiction given in de Smith's 4th ed. (1980), at p. 110.
>
> The appellants err in subdividing the matter before the board. That is a criticism of jurisdictional arguments referred to by Dickson J. in *C.U.P.E., Loc. 963 v. N.B. Liquor Corp.*, ... Paraphrasing

---

62 [1983] 6 W.W.R. 1 (Alta. C.A.).

63 S.A. 1973, c. 33, s. 138 [re-en. 1977, c. 77. s. 11] [later R.S.A. 1980, c. L-1; repealed by Employment Standards Act, R.S.A. 1980 (Supp.), c. E-10.1, s. 121 and by the Labour Relations Act, S.A. 1980, c. 72, s. 182 [now R.S.A. 1980 (Supp.), c. L-1.1].

64 By virtue of s. 138.2(*g*) of the Act and by virtue of art. 34.05 of the collective agreement.

65 *Supra*, note 62 at p. 9.

Dickson J., the question of arbitrability is "plainly confided" to the board here. Had the parties posed only a question of whether this allegation was arbitrable, or themselves divided the questions and put this one forward individually[,] it could not be suggested the board lacked jurisdiction to decide that question.

Stevenson J.A. then distinguished those cases dealing with preliminary or collateral matters, upon which the jurisdiction of a statutory delegate depends: *Jacmain*[66] and *Jarvis*.[67] He also distinguished *Bell v. Ontario Human Rights Commission*[68] on the basis that it involved a determination of a question not remitted or confided to the tribunal,[69] and the *Anisminic*[70] and *Metropolitan Life Insurance*[71] cases. All three of these cases involved the "wrong question" being asked by the statutory delegate in such a way as to deprive it of its jurisdiction. By contrast, in the *U.N.A.* case, the board of arbitration clearly had the authority over the "kind of case" involving arbitrability. In short, as Stevenson J.A. said,[72] "the decision on the question of arbitrability is an exercise of jurisdiction rather than a determination of it".

Stevenson J.A. then directed his attention to whether the decision of the board of arbitration was "patently unreasonable". After reviewing numerous cases[73] going both ways on the matter, he held that they only confirmed that the point subject to determination by the board was an arguable one, and therefore not one in which the court should substitute its opinion.

Moir J.A. concurred in this result, but noted that s. 146 of the Labour Act[74] had not previously been construed by the Court of Appeal as a privative clause, and in any event was considerably less strongly worded than the corresponding provisions in the Public Service Employee Relations Act, 1977[75] dealt with by the Supreme Court of Canada in the *Olds College* case.[76] In particular, Moir J.A. noted that the Court of Appeal had previously interfered for errors of law on the face of the record which were not necessarily

---

66 *Jacmain v. A.G. Can.*, [1978] 2 S.C.R. 15.

67 *Jarvis v. Assoc. Medical Services Inc.*, [1964] S.C.R. 497.

68 [1971] S.C.R. 756.

69 That is, whether a "self-contained domestic establishment" was involved.

70 *Anisminic v. Foreign Comp. Comm.*, [1969] 2 A.C. 147 (H.L.).

71 *Metro. Life Ins. Co. v. Int. Union of Operating Engineers*, [1970] S.C.R. 425.

72 *Supra*, note 62 at p. 10.

73 *Re Int. Chemical Wkrs. Union, Loc. 424; Re A.C. Horn Co. Ltd.*, (1953) 4 L.A.C. 1524; *R. v. Bd. of Arbitration; Ex parte Stevens*, (1970) 12 D.L.R. (3d) 284 (N.B.C.A.); *Re Foothills Prov. Gen. Hosp. and Civic Service Assn. of Alta.*, (1974) 7 L.A.C. (2d) 436; *Re Retail, Wholesale & Dept. Store Union and Hershey Chocolate of Can. (1967) Ltd.*, (1970) 21 L.A.C. 83; *Western Co-op. Fertilizers Ltd. v. Oil, Chemical etc. Int. Union*, (1971) 22 D.L.R. (3d) 99 (Alta. C.A.); *Zeller's (Western) Ltd. v. Retail, Wholesale & Dept. Store Union*, (1973) 40 D.L.R. (3d) 761 (S.C.C.).

74 Labour Act, S.A. 1973, c. 33, ss. 138, 146 [later R.S.A. 1980, c. L-1; repealed by Employment Standards Act, R.S.A. 1980 (Supp.), c. E-10.1, s. 121 and by the Labour Relations Act, S.A. 1980, c. 72, s. 182 [now R.S.A. 1980 (Supp.), c. L-1.1]].

75 S.A. 1977, c. 40 [now R.S.A. 1980, c. P-33].

76 [1982] 21 Alta. L.R. (2d) 104 (S.C.C.), discussed *infra*.

"patently unreasonable" in *Yellow Cab Ltd. v. Board of Industrial Relations (Alberta)*[77] and *Industrial Relations Board (Alberta) v. Stedelbauer Chevrolet Oldsmobile Ltd.*[78] He criticized the decision of another panel of the Court of Appeal in *Suncor*[79] which appeared to restrict the court's ability to review the record under s. 146 of the Labour Act because of the words of a specific clause of the collective agreement in *Suncor*. Moir J.A. noted that the Court of Appeal was not compelled to reach the decision which it did in *Suncor*, but now was bound by it, as well as by the subsequent decision of the Supreme Court of Canada in *Shalansky*.[80]

On a practical level, Moir J.A. was disturbed by the consequence which would result from the application of the "patently unreasonable" test limiting the court's ability to correct an intra-jurisdictional error of law on the face of the record where no privative clause exists. As His Lordship noted, there are numerous identical collective agreements in existence between the United Nurses and all of the hospitals in the province. The contractual rights of the union, its members and the employer should be identical under all of these contracts, and that matter should be determined once and for all. The court was well placed to give a uniform construction to the language used in these contracts.[81] On the other hand, if the same issue could be raised before several different arbitration boards, different results could arise, which could not be made uniform by the courts unless it could be said that all but one of those interpretations was "patently unreasonable". As His Lordship said:[82]

> The result of this decision is to leave the question to the individual arbitration boards who hear grievances under collective agreements. Whatever these boards decide will be protected unless their decisions are "patently unreasonable" or "clearly wrong". To my mind this is not a desirable result but it must follow from the decision in *Suncor* and probably *Shalansky*.

---

77 11 Alta. L.R. (2d) 97, reversed on other grounds [1980] 2 S.C.R. 761.

78 [1969] S.C.R. 137.

79 [1983] 1 W.W.R. 604.

80 *Shalansky v. Regina Pasqua Hosp. Bd. of Gov.*, [1983] 1 S.C.R. 303, affirming 82 C.L.L.C. 14, 186 (*sub nom. Shalansky v. Sask. Union of Nurses, Loc. 105*), which affirmed 10 Sask. R. 225.

81 This argument may be compelling when used to urge the court to issue a prerogative remedy when it has jurisdiction to do so, and not to exercise its discretion to refuse the remedy if the arbitrators' decision is incorrect (even if not patently unreasonable). This reasoning cannot, however, be applied in the *U.N.A.* case, [1983] 6 W.W.R. 1 (Alta. C.A.), where a privative clause did exist (at least after the expiration of the 30-day period during which the legislation specifically permitted *certiorari* to be brought). Query: is it more accurate to characterize this clause as a specific invitation to *certiorari* within 30 days, but thereafter a privative clause? In effect, is it a time-delayed privative clause? If so, reasoning applicable to a case involving a privative clause cannot properly be used to prevent an application for judicial review which has been brought *within* the 30-day period during which the statute expressly permits judicial review.

82 *Ibid.*, p. 6.

7. The "Patently Unreasonable" Doctrine in the Absence of a Privative Clause

The question then arises as to the applicability of the "patently unreasonable" test to protect intra-jurisdictional errors of law on the face of the record, where no privative clause occurs in the legislation. In principle, *certiorari* should be available to correct any and all such errors of law. In fact, the courts have recently retreated from such a bold assertion of their jurisdiction, and have tended to restrict the anomalous use of *certiorari* to correct only certain errors of law. They have done this in two quite distinct ways.

First, as Wade notes,[83] the courts have sometimes held that there is no error of law if the legal conclusion is "within the range of interpretations within which different persons might reasonably reach different conclusions". With respect, there is little to be said for this approach, which simply assumes the problem away. After all, there is only one correct construction of any legal phrase in a particular context, and it is the responsibility of the courts to determine that correct construction. Of course the court may defer to the expertise of a specialized tribunal to arrive at that correct construction, but one cannot conclude from such prudence that there can theoretically be more than one correct legal result.

This brings us to the second basis upon which the courts might decline to correct an error of law in certain circumstances. *Certiorari*, after all, is one of the prerogative remedies, all of which are discretionary in nature. It can be argued that the Canadian courts have recently decided that they can properly exercise their discretion to refuse *certiorari* when the intra-jurisdictional error of law is not patently unreasonable. Such an approach does not prevent or restrict the power of the courts to issue *certiorari*, but rather merely indicates a circumstance where the courts may choose not to do so. At any rate, this rationale is helpful in explaining the recent cases where the courts have adopted the "patently unreasonable" test to refuse to issue *certiorari* to correct an intra-jurisdictional error of law where no privative clause existed. Let us examine these cases closely.

(a) The *Olds College* Case

The decision of the Supreme Court of Canada in *Re Alberta Union of Provincial Employees and Board of Governors of Olds College*[84] is open to two theoretical explanations. On the one hand, the court may have applied the "patently unreasonable" test to prevent judicial review of certain intra-jurisdictional errors of law in the absence of a privative clause. If this reading

---

83 *Administrative Law*, 4th ed., p. 776.
84 (1982) 21 Alta. L.R. (2d) 104, Martland and Beetz JJ. dissenting. See the comment by Mullan in (1983) 5 S.C. Rev. 24.

of the case is correct, the court has greatly restricted the anomalous use of *certiorari* to correct errors of law and it is important to discern the theoretical basis for such a change in the law. On the other hand, it may be possible to construe *Olds College* as simply breathing life into a "final and binding" clause so as to create an effective privative clause which can only be avoided by an error of law which is so patently unreasonable that it deprives the statutory delegate of its jurisdiction. Such an approach would not alter the function of the "patently unreasonable" test discussed in section 6 of this chapter, but it would seriously change conventional thinking by expanding the ambit of privative clauses. So the *Olds College* decision must be reckoned with!

The case dealt with the power of the Public Service Employee Relations Board to certify which items were capable of being arbitrated in a dispute concerning the terms of a collective agreement between an employer and a union. Section 9(1) of the Act[85] gave the board extensive powers to decide whether "a matter in dispute is an arbitral item", and stated that the board's decision was "final and binding". Section 11 of the Act stated that:

> 11. *The Board has exclusive jurisdiction to exercise the powers conferred upon it by or under this Act and to determine all questions of fact or law that arise in any matter before it and the action or decision of the Board thereon is final and conclusive for all purposes*, but the Board may, at any time, reconsider any order, notice, directive, declaration, certificate or other decision made by it and vary or revoke it. [Emphasis added.]

Section 89 of the Act prevented judicial review except by way of an application for *certiorari* or *mandamus* filed within 30 days of the impugned decision:

> 89.(1) No award, proceeding or decision of a tribunal shall be questioned or reviewed in any court, and no order shall be made or process entered or proceedings taken in any court, (whether by way of injunction, declaratory judgment, prohibition, quo warranto or otherwise) to question, review, prohibit or restrain the tribunal in any of his or its proceedings.
>
> (2) Notwithstanding subsection (1), the award, proceeding or decision of a tribunal may be questioned, or reviewed by way of an application for certiorari or mandamus, if an application therefor is filed with the Court not later than 30 days after the date of the award, proceeding or decision of the tribunal.

Chief Justice Laskin had this to say about the relationship between the "final and binding" clauses and the explicit provision for judicial review:[86]

---

85 Public Service Employee Relations Act, 1977 (Alta.), c. 40 [now R.S.A. 1980, c. P-33, s. 9(1)(*m*)].

86 *Supra*, note 84 at p. 107.

In the face of this explicit provision for review, it is impossible to read it out of this statute or to subordinate it [section 89] to ss. 9 and 11 or even to limit it to questions of jurisdiction in the strict sense, as urged by counsel for the union and counsel for the board. That being said, however, it still remains to consider the scope of review on alleged errors of law, and it is my opinion that the commanding terms of s. 9(1) and especially of s. 11 cast a gloss on the extent to which decisions of the board may be overturned by a court. Certiorari, considered in the light of ss. 9(1) and 11, is a long way from an appeal and is subject to restriction in accordance with a line of decisions of this court which, to assess them generally, preclude judicial interference with interpretations made by the board which are not plainly unreasonable. Jurisdictional errors, including want of natural justice, are clearly reviewable and subject to reversal as was conceded by the appellants, but they are not involved here.

It was agreed that none of the alleged legal errors was jurisdictional in nature.[87] Although a majority of the Alberta Court of Appeal had issued *certiorari* to correct these intra-jurisdictional errors, Chief Justice Laskin persuaded a majority of the Supreme Court of Canada not to do so for these reasons:[88]

... [I]t is obvious that Prowse J.A. [in the Alberta Court of Appeal] treated the case before him as more akin to an appeal than to one involving a limited right of review. In so doing, he appears to have misapprehended what was involved in *McLeod v. Egan*, [1975] 1 S.C.R. 517, 74 C.L.L.C. 14,220 (sub nom. *United Steel Wkrs. v. Galt Metal Indust. Ltd.*), 46 D.L.R. (3d) 150, 2 N.R. 443 (sub nom. *Re MacLeod*), and in *Re Bradburn and Wentworth Arms Hotel*, [1979] 1 S.C.R. 846, 79 C.L.L.C. 14,189, 94 D.L.R. (3d) 161. Both these cases, although concerned with grievances under collective agreements, required the arbitration boards (dealing with "rights" arbitrations) to consider applicable public statutes. The interpretation of those statutes did not require so-called curial deference to the views of the arbitration boards.

That, however, is not this case. Here the Public Service Employee Relations Board is operating in its home territory, so to speak. It was concerned with the interpretation and application of provisions confided by its constitutent Act to its exclusive administration, with its decisions stated to have final and conclusive effect. In such circumstances, the proper approach by a reviewing court is not the blunt substitution of judicial opinion for the views of the

---

87 In the narrow sense of the word.
88 *Supra*, note 84 at pp. 109-10.

Board but rather that expressed by Dickson J. in *Can. Union of Public Employees, Local 963 v. N.B. Liquor Corp.*, [1979] 2 S.C.R. 227 at 237, 25 N.B.R. (2d) 237, 79 C.L.L.C. 14,209, 97 D.L.R. (3d) 417, 51 A.P.R. 237, 26 N.R. 341, where he formulated the issue of scope of review as follows:

> . . . was the Board's interpretation so patently unreasonable that its construction cannot be rationally supported by the relevant legislation and demands intervention by the court upon review?

I should note that Dickson J. was also dealing with a public service labour relations Act and with the administration of the Act by a board.

Dickson J.'s approach was adopted in *Volvo Can. Ltd. v. Int. Union, United Automobile, etc. Wkrs.*, [1980] 1 S.C.R. 178, 99 D.L.R. (3d) 193, 27 N.R. 502, in the reasons of Pigeon J. at p. 214, and it is also evident in the reasons of Estey J. speaking for the court in *Douglas Aircraft Co. of Can. v. McConnell*, [1980] 1 S.C.R. 245 at 274, 79 C.L.L.C. 14,221 (sub nom. *Douglas Aircraft Co. v. U.A.W. Loc. 1967*) 99 D.L.R. (3d) 385, 23 L.A.C. (2d) 143n, 29 N.R. 109.

Needless to say, however the scope of review is limited according to the reach of near-privative clauses, there is no complete ouster of review, even on errors of law unless a privative clause clearly enjoins interference on this ground: see *Re Ont. L.R.B. and Bradley*, [1975] O.R. 316, 8 D.L.R. (2d) 65 (C.A.).

His Lordship then examined the arbitrable items in dispute, and concluded that as the board's disposition of them could not be characterized as being "patently unreasonable", *certiorari* would not issue.

(b) The *Suncor* Case

The Alberta Court of Appeal adopted this approach with a vengeance in *Suncor Inc. v. McMurray Independent Oil Workers, Local 1.*[89] The court was required in *Suncor* to determine whether *certiorari* was available to quash an arbitrator's decision for an intra-jurisdictional[90] error of law. At the outset, the court had to determine whether the arbitration was consensual or statutory in nature in order to determine both whether *certiorari* was available at all and also the test for determining which errors of law could be reviewed by the court. The parts of the judgment dealing with non-consensual arbitrations are considered below.

---

89 *Supra*, note 79.
90 No suggestion arises in the case that the error was jurisdictional in nature, unlike the submissions in *C.U.P.E.*, (1979) 97 D.L.R. (3d) 417 (S.C.C.), or *Massicotte*, (1982) 134 D.L.R. (3d) 385 (S.C.C.).

Assuming that the arbitrators were statutory in nature,[91] Kerans J.A. held that the Court of Appeal was bound by the decision of the Supreme Court of Canada in *Olds College* to apply the "patently unreasonable" test to limit the availability of *certiorari* to correct errors of law on the face of the record. His Lordship noted that the wording of the privative clause in section 129 of the Labour Relations Act[92] was almost identical to the one[93] from the Public Service Employee Relations Act at issue in *Olds College*. Section 129 read as follows:

129(1) Subject to subsection (2), no award or proceeding of an arbitrator, arbitration board or other body shall be questioned or reviewed in any court, and no order shall be made or process entered or proceedings taken in any court, whether by way of injunction, declaratory judgment, prohibition, quo warranto or otherwise, to question, review, prohibit or restrain the arbitrator, arbitration board or other body in any of his or its proceedings.

(2) *The decision or proceedings of an arbitrator, arbitration board or other body may be questioned, or reviewed by way of an application for certiorari or mandamus, if an application therefor is filed with the court not later than 30 days after the issuance of the award of the arbitrator, arbitration board or other body.* [Emphasis added.]

Although Kerans J.A. recognized[94] that this explicit provision for judicial review could not be ignored by the Court of Appeal, he nevertheless held that *certiorari* would not issue to correct the arbitrator's impugned error of law.

There is one important difference between the *Olds College* case and the issue in *Suncor*. In the former, two separate provisions[95] of the statute itself made the decision of the Public Service Employee Relations Board "final and binding", and these statutory provisions provided the gloss which permitted Laskin C.J.C. to eviscerate the statutory right to *certiorari*. In *Suncor*, however, the legislation only protected decisions of the Labour Relations Board, and not those of arbitrators appointed pursuant to the Act. Nevertheless, Kerans J.A. reached down to the collective agreement, which provided that[96]

---

91 This assumption appears to have been correct in light of the almost contemporaneous decision of the Supeme Court of Canada in *Roberval Express Ltee. v. Tpt. Drivers, Warehousemen & Gen. Wkrs. Union, Loc. 106*, [1982] 2 S.C.R. 888.

92 R.S.A. 1980, c. L-1.1 (Supp.).

93 S. 89, quoted *supra*, in the discussion on *Olds College*, section 7(a).

94 [1983] 1 W.W.R. 604 at 609.

95 Ss. 9 and 11, quoted *supra*, section 7(a).

96 Article 13.09. Note that the Act does not make the arbitration decision "final and binding"; that provision is purely contractual in nature. Thus the phrase "as set out in *The Alberta Labour Act*" must refer to the provision in the statute which makes a collective agreement

[t]he decision of the Board of Arbitration shall be final and binding upon the parties and upon all affected employees as set out in *The Alberta Labour Act.*

His Lordship held that this contractual provision "casts a like gloss on the power of judicial review" similar to the restriction imposed by the Supreme Court of Canada in *Olds College.* Accordingly, we must now accept that that case of the Supreme Court has overruled the Court of Appeal's decision in *Yellow Cab,*[97] as well as the Supreme Court's own decision in *Stedelbauer.*[98] As Kerans J.A. said, the law must now be taken to be as follows:[99]

> In the result, the combined effect of the decision in *N.B. Liquor Corp.* on the one hand and *Olds College* on the other is this: the position of the appellant can be no higher than that s. 129(1) *prevents* review on any standard other than "patent unreasonableness" and that of the respondent no higher than that s. 129(2) (combined with art. 13.09) *permits* review only by the same standard.

(c) The *U.N.A.* Case

As noted in section 6, *supra,* dealing with cases where privative clauses exist, the *Suncor* case has been criticized subsequently by Moir J.A. in his dissent in the *U.N.A.* case. His Lordship noted that all of the statutes in question in *Olds College,*[100] *Suncor*[101] and *U.N.A.*[102] specifically provided for the availability of *certiorari.* The Court of Appeal had previously used that statutory exception to the privative clause to correct all intra-jurisdictional errors of law, and not just those which were "patently unreasonable": see *Yellow Cab*[103] and *Stedelbauer.*[104] He objected to the use by Kerans J.A. in *Suncor* of the "final and binding" clause in the collective agreement to fortify

---

binding on employees even though only the employer and the union are privy to it. It is extra-ordinary that the court treated a mere contractual "final and binding" clause as though it were equal to the strongest form of privative clause contained in a statute.

97 *Yellow Cab Ltd. v. Indust. Rel. Bd. (Alta.),* (1980) 11 Alta. L.R. (2d) 97 at 103, reversed on other grounds [1980] 2 S.C.R. 761, where the Court of Appeal had ruled that s. 129(2) permitted the issuance of *certiorari* to correct any error in law, and not just patently unreasonable ones.

98 *Indust. Rel. Bd. (Alta.) v. Stedelbauer Chevrolet Oldsmobile,* [1969] S.C.R. 137. Note, however, that Laskin C.J.C. did not refer to either *Yellow Cab, ibid,* or *Stedelbauer* in *Olds College,* (1982) 21 Alta. L.R. (2d) 104 (S.C.C.). He did, however, adopt the reasoning of Estey J. in *Douglas Aircraft Co. of Can. v. McConnell,* [1980] 1 S.C.R. 245, who specifically adopted the views of Martland J. in *Stedelbauer.* Accordingly, it is not at all clear that the statement by Kerans J.A. in *Suncor* is correct with respect to which cases are still good law.

99 [1983] 1 W.W.R. 604 at 610 (Alta. C.A.).

100 *Supra,* note 98.

101 *Supra,* note 99.

102 [1983] 6 W.W.R. 1 (Alta. C.A.).

103 *Supra,* note 97.

104 *Supra,* note 98.

(or "gloss") the terms of the privative clause in the statute, thereby eviscerating the statutory right to *certiorari*.

Although Moir J.A. accepted that the Court of Appeal was bound by *Suncor*, he noted the practical problems arising from using the "patently unreasonable" test to prevent judicial review of intra-jurisdictional errors. As it happens, there are numerous identical collective agreements in existence between the United Nurses and all of the hospitals in the province. The contractual rights of the union, its members and the employer should be identical under all of these contracts. The court was well placed to give a uniform construction to the language used in these contracts. On the other hand, if the same issue could be raised before several different arbitration boards, different results could arise, which could not be made uniform by the courts unless it could be said that all but one of those interpretations was "patently unreasonable". As His Lordship said:[105]

> The result of this decision is to leave the question to the individual arbitration boards who hear grievances under collective agreements. Whatever these boards decide will be protected unless their decisions are "patently unreasonable" or "clearly wrong". To my mind this is not a desirable result but it must follow from the decision in *Suncor* and probably *Shalansky*.

This criticism of the "patently unreasonable" test appears to be unanswerable to the extent that the test limits — as a matter of law — the availability of *certiorari* to correct intra-jurisdictional errors of law where no privative clause exists. On the other hand, if the test is only to be used as a guide for determining the circumstances in which the courts should consider exercising their undoubted discretion to refuse prerogative remedies, the situation may not be as bleak as suggested by Moir J.A. After all, if the latter view is correct, it was open to the court to exercise its discretion to issue *certiorari* to correct an error of law which was not patently unreasonable, and such a discretionary use of *certiorari* would clearly be justified to prevent the chaos referred to by Moir J.A.

(d) The *Shalansky* Case

Finally, it is important to note that the "patently unreasonable" test was also applied by both the Saskatchewan Court of Appeal and the Supreme Court of Canada in *Shalansky v. Board of Governors of Regina Pasqua Hospital*.[106] This case undoubtedly dealt with a consensual arbitration, and will be considered at greater length in a later part of this chapter. Nevertheless, both courts specifically refused to review a decision of the arbitrators

---

105 *Supra*, note 102 at p. 6.
106 (1983) 145 D.L.R. (3d) 413, affirming 15 Sask. L.R. 253 which affirmed 10 Sask. L.R. 225, dismissing an application for judicial review of an arbitration award (S.C.C.).

which was not "patently unreasonable", even if the judges might have preferred a different legal construction of the collective agreement in question. As Chief Justice Laskin said in the Supreme Court's decision:[107]

> As a matter of interpretation, the Chief Justice [of the Saskatchewan Court of Appeal, Bayda C.J.S.] was of the view that the board had interpreted the relevant provisions of the collective agreement incorrectly, with the result that there was an error on the face of the award. This conclusion led him to consider whether the award of this consensual board was impeachable. He was of the opinion that the effect of this court's decisions in *Bell Canada v. Office & Professional Employees' Int'l Union, Local 131* (1973), 37 D.L.R. (3d) 561, [1974] 1 S.C.R. 335; *Metropolitan Toronto Police Ass'n, et al. v. Metropolitan Toronto Board of Com'rs of Police* (1974), 45 D.L.R. (3d) 548, [1975] 1 S.C.R. 630, 2 N.R. 95, and *Volvo Canada Ltd. v. Int'l Union, United Automobile, Aerospace & Agricultural Implement Workers of America, Local 720* (1979), 99 D.L.R. (3d) 193, [1980] 1 S.C.R. 178, 33 N.S.R. (2d) 22, was that the proper issue was not whether the submission to arbitration was of a specific question of law or a general question in the course of which questions of law arose but there was rather a third category, namely, whether the issue submitted to arbitration constituted a grievance in the course of whose determination questions of the construction of the collective agreement arose. In his view, if the issue submitted to arbitration was in this category, an error by the board in its interpretation is not reviewable unless the interpretation is outrageous or patently unjustifiable (words used in the dissent in the *Bell Canada* case) or patently unreasonable (to use the words of Pigeon J. in the *Volvo* case).
>
> I agree with Chief Justice Bayda that there is no significant difference in the meaning of the aforementioned three terms. Indeed, it would be my view that, apart from a question of emphasis, the test of unreasonableness or test of clearly wrong is also not different. Bayda C.J.S. himself concluded that the board was presented with two reasonable constructions and hence was entitled to choose the one it did rather than the one preferred by the Chief Justice. In the result, he dismissed the appeal.
>
> In my opinion, this is the correct approach. Once it is accepted that there are two reasonable interpretations, the suggestion of a reviewable error of law in consensual arbitration disappears. There is no need to construct a third category, namely, reference to an arbitrator involving construction of a collective agreement. The principle on which this so-called third category is founded is the very

---

107 *Ibid.*, pp. 415-16.

principle applicable in all consensual arbitration cases. The decision of the arbitrator can be set aside only if it involves an interpretation which the words of the agreement could not reasonably bear.

(e) Summary

The *Olds College*,[108] *Suncor*,[109] *U.N.A.*[110] and *Shalansky*[111] cases all demonstrate that the courts have adopted the "patently unreasonable" test to restrict the availability of *certiorari* in cases where no privative clause exists. These cases, therefore, are qualitatively different from those involving a privative clause. In the latter category, it is necessary to find that the error of law is "patently unreasonable" in order to characterize it as jurisdictional in nature, and thereby not protected by the privative clause. In other words, the "patently unreasonable" test is used as a sword to defeat the operation of a privative clause. Very oddly, the same words have been used for precisely the opposite purpose by the courts in the *Olds College* line of cases. To protect intra-jurisdictional errors of law where there is no privative clause effectively converts the "patently unreasonable" test into a shield, not a sword. To the extent that this novel use of the test in fact limits the availability of *certiorari as a matter of law and not as a matter of discretion*, the test really amounts to a judicially-constructed privative clause.

8. The English Position: A Comparison

The English approach to correcting errors of law by judicial review differs in some important respects from that adopted by the Canadian courts. On the one hand, both use the reasoning from *Anisminic*[112] to hold that a patently unreasonable error deprives a statutory delegate of jurisdiction, thereby making his decision subject to judicial review — although the English do not use the phrase "patently unreasonable". On the other hand, the English courts (as opposed to the Privy Council) have tended to treat all errors of law in this manner, without regard to the distinction between jurisdictional and intra-jurisdictional errors of law.[113] After all, the concept of an intra-jurisdictional error of law is only important if there is a privative clause which prevents the availability of the anomalous use of *certiorari* recognized in *R. v. Northumberland Compensation Appeal Tribunal; Ex parte Shaw*[114] to correct such errors. As it happens, however, privative clauses have been almost

---

108 *Supra*, note 98.
109 *Supra*, note 99.
110 *Supra*, note 102.
111 *Supra*, note 106.
112 *Anisminic v. Foreign Comp. Comm.*, [1969] A.C. 147.
113 For an extremely persuasive academic argument as to the correctness of this "jurisdictional" view, see B. Gould, "Anisminic and Judicial Review", [1970] P.L. 358.
114 [1951] 1 K.B. 711, affirmed [1952] 1 K.B. 338 (C.A.).

completely abolished in England since the 1958 Tribunals and Inquiries Act, which provides that:[115]

> As respects England and Wales . . . any provision in an Act passed before [the commencement of this Act] that any order or determination shall not be called into question in any court, or any provision in such an Act which by similar words excludes *any* of the powers of the High court, shall not have effect so as to prevent the removal of proceedings into the High Court by order of certiorari or to prejudice the powers of the High Court to make orders of mandamus. . . .

Although there are a few privative clauses still in operation in England, the net result of their general abolition is that English courts almost never have to push an alleged error of law into the category of jurisdictional error before being able to exercise judicial review: there is no need for them to go beyond *Shaw's* case.

In theory, the Canadian courts take the same approach to correcting intra-jurisdictional errors, subject, however, to two qualifications. First, privative clauses are still quite prevalent in Canada.[116] As a result, Canadian courts have had to concentrate on what types of errors take a delegate outside his jurisdiction and therefore outside the protective cloak of a privative clause. Because of the English policy against privative clauses, there has been relatively little need for the English courts to focus on this aspect of the problem. Conversely, the Canadian courts have had relatively few cases where there was no privative clause[117] so that the anomalous use of *certiorari* in *Shaw's* case could be applied pure and simple to correct all errors of law. Secondly, a casual reading of some recent Canadian cases may incorrectly lead one to assume that the availability of this anomalous use of *certiorari* no longer permits the correction of all intra-jurisdictional errors of law, but only those which are "patently unreasonable" — even in the absence of a privative clause. However, the better view is that the Canadian courts have only applied the patently unreasonable test to cases where there is a privative "gloss" so as to place them on the same footing as cases where there is a true privative clause. Alternatively, it may be possible to explain these recent Canadian cases away as examples of the exercise of discretion to refuse judicial review, and not

---

115 6 & 7 Eliz. 2, c. 66. s. 14(1).

116 And virtually no Canadian jurisdiction has adopted an equivalent of s. 14(1) of the 1958 (*ibid.*) and 1971 (c. 62) English Tribunals and Inquiries Acts to eviscerate privative clauses. The only exception is s. 28 of the Federal Court Act, R.S.C. 1970, c. 10 (2nd Supp.), which permits an application for judicial review of certain federal administrative decisions "notwithstanding the provisions of any other Act".

117 Indeed, there was a privative clause involved in all of the Supreme Court of Canada cases discussed in the text of this chapter, except *Olds College (Re A. U.P.E. and Olds College Bd. of Govs.*, [1982] 1 S.C.R. 923) where the Court nevertheless construed the legislation to contain a "privative gloss".

as legal limitations on the availability of *certiorari* to correct intra-jurisdictional errors of law where there is no privative clause or "gloss". There is, nevertheless, the danger that the Canadian courts will incorrectly apply the patently unreasonable test to restrict the availability of *certiorari* to correct all errors of law.

By contrast, the English courts may be in danger of making exactly the opposite mistake. In *obiter* statements in two recent judgments[118] and in a non-curial paper,[119] Lord Diplock appears to accept that all errors of law must be jurisdictional in nature, and therefore always susceptible to judicial review. As he said *Re Racal Communications:*[120]

> The breakthrough made by *Anisminic* was that, as respects administrative tribunals and authorities, the old distinction between errors of law that went to jurisdiction and errors of law that did not was for practical purposes abolished. *Any error of law that could be shown to have been made by them in the course of reaching their decision on matters of fact or of administrative policy would result in their having asked themselves the wrong question* with the result that the decision they reached would be a nullity.

While it would be very appealing to assert that no administrative tribunal should have the authority to make an error of law, such a statement is nevertheless fallacious. In the first place, this view totally ignores the sovereign right of the British Parliament to delegate the determination of legal questions to someone other than the courts. While it is undoubtedly sound policy for Parliament to make sure that all questions of law are determined by the courts[121] — whether by way of appeal or by judicial review — there is no constitutional requirement for legislation to do this. Indeed, even the inherent right of the superior courts to ensure that statutory delegates do not exceed the limits of their jurisdiction must yield to express legislative provision ousting this common law right of the courts.[122] So if it is a matter of statutory con-

---

118 The two cases are: (1) *Re Racal Communications*, [1980] 2 All E.R. 634, (H.L.) which did not deal with judicial review of an administrator's actions but rather with the inability of the Court of Appeal to hear an appeal from the decision of a judge of the High Court not to issue a warrant to search and seize, and whose decision was specifically stated in the legislation to be "unappealable"; and (2) *O'Reilly v. Mackman; Millbanks v. Secretary of State for Home Dept.*, [1983] A.C. 120 (H.L.), which dealt with the unavailability of an action for a declaration where the new "application for judicial review" would also be available.

119 "Administrative Law: Judicial Review Reviewed", [1974] Camb. L.J. 233.

120 *Supra*, note 117 at pp. 638-39, emphasis added.

121 As we believe. See also Wade's 5th ed. at pp. 264-67.

122 Thus, in England there could be no doubt as to the constitutional validity of the privative clause contained in s. 33 of the B.C. Labour Code, R.S.B.C. 1979, c. 212:

> 33. The board has and shall exercise exclusive jurisdiction to determine the extent of its jurisdiction under this Act, a collective agreement or the regulations, to determine a fact or question of law necessary to establish its jurisdiction or to determine whether or in what manner it shall exercise its jurisdiction.

struction whether the courts have authority to review the jurisdiction of a delegate, so also is it a matter of statutory construction whether Parliament intended that delegate to be the sole person to make determinations on certain points of law. In other words, it is simply not correct to assert that all errors of law are jurisdictional in nature.[123] In particular, not all errors of law mean that the delegate has "asked the wrong question" and therefore declined or exceeded his statutory jurisdiction.

One might ask why Lord Diplock has found it necessary to treat all errors of law as being jurisdictional in nature. After all, very few privative clauses are effective in England since the Tribunals and Inquiries Act 1958, so that *Shaw's* case would almost always apply to permit the anomalous use of *certiorari* to correct intra-jurisdictional errors of law. It is true that the *Anisminic* case involved one of the rare privative clauses still in effect in England,[124] but it is also true that the error of law there clearly *was* jurisdictional in nature. Again, with respect, it is wrong to treat *Anisminic* as any authority for the proposition that all errors of law deprive a statutory delegate of his jurisdiction.

Curiously, the Privy Council specifically recognized the existence of intra-jurisdictional errors of law in a case decided just ten days before the House of Lords' decision in the *Racal* case. In *South East Asia Fire Bricks Sdn. Bhd. v. Non-Metallic Mineral Products Manufacturing Employees Union*,[125] the issue was whether a privative clause prevented the courts from reviewing an alleged error of law by the statutory delegate. Although the Privy Council was prepared to assume that the delegate had made an error of law in reaching its decision,[126] it nevertheless held that the error did not *ipso facto* deprive the delegate of its jurisdiction. Their Lordships[127] noted that the correct parties were before the statutory delegate, on a matter which it undoubtedly had jurisdiction to entertain, and it clearly applied its mind to the proper question required for the purpose of making its award. Therefore, the delegate's decision was within its jurisdiction — and indeed neither party contended to the contrary. Accordingly, the Privy Council held that the privative clause was effective to prevent judicial review of the delegate's decision. In the words of Lord Fraser of Tullybelton:[128]

> The decision of the House of Lords in *Anisminic* . . . shows that, when words in a statute oust the power of the High Court to review decisions of an inferior tribunal by certiorari, they must be

---

Query, however, whether this provision breaches s. 96 of the Canadian Constitution Act, 1867.

123 As the Privy Council unequivocally stated in the *South East Asia Firebrick* case, *infra*, note 125.

124 Because the Tribunals and Inquiries Act 1958 did not apply to the Foreign Compensation Commission, in whose Act there was a privative clause.

125 [1981] A.C. 363 (P.C.).

126 *Ibid.*, p. 374.

127 *Ibid.*, p. 373.

128 *Ibid.*, p. 370.

construed strictly, and they will not have the effect of ousting that power if the inferior tribunal has acted without jurisdiction or if "it has done or failed to do something in the course of the inquiry which is of such a nature that its decision is a nullity": *per* Lord Reid at p. 171. But if the inferior tribunal has merely made an error of law which does not affect its jurisdiction, and if its decision is not a nullity for some reason such as breach of the rules of natural justice, then the ouster will be effective. In *Pearlman v. Keepers and Governors of Harrow School*, [1979] Q.B. 56, 70 Lord Denning M.R. suggested that the distinction between an error of law which affected jurisdiction and one which did not should now be "discarded". Their Lordships do not accept that suggestion. They consider that the law was correctly applied to the circumstances of that case in the dissenting opinion of Geoffrey Lane L.J. when he said, at p. 74:

> . . . the only circumstances in which this court can correct what is to my mind the error of the [county court] judge is if he was acting in excess of his jurisdiction as opposed to merely making an error of law in his judgment by misinterpreting the meaning of "structural alteration . . . or addition".

In the result, the Privy Council clearly recognized that not all errors of law are jurisdictional in nature, and that Parliament may validly enact a privative clause preventing judicial review of such intra-jurisdictional errors of law. In other words, the privative clause deprives the courts of their anomalous power under *Shaw's* case to issue *certiorari* to correct intra-jurisdictional errors of law.

With respect, the Privy Council's view is clearly correct to recognize the existence of intra-jurisdictional errors of law. While one may hate privative clauses and fervently hope that Parliament always provided a right of appeal or judicial review to correct all errors of law made by a statutory delegate, Lord Diplock is wrong to assume that *Anisminic* achieves this goal. So far, neither the Privy Council nor the House of Lords has commented on the Supreme Court of Canada's requirement of "patent unreasonability" in determining whether *certiorari* lies to correct an intra-jurisdictional error.

9. The Common Law Action to Quash and Remit the Decision of a Consensual Arbitrator

(a) What Are Consensual Arbitrations?

It is important to note that the superior courts have a separate general superintending and reforming power with respect to all arbitrations, even if they are not statutory in nature, so that certain errors committed by arbitrators are susceptible to judicial review, even if not by way of *certiorari*. In *Association of Radio and Television Employees of Canada (CUPE-CLC) v. Canadian Broadcasting Corporation*,[129] the Supreme Court of Canada (per Laskin J.) dealt with this point as follows:

> However, the Court in the *Howe Sound* case did go on to say that the fact that *certiorari* would not lie did not mean that review *under the common law or under a general arbitration statute* was precluded.
>
> This latter point was restated and expanded by this Court in *Port Arthur Shipbuilding Co. v. Arthurs*, [1969] S.C.R. 85, at pp. 94-95. The effect of what was said there is to deny homage to technicality, and to make it clear that where the proceedings to review a decision of a board of arbitration are made by way of a motion to quash or to set aside the award, dispensing with the issue of a writ of *certiorari*, it matters not whether the board of arbitration is or is not a statutory tribunal in any strict sense. I agree with this view of the issue and would add that it would be equally resolved by the bringing of an action for a declaration. Having regard to the form of the proceedings in the present case, it is unnecessary to consider whether the board of arbitration was a statutory tribunal in the *Rivando* sense or was a non-statutory tribunal in the *Howe Sound* sense. In either case, there was jurisdiction in the Manitoba Court of Queen's Bench. [Emphasis added.]

Other authorities on the inherent jurisdiction of the superior courts to review and reform awards of consensual arbitration boards include: *Re Oil, Chemical & Atomic Workers' International Union, Local 9-14 and Polymer Corporation Ltd.*;[130] *Athabasca Realty Co. v. Merenick*;[131] *Arbitration Act*,[132] and the decision of the Alberta Court of Appeal in *Suncor*[133] (where *only certiorari* was sought, but the court was prepared if necessary to grant another remedy to review the arbitrator's award if it was non-statutory in nature). The technical distinction between statutory and consensual arbitrations should become much less important — at least in the labour field — in light of the Supreme Court's decision in *Roberval*[134] to the effect that the choice of arbitration in fact makes that arbitration board a statutory one, even though the parties under the statute could have chosen some other method for resolving their dispute. Nevertheless, *certiorari* is only available against statutory bodies, and the common law action to quash and remit a decision is only available against

---

129 [1975] 1 S.C.R. 118 at 136-37, a case where arbitration was the only method for settling the differences.
130 (1966) 55 D.L.R. (2d) 198 at 208 (Ont. H.C.).
131 (1982) 36 A.R. 507 (Q.B.).
132 R.S.A. 1980, c. A-43.
133 [1983] 1 W.W.R. 604.
134 *Roberval Express Ltee. v. Tpt. Drivers, Warehousemen & Gen. Wkrs.*, [1982] 2 S.C.R. 888.

a consensual arbitrator: see *Racecourse Betting Control Board v. Secretary of Air*.[135] The two remedies are mutually exclusive, therefore, and some care is necessary in determining which one applies to the particular case at hand.

(b) Is the Test the Same for *Certiorari* for Errors of Law and for the Common Law Action to Quash and Remit?

It may be dangerous to assume that the ambit of the court's power to review the decision of a statutory arbitration board by *certiorari* is identical to the ambit of its inherent power to review awards of consensual arbitration boards. Chouinard J. referred to this distinction in *Roberval*[136] when noting the distinction between the ambit of a direct action in nullity under article 33 of the Quebec Code of Civil Procedure (which closely resembles a declaration or a declaratory order in Alberta), and the grounds for the availability of evocation under article 846 of the Quebec Code of Civil Procedure (which is a statutory amalgamation of the prerogative remedies of prohibition and *certiorari*, both of which continue their separate existences in Alberta).[137]

First, both the Quebec action in nullity and the common law declaration are only available once the arbitrator has rendered his decision, whereas prohibition (that is, an anticipatory *certiorari*) may be available to prevent an error of law being made prior to that point in time.

Secondly, the Quebec action in nullity applies only to cases of excess of jurisdiction or to an injustice amounting to fraud (which probably is a particular example of an action taking the delegate outside his jurisdiction), and cannot be used to correct an error of law *within* the delegate's jurisdiction. Similar restrictions apply to the availability of a declaration under the common law[138] where the error lies *within* the delegate's jurisdiction, because such a decision must be quashed. A declaration quashes nothing; this can only be done by an order of *certiorari*.

Thirdly, the Arbitration Act[139] of Alberta specifically prescribes the standard of judicial review of a decision of a non-statutory arbitrator in terms of "misconduct". Historically, the courts construed "misconduct" to mean corruption or other undue means, which did not include errors of law by the arbitrator. This approach was changed, however, in *Kent v. Elstob*,[140] and "misconduct" was expanded to include all errors of law on the face of the record. The Alberta Court of Appeal recently restated this doctrine in *R.O.M. Construction Ltd. v. Electric Power Equipment Ltd.*,[141] which holds that review

---

135 [1943] Ch. 198, affirmed [1944] Ch. 114 (C.A.).
136 *Supra*, note 133.
137 See also the decision in *Vachon v. A.G. Que.*; *Richard v. A.G. Que.*, [1979] 1 S.C.R. 555; and *Seminary of Chicoutimi v. A.G. Que.*, [1970] Que. C.A. 413, affirmed [1973] S.C.R. 681.
138 See *Punton (No. 2)*, *supra*, note 3.
139 *Supra*, note 132.
140 (1802) 3 East 18, regretted but not reversed in *Hodgkinson v. Fernie*, (1857) 3 C.B.N.S. 189.
141 (1981) 121 D.L.R. (3d) 753, leave to appeal to S.C.C. refused 121 D.L.R. (3d) 753n.

of consensual arbitrations is available for any error of law on the face of the record, and is not restricted only to those errors which are patently unreasonable. Unfortunately, the clarity of this rule has been muddied by *obiter dicta* in the subsequent decision of the Alberta Court of Appeal in the *Suncor* case,[142] where Kerans J.A. indicates that the standard of review is the same for consensual or statutory arbitrations: namely, whether the arbitrator has committed an error of law which is patently unreasonable, and not whether he has committed an error of law pure and simple. Regrettably, Kerans J.A. simply asserts in *Suncor* that consensual arbitrations are subject to the "patently unreasonable" test, relying on the rationale expressed by Dickson J. in *C.U.P.E. Local 963 v. N.B. Liquor Corporation*,[143] as follows:

> It is contended, however, that the interpretation placed upon [the section in dispute] was so patently unreasonable that the Board, although possessing "jurisdiction in the narrow sense of authority to enter upon an inquiry", in the course of that inquiry did "something which takes the exercise of its powers outside the protection of the privative or preclusive clause".... Put another way, was the Board's interpretation so patently unreasonable that its construction cannot be rationally supported by the relevant legislation and demands intervention by the court upon review?

However, it is important to note that the *C.U.P.E.* case undoubtedly dealt with a *statutory* power, so it is difficult to understand why Kerans J.A. relied upon this quotation to assert that the "patently unreasonable" test applies to determine the standard of review to be applied to consensual arbitrators under the court's inherent jurisdiction or under the Arbitration Act's reference to "misconduct". Nevertheless, this new approach has been recently confirmed by the Supreme Court of Canada in *Shalansky v. Board of Governors of Regina Pasqua Hospital*,[144] which clearly dealt with a consensual arbitration. On behalf of a unanimous five-member panel, Laskin C.J.C. specifically stated that[145]

> [o]nce it is accepted that there are two reasonable interpretations, the suggestion of a reviewable error of law in consensual arbitration disappears. ... The decision of the arbitrator can be set aside only if it involves an interpretation which the words of the agreement could not reasonably bear.

(c) Summary

In summary, then, the courts have a general power to issue *certiorari* to

---

142 *Supra*, note 133.
143 [1979] 2 S.C.R. 227 at 237.
144 (1983) 145 D.L.R. (3d) 413 (S.C.C.).
145 *Ibid.*, p. 416.

review certain errors of law made by a statutory delegate in the course of the exercise of his jurisdiction. The error must appear on the face of the record. And recent jurisprudence indicates that the courts will only review such errors if they are patently unreasonable, patently unjustifiable, outrageous, or clearly wrong.[146] Although *certiorari* is not available against consensual arbitrations,[147] the definition of what constitutes a statutory arbitration has been extended considerably by the *Roberval* case.[148] Further, the courts have a parallel common law power to quash and remit the decision of a consensual arbitrator for misconduct, which has been defined to include committing an error of law on the face of the arbitration award. The Supreme Court of Canada in *Shalansky*[149] has recently narrowed this supervisory power to correct only patently unreasonable errors of law made by consensual arbitrators. Although the legal reasoning process involved in getting to this result may be perplexing, the end result makes the rules coincide for judicial review of both statutory delegates and consensual arbitrations, and reflects a certain degree of judicial restraint in reviewing the decisions of delegates to whom either the legislators or adverse parties have remitted the power to make decisions. In principle, this operating rule should apply to judicial review of all discretionary powers, and not just to labour matters which are statutory or consensual in nature. After all, judicial review of labour matters is merely a particular application of the general principles of Administrative Law.

10. Does the "Patently Unreasonable" Test Apply to Shield Jurisdictional Errors?

It is important to recall again that the "patently unreasonable" test performs two quite distinct functions. First, the test is used as a sword to avoid the effect of a privative clause by characterizing any "patently unreasonable" error of law as one which goes to the jurisdiction of the statutory delegate. Secondly, the test has recently been expanded by the *Olds College* case to act as a shield to prevent judicial review of intra-jurisdictional errors of law which are not "patently unreasonable", even where no privative clause is involved. The interesting question then arises whether this form of curial deference will also be applied to protect *jurisdictional* matters which have not been determined in a "patently unreasonable" manner by the statutory delegate. In principle, the answer to this question should be a resounding "no" for the following reasons, although some contrary *dicta* do exist.

---

146 See *Shalansky, ibid.*, pp. 415-16.
147 Unless of course legislation specifically makes *certiorari* available in such a non-statutory context. The Labour Act may do precisely this by specifically making *certiorari* available against the decision of an arbitration tribunal, which (at least prior to *Roberval* and *Suncor*) might be characterized as being consensual in nature.
148 [1982] 2 S.C.R. 888.
149 *Supra*, note 144.

First, no statutory delegate can lawfully extend the jurisdiction delegated to him by the legislative branch. This is the doctrine of *ultra vires*. And the superior courts have made this rule effective by judicial review. To permit a delegate to expand his jurisdiction by committing an error of law (or jurisdictional fact) would subvert this high constitutional principle. The reasonableness of such an error of law is really irrelevant to the jurisdictional question involved. Indeed, Wachowich J. applied this principle in *R. v. Alberta Labour Relations Board*,[150] where he specifically held that the "patently unreasonable" test does not apply to an error on a jurisdictional matter.[151] Veit J. reached the same conclusion in *Allied Communications v. International Brotherhood of Electrical Workers, Local 348*:[152]

> In addition to the points mentioned by the learned authors it appears to me to be reasonable to distinguish between intra-jurisdictional and jurisdictional issues because of the different expertise component in those areas. Curial deference exists as tribunals are appointed for special expertise, for special background which might only be that of the common sense member of the public; it would obviously defeat the purpose of such tribunals if the courts were then to substantively reassess matters requiring expertise. There is, however, no special expertise in matters relating to jurisdiction; it might be said, in another way, that the expertise required for jurisdictional issues is usually legal expertise. The empowering statute will determine the narrowness or the breadth of the tribunal's threshold; so long as the threshold requirement does not contain a special expertise component, the courts are the appropriate interpreting authority.

This approach has recently been resoundingly confirmed by the unanimous Supreme Court of Canada decision in *Le Syndicat des Employés de Production du Québec et de l'Acadie v. Can. L.B.R.*,[153] where Beetz J. said:

> Unquestionably, as has already been noted, it is often difficult to determine what constitutes a question of jurisdiction, and administrative tribunals like the Board must generally be given the benefit of any doubt. Once the classification has been established, however,

---

150 (1983) 27 Alta. L.R. (2d) 338 at 343 (Q.B.).
151 The error dealt with a failure to consider relevant evidence, which His Lordship held constituted a jurisdictional matter (but not "in the narrow sense" so often referred to by Dickson J. See *Service Employees' Int. Union v. Nipawin Dist. Staff Nurses Assn.*, (1973) 41 D.L.R. (3d) 6 at 11-12, and the cases cited therein.) Query: did Wachowich J. correctly characterize this alleged error as being "jurisdictional" in nature? Interestingly, he justified his decision on the alternative basis that the alleged error of ignoring evidence was "patently unreasonable" in any event!
152 [1985] 1 W.W.R. 714 at 723 (Q.B.).
153 [1984] 2 S.C.R. 412 at 441-42.

it does not matter whether an error as to such a question is doubtful, excusable or not unreasonable, or on the contrary is excessive, blatant or patently unreasonable. What makes this kind of error fatal, whether serious or slight, is its jurisdictional nature; and what leads to excluding the rule of the patently unreasonable error is the duty imposed on the Federal Court of Appeal to exercise the jurisdiction conferred on it by s. 28(1)(*a*) of the *Federal Court Act* [to correct jurisdictional errors made by federal tribunals].

When the Federal Court of Appeal, and in general courts with a duty to exercise a superintending and reforming power over administrative tribunals, find that an interpretation given by the latter to an enactment is not patently unreasonable, they are finding that this interpretation is defensible: however, they are not deciding whether the interpretation is correct or incorrect, and are not in general expressing any opinion on the point. . . .

Once a question is classified as one of jurisdiction, and has been the subject of a decision by an administrative tribunal, the superior court exercising the superintending and reforming power over that tribunal cannot, without itself refusing to exercise its own jurisdiction, refrain from ruling on the correctness of that decision, or rule on it by means of an approximate criterion.

This is why the superior courts which exercise the power of judicial review do not and may not use the rule of the patently unreasonable error once they have classified an error as jurisdictional.

Secondly, a close reading of the cases referred to in this chapter indicates that the courts have very definitely maintained the distinction between jurisdictional and intra-jurisdictional errors, although putting the distinction into practice may be difficult. Thus, in *C.U.P.E.* Dickson J. noted that there was no preliminary or collateral question involved which could affect the board's jurisdiction. He characterized the alleged legal error as being intra-jurisdictional in nature, and indicated that the courts should generally do so in cases of doubt:[154]

The question of what is and is not jurisdictional is often very difficult to determine. *The Courts, in my view, should not be alert to brand as jurisdictional, and therefore subject to broader curial review, that which may be doubtfully so.*

This approach recognizes both the possibility of jurisdictional errors and the wider ambit of judicial review to correct such errors. Indeed, Beetz J. specifically recognizes this distinction in the *Syndicat* case:[155]

---

154 [1979] 2 S.C.R. 227 at 233, emphasis added.
155 *Supra*, note 153 at p. 437.

It should be said, first, that the warning given the courts by this Court against over-hasty classification of a question of jurisdiction contains an important qualification: as Dickson J. . . . observed the courts should not be alert to brand as jurisdictional "that which may be doubtfully so." I hope to be able to show that in the case at bar there is no doubt as to such a classification.

This approach to jurisdictional errors allows the courts to distinguish the *Jacmain*,[156] *Parkhill Bedding*,[157] *Jarvis*,[158] *Anisminic*,[159] *Metropolitan Life Insurance*[160] and *Bell*[161] cases on the basis that they deal with jurisdictional errors. Chief Justice Laskin recognized the concept of jurisdictional errors in *Massicotte*,[162] as did Stevenson J.A. in *U.N.A.*,[163] although jurisdictional errors were held not to be involved in either case. Accordingly, one must conclude that judicial review for jurisdictional error has not been affected by the recent use of the "patently unreasonable" test to shield certain intra-jurisdictional errors from judicial review.

Thirdly, the very use of the "patently unreasonable" test as a sword to permit judicial review in the face of a privative clause must demonstrate the continued importance of jurisdictional matters. After all, judicial review can in theory only occur where there is a privative clause *because* a jurisdictional error is involved. The use of the "patently unreasonable" doctrine in this circumstance in effect denotes that what might otherwise have been an intra-jurisdictional error is so objectionable that it has deprived the statutory delegate of his jurisdiction, and hence of the protection of the privative clause. Beetz J. in the recent *Syndicat* case recognizes a number of different types of jurisdictional errors:[164]

> In my opinion it cannot be said that the only jurisdictional error is one affecting the initial jurisdiction, jurisdiction *ratione materiae*, or attributive jurisdiction of an administrative tribunal initiating a hearing. Further, I do not think that anything was said or decided to this effect in *New Brunswick Liquor Corporation* [*v. C.U.P.E.*], where the provision at issue did not confer jurisdiction but, it was wrongly argued, concerned a prerequisite to the exercise of jurisdiction.
>
> It seems to me that if jurisdictional error includes error as to the

---

156 *Jacmain v. A.G. Can.*, [1978] 2 S.C.R. 15.
157 *Parkhill Furniture & Bedding Ltd. v. Int. Molders etc. Union*, (1961) 26 D.L.R. (2d) 589 (Man. C.A.).
158 *Jarvis v. Assoc. Medical Services Inc.*, [1964] S.C.R. 497.
159 *Anisminic v. Foreign Comp. Comm.*, [1969] 2 A.C. 147 (H.L.).
160 *Metro. Life Ins. Co. v. Int. Union of Operating Engineers*, [1970] S.C.R. 425.
161 *Bell v. Ont. Human Rights Comm.*, [1971] S.C.R. 756.
162 (1982) 134 D.L.R. (3d) 385 (S.C.C.).
163 [1983] 6 W.W.R. 1 (Alta. C.A.).
164 *Supra*, note 153 at pp. 438-39.

initial jurisdiction of an administrative tribunal initiating a hearing and its power to resolve by a declaration the question submitted to it, *a fortiori* it covers provisions which confer on it the power to add to its final decision orders arising out of the hearing and intended to give effect to its declarations by injunctions and other means of redress such as those in . . . [The *Canada Labour Code*]. I do not see how it is logical to limit the possibility that an administrative tribunal may make a jurisdictional error to the initial stage, if the tribunal could err and exceed its jurisdiction with impunity at the stage of the conclusion which constitutes the outcome of its hearing and is its ultimate purpose.

The same is generally true, in my view, for errors relating to the executory, if not declaratory, powers which the Board exercises during a hearing, like that of questioning witnesses, requiring the production of documents, entering an employer's premises and so on, conferred on it by s. 118 of the Code. Wide as these powers may be, they do not include, for example, giving the Board the right to punish for contempt. This power continues to belong to the Federal Court, as provided in s. 123 regarding registration of the Board's orders or decisions, exclusive of the reasons therefor, in the Federal Court. That section expressly refers to s. 28 of the *Federal Court Act*, and maintains it in effect. Section 123 therefore assumes by implication that a jurisdictional error may be committed at any stage of a hearing held by the Board.

Additionally, as I have already indicated, s. 28(1)(*a*) of the *Federal Court Act* does not apply to the error as such, but quite apart from any error, to the excess of jurisdiction or refusal to exercise it, that is, the exercise by an administrative tribunal of a power denied to it by the Act or the refusal to exercise power imposed on it by the Act. Section 28(1)(*a*) does not distinguish between types of excess of power, the stages of the hearing at which they occur and the circumstances causing them. It applies to any excess of power. There is therefore no reason to make a distinction where s. 28(1)(*a*) makes none, between on the one hand excess of jurisdiction *ratione materiae* committed at the beginning of a hearing, whether or not resulting from an error, and on the other, an error made during the hearing or in the conclusion of a hearing and the corrective orders attached to it, despite the fact that the administrative tribunal has jurisdiction *ratione materiae*.

It is clear, therefore, that the courts do recognize jurisdictional errors as a category separate from intra-jurisdictional errors of law. Different tests apply to these categories for determining the availability of judicial review.

Fourthly, it is important to remember that certain matters which otherwise would be jurisdictional in nature may by legislation be placed *within* the delegate's jurisdiction. Thus, in the *U.N.A.* case, the question whether an item was arbitrable was specifically stated by the legislation to lie *within* the jurisdiction of the arbitration board, even though in other cases such an issue would be preliminary or collateral to the arbitrator's jurisdiction. The application of the "patently unreasonable" test by the court to prevent judicial review in the *U.N.A.* case, therefore, must not be misread to suggest that that test applies to jurisdictional matters too.

Similarly, some jurisdictional matters are specifically made elastic or subjective by the legislation involved. Thus, in *Liversidge v. Anderson*,[165] the Home Secretary was given power to intern enemy aliens whom he had reason to believe were dangerous to the security of the United Kingdom. The majority of the House of Lords held that the powers granted to the Home Secretary were so subjective in nature that it would be impossible for their exercise to be reviewed by the courts. This does not mean that no jurisdictional question could ever be raised concerning any particular exercise of the Home Secretary's internment powers if, for example, malice, bad faith or an improper purpose could be demonstrated. On the contrary, the subjective nature of the delegated power merely converts some matters which might otherwise be jurisdictional in nature into intra-jurisdictional ones. As a result, the patently unreasonable test may have to be met in order to obtain judicial review of an error of law with respect to such intra-jurisdictional matters. Nevertheless, it would be wrong to suggest that these cases support any attempt to make the patently unreasonable test applicable to matters which clearly go to the jurisdiction of a statutory delegate.

It is important to examine closely the various stray *dicta* which suggest that the courts may apply the "patently unreasonable" test even to jurisdictional questions, contrary to all theory. In his dissenting opinion in *Jacmain*,[166] Dickson J.[167] suggests that judicial review should not issue even on a jurisdictional matter, whether of fact or law, unless the delegate's decision on that matter lacks a rational basis or is manifestly in error — in short, is "patently unreasonable". In *Jacmain*, the issue was whether a probationary employee was dismissed for disciplinary reasons or rejected for inadequacy. In the former case, an appeal lay to an arbitration board, but which had no jurisdiction in the latter case. The board heard evidence on the nature of the dismissal, and took jurisdiction because it held discipline in fact was involved. The majority of the Supreme Court held that the board erred in this conclusion. Laskin, Dickson and Pigeon JJ. dissented, and would have exercised

---

165 [1942] A.C. 206 (H.L.). Note Lord Atkin's vehement dissent, which would have construed the enabling legislation in objective terms, not subjective ones. Such an approach would make judicial review more easily available because the court could determine whether those objective factors existed (*i.e.*, whether there in fact *were* reasonable grounds, instead of whether the minister *believed* there were).

166 *Supra*, note 156.

167 On behalf of himself, Laskin C.J.C. and Spence J.

curial deference to the findings of the board with respect to which its jurisdiction depended:[168]

> The intractable difficulty is this. It is hard to conceive that a
> legislature would create a tribunal with a limited jurisdiction and
> yet bestow on such tribunal an unlimited power to determine the
> extent of its jurisdiction. On the other hand, if the correctness of
> every detail upon which the jurisdiction of the tribunal depends is to
> be subject to re-trial in the Courts and the opinion of a judge substi-
> tuted for that of the tribunal, then the special experience and knowl-
> edge of the members of such a tribunal and the advantage they have
> of hearing and seeing the witnesses may be lost. The power to review
> jurisdictional questions provides the Courts with a useful tool to
> ensure that tribunals deal with the type of issues which the
> Legislature intended. It enables the Courts to check unlawful
> attempts at usurpation of power. But the Courts, in my opinion,
> should exercise restraint in declaring a tribunal to be without juris-
> diction when it has reached its decision honestly and fairly and with
> due regard to the material before it. The Court should allow some
> latitude in its surveillance of jurisdictional findings. It should ask
> whether there is substantial evidence for decisions of fact and a
> rational basis for decisions of law, or mixed decisions of fact and
> law. The error must be manifest. The role of the Court is one of
> review, not trial *de novo*.

This approach no doubt explains Dickson J.'s comments in the *C.U.P.E.*
case[169] urging the courts to characterize alleged errors as being intra-jurisdictional in nature whenever possible, and not jurisdictional. It is also important
to note that the prerogative remedies are discretionary in nature, and may
be refused by the courts even when a jurisdictional point is involved.[170]

---

168 [1978] 2 S.C.R. 15 at 29.
169 [1979] 2 S.C.R. 227.
170 Stevenson J.A. makes a similar comment in the *U.N.A.* case, *supra*, note 163 at p. 10:

> A tribunal necessarily has the authority to decide whether a matter before it comes
> within its jurisdiction. What the courts must decide is what limitations there are on that
> authority. Even if we are to accept the appellants' argument that the matter before the
> board was the question of just cause, and that arbitrability is preliminary or collateral,
> nonetheless the statute and agreement expressly commit this question to arbitrators
> whose decision is final and binding. This is contrasted with cases where the tribunal may
> only act if certain facts exist, a distinction noted by Lord Esher M.R. in *R. v. Income Tax
> Special Purpose Commr.* (1888), 21 Q.B.D. 313 at 319 (C.A.), quoted by Wade,
> Administrative Law, 4th ed. (1977), at p. 244. *Even in such cases curial deference may
> require restraint if it is found that a preliminary fact issue was intended to be resolved by a
> tribunal.* [Emphasis added.]

It is suggested that this *dictum* must be very carefully limited to the type of hypothetical
statutory provisions referred to by Stevenson J.A. at the end of the quotation.

In theory, therefore, the "patently unreasonable" test should have no application to shield any jurisdictional matters from judicial review, and the *Syndicat* case indicates that the Supreme Court of Canada has now unanimously and unequivocally confirmed this point.

11. Rationales for Using the "Patently Unreasonable" Test as a Guide for Exercising Discretion to Refuse Judicial Review of Intra-Jurisdictional Errors

As indicated earlier, some rationale must be found for using the "patently unreasonable" test to restrict judicial review of intra-jurisdictional errors where no privative clause exists, as was done in the *Olds College*,[171] *Suncor*,[172] *U.N.A.*[173] and *Shalansky*[174] cases. It has already been suggested that these cases cannot theoretically be read to prevent *certiorari* from issuing — as a matter of law — to correct such an error, even if it is not patently unreasonable. On the other hand, it has also been suggested that the "patently unreasonable" test may be useful in helping the courts to decide whether to exercise their discretion to refuse judicial review. Let us, therefore, now examine the circumstances to which the courts have hitherto referred to justify such a discretionary refusal of a prerogative remedy, as well as the policy reasons referred to by them in adopting the "patently unreasonable" test to refuse *certiorari* in the absence of a privative clause.

Professor de Smith recognized[175] only three cases in which the courts exercised their discretion to refuse prerogative remedies:

(a) where there is an appeal which provides a more effective remedy;
(b) where the applicant's conduct has disentitled him to relief; and
(c) where it would be pointless to issue the remedy.

The "patently unreasonable" test does not fit in any of these three categories. To be fair, the courts have not attempted to relate the "patently unreasonable" test to any of these categories, and have very seldom even acknowledged that using this test involves their discretion to refuse judicial review. Let us see what their Lordships have said.

Kerans J.A. rationalized the restricted availability of *certiorari* to correct errors of law in light of the summary nature and perceived speed of the arbitra-

---

171 (1982) 21 Alta. L.R. (2d) 104 (S.C.C.).
172 [1983] 1 W.W.R. 604 (Alta. C.A.).
173 [1983] 6 W.W.R. 1 (Alta. C.A.).
174 (1983) 145 D.L.R. (3d) 413 (S.C.C.).
175 J.M. Evans, *de Smith's Judicial Review of Administrative Action*, 4th ed. (1980), pp. 422-28. See D.P. Jones, "Discretionary Refusal of Judicial Review in Administrative Law", (1981) 19 Alta. L. Rev. 483.

tion process. His comments deserve quotation at length to see whether they really bear out the need to restrict *certiorari* in this manner:[176]

> The object of the Labour Relations Act is to require some form of summary resolution of disputes which arise during the currency of a collective agreement. As Pigeon J. said in *Volvo Can. Ltd. v. Int. Union, United Auto. etc., Wkrs.*, [1980] 1 S.C.R. 178, 99 D.L.R. (3d) 193 at 222, 27 N.R. 502:
>
> > the arbitration is not meant to be an additional step before the matter goes before the Courts, the decision is meant to be final.
>
> In my view, there is much to be said for judicial restraint in the face of summary disposition of grievances under collective agreements, whether this disposition is imposed or voluntary. Legislators impose summary process for the same reasons that individuals agree on it: those who choose arbitration in substitution for traditional process perceive themselves as having a greater interest in quickness and cheapness than in "correctness". They select a summary process in the hope that it will be quick and cheap. That this hope is often in vain is not material; nor is it material that this hope is sometimes founded in a simplified procedure and sometimes in the expertise of the substitute tribunal; nor is it material that they may have misjudged the capacity of traditional process fairly to balance the three criteria. *I distinguish summary process from specialized process, where the trier has special knowledge and the hope is that his expertise will produce a result more correct than if considered in the traditional process.*
>
> Of course, the advantage of summary or special disposition never outweighs the disadvantage of a decision which provokes outrage. So all such process is subject at least to minimal review.
>
> The courts sometimes strain at the leash fashioned by a privative clause. Perhaps this is because they do not agree with the legislature that, in the circumstances of the case, the advantages of summary process outweigh the disadvantages. Be that as it may, the process at least of arbitration of grievances under collective agreements is, in this day, one best left largely alone by the courts.
>
> *That this consideration justifies a standard of review so narrow as the "patent unreasonableness" test is a decision which, in my view, has been made for us by the Supreme Court of Canada in Olds College. And it follows that the standard of review is that test, whether the arbitration here can be classified as consensual or compulsory.*

---

176 *Supra*, note 172 at pp. 610-11, emphasis added.

Kerans J.A., therefore, justifies the discretionary[177] refusal of *certiorari* because of the compelling need for speedy decisions, even if incorrect. He notes that this is not the same as exercising curial restraint because of the specialized nature of the statutory delegate, which Dickson J. relied on in *C.U.P.E.*:[178]

> [The privative clause] constitutes a clear statutory direction on the part of the Legislature that public sector labour matters be promptly and finally decided by the Board. Privative clauses of this type are typically found in labour relations legislation. The rationale for protection of a labour board's decisions within jurisdiction is straightforward and compelling. The labour board is a specialized tribunal which administers a comprehensive statute regulating labour relations. In the administration of that regime, a board is called upon not only to find facts and decide questions of law, but also to exercise its understanding of the body of jurisprudence that has developed around the collective bargaining system, as under-stood in Canada, and its labour relations sense acquired from accumulated experience in the area.
>
> The usual reasons for judicial restraint upon review of labour board decisions are only reinforced in a case such as the one at bar. Not only has the Legislature confided certain decisions to the administrative board, but to a separate and distinct Public Service Labour Relations Board. That Board is given broad powers — broader than those typically vested in a labour board — to supervise and administer the novel system of collective bargaining created by the *Public Service Labour Relations Act*. The Act calls for a delicate balance between the need to maintain public services, and the need to maintain collective bargaining. Considerable sensitivity and unique expertise on the part of the Board members is all the more required if the twin purposes of the legislation are to be met. Nowhere is the application of those skills more evident than in the supervision of a lawful strike by public service employees under the Act. Although the New Brunswick Act is patterned closely upon the federal *Public Service Staff Relations Act*, R.S.C. 1970, c. P-35. s. 102(3) is not found in the federal legislation nor, in fact, in any other public sector labour legislation in Canada. The interpretation of s. 102(3) would seem to lie logically at the heart of the specialized jurisdiction confided to the Board. In that case, not only would the Board not be required to be "correct" in its interpretation, but one would think that the Board was entitled to err and any such error would be protected from review by the privative clause in s. 101: see

---

177 Although he nowhere speaks in terms of discretion.
178 (1979) 97 D.L.R. (3d) 417 (S.C.C.) at 423-24.

Farrell et al. v. Workmen's Compensation Board and A.-G. B.C.
(1961), 31 D.L.R. 177, [1962] S.C.R. 48, 37 W.W.R. 39.

In my view, that would be sufficient to dispose of this appeal.

And this passage was quoted with approval by Laskin C.J.C. in *Massicotte*,[179] and again referred to in his judgment in *Olds College*.[180]

Accordingly, it appears that one must add the following two reasons to the list of justifications for refusing judicial review:

(d) where the specialized knowledge of the statutory delegate indicates the courts should not interfere; and

(e) where the advantages of the summary and speedy nature of the administrative process outweigh the public interest in having the law correctly applied in all cases.

It is important to remember that the discretion to refuse prerogative remedies is precisely that: discretionary. Thus, none of these considerations should bind the courts to refuse judicial review where other considerations require it — such as those referred to by Moir J.A. in the *U.N.A.* case.[181] Finally, it is important to remember that not all remedies for illegal administrative action are discretionary in nature.[182]

12. Conclusion: Can an Intra-Jurisdictional Error of Law Still Exist Under the "Patently Unreasonable" Test?

It will be recalled that the purpose of this chapter has been to examine the anomalous availability of *certiorari* to correct intra-jurisdictional errors of law on the face of the record. To do this, it was necessary to examine:

(a) the distinction between errors which deprive a statutory delegate of his jurisdiction;

(b) the general limitations on the availability of *certiorari* as a remedy;

(c) the extent of the "record";

(d) the distinction between errors of "law" and other kinds of errors;[183]

---

179 (1982) 134 D.L.R. (3d) 385 at 394 (S.C.C.).

180 *Supra*, note 171 at p. 110.

181 *Supra*, note 173. A further circumstance in which the court may exercise its jurisdiction to refuse a prerogative remedy may arise when the error would not affect the result: see *Can. Kellogg Co. v. Indust. Rel. Bd. (Alta.)*, [1976] 2 W.W.R. 67 (Alta. T.D.).

182 *E.g.*, the right to damages is not discretionary (although the amount thereof may be). See the discussion of the consequences of this point in D.P. Jones, *supra*, note 175.

183 Consider Dickson J.'s comments on this point in *Jacmain v. A.G. Can.*, [1978] 2 S.C.R. 15 at 30:

It seems to me that, in the present case, nothing turns on the distinction between fact and law; it is immaterial whether the question is classified as one of fact, or law, or a mixed question of fact and law. The key distinction is between jurisdictional questions (whether of fact, or law, or both) and non-jurisdictional questions. An answer beyond

(e) the use of the "patently unreasonable" test to identify jurisdictional errors, in particular to avoid the effect of a privative clause;

(f) the new use of the "patently unreasonable" test to determine whether the court should exercise its discretion to refuse *certiorari* where there is no privative clause to protect an intra-jurisdictional error of law;

(g) the common law action to quash and remit a decision of a consensual arbitrator which is "patently unreasonable";

(h) whether the "patently unreasonable" test should apply to determine whether a statutory delegate has committed an error on a matter which is undoubtedly jurisdictional in nature; and

(i) the rationales used by the courts in adopting the "patently unreasonable" test for curial deference in correcting decisions of statutory delegates.

The law on this subject is complicated, and has moved very rapidly in the past few years.

In one respect, the "patently unreasonable" test is not new at all. The courts have long used the test to identify a jurisdictional error, and thereby avoid the effect of a privative clause. The recent cases on this point — *Volvo*,[184] *C.U.P.E.*,[185] *Massicotte*,[186] and one interpretation of *Olds College*[187] — are therefore only recent applications of previously well-recognized law.

On the other hand, the courts have clearly developed new law in using the "patently unreasonable" test to shield a non-jurisdictional error in the absence of a privative clause. Thus, a second interpretation of *Olds College*,[188] *Suncor*[189] and *U.N.A.*[190] represents new law. Coupled with the *Roberval*[191] decision extending the category of what constitutes a statutory decision, as well as the *Shalansky*[192] case applying the "patently unreasonable" test to

---

the permissible latitudes to a jurisdictional question causes the tribunal either to act beyond its jurisdiction (if it decides to consider the merits when it has no authority to do so), or to refuse to exercise its jurisdiction (if it decides that it does not have authority to consider the merits when actually it does have such authority). Thus, an error is reviewable under s. 28(1)(*a*) of the *Federal Court Act*. Only if a question is non-jurisdictional does the characterization of it as one of fact, or law, become material. If it is a question of law, s. 28(1)(*b*) applies and any error is subject to review. If it is a question of fact, s. 28(1)(*c*) applies and an error is reviewable only if it is made in a perverse or capricious manner, or without regard for the material before the tribunal.

The crucial question, therefore, to be determined may be simply stated — was the adjudicator wrong? Did his decision with respect to jurisdiction fall outside tolerable parameters?

184 (1979) 99 D.L.R. (3d) 193 (S.C.C.).
185 *Supra*, note 178.
186 *Supra*, note 179.
187 (1982) 21 Alta. L.R. (2d) 104 (S.C.C.); on the assumption that there *is* a privative clause.
188 *Ibid.*, *i.e.*, on the assumption that there *is no* privative clause.
189 [1983] 1 W.W.R. 604 (Alta. C.A.).
190 [1983] 6 W.W.R. 1 (Alta. C.A.).
191 *Roberval Express Ltee. v. Tpt. Drivers, Warehousemen & Gen. Wkrs.*, [1982] 2 S.C.R. 888.
192 (1983) 145 D.L.R. (3d) 413 (S.C.C.).

non-statutory arbitrations, the new use of the test may well have become universal. As Kerans J.A. said in *Suncor*:[193]

> In the result, the combined effect of the decision in *N.B. Liquor Corp.* on the one hand and *Olds College* on the other is this: the position of the appellant can be no higher than that s. 129(1) *prevents* review on any standard other than "patent unreasonableness" and that of the respondent no higher than that s. 129(2) (combined with art. 13.09) *permits* review only by the same standard.

The effect of this new use of the "patently unreasonable" test may well be to obliterate the notion of an error of law on the face of the record within jurisdiction. On the one hand, if the error is patently unreasonable, it clearly constitutes a jurisdictional matter. On the other hand, if the courts will not review an intra-jurisdictional error which is not patently unreasonable, *certiorari* will never issue for an error *within* jurisdiction. In short, if the only errors which can be reviewed are those which are patently unreasonable, they must be jurisdictional in nature. What a strange comparison to the statement of the law in the *Shaw* case!

The only possible way to reconcile the new use of the "patently unreasonable" test as a shield with Lord Denning's statement of the law in *Shaw* is to recognize that the courts are using the test as a guideline to determine when to exercise their discretion to refuse a prerogative remedy when a case for judicial review has otherwise been established. As Moir J.A. implies in *U.N.A.*[194] such curial deference should not be absolute, but should yield in the face of more compelling reasons for judicial review to correct an intra-jurisdictional error of law.

In principle, the new use of the "patently unreasonable" test should apply as a shield for all statutory delegates, and not just in the labour context. Certainly, the rationales for curial deference in the recent cases apply throughout Administrative Law.

Finally, it is important to remember that the "patently unreasonable" test should have no application to questions of jurisdiction in the narrow sense of the word. No statutory delegate should be allowed to expand his jurisdiction beyond that granted by legislation. In theory, curial deference has no place in this context.

---

193 *Supra*, note 189 at p. 610.
194 *Supra*, note 190.

13. Selected Bibliography

Abel, A., "Materials for Consideration in Certiorari: 1", (1963-64) 15 U. of T. L.J. 102.

Beatson, J., "The Scope of Judicial Review for Error of Law", 4 Oxford J. of Legal Studies 22.

de Smith, S.A., "Certiorari and Speaking Orders", (1951) 14 Mod. L. Rev. 207.

Lord Diplock, "Administrative Law: Judicial Review Reviewed", [1974] Camb. L.J. 233.

Emery, C.T., and B. Smythe, "Error of Law in Administrative Law", (1984) 100 L.Q. Rev. 612.

Gordon, D.M. "Quashing on Certiorari for Error of Law", (1951) 67 L.Q. Rev. 452.

Gould, B., "Anisminic and Judicial Review", [1970] P.L. 358.

Law Reform Commission of British Columbia, *Report on Arbitration*, May 1982, especially Chapter IX, "Judicial Supervision of Awards", and Chapter X, "Judicial Supervision of Awards: Reform".

McRuer Report, Vol. 1, pp. 302-15.

Morden, D., "Recent Developments in Administrative Law", [1967] Law Soc. of Upper Can. Special Lectures 275 at 295-98.

Mullan, D.J., "Developments in Administrative Law: The 1981-82 Term", (1983) 5 Supreme Court Rev. 1.

Sawer, G., "Error of Law on the Face of the Administrative Record", (1954) 3 U.W. Aust. Ann. L. Rev. 24.

Yardley, D.C.M., "The Grounds for Certiorari and Prohibition", (1959) 37 Can. Bar Rev. 294 at 323-37.

III

REMEDIES

11

Introduction
To Remedies

Because of the common law view that there is generally "no right without a remedy", it is not sufficient to be familiar just with the grounds for seeking judicial review of administrative action: a determination must be made as to whether there is a remedy available to correct the illegal administrative action in question.

There are three broad classes of remedies which might be available in a particular circumstance.

First, the legislature may have provided a specific method of appealing the action or decision taken by its delegate in first instance. In general, the right of appeal does not derive from the common law, but must be expressly provided for by statute. As a result, the legislation in question will determine to whom the appeal lies, the procedure that must be followed, and the scope of the appeal. The existence of an appeal — to whatever body — frequently inclines the superior courts to exercise their discretion to refuse one of the other possible remedies for illegal administrative action. Chapter 12 discusses appeals.

Secondly, one of the "prerogative" remedies may be available from one of the superior courts to correct an administrative illegality. This family of remedies includes *certiorari* (which permits the court to determine whether a statutory delegate's decision has been made within his jurisdiction), prohibition (which prevents the delegate from making a decision which will take him outside his jurisdiction), *mandamus* (which compels a delegate to fulfill his statutory duties), *quo warranto* (which requires a delegate to justify the authority by which he occupies an office), and — probably most famous of them all — *habeas corpus* (which requires the production of a person into the face of the court to explain why he is being detained). These remedies are called "prerogative" because the Crown is nominally the applicant. This is indicated by the style of the cause of action as follows: "*R. v. Delegate; Ex parte Affected Person*". The prerogative remedies are discretionary in nature, and can be refused by the courts in certain circumstances. These circumstances include cases where the applicant has slept on his rights or does not come to court with clean hands, where there is an equally effective appeal provided by statute, where the applicant does not have a sufficient interest or standing to challenge the administrative act in question, and perhaps where the delegate's interpretation of the law is not "patently unreasonable". The prerogative remedies are discussed in chapter 13.

Thirdly, some remedies from private law may be available in the public law context. Thus, certain illegal administrative actions may give rise to an actionable wrong for which the ordinary private law provides an adequate remedy. For example, a delegate acting outside his jurisdiction may well commit a tort — as occurred in *Cooper v. Wandsworth Board of Works*[1] when a partially built house was torn down pursuant to statutory authority without complying with the principles of natural justice. In principle, administrators may be liable for any form of tort or breach of contract unless their actions are justified by specific statutory authority. Similarly, an injunction may be available in certain circumstances to prevent some types of anticipated illegal administrative actions. Further, a declaration or a declaratory order may be available to proclaim the illegality of certain forms of administrative action. Nevertheless, not all illegal administrative actions necessarily give rise to an actionable wrong known to the common law; and illegal administrative action does not *per se* constitute a tort. Therefore, the common law maxim that there is "no right without a remedy" is still very important in attempting to apply the ordinary civil law to some forms of illegal administrative action. On the other hand, some private law remedies, such as a damage action, are not discretionary in nature, and therefore may be available to obtain a remedy in circumstances when the courts would otherwise be inclined to exercise their discretion to refuse a prerogative remedy. Some of the applications of private law remedies to the public law context are discussed in chapter 14.

There have been a number of recent reforms to the procedure for obtaining judicial review of illegal administrative actions. In particular, the 1971 Ontario Judicial Review Procedure Act[2] merged most of the prerogative and private law remedies into one "application for judicial review" — reminiscent of the abolition in the late 1800's of the forms of action in tort. Such a reform minimizes the importance of choosing the correct remedy to rectify a particular type of administrative wrong, and permits the court to determine whether there are *any* grounds for judicial review without regard to the confines of one of the nominate remedies. This type of procedural reform has been widely copied in varying forms throughout much of the English common law world. Indeed, the Institute of Law Research and Reform in Alberta has issued a report recommending amendments to the Rules of Court which would accomplish the same goal, although nothing has yet been implemented.

---

1 (1863) 14 C.B. (N.S.) 180.
2 S.O. 1971, c. 48. [now R.S.O. 1980, c. 224].

In the early 1970's the Federal Parliament took a different approach to reforming judicial review of federal administrative action. The Federal Court Act[3] transferred review of the legality of federal administrative acts from the provincial superior courts to the Trial Division of the Federal Court (with the exception of *habeas corpus*, which remained with the provincial superior courts). The legislation then created an "application for judicial review" which is available from the Federal Court of Appeal — unfortunately, only with respect to activities which are judicial or quasi-judicial in nature, thereby perpetuating an untenable characterization of delegated functions and also creating an important procedural dilemma about which division of the Federal Court has jurisdiction to hear a particular case alleging illegality by a federal administrator.

Other reforms have included legislative expansions of the grounds for judicial review (see, for example, section 28 of the Federal Court Act), the creation of ombudsmen to deal with complaints about maladministration even where there is no illegality involved, the creation in some jurisdictions of a council on tribunals to comment upon the types of powers which should be delegated to administrators and to supervise the rules and procedures which they adopt for exercising those delegated powers.

These recent reforms are referred to in chapter 15.

Sometimes legislation contains a "privative clause" which purports to prevent judicial review of administrative action. Various forms of privative clauses exist, ranging from simple time limits within which applications for judicial review must be brought to more comprehensive attempts to prevent any direct or collateral attempt to challenge the legality or the merits of a delegate's action in any court proceeding whatever. For many years, the courts have resisted giving literal effect to most of these clauses by asserting that an *ultra vires* administrative action is a nullity which does not exist in the eyes of the law, and which therefore cannot attract the protection of a privative clause. To a certain extent, this approach flies in the face of clear parliamentary intent to prevent judicial review of a particular administrator's actions, but the courts' persistence in asserting the principle of legality is now so engrained (and probably so desirable) that the only real questions today revolve around the types of errors that prevent a delegate from acquiring jurisdiction or that subsequently cause him to lose it. Thus, the concept of "jurisdiction" is central to any discussion of the effectiveness of privative clauses. Chapter 16 examines different types of privative clauses, and how the courts have dealt with them.

In chapter 17, we try to identify those areas where we think there may be considerable change and growth in the next few years.

---

3 R.S.C. 1970, c. 10 (2nd Supp.).

12

Appeals from Administrative Decisions

1. Introduction

Unlike judicial review of administrative action, the general rule is that no appeal exists unless specifically provided for by statute. Particular legislation does, of course, very frequently provide for appeals, either within the administrative hierarchy, to the courts, or both. The range of these appeals is very broad, going from a complete new hearing on the one hand to a mere review of the original delegate's jurisdiction and correctness in law on the other hand. In general, judicial review of administrative action is not available where an equally effective appeal exists. It is useful, therefore, to consider some examples of statutory appeals from administrative decisions. It is also useful to consider other possible routes for redress, such as the Ombudsman and direct political intervention in the administrative process. All of these remedies are to be distinguished from those more familiar to Administrative Law: the prerogative remedies (discussed in chapter 13) and private law remedies applied to administrative action (discussed in chapter 14).

2. Examples of Circumstances Where There is No Appeal

There is no legal or constitutional requirement that an appeal should exist from any decision made by a statutory delegate. It is possible, therefore, to find numerous examples where legislation has made no provision for an appeal, whether to the courts or to another step in the administrative hierarchy. In such a circumstance, it may still be possible for the courts to review the jurisdiction and legality of the delegate's decision, but such judicial review is much more limited than an appeal on the merits.

For example, under the Municipal Taxation Act,[1] the Alberta Assessment Appeal Board has the final power to determine the amount of municipal taxes, and no appeal lies from its decision. Accordingly, there is no other person, court or body which has jurisdiction to consider the merits of a particular tax assessment on property, except, in theory, the legislature itself, which could enact legislation altering a particular assessment, even retroactively.[2] By contrast, an application can be made to the courts to review the jurisdiction of the Board in any matter before it, although such judicial review would probably not deal directly with the merits of the case.

The principles of good public administration usually require that at least one level of appeal exist with respect to any delegate's decision. It may happen, therefore, that the administrators will themselves try to fashion an appeal mechanism even where none exists under the legislation. Two such examples can be found in the procedures adopted by the Universities Co-ordinating Council in exercising its powers under the Universities Act[3] to determine what must be done by a non-Alberta trained person in order to enter one of a number of professions. Under the legislation, the Professional Examination Board in Law,[4] for example, is the delegate of the Council for the purpose of determining (a) whether an applicant's law degree is equivalent to those granted by one of the Alberta universities, and (b) which special examinations

---

1 R.S.A. 1980, c. M-31, ss. 56-61. See also the Assessment Appeal Board Act, R.S.A. 1980, c. A-46; and note also s. 8 dealing with the Board's power to act even in the temporary absence of some of its members.

2 See, e.g., the Municipal Taxation Amendment Act, S.A. 1981, c. 26, s. 2, which amends the definition of "improvement" in the parent Act to include huge mobile diggers which the Board had held not to come within the definition and therefore not to be taxable.

3 R.S.A. 1980, c. U-5.

4 Section 64(e) [re-en. 1984, c. 41, s. 2] allows the Universities Co-ordinating Council to establish a board of examiners in a particular profession, which it has done in Law, and to delegate to the board some or all of its powers under ss. 35-45 of the Legal Profession Act, R.S.A. 1980, c. L-9, for determining equivalence of degrees and assessing special examinations.

the applicant will be required to pass in order to demonstrate his competence in particular areas of the law. The legislation provides for no appeal from a decision of the Professional Examination Board, whose decision in law is final.[5] Many years ago, the Council decided that it was desirable to establish a method of appealing determinations by all of the various professional examination boards, and it created the Professional Examination Review Committee. Unfortunately, there is no statutory authority to create this unspecialized appellate body, and several of the professional examination boards complained about its decisions.[6] As a result, the Review Committee was disbanded, but the Council devised another administrative method for effectively creating an appeal. The professional examination boards in fact do most of their work by using their statutory power to sub-delegate to their respective executive committees (who often have a quorum of one person).[7] The executive committees, therefore, have adopted the practice of making provisional determinations, which a dissatisfied applicant can take to the full professional examination board — in effect an appeal, although in strict legal theory the first and only determination of the matter. This two-step process achieves the policy goal of providing for an appeal even in the absence of a legislative provision requiring one.

The creation of an appellate mechanism lies in the gift of the legislature, and considerably more attention ought to be devoted by the legislature to the desirability and format of an appeal in all cases delegating statutory powers.

3. Appeals to Other Administrators

Of course, legislation very frequently does provide a right of appeal from one delegate to another. Thus, section 2 of the Child Welfare Act[8] provides two levels of administrative appeals:

> 2(1) A person affected by a decision of the Director, a child welfare worker or an employee in the Department on any matter under this Act may appeal to the Commission for a review of the decision and the Commission may confirm, reverse or vary the

---

5 No appeal lies to the Council because it has delegated its power to the Board, as it is permitted to do by the statute, and it retains no residual power to hear an appeal. The same situation would arise if the Council had not delegated its powers to the Board, but had made the determinations itself: no appeal would lie therefrom.

6 What would have happened if one of the professional examination boards had refused to implement a decision of the Professional Examination Review Committee allowing an applicant's appeal over the decision and objections of the professional examination board? A *mandamus* against the professional examination board would not have succeeded because of the illegality of the existence of the Professional Examination Review Committee, whose decision would therefore have had no legal effect.

7 *Supra*, note 3, s. 64(*f*) [re-en. 1984, c. 41, s. 2].

8 R.S.A. 1980, c. C-8.

decision as, in its discretion, it considers proper in the circumstances.

(2) Any person affected by a decision of the Commission under
subsection (1) may appeal to the Minister for a review of the
decision and the Minister may confirm, vary or reverse the
decision as, in his discretion, he considers proper in the circumstances.

Similarly, the Planning Act provides for an appeal to the Development
Appeal Board from a decision made by a planning officer with respect to the
proposed development of land,[9] and the Legal Profession Act permits an
appeal to the Benchers from a disposition by the Investigating Committee of a
charge of misconduct against a member,[10] and the Hospitals Act permits an
appeal to the Hospital Privileges Appeal Board by a doctor whose medical
privileges have been cancelled or not renewed by the governing body of a
hospital.[11] The statute books are replete with other examples of administrative
appeals. There does not appear to be any particular logic in whether the
appeal lies from one public servant to another, to a standing board or tribunal,
or to a minister; or from a minister to cabinet, or to a standing board or
tribunal.

Finally, one must remember that more than one level of appeal may be
provided,[12] and that the existence of any right of appeal may affect the availability of the forms of judicial review discussed in this book.[13]

4. Specific Statutory Appeals to the Courts

The general rule that appeals must be specifically created by legislation
also applies with respect to appeals to the courts of law. Of course, legislation
very often does provide for such appeals, although there does not appear to be
a discernible pattern about which level of court should hear such an appeal.

In some cases, an appeal is provided directly to the Court of Appeal from
the decision of a statutory delegate. For example, the Court of Appeal of
Alberta has jurisdiction to hear an appeal from a decision of the Benchers that
a member of the Law Society is guilty of conduct unbecoming.[14] Similarly,
that court is empowered to hear an appeal on any point of law or jurisdiction
arising from a decision of the Development Appeal Board,[15] the Energy
Resources Conservation Board,[16] or the Public Utilities Board[17] (generally

---

9 R.S.A. 1980, c. P-9, ss. 83 to 85.
10 R.S.A. 1980, c. L-9, s. 64(5) [re-en. 1981, c. 53, s. 33].
11 R.S.A. 1980, c. H-11, s. 36.
12 *E.g.*, to the minister under the Child Welfare Act.
13 See the discussion on this point later in this chapter.
14 R.S.A. 1980, c. L-9, s. 70(1) [am. 1981, c. 53, s. 38].
15 Planning Act, R.S.A. 1980, c. P-9, s. 152 [am. 1984, c. 33, s. 8].
16 Energy Resources Conservation Act, R.S.A. 1980, c. E-11, s. 44.
17 Public Utilities Board Act, R.S.A. 1980, c. P-37, s. 62.

with leave of the Court of Appeal). In theory, a further statutory right of appeal lies from the Court of Appeal to the Supreme Court of Canada, generally with leave of the latter court.[18]

Other times, legislation provides for an appeal to the Court of Queen's Bench. Thus, the Engineering and Related Professions Act grants a right of appeal to that superior court to a person who has been refused registration as an engineer on the grounds of bad character;[19] the Chiropractic Profession Act grants a similar right of appeal against the imposition of discipline on a member;[20] and the Surface Rights Act provides for an appeal *de novo* with respect to a compensation order made by the Board for the use of land.[21] For some reason, the legislature of Quebec has adopted the policy of providing that the corresponding rights of appeal in matters of professional discipline go to the Provincial Court, and not to the Superior Court, which may create a problem under section 96 of the Constitution Act, 1867.[22] On the federal level, Parliament has provided a right of appeal to the Trial Division of the Federal Court of Canada against a tax assessment and certain other determinations under the Income Tax Act.[23] In principle, any appellate decision rendered by one of these courts of first instance may itself be appealed further up the court hierarchy to the Court of Appeal[24] and (with leave) to the Supreme Court of Canada.[25]

Sometimes an appeal is provided to a court which has been specially created for this purpose. Thus, the Tax Court of Canada was established to discharge the functions previously performed by the Tax Review Board in hearing appeals from income tax assessments.[26] That court has also recently been given jurisdiction to hear appeals against assessments in unemployment insurance matters,[27] which were previously dealt with by umpires appointed under the Unemployment Insurance Act.[28] Other examples of special appellate courts include the Patent Appeals Tribunal[29] and the Pension

---

18 Supreme Court Act, R.S.C. 1970, c. S-19.
19 R.S.A. 1980, c. E-12, s. 20, replaced by the Engineering, Geological and Geophysical Professions Act, S.A. 1981, c. E-11.1, which removes the right of appeal to a court on this matter, and substitutes a right of appeal to the council of the professional association. In addition, the other appeals under the new Act generally go to the Court of Queen's Bench.
20 R.S.A. 1980, c. C-9, s. 8 [am. 1983, c. 37, s. 11].
21 Surface Rights Act, S.A. 1983, c. S-27.1, s. 24. Note that a further appeal lies with leave to the Court of Appeal. Query whether this appeal is also *de novo*.
22 See the discussion on this problem in chapter 2, *supra*.
23 R.S.C. 1952, c. 148, especially ss. 169 to 180, as amended by S.C. 1970-71-72, c. 63 and subsequent amendments.
24 See s. 3(*b*)(iv) of the Judicature Act, R.S.A. 1980, c. J-1 and R. 501 to 543 of the Rules of Court of Alberta.
25 *Supra*, note 18.
26 Tax Court of Canada Act, S.C. 1980-81-82-83, c. 158.
27 *Ibid.*, s. 53.
28 S.C. 1970-71-72, c. 48.
29 Patent Act, R.S.C. 1970, c. P-4.

Review Board.[30] Again, decisions of any of these specially created courts may sometimes be appealed further up the court hierarchy.[31] The question sometimes arises whether the members of these special courts must be appointed by the Governor in Council under section 96 of the Constitution Act, 1867, especially if there is any attempt to make their decisions final without recourse to further steps in the court hierarchy.[32]

It can readily be seen that no uniform pattern has developed concerning the appropriate court to hear an appeal from a decision of a statutory delegate. Similarly, no uniform procedure is prescribed for taking such an appeal. On the one hand, an appeal to the Court of Queen's Bench under the Chiropractic Profession Act[33] must be taken by an originating notice of motion, whereas no procedure was specified for an appeal to the same court under the Engineering and Related Professions Act.[34] On the other hand, an application for leave to appeal must first be granted on a point of law or jurisdiction by one of the judges of the Court of Appeal against a decision of a Development Appeal Board under the Planning Act,[35] and only thereafter can the appeal be proceeded with to the full Court of Appeal. A similar diversity exists with respect to time limits within which an appeal must be taken to the court.[36] One must, therefore, study the appropriate legislation very carefully to make certain that the proper procedure is taken within the correct time to the court designated to hear the particular appeal.

5. Nature and Scope of Appeals

The exact ambit of an administrative appeal may not be clearly stated in the legislation. On the one hand, administrative appeals are rarely restricted to determining from the record whether the first delegate erred in determining

---

30 Pension Act, R.S.C. 1970, c. P-7, ss. 75-81.1, as amended.
31 *E.g.*, the Income Tax Act permits an appeal from the Tax Court to the Trial Division of the Federal Court, and a further appeal to the Federal Court of Appeal. On the other hand, no *appeal* lies from a decision of the Patent Appeal Tribunal or the Pension Review Board, although they are both susceptible to an application for judicial review to the Federal Court of Appeal under s. 28 of the Federal Court Act, R.S.C. 1970, c. 10 (2nd Supp.), and a further right of appeal lies from that court to the Supreme Court of Canada (with leave).
32 See the discussion on this problem in chapter 2, *supra*.
33 R.S.A. 1980, c. C-9, s. 8(1), which also requires the appeal to be taken within 30 days or such further time as the court orders.
34 R.S.A. 1980, c. E-12, replaced by the Engineering, Geological and Geophysical Professions Act, S.A. 1981, c. E-11.1.
35 R.S.A. 1980, c. P-9.
36 Under s. 62 of the Public Utilities Board Act, R.S.A. 1980, c. P-37, leave to appeal "shall be *obtained* . . . within one month" or "within any further time that the judge under special circumstances allows". By contrast, s. 152 [am. 1984, c. 33, s. 8] of the Planning Act, *ibid*, only requires that the application for leave to appeal be *made* within 30 days of the decision appealed from, not necessarily disposed of within that time. Similarly, under s. 8 [am. 1983, c. 37, s. 11] of the Chiropractic Profession Act, *supra*, note 33, the appeal shall be *filed* "within 30

his jurisdiction or otherwise erred in law.[37] Thus, the scope of administrative appeals is almost always broader than judicial review because the latter generally does not consider the merits of the delegate's decision but only the legality thereof. On the other hand, an appeal on the merits may take many forms. It may involve a complete hearing *de novo*, with there being no reference to the proceedings before the first delegate in the administrative appeal.[38] Alternatively, the appellate body may well be aware of the first delegate's decision,[39] and may treat that decision deferentially, particularly if the delegate has some expertise.[40] On the other hand, the Court of Appeal has asserted its right to hear evidence and decide about the merits of an appeal from a specialized statutory body whose decision did not disclose on its face any reliance on expertise.[41] As Stevenson J.A. said:[42]

> I stress that what has been decided by the *Caswell* and *Lamb* decisions is that it is the board's expertise that is entitled to consideration. Allen J.A. [in *Caswell*] refers to "knowledge" and "experience" . . . while Martland J. in adopting *Caswell* [in his decision in *Lamb*] refers to "expertise". It is that element that is entitled to weight. Martland J. specifically notes that the court must assess the credibility of witnesses called before it on the hearing it holds. It is obvious to me that, even if the evidence before the court is given by the same witnesses that were called before the board, that evidence will invariably differ and no board engaged in a new

---

days . . . or within such further time as the Court may order". The time limit under the Engineering and Related Professions Act, *supra*, note 34, for filing an appeal was 30 days from the date the council *communicated* its refusal to register an engineer to him in writing: s. 20(5). By contrast, the time limit for an appeal by a lawyer who has been found to be guilty of conduct unbecoming is 30 days from the finding of guilt or order of punishment, apparently regardless of when it was communicated to him: s. 70(2) of the Legal Profession Act, R.S.A. 1980, c. L-9. Under s. 21 of the Insurance Act, R.S.A. 1980, c. I-5, an appeal lies "in a summary manner to the Lieutenant Governor in Council, who has power to make all necessary rules for the conduct of appeals under this section" against a ruling of the superintendent as to the admissibility of any asset or liability in calculating the financial strength of an insurance company, provided that the appellant notifies the superintendent of his appeal within 15 days of the decision, and then also notifies the Lieutenant Governor in Council within a further 15 days.

37 See s. 18 of the draft B.C. Planning Act (1983), which limits the powers of the appeal board to a number of legal questions, and s. 40, which specifically states that the appeal board shall not substitute its decision for that of the local government or officer.

38 As occurs when an appeal is taken from the Tax Court to the Trial Division of the Federal Court under ss. 175 to 179 of the Income Tax Act, as amended.

39 See *Dudley v. Alta. Chiropractic Assn.*, (1977) 2 Alta. L.R. (2d) 384 (Dist. Ct.), where there was an appeal on the merits, but the court had the previous decision before it, even though it permitted further evidence to be led on the appeal.

40 *Caswell v. Alexandra Petroleums*, [1972] 3 W.W.R. 706 (Alta. C.A.); *Lamb v. Can. Reserve Oil & Gas Ltd.*, [1977] 1 S.C.R. 517; *Chieftain Dev. Co. v. Lachowich*, [1982] 1 W.W.R. 37 (Alta. Q.B.); *Livingston v. Siebens Oil & Gas Ltd.*, [1978] 3 W.W.R. 484 (Alta. C.A.).

41 *Whitehouse v. Sun Oil Co.*, [1982] 6 W.W.R. 289 (Alta. C.A.).

42 *Ibid.*, p. 295.

hearing can be bound to come to the same conclusion on such matters as credibility and weight. A judge on appeal can only accord the board's expertise weight when he can identify it. The board's scant reasons here do not reveal to what extent, if any, that expertise was called upon. Experts' conclusions are given weight in accordance with their demonstrated reliability and a mere assertion that expertise was employed cannot be given the weight that the carefully considered judgments under scrutiny in *Lamb* and *Caswell* were given. Where little, if any, weight can be given to the board's expertise, the court sitting on appeal will necessarily have to rely upon the evidence before it.

The appellate body may sometimes even permit the delegate to participate in the appellate proceedings. Indeed, legislation sometimes specifically permits such adversarial participation.[43] In the absence of a specific statutory statement as to the form of the appellate hearing, there would appear to be no requirement on the appellate body to hear the appellant in person or through counsel, and it may be difficult to lead further evidence[44] or make additional submissions which were not before the original decision-maker from whom the administrative appeal has been taken. Of course, the rules of natural justice require the appeal to be "fair" in all of the circumstances, but it is impossible to lay down a code of what fairness requires in the absence of a specific statutory provision as to the procedure to be adopted on appeal.

The problem referred to in the previous paragraph is particularly important where legislation creates a board or tribunal to hear an appeal, and one or more members of that body is a judge.[45] The mere presence of a judge on the appellate body does not make it a court, nor should one infer any

---

43 *E.g.*, s. 65 of the Public Utilities Board Act, R.S.A. 1980, c. P-37, entitles the Board "to be heard . . . on the argument of an appeal", although the Supreme Court of Canada construed this provision extremely narrowly in *Re Northwestern Utilities Ltd.; Edmonton v. Pub. Utilities Bd.*, [1979] 1 S.C.R. 684; *Can. L.R.B. v. Transair Ltd.*, [1977] 1 S.C.R. 722; *Central Broadcasting Co. v. L.R.B. (Can.)*, [1977] S.C.R. 112. Compare the subsequent more generous role granted to administrative bodies defending their actions in an appeal enunciated in *Re Sheckter*, (1979) 9 Alta. L.R. (2d) 45 (C.A.) and in *Calgary Reg. Planning Comm. v. Mun. Dist. of Foothills No. 31*, 1979 (unreported) and in *Mun. Dist. of Rockyview No. 44 v. Alta. Planning Bd.*, 1982 (unreported). Curiously, the Supreme Court of Canada permitted the statutory delegate to participate fully in the judicial review proceedings in *L.S.U.C. v. French*, [1975] 2 S.C.R. 767, but a similar adversarial role is specifically prohibited under s. 67 [re-en. 1981, c. 53, s. 33] of the Alberta Legal Profession Act, R.S.A. 1980, c. L-9. This type of overlap could, however, arise under the Alberta Child Welfare Act, R.S.A. 1980, c. C-8, because the Director of Child Welfare is a member of the Commission which hears appeals from his decisions.

44 *E.g.*, the legislation in the *Dudley* case, *supra*, note 39, specifically stated that the appeal was to be "on the merits".

45 See, *e.g.*, s. 20(2) of the Teaching Profession Act, R.S.A. 1980, c. T-3, which makes a judge of the Court of Queen's Bench chairman of the three-member Teaching Profession Appeal Board to hear appeals from teachers found to be guilty of unprofessional or unethical conduct.

restrictions on the ambit of the appeal merely because a judge is involved as a *persona designata.*

Other types of difficulties arise in determining the scope of an appeal to a court. Because the right of appeal must be specifically provided for by statute, it is clearly possible for legislation to prescribe what issues can be appealed, on whom lies the burden of proof, whether new evidence can be led, what procedure is to be adopted by the court in hearing the appeal, what remedies the court can order, whether costs can be awarded, and similar problems. Sometimes legislation does deal with these matters specifically. Thus, the Income Tax Act provides that the Tax Court or the Trial Division of the Federal Court (as the case may be) may "confirm, vary or vacate" any assessment at issue before it.[46]

The Securities Act of British Columbia is even more specific:[47]

> Where an appeal is taken under this section, the Court of Appeal may by its order direct the commission or superindent to make such direction, decision, order, or ruling or to do the other act as the commission or superintendent is authorized and empowered to do under this Act or the regulations and that the Court thinks proper, having regard to the material and submissions before it and to this Act and the regulations, and the commission or superintendent shall make the direction, decision, order or ruling or do the act accordingly.

and the Health Disciplines Act of Ontario provides that:[48]

> Any party to proceedings before a discipline committee may appeal from its decision or order to the Divisional Court . . . and the court may affirm or may rescind the decision of the committee appealed from and may exercise all powers of the committee and may direct the committee or the College to take any action which the committee or the College may take and as the court considers proper, and for such purposes the court may substitute its opinion for that of the committee, or the court may refer the matter back to the committee for rehearing, in whole or in part, in accordance with such directions as the court considers proper.

By contrast, section 153 of the Planning Act limits the powers of the Court of Appeal by providing that:[49]

153(1) On the hearing of the appeal

---

46 R.S.C. 1952, c. 148, as amended by S.C. 1970-71-72, c. 63 and subsequent amendments.
47 R.S.B.C. 1979, c. 380, s. 30(6).
48 R.S.O. 1980, c. 196, s. 13.
49 R.S.A. 1980, c. P-9.

> (*a*) no evidence other than the evidence that was submitted to the . . . development appeal board . . . shall be admitted, but the Court may draw any inferences
>
> > (i) that are not inconsistent with the facts expressly found by the . . . development appeal board . . . and
> >
> > (ii) that are necessary for determining the question of law or the question of jurisdiction,
>
> and
>
> (*b*) the Court shall either confirm, vary, reverse or vacate the order, decision, permit or approval.

Under some legislation (such as the Planning Act[50]), therefore, the court is bound by the findings of fact made by the administrative tribunal from whom the appeal lies, but other legislative provisions (such as the power of either the Tax Court or the Federal Court under the Income Tax Act[51]) impose no such limitations. In many cases, however, the legislative provision granting the appeal is sufficiently vague that litigation is required to determine its precise nature and form in the circumstances: see *Dudley v. Alberta Chiropractic Association*[52] where Stevenson D.C.J. said that "[i]n principle an appeal 'on the merits' authorizes a retrial of the facts" so that "this court is not bound by the fact findings [of the statutory delegate] and is not precluded from hearing evidence to the extent that there are fact issues".

A number of statutes[53] provide for an appeal from the decision of a statutory tribunal to the courts restricted to questions of law or jurisdiction. This effectively means that the courts are unable to inquire into the merits of any decision and therefore constitutes a restriction on the width of the appeal. On the other hand, a "law and jurisdiction" appeal will allow the courts to correct an error of law which might otherwise not be reviewable by judicial review.

As discussed in chapter 10, the Canadian courts have recently restricted the availability of judicial review to correct intra-jurisdictional errors of law. In particular, where legislation contains a privative clause precluding judicial review, intra-jurisdictional errors of law are only reviewable if they can be shown to be "patently unreasonable". Indeed, the courts have indicated that they may be prepared to adopt this restriction even where the legislation contains no privative clause. The result is that totally contradictory decisions — none of which is patently unreasonable — may be allowed to stand side by

---

50 *Ibid.*
51 *Supra*, note 46.
52 (1977) 2 Alta. L.R. (2d) 384 at 386, 388 (Dist. Ct.).
53 *E.g.*, s. 152 [am. 1984, c. 33, s. 8] of the Planning Act, R.S.A. 1980, c. P-9; s. 62 of the Public Utilities Board Act, R.S.A. 1980, c. P-37; and s. 44 of the Energy Resources Conservation Act, R.S.A. 1980, c. E-11.

side. The consequences of such a lack of uniformity have been pointed out forcefully by Moir J.A. in the *U.N.A.* case.[54]

The "patently unreasonable" test has no application in the context of statutory appeals on "law or jurisdiction". In the first place, the legislature has granted an appeal on *all* errors of law, not just those which are patently unreasonable. Accordingly, it is the court's duty to determine the law in every case. Secondly, the very existence of such an appeal provision negates any concept of curial deference to the delegate's expertise, specialization or specific right to determine the matter finally, simply because the courts have been given such an explicit appellate power. Accordingly, there can be no argument that the statutory delegate has any right to make an error of law, however reasonable it might seem. As Beetz J. said in *Le Syndicat des Employés de Production du Québec et de l'Acadie v. Can. L.R.B.*:[55]

> Unquestionably, . . . it is often difficult to determine what constitutes a question of jurisdiction, and administrative tribunals like the Board must generally be given the benefit of any doubt. Once the classification has been established, however, it does not matter whether an error as to such a question is doubtful, excusable or not unreasonable, or on the contrary is excessive, blatant or patently unreasonable. What makes this kind of error fatal, whether serious or slight, is its jurisdictional nature; and what leads to excluding the . . . ["patently unreasonable"] rule . . . is the duty imposed on the Federal Court of Appeal to exercise the jurisdiction conferred on it by s. 28(1)(*a*) of the *Federal Court Act* [to correct jurisdictional errors made by federal tribunals].

This same reasoning applies where the legislature has specifically imposed the duty on the court to correct errors of law. Accordingly, it does not matter whether an error is "doubtful, excusable or not unreasonable", the court has no authority not to correct such errors. This result must arise whether the alleged error is one of law or is jurisdictional in nature, because the legislation in question imposes the duty on the courts to correct all errors of both types. Accordingly, the only type of error which the court cannot correct is one relating solely to the merits of the delegate's decision, involving no question of law or of jurisdiction.

6. Appellate Exercise of Discretion

Finally, one must consider whether the appellate body has the right to exercise a statutory discretion differently from the way chosen by the original statutory delegate. Occasionally, the legislation in question may specifically

54 *United Nurses of Alta., Loc. 11 v. Misericordia Hosp.*, [1983] 6 W.W.R. 1 (Alta. C.A.).
55 [1984] 2 S.C.R. 412 at 441.

prevent the appellate body from doing so, but this would appear to be rare.[56] In principle, the general rule should be the reverse: where an appeal is provided from the exercise of a statutory power which is discretionary in nature, the appellate body itself should be able to exercise the discretion granted by statute on the delegate from whom the appeal lies. This is particularly clear where the only matter capable of being appealed is discretionary in nature, and the appeal is said to be "on the merits". Obviously the legislature intended the appellate body to exercise its own plenipotentiary discretion in a second hearing of the matter. As discussed below, the courts have sometimes taken the view that they themselves should show curial restraint in exercising any appellate powers which they may have from the exercise of a discretionary power. This concept of curial restraint can be criticized if the very matter with respect to which the appeal is provided is a discretionary power; and the doctrine of curial restraint would appear to have no applicability to the situation where the appeal lies to another administrator, board, tribunal, minister, or anyone else who is not a court used to the limitations of judicial review.

The courts have often been very reluctant to substitute their own discretion for that of a statutory delegate, even where that very discretion is capable of being appealed to the court. As Lord Greene said in *Wrights' Canadian Ropes Ltd. v. Minister of National Revenue*,[57] which dealt with an appeal from the minister's discretionary decision to disallow a claim for expenses:

> [U]nless it be shown that the Minister has acted in contravention of some principle of law the Court, in their Lordships' opinion, cannot interfere: the section makes the Minister the sole judge of the fact of reasonableness or normalcy and the Court is not at liberty to substitute its own opinion for his. . . .
>
> The Court is, in their Lordships' opinion, always entitled to examine the facts which are shown by evidence to have been before the Minister when he made his determination. If those facts are in the opinion of the Court insufficient in law to support it the determination cannot stand. In such a case the determination can only have been an arbitrary one. If, on the other hand, there is in the facts shown to have been before the Minister sufficient material to support his determination the *Court is not at liberty to overrule it merely because it would itself on those facts have come to a different conclusion. As has already been said, the Minister is by the subsection made the sole judge of the fact of reasonableness and normalcy* but as in the case of any other judge of fact there must be material sufficient in law to support his decision.

---

56 See the example referred to in note 37, *supra*.
57 [1947] 1 D.L.R. 721 at 730-31 (P.C.), emphasis added.

This reluctance by the courts to substitute their view of how a statutory delegate should exercise his discretion is particularly marked in the case of appeals from the imposition of discipline by governing bodies of a profession.[58]

7. Isolated Reforms to Permit Appeals to the Courts

Although the common law provides no automatic right of appeal to the courts from an administrative decision (so that such a right must be specifically provided for by statute), there have been a number of recommendations and attempts to reverse this rule so as to provide a generalized right of appeal to the courts on various legal matters involved in the exercise of statutory powers. For example, the Franks Committee in England recommended that there should be a general right of appeal on "fact, law and merits". This recommendation was implemented in a more restricted form by the Tribunals and Inquiries Act 1958[59] (replaced without substantial variation by the Tribunals and Inquiries Act 1971[60]), which provides for a right of appeal to the High Court on a point of law only from those specific tribunals enumerated in the schedule to the Act.

In 1965, the Special Committee on Boards and Tribunals appointed by the Legislative Assembly of Alberta was asked to consider whether there should be a greater provision for appeals to the courts from the decisions of such boards and tribunals. The committee made the following observations:

> It has already been noted in this report that a widespread and nearly unanimous desire for a right of appeal to the Courts was expressed to the Committee in submissions which dealt with particular tribunals. . . . It is said that if the recommendations of the Committee respecting minimum uniform standards of procedures are implemented, the occasions would be diminished on which an appeal would be required to obtain justice: this may be so. Nevertheless, there is embedded in the democratic principles of the administration of justice a right to appeal by a person who considers himself aggrieved, and the Committee is of the view that this principle should be more fully recognized in administrative law than it is at present. It would give citizens who are affected by the decisions of

---

58 See *Lazar v. Assn. of Pro. Engineers of Man.*, [1971] 5 W.W.R. 614 (Man. Q.B.); *Marten v. Disciplinary Ctee. of the Royal College of Veterinary Surgeons*, [1965] 1 All E.R. 949 (Q.B.); *Kerster v. College of Physicians and Surgeons of Sask.*, (1970) 72 W.W.R. 321; *Rajasooria v. Disciplinary Ctee.*, [1955] 1 W.L.R. 405; *Re Solicitor; Ex parte Law Soc.*, [1912] 1 K.B. 302 at 312; *Re Weber and Metro. Licencing Comm.*, [1963] 2 O.R. 286, reversed [1964] 1 O.R. 621 (C.A.). See also *Can. Western Natural Gas Co. v. Pub. Utilities Bd.*, (1984) 33 Alta. L.R. (2d) 185, where the Court of Appeal refused to second-guess the discretion exercised by the board not to re-hear a matter.

59 6 & 7 Eliz. 2, c. 66.

60 1971 (Eng.), c. 62.

a tribunal a right comparable to the one they have traditionally had in respect of judgments of the Courts. And, as with the Courts, a right of appeal would impose a measure of discipline on the tribunal and a sense of responsibility in maintaining proper standards in its procedures. The growth and extent of a new system of administration of justice created by Legislatures in administrative law requires that all reasonable steps be taken to assure the society in which it operates that it is indeed doing justice. This is not to say that at the present stage of the development of administrative law in Alberta the Committee as a whole is prepared to recommend a full right of appeal to the Courts in all cases, or to recommend the establishment of an over-all appeal tribunal even if it were constitutionally possible to do so.

The Committee is unanimously and firmly of the view that in every case there should be a right of appeal to the Supreme Court of Alberta on a question of jurisdiction and a question of law. No legitimate reason can be put forward why a tribunal to whom the legislature has delegated certain defined authority should be permitted with impunity to transgress the bounds of the jurisdiction that it was intended it should exercise. Similarly, there should be no excuse for a tribunal misapplying law, or ignoring law, to which all citizens of the Province are subject, in favour of its own views as to what should be applicable to the persons that are affected by its decisions. No leave should be required for such an appeal, and simple and expeditious procedures should be provided. By this stroke there would be cut away the privative clauses still remaining in some statutes whereby the Legislature seeks to protect its tribunals from the disciplines of the Rule of Law; and in place of the old and difficult prerogative writs persons who felt themselves aggrieved by excesses of jurisdiction or misapplication of law would have a simple and easy access to the Courts to determine the point.

Appeals on facts, which might be described as appeals from the quality of decisions, are subject to several considerations. . . .

By statute tribunals are not required to judge the acceptability of evidence by any established standards. If there are no accepted standards for determining facts, then an appeal on facts could be taken, not because a standard has been departed from in the exercise of the judicial function, but in the hope that the appeal tribunal of itself might come to a different result by applying different standards or taking a different approach. It is difficult to see how the ends of justice would be advanced by a contest to have the facts determined on some amorphous basis other than that adopted in the particular case by the tribunal of first instance. This would be so even if, as in Court procedures, the appeal is based on the trial proceedings: that is to say, the oral evidence is transcribed and it, together with whatever documentary evidence is involved, is put before the appeal tribunal. Further than that, if the members of the tribunal of first instance have been appointed because they possess expert knowledge which would promote administrative efficiency in attaining the objective of the legislature, then the appeal tribunal would require to be constituted with members having at least comparable expert knowledge, otherwise this purpose would be stultified. The alternative would be a re-hearing before the appeal tribunal so that expert evidence could be called to inform it on matters for which the tribunal of first instance itself provided the expert knowledge. Thus, considerations of expediency and efficiency that the Legislature had thought desirable in the general interests in establishing such a tribunal would be lost. In the area of administrative law the claims of the public are in reality foremost in the statutory enactments, and the degree to which individual interests must be sacrificed for the general good must be a matter of balance for the legislature to determine. . . .

In the result, the Committee as a whole is of the view that at the present time there cannot be generalizations on the question of appeals on facts. A specific solution should be sought for each specific problem: the nature of the jurisdiction exercised by each tribunal requires examination, a balance must be struck between efficiency of administration and the interests of the individuals having regard to the purpose of the statute, and a conclusion then reached as to whether an appeal to the Courts is on balance warranted, or whether an effective appeal tribunal can be provided. In The Securities Act the Legislature determined that a full appeal is appropriate, and it may be that on close consideration the Legislature might find others in which it would be appropriate also. . . .

Unfortunately, these recommendations have never been implemented in Alberta, even though the subsequent adoption of the Administrative Procedures Act[61] would have provided an appropriate vehicle for a generalized right of appeal (whether restricted to law and jurisdiction, or extending to merits as well), at least with respect to the nine tribunals which have been made subject to it. Frankly, it is unrealistic to expect that the members of the legislature will be able to give reasoned, detailed consideration to the need for an appeal — or its nature and extent — from each statutory power contained in each piece of legislation which they enact. To some extent, the Sovereignty of Parliament could be used to solve this problem if the provincial legislature were to create a Scrutiny Committee on Regulations, such as exists federally and in England.

---

61 R.S.A. 1980, c. A-2.

Such a committee could use its power to review systematically how administrators exercise their statutory powers to insist that rights of appeal be implemented whenever possible in administrative schemes created by delegated legislation. But this goal would be achieved even more effectively if the Scrutiny Committee were given the power, sought by the federal committee, to review the enabling legislation itself to make sure that the question of appeals has been carefully dealt with. Similarly, a Council on Tribunals (such as exists in England) might help concentrate proper attention on the existence and scope of appeals, in at least some contexts. In short, what is required is a commitment, a statement of policy, that Canadian society requires and values the right of appeal, so that the onus should be on our governments to justify why no appeal exists in particular circumstances.

8. The Australian Administrative Appeals Tribunal

This type of reform has been implemented at the federal level in Australia by the creation of the Administrative Appeals Tribunal,[62] which hears appeals from the merits of decisions made from a large number of designated statutory delegates.[63] Professor Mullan has described and criticized the idea and operation of this general administrative appeals tribunal.[64] In particular, some difficulties appear to arise from the wide variety of matters which can be appealed, so that the Appeals Tribunal is not guaranteed to have any particular expertise in the subject matter of each appeal. Similarly, the Australian model appears to have succumbed to an overly judicial procedure which may just encumber the whole administrative process and compete unnecessarily with more conventional routes for judicial review and with the broader powers of the Ombudsman to correct maladministration. It may be, therefore, that considerable care should be given to the format and vehicle for implementing the desirable policy of full right of appeal from every administrative decision,[65] whether that appeal lies to the ordinary courts, to a specially created administrative court, or to an *ad hoc* administrative body.

---

62 Administrative Appeals Tribunal Act, 1975.

63 *Ibid.*, ss. 25 (permitting other statutes to confer appellate jurisdiction on the A.A.T.) and 26 (giving the A.A.T. appellate jurisdiction over the bodies listed in Sched. 1 to the Act).

64 See David J. Mullan, "Alternatives to Judicial Review of Administrative Action — The Commonwealth of Australia's Administrative Appeals Tribunal" in *Judicial Review of Administrative Rulings* (Montreal: Les Editions Yvon Blais, Inc., 1983), pp. 441-66, for The Canadian Institute for the Administration of Justice; also found at (1983) 43 Revue du Barreau 569. This article contains a large number of references to extremely good articles on the whole gamut of recent reforms to Australian Administrative Law.

65 Thus, Mullan suggests not only the creation of a federal Ombudsman, but also the need to rationalize existing statutory appeal procedures, making them as uniform as possible, and grouping them under a single umbrella whenever common issues are involved (such as Quebec tried in its Tribunal on the Professions): *ibid.*, p. 465.

9. The Ombudsman

Another possible route for preventing abuse of delegated powers is to invoke the help of the Ombudsman. Borrowed in 1962 by New Zealand[66] from the Scandinavian countries, the idea of the Ombudsman has spread throughout the British Commonwealth[67] and beyond. Alberta[68] was the first province in Canada to create an Ombudsman, and now they exist everywhere[69] except in Prince Edward Island, the Territories, and federally.

Section 11 of the Alberta Act sets out the functions of the Ombudsman, which are almost the same in all jurisdictions:

11(1) It is the function and duty of the Ombudsman to investigate any decision or recommendation made, including any recommendation made to a Minister, or any act done or omitted, relating to a matter of administration and affecting any person or body of persons in his or its personal capacity, in or by any department or agency, or by any officer, employee or member thereof in the exercise of any power or function conferred on him by any enactment.

(2) The Ombudsman may make an investigation either on a complaint made to him by any person or of his own motion, and he may commence an investigation notwithstanding that the complaint may not on its face be against a decision, recommendation, act or omission as mentioned in subsection (1).

(3) The powers and duties conferred on the Ombudsman by this Act may be exercised and performed notwithstanding any provision in any Act to the effect

(a) that any decision, recommendation, act or omission mentioned in subsection (1) is final,

(b) that no appeal lies in respect thereof, or

(c) that no proceeding or decision of the person or organization whose decision, recommendation, act or omission it is shall be challenged, reviewed, quashed or called in question. . . .

---

66 Parliamentary Commissioner (Ombudsman) Act, 1962 (N.Z.).
67 Note the work of the International Ombudsman Institute, located at the University of Alberta.
68 S.A. 1967, c. 59; now R.S.A. 1980, c. O-7.
69 New Brunswick: S.N.B. 1967, c. 18 (now R.S.N.B. 1973, c. O-5); Quebec: *Public Protector Act*, S.Q. 1968, c. 11 (now R.S.Q. 1977, c. P-32); Manitoba: S.M. 1969 (2nd Sess.), c. 26 (now C.C.S.M., c. O45); Nova Scotia: S.N.S. 1970-71, c. 3; Saskatchewan: S.S. 1972, c. 87 (now R.S.S. 1978, c. O-4); Ontario: S.O. 1975, c. 42 (now R.S.O. 1980, c. 325); Newfoundland: Parliamentary Commissioner (Ombudsman) Act, R.S.N. 1970, c. 285; British Columbia: S.B.C. 1977, c. 58 (now R.S.B.C. 1979, c. 306).

The Ombudsman does not have jurisdiction whenever there is a right of appeal, objection or review on the merits of a case to a court or statutory tribunal,[70] so his role is complementary to rights of appeal provided under legislation.

The real powers of the Ombudsman lie in his right to investigate the propriety of governmental action, even if it is not *ultra vires* in Administrative Law terms. Section 20 of the Alberta Act demonstrates the width of these powers in a somewhat convoluted way:

20(1) This section applies when, after making an investigation under this Act, the Ombudsman is of the opinion that the decision, recommendation, act or omission that was the subject matter of the investigation

   (*a*) appears to have been contrary to law,

   (*b*) was unreasonable, unjust, oppressive or improperly discriminatory or was in accordance with a rule of law, a provision of any Act or a practice that is or may be unreasonable, unjust, oppressive or improperly discriminatory,

   (*c*) was based wholly or partly on a mistake of law or fact, or

   (*d*) was wrong.

(2) This section also applies when the Ombudsman is of the opinion

   (*a*) that in the making of the decision or recommendation, or in the doing or omission of the act, a discretionary power has been exercised

      (i) for an improper purpose,

      (ii) on irrelevant grounds, or

      (iii) on the taking into account of irrelevant considerations,

   or

   (*b*) that in the case of a decision made in the exercise of a discretionary power, reasons should have been given for the decision.

(3) If, when this section applies, the Ombudsman is of the opinion

   (*a*) that the matter should be referred to the appropriate authority for further consideration,

---

70 See s. 12 of the Alberta Act. Note, however, that the Ombudsman will gain jurisdiction once an appeal has been exercised (unsatisfactorily?) or the right to appeal has lapsed. Further, note that s. 12 does not require a person to seek judicial review — as opposed to an appeal — before going to the Ombudsman.

(b) that the omission should be rectified,

(c) that the decision should be cancelled or varied,

(d) that any practice on which the decision, recommendation, act or omission was based should be altered,

(e) that any law on which the decision, recommendation, act or omission was based should be reconsidered,

(f) that reasons should have been given for the decision, or

(g) that any other steps should be taken,

the Ombudsman shall report his opinion and his reasons for it to the appropriate Minister and to the department or agency concerned, and may make any recommendations he thinks fit and in that case he may request the department or agency to notify him within a specified time of the steps, if any, that it proposes to take to give effect to his recommendations.

(4) If within a reasonable time after the report is made no action is taken which seems to the Ombudsman to be adequate and appropriate, the Ombudsman, in his discretion after considering the comments, if any, made by or on behalf of the department or agency affected, may send a copy of the report and recommendations to the Lieutenant Governor in Council and may thereafter make any report to the Legislature on the matter that he thinks fit.

(5) The Ombudsman shall attach to every report sent or made under subsection (4) a copy of any comments made by or on behalf of the department or agency concerned.

Thus, the Ombudsman is empowered to ask very searching questions about the way statutory delegates exercise their powers. Merely having the Ombudsman ask questions and make recommendations will very often cause a statutory delegate to revise a questionable action or policy: the effectiveness of the Ombudsman's function is not to be underestimated.[71] On the other hand, in the final analysis the Ombudsman has no legal means for compelling a recalcitrant administrator to correct maladministration or to avoid it in the future: his sole sanction is to make a public report to the legislature.[72] To this extent, therefore, the Ombudsman does not have the same legal power as the

---

71 As demonstrated by a review of any of the annual reports filed by the various Ombudsmen. For litigation concerning the Ombudsman's powers under their respective Acts, see the decision of the Supreme Court of Canada in *B.C. Dev. Corp. v. Ombudsman*, [1985] 1 W.W.R. 193; *Re Ombudsman Act*, (1970) 72 W.W.R. 176; *Re Ont. Ombudsman and Ont. Health Disciplines Bd.*, (1979) 26 O.R. (2d) 105 (C.A.); *Re Ont. Ombudsman and Ont. Min. of Housing*, (1979) 26 O.R. (2d) 434, affirmed 30 O.R. (3d) 768 (sub nom. *Re Ombudsman of Ont. and R.*); *Re Ombudsman Act*, [1974] 5 W.W.R. 176 (Sask.); *Ombudsman N.S. v. Sydney Steel Corp.*, (1976) 17 N.S.R. (2d) 361 (C.A.).

72 See s. 20 of the Alberta Act.

Australian Administrative Appeals Tribunal, or any other appellate mechanism, to implement the results of his investigation.

10. The Effect of an Appeal on the Availability of Judicial Review

The existence of an appeal may have the effect of causing the courts to exercise their discretion to refuse to grant judicial review of an administrator's decision by way of one of the prerogative remedies, a declaration or an injunction.[73] As McDermid J.A. stated in *Re Chad Investments Ltd. and Longson, Tammets & Denton Real Estate Ltd.*:[74]

> It is a wrongful exercise of judicial discretion, unless there are special circumstances, to grant an order of *certiorari* where the party aggrieved has been given an effective right of appeal which the party has not taken advantage of and which has expired. I think this is supported by the majority of the authorities.
>
> Here the Legislature has given the right of appeal upon a question of jurisdiction or law, but has provided that application for leave must be made within 30 days after the making of the decision, and that the Appellate Division shall hear the appeal as speedily as practicable. Under the Alberta Rules of Court an application for *certiorari* must be made within six months of the decision. To grant *certiorari* in a situation such as this would, in effect, circumvent the clear intention of the Legislature that time is a critical and important factor in planning matters.
>
> *A Court, therefore, should not exercise its discretion* which would effect such a result *unless there are special circumstances*, and I do not find any such special circumstances in this case.

Thus, the Appellate Division held that the trial judge had erred in granting *certiorari* to quash the issuance of a development permit after the 30-day appeal period had elapsed.

The policy of refusing judicial review appears now to apply whether the appeal lies to the courts or to another administrative body. In *Harelkin v. University of Regina*,[75] the Supreme Court of Canada refused to issue a prerogative remedy to quash the decision that a student be required to withdraw from the University because the Supreme Court held that his right to

---

73 There is a *right* to damages, however, the court has no discretion to refuse damages if a case is made out, although it may have a discretion as to the amount. In England, there appears to be no requirement for an applicant to exhaust alternative remedies before applying for judicial review: see Wade's 5th ed., pp. 593 *ff.* and Viscount Simonds' dicta in *Pyx Granite Co. v. Min. of Housing and Loc. Govt.*, [1960] A.C. 260 at p. 286 (H.L.).

74 (1971) 20 D.L.R. (3d) 627 at 631-32 (Alta. C.A.).

75 (1979) 96 D.L.R. (3d) 14 (S.C.C.).

appeal to a committee of the University Senate would constitute an "adequate alternative remedy" to judicial review. Until the *Harelkin* case, a credible argument could be made that appeals to another administrative body should not be treated with the same deference as appeals to the courts, so that a greater claim to judicial review would exist in the former case notwithstanding the existence of an appeal in the legislation in question.[76] However, the decision of the majority of the Supreme Court in *Harelkin* clearly focuses on whether the appeal — to whatever body — is an adequate remedy in the circumstances.

It may be difficult to second-guess the courts' view on whether a particular appeal is or is not an adequate alternative remedy to judicial review.[77] Beetz J. set out the following criteria in his decision for the majority in *Harelkin*:[78]

> In order to evaluate whether appellant's right of appeal to the senate committee constituted an adequate alternative remedy and even a better remedy than a recourse to the Courts by way of prerogative writs, several factors should have been taken into consideration among which[:] the procedure on the appeal, the composition of the senate committee, its powers and the manner in which they were probably to be exercised by a body which was not a professional Court of appeal and was not bound to act exactly as one nor likely to do so. Other relevant factors include the burden of a previous finding, expeditiousness and costs.

On the one hand, the courts have concluded that it would be unfair to prevent judicial review where the applicant was not a party to the proceedings in question, had not received notice of the decision, and therefore could not in practice take advantage of the statutory right of appeal;[79] or where the material which would be available to the appellate body would be less complete than that before the court in an application for *certiorari*;[80] where the appeal procedure did not provide for a hearing *de novo*;[81] and possibly in circumstances of bias or improperly obtained evidence which would eviscer-

---

76 See *Re Chad Invt. Ltd. and Longson, Tammets & Denton Real Estate, supra,* note 74, p. 632; *Madison Dev. Corp. v. St. Albert,* [1975] 6 W.W.R. 345 (Alta. S.C.); *Re Min. of Educ. and Civil Service Assn. (Alta.),* (1976) 70 D.L.R. (3d) 696 (Alta. C.A.); *Re Spalding,* (1955) 16 W.W.R. 157 (B.C.C.A.); *R. v. Postmaster-Gen., Ex parte Carmichael,* [1928] 1 K.B. 291 at 299 (D.C.); *cf. Alta. Giftwares Ltd. v. Calgary,* (1979) 10 Alta. L.R. (2d) 221 (Q.B.).

77 See how the various courts dealt with *Harelkin*.

78 *Supra,* note 75, at p. 51. A similar list was adopted by the Alberta Court of Appeal in *Edith Lake Service Ltd. v. Edmonton,* (1981) 20 Alta. L.R. (2d) 1, leave to appeal to S.C.C. refused 42 N.R. 358.

79 See *Can. Indust. Ltd. v. Dev. App. Bd. of Edmonton,* (1969) 71 W.W.R. 635 (Alta. C.A.); *Harvie v. Prov. Planning Bd.,* (1977) 5 A.R. 445 (T.D.).

80 *Re Solicitor,* (1967) 60 W.W.R. 705 (Alta. C.A.).

81 *Fooks v. Alta. Assn. of Architects,* (1982) 21 Alta. L.R. (2d) 306 (Q.B.).

ate the appeal.[82] By contrast, the courts have held that the following factors do not prevent the appeal route from being effective, adequate and exclusive: difficulty in getting a lawyer within the appeal period;[83] being lulled into not appealing because legislative or administrative changes would be made to permit the application to be granted;[84] or the mere fact that the original administrator made an error of law.[85]

On the other hand, difficult conceptual problems arise if there is a jurisdictional defect in the administrative proceedings from which an appeal lies. In the first place, it may be extremely efficient and speedy to use judicial review to identify and determine the effect of a jurisdictional error, particularly if it involves a preliminary or collateral matter so that the delegate has no jurisdiction whatever. To force a party to exhaust his statutory appeals instead of applying for judicial review not only undercuts the *ultra vires* principle by breathing life into a void decision, it may well delay the clarification of an important point of law.[86] The same argument for expeditious judicial review can be made — with less force — when it is alleged that the statutory delegate has committed an error (like a breach of natural justice[87]) which causes him to lose the jurisdiction which he undoubtedly had. In such a circumstance, it may well be the case that a robust right of appeal would provide ample opportunity to correct any such error made by the original delegate.[88] At least, this reasoning was accepted by the majority of the Supreme Court of Canada in the *Harelkin* case to deny judicial review when there was a right of appeal from a

---

82 *Obiter* in *Rozander v. Energy Resources Conservation Bd.*, (1979) 8 Alta. L.R. (2d) 203, leave to appeal to S.C.C. refused 14 A.R. 540. See *Connor v. Law Soc. of B.C.*, [1980] 4 W.W.R. 638 (B.C.S.C.) for a case involving an allegation of bias, and where there was some doubt as to the existence of an appeal in any event.

83 Though note that this may cause the court to extend the appeal period if it can do so under the legislation. See also *Rozander v. Energy Resources Conservation Bd., supra,* note 82; *N. Amer. Montessori Academy Ltd. v. Dev. App. Bd. (Edmonton),* (1977) 7 A.R. 39 (C.A.).

84 The *Montessori* case, *supra,* note 83.

85 *Re Saratoga Processing Co.*, (1979) 10 Alta. L.R. (2d) 193 (Alta. Q.B.). *Cf. Winter v. Residential Tenancies Bd.*, (1980) 31 Nfld. & P.E.I.R. 148 (Nfld. T.D), where the court held that the jurisdictional nature of the alleged error committed by the delegate constituted a special circumstance for permitting judicial review rather than forcing the citizen through the appellate process.

86 Of course, it may be that the delegate will be able — and will agree — to state a case to the courts at the outset, instead of compelling the parties to complete a hearing before him — and perhaps other statutory appeals — before finally being able to get the matter before a court, if an appeal is provided to the court: see the *Committee for Justice and Liberty v. Nat. Energy Bd.* case, [1978] 1 S.C.R. 369, for an example of the use of this sensible procedure. For an example of the opposite approach, see the *Saratoga* case, *supra,* note 85.

87 Beetz J. heretically suggests in *Harelkin* that a breach of the principles of natural justice may not constitute a jurisdictional error. This reasoning is insupportable, and has been criticized by D.P. Jones, "Discretionary Refusal of Judicial Review in Administrative Law", (1981) 19 Alta. L. Rev. 483 at 485-87.

88 On the other hand, it also has the effect of expropriating the appellant's right to two proper hearings. Using a criminal law paradigm, a procedural irregularity at trial is grounds for appeal, which would result in the whole matter being remitted for a complete re-hearing to the

decision made in breach of natural justice.[89] By contrast, the minority of the court dissented strongly on this point, as demonstrated by the following quotation from Dickson J.:[90]

> This point raises the general issue of the discretionary nature of *certiorari*. In this context the authorities . . . draw a distinction between jurisdictional and non-jurisdictional error and between a right of appeal to an administrative or domestic tribunal and a right of appeal to the Courts. Generally speaking, the rule is that, if the error is jurisdictional, *certiorari will* issue *ex debito justitiae*, but if the error is error in law, then in the absence of a privative clause, *certiorari may* issue. The discretion is broad when the error is non-jurisdictional and there is an appeal to the Courts, but virtually disappears when the error is jurisdictional and the right of appeal, if any, is to an administrative or domestic tribunal sitting in a purely appellate role.

> Professor de Smith expresses the point admirably . . . :

>> Nor will a person aggrieved by an invalid decision be required first to exhaust administrative or domestic appellate remedies as a condition precedent to impugning that decision in the courts.

>> The loosely-formulated American doctrine of exhaustion of remedies has simply no Canadian or English counterpart. . . .

Accordingly, the argument is about the width of the court's discretion to refuse judicial review of a jurisdictional error in a delegate's decision if an adequate alternative remedy is provided in the legislation. It is important to note again that the policy of refusing judicial review where there is an adequate right of appeal is not an inflexible rule of law but is the result of the court's discretion to refuse certain remedies. Further, the applicability of the policy does not depend upon the presence of a privative clause in the legislation to protect the decision from which the appeal is to be taken,[91] which would clearly indicate the legislature's intention to provide the appeal *instead of* judicial review. Nevertheless, the implied legislative intention to oust

---

trial court, from which a further appeal on the merits would lie to the court of appeal. In *Harelkin*, the problem was that the appellate body not only would be unlikely to understand the procedural defects of the first proceedings, but would not then remit the matter back for re-hearing by the Council. Rather, the appeal body would simply dispatch the case on its own merits, thereby expropriating the student of his right to two complete hearings.

89 See also *Montessori, supra*, note 83; *Dierks v. Altermatt*, [1918] 1 W.W.R. 719 (Alta. C.A.); *S. (Smith) v. R.* [1959] S.C.R. 638; *Re Wilfong; Cathcart v. Lowery*, (1962) 37 W.W.R. 612 (Sask. C.A.), *Rozander v. Energy Resources Conservation Bd., supra*, note 82; *Re Saratoga Processing Co., supra*, note 85.

90 (1979) 96 D.L.R. (3d) 14 at 27 (S.C.C).

91 *E.g.*, see *Pringle v. Fraser*, [1972] S.C.R. 821.

judicial review must underlie the existence of the court's discretion to refuse judicial review even where there is no privative clause to highlight the exclusivity of the appeal. Yet, this very assumption points to the fallacy inherent in the discretionary nature of the policy. For either the legislature intended the appeal to be exclusive, or it did not; either judicial review should be precluded in all cases where there is an appeal, or in none.

How can one appeal from a void decision? The courts have dealt with this intellectual conundrum by holding that a statutory right of appeal must be intended to permit an appeal from *all* determinations, whether valid or void. As Beetz J. said for the majority in *Harelkin*:[92]

> [E]ven if it can be said that the decision of the council committee was a nullity, I believe it was still appealable to the senate committee for the simple reason that the senate committee was given by statute the power to hear and decide upon appeals from the decisions of the council, whether or not such decisions were null.

and referred to the earlier decision of the court in *Provincial Secretary of Prince Edward Island v. Egan*:[93]

> The fact that the County Judge has acted without jurisdiction does not, in my opinion, affect this right of appeal. Once the conclusion is reached that the section intends to give an appeal to the Supreme Court . . . I can see no reason for limiting the scope of the appeal in such a way as to exclude questions of jurisdiction. As the Attorney-General observed in the course of his argument, lawyers are more familiar with the practice of dealing with questions of jurisdiction raised by proceedings by way of *certiorari* and prohibition. A tribunal exercising a limited statutory jurisdiction has no authority to give a binding decision upon its own jurisdiction and where it wrongfully assumes jurisdiction it follows, as a general rule, that, since what he has done is null, there is nothing to appeal from. But here we have a statute and this is only pertinent on the point of the meaning and effect of the statute.
>
> It has always seemed to me that the proceeding by way of appeal would be the most convenient way of questioning the judgment of any judicial tribunal whose judgment is alleged to be wrong, whether in point of wrongful assumption of jurisdiction, or otherwise. There is no appeal, of course, except by statute and, I repeat, the question arising upon this point is entirely a question of the scope and effect of this statute.

---

92 *Supra*, note 90, p. 49.
93 *Ibid.*, p. 50 (per Sir Lyman Duff C.J.C.).

This approach clears away a great deal of pointless abstruse learning about whether there can be an appeal from a void decision,[94] and permits one to focus on whether the appeal is or is not a more efficient way of correcting errors than judicial review.

11. Conclusion

The discussion in this chapter indicates that our legislators have not developed a comprehensive philosophy concerning the desirability and establishment of appeals from administrative decisions. It is apparent that there is no rationale to whether an appeal lies to another statutory tribunal or whether it lies to a court (and, if so, to which level of court), whether the appeal is to be *de novo* (with or without the appellate body knowing the result of the lower decision) or whether it is to be limited to a question of law or jurisdiction. This state of affairs is unsatisfactory. The legislative branch should give considerably more attention to whether there should be an appeal, to whom it is to lie, and upon what basis it is to be heard; and these decisions should be based on discernible policy considerations and should constitute a rational scheme.

The nature of modern society necessitates that legislators will delegate a wide range of governmental powers simply because the process of modern government cannot be handled in any other way. Thus, persons other than judicial officers are given the responsibility of making decisions which affect people's lives in significant ways. In most cases, the decisions made by these delegates affect people quite directly, and range from minutiae which hardly make a ripple on the consciousness of the citizenry to comprehensive legislation which directly affects their lives and livelihoods and which may be the subject of intensive public and media attention. Within this vast range, the legislators must decide whether there is to be an appeal to another level of decision-maker. Generally speaking, the more directly an administrative decision affects a person's life, the greater the moral claim to a right of appeal, and the more likely that one will in fact be provided by statute. As the Special Committee on Boards and Tribunals reported in 1965:[95]

> Nevertheless, there is embedded in the democratic principles of the administration of justice a right to appeal by a person who considers himself aggrieved, and this Committee is of the view that this principle should be more fully recognised in administrative law than it is at present. It would give citizens who are affected by the decisions of a tribunal a right comparable to the one they have traditionally had in respect of judgments of the Courts.

---

94 For an excellent discussion of this problem, see H.W.R. Wade, "Unlawful Administrative Action: Void or Voidable?", Part I at (1967) 83 L.Q.R. 499; Part II at (1968) 84 L.Q.R. 95.
95 Pp. 12-14.

However, this democratic principle is difficult to apply to administrative agencies which have been created precisely to keep matters out of the courts. On the one hand, any presumption that the delegate has specialized knowledge implies that an appeal should go to someone else who also possesses that specialized knowledge, and not to a generalist judge. On the other hand, judges are specialists in the area of errors of law and jurisdiction. Indeed, this has always been the role of the superior courts. No statutory delegate can be said to have greater competence in this area. Accordingly, there should be no requirement upon an applicant to appeal through the hierarchy of statutory appeals on a question of law or jurisdiction before gaining access to a court which is the proper forum for such questions. Rather, it should be possible to have such legal questions determined immediately by a court (whether using traditional judicial review or through a specific legislative right of appeal to the courts on such questions). Further, such legal determinations should be done preferably at the Queen's Bench level, which would be simple, expeditious, and efficient, and would also allow for a normal further appeal — perhaps only with leave — to the Court of Appeal.

There can be no reasoned argument against such judicial review of legal questions. There can be no support for any argument that a statutory tribunal should be allowed to transgress its jurisdictional bounds with impunity or should be able to determine the law wrongly, nor that another administrative tribunal is better able to judge such legal matters than a court of law.

Appeals on the merits of decisions should, however, lie to other statutory bodies and not to the courts. (In any given case, the legislature might determine that a court is the proper forum for an appeal, perhaps because of the prestige or perceived independence of judges; but it is suggested that this would be the exception and not the rule and that it would be done after proper consideration of the subject area in question and not, as it now appears, by default.) In principle, appeals on the merits would progress up the statutory appeal chain. Whether such appeals would be strictly *de novo* or on the merits should be determined in every case. Proper considerations might include whether the first decision-maker was only one person or a multiple-member board, his (or their) competence, the specialized nature of the decision being made, what procedure is to be used in reaching the decision, whether reasons are to be given, and how directly a person might be affected by the decision.

This then makes some sense of the problem of "appealing" a void decision. A decision that is void for error of law or lack of jurisdiction would not be appealed under this scheme but would be reviewed judicially instead. If there has been an error, the decision will be quashed and remitted to the tribunal to be made again properly, according to law. If there has not been an error of law, then the tribunal's decision will stand and the applicant may exercise his right of a statutory appeal on the merits. This would particularly make sense of the present absurdity of requiring that an applicant who alleges that a tribunal has made an error on a preliminary point of law exhaust the statutory route of appeals on the merits.

This is obviously an area for considerable further thought and rationalization by the legislature when it creates administrative schemes for implementing governmental objectives.

12. Selected Bibliography

Giles, Jack, "Should there be Judicial Review where there is an Adequate Right of Appeal?", (1983) 43 Revue du Barreau 497; also published as a chapter in *Judicial Review of Administrative Rulings*, (Montreal: Les Editions Yvon Blais, Inc., 1983).

Jones, D.P., "Discretionary Refusal of Judicial Review in Administrative Law", (1981) 19 Alta. L. Rev. 483.

Katz, L., "Australian Federal Administrative Law Reform", (1980) 58 Can. Bar Rev. 341.

Williams, D.G.T., "The Council on Tribunals: The First Twenty-Five Years", [1984] P.L. 73.

13

Prerogative Remedies

1. Introduction

The prerogative remedies have an ancient history,[1] and are some of the primary vehicles through which the superior courts review the legality of

---

1 See S.A. de Smith, *Judicial Review of Administrative Law*, 4th ed. (1980), App. 1, for a historical description of the various prerogative writs. See also E. Jenks, "The Prerogative Writs in English Law", (1923) 32 Yale L.J. 532; and A. Rubinstein, "On the Origins of Judicial Review", (1964) 1 U.B.C.L. Rev. 1.

government actions. The five prerogative remedies still in use[2] today are *habeas corpus, certiorari*, prohibition, *mandamus* and *quo warranto*. Each of these is used for a specific purpose. *Habeas corpus* requires a person to justify his lawful authority to detain the applicant. *Certiorari* permits the court to review the legality of the decision of an administrative tribunal, and to quash it if defective. Prohibition is used anticipatorily to prevent a delegate from committing certain kinds of errors. *Mandamus* compels a delegate to perform statutory duties imposed upon him. Finally, *quo warranto* is used to determine the right of the respondent to occupy a public office.

The "prerogative" nature of the remedies derives from the fact that they were issued by the Crown to control the actions of its servants taken in its name.[3] In time, the Crown delegated these remedies to the superior courts to exercise on its behalf. Royal writs[4] were used to compel the administrators to come before the courts to justify their actions. Hence the proper nomenclature for a prerogative remedy is "*R. v. Delegate; Ex parte Applicant*". The applicant applied for the writ *ex parte*, which was accompanied by an affidavit indicating his knowledge, information or belief about the invalidity of the delegate's decision.[5] The writ was issued if there was a *prima facie* case of illegality (although even this was not required if the Crown itself was the applicant[6]). The delegate was thus required to come to court to justify his actions. The procedure then entered a second stage involving both the applicant and the delegate, at which the court determined the issue of illegality. If illegality was demonstrated, the court would then generally issue an order for the respective prerogative remedy, although the court always retained the discre-

---

2 De Smith identifies three other writs which are probably now obsolete: (a) *de non procedendo rege inconsulto* to prevent the common law courts from dealing with matters in which the King had an interest; (b) *scire facias* for the purpose of rescinding royal grants, charters and franchises; and (c) *ne exeat regno* to prevent subjects leaving the Kingdom. *Ibid.*, p. 585.

3 Because the writs issue in the name of the Crown, they are not available against the Crown: *Min. of Finance (B.C.) v. R.*, [1935] S.C.R. 278 at 285; *R. v. Treasury Lords Commrs.*, (1872) L.R. 7 Q.B. 387. But see the discussion in chapter 16 about who constitutes "the Crown".

4 We sometimes still refer to the "prerogative writs" when we really mean the corresponding modern *orders* issued by the court.

5 Because the writ was the first step in a two-step procedure, it was not a final order. Therefore, the affidavit did not have to be on the applicant's personal knowledge but could be on information and belief. Query whether the conversion in Alberta to a one-step procedure which might result in a final order makes R. 305(1) applicable so that the affidavit must be based on the applicant's knowledge, not merely on information and belief. D.C. McDonald J. adopted this view in *R. in Right of Alta. v. Beaver*, [1982] 4 W.W.R. 344, reversed on another point [1984] 4 W.W.R. 371 (Alta. C.A.). See also *Edmonton v. Riemer*, (1979) 10 Alta. L.R. (2d) 92 (Dist. Ct.), which involved an injunction; and *Re Swansea Election*, [1963] 2 O.R. 525 (C.A.), which involved a statutory application to the court instead of a prerogative remedy.

6 Because the Crown has a right to the initial writ — as opposed to the final order — as of right. See D.P. Jones, "Comment on *P.P.G. Industries Canada Ltd. v. A.G. Canada*", (1977) 55 Can. Bar Rev. 718, for a discussion of this distinction.

tion to refuse to issue such an order even if the case was made out by the applicant.[7]

In Alberta, this two-step procedure was abolished a number of years ago,[8] in favour of a one-step procedure involving a notice of motion[9] for the particular order sought. In effect, this streamlined procedure assumes that the writ has always been issued. Perhaps as a result of this change, the style of cause for prerogative remedies in Alberta often (incorrectly) shows the action as being between the person aggrieved (as applicant) and the decision-maker (as respondent), without the intervention of the Crown. Similarly, this change has erroneously caused some judges to insist that the affidavit accompanying the notice of motion refer to personal knowledge, and not merely information or belief, on the incorrect assumption that the affidavit is sworn for the purpose of obtaining the final order.[10] These points can be illustrated by referring to the unreformed two-step procedure which still exists in Quebec.[11]

There are a number of limitations on the availability of prerogative remedies to correct illegal governmental action. In the first place, it is now necessary in our federal system to determine whether the Federal Court or a provincial superior court has authority to issue a prerogative remedy to supervise the particular delegate's actions. Secondly, while the Crown always has the right to apply for a prerogative remedy, the standing of a private person to do so may be problematic. Thirdly, the courts have a discretion to refuse to issue a prerogative remedy even where the applicant has otherwise demonstrated his entitlement thereto. Fourthly, the prerogative remedies are a family unto themselves, and cannot be joined with the private law remedies discussed in chapter 14. Finally, there have been a number of recent procedural and substantive reforms affecting the prerogative remedies, and these are discussed in chapter 15.

Let us now, therefore, consider each of the prerogative remedies in more detail, and then look at the limitations on their availability.

---

7 There is some suggestion that this discretion should never be exercised: (1) against the Crown, if it is the applicant; (2) whenever a jurisdictional defect is involved; or (3) in *habeas corpus* proceedings.

8 Under the 1914 R. 824, borrowed in turn from Ontario's 1897 R. 1294.

9 Not an *originating* notice of motion. Hence, only two days' notice need be given instead of ten, and no fee is payable on filing the notice with the court.

10 See *supra*, note 5.

11 Quebec retains the old two-step system of writs, but has merged *certiorari* and prohibition into a remedy called "evocation". See arts. 834-50 of the Code of Civil Procedure, R.S.Q. 1977, c. C-25. See also G. LeDain, "The Supervisory Jurisdiction in Quebec", (1957) 35 Can. Bar Rev. 788; and D. Lemieux, "Supervisory Judicial Control of Federal and Provincial Public Authorities in Quebec", (1979) 17 Osgoode Hall L.J. 133. As discussed in chapter 15, Ontario, British Columbia and Nova Scotia have changed the procedure for obtaining the prerogative remedies by creating an "application for judicial review", and a similar reform has occurred on a more limited scale federally under ss. 18 and 28 of the Federal Court Act, R.S.C. 1970, c. 10 (2nd Supp.).

2. *Habeas Corpus*

Habeas corpus has probably the greatest constitutional importance of all of the prerogative remedies.[12] It is mentioned in the Magna Carta and has become synonymous with legal systems in which the state must justify the detention of citizens to the courts.

In Administrative Law, *habeas corpus* is most frequently used in cases dealing with immigration,[13] prisoners,[14] custody of children,[15] and in detention of mentally incapacitated persons.[16] The detention of the applicant is quashed by the issue of *habeas corpus*. In reviewing such a detention, the courts are reviewing for errors of law or jurisdiction such as to make the decision *ultra vires*; *habeas corpus* is not an appeal procedure on the merits. In *Armah v. Govt. of Ghana*[17] the House of Lords confirmed that the *habeas corpus* extends to include errors of law on the face of the record. The courts have treated the issue of the order as not being discretionary once a defect has been found in the legality of the detention of the applicant.[18]

Status to apply for *habeas corpus* is confined to the person detained or someone acting on his authority where he cannot act.[19] The burden of proof is on the respondent, who will normally be the person who is actually detaining the applicant. Unlike the other prerogative remedies, *habeas corpus* lies against anyone, and not just someone purporting to act under statutory authority.

Because *habeas corpus* has acquired such constitutional importance, it has generally not been included in the various procedural reforms which have replaced the other prerogative remedies with a new procedure for "judicial review".[20] There appears to be a fear that replacing *habeas corpus* by judicial review might cause the loss of some essential element of the remedy.

---

12 See S.A. de Smith, *Judicial Review of Administrative Law*, 4th ed., (1980) App. 2, for a detailed discussion of *habeas corpus*; as well as R.J. Sharpe, *The Law of Habeas Corpus*, (Oxford Univ. Press, 1976); and M. Cohen, (1938) 16 Can. Bar Rev. 92, and (1940) 18 Can. Bar Rev. 10 and 172. Note that *habeas corpus* may effectively be suspended under the War Measures Act, R.S.C. 1970, c. W-2, and this was done during the October Crisis in 1970.

13 *Azam v. Secretary of State for Home Dept.*, [1974] A.C. 18 (H.L.); *De Marigny v. Langlais*, [1948] S.C.R. 155.

14 *Cardinal v. Kent Inst., Dir.*, [1982] 3 W.W.R. 593 (B.C.C.A.); *Mitchell v. R.*, [1976] 2 S.C.R. 570; *Hicks v. R.*, [1982] 1 W.W.R. 71 (Alta. C.A.).

15 *Re Stawiarski*, (1970) 13 D.L.R. (3d) 507 (N.B.C.A.); *Ex parte D.*, [1971] 1 O.R. 311; *Kovacs v. Graham*, (1981) 16 Alta. L.R. (2d) 396 (Q.B.).

16 *Re Brooks*, (1961) 38 W.W.R. 51 (Alta. S.C.); *Re Perry and Steele*, (1959) 129 C.C.C. 206 (P.E.I.C.A.).

17 [1968] A.C. 192 (H.L.).

18 It may be academic whether this is an exception to the general rule that all prerogative remedies are discretionary, or is merely a strong guideline as to how the courts will exercise their discretion.

19 *E.g.*, in cases of legal or mental incapacity, by someone with a special interest such as the parent or guardian.

20 *E.g.*, s. 18 of the Federal Court Act, R.S.C. 1970, c. 10 (2nd Supp.), does not transfer *habeas corpus* from the provincial superior courts to the Trial Division of the Federal Court.

Similarly, section 18 of the Federal Court Act[21] does not transfer *habeas corpus* from the provincial superior courts to the Federal Court with respect to detentions by a federal board, tribunal or commission. While this has the geographic advantage of keeping *habeas corpus* available from the local superior court instead of from the itinerant Federal Court, it has the disadvantage of making it procedurally impossible to join an application for any other prerogative remedy (such as *certiorari* in aid[22]) with one for *habeas corpus*.

3. *Certiorari* and Prohibition

Certiorari and prohibition are discussed together because of their similarity and the fact that they are the reverse face of each other. On the one hand, *certiorari* is used to quash decisions of lower tribunals where they have acted without jurisdiction, or where they have made an intra-jurisdictional error on the face of the record.[23] On the other hand, prohibition is issued to prevent a tribunal from embarking or continuing upon a procedure for which it has no jurisdiction or to prevent it from making an intra-jurisdictional error of law. Prohibition is forward-looking, designed to prevent something from being done, and is therefore invoked earlier in the proceedings than *certiorari*, which only comes into play once an erroneous decision has been made. As Atkin L.J. said in *R. v. Electricity Commissioners; Ex parte London Electricity Joint Committee Co.*:[24]

> I can see no difference in principle between certiorari and prohibition, except that the latter may be invoked at an earlier stage. If the proceedings establish that the body complained of is exceeding its jurisdiction by entertaining matters which would result in its final decision being subject to being brought up and quashed on certiorari, I think that prohibition will lie to restrain it from so exceeding its jurisdiction.

The history of how these remedies were extended to control a wide range of *ultra vires* governmental actions that are not strictly "judicial" in nature has been described in detail in chapter 8. The superior courts originally supervised the lower courts acting judicially in the traditional sense, and continued that

---

Similarly, s. 12(2) of the Ontario Judicial Review Procedure Act, R.S.O. 1980, c. 224, specifically provides that the "application for judicial review " does not affect the right to apply for *habeas corpus*. The reforms in British Columbia, New Zealand and England do not merge *habeas corpus* into their new procedures for judicial review either. The proposed Alberta reforms would permit either procedure to be used: see chapter 15.

21 *Ibid.*
22 *Mitchell v. R.*, [1976] 2 S.C.R. 570.
23 The concept of an intra-jurisdictional error of law is discussed in detail in chapters 10 and 16; and what constitutes the "record" is discussed in section 2 of chapter 10.
24 [1924] 1 K.B. 171 at 206 (C.A.).

supervisory role as the lower courts came to perform much wider and non-judicial functions in the administration of government. As the duties of the magistrates in the administration of local government were subsequently transferred to a multitude of local government authorities and other statutory delegates in the late 19th century, the traditional supervisory role of the superior courts nevertheless remained available. Where Parliament had made no other provision, the common law remedies of *certiorari* and prohibition continued to be used to ensure that these statutory authorities acted within their jurisdiction. Thus these prerogative remedies came to be used outside the traditional judicial context.

As previously described in chapter 8, the courts were later led astray by the heresy that *certiorari* and prohibition would only be available if the nature of the impugned decision could be characterized as "judicial" or "quasi-judicial". As Atkin L.J. said in the *Electricity Commissioners* case:[25]

> Wherever any body of persons having legal authority to determine questions affecting the rights of subjects *and having the duty to act judicially*, act in excess of their legal authority they are subject to the controlling jurisdiction of the King's Bench Division exercised in these writs.

Whether or not the decision-maker was "acting judicially" (or "quasi-judicially") came to be the rock upon which many litigants foundered who sought to have the wrongs which had been done to them corrected. *Certiorari* and prohibition were held not to be applicable to actions which could be described as being merely "administrative" in nature. This entirely misread the *Electricity Commissioners* case, which undoubtedly involved an administrative act, that is, one performed by statutory delegates who were not judges; and, on the other hand, ignored the long history of supervision by the courts of all kinds of governmental action which although exercised by judicial officers, could not be said to be judicial in nature. The courts have long asserted their right to step in to supervise both "judicial" and "administrative" actions. Nevertheless, the course of administrative law was severely skewed for many years by the adoption of the "quasi-judicial" terminology. Although it has been suggested that the quasi-judicial restriction only applied to determine the applicability of the principles of natural justice to the exercise of a statutory power, in fact it also seriously restricted the ambit of *certiorari* and prohibition as vehicles for judicial review of the legality of governmental action on grounds which either did not include or went beyond breaches of natural justice.[26]

---

25 *Ibid.*, p. 205, emphasis added. The quasi-judicial terminology was clearly accepted by the Supreme Court of Canada in *Calgary Power Ltd. v. Copithorne*, [1959] S.C.R. 24.

26 This is explained in chapter 8. For a good example of the distinction between what constitutes grounds of judicial review (*e.g.*, breach of natural justice) and the availability of *certiorari*, see D.C. McDonald J.'s judgment in *R. in Right of Alta. v. Beaver*, [1982] 4 W.W.R. 344, reversed on another point [1984] 4 W.W.R. 371 (Alta. C.A.).

The courts started to abandon the quasi-judicial heresy after *Ridge v. Baldwin*[27] in England and *Nicholson*,[28] *McCarthy*[29] and *Martineau (No. 2)*[30] in Canada. The close parallel between the applicability of natural justice and the availability of *certiorari* and prohibition means that the reasonings in these natural justice cases also applies to the availability of *certiorari* and prohibition, and it is quite clear that they are now also available to control purely administrative actions.

There must have been a decision or determination of some kind before *certiorari* will issue. A mere recommendation or report not constituting a determination will not attract the remedy.[31] When a decision is quashed, the effect is as if it had not been made and no one need follow it. To the extent that the quashed decision involved a jurisdictional error,[32] it was always void[33] *ab initio* and could have been ignored with impunity, although it is generally safer to get an order of *certiorari* to that effect.

Today, *certiorari* and prohibition are used exclusively to control the exercise of statutory authority,[34] and are confined to the public law field. They play no part in private law and thus, for example, will lie neither to compel compliance with a private right[35] nor to review the award of a consensual arbitrator.[36] On the other hand, a person may sometimes[37] seek one of the private law remedies discussed in chapter 14 in the context of an illegal governmental action, instead of obtaining *certiorari* or prohibition.

---

27 [1964] A.C. 40 (H.L.).

28 *Nicholson v. Haldimand-Norfolk Police Commr. Bd.*, [1979] 1 S.C.R. 311.

29 *McCarthy v. R.C. Sep. Sch. Dist. No. 1 Bd. of Trustees*, [1979] 4 W.W.R. 725 (Alta. T.D.).

30 *Martineau v. Matsqui Inst. Disciplinary Bd.*, [1980] 1 S.C.R. 602.

31 Thus, a coroner's inquest is generally not subject to *certiorari*: *Wolfe v. Robinson*, [1962] O.R. 132 (C.A.); *R. v. Farley*, (1865) 24 U.C.Q.B. 384; *Re Daws*, (1838) 8 Ad. & El. 936; *Ex parte Scratchley*, (1844) 2 Dowl. & L. 29; *Young v. A.G. Man.*, (1960) 33 W.W.R. 3 (Man. C.A.).; *cf. Mahon v. Air New Zealand*, [1984] 3 All E.R. 201 (P.C.), where an application for judicial review was granted against a royal commission of inquiry.

32 The law may differ with respect to an intra-jurisdictional error of law.

33 See H.W.R. Wade, "Unlawful Administrative Action: Void or Voidable?", Pt. I at (1967) 83 L.Q. Rev. 499; Pt. II at (1968) 84 L.Q. Rev; Wade's *Administrative Law*, 5th ed. (1982), pp. 310ff.; M.B. Akehurst, (1968) 31 Mod. L. Rev. 2; J.F. Northey, [1977] N.Z.L.J. 284; G.L. Peiris, "Natural Justice and Degrees of Invalidity of Administrative Action", [1983] P.L. 634; *Harelkin v. Univ. of Regina*, [1979] 2 S.C.R. 561, and comment by D.P. Jones, "Discretionary Refusal of Judicial Review in Administrative Law", (1981) 19 Alta. L. Rev. 483.

34 Although they have been applied to prerogative powers: *R. v. Criminal Injuries Comp. Bd.; Ex parte Lain*, [1967] 2 Q.B. 864.

35 *Vanek v. Univ. of Alta. Gov.*, [1975] 5 W.W.R. 429 (Alta. C.A.); *Re Min. of Educ. and Civil Service Assn.* (Alta.), (1976) 70 D.L.R. (3d) 696 at 699 (Alta. C.A.).

36 *Howe Sound Co. v. Int. Union of Mine etc Wkrs.*, [1962] S.C.R. 318; *cf. Port Arthur Shipbldg. v. Arthurs*, [1969] S.C.R. 85. The Supreme Court of Canada has greatly expanded the category of statutory arbitrations: see *Roberval Express Ltée v. Tpt. Drivers, Warehousemen and Gen. Wkrs. Union, Loc. 106*, [1982] 2 S.C.R. 888.

37 But a private law remedy will only lie against the government if it would lie against a private defendant for the same act; and even then the Crown has more extensive immunities and defences from suit. Accordingly, private law remedies cannot always be substituted for prerogative remedies. See chapter 14.

It is also important to recognize a number of limitations on the availability of *certiorari* or prohibition even in the context of controlling illegal
governmental action. First, although the areas of judicial and administrative
decisions are fully within the sphere of *certiorari* and prohibition, legislative
decisions are still not.[38] This limitation also seems to apply to delegated legislation.[39] Secondly, *certiorari* and prohibition lie only against public bodies
whose authority normally is derived from statute.[40] Thirdly, these remedies do
not lie against the Crown,[41] although they do lie against the Crown and her
ministers when exercising statutory functions.[42] Fourthly, visitors to
universities may perform the same function as *certiorari* and prohibition,
thereby effectively preventing the application of these remedies to universities.[43] Fifthly, *certiorari* and prohibition do not lie to enforce contractual
or other private law rights — perhaps even where there is a "public law" back-

---

38 *Campeau Corp. v. Calgary (No. 2)*, (1980) 12 Alta. L.R. (2d) 379 (C.A.); *R. in Right of Alta.
    v. Beaver*, (1982) 20 Alta. L.R. (2d) 78, reversed (1984) 31 Alta. L.R. (2d) 174 (C.A.); *cf. Bates
    v. Lord Hailsham of St. Marylebone*, [1972] 1 W.L.R. 1373 (Ch.D.). See section 5 of chapter 8.

39 Both *Campeau (No. 2)* and the *Beaver* cases dealt with municipal by-laws, which are a form
    of delegated legislation.

40 Or from the Royal Prerogative? See *Ex parte Lain*, *supra*, note 34. For a discussion of
    whether this case really involved the prerogatives of the Crown or merely a non-statutory
    executive scheme, see Wade's *Administrative Law*, 5th ed. (1982), pp. 213ff.

41 See *supra*, note 3. See also *Loc. Govt. Bd. v. Arlidge*, [1915] A.C. 120 (H.L.), where *certiorari*
    was issued.

42 *Commr. of Prov. Police v. R.*, [1940] 3 W.W.R. 39, affirmed [1941] S.C.R. 317; *R. v. W.C.B.*,
    [1942] 2 W.W.R. 129 (B.C.C.A.); *R. v. Leong Ba Chai*, [1954] S.C.R. 10.

43 See the decision of the Alberta Court of Appeal in *Vanek v. Univ. of Alta. Gov.*, [1975] 5
    W.W.R. 429, where *certiorari* was refused because s. 5 of the Universities Act made the
    Lieutenant Governor the visitor to the University. In a subsequent unreported decision (23rd
    September 1975), Steer J. granted an order of *mandamus* compelling the Lieutenant
    Governor to perform his statutory visitatorial function; and a similar *mandamus* order was
    issued in *McWhirter v. Univ. of Alta. Gov.*, (1975) 63 D.L.R. (3d) 684. The Legislature
    subsequently abolished the office of visitor: S.A. 1976, c. 88, s. 2. In effect, all remedies
    against illegal actions by the University against its staff or students now lie in the civil courts.
      In *King v. Univ. of Sask.*, the trial judge recognized the exclusive jurisdiction of the
    visitor: (1968) 66 W.W.R. 505; but both the Court of Appeal and the Supreme Court of
    Canada dealt with the merits of the case themselves: see (1968) 67 W.W.R. 126, and [1969]
    S.C.R. 698 respectively. See also *Re Univ. of Sask. and MacLaurin*, [1920] 2 W.W.R. 823
    (Sask. C.A.).
      The visitor to the University of Toronto was effectively abolished in 1906: *Re Polten and
    Univ. of Toronto Governing Council*, (1975) 8 O.R. (2d) 749 (Ont. H.C.).
      Although the Governor General is visitor to McGill University, the Quebec Superior
    Court expressed surprise at the suggestion that his jurisdiction was exclusive in *Fekete v. The
    Royal Institution for the Advancement of Learning*, [1969] B.R. 1, but nevertheless upheld this
    exclusivity in *Langlois v. Rector & Members of Laval University*, (1973) 47 D.L.R. (3d) 674
    (Que. C.A.).
      For a discussion of the law in Canada, see G.H.L. Fridman, (1973) 21 Chitty's L.J. 181;
    and more generally: J.W. Bridge, (1969) 85 L.Q. Rev. 468; P.M. Smith, (1981) 97 L.Q. Rev.
    610; and for a thorough review of the English cases: *Patel v. Univ. of Bradford Senate*, [1978] 1
    W.L.R. 1488, affirmed [1979] 1 W.L.R. 1066 (C.A.).

drop to these rights.[44] Sixthly, the anomalous use of *certiorari* to correct an intra-jurisdictional error of law on the face of the record may be subject to the "patently unreasonable" test.[45] Finally, legislation frequently attempts to oust the availability of *certiorari* or prohibition to review the legality of particular governmental action. The effectiveness of these "privative clauses" is discussed in chapter 16.[46]

Section 18 of the Federal Court Act[47] transfers the jurisdiction to issue *certiorari* and prohibition against a "federal board, commission or other tribunal"[48] from the provincial superior courts to the Trial Division of the Federal Court. In turn, section 28 of the Federal Court Act replaces *certiorari* and prohibition (and other remedies[49]) with an "application for judicial review" of the exercise of judicial or quasi-judicial powers. This anachronistic reference has the effect of leaving a residual jurisdiction in the Trial Division of the Federal Court to issue *certiorari* and prohibition where a quasi-judicial function is not involved.[50] The jurisdiction of the Federal Court is limited by the terms of its statute; it does not have the same inherent jurisdiction possessed by the provincial superior courts to correct all governmental illegalities. One example of the difficulties arising from the creation of the Administrative Law jurisdiction of the Federal Court is the procedural inability to join an application for *habeas corpus* (which was left in the provincial superior courts) against a federal body with an application for any other prerogative remedy under section 18 or for judicial review under section 28 of the Federal Court Act.[51]

---

44 See notes 35 and 36, *supra*. The distinction between "private law" and "public law" has become very important in England after the reform of the remedies there. See *O'Reilly v. Mackman; Millbanks v. Secretary of State for Home Dept.*, [1983] A.C. 120 (H.L.); *Cocks v. Thanet Dist. Council*, [1983] A.C. 286 (H.L.); *Davy v. Spelthorne Borough Council*, [1983] 3 All E.R. 278 (H.L.); *Law v. Nat. Greyhound Racing Club Ltd.*, [1983] 3 All E.R. 300 (C.A.). See also C. Harlow, " 'Public' and 'Private' Law: Definition with out Distinction", (1980) 43 Mod. L. Rev. 241.

45 See chapter 10, *supra*.

46 See section 4 of chapter 16, *infra*.

47 R.S.C. 1970, c. 10 (2nd Supp.).

48 Section 2 defines a "federal board, commission or other tribunal" to mean:

> . . . any body or any person or persons having, exercising or purporting to exercise jurisdiction or powers conferred by or under an Act of the Parliament of Canada, other than any such body constituted or established by or under a law of a province or any such person or persons appointed under or in accordance with a law of a province or under section 96 of the Constitution Act, 1867.

For a discussion of this definition, see D.J. Mullan's study for the Law Reform Commission of Canada entitled *The Federal Court Act: A Study of the Court's Administrative Law Jurisdiction* (1977), pp. 17-22.

49 But not *habeas corpus*.

50 *Martineau v. Matsqui Inst. Disciplinary Bd. (No. 2)*, [1980] 1 S.C.R. 602; *Howarth v. Nat. Parole Bd.*, [1976] 1 S.C.R. 453.

51 *Mitchell v. R.*, [1976] 2 S.C.R. 570.

4. *Mandamus*

An order of *mandamus* compels the performance of a statutory duty owed to the applicant.[52] Unlike *certiorari* and prohibition, which prevent statutory delegates from exercising a power unlawfully, *mandamus* is used where the statutory delegate refuses to exercise a power he is compelled to use. In legal theory, an order of *mandamus* is a royal command to perform a public duty; failure to obey is contempt of court. Like *certiorari* and prohibition, *mandamus* is a discretionary remedy which might be refused by the court even though the applicant otherwise makes out his case.[53] Examples of reasons for refusal might be that there is an alternative remedy available, delay by the applicant, or that the delegate performed his obligations prior to the hearing for *mandamus*. The remedy has never been confined to judicial or quasi-judicial functions but has always covered all forms of administrative action (or, more properly, inaction). *Mandamus* only operates in the public law arena, and cannot be used to enforce private contractual rights.[54]

Whether or not a statutory duty exists can only be determined from the legislative language. In some cases, the answer is fairly obvious, especially where mandatory words such as "shall" or "must" are used. The absence of such language is, however, not conclusive of the issue and words which apparently are merely directory may still carry with them a duty to act.[55]

A difficulty may arise in determining whether legislation imposes a duty on the delegate or merely grants a power instead. The problem is compounded if the delegation permits the delegate to exercise discretion. In general, *mandamus* will issue to compel the delegate to exercise his discretion, but the courts will not dictate *how* he is to do so, for that is the very essence of the discretion granted to the delegate.[56] In some cases, however, there is only one legal way in which the delegate can exercise his discretion in the particular circumstances, and the courts have been known to order this result.[57] At the

---

52 Normally, the applicant for *mandamus* will be a private citizen. It may sometimes happen, however, that one public body will seek to enforce a duty lying upon another public body, as occurred in *P.P.G. Indust. Can. Ltd. v. A.G. Can.*, (1976) 65 D.L.R. (3d) 354 (S.C.C.); and *R. in right of Alta. v. Beaver*, (1982) 20 Alta. L.R. (2d) 78, reversed (1984) 31 Alta. L.R. (2d) 174 (C.A.).

53 *McLeod v. Salmon Arm Sch. Trustees*, (1951) 4 W.W.R. 385 (B.C.C.A.); *Seabee Homes Ltd. v. Georgetown*, [1962] O.R. 286, affirmed without written reasons [1962] O.R. 621; *Commr. of Prov. Police v. R.*, [1940] 3 W.W.R. 39, affirmed [1941] S.C.R. 317.

54 A mandatory injunction or an order of specific performance would be the appropriate private law remedies.

55 See the discussion on the distinction between a mandatory and a merely directory statute provision in section 4 of chapter 6, *supra*.

56 *R. v. Gloucester (Bishop)*, (1831) 2 B. & Ad. 158 at 163; *Pecover v. Bowker and Gov. of Univ. of Alta.*, (1957) 20 W.W.R. 561 (Alta. C.A.); *Fahlman v. Law Soc. of Alta.*, [1982] 6 W.W.R. 75 (Q.B.); *Campeau Corp. v. Calgary*, (1979) 7 Alta. L.R. (2d) 294 (C.A.).

57 *Vic Restaurant Inc. v. Montreal*, [1959] S.C.R. 58; *R. v. Baker*, [1923] 1 W.W.R. 1430 at 1434 (Alta. C.A.); *Brampton Jersey Ent. Ltd. v. Milk Control Bd. of Ont.*, [1956] O.R. 1 (C.A.); *R. ex rel Lee v. W.C.B.*, [1942] 2 W.W.R. 129 (B.C.C.A); *R. v. London Licensing Justices; Ex parte*

other extreme, the delegate may have discretion whether to act at all, and no *mandamus* can lie because there is no duty to act at all.[58]

Certain conditions must be fulfilled before a court will issue an order of *mandamus*. First, there must be a public[59] duty to act and this duty must be owed to this particular applicant. In other words, the applicant will have to satisfy the *locus standi* requirements described below. Secondly, there must have been an express demand made to the delegate that he act and he must have refused to do so.[60] In some cases, the delegate's conduct or lack of action may, by implication, be sufficient evidence of the refusal.[61] Thirdly, *mandamus* does not lie against the Crown or its agents.[62] This reflects the general rule that none of the prerogative remedies is available against the Crown, because in theory the court cannot treat the monarch as both applicant and respondent in the same action at the same time, nor could it commit itself in contempt for disobedience.[63] On the other hand, the number of people entitled to this immunity is quite restricted. In particular, it does not apply to the Queen, the Lieutenant Governor, cabinet ministers or public servants when they are exercising a power conferred by statute, for then they are *personae designatae*.[64]

The Alberta Rules of Court contain one important procedural pitfall in applying for *mandamus*. Rule 751 states:

> No order in the nature of *mandamus* shall be granted unless at the time of the application an affidavit is produced by which some person deposes that the application is made at his instance as prose-

---

Stewart, [1954] 1 W.L.R. 1325; *R. v. Newcastle-upon-Tyne Corporation*, (1889) 60 L.T. 963; *R. v. Ormesby Loc. Bd. of Health*, (1894) 43 W.R. 96.

58 *Re Fletcher*, [1970] 2 All E.R. 527n; *Poizier v. Ward*, [1947] 2 W.W.R. 193 (Man. C.A.); *R. v. B.C. Lab. Rel. Bd.*, [1949] 2 W.W.R. 873 (B.C.S.C.); *R. v. Marshland Smeeth and Fen. Dist. Commrs.*, [1920] 1 K.B. 155 at 165.

59 As opposed to a private duty. See the *Vanek* case, *supra*, note 43, and *Dombrowski v. Dalhousie Univ. Bd. of Gov.*, (1974) 55 D.L.R. (3d) 268, affirmed 79 D.L.R. (3d) 355 (N.S.C.A.).

60 *Re Hamilton Dairies Ltd. and Dundas*, (1927) 33 O.W.N. 113 at 114; *Hughes v. Henderson*, (1963) 46 W.W.R. 202 (Man. Q.B.).

61 *Re Civil Service Assn. and Alta. Human Rights Comm.*, (1975) 62 D.L.R. (3d) 531 (Alta. T.D.); *R. v. Highway Traffic Bd.*, [1947] 2 D.L.R. 373 (Alta. T.D.).

62 But "the Crown" must be distinguished from the Governor (alone or in Council), the Cabinet, a Minister, or any other public servant to whom the legislature has delegated a statutory duty. In the latter case, *mandamus* will lie: see *Vanek* and *McWhirter*, *supra*, note 43; *R. ex rel. Lee v. W.C.B.*, [1942] 2 W.W.R. 129 (B.C.C.A.); *Re Central Can. Potash Co. and Min. of Mineral Resources*, [1973] 2 W.W.R. 672 (S.C.C.); and the excellent analysis of the rule in the Report by the Law Reform Commission of B.C. on Civil Rights, Pt. I: "Legal Position of the Crown", (1972), pp. 32-34.

63 *Re Massey Mfg. Co.*, (1886) 13 O.A.R. 446; *C.B.C. v. A.G. Ont.*, [1959] S.C.R. 188 at 204; *R. v. Powell*, (1841) 1 Q.B. 352 at 361. See the powerful criticisms of these justifications for Crown immunity in the Report of the B.C. Law Reform Commission, *supra*, note 62.

64 *Supra*, note 62.

cutor and the name of that person shall appear as the person at whose instance it is made.

This rule causes problems when the applicant is a corporation, because it cannot swear an affidavit, but the individual deponent will not be the applicant.[65] The obvious solution is to remember that all corporations must act through agents, and to treat the agent's affidavit as the corporation's in law so that it can be the applicant (or "prosecutor") for the order of *mandamus*.

Again, it is important to remember that section 18 of the Federal Court Act transfers the authority to grant *mandamus* against a "federal board, commission or other tribunal" from the provincial superior courts to the Trial Division of the Federal Court. Because there is no relationship between the characterization of a function as quasi-judicial and the ambit of *mandamus*, section 28 does not operate to transfer the authority to issue *mandamus* from the Trial Division to the Appellate Division of the Federal Court.[66]

5. *Quo Warranto*

Quo warranto is used to challenge the right of a person to hold a public office, whether created by the Crown, by charter or by statute.[67] The Alberta Rules of Court[68] provide that no application for *quo warranto* shall proceed without the leave of the court, except for an *ex officio* one.[69] The Rules of Court govern the procedure, except that the courts will exercise their discretion to refuse the remedy to the extent that such an equivalent application is provided by statute.[70]

---

65 *R. v. United Grain Growers Ltd.*, (1977) 3 Alta. L.R. (2d) 387 (T.D.). See the similar provisions in RR. 834-36 relating to applications for *mandamus* under s. 424 of the *Criminal Code*.

66 See Mullan, *supra*, note 48.

67 See *Sargent v. McPhee*, (1967) 60 W.W.R. 604 (B.C.C.A.), challenging the appointment of a member of a public inquiry; *cf. R. v. Trainor*, (1967) 66 D.L.R. (2d) 605 (P.E.I.C.A.); *R. v. Gee*, (1965) 51 W.W.R. 705 (Alta. T.D.) but *cf. R. v. Clark*, [1943] O.R. 501 (C.A.), and *R. v. Steinkopf*, (1964) 49 W.W.R. 759, reversed 50 W.W.R. 643 (Man. C.A.), and the comment thereon by F. Muldoon, "Quo Warranto and the Legislator: *Stubbs and Steinkopf Revisited*", (1970) 4 Man. L.J. 178.

68 Rules 745-50.

69 Query what constitutes "an *ex officio* application"?

70 *E.g.*, under Pt. 2 of the Municipal Election Act, R.S.A. 1980, c. M-25 ("Controverted Elections"); see also *R. v. Stevens*, (1969) 3 D.L.R. (3d) 668 (N.S.S.C.).

6. *Locus Standi*

An applicant must be "aggrieved",[71] "affected"[72] or have some other "sufficient interest"[73] in order to possess standing to obtain one of the prerogative remedies; mere busy-bodies need not apply.[74] The courts have had considerable difficulty over the years in determining who qualifies under these terms, and one can detect both a wide and a narrow approach to standing. To some extent, the different tests for standing can be explained by noting which prerogative remedy was being sought,[75] as well as by noting the type of defect being attacked.[76] Theoretically, the applicant's standing should be determined as a preliminary matter at the outset of the proceedings,[77] but the English courts have recently adopted the better approach of leaving the issue to the end of the hearing so as to permit them to treat lack of standing as one of the grounds for exercising their discretion to refuse a prerogative remedy.[78] Difficulties sometimes arise in determining whether the applicant has sufficient legal personality to participate in legal proceedings; and the reverse problem sometimes arises in identifying the correct legal entity to be the respondent. A related issue involves the standing or role of the administrative agency to

---

71 *R. v. Surrey Justices*, (1870) L.R. 5 Q.B. 466, per Blackburn J. at p. 473:

> In other cases where the application is by the party grieved . . . we think that it ought to be treated . . . as ex debito justitiae; but where the applicant is not a party grieved (who substantially brings error to redress his private wrong), but comes forward as one of the general public having no particular interest in the matter, the Court has a discretion, and if it thinks that no good would be done to the public by quashing the order, it is not bound to grant it at the instance of such a person.

On standing generally, see the Report of the English Law Commission on Remedies in Administrative Law, Cmnd. 6407, 1976.

See also *Wolfe v. Robinson*, [1962] O.R. 132 (C.A.) where a person "interested" in the outcome of a coroner's inquiry was not "aggrieved" because it made no finding.

72 Compare *Harvie v. Calgary Regional Planning Comm.*, (1977) 5 Alta. L.R. (2d) 301, reversed 8 Alta. L.R. (2d) 166 (C.A.), dealing with a statutory right of review.

73 *R. v. Manchester Corp.*, [1911] 1 K.B. 560. See also S.M. Thio, [1966] P.L. 133.

74 *Gouriet v. Union of Post Office Wkrs.*, [1978] A.C. 435 (H.L.), dealing with an injunction; *Blackburn v. A.G.*, [1971] 1 W.L.R. 1037 (C.A.); *McWhirter v. A.G.*, [1972] C.M.L.R. 882 (C.A.).

75 Although there may previously have been different tests for standing for different rules, a majority of the House of Lords has held that there is now only one rule: *R. v. Inland Revenue Commr; Ex parte Nat. Fed. of Self-Employed and Small Businesses Ltd.*, [1982] A.C. 617; *cf. Lord Nelson Hotel Ltd. v. Halifax*, (1972) 33 D.L.R. (3d) 98 (C.A.).

76 *Supra*, note 71.

77 Indeed, English O. 53, R. 3(5) (now incorporated in the Supreme Court Act 1981, c. 54, s. 31(3)) provides:

> The Court shall not grant leave unless it considers that the applicant has a sufficient interest in the matter to which the application relates.

This implies that standing is a question to be determined at the initial stage of the reformed English procedure, when leave is sought *ex parte*.

78 See the *Inland Revenue* case, *supra*, note 75.

participate in the proceedings for judicial review before the various courts. These problems will now be considered.

Although the whole world obviously had the right to make an application for a prerogative writ,[79] the courts would only issue this first step to a person so "aggrieved" or "affected" by the governmental action that he had a "sufficient interest" to have standing to require the delegate to come to court to explain the legality of his actions. The courts have vacillated between a wider and a narrower concept of standing.

Under the wider view, standing was granted in the following cases: to a brewer who sought to quash the provisional licence of trade rivals;[80] to an adjoining landowner and ratepayer who objected to the granting of interim development permission;[81] to a ratepaying corporation to challenge valuations on assessment rolls, although the financial consequence of a change would be minimal to the applicant;[82] to a prospective defendant to challenge the granting of a legal aid certificate to the plaintiff;[83] and to the vicar of a parish who objected to the transfer of a liquor licence.[84]

The narrower view denied standing in the following circumstances: to the mayor of a local council which had been dissolved by the Minister without compliance with the principles of natural justice;[85] to a contractor objecting to an improper tendering process;[86] to one governmental agency trying to force another agency to enforce the provisions of the Vaccination Acts;[87] to one bookmaker trying to put competitors out of business;[88] and to local ratepayers trying to force the municipality to enforce a development agreement with a developer of nearby property.[89]

These cases are not easily reconcilable. In theory, the question of standing is a preliminary matter which should be determined at the outset of the application for a prerogative remedy,[90] even under the modern procedure which has been telescoped into one step.[91] In practice, however, the courts very often exercise considerable discretion in determining who should be granted standing; indeed, the House of Lords has recently specifically recog-

---

79 But not necessarily to obtain it.

80 *R. v. Groom; Ex parte Cobbold*, [1901] 2 K.B. 157.

81 *R. v. Hendon R.D.C.; Ex parte Chorley*, [1933] 2 K.B. 696; *cf. Harvie v. Calgary Regional Planning Commission, supra*, note 72.

82 *R. v. Paddington Valuation Officer; Ex parte Peachey Property Corp.*, [1966] 1 Q.B. 380 (C.A.).

83 *R. v. Manchester Legal Aid Committee; Ex parte R.A. Brand & Co.*, [1952] 2 Q.B. 413.

84 *R. v. Cotham*, [1898] 1 Q.B. 802.

85 *Durayappah v. Fernando*, [1967] 2 A.C. 337 (P.C.).

86 *R. v. Hereford Corp; Ex parte Harrower*, [1970] 1 W.L.R. 1424; *cf. Hughes v. Henderson*, (1964) 46 W.W.R. 202 (Man. Q.B.).

87 *R. v. Lewisham Union*, [1897] 1 Q.B. 498.

88 *R. v. Customs & Excise Commr.; Ex parte Cook*, [1970] 1 W.L.R. 450.

89 See Wade, 5th ed. (1982), chapter 9, especially pp. 272*ff.*

90 See *supra*, notes 77 and 78.

91 See the discussion of the Alberta procedure in section 1 of this chapter, *supra*.

nized the propriety of this approach.[92] It has sometimes been suggested that standing should not be denied when a jurisdictional defect is alleged,[93] as (incorrectly) opposed to a breach of natural justice[94] or perhaps an intra-jurisdictional error of law. Two clear extremes can be identified. On the one hand, the courts will always grant standing to a private citizen in constitutional cases,[95] as well as to the Crown in all cases.[96] On the other hand, standing will not be granted to mere busy-bodies.[97]

In general, the applicant for a prerogative remedy must be recognized as a person in law. Thus, unincorporated associations have been held to lack standing both in administrative proceedings[98] and in applications for a prerogative remedy to verify the legality of such proceedings.[99] Nevertheless, there are a number of cases, principally dealing with labour unions, which go the other way.[100]

The courts have also had to consider the reverse question of the necessity for the respondent administrator to have legal personality.[101] Almost all of the cases dealing with this point do not involve a prerogative remedy, but rather one of the private law actions discussed in chapter 14 — which explains why the legal personality of the defendant is important in those cases. In the public law context of the prerogative remedies, however, the legal personality of the respondent is irrelevant. After all, the prerogative remedies supervise the exercise of statutory power. If Parliament has seen fit to grant such powers to boards, tribunals or other entities which are not legally persons, then that fact alone is sufficient to permit the courts to recognize their existence for the purpose of the prerogative remedies.[102]

---

92 The *Inland Revenue* case, *supra*, note 75.

93 *R. v. Surrey Justices*, (1870) L.R. 5 Q.B. 466. See also the conflicting judgments on this point in *Harelkin v. Univ. of Regina*, [1979] 2 S.C.R. 561.

94 Per Beetz J. in *Harelkin, supra*, note 93. *Cf.* McRuer C.J.H.C. in *R. v. Lab. Rel. Bd. (Ont.); Ex parte Dunn*, [1963] 2 O.R. 301 (Ont. H.C.).

95 *Thorson v. A.G. Can.*, [1975] S.C.R. 138; *MacNeil v. N.S. Bd. of Censors*, [1976] 2 S.C.R. 265; *Min. of Justice, Can. v. Borowski*, [1982] 1 W.W.R. 97 (S.C.C.).

96 *P.P.G. Indust. Can. Ltd. v. A.G. Can.*, (1976) 65 D.L.R. (3d) 354 (S.C.C.); *R. in Right of Alta. v. Beaver*, (1982) 20 Alta. L.R. (2d) 78, reversed on other grounds (1984) 31 Alta. L.R. (2d) 174 (C.A.), citing *R. v. Berkley and Bragge*, (1754) 96 E.R. 923 at 932, and *R. v. Thomas*, (1815) 4 M. & S. 442.

97 See *supra*, note 74.

98 *Ladies of the Sacred Heart v. Armstrong's Point Assn.*, (1961) 36 W.W.R. 264 (Man. C.A.).

99 *Sisters of Charity, Providence Hosp. v. Lab. Rel. Bd. (Sask)*, [1950] 2 W.W.R. 1046, affirmed 2 W.W.R. 66 (Sask. C.A.); *Can. Morning News Co. v. Thompson*, [1930] S.C.R. 338 at 342.

100 *Can. Seamen's Union v. Lab. Rel. Bd. (Can.) and Branch Lines Ltd.*, [1951] O.R. 178; *R. v. Lab. Rel. Bd. (Sask.)*, (1966) 55 W.W.R. 133 (Sask. Q.B.); and *Regina Grey Nuns' Hosp. Employees' Assn. v. Lab. Rel. Bd. (Sask).*, [1950] 2 W.W.R. 659 (Sask. K.B.).

101 *MacLean v. Liquor Licence Bd. of Ont.*, (1975) 9 O.R. (2d) 597 (Div. Ct.); *Westlake v. R.*, [1971] 3 O.R. 533, affirmed [1972] 2 O.R. 605, which was affirmed [1973] S.C.R. vii; *Nor. Pipeline Agency v. Perehinec*, [1981] 2 W.W.R. 566, affirmed [1983] 2 S.C.R. 513; *Nat. Harbours Bd. v. Langelier*, (1968) 2 D.L.R. (3d) 81 (S.C.C.).

102 See the *Nor. Pipeline* case, *ibid*.

Finally, the issue arises as to the standing of a statutory delegate to participate in proceedings for a prerogative remedy against the validity of his decision, or to appeal from an adverse ruling of a lower court on this point. In England, it seems that all delegates have standing to participate fully at every level of judicial review of their decisions, even to the point of defending the merits of their actions.[103] In Canada, however, the Supreme Court has unmistakably restricted statutory delegates to the more neutral role of making representations about jurisdictional matters only in proceedings for judicial review, almost like an *amicus curiae*.[104] The Canadian courts, however, have recognized the right of one administrative body to participate in hearings by another statutory delegate.[105] Legislation sometimes specifically grants this right[106] and the right to third parties to intervene in administrative proceedings.[107]

7. Discretionary Nature of the Prerogative Remedies

The discretionary nature of the prerogative remedies in effect amounts to a restriction on a citizen's right to obtain redress for illegal governmental action. The courts have recognized the following broad categories in which they have sometimes exercised their discretion to refuse one of the prerogative remedies: (a) where the applicant has waived his right to object to the defect in the statutory delegate's proceedings, or acquiesced in them; (b) where there is unreasonable delay in bringing the application to the court; (c) where the applicant's conduct disentitles him to the remedy; (d) where granting the

---

103 *E.g., Bd. of Educ. v. Rice*, [1911] A.C. 179 (H.L.). The authors understand the text to reflect the state of English law, although Wade's 5th ed. does not appear to deal with this point specifically.

104 *Re Northwestern Utilities Ltd.; Edmonton v. Pub. Utilities Bd.*, [1979] 1 S.C.R. 684, discussed more fully in chapter 12, *supra*; *Central Broadcasting Co. v. Lab. Rel. Bd. (Can.)*, [1977] 2 S.C.R. 112; *Lab. Rel. Bd. (N.B.) v. Eastern Bakeries Ltd.*, [1961] S.C.R. 72; *Lab. Rel. Bd. (Sask.) v. Dom. Fire Brick Ltd.*, [1947] S.C.R. 336; *Int. Assn. of Machinists v. Genaire Ltd.*, (1958) 18 D.L.R. (2d) 588 (Ont. C.A.); *Can. Lab. Rel. Bd. v. Transair Ltd.*, [1977] 1 S.C.R. 722; D.J. Mullan, "Recent Developments in N.S. Administrative Law", (1978) 4 Dalhousie L.J. 467 at 486-97.

105 *E.g., Rockyview and Alta. Planning Bd.*, (1983) 22 Alta. L.R. (2d) 87 (C.A.); *Re Bennett and Emmott Ltd.; Calgary v. Prov. Planning Bd.*, (1979) 9 Alta. L.R. (2d) 373 (C.A.); *Re Sheckter*, (1979) 9 Alta. L.R. (2d) 45 (C.A.); *O'Hanlon v. Foothills Mun. Dist. No. 31*, [1979] 6 W.W.R. 709, affirmed [1980] 1 W.W.R. 304 (Alta. C.A.); *Northland Fisheries v. Motor Tpt. Bd.*, (1980) 5 Man. R. (2d) 100 (C.A.); *Re Crosbie Offshore Services Ltd.*, (1981) 34 Nfld. & P.E.I.R. 456 (Nfld. T.D.).

106 See Reid and David, *Administrative Law and Practice*, 2nd ed. (1978), chapter 10, "Appearances by Tribunals in Court".

107 *E.g.*, as occurred in *Committee for Justice & Liberty v. Nat. Energy Bd.*, [1978] 1 S.C.R. 369; see also *Morgentaler v. R.*, [1976] 1 S.C.R. 616; *Re Clark and A.G. Can.*, (1977) 17 O.R. (2d) 593 (H.C.); *Solosky v. R.*, [1978] 1 F.C. 609 (C.A.); *Can. Broadcasting League v. C.R.T.C.*, (1980) 101 D.L.R. (3d) 669 (Fed. C.A.); and see s. 31 [re-en. 1981, c. 47, s. 2] of the Energy Resources Conservation Act, R.S.A. 1980, c. E-11, for a statutory recognition of intervenors.

remedy would be futile; (e) where there is an equally effective alternative remedy; and, possibly, (f) where an intra-jurisdictional error of law is not "patently unreasonable". By contrast, the discretionary nature of the prerogative remedies should be compared with the right to a judgment for damages if the plaintiff otherwise meets all the tests of tort law.[108]

(a) Waiver and Acquiescence

The parties cannot validly confer jurisdiction on an administrative body which is lacking under its constituent legislation.[109] Where a tribunal commits a jurisdictional error, its decision is void; and no amount of acquiescence by the parties can legally validate its non-decision. Nevertheless, because the prerogative remedies are discretionary, it does not follow that a person who acquiesced in the invalid proceedings will necessarily be granted relief; his conduct may disentitle him to it. Such a discretionary withholding of the remedy, however, will not make the tribunal's proceedings valid.[110] It simply means that a particular applicant's conduct was such that the court decided to exercise its discretion to refuse him a remedy.

Acquiescence or implied waiver may occur when no objection is made to the tribunal's jurisdiction although the defect was apparent. Where there is a breach of the rules of natural justice or procedural fairness, continued participation in the proceedings may deprive the applicant of his right to a prerogative remedy. For example, the court may refuse relief where the applicant raises an allegation of bias after the proceedings have gone against him, but knew of all the facts relating to bias before or at the time of the hearing.[111]

(b) Unreasonable Delay

Where an applicant is guilty of unreasonable delay in bringing his application before a court, he may find the remedy barred to him. This is especially true where the delay would result in hardship or prejudice to third

---

108 An important aspect of *Cooper v. Wandsworth Bd. of Works*, (1863) 14 C.B. (N.S.) 180; and *Roncarelli v. Duplessis*, [1959] S.C.R. 121.

109 Because the delegate's action would still be *ultra vires* the legislative authority granted to him. But the parties may waive this defect, and this waiver may cause the courts to exercise their discretion to refuse a prerogative remedy. See Rogers, *The Law of Muncipal Corporations*, p. 374.

110 See Wade's *Administrative Law*, 5th ed. (1982), pp. 236, 430, 440, 478, and 807.

111 *Camac Exploration Ltd. v. Oil & Gas Conservation Bd. of Alta.*, (1964) 47 W.W.R. 81 (Alta.); *R. v. Can. Lab. Rel. Bd.; Ex parte Martin*, (1966) 58 D.L.R. (2d) 134 (Ont. C.A.); *Seaside Real Estate Ltd. v. Halifax-Dartmouth Real Estate Bd.*, (1964) 44 D.L.R. (2d) 248 (N.S.C.A.); *Wyman & Moscrop Realty v. Vancouver Real Estate Bd.*, (1959) 19 D.L.R. (2d) 336 (B.C.S.C.); *Re Polten and Univ. of Toronto Governing Council*, (1975) 8 O.R. (2d) 749 (H.C.); *Re Thompson and Loc. 1026 of Int. Union of Mine etc. Wkrs.*, (1962) 35 D.L.R. (2d) 333 (Man. C.A.) (bias); *Can. Air Line Pilots Assn. v. C.P. Air Lines Ltd.*, (1966) 57 D.L.R. (2d) 417 (B.C.C.A.) (bias); *cf. Committee for Justice & Liberty v. Nat. Energy Bd.*, [1978] 1 S.C.R. 369.

parties who have acted in good faith on the strength of the delegate's apparently valid decision.[112] Rule 742 of the Alberta Rules of Court provides that an application for *certiorari* shall be filed and served within six months after the order to which it relates and further expressly provides that the court cannot enlarge or abridge this time limitation.[113] It does not necessarily follow, however, that an application can safely wait for six months without running the risk of the court finding there to have been an unreasonable delay.[114] What constitutes unreasonable delay is a question to be decided in each case. One primary consideration must be the need for effective and reliable administration, which must entail the notion of finality in decision-making.

Delay in bringing an application for prohibition may mean that the tribunal has reached its decision and there is nothing that the court can prohibit; an attempt would have to be made to quash the decision by *certiorari* instead.

(c) Clean Hands and the General Conduct of the Applicant

Apart from the two examples already described where the applicant's conduct may lead to a refusal of the remedy, other forms of conduct may also be taken into consideration. For instance, the court may exercise its discretion to refuse a prerogative remedy if the applicant has dealt with the tribunal in bad faith, been deceitful, withheld evidence or conducted himself fraudulently.[115] Where the applicant's motives can be called into question, he may fail in his application.[116] Thus, a remedy may be refused where the motive behind the application is really to further the applicant's own pecuniary interests or for some other purely personal motive considered improper by the court.[117]

(d) Futility

Prerogative remedies will not be issued where it would be futile to do so. For instance, once a tribunal has made a decision, prohibition is no longer useful.[118] Similarly, *mandamus* is unnecessary where the tribunal has agreed to perform its statutory duty. Minor procedural irregularities which in fact or which in all likelihood had no effect on the ultimate decision have been

---

112 *E.g.*, the injustice which resulted in *Welbridge Hldg. Ltd. v. Winnipeg*, [1971] S.C.R. 957; and *Wiswell v. Winnipeg*, [1965] S.C.R. 512.

113 Query whether the six-month rule applies to an application by the Crown for *certiorari*.

114 *R. v. Stafford Justices; Ex parte Stafford Corp.*, [1940] 2 K.B. 33 at 46-47 (C.A.).

115 *Cock v. Lab. Rel. Bd. (B.C.)*, (1960) 33 W.W.R. 429 (B.C.C.A.); *Re Burgin and King*, [1973] 3 O.R. 174 (Div. Ct.); *Rodd v. Essex*, (1910) 44 S.C.R. 137; *Ex parte Fry*, [1954] 1 W.L.R. 730 (C.A.); *Glynn v. Keele Univ.*, [1971] 1 W.L.R. 487.

116 *Ex parte Swim*, (1921) 49 N.B.R. 207 (C.A.).

117 *Homex Realty & Dev. Co. v. Wyoming*, [1980] 2 S.C.R. 1011.

118 Although *certiorari* may be used to quash an improper decision that has been made.

ignored by the courts.[119] On the other hand, it is not the court's task to second-guess the result if the statutory delegate has performed its function correctly, so that the court generally will not exercise its discretion to refuse a prerogative remedy where a breach of natural justice has occurred.[120]

(e) Availability of Alternative Remedies

The courts have sometimes exercised their discretion to refuse a prerogative remedy when an equally effective alternative remedy (such as an appeal) is, or was,[121] available to the applicant. The courts' approach on this aspect of discretion has diverged in recent years in England and in Canada. The English courts have tended to assert their right to issue prerogative remedies to correct illegality without requiring the applicant to exhaust his statutory or administrative rights of appeal.[122] By contrast, the decision of the majority of the Supreme Court of Canada in *Harelkin v. University of Regina*[123] is a clear indication to Canadian courts to give precedence to the alternative remedy prescribed by the legislators. This topic is discussed in greater detail in chapter 12.

(f) Intra-jurisdictional Errors of Law

The Canadian courts have recently indicated that they will not use *certiorari* to review an intra-jurisdictional error of law on the face of the record[124] unless it is "patently unreasonable". As discussed in chapter 10, the better view is to treat this development as a circumstance in which the courts will exercise their discretion to refuse judicial review, and not as a limitation on the availability of a remedy as a hard-and-fast matter of law.

8. The Federal Court Act

As noted in the discussion above of each of the prerogative remedies, it is extremely important to take an application against a "federal board, commission or other tribunal" in the correct court, whether the superior court of a province on the one hand, or one of the divisions of the Federal Court on the other.

---

119 *Pringle v. Victoria*, (1951) 3 W.W.R. (N.S.) 570 (B.C.S.C.); *Invictus Ltd. v. Man. Lab. Bd.*, (1967) 62 W.W.R. 150 (Man. Q.B.); *R. v. Bd. of Broadcast Gov.; Ex parte Swift Current Telecasting Co.*, [1962] O.R. 657 (C.A.).

120 See Dickson J.'s dissenting judgment in *Harelkin v. Univ. of Regina*, [1979] 2 S.C.R. 561.

121 As was the case in *N. Amer. Montessori Academy Ltd. v. Dev. App. Bd. (Edmonton)*, (1978) 7 A.R. 39 (C.A.), and *Rozander v. Energy Resources Conservation Bd.*, (1978) 8 Alta. L.R. (2d) 203 (C.A.).

122 See Wade's *Administrative Law*, 5th ed. (1982), pp. 593*ff*.

123 *Supra*, note 120.

124 For a discussion of what constitutes the "record", see section 4 of chapter 10, *supra*.

For convenience, sections 18 and 28 of the Federal Court Act are reproduced here:[125]

18. The Trial Division has exclusive original jurisdiction

  (*a*) to issue an injunction, writ of *certiorari*, writ of prohibition, writ of *mandamus* or writ of *quo warranto*, or grant declaratory relief, against any federal board, commission or other tribunal; and

  (*b*) to hear and determine any application or other proceeding for relief in the nature of relief contemplated by paragraph (*a*), including any proceedings brought against the Attorney General of Canada, to obtain relief against a federal board, commission or other tribunal. . . .

28.(1) Notwithstanding section 18 or the provisions of any other Act, the Court of Appeal has jurisdiction to hear and determine an application to review and set aside a decision or order, other than a decision or order of an administrative nature not required by law to be made on a judicial or quasi-judicial basis, made by or in the course of proceedings before a federal board, commission or tribunal, upon the ground that the board, commission or tribunal

  (*a*) failed to observe a principle of natural justice or otherwise acted beyond or refused to exercise its jurisdiction;

  (*b*) erred in law in making its decision or order, whether or not the error appears on the face of the record; or

  (*c*) based its decision or order on an erroneous finding of fact that it made in a perverse or capricious manner or without regard for the material before it.

  (2) Any such application may be made by the Attorney General of Canada or any party directly affected by the decision or order by filing a notice of the application in the Court within ten days of the time the decision or order was first communicated to the office of the Deputy Attorney General of Canada or to that party by the board, commission or other tribunal, or within such further time as the Court of Appeal or a judge thereof may, either before or after the expiry of those ten days, fix or allow.

  (3) Where the Court of Appeal has jurisdiction under this section to hear and determine an application to review and set aside a decision or order, the Trial Division has no jurisdiction to entertain any proceeding in respect of that decision or order.

---

125 R.S.C. 1970, c. 10 (2nd Supp.). For a detailed discussion of the Federal Court Act see D.J. Mullan's Study for the Law Reform Commission, *supra*, note 48.

(4) A federal board, commission or other tribunal to which subsection (1) applies may at any stage of its proceedings refer any question or issue of law, or jurisdiction or of practice and procedure to the Court of Appeal for hearing and determination.

(5) An application or reference to the Court of Appeal made under this section shall be heard and determined without delay in a summary way.

(6) Notwithstanding subsection (1), no proceeding shall be taken thereunder in respect of a decision or order of the Governor in Council, the Treasury Board, a superior court or the Pension Appeals Board or in respect of a proceeding for a service offence under the *National Defence Act*.

9. Conclusion

The prerogative remedies have a long history of being used to control illegal governmental action. However, the differentiation of the family into separate remedies directed to different types of illegalities has resulted in an undesirable number of technical pitfalls to trap the unwary litigant. It is not surprising, therefore, that the private law remedies discussed in chapter 14 have also been used to control illegal governmental action. Nor is it surprising that there have been numerous recent attempts and proposals to reform all administrative law remedies into a more efficient system, as discussed in chapter 15.

10. Selected Bibliography

Cohen, M., "Habeas Corpus Cum Causa — The Emergence of the Modern Writ", (1940) 18 Can. Bar Rev. 10 and 172.

Cohen, M., "Some Considerations on the Origins of Habeas Corpus", (1938) 16 Can. Bar Rev 92.

de Smith, S.A., "The Prerogative Writs: Historical Origins", published as App. 1 to *Judicial Review of Administrative Action*, 4th ed. (1980) ed. J.M. Evans.

Heuston, R.F.V., "Habeas Corpus Procedure", (1950) 66 L.Q. Rev. 79.

Jenks, E., "The Prerogative Writs in English Law", (1923) 32 Yale L.J. 523.

Law Commission (England), *Remedies in Administrative Law*, Working Paper No. 40, 1971.

Law Commission (England), *Report on Remedies in Administrative Law*, Law Com. No. 73, Cmnd. 6407, 1976.

Le Dain, G., "The Supervisory Jurisdiction in Quebec", (1957) 35 Can. Bar Rev. 788.

Lemieux, D., "Supervisory Judicial Control of Federal and Provincial Public Authorities in Quebec", (1979) 17 Osgoode Hall L.J. 133.

Letourneau, G., *The Prerogative Writs in Canadian Criminal Law and Procedure*, 1976.

Mercer, P.P., "The *Gouriet* Case: Public Interest Litigation in Britain and Canada", [1979] P.L. 214.

Mullan, D.J., *The Federal Court Act: A Study of the Court's Administrative Law Jurisdiction*, prepared for the Law Reform Commission of Canada, 1977.

Rubinstein, A., "On the Origins of Judicial Review", (1964) 1 U.B.C. L. Rev. 1.

Sharpe, R.J., *The Law of Habeas Corpus*, 1976.

Thio, S.M., *Locus Standi and Judicial Review*, 1971.

Thio, S.M., "Locus Standi in Relation to Mandamus", [1966] P.L. 133.

14

Private Law Remedies

1. Introduction

In addition to statutory appeals[1] and prerogative remedies,[2] private law actions for damages, injunctions and declarations may sometimes be available to redress illegal governmental action. These private law remedies may be sought together within the same action, but they cannot be joined with either a statutory appeal or an application for a prerogative remedy.[3] Whole books have been written upon each of these private law remedies, and it is not desirable to try to duplicate that type of comprehensive tréatment here. Nevertheless, because illegal governmental action can sometimes give rise to a wrong recognized by private law, it is important to canvas some of the circumstances in which these private law remedies may give effective redress to an aggrieved person, as well as some of the limitations inherent in them.

2. Damages

In theory, there is no reason why public authorities should not be as responsible for their tortious actions as any other member of the public. Just as a private citizen can be sued in damages for his intentional or negligent actions which cause harm to others, so should governmental activity be similarly actionable where people or property have suffered loss as a result of it. In many circumstances, government officials are liable for their torts. However, the analogy to private law breaks down very quickly. First, not all injurious governmental actions fit into the recognized categories of actionable torts. In these cases, no remedy may be available. Nevertheless, it may be possible to identify an emerging new head of damage applicable only in the public law field, which is sometimes called "misfeasance in a public office". Secondly, a public official will often be able to rely upon the complete defence of valid statutory authority to do the injurious act, which will protect him from suit despite any loss caused. This immunity may be lost, however, where his actions are so unreasonable or careless as to take him outside his authority. Thirdly, there is the recognized immunity of judicial officers and of those officials said to be acting in a legislative or quasi-judicial manner, despite the fact that their actions would otherwise be actionable without this immunity. The cases on damages in the public law field illustrate the courts' struggle to balance two competing and legitimate interests: on the one hand, the wish to compensate an individual who has suffered loss at the hands of illegal official action and the desire to curb such action; and, on the other hand, the wish to preserve independence in government action even in the face of unpopularity

---

1 See chapter 12.

2 See chapter 13.

3 However, some of the procedural reforms discussed in chapter 15 do permit joinder of the different forms of remedies.

and the need to encourage worthy individuals to enter the public service without fear of incurring devastating legal liability.

(a) General Liability for Nominate Torts and Negligence

In principle, public officials are liable for the torts committed by them on the same basis as in private tort law. Therefore, a public official is liable where the action is *ultra vires* and otherwise falls into one of the nominate torts (such as trespass, nuisance, assault and battery, or false imprisonment), or where the action is *ultra vires* and is found to be negligent in relation to a person to whom the public official owes a duty of care. An injured party may seek his remedy by way of damages.[4] A necessary precondition to liability, however, is that the governmental action must be illegal. *Intra vires* actions are completely protected from suit. Hence, this type of damage action in effect constitutes a form of judicial review of the legality of governmental action. Once it is established that the action is illegal, then it must be established further that the action is tortious before it becomes actionable.

These principles can be seen from three cases: the first involves a nominate tort; the last two involve actions for damages arising out of negligence.

In *Cooper v. Wandsworth Board of Works*,[5] the plaintiff recovered damages for trespass. The board had demolished the plaintiff's house purporting to act under the authority given to it in the Metropolis Management Act, 1855,[6] which provided that a person had to give seven days' notice to the board of his intention to build a house. Failure to give the notice made it lawful for the board to demolish the structure. Mr. Cooper gave no notice. However, the court held that the board's act was in fact *ultra vires* because the board had failed to give Mr. Cooper an opportunity to be heard before taking action although the legislation did not expressly require this. Thus the board's act was illegal[7] and the demolition of the house constituted a trespass, an actionable wrong. *Cooper* is an example of an *ultra vires* administrative action which constituted one of the nominate torts. Damage actions sometimes also succeed against public authorities which have been negligent. The leading

---

4 This common law right is not restricted unless the injurious public action is permitted by statute. Then the injured party is restricted to the statutory remedy provided in the legislation: *Von Thurn Und Taxis Johannes Prinz v. Edmonton*; *Heemeryck v. Edmonton*, [1982] 4 W.W.R. 457 (Q.B.). See also *Marriage v. East Norfolk Rivers Catchment Bd.*, [1950] 1 K.B. 284 (C.A.); *Raleigh Corp. v. Williams*, [1893] A.C. 540 (P.C.); *C.N.R. v. Trudeau*, [1962] S.C.R. 398; *Leighton v. B.C. Elec. Ry.*, (1914) 6 W.W.R. 1472 (B.C. C.A.); *North Vancouver v. McKenzie Barge & Marine Ways Ltd.*, [1965] S.C.R. 377; *Groat v. Edmonton*, [1928] S.C.R. 522; *Portage la Prairie v. B.C. Pea Growers Ltd.*, [1966] S.C.R. 150; *Klimenko v. Winnipeg*, (1965) 55 W.W.R. 180 (Man. C.A.).
5 (1863) 14 C.B. (N.S.) 180.
6 18 & 19 Vict., c. 120.
7 And therefore void, not voidable.

English case, *Anns v. Merton London Borough Council*,[8] involved liability for defective foundations of a two-storey block of flats which had been approved by the council surveyor although they did not conform to the approved plans. Lord Wilberforce described the nature of actions which would create a duty of care and those which would not by making the distinction between policy areas and operational areas:[9]

> Most, indeed probably all, statutes relating to public authorities or public bodies, contain in them a large area of policy. The courts call this "discretion" meaning that the decision is one for the authority or body to make, and not for the courts. Many statutes also prescribe or at least presuppose the practical execution of policy decisions: a convenient description of this is to say that in addition to the area of policy or discretion, there is an operational area. Although this distinction between the policy area and the operational area is convenient, and illuminating, it is probably a distinction of degree; many "operational" powers or duties have in them some element of "discretion". It can safely be said that the more "operational" a power or duty may be, the easier it is to superimpose on it a common law duty of care.

Thus, the duty is one of "taking care to avoid harm to those likely to be affected".[10] In the area of policy decision-making the public body must exercise its discretion by giving proper consideration to whether it will or will not perform some power given to it, for example, whether or not to inspect. In doing so, a public body must make its discretionary decisions responsibly, having in mind the public interest which the statute contemplates. It cannot simply decide not to exercise the power. If the public body has the power to act in ways to promote public safety, then it cannot abdicate its responsibilities by deciding not to act at all for fear that its actions might then be negligent and it may be found liable. Once the public authority decides to act (for example, by inspecting), then the scope of its duty in the operational area is to exercise reasonable care. One difficulty is that, even in the operational area, there are elements of discretion, for instance, when to inspect and how often. In such a case, a plaintiff must first establish that the action was "not within the limits of a discretion bona fide exercised . . .".[11] Then he may rely on a breach of the duty of care.

A similar case involving an action for damages resulting from negligent government activity has recently been considered by the Supreme Court of Canada in *Kamloops v. Nielsen*.[12] The issue was whether a municipality can be

---

8 [1978] A.C. 728 (H.L.).
9 *Ibid.*, p. 754.
10 *Ibid.*
11 *Ibid.*, p. 755.
12 [1984] 5 W.W.R. 1 (S.C.C.).

held liable in negligence for failure to prevent the construction of a house with defective foundations. The house builder had ignored the city's stop-work orders. Although the city knew that construction was still going on, it took no steps to enforce its orders either because (a) the owner was an alderman, or (b) the city employees had gone on strike and the department was short of man-power. No further inspections were made and no occupancy permit was issued. The defect was not uncovered in a general inspection made for Nielson before purchase. Some time later, the defective foundations were discovered by chance by the new owner, Nielsen. Nielsen alleged that the city was negligent for failing to enforce the stop-work order or, alternatively, for failing to condemn the building as unfit for habitation. The city was found 25 per cent liable in negligence at trial. This was upheld by the British Columbia Court of Appeal and by the Supreme Court of Canada in a three-to-two decision.

Wilson J., writing for the majority of the Supreme Court, relied on the decision of the House of Lords in the *Anns* case to establish that the city owed a duty of care to the plaintiff and that it was liable in damages where it had breached that duty. Wilson J. applied the policy/operational test developed in the *Anns* case to the facts before her in *Kamloops*:[13]

> It seems to me that, applying the principle in *Anns*, it is fair to say that the City of Kamloops had a statutory power to regulate construction by by-law. It did not have to do so. It was in its discretion whether to do so or not. It was, in other words, a "policy" decision. However, not only did it make the policy decision in favour of regulating construction by by-law, it also imposed on the city's Building Inspector a duty to enforce the provisions of the by-law. This would be Lord Wilberforce's "operational" duty.

The city was thus held negligent by virtue of the breach of its duty to the plaintiff to protect him against the builder's negligence by its system of inspections.[14]

The question then arose as to whether the principle in *Anns* should be confined to cases of misfeasance, as opposed to nonfeasance. The Supreme Court appears to have rejected the nonfeasance/misfeasance dichotomy: if a public official fails to do that which he has a duty to do, his breach gives rise to liability where the breach causes damage to the plaintiff; if he has no duty to act and does not do so, there can be no liability. The question of nonfeasance or misfeasance does not arise.

In the *Kamloops* case, the building inspector was called upon to perform operational decisions. He had no discretion to decide whether or not to

---

13 *Ibid.*, p. 27.
14 Note, however, that the builder was considered to be primarily responsible (75 per cent) for the damage.

enforce the by-law. He did, however, have a discretion to determine the manner of enforcement. This involved policy considerations. The distinction then becomes very fine in identifying the "policy" versus the "operational" content of the decision. The City of Kamloops was held liable, not because it had weighed the policy considerations and had made the wrong choice, but rather because it had failed to consider the options at all. The city had to make a policy decision whether to seek legal means to enforce its by-law, a legitimate exercise of discretion within the operational area. It may well be that a policy decision not to prosecute could not be faulted. But the evidence indicated that the city, far from entering upon a *bona fide* exercise of its discretion within the proper limits, dropped the whole matter because one of its aldermen was involved:[15]

> In my view, inaction for no reason or inaction for an improper reason cannot be a policy decision taken in the bona fide exercise of discretion. Where the question whether the requisite action should be taken has not even been considered by the public authority, or at least has not been considered in good faith, it seems clear that for that very reason the authority has not acted with reasonable care.

In summary, policy decisions made *bona fide* in the exercise of a discretion provided by statute will not establish the duty of care necessary to attract liability in negligence even where damage has resulted. The courts will not inquire into the merits of such primary policy decisions. However, in the operational area, public officials will be liable for their negligent actions upon the same principles which operate in the law of torts.

The difficulty arises where operational decisions contain within them some element of discretion — what Wilson J. calls "policy considerations at the secondary level".[16] The majority of the Supreme Court did not deal with this difficulty in reaching its decision because it found that there had been a complete lack of review of any of the policy considerations at the operational level. Therefore the city was liable.[17]

The dissenting members of the Supreme Court did deal with this difficulty. They held that the building inspector had properly fulfilled his duties because, for any action in negligence to succeed, the plaintiff would have to show that the city was under a duty to prosecute to enforce its by-law. However, since this decision lay within the competence of the council to decide in its discretion, it was an area with which the court should not interfere.

It is difficult to understand why the element of discretion should make the duty of care so difficult to establish. If the city had considered whether to

---

15 *Supra*, note 12 at p. 37.
16 *Ibid.*, p. 38.
17 This reasoning — that total disregard of policy considerations should lead to liability — should also operate at the primary level of policy decision-making.

prosecute and had not done so for economic reasons,[18] yet the house had still been defective causing damage to the plaintiff, should the city be able to hide behind this? Surely the purpose of the statute was to ensure the safety of citizens. If the city, having decided to embark upon a scheme of inspection, failed to maintain safety, why should it be able to escape liability because of an artificial distinction between policy and operations? If an architect had known of the defect yet failed to act, he would certainly have been liable; indeed, the builder here was held 75 per cent liable. Why is a municipality so protected? In principle, we think the better distinction is to speak of "political" decisions in the broad context affecting all citizens and giving rise to no liability, as distinct from decisions taken in the area where a direct lineal relationship between the citizen and the municipality operates, thereby surely establishing a duty of care.

(b) Immunities

(i) Members of Parliament and provincial legislatures

All members of the Federal Parliament and of the provincial legislatures enjoy many legal privileges and immunities. These immunities emerged from the constitutional struggles between Parliament and the King in England in the 17th century. No member can be held liable in the courts for his tortious actions committed in the House or while on parliamentary business.[19] Disciplinary proceedings can only be taken against him by Parliament and Parliament retains the power to impose appropriate sanctions against its members for such behaviour.

(ii) Judicial officers

Judges of all[20] the properly constituted courts in Canada are immune from liability for any tortious actions committed by them when acting in their judicial capacity. This is a long-standing principle in the common law. It has long been considered desirable in order to protect the independence of the judiciary and to free judges from fear of personal calumny from those who, having appeared before them, considered themselves harshly judged. The immunity operates even where a judge's actions are malicious. Lord Denning M.R. in *Sirros v. Moore*[21] considered that in this modern age when the judicial system has changed out of all recognition, as a matter of principle there should be no greater immunity for the judges of the superior courts than of the lower

---

18 Which the majority of the Supreme Court thought would be legitimate, and not give rise to liability.

19 *Re Ouellet (Nos. 1 and 2)*, (1977) 72 D.L.R. (3d) 95 (Que. C.A.); *Roman Corp. v. Hudson's Bay Oil & Gas Co.*, [1973] S.C.R. 820.

20 Some commentators say that the immunity applies only to superior court judges: see A. Rubinstein, "Liability in Tort of Judicial Officers", (1963-64) 15 U.T.L.J. 317.

21 [1975] Q.B. 118.

courts. All should be protected to the same extent, including justices of the peace, so that:[22]

> Each should be able to do his work in complete independence and free from fear. . . . So long as he does his work in the honest belief that it is within his jurisdiction, then he is not liable to an action. He may be mistaken in fact. He may be ignorant in law. What he does may be outside his jurisdiction — in fact or in law — but so long as he honestly believes it to be within his jurisdiction, he should not be liable. Once he honestly entertains this belief, nothing else will make him liable. He is not to be plagued with allegations of malice or ill-will or bias or anything of the kind. Actions based on such allegations have been struck out and will continue to be struck out. Nothing will make him liable except it be shown that he was not acting judicially, knowing that he had no jurisdiction to do it.

(iii) Public officials acting legislatively

A public body engaged in a legislative activity is immune from suit, even though acting negligently. The leading case in Canada of immunity from the consequences of a legislative action negligently done is *Welbridge Holdings Ltd. v. Winnipeg*,[23] where the Metropolitan Corporation of Greater Winnipeg had passed a by-law re-zoning certain property. Welbridge then spent large sums of money on the development and partial construction of the building. Wiswell and other adjacent property owners had challenged the validity of the by-law on the grounds of lack of notice and the denial of a proper hearing. The Supreme Court of Canada declared the by-law invalid.[24] Stop-work orders were issued against Welbridge which suffered considerable financial loss as a result. Welbridge sued in negligence for damages but was unsuccessful.

Welbridge argued that the council owed it a duty of care to ensure that the proper procedures were followed when enacting the by-law. Furthermore, the case for the existence of a duty of care was even stronger because there was a direct link between this by-law affecting this property and those with an interest in the property. The duty was not merely to the citizens of the municipality in general. Nevertheless, the court held that there was no responsibility in negligence when the statutory body was exercising a legislative power.[25] Nor would the principle in *Hedley Byrne & Co. v. Heller & Partners*[26] apply where the action was legislative in nature.[27] Although a

---

22 *Ibid.*, p. 136.

23 [1971] S.C.R. 957.

24 *Wiswell v. Winnipeg*, [1965] S.C.R. 512.

25 *Kwong v. R.*, [1979] 2 W.W.R. 1, affirmed [1979] 2 S.C.R. 1010. See also *Berryland Canning Co. v. R.*, [1974] 1 F.C. 91 (T.D.).

26 [1964] A.C. 465.

27 *Hedley Byrne* was applied in *Windsor Motors Ltd. v. Powell River Corp.*, (1969) 68 W.W.R. 173 (B.C.C.A.), where the municipality was held vicariously liable for the administrative action of

municipality may be liable in tort at the operational level or in the exercise of business powers, its legislative activities do not attract tortious liability. As Laskin J. said:[28]

> In exercising such [legislative] authority, a municipality (no less than a provincial Legislature or the Parliament of Canada) may act beyond its powers in the ultimate view of a Court, albeit it acted on the advice of counsel. It would be incredible to say in such circumstances that it owed a duty of care giving rise to liability in damages for its breach. "Invalidity is not the test of fault and it should not be the test of liability": see Davis, 3 *Administrative Law Treatise* (1958), at p. 487.

The policy behind the Supreme Court of Canada's decision in *Welbridge* appears to be that the risk of loss from the exercise of legislative powers is a general public one and that no private duty of care can arise in these circumstances. It should be noted that the immunity applies to negligent legislative action itself, not to negligent actions taken to implement the legislation which are then negligent.[29]

(iv) Public officials acting quasi-judicially

The Supreme Court specifically stated in *Welbridge* that the immunity enjoyed by a public body acting legislatively applied equally to such a body when acting quasi-judicially. Although in *Welbridge* the re-zoning function seems to have been characterized as legislative with a quasi-judicial element, Laskin J. also specifically stated that the immunity applies to a quasi-judicial function taken in isolation.[30]

This principle was applied in the case of *Bowen v. Edmonton*,[31] where the city had authorized a re-plot of land to create smaller residential lots in an existing subdivision. The Provincial Planning Advisory Board had advised the city that soil stability tests were necessary before any subdivision should be approved but no tests were made. The plaintiffs purchased one of the lots after which soil stability tests were done which showed that the land was unstable and unsuitable for building. The city forbade building. The plaintiffs could neither build nor sell. However, their action for damages against the city for negligently authorizing the re-plot failed.

Although the court found that the city had been negligent in failing to have regard to the soil stability tests before authorizing the re-plot, it also

---

its licence inspector in giving negligent advice and issuing a licence for a used car business on land whose zoning forbade such a use. The plaintiff had relied on the advice and the inspector's special knowledge and had suffered loss as a result.

28 *Welbridge Holdings, supra*, note 23 at p. 969.
29 *Ibid.*, p. 970.
30 *Ibid.*, p. 969.
31 [1977] 6 W.W.R. 344 (Alta. T.D.).

found that there was no duty of care owed by the city to the plaintiffs because the city had been acting quasi-judicially. As such, the city was immune from liability. The court found a strong analogy between a zoning function as in *Welbridge*, considered by the Supreme Court to be legislative in nature with a quasi-judicial element, and a subdivision function as in *Bowen*, considered by the Alberta Court of Appeal to be quasi-judicial in nature.

With respect, it is hard to justify this result, and it may be wrong in light of the Supreme Court of Canada's subsequent decision in *Kamloops*.[32] Failure to conduct soil stability tests when their necessity was already known to the city did not require a policy decision to be made nor involve an element of discretion. With the possibility of land instability known to it, the city ought to have had potential purchasers such as the plaintiffs reasonably in mind before allowing the re-plot. If there was an element of discretion involved, the city nevertheless should have been liable because it exercised its discretion so carelessly or unreasonably as to amount to no real exercise of its discretion at all.[33]

In other cases, the courts have similarly allowed an immunity to public bodies exercising purely quasi-judicial functions. In many cases, the argument has centred on whether the function was quasi-judicial and therefore immune, or merely administrative, thus giving rise to a duty of care.[34] In such cases, the classification of the function determined the issue of whether or not a duty of care existed. It did not depend on whether the action was *ultra vires* or not. The conclusion must be that any legislative or quasi-judicial action (now called policy decision-making) is immune; actions which are ministerial or merely administrative (now called operational) are not. The grey area lies in administrative or operational acts which contain an element of discretion. Nevertheless, the English courts in *Dorset Yacht*[35] and *Anns*[36] suggest that a duty of care may arise even in the policy area where the decision is negligently made by a public body acting outside the limits of its discretion. In other words, an *ultra vires* action might remove the usual immunity — even to legislative or quasi-judicial functions.[37] Following *Anns*, Canadian courts are now moving towards the planning/policy versus operational approach.[38]

---

32 *Kamloops v. Nielsen*, [1984] 5 W.W.R. 1 (S.C.C.).

33 This would also have followed the judgment of Lord Reid in *Home Office v. Dorset Yacht Co.*, [1970] 2 All E.R. 294 (H.L.).

34 *E.g., French v. L.S.U.C.*, (1975) 9 O.R. (2d) 473 (C.A.), where the investigative proceedings of the law society preliminary to the institution of disciplinary hearings were held to be quasi-judicial in nature, as were the activities of the secretary of the law society in his initial investigation of the complaint. See also *Partridge v. Gen. Council of Medical Educ. & Registration*, (1890) 25 Q.B.D. 90; *Harris v. Law Soc. of Alta.*, [1936] S.C.R. 88.

35 *Supra*, note 33.

36 [1978] A.C. 728 (H.L.).

37 This approach has been followed in the New Zealand Court of Appeal in *Takaro Properties Ltd. (In Receivership) v. Rowling*, [1978] 2 N.Z.L.R. 314.

38 See *Barratt v. North Vancouver*, [1980] 2 S.C.R. 418, where the manner and frequency of inspection for potholes was held to be within the policy area to be determined in the discretion

(c) Misfeasance in a Public Office

This is not yet a recognized head of liability either in tort law or in Administrative Law. It refers to an *ultra vires* action on the part of a statutory body which does not give rise to an actionable wrong known to tort law but which nevertheless causes injury to someone. For the moment the action cannot be successful without there being present some element of malice or bad faith. On the one hand, it is not clear from the cases whether the presence of malice or bad faith by itself is enough to establish liability, on the basis that malice or bad faith is sufficient to render the action *ultra vires* and that no more is needed to justify compensation for any loss occasioned. On the other hand, it may be that malice or bad faith are just one of many elements necessary to maintain a successful action against a public body for compensation for injury suffered as a result of *ultra vires* action. In any event, where a statutory tribunal acts *ultra vires* but in good faith, it will not in general be held liable for losses suffered as a consequence of its *ultra vires* action, unless those actions otherwise constitute a tort.[39]

The case most often cited in this area is *Roncarelli v. Duplessis*.[40] Roncarelli owned a restaurant in Montreal which had had a liquor licence for many years. He was also a Jehovah's Witness and during a time when many Witnesses were arrested for their religious activities, Roncarelli posted bail for several of them. The liquor commissioner advised Duplessis of this. Duplessis, who was Premier and Attorney General, ordered the commissioner to refuse to renew Roncarelli's liquor licence. Roncarelli suffered considerable economic loss. The relevant legislation gave the commissioner power to grant or cancel licences "at its discretion".

Roncarelli sued in damages for the illegal cancellation of his licence. Duplessis defended by saying that he had acted in good faith and that he had only recommended to the commissioner. However, the Supreme Court of Canada decided otherwise. By a majority decision, the court held that the commissioner had not exercised his discretion in determining to cancel the

---

of the public body; liability would only arise from the negligent operational implementation of the policy. See also *Hugh v. Vancouver*, [1981] 5 W.W.R. 250 (B.C.S.C.), where the frequency of inspecting sidewalks was held to be a policy matter, so that no liability arose for injuries sustained from a dangerous sidewalk. *Cf. Malat v. Bjornson*, [1978] 5 W.W.R. 429, affirmed [1981] 2 W.W.R. 429 (B.C.C.A.), where the decision to replace an 18-inch highway median with a 30-inch one was held to be an operational action, so that a duty of care arose to a user of the highway injured because of the delay in implementing the change; and *Toews v. Mackenzie*, [1980] 4 W.W.R. 108 (B.C.C.A.), where the court held that the decision to issue a temporary day pass to an inmate of a penitentiary was a policy or planning matter, and thus did not give rise to tortious liability where the inmate harmed a third party.

39 See *Harris v. Law Soc. of Alta.*, [1936] S.C.R. 88, where the benchers were exercising a quasi-judicial function and were therefore not liable for the economic harm arising from the disbarment of a member without holding a hearing; *Hlookoff v. Vancouver*, (1968) 63 W.W.R. 129 (B.C.S.C.), where no damages were awarded when the chief licensing inspector suspended the plaintiff's licence as a street vendor (no fraud, collusion or malice having been shown).

40 [1959] S.C.R. 121.

licence but had followed orders. Duplessis should have limited himself to giving advice as to whether any cancellation was valid for any reason or purpose. His action, however, went beyond the scope of his office and turned the act into a personal one. Liability arose, not merely because his action was *ultra vires*, but because his motivation was wrongful and improper. Although the action was discretionary in nature, this necessarily implies good faith in exercising that discretion and it cannot exceed those bounds. In other words, it was an *ultra vires* action maliciously done. It was, in the words of Rand J., "a gross abuse of legal power expressly intended to punish him for an act wholly irrelevant to the statute. . . ."[41] This "malice" means not only spite and ill-will, but also includes the intentional exercise of discretionary authority for an improper purpose. However, caution must be exercised in using this case to establish a new cause of action, because the Supreme Court allowed recovery on the basis of the Quebec Civil Code, which may define the scope of delictual liability more widely than the ambit of torts in common law.

Whereas *Roncarelli* used an excess of jurisdiction as a ground for establishing liability, there are also authorities which deal with a total absence of jurisdiction to found liability. In *McGillivray v. Kimber*,[42] the plaintiff's harbour pilot's licence was forfeited without a hearing being afforded to him. The legislation provided that a licence could be forfeited where it was proven on oath that a holder was incapacitated. The Supreme Court of Canada held that the necessary proof could only be established by sworn testimony at a hearing. Without a hearing the authority acted totally without jurisdiction and was thus liable. The decision does not appear to rest on a finding of malice although there is some indication that the court found some evidence of malice in the authority's action.[43]

3. Injunctions

(a) Nature of Injunctions

Injunctions may be of two kinds: prohibitory and mandatory. Prohibitory injunctions forbid the taking of some illegal act or stop an unlawful action already embarked upon. Mandatory injunctions, which are rarer, require performance of some action (and therefore to a degree resemble an order of *mandamus*). Both are available to restrain unauthorized governmental action even where the action would not give rise to a tort or other actionable wrong.

---

41 *Ibid.*, p. 141.
42 (1915) 52 S.C.R. 146.
43 For other cases in this area, see *Smith v. East Elloe Rural Dist. Council*, [1956] A.C. 736 (H.L.); *David v. Abdul Cader*, [1963] 1 W.L.R. 834 (P.C.); *Farrington v. Thomson*, [1959] V.R. 286 (Vict. S.C.); *Sirros v. Moore*, [1975] Q.B. 118 (C.A.); *MacKenzie v. MacLachlin*, [1979] 1 N.Z.L.R. 670 (S.C.).

Injunctions may be interim in nature, thus preserving the *status quo* until the merits of the action are determined. In an application for an interim injunction, the plaintiff must show a *prima facie* case and that, on the balance of convenience, the interim injunction should be granted rather than requiring the plaintiff to wait for the outcome of the trial at which time he could equally well be compensated in damages. Usually the plaintiff is required to provide an undertaking that he will pay damages to the defendant if it is subsequently proven that the interim injunction should not have been given. Interlocutory injunctions can be granted *ex parte*, for example in cases where either the fact of notice to the defendant or the time taken to give such notice would lead to irreparable harm. Normally, however, the defendant is given an opportunity to challenge the interim injunction within a short period of time and does not have to wait until the time of trial.

Injunctions may also be permanent in nature and then are definitive of rights. They are granted at the end of a trial as a final remedy although they may include a time limitation. For example, they may be granted for a fixed period of time only, or be in effect only until the fulfillment of certain conditions.

Injunctions are an equitable remedy and discretionary in nature. Generally speaking, all the reasons why a court may exercise its discretion to refuse one of the prerogative remedies[44] apply to injunctive relief also.

(b) Procedure

In Alberta, the action is commenced by issuing a statement of claim,[45] and follows the usual course of trial procedure allowing for interlocutory applications and discovery. This procedure can be lengthy and an application for one of the faster prerogative remedies may be more satisfactory. A plaintiff may serve notice that he intends to apply for an interim injunction,[46] and the plaintiff can seek his interim injunction *ex parte* where the court is satisfied that no notice is necessary or where notice might entail serious mischief.[47]

A claim for an injunction cannot be joined with an application for one of the prerogative remedies,[48] and there are other procedural difficulties inherent in the different natures of the prerogative and private law remedies.[49] As a

---

44 See the discussion on this point in chapter 13.
45 Alberta Rules of Court, R. 6(1).
46 *Ibid.*, R. 392(1).
47 *Ibid.*, R. 387(1).
48 *Re Oil etc. Wkrs. Int. Union and Polymer Corp.*, [1966] 1 O.R. 774 (H.C.); *McCarthy v. Bd. of Trustees, Calgary R.C. Sep. Sch. Dist. No. 1*, [1979] 4 W.W.R. 725 (Alta. T.D.).
49 *E.g.*, different time limitation; the fact that private law remedies can be granted against non-statutory or private authorities but prerogative remedies cannot: *Howe Sound Co. v. Int. Union of Mine etc. Wkrs.*, [1962] S.C.R. 318; prerogative remedies may be granted against entities which do not have the capacity to be sued, whereas injunctions and declarations cannot: *Hollinger Bus Lines Ltd. v. Lab. Rel. Bd. (Ont.)*, [1952] O.R. 366 (C.A.).

result, several jurisdictions have reformed their procedures to allow applications for all the prerogative and private law remedies (sometimes with the exception of damages[50]) under one "application for judicial review". These reforms are discussed more fully in chapter 15.

(c) *Locus Standi*

A private person appears to have personal capacity to sue for an injunction in the area of public law: first, where the interference with a public right also interferes with a private right of his own; and, secondly, where he has no private right but has suffered special damage as a result of interference with a public right.[51] However, some authorities suggest that merely suffering special damage is insufficient; the plaintiff must also be able to show an actionable wrong.[52] Certainly, where illegal government action would result in the plaintiff suffering an actionable wrong (such as trespass or breach of contract), he has standing to seek an injunction.

Where the harm done by the unlawful action is suffered by the public generally, then a private individual has no capacity to sue for an injunction to restrain the wrongful action. This is the function of the Attorneys General who have standing to restrain illegal government action over a broad field.[53] In such cases, the Attorney General represents the general public and has in mind the public's interest in ensuring that excesses of statutory authority or breaches of statutory duties are restrained.

(d) Relator Actions

These actions are brought by the Attorney General at the relation of a private individual who agrees to bear the costs and who takes the benefit of the remedy. Usually the relator's counsel conducts the proceedings, although the Attorney General has complete control over the action. The Attorney General's decision to take the case or not is unfettered, and cannot be questioned by the courts.[54]

---

50 Damages may be joined in England, but not in Ontario nor under the proposed Alberta reforms. See chapter 15.
51 *Boyce v. Paddington Corp.*, [1903] 1 Ch. 109, reversed [1903] 2 Ch. 556, which was reversed [1906] A.C. 1 (H.L.); *Halsey v. Esso Petroleum Co.*, [1961] 1 W.L.R. 683 (Q.B.); *Birmingham & Midland Motor Omnibus Co. v. Worcestershire County Council*, [1967] 1 W.L.R. 409 (C.A.). These cases deal with public nuisances, but their reasoning appears to establish generally the guidelines for standing with regard to injunctions.
52 *Stockport Dist. Waterworks Co. v. Manchester Corp.*, (1863) 7 L.T. 545; *Pudsey Coal Gas Co. v. Bradford Corp.*, (1873) L.R. 15 Eq. 167.
53 In most of the reform legislation discussed in chapter 15, specific mention is made of the Attorney General's right to bring or appear on any application for judicial review.
54 *London County Council v. A.G.*, [1902] A.C. 165 (H.L.); *A.G. v. Parish*, [1913] 2 Ch. 444 (C.A.); *A.G. v. Westminster City Council*, [1924] 2 Ch. 416 (C.A.); *Gouriet v. Int. Union of Post Office Wkrs.*, [1978] A.C. 435 (H.L.).

(e) Availability

Proceedings of the Federal Parliament and the provincial legislatures are completely privileged against injunctive proceedings and any other judicial intervention. However, the constitutionality of any Act may be challenged by the special reference procedure, and in this way the courts are able to pronounce on the lawfulness of any parliamentary action, at least insofar as its constitutional validity is concerned.[55]

Delegated legislation may, however, be challenged in the courts in order to determine its legality. A private individual who is adversely affected may bring such proceedings once the delegated legislation is passed. In addition, where there is a defect in the procedure, it might be possible to obtain injunctive relief before final passage of the delegated legislation.

In quasi-judicial proceedings, an injunction is available to stop a statutory tribunal from embarking on or continuing proceedings which are *ultra vires*. It may be, however, that the remedy of prohibition is equally or perhaps more effective, particularly if the statutory tribunal lacks sufficient legal personality to be a defendant in an action at private law.[56]

(f) Crown Immunity

(i) At common law

It is generally thought that an injunction cannot issue against the Crown .at common law. However, in *Carlic v. R.*,[57] the Manitoba Court of Appeal granted an injunction against the Crown and other defendants. The court held that the reason for Crown immunity was based not so much on the notion of the inviolability of the Sovereign as on the practical problem that the order could not be enforced in the face of the Crown's — albeit unlikely — disobedience. Disobedience by the other defendants could, however, be enforced. Commenting on this case, the Law Reform Commission of British Columbia remarks:[58]

> Confronting the Crown with such bold pragmatism is a very refreshing change from the usual obsequious mysticism that surrounds the prerogatives of the Queen, although to give the right to enjoin the Crown without the right to enforce the injunction is not perhaps an act of courage — it is a right without a remedy.

It may be, therefore, that injunctions are available against the Crown at least when there are other defendants.

---

55 *E.g.*, the reference to the Supreme Court of Canada over the constitutionality of the federal government's proposed patriation of the B.N.A. Act (*A.G. Man. v. A.G. Can.; A.G. Can. v. A.G. Nfld.; A.G. Que. v. A.G. Can.; A.G. Can. v. A.G. Que.*, [1981] 1 S.C.R. 753).

56 See the discussion on this point in chapter 13.

57 (1967) 62 W.W.R. 229 (Man. C.A.).

58 Pt. 1 of the *Report on Civil Rights*, "Legal Position of the Crown", (1972), p. 24. See also the reforms proposed in Working Paper 40 of the Law Reform Commission of Canada entitled *The Legal Status of the Federal Administration* (1985).

The law is similarly unclear with regard to the availability of injunctions against Crown agents and servants. Injunctions have been issued in four situations involving Crown agents:

(a) when they were acting in their personal capacity;[59]
(b) when they were acting *ultra vires* their authority even although acting in an official capacity;[60]
(c) when they are acting as "agents of the Legislature", on the basis that they are then agents of Parliament, not agents of the Crown;[61]
(d) when the subject matter of the litigation concerns private, not public, rights.[62]

Frankly, these distinctions are sometimes hard to draw.

(ii) Under legislation

In 1947, the English Crown Proceedings Act expressly prohibited the granting of injunctions against the Crown.[63] Most Canadian provinces subsequently followed this model.[64] In these provinces, injunctive relief is replaced by an order delcaring the rights of the parties. In general, a declaration may be almost as effective as an injunction, although one disadvantage is that no interim relief can be granted by way of a declaration.[65]

4. Declarations

(a) Nature of Declarations

Declarations are pronouncements by the court on an issue of law. The suit is usually brought by a private litigant against a statutory delegate, although the Attorney General may also seek a declaration on a point of public interest. The Attorney General may also lend his name to a private

---

59 *Nat. Harbours Bd. v. Langelier*, (1968) 2 D.L.R. (3d) 81 (S.C.C.).
60 *Rattenbury v. Land Settlement Bd.*, [1929] S.C.R. 52, on the basis that a Crown officer acting illegally is not really a Crown officer and therefore is subject to liability in his personal capacity.
61 *Min. of Fin. (B.C.) v. R.*, [1935] S.C.R. 278; *C.P.R. v. A.G. Sask.*, (1951) 1 W.W.R. 193, reversed in part on other grounds (1951) 2 W.W.R. 424, restored [1952] 2 S.C.R. 231; *Duplain v. Cameron*, (1960) 33 W.W.R. 38 (Sask. Q.B.); *Taal v. Sask. Medical Care Ins. Comm.*, (1962) 40 W.W.R. 8 (Sask. Q.B.).
62 *Baton Broadcasting Ltd. v. CBC*, [1966] 2 O.R. 169 at 176, 179 (H.C.).
63 10 & 11 Geo. 6 c. 44, s. 21.
64 R.S.N.S. 1967, c. 239, s. 15; R.S.N.B. 1952, c. 176, s. 14 [now R.S.N.B. 1973, c. P-18, s. 15]; S.Q. 1965, c. 80 [now R.S.Q. 1977, c. C-25], ss. 94, 100 [both am. 1966, c. 21, s. 5]; R.S.O. 1970, c. 365, s. 18 [now R.S.O. 1980, c. 393, s. 18]; C.C.S.M., c. P140, s. 17; R.S.S. 1965, c. 87, s. 17 [now R.S.S. 1978, c. P-2, s. 17], R.S.A. 1980, c. P-18, s. 17. There is no such prohibition in British Columbia or in federal legislation. See generally, C.H.H. McNairn, *Governmental and Inter-governmental Immunity* (U. of Toronto Press, 1977).
65 *Int. Gen. Elec. Co. v. Customs and Excise Commr.*, [1962] Ch. 784 (C.A.).

person in a relator action where that person would otherwise not have standing to sue. Some statutory delegates may also have standing to sue in their own name.[66]

A declaration declares the rights as between the parties to litigation but grants no consequential relief. As a result, there is no penalty which can be imposed on a defendant who fails to act on the declaration. Generally speaking, however, it is unheard of for a statutory delegate to ignore the court's pronouncement concerning a matter before it. Declarations may be granted where real, but not fictitious or academic, issues are raised.[67] A declaration may be granted about future rights,[68] but not about hypothetical future events.[69] Declarations are sometimes considered to be a form of equitable relief, but Wade points out that declarations originated in England with the rules of court of 1883, so that they should be considered a statutory remedy.[70]

Declarations are widely used in Administrative Law to establish whether a statutory tribunal is acting within its jurisdiction or has exceeded it. If the applicant obtains a declaration that the tribunal is acting *ultra vires*, then in the face of such continued illegal action by the tribunal, he may seek to restrain the tribunal by other remedies or he may safely refuse to comply with its illegal decision. A declaration can be obtained against the Crown,[71] which makes it extremely useful in an area where the Crown is generally immune. One of its disadvantages is that no interim declaratory relief can be obtained,[72] nor can it quash a decision.[73]

The leading case on declarations in Administrative Law is *Dyson v. Attorney General*.[74] The Commissioners of Inland Revenue were authorized to obtain information from owners of land to enable the commissioners to value land which was newly subject to tax. One of their demands from landowners was a statement of the annual value of the land. This was not authorized by the Act. Dyson sought and obtained a declaration against the Attorney General that this demand was *ultra vires* and therefore ineffective.

Dyson's case established a number of important principles. First, it is appropriate to seek such a remedy as an offensive response against illegal

---

66 *E.g.*, municipal corporations.
67 *Russian Commercial & Indust. Bank v. British Bank for Foreign Trade Ltd.*, [1921] 2 A.C. 438 (H.L.).
68 *Solosky v. Can.*, [1980] 1 S.C.R. 821.
69 *Mellstrom v. Garner*, [1970] 1 W.L.R. 603 (C.A.).
70 *Administrative Law*, 5th ed. (Oxford: Clarendon Press, 1982), p. 523. Declarations had previously been granted, however, in connection with petitions of right and in the Court of Exchequer. Power was given to the Court of Chancery to make declarations of right in Acts in 1850 and 1852, but the power was narrowly interpreted.
71 Unlike an injunction.
72 But many of the reforms referred to in chapter 15 will permit interim declarations.
73 *Punton v. Min. of Pensions and Nat. Ins. (No. 2)*, [1964] 1 W.L.R. 226 (C.A.); *cf. Pyx Granite Co. v. Min. of Housing and Loc. Gov.*, [1960] A.C. 260 (H.L.).
74 [1911] 1 K.B. 410 (C.A.) and [1912] 1 Ch. 158 (C.A.).

action. The Court of Appeal found that a declaration was "the most convenient method of enabling the subject to test the justifiability of proceedings on the part of permanent officials purporting to act under statutory provisions".[75] Secondly, there is no need for an applicant to wait until he is sued for failure to comply with an administrative order before bringing any action. Thirdly, it is an example of a situation where the applicant had no other cause of action available to him which would have established the validity or otherwise of the commissioners' demand.

(b) Procedure

Under the Alberta Rules of Court, there are two ways to apply for a declaration.

First, proceedings may be commenced under Rule 410 by originating notice in certain circumstances.[76] This is a chambers application, which has the advantage of speed but has the disadvantage of no pre-trial discovery. Evidence is led by way of affidavits, although the court may permit oral evidence.[77]

Secondly, a regular action may be commenced by way of statement of claim which allows all the usual interlocutory steps leading to trial, but this process can take a long time before a final determination is reached.

A declaration on its own may not be enough. If the applicant wishes to quash a decision of a tribunal or if he wishes to stop a tribunal from proceeding, a declaration will not help him.[78] *Certiorari* or prohibition is required and these must be the subject of a separate application. However, a declaration has the procedural advantage that there is no time limitation within which the action must be brought, unlike *certiorari* and prohibition, and does allow for the discovery of documents which may bring facts to light not previously within the knowledge of the applicant.

(c) *Locus Standi*

The applicant must have a private legal right in issue which directly affects him in order to have standing. He does not, however, have to have some other independent cause of action. Merely wishing to inquire as to the state of the law generally is not enough; such questions of general interest must be left to action by the Attorney General,[79] either acting on his own motion or lending his name and standing to a private person in a relator action. Where the applicant is one of several people whose legal rights are affected, he may

---

75 [1911] Ch. 158 at 168, per Fletcher Moulton L.J.
76 R. 410(*d*) and (*e*).
77 R. 407.
78 *Supra*, note 73.
79 *Gouriet v. Int. Union of Post Office Wkrs.*, [1978] A.C. 435 (H.L.).

still bring the application individually.[80] This allows a challenge to legislation which affects more than one person in its scope. Even legislation of broad applicability may be challenged in certain circumstances. For example, in *Thorson v. Attorney General of Canada (No. 2)*,[81] the Supreme Court of Canada gave standing to Thorson to challenge the validity of the Official Languages Act[82] in his capacity as a taxpayer. Laskin C.J.C. held that where the issue was justiciable and where the nature of the legislation was such that all members of the public (and not just particular persons or classes of persons) were similarly affected, then standing could be given to such an applicant, in the court's discretion. One reason to exercise this discretion favourably was the lack of any other way to test the validity of the legislation in court. Interestingly, the Attorney General had refused to permit Thorson to bring a relator action.

(d) Relator Actions

The problem of standing can be solved by the use of the relator action. This is an action for a declaration or an injunction or both brought in the name of the Attorney General at the relation of an individual. It allows a private individual to have standing in a matter of general public interest where standing would otherwise be denied to him because no personal legal right of his was affected. The courts cannot inquire into why the Attorney General has lent his name in any given case,[83] nor why he has refused.[84] It is a matter entirely within his discretion. However, where the Attorney General has refused to lend his name in a matter where the applicant cannot demonstrate a personal legal right, the courts have sometimes asserted their discretion to give standing to a private individual because otherwise allegedly illegal governmental action would go unchecked.[85] In such cases, the discretion of the court to refuse standing is sufficient to prevent a proliferation of unworthy actions.

Having lent his name, the Attorney General then leaves the carriage of the proceedings to the relator, who is responsible for costs and for all other aspects of the litigation as if it were a private suit.

(e) Availability

A declaration is a discretionary remedy. However, the considerations which might lead a court to refuse an equitable remedy are not always applied

---

80 *Dyson, supra*, note 74; *Gouriet, ibid.*; *MacNeil v. N.S. Bd. of Censors*, [1976] 2 S.C.R. 265.

81 (1974) 43 D.L.R. (3d) 1 (S.C.C.).

82 R.S.C. 1970, c. O-2.

83 *London County Council v. A.G.*, [1902] A.C. 165 (H.L.).

84 *A.G. ex rel. McWhirter v. Independent Broadcasting Authority*, [1973] Q.B. 629 (C.A.); *Gouriet, supra*, note 79. The House of Lords' latest pronouncement on standing can be found in *R. v. Inland Revenue Comrs.; Ex parte National Federation of Self-Employed and Small Businesses Ltd.*, [1982] A.C. 617.

85 *Thorson v. A.G. Can. (No. 2), supra*, note 81.

to declarations. Questions of *locus standi* will affect their availability, as will the availability of adequate alternative remedies.[86]

A further limitation on the availability of a declaration appears in the decision of the English Court of Appeal in *Punton v. Ministry of Pensions and National Insurance (No. 2)*,[87] where the court held that it had no jurisdiction to issue a declaration to correct an intra-jurisdictional error of law on the face of the record. By contrast, a declaration is available to correct an excess of jurisdiction (including breaches of the principles of natural justice).[88]

(f) Crown Liability

In contrast to the general rule, declarations are available against the Crown. This has been accepted since *Dyson*'s case and has been applied in Canada.[89] Presumably the reason is that since no consequential relief can be granted, the Crown cannot be held in contempt of court for failure to obey, nor can its property be sequestrated.

A problem may arise as to the identity of the proper defendant when a statutory body is not granted sufficient legal personality to be sued in its own right.[90] Thus, in *B. v. Department of Manpower and Immigration Commission of Inquiry*,[91] the Federal Court held that a declaration is not available against a federal board or tribunal unless its enabling legislation expressly states it to be a suable entity. Therefore, such a delegate cannot be touched by a declaratory judgment (although it may be amenable to *certiorari* or prohibition). The proper course of action in such a case is to name either the Crown or the Attorney General acting on behalf of the Crown as the defendant.

A different approach to this problem was taken in *Klymchuk v. Cowan*,[92] where the court granted declaratory relief on the basis that there was no other adequate remedy available, without considering the legal status of the defendant.

Of course, when the delegate is stated to be a suable entity, it is the proper defendant.

5. Conclusion

This chapter indicates the general areas in which private law remedies may be used to redress illegal governmental action. These private law

---

86 See the discussion on the effect of alternative remedies in chapter 12.

87 *Supra*, note 73.

88 *Anisminic Ltd. v. Foreign Compensation Comm.*, [1969] 2 A.C. 147 (H.L.); *Fullbrook v. Berkshire Magistrates' Courts Committee*, (1970) 69 L.G.R. 75; and the recent decision of the Supreme Court of Canada in *Blanchard v. Control Data Canada Ltd.*, [1984] 2 S.C.R. 476.

89 *Greenlees v. A.G. Can.*, [1946] S.C.R. 462; *Great West Life Assur. Co. v. Baptiste*, [1924] 2 W.W.R. 920 (Alta. C.A.); and see the reforms proposed in Working Paper 40 of the Law Reform Commission of Canada entitled *The Legal Status of the Federal Administration* (1985).

90 See the discussion on this problem in chapter 13.

91 (1975) 60 D.L.R. (3d) 339 (Fed. T.D.).

92 (1964) 47 W.W.R. 467 (Man. Q.B.).

remedies may in some circumstances overlap the prerogative remedies, but in other circumstances they supplement each other. Thus, declarations and all of the prerogative remedies are extremely useful to settle disputes about the legality of governmental action. Although declarations apply to a much wider range of governmental activity, the inability of declarations to quash illegal actions may make them less effective in some cases than an order of *certiorari*. On the other hand, the interlocutory proceedings available with an action for a declaration may make it more productive than a prerogative remedy in discovering precisely how the statutory delegate made an error. Similarly, an injunction may be used interchangeably with an application for prohibition in some circumstances, and a mandatory injunction may do the work of a *mandamus*. Nevertheless, the usefulness of injunctions in administrative law is both wider and narrower than the availability of these two prerogative remedies. On the one hand, injunctions bring with them all interlocutory proceedings, and there is the possibility of an interim injunction to preserve the *status quo* pending determination of the final outcome of the litigation. On the other hand, injunctions are not available against the Crown. Damages have no clear analogue in the prerogative remedies, and in some ways provide a real way to recompense a citizen aggrieved of wrongful governmental action. However, not all illegal governmental actions constitute torts (particularly if the Crown is involved), and therefore it may be necessary to resort to other remedies in order to determine the rights of the parties.

Because the private law and prerogative remedies are not always interchangeable, differ so considerably from each other, and involve incompatible procedures, the choice of remedy is a matter requiring considerable care. Chapter 15 examines a number of recent and proposed reforms to minimize the pitfalls arising from these procedural difficulties.

6. Selected Bibliography

Bridge, M.G., "Governmental Liability, The Tort of Negligence and The House of Lords' Decision in *Anns v. Merton London Borough Council*", (1978) 24 McGill L.J. 277.

Buckley, R.A., "Liability in Tort for Breach of Statutory Duty", (1984) 100 L.Q. Rev. 204.

Craig, P.P., "Negligence in the Exercise of Statutory Power", (1978) 94 L.Q. Rev. 428.

Dussault, R., and Carrier, D., "Le contrat administratif en droit canadien et quebecois", (1970) 48 Can. Bar Rev. 439.

English Law Commission, *Report No. 73*, on "Remedies in Administrative Law", 1976, Cmnd. 6407.

English Law Commission, Working Paper No. 40, *Remedies in Administrative Law* (1971).

Ganz, G., "Compensation for Negligent Administrative Action", [1973] P.L. 85.

Gould, B.C., "Damages as a Remedy in Administrative Law", (1972-73) 5 N.Z.U.L. Rev. 105.

Harlow, C., *Compensation and Government Torts* (London: Sweet & Maxwell, 1982).

Hogg, P., *Liability of the Crown* (Sydney: The Law Book Co., 1971).

Jamieson, D.P., "Proceedings By and Against the Crown in Canada", (1948) 26 Can. Bar Rev. 373.

Kennedy, W.P.M., "Suits by and Against the Crown", (1928) 6 Can. Bar Rev. 387.

Laskin, B., "Crown Companies and Civil Liability", (1944) 22 Can. Bar Rev. 927.

Law, J.M., "Damages in Administrative Law — An Old Remedy with New Potential", prepared for the Administrative Law Seminar jointly sponsored by the Faculty of Law at the University of Alberta and the Legal Education Society of Alberta, March 1984.

Law Reform Commission of British Columbia, *Report on Civil Rights, Part I*, "Legal Position of the Crown", 1972.

Law Reform Commission of Canada, *The Legal Status of the Federal Administration*, Working Paper No. 40 (1985).

Linden, A.M., "Public Law and Private Law: The Frontier from the Perspective of a Tort Teacher", (1976) 17 Cahiers de Droit 865.

McBridge, J., "Damages as a Remedy for Unlawful Administrative Action", (1979) 38 C.L.J. 323.

Molot, H.L., "Administrative Bodies, Economic Loss, and Tortious Liability", ch. 12 in *Studies in Canadian Business Law*, (Toronto: Butterworths).

Moore, W.H., "Misfeasance and Nonfeasance in the Liability of Public Authorities", (1914) 30 L.Q. Rev. 415.

Mueller, W.H.O., "The Liability of the Ontario Government in Tort", (1967) 25 U.T. Fac. L. Rev. 3.

Mullan, D.J., "The Declaratory Judgment: Its Place as an Administrative Law Remedy in Nova Scotia", (1975) 2 Dalhousie L.J. 91.

Phegan, C.S., "Damages for Improper Exercise of Statutory Powers", (1980) 9 Sydney L. Rev. 93.

Rubinstein, A., "Liability in Tort of Judicial Officers", (1963-64) U.T.L.J. 317.

Slutsky, B., "The Liability of Public Authorities for Negligence: Recent Canadian Developments", (1973) 36 Mod. L. Rev. 656.

Smith, A., "Liability to Suit of an Agent of the Crown", (1950) U.T.L.J. 218.

Strayer, B., "Injunctions Against Crown Officers", (1964) 42 Can. Bar Rev. 1.

Warren, D.T., "The Declaratory Judgment: Reviewing Administrative Action", (1966) 44 Can. Bar Rev. 610.

Williams, Glanville, *Crown Proceedings Act, 1947*, (1948).

Zamir, A., *The Declaratory Judgment*, (1962).

15

Recent and Proposed Procedural Reforms

1. Problems with the Present Remedies

There have been numerous proposals and attempts in recent years to rationalize the procedural aspects of judicial review of administrative action. In addition, there have been attempts to codify the substantive grounds for judicial review. The purpose of this chapter is to identify the defects in the present prerogative and private law remedies against illegal governmental action, and to outline the reforms which have been implemented in some jurisdictions — with particular reference to those proposed in Alberta by the Institute of Law Research and Reform.

The Institute of Law Research and Reform has identified[1] two principal defects in the existing prerogative and private law remedies against illegal governmental action. First, different rules govern the availability of different

---

1 *Judicial Review of Administrative Action: Application for Judicial Review* (Report No. 40, March 1984).

remedies, so that there are differences with respect to standing to commence proceedings, the time within which different remedies must be commenced, and the grounds which must be proved in order to obtain the different remedies. Although more than one remedy may be available in certain circumstances, the existing remedies are not completely fungible and care must frequently be taken to choose the correct one. Secondly, an application for one or more prerogative remedies cannot be joined with an action at private law.[2]

The institute gives the following examples of difficulties caused by differences in the legal rules applicable to the various remedies:[3]

(a) Courts sometimes hold that a claimant who could have obtained a prerogative remedy cannot obtain a private law remedy.[4] For example, a court might hold that a claimant who could have obtained an order for *certiorari* cannot obtain a declaration that the decision is invalid.

(b) A declaration is often an alternative to *certiorari*, but covers a much wider range of acts of public authorities. Previously, *certiorari* was thought to apply only to decisions which were similar enough to those made by courts to be characterized as "judicial" or "quasi-judicial,"[5] but it now applies to merely administrative or ministerial decisions to enforce compliance with the duty to be fair.[6] Similarly, an injunction is also an alternative to prohibition, but covers a much wider range of acts of public authorities.

(c) A declaration or injunction may be granted against a private authority or non-statutory authority such as the executive of a club or a trade union, but a prerogative remedy will not be granted against such a body.[7]

(d) The prerogative remedies may be granted against entities which do not have the capacity to be sued, whereas declarations and injunctions may not.[8]

(e) The prerogative remedies are rarely available against the Crown,[9] and an

---

2 *Re Oil, etc. Wkrs. Int. Union and Polymer Corp.*, [1966] 1 O.R. 774 (H.C.); and see also *McCarthy v. Calgary R.C. Sep. Sch. Dist. No. 1 Bd. of Trustees*, [1979] 4 W.W.R. 725 at 730 (Alta. T.D.).

3 *Supra*, note 1 at pp. 24*ff.*; see also Report No. 18 of the British Columbia Law Reform Commission, *A Procedure for Judicial Review of the Actions of Statutory Agencies*, 1974, pp. 24-25; and Report No. 79 of the English Law Commission, *Report on Remedies in Administrative Law*, Cmnd. 6407, 1976, pp. 15-16.

4 *Hollinger Bus Lines Ltd. v. Lab. Rel. Bd. (Ont.)*, [1952] O.R. 366 (C.A.), but *cf. Driver Salesmen etc. Union Loc. 987 v. Bd. of Indust. Rel. (Alta.)*, (1967) 61 W.W.R. 484 (Alta. T.D.).

5 *Calgary Power v. Copithorne*, [1959] S.C.R. 24.

6 *Martineau v. Matsqui Inst. Disciplinary Bd. (No. 2)*, [1980] 1 S.C.R. 602.

7 *Howe Sound Co. v. Int. Union of Mine etc. Wkrs.*, [1962] S.C.R. 318.

8 *Hollinger Bus Lines v. Lab. Rel. Bd. (Ont.)*, *supra*, note 4; *Westlake v. R.*, [1971] 3 O.R. 533, affirmed [1972] 2 O.R. 605, which was affirmed [1973] S.C.R. vii.

9 See *Gooliah (Goolia) v. R.*, (1967) 59 W.W.R. 705 (Man. C.A.); *Border Cities Press Club v. A. G. Ont.*, [1955] O.R. 14 (C.A.).

injunction is not available at all.[10] A declaration is the only effective remedy,[11] and in an action for a declaration against the Crown there is no interim remedy to preserve the situation until the final decision is made.

(f) Declarations and injunctions are obtained in ordinary civil actions in which a range of interlocutory procedures are available to assist the claimant; for example, examinations for discovery, production of documents, and interim injunctions preserve the situation until the final decision is made. Prerogative remedies are more summary in nature and the interlocutory procedures are not readily available.

(g) Damages may be obtained in conjunction with private law relief but not with a prerogative remedy.

(h) An order of *certiorari* quashes a decision and renders it ineffective. A declaration merely states the legal position that the decision is unauthorized or otherwise invalid; it does not quash the decision, nor does it order or prohibit any action.[12]

(i) A notice of motion for *certiorari* must be brought within six months from the date of the decision impugned. A declaration may be sought within no fixed limit of time, although an unreasonable delay may operate as a discretionary bar.

(j) Historically, any member of the public could apply for and, in the discretion of the court, be granted prerogative relief.[13] The extent of the connection with the proceedings which is required of the applicant for non-prerogative relief is uncertain.

A number of reforms to administrative law have been implemented in various Commonwealth jurisdictions over the past few years. Some of these reforms are procedural in nature, while others attempt to codify substantive grounds for judicial review of unlawful administrative action.

2. The Ontario Model

Ontario pioneered the reforms in administrative law by enacting two pieces of legislation in 1971 to implement the recommendations of the McRuer Commission's *Inquiry into Civil Rights*:[14] (a) the Statutory Powers Procedure Act,[15] which attempts to codify the procedure to be used by

---

10 But see Part 1 of the B.C. Law Reform Commission's Report on Civil Rights entitled "Legal Position of the Crown", 1972, which recommends that the Crown should be subject to injunctive relief.

11 Proceedings Against the Crown Act, R.S.A. 1980, c. P-18, s. 17.

12 See *Punton v. Min. of Pensions & Nat. Ins. (No. 2)*, [1964] 1 W.L.R. 226 (C.A.); *cf. Pyx Granite Co. Ltd. v. Min. of Housing and Loc. Govt.*, [1960] A.C. 260 (H.L.).

13 See *Martineau (No. 2), supra*, note 6 at p. 619, per Dickson J.

14 The "McRuer Report".

15 S.O. 1971, c. 47 [now R.S.O. 1980, c. 484].

statutory delegates in the exercise of their "statutory powers";[16] and (b) the Judicial Review Procedure Act,[17] which in effect amalgamates the prerogative and private law remedies against illegal governmental action into one procedure called an "application for judicial review" to a three-member Divisional Court of the Ontario High Court.[18] An appeal lies to the Court of Appeal, and then (with leave) to the Supreme Court of Canada.

The Judicial Review Procedure Act does not, in terms, abolish the old prerogative remedies, but rather states[19] that *certiorari*, prohibition and *mandamus* shall be treated as "applications for judicial review". Thus, *habeas corpus* is not brought under the new regime.[20] Similarly, the Act does not abolish the availability of declarations or injunctions with respect to the exercise of statutory powers, but allows[21] a judge of the High Court to order such actions to be treated as "applications for judicial review" instead. This leaves open the possibility of an application for a declaration or an injunction continuing to proceed as an action under the old common law form where it would be more convenient to do so, for example, where an interlocutory proceeding such as discoveries are desirable, or where these remedies are coupled with an action for damages.[22] The Act does not permit the court to award damages in the context of an "application for judicial review". On the other hand, interim relief can be granted in an "application for judicial review". This is a marked change from the situation with respect to the old prerogative remedies, which could only be issued in a final form. However, the Act does not bind the Crown, so this provision probably does not permit an interim injunction or similar declaratory order against the Crown. The Act does, however,[23] grant the court power to use a declaration to quash an impugned decision — which at common law was one of the defects of a declaration as opposed to *certiorari*.[24] The court is also given power to use any remedy (and not just *certiorari*) to correct an error of law on the face of the record. This includes the power to review both the existence and the adequacy

---

16 See the definition in s. 1(1)(*d*) of the Ontario Act, *ibid.*, and the Alberta Institute of Law Research and Reform's comments, *Judicial Review of Administrative Action: Application for Judicial Review.* (Report No. 40, March 1984), on the problems raised by such a definition.
17 S.O. 1971, c. 48 [now R.S.O. 1980, c. 224].
18 Note, however, that s. 6 grants the judge discretion to permit the application to proceed before a single judge instead of going to the Divisional Court.
19 Section 7.
20 See s. 12(2); compare the Alberta proposal (discussed, *infra*) to permit *habeas corpus* to be obtained either under the present procedure or under the "application for judicial review".
21 Section 8.
22 It may be that s. 8 would permit damages in certain circumstances, but not generally.
23 Section 2(4).
24 See *Punton v. Min. of Pensions & Nat. Ins. (No. 2)*, [1964] 1 W.L.R. 226 (C.A.); *cf. Pyx Granite Co. Ltd. v. Min. of Housing and Loc. Govt.*, [1960] A.C. 260 (H.L.).

of the evidence upon which the statutory delegate has acted.[25] However, the Act unfortunately maintains the effectiveness of privative clauses.[26]

The Ontario model has been followed in New Zealand,[27] which had previously created a specialized administrative law division of its courts, and in British Columbia.[28]

3. The English Reforms

The English reforms took place in two steps, with results that both resemble and differ from the Ontario model. The first step took place in 1977 by amendments to Order 53 of the Rules of the Supreme Court, which incorporated many of the recommendations of the Law Commission's 1976 *Report on Remedies in Administrative Law*.[29] The amendments created a new "application for judicial review", and provided that all applications for *certiorari*, prohibition and *mandamus* should be made using the new procedure. It also provided that declarations and injunctions in the administrative law context should be brought by the same new procedure.[30] The revised rule went much further than the Ontario model by expressly permitting a claim for damages to be joined with an "application for review" and provided for discoveries and cross-examinations of applications.

On the other hand, the revised English rule required an applicant for judicial review to obtain leave of the court on an *ex parte* basis[31] before proceeding with the application. The court was required to determine at the outset whether the applicant had "a sufficient interest in the matter to which the application relates" in order to grant leave, which had the effect of making the rules on standing uniform for all forms of judicial review. The rule also provided that the granting of leave operated as a stay of the impugned administrative decision, unless the court directed otherwise. Unlike the three-member Divisional Court instituted in Ontario, however, the revised English rule left each step to a single judge. The new rule also required the applicant to apply for judicial review "promptly", which the courts implied to mean at least within three months from the date on which grounds for judicial review

---

25 Section 2(3).

26 Section 2(2).

27 Judicature Amendment Act, 1972, amended by the Judicature Amendment Act, 1977. With respect to the Administrative Division of the Supreme Court, see Judicature Amendment Act, 1968.

28 Judicial Review Procedure Act, S.B.C. 1976, c. 25 [now R.S.B.C. 1979, c. 209].

29 Report No. 79, Cmnd. 6407. Nova Scotia had previously implemented a general "application for judicial review" by amending its rules of court in 1972.

30 Thus not making the new procedure available for all declaratory or injunctive relief against defendants who just happen to be public authorities.

31 There is a recent proposal to abolish the right to appeal to the Court of Appeal against the refusal of leave to proceed with an "application for judicial review": see Patrick Browne's letter to *The Times*, 30th January 1985.

arose, although the court was given discretion to extend this three-month limitation period in appropriate circumstances.[32]

In order to quell doubts about the authority to enact such sweeping changes by a mere amendment to the rules of court, many aspects of the revised rule were incorporated into statutory form in the Supreme Court Act 1981.[33] The Act retains the requirement that an applicant obtain leave of the court *ex parte* to proceed with the application for judicial review, and it reiterates that the requirement of "a sufficient interest" shall be determined at the leave stage.[34] Unfortunately, the wording of the Act has created doubt whether an applicant must proceed by way of an "application for judicial review" in the nature of a declaration or an injunction, or has the alternative of starting a private law action for the normal form of these remedies.[35] Further, the Act states that the court may refuse either leave or final relief where there has been undue delay in bringing the application, if it considers that granting the relief would cause substantial hardship to (or substantially prejudice the rights of) any person, or would be detrimental to good administration.[36]

One of the questionable effects of the reforms based on the Ontario model has been the development of the distinction between "public law" and "private law", and the concomitant need to choose between the "applications for judicial review" which govern public law matters and the normal forms of action which govern private law matters. A similar problem, of course, has been created in Ontario, New Zealand and British Columbia because all of their reform Acts contain definitions of those "statutory powers"[37] with respect to which the unified procedure is available.

4. The Federal Court Act

In some ways, the reforms to federal administrative practice in Canada were far more extensive than the Ontario model.

First, almost all aspects of judicial review of most federal administrative actions were transferred from the provincial superior courts to the newly created Federal Court.[38]

---

32 Unlike the current six month limitation on *certiorari* in Alberta.

33 (Eng.), c. 54.

34 The most recent English statement on the law of standing is contained in *R. v. Inland Revenue Commr.; Ex parte Nat. Fed. of Self-Employed and Small Business Ltd.*, [1982] A.C. 617.

35 *O'Reilly v. Mackman: Millbanks v. Secretary of State for Home Dept.*, [1983] A.C. 120 (H.L.), but *cf. Wandsworth London Borough Council v. Winder*, [1984] 3 All E.R. 83 (C.A.).

36 Although there may be differing views of what constitutes "good administration".

37 See the definition in s. 1(1)(d) of the Ontario Act, *ibid.*, and the Alberta Institute of Law Research and Reform's comments, *Judicial Review of Administrative Action: Application for Judicial Review* (Report No. 40, March 1984) on the problems raised by such a definition.

38 See s. 18 of the Federal Court Act, R.S.C. 1970, c. 10 (2nd Supp.). Note that *habeas corpus* was not transferred from the provincial superior courts to the Federal Court: *Mitchell v. R.*, [1976] 2 S.C.R. 570.

Secondly, section 28 of the Federal Court Act permits (and requires) an "application to review" in the Federal Court of Appeal against "a decision or order . . . required by law to be made on a judicial or quasi-judicial basis, made by or in the course of proceedings before a federal board, commission or other tribunal . . .". This resembles the Ontario "application for judicial review" in some respects, because there is a unified procedure taken to a three-member court. However, an appeal lies from the Ontario Divisional Court to the Court of Appeal and then to the Supreme Court of Canada (with leave) in the normal way; but an appeal from a decision of the Federal Court of Appeal on an "application for judicial review" only lies to the Supreme Court of Canada (with leave). Further, the Ontario procedure is not restricted to judicial or quasi-judicial decisions, and this restriction in section 28 of the federal Act has created confusion in determining whether to apply for judicial review in the Court of Appeal or to apply for one of the nominate prerogative remedies or a declaration in the Trial Division — particularly in light of the subsequent judicial extension of the principles of natural justice in circumstances which cannot be characterized as being judicial or quasi-judicial in nature.[39]

Thirdly, section 28 of the Federal Court Act specifically enumerates the grounds for granting an "application for judicial review" against judicial or quasi-judicial decisions. This list in some respects probably extends the grounds previously known to common law. The statutory grounds are that the federal board, commission or tribunal:

(a) failed to observe a principle of natural justice or otherwise acted beyond or refused to exercise its jurisdiction;
(b) erred in law in making its decision or order, whether or not the error appears on the face of the record;[40] or
(c) based its decision or order on an erroneous finding of fact that it made in a perverse or capricious manner or without regard for the material before it.

Fourthly, unlike the English reforms, however, there is no provision to join an action for damages either with the federal unified "application for judicial review" under section 28, or with the prerogative remedies or declaratory relief under section 18. On the contrary, section 17 of the Act treats damage actions against the federal Crown[41] quite separately from other aspects of judicial review of administrative action.

Fifthly, there is no provision for discoveries or cross-examination under either section 18 or 28 of the Federal Court Act — again unlike the situation under the English reforms.

---

39 See *Martineau v. Matsqui Inst. Disiplinary Bd. (No. 2)*, [1980] 1 S.C.R. 602.
40 Not only does this provision extend the concept of reviewing intra-jurisdictional errors beyond those which appear on the face of the record, it arguably requires the court to correct all errors of law, whether "patently unreasonable" or not. See chapters 10 and 12 for further elaboration on this point.
41 As opposed to all other federal emanations?

Sixthly — and perhaps most importantly in the Canadian context — section 28 of the Federal Court Act operates "notwithstanding . . . the provisions of any other Act" which has the effect of nullifying almost all privative clauses at the federal level.[42] This is in stark contrast to the Ontario model, which specifically recognizes and preserves the effect of privative clauses.[43]

5. The Proposed Reforms in Alberta

In 1984, the Alberta Institute of Law Research and Reform proposed a number of reforms to streamline and rationalize the remedies in administrative law.[44] Although these proposals have not yet been implemented, it is useful to consider the proposed changes and how they are to be achieved.

In the first place, the institute contemplates amendments to the Rules of Court (as Nova Scotia did in 1972), and not an Act of the legislature. This necessarily contemplates purely procedural reforms (which would be within the powers of the Rules Committee to make under the powers delegated to it), leaving reforms to substantive areas of Administrative Law to a later date.

Secondly, the Alberta proposals would follow the generally accepted model of creating a new "application for judicial review". The new procedure would lie to a single judge sitting in chambers in the Court of Queen's Bench, following the English model, and not following the Ontario or federal model of a three-member court. The new remedy would be instituted by an originating notice of motion (like the procedure now used for a declaratory order under Rule 410), instead of by the simple notice of motion now required for a prerogative remedy. Although this procedural change would theoretically have the effect of lengthening the period between service of the notice and the date of the hearing in court, a judge in appropriate circumstances can dispense with all or any part of the ten-day notice. In any event, the general practice now in Alberta is to schedule applications for judicial review at a special hearing of the court in chambers at some relatively remote point in time, because very few cases have to be dealt with on an extremely urgent basis. The institute also proposes to correct a number of Alberta cases which imply that the affidavit supporting an application for a prerogative remedy must be made on personal knowledge:[45] affidavits on information and belief are specifically stated to be appropriate and admissible.[46]

---

42 See *Howarth v. Nat. Parole Bd.*, [1976] 1 S.C.R. 453 at 475; and *A.G. Can. v. Pub. Service Staff Rel. Bd.*, [1977] 2 F.C. 663 (C.A.).

43 Thus, the federal position is similar to that in England after the Tribunals and Inquiries Act 1958 (6 & 7 Eliz. 2, c. 66).

44 *Supra*, note 37.

45 See *R. in Right of Alta. v. Beaver*, [1982] 4 W.W.R. 344, reversed on another point [1984] 4 W.W.R. 371 (Alta. C.A.); *Edmonton v. Riemer*, (1979) 10 Alta. L.R. (2d) 92 (Dist. Ct.), criticized in chapter 13 at note 5.

46 *Supra*, note 44 at pp. 71-72.

Thirdly, the proposed Alberta "application for judicial review" would be available for applications in the nature of the present *habeas corpus*, even though the present prerogative remedy of *habeas corpus* would not be abolished. This differs from the situation in Ontario, British Columbia, and under the Federal Court Act, but it has the clear advantage of preventing an applicant from making a mistake by choosing the wrong remedy.

Fourthly, the new "application for judicial review" can be used whenever a declaration or injunction could formerly have been obtained. The effective ambit of a declaratory order would be extended by permitting the court to set aside the impugned administrative act or decision. The court would be given discretion to convert either an action or a motion for a declaration into an "application for judicial review", or vice versa.

Fifthly, the institute proposes to give the court power to determine who has standing to participate in proceedings for judicial review, and therefore eliminate much of the technicality associated with standing.[47]

Sixthly, the proposals require an "application for judicial review" to be filed and served within six months after the date or decision attacked, and the court would be prevented from extending this time.[48] In effect, this would make the six-month limitation currently applicable to *certiorari* extend to all other forms of judicial review. This generalization of the limitation period occurs under most of the reforms in other jurisdictions. However, the Alberta proposals are diametrically opposed to the English position, where the court is given unlimited discretion in a proper case to extend the time limit for applying for judicial review.[49]

Seventhly, the new uniform procedure contemplates that a statutory delegate may be required to file a return with the court in all types of "applications for judicial review", and not just those resembling the present *certiorari*.[50]

Eighthly, the court is entitled to make "such interim order as it considers proper upon motion made either in the application for judicial review or at any time pending the final determination of the application . . .", except as against the Crown.[51]

Finally, the institute recommends retaining an appeal as of right to the Court of Appeal from any order granted by the Court of Queen's Bench on an "application for judicial review".

It is also interesting to note some of the areas which are not included in the institute's package of proposed reforms. Perhaps the most important is the

---

47 *Ibid.*, pp. 75-77.
48 *Ibid.*, p. 67.
49 Although in England the general time frame within which the application must be brought is three months.
50 Institute of Law Research and Reform, *Judicial Review of Administrative Action: Application for Judicial Review* (Report No. 40, March 1984), pp. 78-79.
51 *Ibid.*, p. 83.

institute's decision not to attempt either to define a "statutory power" or to delineate those areas of "public law" to which the new "application for judicial review" would apply — thereby skirting the difficult issues which have arisen under similar reforms in Ontario, British Columbia, New Zealand and England.[52] Secondly, the institute did not detect a wide enough consensus to follow the English model of including the possibility of obtaining damages under the new "application for judicial review".[53] Thirdly, the institute did not find it necessary to include a specific provision retaining the court's discretion to refuse judicial review, adopting the position that the suggested reforms are only procedural in nature and do not purport to extend, restrict or alter the court's existing discretion. This differs from the position under the Federal Court Act,[54] as well as the position in England.[55] Fourthly, the Alberta proposals do not make provision for discoveries or other interlocutory proceedings in the course of an "application for judicial review". It is obviously a matter of judgment how far any particular set of reforms should go.

6. Conclusion

The last few years have seen the implementation of extensive reforms to the procedural aspects of administrative law. The most important common theme has been the unification of the prerogative remedies, declarations (and sometimes damages) and injunctions into a new procedure called an "application for judicial review". There has been no uniformity, however, in the appropriate level or composition of the court to whom this application lies — whether a single judge of the lowest court of general superior jurisdiction,[56] a judge of a specialized administrative law division of that court,[57] a three-member panel of that court (whether specialized or not),[58] or directly to the Court of Appeal.[59] Further, there has been no uniformity in determining whether an applicant should be able to seek judicial review as of right,[60] or only with leave;[61] and there is considerable diversity concerning the availability of interlocutory process.[62] Finally, most of the reforms try — more or less successfully — to define some area of "public law" or "statutory power" within which the application for judicial review is available, although the Alberta proposals avoid this approach.

---

52 *Ibid.*, Appendix A.
53 *Ibid.*, pp. 55-57.
54 See s. 28(4) of the Federal Court Act, R.S.C. 1970, c. 10 (2nd Supp.).
55 See the text accompanying note 36, *supra.*
56 As in England, and as proposed in Alberta.
57 As in New Zealand.
58 As in Ontario.
59 Under s. 28 of the Federal Court Act.
60 As in most jurisdictions.
61 As in England.
62 The English reforms appear to be the most extensive in this area.

Almost none[63] of the recent or proposed reforms deal squarely with more substantive grounds for judicial review of administrative action, nor with compensating a victim of (or preventing) "bad government" or "maladministration". Accordingly, there is considerable work still to be done in reforming administrative law.

The increasing diversity of the procedural rules for obtaining judicial review may well militate against a uniform development of Administrative Law throughout the Commonwealth. Unfortunately, as in so many other areas of law, substantive rights are very often affected by procedural matters. In the long run, the only way to evaluate the desirability of the various types of reform is to determine whether judicial review of administrative action has in fact operated efficiently in each respective jurisdiction. After all, the purpose of Administrative Law is to achieve better government, coupled with a sense of justice to the individual.

7. Selected Bibliography

Alberta Institute of Law Research and Reform, Report No. 40, *Judicial Review of Administrative Action: Application for Judicial Review* (1984).

Beatson & Matthews, "Reform of Administrative Law Remedies: The First Step", (1978) 41 Mod. L. Rev. 437.

British Columbia Law Reform Commission, Report No. 18, *A Procedure for Judicial Review of the Actions of Statutory Agencies* (1974).

English Law Commission, *Report on Remedies in Administrative Law*, No. 73, Cmnd. 6407, 1976.

English Law Commission, *Remedies in Administrative Law*, Working Paper No. 40, 1971.

Evans, J.M., "Judicial Review in Ontario — Some Problems of Pouring Old Wine Into New Bottles", (1977) 55 Can. Bar Rev. 148.

Katz, L., "Australian Federal Administrative Law Reform", (1980) 57 Can. Bar Rev. 341.

Law Reform Commission of Canada, Report No. 14, *Judicial Review and the Federal Court* (1980).

Northey, J.F., "An Administrative Law Division of the New Zealand Supreme Court — A Proposal for Law Reform", (1969) 7 Alta. L. Rev. 62.

Northey, J.F., "The Administrative Division of the New Zealand Supreme Court — A Postscript", (1977) 17 Alta. L.R. 186.

---

63 Section 28 of the Federal Court Act sets out the statutory grounds on which the Court of Appeal can grant an application for review. See also s. 5 of the Australian Administrative Decisions (Judicial Review) Act, 1977 (proclaimed in force in 1980) which lays out extensive grounds for judicial review.

16

Restrictions on Judicial Review

1. Introduction

There are a number of limitations on the inherent power of the superior courts to review the legality of actions taken by statutory delegates. First, judicial review uses the doctrine of *ultra vires* to make sure that delegates act within the ambit of the power granted to them by legislation. Effective judicial review, therefore, can be precluded by the enactment of enabling legislation in such broad or subjective terms that it would be virtually impossible ever to determine that the delegate has transgressed the limits of his jurisdiction. Secondly, the legislative branch sometimes specifically incorporates the delegate's actions into legislation, where the doctrine of parliamentary sovereignty prevents the court's scrutiny. Thirdly, the doctrine of Parliamentary Sovereignty also means that clearly worded legislation can oust the court's inherent jurisdiction to review the legality of a delegate's actions. Because our constitution provides relatively few guarantees protecting the existence of the courts, or any part of their jurisdiction, such "privative clauses" are theoretically valid. Fourthly, the common law has perversely persisted in preserving many of the Crown's historical immunities from the general law of the land. Further, legislation sometimes specifically grants immunity from suit to certain statutory delegates who have acted illegally. This has the effect of potentially preventing judicial review against a restricted number of governmental actions. Finally, evidentiary problems may prevent an aggrieved citizen from obtaining redress for illegal administrative action. All of these problems are important for a complete understanding of Administrative Law.

2. Granting Delegated Powers in Broad or Subjective Terms

The doctrine of *ultra vires* means that a statutory delegate can only act within the ambit specifically granted by legislation, and judicial review is generally available to determine the legality of the delegate's action. This implies a defined area within which the delegate is authorized to act. Obviously, the broader the area granted, the more likely that the delegate will act within that area. Sometimes, however, it is not possible to determine objectively the limits of the delegated power because the legislation is written in very subjective terms. As long as the delegate acts *bona fide*, the courts will generally be very reluctant to second-guess his opinion, with the result that it is impossible to assert that the delegate's action is *ultra vires*. For example, the sweeping powers of the War Measures Act[1] permit the Governor in Council to

> do and authorize such acts and things, and make from time to time
> such orders and regulations, as he may by reason of the existence of
> ... apprehended ... insurrection deem necessary or advisable for the
> security, defence, peace, order and welfare of Canada. . . .

This provision really contains two elements. The first is the existence of an "apprehended insurrection". The very use of the word "apprehended" implies a subjective determination, and that subjective determination is to be

---

1 R.S.C. 1970, c. W-2, s. 3.

made by the Governor in Council and not by the courts. The second element is the determination of the action to be taken for the security, defence, peace, order and welfare of Canada. Again, the legislation contemplates this to be a subjective determination because it authorizes all acts and things which the Governor in Council "deem[s to be] necessary or advisable" to achieve these goals. This subjective grant of power makes it very difficult to obtain judicial review on the basis that the delegate has acted outside of the ambit of his power.[2]

A similar problem was presented in the famous case of *Liversidge v. Anderson*,[3] where the Secretary of State was authorized to order the detention of any person whom he had "reasonable cause to believe to be of hostile origin or association . . . and that by reason thereof it is necessary to exercise control over him . . .". The majority of the House of Lords held that they could not review the *bona fide* exercise of this delegated power because it was couched in terms of the Secretary of State's subjective belief as to Liversidge's hostile origins, as well as his subjective determination of the necessity to detain Liversidge. Lord Atkin dissented strongly from this subjective construction of the enabling legislation, preferring to construe the grant of power in much more objective terms which would permit the courts to determine the reasonability of the evidence upon which the Secretary of State made the decision to intern Liversidge.

Although both of these examples deal with emergency legislation which might naturally cause the courts to strain to uphold the validity of governmental action, it is nevertheless clear that there is no constitutional limitation on the ability of the legislative branch to use very subjective terms in defining the ambit of administrative powers, even in peacetime. Indeed, the statute books are full of less awesome examples of delegated powers granted in subjective terms. For example, under section 31 of the Energy Resources Conservation Act[4] the board is entitled to make quite wide subjective determinations about who qualifies as a "local intervenor" entitled to have his costs paid for participating in the board's proceedings. The statute reads as follows:

31(1) In this section, "local intervenor" means a person or group or association of persons who, *in the opinion of the Board,*

(a) has an interest in, or

(b) is in actual occupation of or is entitled to occupy

---

2 The courts declined to review the government's proclamation of apprehended insurrection during the 1970 October Crisis in Quebec on this ground. See Marx, (1972) 7 U.B.C. L. Rev. 55; Lyon, (1972) 18 McGill L.J. 136.

3 [1942] A.C. 206 (H.L.); and Heuston, "*Liveridge v. Anderson* in Retrospect", (1970) 86 L.Q. Rev. 33 for an interesting postscript on the controversy caused by this case.

4 R.S.A. 1980, c. E-11 [re-en. 1981, c. 47, s.2], emphasis added.

land that is or may be directly and adversely affected by a decision of the Board. . . .

This legislative reference to the board's opinion greatly broadens the scope within which it can legally exercise its power, and correspondingly reduces the ambit of judicial review.

Another example of the subjective grant of power is contained in section 41(1) of the Public Utilities Board Act (and many other similar provisions for other delegates), which authorizes the board to issue subpoenas to compel testimony before it:[5]

> 41(1) The Board may, *when in its opinion* the attendance of any witness before the Board is desirable, cause to be served on the witness a notice requiring his attendance before the Board. . . .

This type of wording makes it very difficult to obtain a court order striking down the validity of the notice to attend, simply because it will generally be impossible to attack the board's opinion that the witness's testimony is desirable.

While there is no constitutional or other prohibition against the delegation of subjective powers, it is probably true to say that the courts strain against construing delegated powers in subjective terms if the language can also be construed objectively. Construing enabling legislation in objective terms has the result of extending the applicability of the *ultra vires* doctrine and therefore the ambit of judicial review of the legality of the delegate's actions. Conversely, a conscious and clearly-worded decision by the legislature to use a subjective grant of power has the effect of widening the delegate's jurisdiction and therefore narrowing the ambit of judicial review of the legality of his actions.

3. Incorporating the Delegate's Actions Into Legislation

Another way of restricting judicial review is to incorporate the delegate's actions into legislation. Because the doctrine of Parliamentary Sovereignty prevents the courts from reviewing the contents of legislation itself (except for constitutional validity), administrative action which is incorporated into parent legislation is thereby also entitled to the protection of Parliamentary Sovereignty. As a result, no question can arise as to whether the delegate is acting within or outside the ambit of power granted to him by the legislature. In effect, the legislators adopt the delegate's actions as their own. Such legislative validation of a delegate's actions can occur at any point in time. Thus, the legislature may retroactively confirm or validate administrative action which has already occurred, or it may incorporate future actions by the delegate. In any event, this legislative structure makes it very difficult to apply

---

5 R.S.A. 1980, c. P-37, emphasis added.

the *ultra vires* principle to strike down the validity of the governmental action in question.

A striking example can be given of the effectiveness of incorporation legislation as a means of preventing judicial review of the legality of administrative action. In *Institute of Patent Agents v. Lockwood*,[6] the Board of Trade was given power to make general rules regulating the registration of patents and trade marks, and these general rules were to have "the same effect as if they were contained in this Act, and shall be judicially noticed". The rules were also required to be laid before both Houses of Parliament where they could be annulled by positive resolution of either house within forty days; otherwise they came into effect. One of the rules made it illegal to act as a patent agent without being registered, and Mr. Lockwood was prosecuted for breaching this regulation. When the question arose about the validity of this rule, the House of Lords initially considered whether the rule was valid without regard to the statutory provision purporting to incorporate all of the rules into the parent legislation. They went on, however, to hold that the incorporation clause necessarily prevented judicial scrutiny of the validity of the regulations. As Lord Herschell L.C. said:[7]

> [The rules] are to be "of the same effect as if they were contained in this Act." My Lords, I have asked in vain for any explanation of the meaning of those words or any suggestion as to the effect to be given to them if, notwithstanding that provision, the rules are open to review and consideration by the Courts. The effect of an enactment is that it binds all subjects who are affected by it. They are bound to conform themselves to the provisions of the law so made. The effect of a statutory rule if validly made is precisely the same that every person must conform himself to its provisions, and, if in each case a penalty be imposed, any person who does not comply with the provisions whether of the enactment or the rule becomes equally subject to the penalty. But there is this difference between a rule and an enactment, that whereas apart from some such provision as we are considering, you may canvass a rule and determine whether or not it was within the power of those who made it, you cannot canvass in that way the provisions of an Act of Parliament. Therefore, there is that difference between the rule and the statute. There is no difference if the rule is one within the statutory authority, but that very substantial difference, if it is open to consideration whether it be so or not.
>
> I own I feel very great difficulty in giving to this provision that they "shall be of the same effect as if they were contained in this Act," any other meaning than this, that you shall for all purposes of

---

6 [1894] A.C. 347 (H.L.).
7 *Ibid.*, pp. 359-60.

construction or obligation or otherwise treat them exactly as if they were in the Act. No doubt there might be some conflict between a rule and a provision of the Act. Well, there is a conflict sometimes between two sections to be found in the same Act. You have to try and reconcile them as best you may. If you cannot, you have to determine which is the leading provision and which the subordinate provision, and which must give way to the other. That would be so with regard to the enactment and with regard to rules which are to be treated as if within the enactment. In that case probably the enactment itself would be treated as the governing consideration and the rule as subordinate to it. Those are points which I need not dwell upon on the present occasion.

And Lord Russell reached the same conclusion:[8]

I think that if the rules are to be read as part of the Act (as I think they ought to be) it is not, in this case, competent to judicial tribunals to reject them. Such effect must be given to them by judicial construction as can properly be given to them taking them in conjunction with the general provisions of the Act or Acts of Parliament in connection with which they have been formulated.

These quotations demonstrate some judicial disquiet about how far an incorporation clause can go to prevent judicial review of the legality of a delegate's actions. Two quite distinct approaches to this problem arose in subsequent cases. In *Minister of Health v. R.; Ex parte Yaffe*,[9] the House of Lords held that it had power to determine whether the delegate's actions were inconsistent with the Act, and therefore were not capable of being incorporated into it pursuant to a statutory provision that "the order of the Minister when made shall have effect as if enacted in this Act". This approach was adopted by the British Columbia Court of Appeal in *Minister of Finance v. Woodward*,[10] when it held that a decision which breached the principles of natural justice was void and therefore was incapable of being protected by legislation which purported to validate it retroactively. The Supreme Court of Canada, however, held that the proper construction of the legislation in question indicated that the legislature clearly intended to ratify and validate the previous decision of the Minister, notwithstanding the fact that it might otherwise have been invalid.

The proper approach, therefore, is to construe the parent legislation to determine how broadly it intends to protect or incorporate the delegate's actions. If one concludes that the legislation does incorporate the delegate's impugned actions, they are protected by the doctrine of Parliamentary

---

8 *Ibid.*, p. 367.
9 [1931] A.C. 494 (H.L.).
10 [1971] 3 W.W.R. 645, affirmed [1973] S.C.R. 120.

Sovereignty from judicial review because by definition they cannot be *ultra vires*.[11]

4. Privative Clauses

A "privative clause" is a statutory provision which purports to oust the inherent jurisdiction of the superior courts to review the legality of actions taken by statutory delegates. In theory, the doctrine of Parliamentary Sovereignty means that the courts must give effect to such legislative provisions. On the other hand, the courts have been quite creative in finding ways to evade the effect of privative clauses: largely by holding that the legislature could not have intended to confer power on a statutory delegate to exceed the bounds of the jurisdiction which the legislature has conferred on him. If the statutory delegate exceeds his jurisdiction, then his decision is void, and there is therefore no lawful action which can be protected by the privative clause. Accordingly, the distinction between jurisdictional and intra-jurisdictional errors is extremely important in understanding the courts' approach to privative clauses. Because Parliament can lawfully exclude the courts' inherent power to review the legality of the delegate's actions, most cases involve a quite detailed examination of the wording used by Parliament to achieve this end. Although each privative clause must be construed in light of its own wording, four general types may be identified.

(a) Final and Binding Clauses

Many statutes contain provisions which state that the delegate's decision shall be "final", "binding", "conclusive", "not subject to appeal", "unappealable" or "not subject to be questioned". The courts have almost universally treated such provisions as meaning that no appeal lies from the delegate's decision, which merely reiterates the common law rule that no appeal lies without being specifically created by statute.[12] Accordingly, such clauses do not have the effect of depriving the superior courts of their inherent jurisdiction to review the legality of a delegate's actions. The courts' power in this regard undoubtedly extends to correct any jurisdictional defects in the delegate's actions, and the better view is that "final and binding" clauses do not affect the courts' right to correct intra-jurisdictional errors of law as well. However, Laskin C.J.C. in *Alberta Union of Provincial Employees v. Alberta Public Service Employees' Relation Board* indicated that the privative "gloss" of a final and binding clause should restrict the courts to correcting only those intra-jurisdictional errors of law which are "patently unreasonable":[13]

---

11 The same types of problems arise with respect to statutory provisions which deem certain certificates or actions to be "conclusive for all purposes": see Vol. 1 of the McRuer Report, pp. 273-74.

12 See the discussion on this point in chapter 12.

13 [1982] 1 S.C.R. 923 at 927, emphasis added.

In the face of this explicit provision for review [by certiorari within 30 days of the decision], it is impossible to read it out of this statute or to subordinate it to ss. 9 and 11 [which provided that the action or decision of the Board was "final and conclusive for all purposes"] or even to limit it to questions of jurisdiction in the strict sense, as urged by counsel for the union and counsel for the Board. That being said, however, *it still remains to consider the scope of review on alleged errors of law, and it is my opinion that the commanding terms of s. 9(1) and especially of s. 11 cast a gloss on the extent to which decisions of the Board may be overturned by a court. Certiorari, considered in the light of ss. 9(1) and 11, is a long way from an appeal and is subject to restriction in accordance with a line of decisions of this court which, to assess them generally, preclude judicial interference with interpretations made by the Board which are not plainly unreasonable.* Jurisdictional errors, including want of natural justice, are clearly reviewable and subject to reversal as was conceded by the appellants, but they are not involved here.

For the reasons set out in chapter 10, the better view is that the patent unreasonability test has no application in a case such as this where no jurisdictional defect is alleged in the delegate's actions.[14] Accordingly, a "final and binding" clause does not have the effect of restricting the ambit of the superior court's supervisory powers over inferior tribunals, whether by restricting the availability of *certiorari* or of any other remedies. At most, it may indicate the legislature's intention that some credence and deference be given to its delegate when the courts decide whether to exercise their discretion to refuse judicial review, even in circumstances where the applicant has shown the illegality of the delegate's actions.

(b) Exclusive Jurisdiction Clauses

A great deal of legislation goes further than stating that the delegate's decisions are final and binding by going on to provide that the delegate has exclusive jurisdiction to determine those matters remitted to him. This implies that the courts have no jurisdiction to deal with any of those matters. Such a provision undoubtedly prevents an appeal to the courts on the merits. It also prevents judicial review for an intra-jurisdictional error of law. But it does not confer on the delegate the authority to determine which matters are within or outside of his jurisdiction: the courts assert the right to make such determinations,[15] notwithstanding such an "exclusive jurisdiction" clause. The courts

---

14 See section 7 of chapter 10.

15 See the clear reasoning to this effect by Beetz J. in the recent decision of the Supreme Court of Canada in *Le Syndicat des Employés de Production du Québec et de l'Acadie v. C.B.C.*, [1984] 2 S.C.R. 412.

use the same legal reasoning to reach this result as they apply to "no *certiorari*" clauses.

(c) No-*Certiorari* Clauses

Legislation also frequently contains a provision preventing the issuance of any prerogative remedy, declaration or other court order to call into question the validity of the delegate's actions.[16] The courts have generally treated this type of clause as effective to prevent judicial review of any intra-jurisdictional error of law, but not effective to prevent judicial review of any jurisdictional defect in the delegate's actions. The constitutional rationale for holding that these clauses do not oust the courts' right to scrutinize juris-dictional defects is the assumption that Parliament cannot ever have intended inferior delegates to act outside their jurisdiction; any such action is *ultra vires* and void; and therefore there is in law nothing to be protected by the privative clause. As Lord Morris put it in the *Anisminic* case:[17]

> The control which is exercised by the High Court over inferior tribunals . . . is of a supervisory but not of an appellate nature. It enables the High Court to correct errors of law if they are revealed on the face of the record. The control cannot, however, be exercised if there is some provision (such as a "no certiorari" clause) which prohibits removal to the High Court. But it is well settled that even such a clause is of no avail if the inferior tribunal acts without jurisdiction or exceeds the limits of its jurisdiction.

To the extent that "no *certiorari*" clauses are still prevalent in Canada, the supervisory power of the courts depends upon the ability to characterize any alleged error by the delegate as being jurisdictional in nature. On the one hand, both the English and the Canadian courts recognize that a jurisdictional defect can occur at the very beginning of a delegate's functions (either because he has no statutory authority whatever to do the act in question, or because some matter preliminary or collateral to his jurisdiction does not obtain[18]), in the course thereof (either because he has breached the principles of natural jutice and procedural fairness, or because he has in some manner abused his discretion[19]) or at the very moment he makes his determination[20]. In general, all of these jurisdictional errors will not be protected by a no *certiorari* clause from judicial review. On the other hand, there may be considerable difficulty in determining the precise ambit of the power which Parliament granted to the statutory delegate. As a result, it may not be easy to determine whether the

---

16 *E.g.*, s. 45 of the Energy Resources Conservation Act, R.S.A. 1980, c. E-11.
17 *Anisminic v. Foreign Comp. Comm.*, [1969] 2 A.C. 147, [1969] 1 All E.R. 208 at 222 (H.L.).
18 See chapter 6.
19 See chapters 7, 8 and 9.
20 *E.g.*, as occurred in the *C.B.C.* case, *supra*, note 15.

delegate has made an error within or outside his jurisdiction. As Lord Morris put it in *Anisminic*:[21]

> it becomes necessary, therefore, to ascertain what was the question submitted for the determination of a tribunal. What were its terms of reference? What was its remit? What were the questions left to it or sent to it for its decision? What were the limits of its duties and powers? Were there any conditions precedent which had to be satisfied before its functions began? If there were, was it or was it not left to the tribunal itself to decide whether or not the conditions precedent were satisfied? If Parliament has enacted that provided a certain situation exists then a tribunal may have certain powers, it is clear that the tribunal will not have those powers unless the situation exists. The decided cases illustrate the infinite variety of the situations which may exist and the variations of statutory wording which have called for consideration. Most of the cases depend, therefore, upon an examination of their own particular facts and of particular sets of words. It is, however, abundantly clear that questions of law as well as of fact can be remitted for the determination of a tribunal.

The cases referred to in chapter 10 clearly demonstrate the difficulties which the Canadian courts have experienced in drawing the line between intra-jurisdictional errors which are protected by no *certiorari* clauses and jurisdictional errors which are not immune from judicial review.

(d) Elastic Jurisdiction Clauses

In theory, Parliament might delegate the power to an inferior tribunal to determine the limit of its own jurisdiction. If coupled with a no *certiorari* clause, such an elastic delegation of jurisdiction appears to prevent all forms of judicial review. Precisely because the statutory delegate has the power to determine his own jurisdiction, none of his actions can ever be *ultra vires*. Because of the strong form in which the doctrine of Parliamentary Sovereignty exists in England, the British courts would have to give effect to such legislation, and would not be able to review the legality of such a delegate's actions for any reasons, including jurisdictional defects.

The only example of a strong clause, to the authors' knowledge, is contained in section 33 of the Labour Code of British Columbia:[22]

> 33. The board has and shall exercise exclusive jurisdiction to determine the extent of its jurisdiction under this Act, a collective agreement or the regulations, to determine a fact or question of law necessary to establish its jurisdiction and to determine whether or in what manner it shall exercise its jurisdiction.

---

21 *Supra*, note 17 at [1969] 1 All E.R. 222-23.
22 R.S.B.C. 1979, c. 212, s. 33.

(e) Constitutional Limitations on Privative Clauses in Canada

As explained in greater detail in chapter 2, there are certain constitutional limitations in Canada affecting the validity of privative clauses. The most important is section 96 of the Constitution Act, 1867, which requires the judges of all superior, district and county courts to be appointed by the federal Governor in Council. This has the effect of limiting the range of persons to whom certain judicial powers can be granted. It also has the effect of preventing the legislative branch from granting unlimited or unreviewable jurisdiction to a statutory delegate, because one of the hallmarks of a superior court is its inherent power to determine the jurisdiction of statutory (or "inferior") tribunals. This proposition can be used to argue that a privative clause which purports to oust the ordinary superior court's inherent power to review a decision of an administrative tribunal effectively gives that tribunal power to determine its own jurisdiction, and thus makes that tribunal into a superior court whose members must be appointed in accordance with section 96. This argument allows the courts either to strike down the validity of such a privative clause, or to strike down every action taken by the administrative tribunal because its members have not been appointed correctly in accordance with section 96.

On the one hand, the latter view appears to be more correct in theory, because there is no doubt that the legislative branch could lawfully enact a stringent privative clause provided the members of the administrative tribunal are appointed by the federal Governor in Council under section 96. Thus, the privative clause would appear to be valid; only the appointment of the delegates could be questioned.

On the other hand, the Supreme Court of Canada has recently used section 96 to strike down the validity of a privative clause. In *Crevier v. Attorney General of Quebec*,[23] sections 194 and 195 of the Professional Code of Quebec[24] purported to preclude the availability of any of the remedies normally available from the Superior Court for the purpose of questioning the validity of any action taken by a wide range of officials and tribunals to whom various powers had been granted under the Code. Laskin C.J.C. held that the mere attempt to deprive the superior courts of their traditional supervisory function over the jurisdiction of these inferior delegates itself contravenes the spirit of section 96. In other words, the Supreme Court of Canada has recognized that our Constitution protects some of the administrative law jurisdiction of the superior courts against privative clauses, and to that extent thereby limits the legislative sovereignty of both Parliament and the legislatures. As Laskin C.J.C. said:[25]

---

23 [1981] 2 S.C.R. 220; *cf.* the recent decision of the Supreme Court of Canada in *A.G. Que. v. Udeco Inc.*, [1984] 2 S.C.R. 502.

24 L.R.Q. 1977, c. C-26, ss. 194 [re-en. 1982, c. 16, s. 2], 195 [re-en. 1982, c. 16, s. 3].

25 *Supra*, note 23, at [1981] 2 S.C.R. 236-37.

It is true that this is the first time that this Court has declared unequivocally that a provincially constituted statutory tribunal cannot constitutionally be immunized from review of decisions on questions of jurisdiction. In my opinion, this limitation, arising by virtue of s. 96, stands on the same footing as the well-accepted limitation on the power of provincial statutory tribunals to make unreviewable determinations of constitutionality. There may be differences of opinion as to what are questions of jurisdiction but, in my lexicon, they rise above and are different from errors of law, whether involving statutory construction or evidentiary matters or other matters. It is now unquestioned that privative clauses may, when properly framed, effectively oust judicial review on questions of law, and, indeed, on other issues not touching jurisdiction. However, given that s. 96 is in the *British North America Act* and that it would make a mockery of it to treat it in non-functional formal terms as a mere appointing power, I can think of nothing that is more the hallmark of a superior court than the vesting of power in a provincial statutory tribunal to determine the limits of its jurisdiction without appeal or other review.

As discussed at length in chapter 10, it may be exceedingly difficult to determine which matters go to jurisdiction, as opposed to those which lie within it. Nevertheless, it is clear that the *Crevier* decision elevates and reinforces the importance of section 96 as a weapon against the unfettered ability of the legislative branch — whether federal or provincial — to enact broad privative clauses ousting judicial review of administrative actions. It is also clear that this case now casts grave doubts on the validity of legislation which purports to give a statutory delegate jurisdiction to determine the limits of his own jurisdiction — legislation so clearly epitomized by the "elastic jurisdiction" clause contained in section 33 of the Labour Code of British Columbia.[26] In effect, the *Crevier* decision must be taken to have silently reversed Laskin J.'s earlier decision for the Supreme Court of Canada in *Pringle v. Fraser*,[27] which upheld Parliament's right to enact legislation depriving the courts of their inherent jurisdiction to review a decision of the Immigration Appeal Board because the latter was given "sole and exclusive jurisdiction to hear and determine all questions of fact and law, including questions of jurisdiction".

(f) Statutory Abolition of Privative Clauses

Some governments have had the courage to eschew their reliance on privative clauses. As early as 1932, the Donoughmore Committee on Ministers' Powers in England recommended the abandonment of such

---

26 *Supra*, note 22.
27 [1972] S.C.R. 821.

clauses.[28] In 1957, the Franks Committee recommended that no statute should purport to preclude judicial review,[29] and this recommendation has been incorporated in both the 1958 and 1971 Tribunals and Inquiries Acts in the following terms:[30]

> [A]ny provision in an Act passed before 1st August 1958 that any order or determination shall not be called into question in any court, or any provision in such an Act which by similar words excludes any of the powers of the High Court, shall not have effect so as to prevent the removal of the proceedings into the High Court by order of certiorari or to prejudice the powers of the High Court to make orders of mandamus.

Only a very few privative clauses were excepted from this general provision, including the one protecting decisions of the Foreign Compensation Commission which gave rise to the famous *Anisminic* decision,[31] as well as certain time-delayed ouster clauses.[32] In general, the British government has not relied on privative clauses for more than twenty-five years, with no obvious impediment to the efficiency of their administrative machinery.

A similar disavowal of privative clauses has been enacted by the federal Parliament in Canada. Section 28 of the Federal Court Act[33] creates a statutory "application for judicial review" against most federal boards, commissions and other tribunals "notwithstanding the provisions of any other Act". This has been held to nullify the effect of privative clauses in statutes enacted before the Federal Court Act came into force, as well as in subsequent statutory re-enactments which the Interpretation Act[34] does not treat as being "new law".[35] Unfortunately, this form of drafting implies that a privative clause contained in any "new law" enacted after the Federal Court Act will be valid because Parliament must be taken to have intended to overrule the operation of section 28 to permit an application for judicial review. This problem of statutory construction will always arise unless a provision is entrenched in the Constitution guaranteeing the right to judicial review of the legality of administrative action.[36]

---

28 Cmd. 4060 (1932), p. 65.
29 Cmnd. 218 (1957), para. 117.
30 6 & 7 Eliz. 2, c. 66; 1971 (Eng.) c. 62. Reproduced here is s. 14 of the 1971 Act.
31 *Supra*, note 17; this privative clause has now been repealed by s. 3(2) and (10) of the Foreign Compensation Act 1969.
32 *E.g.*, see *Smith v. East Elloe Rural Dist. Council*, [1956] A.C. 736 (H.L.). Compare the similar legislative provision in the *Olds College* case (*Alta. Union of Prov. Employees v. Alta. Public Service Employees' Relation Bd.*, [1982] 1 S.C.R. 923).
33 R.S.C. 1970, c. 10 (2nd Supp.).
34 R.S.C. 1970, c. I-23.
35 See *Howarth v. Nat. Parole Bd.*, [1976] 1 S.C.R. 453 at 475; *A.G. Can. v. Pub. Service Staff Rel. Bd.*, [1977] 2 F.C. 663 (C.A.).
36 See David Phillip Jones, "A Constitutionally Guaranteed Role for the Courts", (1979) 57 Can. Bar Rev. 669.

Regrettably, it appears that none of the Canadian provinces has enacted similar provisions to eviscerate the effectiveness of privative clauses, nor has the practice of enacting sweeping privative clauses fallen into disuse.

(g) Summary on Privative Clauses

The courts' treatment of privative clauses illustrates the tension which exists in our constitutional system of government between the doctrine of Parliamentary Sovereignty and the presumed right of the courts to rule on the legality of governmental action. The courts have generally used the *ultra vires* doctrine quite effectively to prevent statutory delegates from exceeding their jurisdiction. As a result, the effect of most privative clauses has been restricted by the courts to protecting intra-jurisdictional errors of law. On the other hand, Parliament is perfectly entitled to use clear words to define which matters lie within the jurisdiction of its statutory delegates. The real question is why Parliament would ever choose to oust the courts' historic role of determining questions of law. For more than twenty-five years, England has accepted the desirability of having the courts determine almost all questions of law arising in the course of administrative action — whether intra-jurisdictional or jurisdictional in nature — with no obvious impediment to the efficiency of government. Why do Canadian legislators so fear judicial review that they insist — often futilely — on inserting privative clauses in almost all important pieces of legislation?

5. Discretionary Refusal of Remedies

The discretionary nature of some[37] of the remedies available in Administrative Law in effect amounts to a restriction on a citizen's right to obtain redress for illegal governmental action. This topic is considered in greater detail in the discussion on remedies in chapters 13 and 14. Nevertheless, it is useful to reiterate here the broad categories in which the courts have sometimes exercised their discretion to refuse one of the prerogative remedies, a declaration or an injunction: (a) where there is an appeal which provides a more efficient remedy;[38] (b) where the applicant's conduct has disentitled him to relief; (c) where it would be pointless to issue the remedy; and, possibly, (d) where an intra-jurisdictional error of law is not "patently unreasonable". By contrast, damages are not discretionary but must be awarded as of right if the plaintiff otherwise meets all the tests of tort law.[39]

---

37 Damages are not discretionary: see chapter 14.
38 See the discussion on this point in chapter 12. See also s. 29 of the Federal Court Act.
39 See chapter 14.

6. Crown and Other Immunities From Suit

At common law, the Crown and her agents were not bound by legislation unless it specifically indicated the contrary, were not capable of being sued and were not subject to the prerogative remedies. Although these three rules have been greatly amended over the years, "Crown law" is a dangerous minefield to be negotiated by a person wronged by illegal actions of the Crown or her agents. Similarly, legislation sometimes provides immunity to statutory delegates from any liability for their actions. A complete discussion of these topics would require a text of its own, but the following is an outline of some of the problems involved in this area.

(a) The Presumption that Statutes do not Bind the Crown

The rules of statutory construction presume that legislation does not bind the Crown unless there are clear words to the contrary.[40] Accordingly, a citizen may not have an action against the Crown for any liability which legislation imposes upon other private citizens, and conversely certain statutory defences may not be available against the Crown which could otherwise be asserted against other private citizens.[41] The presumption that the Crown is not affected by statutes has been enshrined in the federal and most provincial Interpretation Acts.[42] The resultant preferred position of the Crown is incapable of justification in our society, and reform is long overdue.[43] British Columbia has reformed the rule by simply enacting the reverse rule in its Interpretation Act:[44] in that province, the Crown is presumed to be bound by every Act of the legislature unless the clear words of the legislation grant an exemption.[45]

(b) Crown Immunity From Suit

At common law, the Crown was immune from suit: "The Crown can do no wrong" in one sense, therefore, meant that no court was competent to judge the Crown. On the other hand, it was beneath the Crown's dignity not to make amends for wrongs done by it or its servants, and the Crown accepted petitions to it directly to right such wrongs. In due course, the Crown delegated the determination of these Petitions of Right to the courts to advise

---

40 See Driedger, *The Construction of Statutes*, pp. 162*ff.*

41 It is a nice question, however, whether the Crown can take advantage of part of a statute without being subject to the burden of it. For a good discussion of this problem, see Driedger, *ibid.*, and McNairn, *Governmental and Intergovernmental Immunity*, chapters 1 and 3.

42 For a discussion of the position in different Canadian jurisdictions, see McNairn, *ibid.*, p. 7.

43 See the excellent Report of the British Columbia Law Reform Commission on Civil Rights, Pt. I: *Legal Position of the Crown*, 1972, and the authorities quoted therein.

44 R.S.B.C. 1979, c. 206, s. 14.

45 See art. 9 of the Quebec Civil Code, which reflects the traditional common law rule that the Crown is not bound by statutes in the absence of clear words to the contrary.

the Crown what (if any) remedy should be granted. Subsequent legislation[46] enshrined the Petition of Right procedure, but reserved to the Crown the unfettered discretion to grant or withhold its fiat to permit the courts to determine such claims against the Crown.[47]

With the great expansion of governmental activity in all aspects of society in this century, a move came to put Crown (or, really, governmental) liability on a more solid foundation, particularly in the area of vicarious liability for torts committed by public servants. As Dicey pointed out,[48] some public servant was always liable personally for any actionable wrong committed in the name of the Crown, but this alone would not make the much deeper pocket of the Crown available to pay any damages resulting from such a judgment. Accordingly, the Federal Parliament and most Canadian provinces[49] followed the English solution of adopting new legislation expanding the ambit of Crown liability. Sections 4 and 5 of the Alberta Proceedings Against the Crown Act demonstrate the model:[50]

> 4   A claim against the Crown that, if this Act had not been passed, might be enforced by petition of right, subject to the grant of a fiat by the Lieutenant Governor, may be enforced as of right by proceedings against the Crown in accordance with this Act, without the grant of a fiat by the Lieutenant Governor.
>
> 5(1) Except as otherwise provided in this Act and notwithstanding section 14 of the Interpretation Act [which states that legislation does not bind Her Majesty], the Crown is subject to all those liabilities in tort to which, if it were a person of full age and capacity, it would be subject,
>
> > (a) in respect of a tort committed by any of its officers or agents,
> >
> > (b) in respect of any breach of those duties that a person owes to his servants or agents by reason of being their employer,

---

46 *E.g.*, see: Petition of Right Act, R.S.A. 1922, c. 94; Crown Procedure Act, R.S.B.C. 1960, c. 89; Petition of Right Act, R.S.C. 1970, c. P-12 [repealed R.S.C. 1970, c. 10 (2nd Supp.), s. 64(1); see now the Federal Court Act, R.S.C. 1970, c. 10 (2nd Supp.)]. Curiously, there has never been any difficulty in Quebec with suits against the Crown, because arts. 94-100 of the Code of Civil Procedure, L.R.Q. 1977, c. C-25, essentially puts the Crown in the same position as any private individual. See the reforms proposed in Working Paper 40 of the Law Reform Commission of Canada entitled *The Legal Status of the Federal Administration* (1985).

47 *B.C. Power Corp. v. B.C. Elec. Co.*, [1962] S.C.R. 642. See also the cases cited by the British Columbia Law Reform Commission, *supra*, note 43. For a discussion of the similar requirement of a fiat formerly contained in s. 24 of the Judicature Act in Alberta, see Report No. 13 of the Institute of Law Research and Reform, 1974.

48 *An Introduction to the Study of the Law of the Constitution*, 10th ed. by E.C.S. Wade (London: Macmillan Papermac, 1961).

49 See McNairn, *supra*, note 41, chapter 3.

50 R.S.A. 1980, c. P-18. See also the equivalent Crown Proceeding Act, R.S.B.C. 1979, c. 86.

> (c) in respect of any breach of the duties attaching to the ownership, occupation, possession or control of property, and
>
> (d) under any statute or under any regulation or by-law made or passed under the authority of any statute.
>
> (2) No proceedings lie against the Crown under subsection (1)(a) in respect of an act or omission of any officer or agent of the Crown unless the act or omission would, apart from this Act, have given rise to a cause of action in tort against that officer or agent or his personal representative.

It must be realized that these provisions do not impose any primary responsibility on the Crown, but only vicarious liability. Accordingly, Her Majesty cannot be found liable for Her own torts. The question then arises whether Crown agents can be found liable for their torts, or whether they are entitled to the immunity from suit afforded to the Queen Herself. The answer necessarily entails a determination of what constitutes a "Crown agent", which the courts have held to involve a great deal of control by the Crown directly as opposed to statutory powers which the delegate (whether governor, cabinet minister, public servant, Crown corporation, independent board or other delegate) is entitled to exercise in its own right. However, even if the delegate is held to be an agent of the Crown, the Crown's immunity will not protect the agent from personal liability for illegal actions — actions which immunity will not protect. As Martland J. put it in *National Harbours Board v. Langelier:*[51]

> [The cases] illustrate that, where a Crown agent is properly exercising its function as such, its acts, being those of its principal, the Crown, are to be dealt with on that basis.
>
> What is in issue here is the responsibility of a person, whether individual or corporate, who, though a Crown agent, and purporting to act as such, commits an act which is unlawful. My understanding of the law is that a personal liability will result. The liability arises, not because he is an agent of the Crown, but because, though he is an agent of the Crown, the plea of Crown authority will not avail in such event.
>
> There are some authorities which have stated, in terms which I consider to be too broad, the proposition that an instrumentality of the Crown enjoys the same immunity, from an action in tort, as does the Crown itself.

Accordingly, the better view is that merely being an agent of the Crown does not entitle a delegate to the Crown's immunities from suit.

---

51 [1969] S.C.R. 60 at 70. See also the discussion of "crown agents" by the B.C. Law Reform Commission, *supra*, note 43.

(c) Non-Suable Entities

Not all governmental agencies have sufficient legal personality to be sued for damages. If the agency cannot be sued itself, no vicarious liability can arise in the Crown and the plaintiff will have no recourse unless he can go against the individual members of the agency personally. Houlden J. dealt with the ability of statutory delegates to be sued in *Westlake v. R.*[52] by identifying the following categories:

> (1) There are bodies corporate which are not expressly declared to be suable [but which the *Interpretation Act* deems to be capable of suing and being sued in their own name] . . .
>
> (2) There are bodies corporate which are expressly declared to be suable. . . .
>
> (3) There are bodies corporate which are expressly declared [by statute] not to be suable. . . .
>
> (4) There are non-corporate bodies which are, by the terms of the statute creating them, expressly liable to suit. . . .
>
> (5) There are non-corporate bodies which are not by the terms of the statute creating them expressly liable to suit but which are by necessary implication liable to be sued in an action for damages. . . .
>
> (6) . . . [there] are non-corporate bodies which are not by the terms of the statute incorporating them or by necessary implication liable to be sued in an action for damages, but who are legal entities in that their actions may be reviewed in proceedings brought against them by way of the extraordinary remedies of *certiorari, mandamus* and prohibition.

Thus, any problem with the legal personality of a statutory delegate is only relevant in the context of an action for damages or perhaps a declaration against the administrative tribunal itself. It is not relevant to an action for damages or a declaration against the persons who together constitute the administrative tribunal. Similarly, it is never relevant to a prerogative remedy to determine the legality of the statutory delegate's actions.

(d) Statutory Immunity From Suit

Sometimes legislation grants specific immunity from suit to members of a statutory tribunal. For example, section 35(1) of the Alberta Public Utilities Board Act states that:[53]

> 35(1) Neither the members, nor the secretary of the Board, nor any employee of the Board, is personally liable for anything done

---

52 [1971] 3 O.R. 533 at 534-38, affirmed [1972] 2 O.R. 605, which was affirmed [1973] S.C.R. vii.
53 R.S.A. 1980, c. P-37.

by the Board or by him or under the authority of this or any other Act of the Legislature.

This provision will not, of course, protect the delegate from personal liability for a tortious act which is *ultra vires* the statutory powers granted to the Board or its employees. This result would appear to be excluded by the stronger wording of section 46 of the Energy Resources Conservation Act:[54]

> 46 No action or proceeding may be brought against the Board or a member of the Board or an officer, assessor or employee of the Board *in respect of any act or thing done purportedly in pursuance of this Act*, or any Act that the Board administers, the regulations under any of those Acts or an order or direction of the Board.

In such a case, the delegate is immune from suit for even a tortious *ultra vires* action, and neither does section 5 of the Proceedings Against the Crown Act make the Crown vicariously liable for the tort.

7. Crown Privilege and Other Evidentiary Problems

Evidentiary problems may effectively restrict the availability of a remedy for illegal governmental action.

On the one hand, there is no interrogatory or discovery process associated with an application for one of the prerogative remedies. Accordingly, it may be impossible for an applicant to discover defects in the legality of administrative action affecting him. This is true even if a jurisdictional defect is alleged so that affidavit evidence is admissible to permit the court to scrutinize more than just the formal record of the delegate's proceedings for an error.[55] The applicant must still have the knowledge before the proceedings in order to swear the affidavit.[56] This contrasts with the discovery mechanisms normally available in an action for a private law remedy, as was demonstrated so clearly in *Roncarelli v. Duplessis*,[57] where the premier admitted in discovery that he had ordered the Liquor Commission to revoke Roncarelli's licence and why.

On the other hand, discovery may not always be available even in private law actions. In general, the Crown is not subject to the Rules of Court, and therefore is not bound to be discovered in an action to which it is either plain-

---

54 R.S.A. 1980, c. E-11, emphasis added.

55 All types of evidence are admissible to show a jurisdictional error committed by a statutory delegate, whereas an intra-jurisdictional error of law must be apparent on the face of the record (however broad the "record" is). See the discussion on this point in Pt. 5 of chapter 9, and in Pt. 2 of chapter 10.

56 For a discussion of whether the affidavit must be sworn on the applicant's personal knowledge or mere information and belief, see the discussion in chapter 13 on the decision in *R. in Right of Alta. v. Beaver*, [1982] 4 W.W.R. 344, reversed on another point [1984] 4 W.W.R. 371 (C.A.).

57 [1959] S.C.R. 121.

tiff or defendant.[58] Even more far-reaching, however, is the doctrine of Crown Privilege, which prevents the disclosure of certain types of documents which would be contrary to the public interest, even in litigation between private parties not involving the Crown. The most striking case is *Duncan v. Cammell Laird*[59] where the application of Crown Privilege effectively prevented the widow of a sailor from obtaining the evidence she required to demonstrate that the shipbuilders' negligence had caused the submarine *Thetis* to sink with the loss of all lives.

It is not possible to discuss here the exact limits of these evidentiary problems, but they may well provide real limitations on the ability to redress governmental — or other — wrongs.

8. Conclusion

The adage that there is "no right without a remedy" clearly applies to Administrative Law. Because of the limitations on the various vehicles for judicial review of administrative action, many cases will occur where there is no effective remedy for illegal governmental action. Further, the variety of these limitations means that considerable care must be taken to choose the appropriate remedy for the circumstances. In an ideal world, this type of technical pitfall would not exist, and one might hope for future reforms, whether statutory or from the evolution of the common law, which would permit illegal governmental action to be corrected easily and without technicality.

9. Selected Bibliography

Arthurs, H.W., "Protection against Judicial Review", (1983) 43 Revue du Barreau 277; also published in *Judicial Review of Administrative Rulings*, by Canadian Institute for the Administration of Justice (Les Editions Yvon Blais Inc.), p. 149.

Arthurs, H.W., "Rethinking Administrative Law: A Slightly Dicey Business", (1979) 17 Osgoode Hall L.J. 1.

Chumir, S., "Administrative Law — Privative Clauses — The *Rammell* and *Farrell* Cases", (1963) 3 Alta. L. Rev. 124.

---

58 But see s. 11 of the Proceedings Against the Crown Act, R.S.A. 1980, c. P-18; *A.G. v. Newcastle-upon-Tyne*, [1897] 2 Q.B. 384 (C.A.); *Anthony v. A.G. Alta. and Min. of Lands and Mines*, [1942] 1 W.W.R. 545 (Alta. T.D.); *Central Can. Potash Co. v. A.G. Sask.*, [1974] 4 W.W.R. 179, affirmed [1974] 6 W.W.R. 379 (Sask. C.A.).

59 [1942] A.C. 624 (H.L.). But see also *Conway v. Rimmer*, [1968] A.C. 910 (H.L.); *A.G. Que. v. A.G. Can.*, [1979] 1 S.C.R. 218; *Re Human Rights Comm. and Solicitor-Gen. of Can.*, (1978) 93 D.L.R. (3d) 562 (Que. C.A.); *R. v. Mannix*, 119 D.L.R. (3d) 722, affirmed [1981] 5 W.W.R. 343 (Alta. C.A.); and s. 41 of the Federal Court Act, R.S.C. 1970, c. 10 (2nd Supp.) [repealed 1980-81-82-83, c. 111, s. 3; see now the Access to Information Act, 1980-81-82-83, c. 111].

Garant, P., "La qualité d'agent de la Couronne ou de mandatoire du gouvernement", (1979) 20 Cahiers de droit 485.

Hogg, P.W., "Is Judicial Review of Administrative Action Guaranteed by the British North America Act?" (1976) 54 Can. Bar Rev. 716.

Jones, D.P., "A Constitutionally Guaranteed Role for the Courts", (1979) 57 Can. Bar Rev. 669.

Jones, D.P., "Discretionary Refusal of Judicial Review in Administrative Law", (1981) 19 Alta. L. Rev. 483.

Laskin, B., "Certiorari to Labour Boards: the Apparent Futility of Privative Clauses", (1952) 30 Can. Bar Rev. 986.

Law Reform Commission of Canada, *The Legal Status of the Federal Administration*, Working Paper No. 40 (1985).

Lederman, W.R., "The Independence of the Judiciary", (1956) 34 Can. Bar Rev. 1130.

Lyon, J.N., *Note* on the *Metropolitan Life* Decision, (1971) 49 Can. Bar Rev. 365.

McNairn, C., "The Ontario *Crown Agency Act*", (1973) 6 Ottawa L. Rev. 1.

McRuer Report, Vol. 1, pp. 267-79.

Strayer, B., "Injunctions Against Crown Officers", (1964) 42 Can. Bar Rev. 1.

Wade, H.W.R., "Constitutional and Administrative Aspects of the *Anisminic* Case", (1969) 85 L.Q. Rev. 198.

17

A Look
to the Future

The reader of this text will realize that the principles of Administrative Law are not written in stone, but rather are subject to a considerable degree of change. There is a trend throughout the Western world to make governments more open and accountable for their actions. We think that this will increase the importance and relevance of Administrative Law in the coming years. It is, of course, impossible to know exactly how Parliament and the courts will deal with the perpetual tension between individual liberty and the pressure for governmental intervention in virtually all spheres of human activity. Who would have foreseen the developments over the last decade concerning the "duty to be fair" or the adoption of the "patently unreasonable" test to determine which intra-jurisdictional errors of law are subject to judicial review? Nevertheless, we think the following areas may show marked changes in the future.

Undoubtedly, the Charter of Rights and Freedoms will have the greatest impact on all aspects of Canadian public law. The courts have already indicated their willingness to breathe life into the principles set forth in this document, and to make it not only an effective statement of the values which we expect our government to observe but also an effective weapon to limit and strike down unacceptable governmental activity. Accordingly, one can readily state that the Charter will be used extensively in Administrative Law as a ground for attacking the validity of all forms of governmental action, whether legislative, judicial or merely administrative in nature. In particular, section 7 of the Charter will undoubtedly be used to extend the principles of natural (or fundamental) justice to any law or governmental action which deprives a person of life, liberty or security of the person. Similarly, the Supreme Court of Canada's interpretation in the *Southam*[1] case of the prohibition in section 8 against unreasonable searches will almost certainly require extensive revisions to the format of investigative powers granted to a host of administrative agencies. It is foreseeable that the Charter will affect many other legislative

---

1 *Dir. of Investigation and Research of the Combines Investigation Br. v. Southam Inc.*, [1984] 6 W.W.R. 577 (S.C.C.).

and governmental practices, but it is still too early to predict precisely how all of these issues will arise or be resolved over the next few years.

Secondly, one might anticipate that the Canadian legislatures will continue to implement structural and institutional means for supervising the way statutory delegates exercise their powers. Whether legislative, judicial or merely administrative in nature, the legality of these powers is too often protected by the cloak of Parliamentary Sovereignty without any real accountability to the elected representatives of the people. Thus, one might expect the provincial legislatures to adopt standing committees along the lines of the federal Joint Standing Committee on Regulations and other Statutory Instruments to act as a watchdog both on the types of powers delegated in enabling legislation, and how the administration in fact uses those powers. Progress in this area requires a general reassertion of the rights of Parliament over the executive.

Thirdly, the courts may possibly extend their supervision over delegated legislative powers. The recent abandonment of the necessity to characterize a function as "judicial or quasi-judicial" in order for *certiorari* to be available to correct a breach of the principles of natural justice and procedural fairness has enormously increased the ambit of judicial review over merely administrative functions. Nevertheless, the courts have so far drawn up short of applying these same principles of fairness to delegated legislation. There is, however, no inherent reason why some powers are delegated in a legislative form while others are discretionary or administrative in nature. The mere characterization of a delegated function as being legislative in nature does not remove the sense of injustice created when such a power is exercised unfairly or negligently, and we think the courts will have an increasingly difficult time in refusing to extend natural justice to the way in which delegated legislative powers are exercised.

Similarly, the overwhelming degree of governmental regulation of all aspects of society has the corresponding effect of increasing expectations that the government will be liable for harm caused to individual citizens — particularly if the government is perceived to have been negligent. Although the courts have recently recognized the existence of a duty of care not to be negligent lying on public servants in the course of their "operational" governmental duties,[2] we think that tort liability will inevitably be extended beyond this range, and will include negligently adopted policy. Again, the mere characterization of a delegate's function as being legislative in nature should not provide a shield from liability for negligence.

Fourthly, we think there is room for the legislative branch to come to terms with the existence and the desirability of judicial review of the legality of

---

2 *Kamloops v. Nielsen*, [1984] 5 W.W.R. 1 (S.C.C.). See also the reforms proposed in Working Paper 40 of the Law Reform Commission of Canada entitled *The Legal Status of the Federal Administration* (1985).

administrative action. This will require the development of some comprehensive policy concerning the nature and availability of appeals from every power delegated by legislation. It also will require some co-ordination between statutory appeals and judicial review.

Fifthly, there can be no valid policy reason why Canadian legislatures have not abandoned the use of privative clauses to try to protect illegal actions taken by statutory delegates from judicial review. Whatever the theoretical right of Parliament to abolish the courts or to oust their jurisdiction over administrative bodies, both the federal and the English experience in eschewing privative clauses indicate that they simply are not necessary for the efficient or good administration of government. We submit, therefore, that there is a strong need for legislation to embrace the expectation our citizens so strongly hold — rightly or wrongly in point of a purely positivistic constitutional theory — that the courts are a safety valve against illegal governmental action.

Sixthly, on a more technical level, we think that Canadian law is not yet clearly settled with respect to the right of the courts to review all errors of law. Accordingly, we anticipate further consideration of whether the "patently unreasonable" test applies to prevent judicial review of intra-jurisdictional errors of law (even in the absence of a privative clause). The law of England has not adopted this test, and there is some indication that English courts may treat all errors of law as being jurisdictional in nature. Somehow, our courts will have to deal with this problem.

Finally, we think that there should be irresistible pressure to abolish the preferred position of the Crown.

In summary, therefore, we do not anticipate that Administrative Law will be static, and we look forward to incorporating new developments into future editions of this work.

Appendix 1

Alberta
Administrative Procedures Act
R.S.A. 1980, c. A-2

HER MAJESTY, by and with the advice and consent of the Legislative Assembly of Alberta, enacts as follows:

1 In this Act,

(a) "authority" means a person authorized to exercise a statutory power;

(b) "party" means a person whose rights will be varied or affected by the exercise of a statutory power or by an act or thing done pursuant to that power;

(c) "statutory power" means an administrative, quasi-judicial or judicial power conferred by statute, other than a power conferred on a court of record of civil or criminal jurisdiction or a power to make regulations, and for greater certainty, but without restricting the generality of the foregoing, includes a power

   (i) to grant, suspend or revoke a charter or letters patent,

   (ii) to grant, renew, refuse, suspend or revoke a permission to do an act or thing which, but for the permission, would be unlawful, whether the permission is called a licence or permit or certificate or is in any other form,

   (iii) to declare or establish a status provided for under a statute for a person and to suspend or revoke that status,

   (iv) to approve or authorize the doing or omission by a person of an act or thing that, but for the approval or authorization, would be unlawful or unauthorized,

   (v) to declare or establish a right or duty of a person under a statute, whether in a dispute with another person or otherwise, or

(vi) to make an order, decision, direction or finding prohibiting a person from doing an act or thing that, but for the order, decision, direction or finding, it would be lawful for him to do,

or any combination of those powers.   RSA 1970 c2 s2

Application of Act

2 The Lieutenant Governor in Council may, by order,

(a) designate any authority as an authority to which this Act applies in whole or in part,

(b) designate the statutory power of the authority in respect of which this Act applies in whole or in part, and

(c) designate the provisions of this Act which are applicable to the authority in the exercise of that statutory power, and the extent to which they apply,

and this Act only applies to an authority to the extent ordered under this section.   RSA 1970 c2 s3

Notice to parties

3 When

(a) an application is made to an authority, or

(b) an authority on its own initiative proposes

to exercise a statutory power, the authority shall give to all parties adequate notice of the application which it has before it or of the power which it intends to exercise.   RSA 1970 c2 s4

Evidence and representations

4 Before an authority, in the exercise of a statutory power, refuses the application of or makes a decision or order adversely affecting the rights of a party, the authority

(a) shall give the party a reasonable opportunity of furnishing relevant evidence to the authority,

(b) shall inform the party of the facts in its possession or the allegations made to it contrary to the interests of the party in sufficient detail

(i) to permit him to understand the facts or allegations, and

(ii) to afford him a reasonable opportunity to furnish relevant evidence to contradict or explain the facts or allegations,

and

(c) shall give the party an adequate opportunity of making representations by way of argument to the authority.   RSA 1970 c2 s5

5 When an authority has informed a party of facts or allega- Cross-
tions and that party   examination

(a) is entitled under section 4 to contradict or explain them, but

(b) will not have a fair opportunity of doing so without cross-examination of the person making the statements that constitute the facts or allegations,

the authority shall afford the party an opportunity of cross-examination in the presence of the authority or of a person authorized to hear or take evidence for the authority.   RSA 1970 c2 s6

6 Where by this Act a party is entitled to make representations When certain
to an authority with respect to the exercise of a statutory power, representations
the authority is not by this Act required to afford an opportun- not permitted
ity to the party

(a) to make oral representations, or

(b) to be represented by counsel,

if the authority affords the party an opportunity to make representations adequately in writing, but nothing in this Act deprives a party of a right conferred by any other Act to make oral representations or to be represented by counsel. RSA 1970 c2 s7

7 When an authority exercises a statutory power so as to Written
adversely affect the rights of a party, the authority shall furnish decision with
to each party a written statement of its decision setting out reasons

(a) the findings of fact on which it based its decision, and

(b) the reasons for the decision.   RSA 1970 c2 s8

8 Nothing in this Act relieves an authority from complying Requirements
with any procedure to be followed by it under any other Act of other Acts
relating to the exercise of its statutory power.   RSA 1970 c2 s9

9 Nothing in this Act

(a) requires that any evidence or allegations of fact made to Rules of
an authority be made under oath, or   evidence

(b) requires any authority to adhere to the rules of evidence applicable to courts of civil or criminal jurisdiction.   RSA 1970 c2 s10

10 The Lieutenant Governor in Council may make regulations

Regulations

(a) to prescribe the length of time that is reasonable for the giving of a notice in accordance with this Act, with respect to authorities generally or with respect to a specified authority;

(b) to prescribe forms of notices for the purposes of this Act;

(c) to carry into effect the purposes of this Act.   RSA 1970 c2 s11

Appendix 2

Ontario
Statutory Powers Procedure Act
R.S.O. 1980, c. 484

1.—(1) In this Act,

(*a*) "Committee" means the Statutory Powers Procedure Rules Committee;   Interpretation

(*b*) "licence" includes any permit, certificate, approval, registration or similar form of permission required by law;

(*c*) "municipality" has the same meaning as in the *Municipal Affairs Act*, and includes a district, metropolitan and regional municipality and their local boards;   R.S.O. 1980, c. 303

(*d*) "statutory power of decision" means a power or right, conferred by or under a statute, to make a decision deciding or prescribing,

    (i) the legal rights, powers, privileges, immunities, duties or liabilities of any person or party, or

    (ii) the eligibility of any person or party to receive, or to the continuation of, a benefit or licence, whether he is legally entitled thereto or not;

(*e*) "tribunal" means one or more persons, whether or not incorporated and however described, upon which a statutory power of decision is conferred by or under a statute.

(2) A municipality, an unincorporated association of employers, a trade union or council of trade unions who may be a party to proceedings in the exercise of a statutory power of decision under the statute conferring the power, shall be deemed to be a person for the purpose of any provision of this Act or of any rule made under this Act that applies to parties.   1971, c. 47, s. 1; 1972, c. 1, s. 104 (6).   Meaning of "person" extended

PART I

MINIMUM RULES FOR PROCEEDINGS OF CERTAIN TRIBUNALS

Interpretation

2. In this Part,

(*a*) "hearing" means a hearing in any proceedings;

(*b*) "proceedings" means proceedings to which this Part applies.   1971, c. 47, s. 2.

Application of Part I

3.—(1) Subject to subsection (2), this Part applies to proceedings by a tribunal in the exercise of a statutory power of decision conferred by or under an Act of the Legislature, where the tribunal is required by or under such Act or otherwise by law to hold or to afford to the parties to the proceedings an opportunity for a hearing before making a decision.

Where Part I does not apply

(2) This Part does not apply to proceedings,

(*a*) before the Assembly or any committee of the Assembly;

(*b*) in or before,

    (i) the Supreme Court,

    (ii) a county or district court,

    (iii) a surrogate court,

R.S.O. 1980, c. 398

    (iv) a provincial court or a provincial offences court established under the *Provincial Courts Act*,

    (v) the Unified Family Court,

    (vi) a small claims court, or

    (vii) a justice of the peace;

(*c*) to which the Rules of Practice and Procedure of the Supreme Court apply;

R.S.O. 1980, cc. 25, 228

(*d*) before an arbitrator to which the *Arbitrations Act* or the *Labour Relations Act* applies;

(*e*) at a coroner's inquest;

R.S.O. 1980, c. 411

(*f*) of a commission appointed under the *Public Inquiries Act*;

(*g*) of one or more persons required to make an investigation and to make a report, with or without recommendations, where the report is for the information or advice of the person to whom it is made and does not in any way

legally bind or limit that person in any decision he may
have power to make; or

(*h*) of a tribunal empowered to make regulations, rules or
by-laws in so far as its power to make regulations, rules
or by-laws is concerned.   1971, c. 47, s. 3, *revised.*

4. Notwithstanding anything in this Act and unless otherwise provided in the Act under which the proceedings arise, or
the tribunal otherwise directs, any proceedings may be disposed
of by,

(*a*) agreement;

(*b*) consent order; or

(*c*) a decision of the tribunal given,

    (i) without a hearing, or

    (ii) without compliance with any other requirement of
this Act,

where the parties have waived such hearing or compliance.
1971, c. 47, s. 4.

Disposition of
proceedings
without a hear-
ing

5. The parties to any proceedings shall be the persons
specified as parties by or under the statute under which the
proceedings arise or, if not so specified, persons entitled by law
to be parties to the proceedings.   1971, c. 47, s. 5

Parties

6.—(1) The parties to any proceedings shall be given reasonable notice of the hearing by the tribunal.

Notice of
hearing

(2) A notice of a hearing shall include,

Idem

(*a*) a statement of the time, place and purpose of the hearing;

(*b*) a reference to the statutory authority under which the
hearing will be held; and

(*c*) a statement that if the party notified does not attend at
the hearing, the tribunal may proceed in his absence and
he will not be entitled to any further notice in the
proceedings.   1971, c. 47. s. 6.

7. Where notice of a hearing has been given to a party to any
proceedings in accordance with this Act and the party does not
attend at the hearing, the tribunal may proceed in his absence
and he is not entitled to any further notice in the proceedings.
1971, c. 47, s. 7.

Effect of non-
attendance at
hearing after
due notice

Where character, etc., of a party is in issue

8. Where the good character, propriety of conduct or competence of a party is an issue in any proceedings, the party is entitled to be furnished prior to the hearing with reasonable information of any allegations with respect thereto.   1971, c. 47, s. 8.

Hearings to be public, exceptions

9.—(1) A hearing shall be open to the public except where the tribunal is of the opinion that,

(*a*) matters involving public security may be disclosed; or

(*b*) intimate financial or personal matters or other matters may be disclosed at the hearing of such a nature, having regard to the circumstances, that the desirability of avoiding disclosure thereof in the interests of any person affected or in the public interest outweighs the desirability of adhering to the principle that hearings be open to the public,

in which case the tribunal may hold the hearing concerning any such matters *in camera*.

Maintenance of order at hearings

(2) A tribunal may make such orders or give such directions at a hearing as it considers necessary for the maintenance of order at the hearing, and, if any person disobeys or fails to comply with any such order or direction, the tribunal or a member thereof may call for the assistance of any peace officer to enforce the order or direction, and every peace officer so called upon shall take such action as is necessary to enforce the order or direction and may use such force as is reasonably required for that purpose.   1971, c. 47, s. 9.

Rights of parties to counsel, to examine witnesses, etc., at hearings

10. A party to proceedings may at a hearing,

(*a*) be represented by counsel or an agent;

(*b*) call and examine witnesses and present his arguments and submissions;

(*c*) conduct cross-examinations of witnesses at a hearing reasonably required for a full and fair disclosure of the facts in relation to which they have given evidence. 1971, c. 47, s. 10.

Rights of witnesses to counsel

11.—(1) A witness at a hearing is entitled to be advised by his counsel or agent as to his rights but such counsel or agent may take no other part in the hearing without leave of the tribunal.

(2) Where a hearing is *in camera*, a counsel or agent for a witness is not entitled to be present except when that witness is giving evidence.   1971, c. 47, s. 11. Idem

12.—(1) A tribunal may require any person, including a party, by summons, Summonses

(*a*) to give evidence on oath or affirmation at a hearing; and

(*b*) to produce in evidence at a hearing documents and things specified by the tribunal,

relevant to the subject-matter of the proceedings and admissible at a hearing.

(2) A summons issued under subsection (1) shall be in Form 1 and, Form and service of summonses

(*a*) where the tribunal consists of one person, shall be signed by him; or

(*b*) where the tribunal consists of more than one person, shall be signed by the chairman of the tribunal or in such other manner as documents on behalf of the tribunal may be signed under the statute constituting the tribunal; and

(*c*) shall be served personally on the person summoned who shall be paid the like fees and allowances for his attendance as a witness before the tribunal as are paid for the attendance of a witness summoned to attend before the Supreme Court.

(3) Upon proof to the satisfaction of a judge of the Supreme Court of the service of a summons under this section upon a person and that, Bench warrants

(*a*) such person has failed to attend or to remain in attendance at a hearing in accordance with the requirements of the summons;

(*b*) a sufficient sum for his fees and allowances has been duly paid or tendered to him; and

(*c*) his presence is material to the ends of justice,

the judge may, by his warrant in Form 2, directed to any sheriff, police officer or constable, cause such witness to be apprehended anywhere within Ontario and forthwith to be brought before the tribunal and to be detained in custody as the judge may order until his presence as a witness before the tribunal is no longer required, or, in the discretion of the judge, to be released on a recognizance (with or without sureties) conditioned for appearance to give evidence.

Proof of
service

(4) Service of a summons and payment of tender of fees or allowance may be proved by affidavit in an application under subsection (3).

Certificate
of facts

(5) Where an application under subsection (3) is made on behalf of a tribunal, the person constituting the tribunal, or where the tribunal consists of two or more persons, the chairman thereof may certify to the judge the facts relied on to establish that the presence of the person summoned is material to the ends of justice and such certificate may be accepted by the judge as proof of such facts.

Idem

(6) Where an application under subsection (3) is made by a party to the proceedings, proof of the facts relied on to establish that the presence of the person summoned is material to the ends of justice may be by affidavit of such party.   1971, c. 47, s. 12.

Contempt
proceedings

13. Where any person without lawful excuse,

(a) on being duly summoned under section 12 as a witness at a hearing makes default in attending at the hearing; or

(b) being in attendance as a witness at a hearing, refuses to take an oath or to make an affirmation legally required by the tribunal to be taken or made, or to produce any document or thing in his power or control legally required by the tribunal to be produced by him or to answer any question to which the tribunal may legally require an answer; or

(c) does any other thing that would, if the tribunal had been a court of law having power to commit for contempt, have been contempt of that court,

the tribunal may, of its own motion or on application of a party to the proceedings, state a case to the Divisional Court setting out the facts and that court may, on application on behalf of and in the name of the tribunal or by such party, inquire into the matter and, after hearing any witnesses who may be produced against or on behalf of that person and after hearing any statement that may be offered in defence, punish or take steps for the punishment of that person in like manner as if he had been guilty of contempt of the court.   1971, c. 47, s. 13.

14.—(1) A witness at a hearing shall be deemed to have objected to answer any question asked him upon the ground that his answer may tend to criminate him or may tend to establish his liability to civil proceedings at the instance of the Crown, or of any person, and no answer given by a witness at a hearing shall be used or be receivable in evidence against him in any trial or other proceedings against him thereafter taking place, other than a prosecution for perjury in giving such evidence.

Protection for witnesses

(2) A witness shall be informed by the tribunal of his right to object to answer any question under section 5 of the *Canada Evidence Act.*   1971, c. 47, s. 14.

Right to object under R.S.C. 1970, c. E-10

15.—(1) Subject to subsections (2) and (3), a tribunal may admit as evidence at a hearing, whether or not given or proven under oath or affirmation or admissible as evidence in a court,

What is admissible in evidence at a hearing

(*a*) any oral testimony; and

(*b*) any document or other thing,

relevant to the subject matter of the proceedings and may act on such evidence, but the tribunal may exclude anything unduly repetitious.

(2) Nothing is admissible in evidence at a hearing,

What is inadmissible in evidence at a hearing

(*a*) that would be inadmissible in a court by reason of any privilege under the law of evidence; or

(*b*) that is inadmissible by the statute under which the proceedings arise or any other statute.

(3) Nothing in subsection (1) overrides the provisions of any Act expressly limiting the extent to or purposes for which any oral testimony, documents or things may be admitted or used in evidence in any proceedings.

Conflicts

(4) Where a tribunal is satisfied as to their authenticity, a copy of a document or other thing may be admitted as evidence at a hearing.

Copies

(5) Where a document has been filed in evidence at a hearing, the tribunal may, or the person producing it or entitled to it may with the leave of the tribunal, cause the document to be photocopied and the tribunal may authorize the photocopy to be filed in evidence in the place of the document filed and release the document filed, or may furnish to the person producing it or the person entitled to it a photocopy of the document filed certified by a member of the tribunal.

Photocopies

Certified copy admissible in evidence

(6) A document purporting to be a copy of a document filed in evidence at a hearing, certified to be a true copy thereof by a member of the tribunal, is admissible in evidence in proceedings in which the document is admissible as evidence of the document.   1971, c. 47, s. 15.

Notice of facts and opinions

16. A tribunal may, in making its decision in any proceedings,

(*a*) take notice of facts that may be judicially noticed; and

(*b*) take notice of any generally recognized scientific or technical facts, information, or opinions within its scientific or specialized knowledge.   1971, c. 47, s. 16.

Decision

17. A tribunal shall give its final decision and order, if any, in any proceedings in writing and shall give reasons in writing therefor if requested by a party.   1971, c. 47, s. 17.

Notice of decision

18. A tribunal shall send by first class mail addressed to the parties to any proceedings who took part in the hearing, at their addresses last known to the tribunal, a copy of its final decision and order, if any, in the proceedings, together with the reasons therefor, where reasons have been given, and each party shall be deemed to have received a copy of the decision or order on the fifth day after the day of mailing unless the party did not, acting in good faith, through absence, accident, illness or other cause beyond his control receive the copy of the decision or order until a later date.   1971, c. 47, s. 18.

Enforcement of decision

19.—(1) A certified copy of a final decision and order, if any, of a tribunal in any proceedings may be filed in the office of the Registrar of the Supreme Court by the tribunal or by a party and, if it is for the payment of money, it may be enforced at the instance of the tribunal or of such party in the name of the tribunal in the same manner as a judgment of that court, and in all other cases by an application by the tribunal or by such party to the court for such order as the court may consider just.

Idem

(2) Where a tribunal having power to do so makes an order or decision rescinding or varying an order or decision previously made by it that has been filed under subsection (1), upon filing in accordance with subsection (1) the order or decision rescinding or varying the order or decision previously made,

(*a*) if the order or decision rescinds the order or decision previously made, the order or decision previously made ceases to have effect for the purposes of subsection (1); or

(b) if the order or decision varies the order or decision previously made, the order or decision previously made as so varied may be enforced in a like manner as an order or decision filed under subsection (1).   1971, c. 47, s. 19.

20. A tribunal shall compile a record of any proceedings in which a hearing has been held which shall include,

Record of proceedings

(a) any application, complaint, reference or other document, if any, by which the proceedings were commenced;

(b) the notice of any hearing;

(c) any intermediate orders made by the tribunal;

(d) all documentary evidence filed with the tribunal, subject to any limitation expressly imposed by any other Act on the extent to or the purposes for which any such documents may be used in evidence in any proceedings;

(e) the transcript, if any, of the oral evidence given at the hearing; and

(f) the decision of the tribunal and the reasons therefor, where reasons have been given.   1971, c. 47, s. 20.

21. A hearing may be adjourned from time to time by a tribunal of its own motion or where it is shown to the satisfaction of the tribunal that the adjournment is required to permit an adequate hearing to be held.   1971, c. 47, s. 21.

Adjournments

22. A member of a tribunal has power to administer oaths and affirmations for the purpose of any of its proceedings and the tribunal may require evidence before it to be given under oath or affirmation.   1971, c. 47, s. 22.

Administration of oaths

23.—(1) A tribunal may make such orders or give such directions in proceedings before it as it considers proper to prevent abuse of its processes.

Abuse of processes

(2) A tribunal may reasonably limit further cross-examination of a witness where it is satisfied that the cross-examination of the witness has been sufficient to disclose fully and fairly the facts in relation to which he has given evidence.

Limitation on cross-examination

(3) A tribunal may exclude from a hearing anyone, other than a barrister and solicitor qualified to practise in Ontario, appearing as an agent on behalf of a party or as an adviser to a witness if it finds that such person is not competent properly to represent or to advise the party or witness or does not

Exclusion of agents

understand and comply at the hearing with the duties and responsibilities of an advocate or adviser.   1971, c. 47, s. 23.

Notice, etc.   **24.**—(1) Where a tribunal is of opinion that because the parties to any proceedings before it are so numerous or for any other reason, it is impracticable,

    (*a*) to give notice of the hearing; or

    (*b*) to send its decision and the material mentioned in section 18,

to all or any of the parties individually, the tribunal may, instead of doing so, cause reasonable notice of the hearing or of its decision to be given to such parties by public advertisement or otherwise as the tribunal may direct.

Contents of notice   (2) A notice of a decision given by a tribunal under clause (1) (*b*) shall inform the parties of the place where copies of the decision and the reasons therefor, if reasons were given, may be obtained.   1971, c. 47, s. 24.

Appeal operates as stay, exception   **25.**—(1) Unless it is expressly provided to the contrary in the Act under which the proceedings arise, an appeal from a decison of a tribunal to a court or other appellate tribunal operates as a stay in the matter except where the tribunal or the court or other body to which the appeal is taken otherwise orders.

Idem R.S.O. 1980, c. 224   (2) An application for judicial review under the *Judicial Review Procedure Act*, or the bringing of proceedings specified in subsection 2 (1) of that Act is not an appeal within the meaning of subsection (1).   1971, c. 47, s. 25.

PART II

STATUTORY POWERS PROCEDURE RULES COMMITTEE

Rules Committee, composition   **26.**—(1) The committee known as the Statutory Powers Procedure Rules Committee is continued and shall be composed of,

    (*a*) the Deputy Attorney General who shall be chairman of the Committee, but in his absence or at his request his nominee shall act in his place;

    (*b*) the chairman of the Ontario Law Reform Commission;

    (*c*) a judge of the Supreme Court, appointed by the Lieutenant Governor in Council;

(*d*) a senior official in the public service of Ontario who is or has been a member of a tribunal to whose proceedings Part I applies, appointed by the Lieutenant Governor in Council;

(*e*) a member of the Law Society of Upper Canada, appointed by the Lieutenant Governor in Council;

(*f*) a representative of the public who is not a member of the public service of Ontario, appointed by the Lieutenant Governor in Council; and

(*g*) a professor of administrative law on the law faculty of a university in Ontario, appointed by the Lieutenant Governor in Council.

(2) A majority of the members of the Committee may exercise all the powers of the Committee.   1971, c. 47, s. 26; 1972, c. 1, s. 9 (7).   *Quorum*

27. It is the duty of the Committee,   *Duties*

(*a*) to maintain under continuous review the practice and procedure in proceedings to which Part I applies;

(*b*) to maintain under continuous review the practice and procedure, before,

   (i) tribunals upon which a statutory power of decision is conferred by or under an Act of the Legislature but which is not required under such Act or otherwise by law to afford to the parties to the proceedings an opportunity for a hearing before making a decision, and

   (ii) a body coming within clause 3 (2) (*e*) or (*g*).   1971, c. 47, s. 27.

28. No rules of procedure to govern the proceedings of a tribunal to which Part I applies shall be made or approved except after consultation with the Committee.   1971, c. 47, s. 28.   *Rules to be made only after consultation with Committee*

29. The Committee may require a tribunal to which Part I applies or coming within clause 27 (*b*) to report to the Committee the rules of procedure governing its proceedings or, where there are no such rules, information as to the procedure followed by it and to formulate and report to the Committee rules to govern its proceedings.   1971, c. 47, s. 29.   *Report of rules to Committee*

Additional powers of tribunals to make rules

30. Where power is conferred to make rules of procedure governing the proceedings of a tribunal to which Part I applies, such power shall include power,

(*a*) notwithstanding section 15, to require that findings of fact of the tribunal be based exclusively on evidence admissible under the law of evidence and on matters that may be judicially noticed or of which notice may be taken under section 16 or on evidence admissible under section 15 and on matters of which notice may be taken under section 16;

(*b*) to require the oral evidence admitted at a hearing before the tribunal to be recorded;

(*c*) to limit investigation or consultation concerning the subject-matter of any proceedings by members of the tribunal prior to the hearing;

(*d*) to require that any member of the tribunal participating in a decision of the tribunal shall have been present throughout the hearing.   1971, c. 47, s. 30.

Secretary to Committee

31. The Attorney General may assign one or more members of the staff of the Ministry of the Attorney General to be secretary or secretaries of the committee and the committee may prescribe the duties of the secretary or secretaries.   1971, c. 47, s. 31; 1972, c. 1, s. 9 (7).

Conflict

32. Unless it is expressly provided in any other Act that its provisions and regulations, rules or by-laws made under it apply notwithstanding anything in this Act, the provisions of this Act and of rules made under section 33 prevail over the provisions of such other Act and over regulations, rules or by-laws made under such other Act which conflict therewith. 1971, c. 47, s. 32.

Rules respecting publication of decisions

33. Subject to the approval of the Lieutenant Governor in Council, the Committee may make rules respecting the reporting, editing and publication of decisions of the tribunals to which Part I Applies.   1971, c. 47, s. 33.

Annual report

34. The Committee shall report annually to the Attorney General.   1971, c. 47, s. 34; 1972, c. 1, s. 9 (7).

FORM 1

(Section 12(2))

(Name of Act under which proceedings arise)

SUMMONS TO A WITNESS BEFORE .... *(name of tribunal)* ..

RE:

TO:

You are hereby summoned and required to attend before the

.... *(name of tribunal)* ....

at a hearing to be held at .... in the ...... of ...... on .... day, the ...... day of ...... 19 ..... , at the hour of .... o'clock in the .... noon (local time), and so from day to day until the hearing is concluded or the tribunal otherwise orders, to give evidence on oath touching the matters in question in the proceedings and to bring with you and produce at such time and place ....

....

....

Dated this .... day of .... , 19 ......

(name of tribunal)

....

Member of Tribunal

NOTE:

You are entitled to be paid the same personal allowances for your attendance at the hearing as are paid for the attendance of a witness summoned to attend before the Supreme Court.

If you fail to attend and give evidence at the hearing, or to produce the documents or things specified, at the time and place specified, without lawful excuse, you are liable to punishment by the Supreme Court in the same manner as if for contempt of that court for disobedience to a subpoena.

1971, c. 47, Form 1.

FORM 2

(Section 12 (3))

BENCH WARRANT

PROVINCE OF ONTARIO

To   *A.B.*, Sheriff, etc.

WHEREAS proof has been made before me that *C.D.* was duly summoned to appear before the *(name of tribunal)* .... at the hearing of the said tribunal at Toronto (*or as the case may be*) on the .... day of ...., 19 ....; that the presence of the said *C.D.* is material to the ends of justice, and that the said *C.D.* has failed to attend in accordance with the requirements of the summons.

THESE are therefore to command you to take the said *C.D.* to bring and have him before the said tribunal at Toronto (*or as the case may be*) there to testify what he may know concerning the matters in question in the proceedings before the said tribunal, and that you detain him in your custody until he has given his evidence or until the said sittings have ended or until other orders may be made concerning him.

GIVEN UNDER MY HAND this .... day of .... , 19 ...., at ....

....
Judge, S.C.O.

1971, c. 47, Form 2.

Appendix 3

Ontario
Judicial Review Procedure Act
R.S.O. 1980, c. 224

1. In this Act, Interpretation

(*a*) "application for judicial review" means an application under subsection 2 (1);

(*b*) "court" means the Supreme Court;

(*c*) "licence" includes any permit, certificate, approval, registration or similar form of permission required by law;

(*d*) "municipality" has the same meaning as in the *Municipal Affairs Act*, and includes a district, metropolitan and regional municipality and their local boards; R.S.O. 1980, c. 303

(*e*) "party" includes a municipality, association of employers, a trade union or council of trade unions which may be a party to any of the proceedings mentioned in subsection 2 (1);

(*f*) "statutory power of decision" means a power or right conferred by or under a statute to make a decision deciding or prescribing,

    (i) the legal rights, powers, privileges, immunities, duties or liabilities of any person or party, or

    (ii) the eligibility of any person or party to receive, or to the continuation of, a benefit or licence, whether he is legally entitled thereto or not,

and includes the powers of an inferior court;

(*g*) "statutory power" means a power or right conferred by or under a statute,

    (i) to make an regulation. rule. by-law or order, or to give any other direction having force as subordinate legislation,

(ii) to exercise a statutory power of decision,

(iii) to require any person or party to do or to refrain from doing any act or thing that, but for such requirement, such person or party would not be required by law to do or to refrain from doing,

(iv) to do any act or thing that would, but for such power or right, be a breach of the legal rights of any person or party.   1971, c. 48, s. 1; 1972, c. 1, s. 104 (6).

Applications
for judicial
review

2. —(1) On an application by way of originating notice, which may be styled "Notice of Application for Judicial Review", the court may, notwithstanding any right of appeal, by order grant any relief that the applicant would be entitled to in any one or more of the following:

1. Proceedings by way of application for an order in the nature of mandamus, prohibition or certiorari.

2. Proceedings by way of an action for a declaration or for an injunction, or both, in relation to the exercise, refusal to exercise or proposed or purported exercise of a statutory power.

Error of law

(2) The power of the court to set aside a decision for error of law on the face of the record on an application for an order in the nature of certiorari is extended so as to apply on an application for judicial review in relation to any decision made in the exercise of any statutory power of decision to the extent it is not limited or precluded by the Act conferring such power of decision.

Lack of
evidence

(3) Where the findings of fact of a tribunal made in the exercise of a statutory power of decision are required by any statute or law to be based exclusively on evidence admissible before it and on facts of which it may take notice and there is no such evidence and there are no such facts to support findings of fact made by the tribunal in making a decision in the exercise of such power, the court may set aside the decision on an application for judicial review.

Power to
set aside

(4) Where the applicant on an application for judicial review is entitled to a judgment declaring that a decision made in the exercise of a statutory power of decision is unauthorized or otherwise invalid, the court may, in the place of such declaration, set aside the decision.

(5) Where, in any of the proceedings enumerated in subsection (1), the court had before the 17th day of April, 1972 a discretion to refuse to grant relief on any grounds, the court has a like discretion on like grounds to refuse to grant any relief on an application for judicial review.

Power to refuse relief

(6) Subsection (5) does not apply to the discretion of the court before the 17th day of April, 1972 to refuse to grant relief in any of the proceedings enumerated in subsection (1) on the ground that the relief should have been sought in other proceedings enumerated in subsection (1).   1971, c. 48, s. 2.

Where subs. (5) does not apply

3. On an application for judicial review in relation to a statutory power of decision, where the sole ground for relief established is a defect in form or a technical irregularity, if the court finds that no substantial wrong or miscarriage of justice has occurred, the court may refuse relief and, where the decision has already been made, may make an order validating the decision, notwithstanding such defect, to have effect from such time and on such terms as the court considers proper. 1971, c. 48, s. 3

Defects in form, technical irregularities

4. On an application for judicial review, the court may make such interim order as it considers proper pending the final determination of the application.   1971, c. 48, s. 4.

Interim order

5. Notwithstanding any limitation of time for the bringing of an application for judicial review fixed by or under any Act, the court may extend the time for making the application, either before or after expiration of the time so limited, on such terms as it considers proper, where it is satisfied that there are *prima facie* grounds for relief and that no substantial prejudice or hardship will result to any person affected by reason of the delay.   1971, c. 48, s. 5.

Extension of time for bringing application

6.—(1) Subject to subsection (2), an application for judicial review shall be made to the Divisional Court.

Application to Divisional Court

(2) An application for judicial review may be made to the High Court with leave of a judge thereof, which may be granted at the hearing of the application, where it is made to appear to the judge that the case is one of urgency and that the delay required for an application to the Divisional Court is likely to involve a failure of justice.

Application to judge of High Court

Transfer to Divisional Court

(3) Where a judge refuses leave for an application under subsection (2), he may order that the application be transferred to the Divisional Court.   1971, c. 48, s. 6 (1-3).

Appeal to Court of Appeal

(4) An appeal lies to the Court of Appeal, with leave of the Court of Appeal, from a final order of the High Court disposing of an application for judicial review pursuant to leave granted under subsection (2).   1976, c. 45, s. 1.

Summary disposition of mandamus, etc.

7. An application for an order in the nature of mandamus, prohibition or certiorari shall be deemed to be an application for judicial review and shall be made, treated and disposed of as if it were an application for judicial review.   1971, c. 48, s. 7.

Summary disposition of actions

8. Where an action for a declaration or injunction, or both, whether with or without a claim for other relief, is brought and the exercise, refusal to exercise or proposed or purported exercise of a statutory power is an issue in the action, a judge of the High Court may on the application of any party to the action, if he considers it appropriate, direct that the action be treated and disposed of summarily, in so far as it relates to the exercise, refusal to exercise or proposed or purported exercise of such power, as if it were an application for judicial review and may order that the hearing on such issue be transferred to the Divisional Court or may grant leave for it to be disposed of in accordance with subsection 6 (2).   1971, c. 48, s. 8.

Sufficiency of application

9.—(1) It is sufficient in an application for judicial review if an applicant sets out in the notice the grounds upon which he is seeking relief and the nature of the relief that he seeks without specifying the proceedings enumerated in subsection 2 (1) in which the claim would have been made before the 17th day of April, 1972.

Exerciser of power may be a party

(2) For the purposes of an application for judicial review in relation to the exercise, refusal to exercise or proposed or purported exercise of a statutory power, the person who is authorized to exercise the power may be a party to the application.

Idem

(3) For the purposes of subsection (2), any two or more persons who, acting together, may exercise a statutory power, whether styled a board or commission or by any other collective title, shall be deemed to be a person under such collective title.   1971, c. 48, s. 9 (1-3).

(4) Notice of an application for judicial review shall be served upon the Attorney General who is entitled as of right to be heard in person or by counsel on the application.   1971, c. 48, s. 9 (4); 1972, c. 1, s. 9 (7).

Notice to Attorney General

10. When notice of an application for judicial review of a decision made in the exercise or purported exercise of a statutory power of decision has been served on the person making the decision, such person shall forthwith file in the court for use on the application, the record of the proceedings in which the decision was made.   1971, c. 48, s. 10.

Record to be filed in S.C.O.

11. [Repealed 1984, c. 11, s. 188.]

12.—(1) Subject to subsection (2), where reference is made in any other Act or in any regulation, rule or by-law to any of the proceedings enumerated in subsection 2 (1), such reference shall, after the 16th day of April, 1972, be read and construed to include a reference to an application for judicial review.

References in other Acts, etc.

(2) Nothing in this Act affects proceedings under the *Habeas Corpus Act* or the issue of a writ of certiorari thereunder or proceedings pursuant thereto, but an application for judicial review may be brought in aid of an application for a writ of *habeas corpus*.   1971, c. 48, s. 12.

Proceedings under R.S.O. 1980, c. 193

Appendix 4

Proposed Amendments to the Alberta Rules of Court

The following are amendments to the Alberta Rules of Court proposed by the Alberta Institute of Law Research and Reform (Report 40, March 1984 reproduced with permission). The amendments would provide a new uniform procedure for obtaining judicial review.

Rules to Amend the Alberta Rules of Court

1. The Alberta Rules of Court (Alta. Reg. 390/68) are amended by this regulation.

2. The following is added after Part 56:

PART 56.1

JUDICIAL REVIEW IN CIVIL MATTERS

753.1 In this Part,   Definitions

"person" includes a board, commission, tribunal or other body whose decision, act or omission is subject to judicial review, whether comprised of one person or of two or more persons acting together and whether or not styled by a collective title.

753.2 A proceeding under this Part shall be known as an application for judicial review.   Application for judicial review

753.3 An application for judicial review shall be taken by originating notice.   Initiation of application

753.4 (1) On an application for judicial review, the court may grant any relief that the applicant would be entitled to in proceedings for any one or more of the following remedies: Scope of application

(*a*) an order in the nature of mandamus, prohibition, certiorari, quo warranto or habeas corpus; or

(*b*) a declaration or injunction.

(2) the court may grant a declaration or injunction if it considers that the judicial review procedure is just and convenient having regard to all the circumstances of the case including

(i) the nature of the matters in respect of which relief may be granted by orders of mandamus, prohibition, certiorari or quo warranto, and

(ii) the nature of the persons from whose decisions, acts or omissions relief may be granted by such orders.

(3) Subrule (1) applies whether the remedy under which the applicant would be entitled to the relief is or is not specifically named in an application.

(4) Before the court may grant relief under subrule (1), it must be satisfied that the grounds for the remedy under which the applicant would be entitled to the relief have been established.

Setting aside in lieu of declaration
753.5 Subject to Rule 753.11, where the applicant on an application for judicial review is entitled to a declaration that a decision or act is unauthorized or invalid the court may, instead of making a declaration, set aside the decision or act.

Remission of matter for reconsideration
753.6 (1) On an application for judicial review the court may direct the person from whose decision, act or omission relief is claimed to reconsider and determine, either generally or in respect of a specified matter, the whole or any part of a matter to which the application for judicial review relates.

(2) In giving a direction under subrule (1), the court shall

(*a*) advise the person from whose decision, act or omission relief is claimed of its reasons, and

(*b*) give that person such directions as it thinks appropriate.

(3) Where the person from whose decision, act or omission relief is claimed has made a decision, the court may direct a reconsideration and determination under subrule (1) only if the decision has been set aside.

Validation of a minor technical defect
753.7 On an application for judicial review, where the sole ground for relief established is a defect in form or a technical irregularity, if the court finds that no substantial wrong or miscarriage of justice has occurred, the court may refuse relief and, where a decision has been made, may make an order validating the decision, notwithstanding such defect, to have effect from such time and on such terms as the court considers proper.

753.8 (1) An originating notice taken under this Part shall be in Form G.1 modified in such manner as may be necessary having regard to the nature of the application.   Contents of application

(2) Every originating notice taken under this Part shall include a concise statement of the grounds upon which relief is claimed in the proceedings and the nature of the relief claimed.

(3) Every originating notice taken under this Part shall be supported by an affidavit or affidavits or other evidence, including the evidence of the record, verifying the facts relied on in the application for judicial review.

(4) Affidavits containing statements as to the belief of the deponent with the source and grounds thereof may be admitted for the purpose of subrule (3).

753.9 (1) The application for judicial review shall be served upon   Service

    (*a*) the person from whose decision, act or omission relief is claimed,

    (*b*) the Attorney General,

    (*c*) every person who appears to be interested in or likely to be affected by the proceedings.

(2) The court may require the application for judicial review to be served upon any person not previously served.

753.10 (1) The court may direct any person to be added or struck out as a party to proceedings for judicial review.   Right to be heard on application

(2) The Attorney General is entitled as of right to be heard in person or by counsel on the application.

(3) Any person not served with the application for judicial review may show that he is affected by the proceedings and thereupon may, in the discretion of the court, take part in the proceedings as though served.

753.11 (1) Where the relief sought is an order to set aside a decision or act, the application for judicial review shall be filed and served within six months after the decision or act to which it relates.   Time for bringing application

(2) Rule 548 does not apply to this Rule.

Demand for record on application for order to set aside

753.12 (1) Where the relief claimed on an application for judicial review is an order to set aside a decision or act, the applicant shall demand the return of the record.

(2) The demand for the return of the record shall take the form of an endorsement on the application for judicial review addressed to the person from whose decision or act relief is claimed and it shall be to the following effect, adapted as may be necessary:

"You are required forthwith after service of this notice to return to the clerk of the Court of Queen's Bench at .... (as the case may be) the judgment, order or decision (or as the case may be) to which this notice refers and reasons therefor together with the process commencing the proceedings, the evidence and all exhibits filed, if any, and all things touching the matter as fully and entirely as they remain in your custody, together with this notice.

"Date ....

"To A.B., provincial judge at ....
(or as the case may be)

"Signed C.D. ....
(Solicitor for the Applicant)."

(3) All things required by this Rule to be returned to the clerk of the Court of Queen's Bench shall for the purposes of the application constitute part of the record.

Return of record on application for order to set aside.

753.13 (1) Upon receiving the application for judicial review endorsed in accordance with rule 753.12 the person from whose decision or act relief is claimed shall return forthwith to the office mentioned therein the judgment, order or decision (or as the case may be) together with the process commencing the proceedings, the evidence and all exhibits filed, if any, and all things touching the matter and the notice served upon him with a certificate endorsed thereon in the following form:

"Pursuant to the accompanying notice I hereby return to the Honourable Court the following papers and documents, that is to say

"(*a*) the judgment, order, decision (or as the case may be) and the reasons therefor;

"(*b*) the process commencing the proceedings;

"(*c*) the evidence taken at the hearing and all exhibits filed;

"(*d*) all other papers or documents touching the matter.

"And I hereby certify to this Honourable Court that I have above truly set forth all the papers and documents in my custody and power relating to the matter set forth in the originating notice."

(2) The certificate prescribed in subrule (1) has the same effect as a return to a writ of certiorari.

(3) If the proceedings are not in the possession of the person required to transmit them, he shall, in lieu of the certificate, so state and explain the circumstances.

(4) If the proceedings have not been received by the officer to whom or the clerk of the office to which they are by law required to be transmitted, that officer or clerk shall return a certificate of the fact.

(5) The parties to an application for judicial review may agree as to the contents of the return of the record of the proceedings in which the decision was made or act done.

(6) The court may, by direction, override an agreement made between parties pursuant to subrule (5).

(7) The court may dispense with the return of the evidence or exhibits or part of them.

(8) A copy of this rule shall appear upon or be annexed to the application for judicial review served upon the person from whom the return is required.

753.14 (1) Where relief other than an order to set aside a decision or act is claimed on an application for judicial review and the applicant is of the opinion that the record is necessary to establish the claim, he may demand the return of the record by endorsing the application for judicial review in accordance with subrule (2) of Rule 753.12.

Demand for and return of record on application for other relief

(2) Upon receiving the application for judicial review endorsed in accordance with subrule (1), the person from whose decision or act relief is claimed may

(*a*) return the record in which case subrule 753.12(3) and Rule 753.13 apply, or

(*b*) apply to the court to dispense with the requirement to make the return.

(3) Where objection is taken under clause (*b*) of subrule (2), the court may in its discretion order or refuse to order the return of the record or any part thereof.

(4) Where the court orders the return of the record, subrule 753.12(3) and Rule 753.13 apply except as altered by the order of the court.

Interim orders **753.15** The court may make such interim order as it considers proper upon motion made either in the application for judicial review or at any time pending the final determination of the application for judicial review.

Conversion of procedure **753.16** (1) If the relief claimed in a proceeding begun by statement of claim or originating notice under Rule 410 or another procedure ought to be claimed on an application for judicial review, the court, on application or its own motion, may direct that the proceeding be continued as an application for judicial review.

(2) If the relief claimed on an application for judicial review ought to be claimed in a proceeding begun by statement of claim or originating notice under Rule 410 or another procedure, the court, on application or its own motion, may direct that the proceeding be continued under that other procedure.

(3) The court may give such further directions as are necessary to cause the proceedings to conform to the procedure by which they are to be continued.

Appeal to Court of Appeal **753.17** An appeal from an order granted on an application for judicial review lies to the Court of Appeal.

Direction by judge of Court of Appeal **753.18** Any direction required to give effect to an order of the Court of Appeal may be made by a judge of the Court of Appeal.

General rules to apply **753.19** Except where provided specially in this Part, the general rules, including the originating notice Rules in Part 33 and those relating to abridgment or extension of time, apply to all matters under this Part.

3. Rule 738 is amended

(a) in subrule (1) by striking out

"mandamus, prohibition, certiorari" *and* "or quo warranto";

(b) by renumbering subrule (2) as subrule (3); and

(c) by adding the following after subrule (1):

(2) An order in the nature of mandamus, prohibition, certiorari, quo warranto or habeas corpus may be granted upon application for judicial review under Part 56.1.

4. Rules 742 to 753 are repealed.

FORM G.1
(RULE 753.8)

ORIGINATING NOTICE
OF APPLICATION FOR JUDICIAL REVIEW
IN THE COURT OF QUEEN'S BENCH OF ALBERTA

BETWEEN:

A.B.

Applicant,

— and —

C.D.

Respondent.

TO: (the person or persons on whom service is to be made)

TAKE NOTICE that an application for judicial review will be made on behalf of A.B. of the .... of .... in the Province of .... (occupation), the above-named applicant, before the presiding Justice in Chambers at the Court House (or Law Courts) in the City of ...., on .... day, the ..... day of .... 19 ..., at the hour of .... o'clock in the .... noon or so soon thereafter as counsel may be heard for an Order that:

(here set out a concise statement of the grounds upon which relief is claimed and of the nature of the relief claimed).

AND FURTHER TAKE NOTICE that in support of the application will be read the affidavit (or affidavits) of ...., copies of which are served herewith;

Dated at the .... of ...., in the Province of Alberta, the .... day of ...., 19 ...

_____

Clerk of the Court (SEAL)

This originating notice was taken out by ....
solicitor for the applicant whose address for service is

....

(OR — if the applicant sues in person)

This originating notice was taken out by the applicant whose address for service is ....

....

Act to Amend Judicature Act

1. The Judicature Act is amended by this Act.

2. Section 47(1) is amended by adding "and the amendments thereto filed as Alberta Regulation [here insert number of Regulation promulgating Part 56.1 of the Alberta Rules of Court]" *after* "November 4, 1976."

INDEX

APPEAL(S) — *Continued*
    judicial review, effect of appeal on, 348-53
    "jurisdiction", on, 338-39
    "law", on, 338-39
    law, error of on face of record, contrasted with, 338-39
    merits, on, 335
    nature of, 334-39
    ombudsman, relationship to, 346
    participation of first decision-maker in, 336. *See also* BIAS.
    proof, burden of, 337
    provisional determinations, 331
    rationalization, need for, 354
    reforms in England, 341
    reforms proposed in Alberta, 341-44
    re-hearing as a form of, 237-39
    void decisions, from, 354

APPLICATION FOR JUDICIAL REVIEW
    Alberta proposals for reform, 326, 404n, 408-410
    bibliographies on, 377-78, 411
    British Columbia, 405
    damages and, 392, 404, 410
    discoveries, 405, 409
    Divisional Court (Ont.), 404, 405
    England, 405-406
    Federal Court Act, s. 28, 327, 407-408. *See also* FEDERAL COURT ACT.
    injunctions and, 392
    leave required in England, 405
    New Zealand, 405
    Nova Scotia, 405
    Ontario, 326, 403-405, Appendix 3
    standing, 409
    time limit for application, 405, 409

APPOINTMENT, 108-109

ARBITRATION BOARDS
    certiorari, availability against, 276
    common law action to quash and remit decisions of, 305ff., 322
    statutory in nature, whether, 276

ATTORNEY GENERAL
    declarations and, 394
    relator actions, 392, 394
    standing, always has, 394

ATTORNEY GENERAL'S COMMITTEE ON ADMINISTRATIVE PROCEDURES (U.S.). *See* ACHESON REPORT.

AUDI ALTERAM PARTEM. See NATURAL JUSTICE.

AUSTRALIA
    reforms, 13n, 344n

AUSTRALIAN ADMINISTRATIVE APPEALS TRIBUNAL, 344

BAD FAITH, 120, 121, 125-26

BIAS, RULE AGAINST
    actual bias, 244
    administrators, applied to, 244